P9-CEX-092

Everyday SOCIOLOGY
An Introduction

StarPoint Press

C. Michael Botterweck
Triton College
River Grove, IL

Sue Greer-Pitt
Southeast Community College
Whitesburg, KY

Nancy Lee
Salem Community College
Carney's Point, NJ

Nabil Marshood
Hudson County
Community College
Jersey City, NJ

Victor McCullum
Triton College
River Grove, IL

Ron Penton, Sr.
Gulf Coast State College
Panama City, FL

Roy Silver
Southeast Community College
Cumberland, KY

Design and Production: StarPoint Press
Typeface: New Century Schoolbook
Photos: Special thanks to photographers on flickr.com
Executive Editor: Beatrice Kwidd
Project Managers: Beatrice Kwidd and C. Michael Botterweck

Cover: The cover art of this edition of Everyday Sociology is the work of painter, writer, and musician Robert V. Rimmel (1922-1998), beloved husband, father, grandfather, brother, and friend of countless many who crossed his path somewhere along the stretches of Lake Michigan in Chicago, the trails of Mount Hood in Portland, in the moutains and hamlets of Switzerland, or along the beaten paths anywhere in between.

Heb di sorg, Babe.

Graphic Design: Edward Finke

Seventh Edition, 2011
Translation rights reserved by Publisher
ISBN 978-1-886202-21-4

Copyright © by Starpoint Press, 297 May St., Elmhurst, IL 60126 Tel. 630-235-6172

All rights reserved. No part of the material protected by the copyright notice may be reproduced or utilized in any form or by any means, electronic or mechanical, including photocopying, recording, or by any information storage and retrieval system, without written permission from the copyright owner. Printed in China.

Acknowledgments

Anyone who has ever laid words to paper for the purpose of creating a book knows that the journey can be very humbling. Certainly, the writing is important, but we writers also understand that our words would never see the light of day without the professional and thoughtful efforts of others. This book is no exception. It is impossible to name everyone who has contributed in one way or another to the successful completion of this project.

Of course, first we must mention our families and friends—husbands, wives, children, mothers, fathers, sisters, brothers—you know who you are. Without your understanding and patience, we wouldn't have been able to accomplish our task.

Professionally, we extend our gratitude to Edward Finke (InDesign genius) for the countless hours spent in helping to bring this book to print–again!

And finally, we wish to thank our students. Throughout the writing process they were handed bits and pieces to read and evaluate for clarity and interest. It goes without saying that the student is the best and final judge of what does or does not work in print. We thank all of you.

Authors

Dr. C. Michael Botterweck is semi-retired and spends time in Chicago and in the foothills of the Blue Ridge Mountains in North Carolina with his wife, Alaska, and their dog, Traveler. He served 35 years at Triton College where he taught a variety of courses related to sociology and political science and spent two years as the VP for Academic Affairs. He has published a number of professional texts and teaching materials and is active in numerous professional associations. He is a past president of the National Social Science Association and has presented at conferences across the nation. He continues to teach and actively pursues professional writing. He is a strong advocate of critical thinking and decision-making skills, both of which he incorporates in his teaching and writing.

Dr. Sue Greer-Pitt has been teaching sociology at colleges and universities since 1979. She currently teaches full-time for Southeast Kentucky Community and Technical College in Whitesburg, Kentucky where she has been part of the Kentucky Community and Technical College's on-line teaching initiative for the past eleven years. Dr. Greer-Pitt has contributed chapters to scholarly books and articles to scholarly journals. She has been a paid columnist for the Lexington-Herald Leader and has had poetry published in several poetry journals. Dr. Greer-Pitt is also an artist whose 10' x 17' mural of academic life graces a wall at Southeast Kentucky CTC. She lives in rural Kentucky with her husband, two dogs–Rosie and Molly–and 11 indoor cats.

Dr. Nancy Lee is a graduate of Rutgers University and has been teaching for 23 years. In addition, she is the director of Family Matters, a counseling service that works with victims of sexual assault. She balances her teaching and counseling with a love of hiking, canoeing, and training service dogs at the home she built on the Chesapeake Bay. She is an award winning juried artist and is currently writing a novel. Almost ready to retire, she plans to follow a lifelong dream and join her daughter, her son, and son in law and form a rock band. She has two outstanding philosophies: "It's never too late" and "Never lie to your dog".

Dr. Nabil Marshood is a Fulbright scholar and a professor of sociology at Hudson County College in New Jersey. He teaches principles of sociology, sociology of the family, race and ethnic relations, and religion & society. He received his BA and MA degrees from the Hebrew University in Jerusalem, and his doctorate from Columbia University School of Social Work. Dr. Marshood is a recipient of a Mid-Career Fellowship from Princeton University, concentrating on social theory and sociology of religion; and a number of grants offering peace and conflict resolution, and religious pluralism. In addition to writing articles on higher education in community colleges and religious pluralism, he is the author of *Palestinian Teenage Immigrants and Refugees Speak Out,* published by Rosen Publishing Group and *Voices from the Camps: People*'s *History of Palestinian Refugees in Jordan, 2006,* published by University Press of America.

Professor Victor McCullum teaches at Triton Community College outside of Chicago. He earned a B.S. in Criminal Justice from Illinois State University and a M.A. from DePaul University in Sociology. He has completed course work at the doctoral level at Loyola University in Chicago. He has taught for several years as a sociology faculty member at Triton College. Currently, he remains an active member of various professional sociological associations. He has taught an array of courses including, Introduction to Sociology; Race and Ethnicity; Courtship and Marriage, as well as others. He is interested in the green movement and has just developed a course that combines sociology with the Green Revolution. He is a dedicated believer that one's desire and passion for education will produce a positive outcome.

Ron Penton Sr. is the Associate Professor of Sociology at Gulf Coast State College where he has managed the Sociology and Social Work programs for 23 years. He currently serves as the Region 1 Director for the Association of Florida Colleges. A retired Air Force Captain, he served 11 and a half years in the Far East, including a tour in Viet Nam. He is a proud Community College graduate and has earned degrees from the University of Maryland, Pepperdine University. His also did post-graduate work in Organizational Leadership and Multi-Cultural Diversity. He advocates for political, religious, and moral tolerance and firmly believes that if the more than 325 million Americans were genuinely socially integrated and woven into the fabric of our communities...the World Trade Center would still be standing. When not in the classroom or advising, he writes, spends time with his wife and grandchildren and plays golf.

Roy Silver has been a Professor of Sociology at Southeast Kentucky Community and Technical College since 1989. He has a Ph.D. in Educational Theory and Sociological Foundations of Education from the University of Toledo and a Master of Arts in Urban Studies from Queens College, City University of New York. Besides authoring chapters for books and writing journal articles, he has had numerous guest editorials published in newspapers. He is active in a number of community development initiatives and many grassroots citizen groups. Professor Silver and his wife Elaine Conradi–a professional potter and artist–live with their dog, Buddy, in Benham, Kentucky. Benham is nestled at the foot of Black Mountain, the tallest mountain in Kentucky. This Harlan County community is found in the heart of the Central Appalachian coal fields.

Brief Contents

Table of Contents

Preface

The time has come for the seventh edition of *Everyday Sociology*. Our primary goal in writing the original script was to create a student-oriented text—one that was concise, informative, and intriguing to read. From all of the comments from students and professors over the years who have read *Everyday Sociology*, we believe that we have achieved our goal. For that we are thankful and encouraged to continue our work. However, that said, we understand that you might be thinking, "That's nice. Now tell me why I have to take this course?" This is a very interesting question and one we would like to address before you begin your work with us.

Like most students you have signed up for a great number of classes to complete your degree. If you are in the norm, you have no intentions of becoming a sociologist. This class simply fills one of your social science requirements. Believe it or not, that's ok with us; we're sociologists, we welcome diversity. But of course, you may wonder why you have to take courses that are not in your major. We cannot speak for each and every course, but in terms of sociology, we feel that this could well be one of the most important, if not the most important, non-major courses of your college career. Now you may think that we're "tooting our own horn" here but we do have our reasons for saying this. First, by taking this course you will learn about the society in which you live. This is important because although most people think they know about society, they in fact, have very little understanding of how it *really* works. How is it possible? Simple. The very fact that we live in society blinds us to its reality. We become so familiar with our social environment and our way of doing things that we fail to see what's going on. We accept, and in doing so, fail to "see the forest for the trees," as the proverbial expression goes. To this you could respond, "So what—I'm getting along just fine." This, of course, is a half-truth. As we know, everyone has problems in life, some are small and some are big. But nobody, and we do mean nobody, goes through life without problems. And problems, as we know, are like the Cheerios in your cereal bowl—you keep pushing them down and they keep popping back up! Now, taking this course isn't going to solve the Cheerio dilemma but it will help you to better understand life's problems and by understanding them you will be better equipped to solve them.

This brings us to our second reason this course in so important. As you will soon learn, we are a product of our environment. Unlike other of life's creatures, humans are ill-equipped in the instinct department. Who we are and what we become is largely a matter of socialization. This raises the question of how free are we? The answer to this varies. As you might guess, some people are more in control of their lives than others. Why? Because some people are more knowledgeable. Knowledge is power. In taking this course (and reading *Everyday Sociology*) you are going to gain new insights and, in turn, these insights will lead to more choices. This is what freedom is all about!

The third reason sociology is important is that it can lead to a happier, more fulfilling life. Unfortunately, while we gain many great things from our parents and friends, we also end up with some negative baggage. This is not a slam of your family and friends, it's just recognizing that no one is perfect. We all have fears, insecurities, and prejudices. We acquire these at a very young age when we are too vulnerable to think for ourselves. This affects how we see and feel about others. In sociology, we term these negative projections "stereotypes." Stereotypes blind us from the ability to see the beauty in human diversity. Sociology allows us to transcend stereotypes and in doing so it gives us a greater appreciation for our own life and for the lives of those about us. Similarly, sociology provides us with the ability to understand the faults and the destructive behaviors of those who are less fortunate than we are. This is not to say that we should condone destructive behavior in others (and you thought we are just a bunch of "hugs-and-kisses" liberals). We are only suggesting that by understanding the conditions that make people behave destructively, we can more easily move away from blame and focus our attention on solutions. In the end, it will be the solutions and not the blaming that will make this a better world.

Before we rap this up, we need to cover one last topic, namely how to approach this course. Sociology is not a "blow-off" course. As we alluded to earlier, many students already believe they understand the world in which they live. Nothing could be further from the truth. In fact, much of what you think you know is going to be challenged in this book and in class by your professor and other students. Don't be alarmed by this. Take this as an opportunity to open your mind and look at society with an objective eye. This is what we refer to as using your "sociological imagination." Even as professional sociologists, we discover new things about society everyday of our lives. It is for this reason we chose the title "Everyday Sociology" for our text. Our second suggestion comes more in the form of a warning. Sociology deals with some sensitive topics. Throughout this course you will hear and read things that will make you unhappy, even angry. Sorry, but this is the nature of the study of sociology—it's about life and life isn't always hugs and kisses. By forewarning you, it is our hope that you can put aside your anger and learn from the experience. Eventually, someone in class is going to say something they believe to be true but you see as blatantly wrong and offensive. Relax, take a couple of deep breaths and try to remember everyone, including yourself, is a victim of misunderstanding. Try to view the situation as a teaching opportunity, a chance to make a small improvement in the world by sharing your opposing thoughts on the subject. To us, this is what education is all about. We hope you'll join us in this endeavor.

We conclude with this final thought. We know that *Everyday Sociology* is not going to make the *New York Times* top ten list. We confess to being egotists, but even for us there are limits. Likewise, we realize our textbook will never be as sensational as the *National Enquirer* (We did think about telling you that Elvis is alive and well and teaching sociology in Kansas). But we do believe that after reading this book you will know a great deal more about yourself and the world in which you live. Not only will this lead, as we stated earlier, to a sense of empowerment, but a sense of appreciation for the diversity, complexity, and yes, the wonder of life. This is our fondest hope for you this semester. It is the reason we wrote, *Everyday Sociology*.

Part One

Foundations of Sociology

Chapter One: ***Thinking Sociologically***

Chapter Two: ***Social Research Methods***

We live our lives in comfortable patterns. Each day we get up from our beds and begin life anew. We dress, eat our breakfast (one should always eat breakfast), and then hurry out into the world to face a variety of challenges. Along the way we interact with others we meet. After the day is over, we return home to our loved ones, nourish ourselves with dinner, relax, and then head off to bed to start the whole process anew. Rarely, perhaps because we are so busy living life, do we have the opportunity or take the time to analyze what has happened to us throughout our day. We just, as the saying goes, go with the flow.

Hopefully, this will change now that you are enrolled in this course. Throughout this semester we will challenge you to look closely and critically at your life—how you interact with others and how the forces of society help to shape your decisions and as a result, your life. As stated in the preface, this is a challenging and daunting undertaking. But in the end, when you have finished your time with us, we are confident that you will not only be more enlightened, but also better prepared to face life's little (and not so little) ups and downs.

In this section we begin by laying the foundation for our study. We first take a look at exactly what this discipline of sociology is all about. We learn that in many cases the way we think the world works or why we behaved in the manner that we do, might be a bit more complicated than we imagine. We will learn that to truly understand human interaction we must investigate and think in a critical and unbiased fashion. This is what we will refer to as our sociological imagination. Also, we will discover that not all sociologists think alike; so be prepared for ambiguity. Alas, life is not as neat as we would like it to be.

In our second chapter we will consider the tools and methods of the sociologist. We will see that this discipline is a science. As such, our investigations must adhere to scientific principles. In this chapter you will be introduced to the scientific method employed by sociologists in their attempt to explain social interaction.

Copyright: Roger Freedman

Everyday Sociology 7th Edition

Chapter 1

Thinking Sociologically

By all accounts, Hope Wisell was a typical 13-year-old girl just beginning her life as a teenager in the small rural community of Sundance, Florida. Like most girls her age she had group of close friends, was desperately in love with Robert Patterson, the heartthrob in the Twilight movies, of whom she hung a poster on her bedroom wall, loved plants and flowers, and dreamed of a successful career in landscaping.

Life was wonderful for Hope, at least until she made an ill-fated mistake. Smitten by a boy in her class, Hope sent a semi-nude picture of herself over her cell phone to him. Termed "sexting," the practice is a fast-growing craze among many teens today. Studies have shown that almost ten percent of 13 year-old-girls have engaged in sexting. And, fully one in five teenagers have admitted to having engaged in the practice. Unfortunately for Hope, the boy to whom the picture was meant had loaned his phone to a friend who intercepted the message. In a typical juvenile act, the boy then circulated the picture among a group of his own friends who, in turn, relayed it their friends. In a matter of hours, the entire student body was gawking at Hope's body.

Life for Hope quickly turned into a nightmare. Teachers at Beth Shields Middle School noticed the commotion among students, investigated, and alerted school administrators to the picture. Calling in her parents, they informed them that since the school term was at an end, Hope would be suspended for the first week of the new school year. Her parents acted decisively by grounding her and suspending her cell phone privileges. But, the worst was yet to come.

Upon returning to school, Hope was met with a barrage of vicious attacks. Walking the hallways of school, kids openly attacked her by shouting out slurs of whore, slut, and a variety of other sexual obscenities. Her friends rallied around her, encasing her in the middle of the group as they made their way to classes. But they couldn't fully isolate her. As one friend stated for the papers, "she would walk into a class and someone in the class would shout 'here comes the slut!'" As students talked to their parents, word quickly spread through the town about the incident. She soon became a social outcast in her own community. In her journal Hope wrote, "Tons of people are talking about me behind my back."

As the pressure mounted and the attacks grew more openly vicious, Hope began to slip into depression. She finally opened up to her parents about the abuse and bullying she was subjected to at school. In a private meeting with school counselors, it was discovered that Hope had begun cutting herself, a practice some extremely depressed individuals develop to cope with psychological pain. The school's response was to force her to sign a "no-harm contract" in which she promised to talk to an adult if the urge to hurt herself reoccurred. The school did not inform her parents of the contract or the extent to which they believed she was at risk. In her journal the following day she wrote: "I'm done for sure now. I can feel it in my stomach. I'm going to try and strangle myself. I hope it works."

That night, Hope knotted one end of a pink scarf around the canopy of her bed and the other around her neck. Found later in the evening when her mother went up to give her a good night kiss, Hope was rushed to the local hospital where she was pronounced dead (Meacham, 2009).

Picked-up by the media, Hope Wisell's death ignited a national firestorm. Numerous articles were written and local and national talk hosts hit the airwaves with the story. The responses were wide-ranging. Some decried the manner in which Hope was treated by her classmates, school officials, and town citizens, even demanding that criminal proceeding be brought by the state against the offending students and school administrators. Their view was that bullying, especially over the electronic media, was out-of-hand and new laws were needed to protect children from such abuse. Others fiercely opposed the creation of new laws stating that not only would it be an infringement on free speech but an intrusion of government into the private lives of citizens. On a different note, some blamed Hope's parents for their daughter's death suggesting they were negligent in their parental duties. Others castigated Hope herself, even going as far as to state that she, "got what she deserved." Some religious fanatics even went so far as to declare it was God's righteous punishment for Hope's sins.

While on a personal level, sociologists would certainly recognize and empathize with the tragedy of Hope's death, on a professional level they would be concerned with both the personal and structural forces that precipitated the incident as well as the impact of technology on behavior at the individual and group levels. Here are some of the questions they might ask:

- What were Hope's personal beliefs and values and how did she come to possess them? How did they contribute to her actions?
- Did Hope's beliefs and values differ from or were they similar to those of her parents? How about those of her classmates?
- To what social economic class did Hope and her parents belong to?
- Were the religious values of the community a contributing factor to Hope's suicide?
- How similar or different was the social culture of Sundance, Florida from other regions of the country?
- Is bullying a common occurrence in schools?
- What are the characteristics of students most likely to be bullied? What are the characteristics do bullies have in common?
- How successful have anti-bullying programs been?
- Does social or economic class have any influence on which students are most likely to develop into bullies or their victims?
- Do parents of bullies share common characteristics?
- What societal factors have contributed to the rise in sexting among teenagers and what has been the response of the political, social, and religious institutions to bullying and sexting?
- How has the development of new technologies affected social values and beliefs?

As you can see, the interests of sociologists are much broader than the individual or an individual act. Sociologists seek to understand human interaction on a societal level. To do so, they must study the culture and institutions of the society and their relationship to social interaction. Sociologists are interested in the diversity of groups in society and how they interact with each other. Also, sociologists are interested in change and study conditions that allow for change and investigate those conditions that resist change. Although not historians, sociologists seek to understand past cultures as they relate to present-day social interaction. With all of this in mind, we simply define sociology as the scientific and systematic study of society and social interaction.

SOCIOLOGY EVERYWHERE

Characteristics

In thinking about sociology three characteristics stand out. *First*, sociology is a science. As a science it attempts to study the behavior of people and institutions in an unbiased manner. By this we mean that the sociologist must avoid personal involvement in the findings. The studies of the tobacco industry are a good example. In an attempt to convince people that their product was harmless, the tobacco industry employed a number of scientists to conduct experiments. These scientists were very well paid and under pressure to design experiments that concluded that tobacco is harmless. Are you surprised that this is exactly what happened? The results of the studies provided the proof that the tobacco industry needed to disavow any negative consequences associated with smoking. Needless to say, other scientists easily debunked these studies. The point is that the studies were flawed because the researchers were biased.

The *second* characteristic is that sociology must be systematic and utilize scientific principles in its investigations. We have all heard of the scientific method (see Chapter Two). Sociologists use the same methods and tools employed by other social scientists (psychologists, economists, anthropologists, political scientists, etc.). Systematic in their approach, these methods lead to unbiased results that can be duplicated by other sociologists. The ability to duplicate research and then to reach the same conclusions is a crucial requirement of scientific research.

Our *third* characteristic is that sociology is concerned with behavior on a larger scale than that of the individual. In fact, it is this characteristic that distinguishes sociology from psychology. Psychologists are interested in individual behavior: what motivates individuals, what produces abnormal behavior, and how to change behavior and treat abnormalities. Sociologists, on the other hand, are interested in group behavior. Keep in mind, however, that all of the social science disciplines intersect to some extent and draw upon the theories and works of each other. For example, one might think that suicide is the domain of psychologists, right? Not necessarily. Emile Durkheim, a famous sociologist, carefully detailed a sociological explanation for why individuals choose to take their lives. Likewise, one might consider political power the exclusive domain of political scientists. But again, sociologists have made important contributions by implicating societal forces such as class, race, sex, and religion in the formation of governmental institutions and the exercise of political power.

Two categories of social research exist to study group behavior and trends. Investigation at the **micro level** concerns direct interaction of individuals such as family, friends, coworkers, and students. Studies designed for the **macro level** center on larger arenas, including institutions, culture, cross-cultural comparison, and global issues.

Who is a Sociologist?

This is an interesting question. The fact is that all of us are sociologists to some extent. Have you ever gone to a party, a game, or some other event, not so much because you were interested in the activity but rather because you enjoy watching people? People-watching is perhaps the most common and most enjoyable of all human pastimes. And when you watch people, do you not make comparisons and draw conclusions? Also, how many times when you were growing-up did your mother or father say to you, "If you hang around with those kids, you're gonna be just like them!"? Would it surprise you that this is a major sociological concept? Edwin H. Sutherland and Donald R. Ressey, in studying criminal behavior, devised a theory termed "differential association" that incorporated much of your parent's warning. See, your parents were sociologists and didn't even know it! To them, it was just **common sense.**

This issue of common sense is an interesting one for sociologists and other scientists. Exactly how much of our observations and conclusions are just a matter of common sense? First, let's define what we mean by common sense. Almost daily we hear someone express that, "it's just a matter of common sense," or they speculate that the reason your friend got into trouble is because he/she lacks common sense. What we mean by this is that common sense is a way of seeing and understanding the obvious. So we ask, is this what sociology is all about — seeing and understanding the obvious? Unfortunately, the answer to the question is no.

While common sense is important in everyday decision-making, it can be a fatal error in sociological investigations. Let's look at a couple of examples. First, would you consider it a matter of common sense to say that if you expanded sex education classes and distributed condoms to teenagers it would result in an increase of sexual activity? Or, what if the society suddenly decided to legalize all drugs and distribute them free of charge? Wouldn't the number of drug addicts increase? Take a moment to think about this. What would your answers be? Sociologists have surveyed people and found that they generally agree that sexual activity and drug addiction would increase. However, scientific investigations of other societies who did precisely that, such as the Dutch, found that sexual activity and drug addition declined.

What this means is that sociology is more than stating the obvious; it is more than common sense. In fact, we take many things for granted as being obvious that, in fact, are not. This is what the science of sociology is all about—investigating human interaction from an unbiased point of view, discovering new information, and then using this information to improve our lives and the society we live in. This is precisely the point of studying sociology: to provide you with the tools and means to look at your life and that of others in a new light.

Divergence of Sociological Thought

Many students beginning their study of sociology are surprised to find how much disagreement there is among sociologists. In fact, after finishing this course, some students confess that they are more confused about society and social issues then when they started it. As the writers of your text, we have to admit that this is one of the pitfalls of our discipline. However, it is certainly not a lethal one and, perhaps, not even a bad one.

First, before beginning your study of sociology, you should keep in mind that the social and natural sciences are similar, yet different. Unlike the natural sciences, sociologists do not have instruments that provide an absolute measurement of the phenomenon we are studying. For example, the physicist investigating the relationship between force and speed has a host of instruments capable of providing accurate measures. From these measurements the physicist can then provide definitive answers to the relationship between the two variables. Furthermore, under exactly the same conditions, the results will never vary. For social scientists studying human behavior and interaction, no instruments exist that can provide absolute answers. So, how do we approach the study of human behavior? Like all scientists, we collect and analyze data from a variety of sources like observations, interviews, surveys, and others. From this data, theoretical perspectives are developed. The perspectives are, in essence, models that allow us to generalize and make predictions. However, since behavior is so complex and difficult to interpret, it is only natural that disagreement will exist as to what the data means. This, of course, leads to the development of different perspectives and theories.

A *second* problem of studying sociology is that many students approach the discipline with a **belief system** firmly entrenched. For nearly two decades (more for older members of the class), students have lived in families and communities. They have associated with a wide range of people; they have worked, played—lived. Their socialization experiences and observations of others have led them to conclusions they accept as fact. For the discipline of sociology this is a problem. As one sociologist so aptly notes:

> Deeply immersed in our daily routines, though, we hardly ever pause to think about the meaning of what we have gone through; even less often have we the opportunity to compare our private experience with the fate of others, to see the *social* in the individual, the *general* in the *particular*; this is precisely what sociologists can do for us (Bauman, 1990).

A *third* problem students face with the study of sociology is dealing with their own emotions as they discover that what they have always accepted as right and orderly may, in fact, be less than right and orderly and often be just plain wrong and disorderly. Nothing is as threatening as having the foundations of our belief system questioned. For if we suddenly discover that what we thought was right, is in fact, wrong, what do we replace it with? While we admit that this can be frightening, we also offer that it can be exhilarating, challenging, and an opportunity to rethink your life. It is with this thought in mind that we ask you to begin your study of sociology.

ORIGINS AND EVOLUTION OF SOCIOLOGY

Curiosity is a natural trait of human beings. As we pass through our lives we see things and wonder about their cause. Since the beginning of our species, humans have speculated about natural events in their lives. For most of history, mysticism and religion were used to explain the seemingly unexplainable. Slowly, and in many cases with great resistance, science began to replace traditional religious explanations for the world and its creation and evolution. This is also true of the study of human behavior. In the section below we review some early scientists who made major contributions to the discipline of sociology.

Abdel Rahman Ibn-Khaldun (1332-1406). Abd al-Rahman Ibn Mohammad is generally known as Ibn Khaldun. His parents, originally Yemenite Muslim Arabs, had settled in Spain, but after the fall of Seville, had migrated to Tunisia. He was born in Tunisia, where he received his early education and where, still in his teens, he entered the service of the Egyptian ruler Sultan Barquq. His thirst for advanced knowledge and a better academic setting soon made him leave this service and migrate to Fez. This turbulent political period also included a three-year refuge in a small village in Algeria, which provided him with the opportunity to write *Muqaddimah*, the first volume of his world history that won him an immortal place among historians, sociologists and philosophers. The uncertainty of his career still continued, with Egypt becoming his final abode where he spent his last 24 years. Here he lived a life of fame and respect, marked by his appointment as the Chief Malakite Judge and lecturing at *Al-Azhar* University.

Ibn Khaldun's chief contribution lies in philosophy of history and sociology. He sought to write a world history aimed at an analysis of historical events. This volume, commonly known as *Muqaddimah* or 'Prolegomena', was based on Ibn Khaldun's unique approach and original contribution and became a masterpiece in literature on philosophy of history and sociology. The chief concern of this monumental work was to identify psychological, economic, environmental and social facts that contribute to the advancement of human civilization and the currents of history. In this context, he analyzed the dynamics of group relationships and showed how group-feelings, *al-'Asabiyya*, give rise to the ascent of a new civilization and political power. He identified an almost rhythmic repetition of rise and fall in human civilization, and analyzed factors contributing to it. His contribution to history is marked by the fact that, unlike earlier writers interpreting history largely in a political context, he emphasized environmental, sociological, psychological and economic factors governing the apparent events. This revolutionized the science of history and also laid the foundation of *Umraniyat* (sociology).

Auguste Comte (1798-1859). Frenchman, Auguste Comte, coined the word sociology. Considered by many to be the father of modern sociology, he established a new line of thought that greatly influenced the thinking and direction of future sociologists. Comte's main contribution to the field of sociology was his recognition that society contained two equal and opposing forces. The first, which he termed **social statics**, sought to maintain the existing status quo (that which currently exists). The second, he called **social dynamics**, the forces for change and conflict. The importance of the recognition of these two diametrically opposed forces is seen today in that contemporary sociologists have a tendency to fall into one of two perspectives in explaining human interaction: those stressing the forces for stability (structural functional perspective), and those who emphasize the forces for change (social conflict perspective). As you will soon see, the disagreement between the structural functional perspective and the social conflict perspective dominates not only the discussion in this book, but all of sociology. As such, it is imperative that you work hard very early in your study of sociology to grasp the basic positions and arguments of both perspectives.

Auguste Comte (1789-1857) The theorist who coined the term sociology.

For Comte, the responsibility of the sociologist was greater than just gaining knowledge for its own sake. Deeply involved in the turbulence of his time, he believed that the knowledge gained from the study of sociology could be used to equip people with the ability to build better societies and improve the human condition.

Harriet Martineau (1802-1876). Harriet Martineau was a British sociologist and a woman in a male-dominated field. As such, she received little recognition during her time even though she made many early contributions to the field of sociology. Many scholars today would argue that her place in sociology should be that of a founding member of the discipline.

Like many of her contemporaries, Martineau was very much interested in the consequences of industrialization and capitalism. In her works, she paid particular attention to social distinctions based on class, gender, and race. Throughout her writings she advocated racial and gender equality. She argued vehemently that a better society could be created if racial and gender barriers were removed. Although passionate in her views, she was committed to creating a science of sociology grounded on impartial, empirical research. To the end of her life, she remained convinced that sociology, the "true science of human nature," would replace ignorance and prejudice to create a better society for all.

Karl Marx (1818-1883). Karl Marx was an economist and political philosopher as well as a sociologist. It would be fair to say that no single individual has had a more profound affect on world politics, as did Marx. Although Marx might not have considered himself a sociologist, he has greatly influenced the discipline and scores of social thinkers.

Karl Marx. Foremost intellectual social thinker of his time, believed that the conflict between the capitalist and the working class was the driving force in modern industrial society.

Marx was born and educated in Germany where he was awarded a doctorate of philosophy, no small achievement in the German University system. Like Comte, and later Durkheim, Marx sought to change the condition of society for the better. However, as his views evolved he quickly found himself at odds with the political elite and was forced into exile. After a brief stay in France, where more trouble developed, he landed in England and remained there until his death.

Like Comte and Durkheim, Marx was profoundly influenced by the turbulence of the Industrial Revolution. Where Comte and Durkheim saw elements of common interest and cooperation, Marx saw only discord and exploitation. It was this that ultimately led to his economic theme in which he saw the entirety of society being shaped by a class conflict between the **bourgeoisie** (owners) and the **proletariat** (workers). The bourgeoisie owned the means of production (what is needed to produce goods to be sold) and the proletariat supplied the necessary labor to produce those goods. The very nature of capitalism - that of intense competition - forced the bourgeoisie to maximize profits to remain competitive in the marketplace. This in turn inevitably led to exploitation of workers. Thus, while the bourgeoisie lived in splendor, workers lived in squalor. Additionally, Marx identified yet another source of discontent for proletariats, that of **alienation** from their work. Prior to the Industrial Revolution, workers were highly skilled craftsmen who took pride in starting and finishing a product. With the advent of the assembly line, this was no longer possible. This, Marx claimed, robbed the workers of their creativity and imagination and ultimately, led to despair.

Why did the workers accept this arrangement? Marx attributed it to **false consciousness**, a process whereby the worker is led to believe that his/her share in life is the outcome of a just and fair competitive system—capitalism. However, Marx pointed out, it was only a matter of time before the competitive, dog-eat-dog condition of the marketplace would place work-

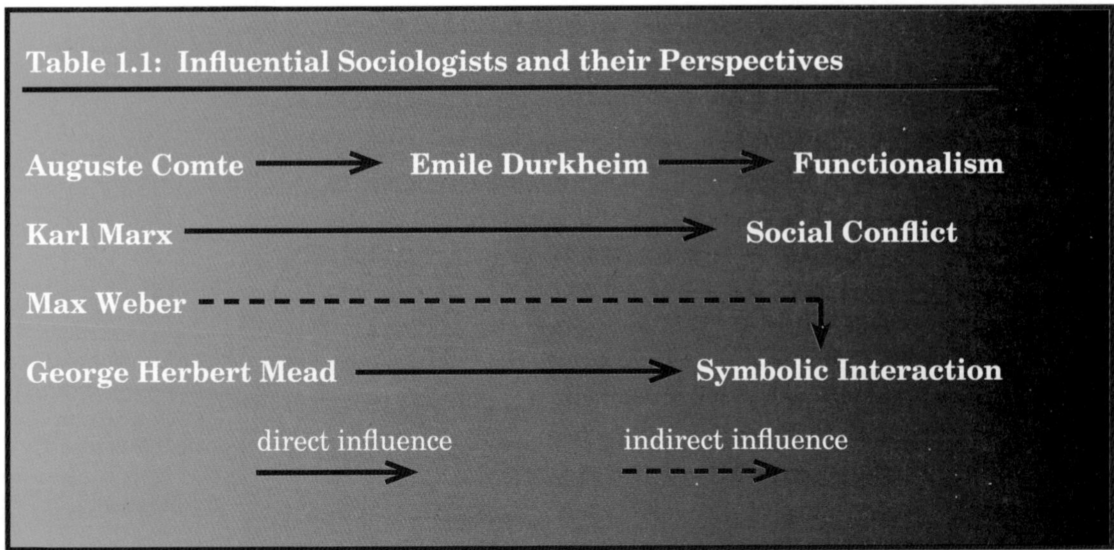

ers in such deplorable conditions that they would rise up in rebellion and take control of the society. After a brief period of time in what he termed would be the **dictatorship of the proletariat**, the workers would create a classless society characterized by harmony and equality.

The above is a major source of difference between the theories of Marx and his contemporaries. For Comte and Durkheim, ideas and values were the driving force of change in the human condition. Marx rejected this. He believed that social change was dictated by economic forces and that this held true for all values and social institutions as well—all flowed from the economy. He termed his theory **historical materialism**.

Emile Durkheim (1858-1917). This famous Frenchman drew heavily on the works of Auguste Comte. Durkheim's criticism of Comte's work, however, was that it was too vague and relied too heavily on speculation. Durkheim believed that sociology needed to align itself more with the scientific methods of the natural sciences. He was the first to carry out an investigation utilizing a large-scale collection of data. Many sociologists consider him to be the first social researcher.

In one of the first classical sociological studies, Durkheim undertook the examination of suicide. Drawing on data available to him at the time, he noticed that a higher percentage of French Protestants committed suicide than did their Roman Catholic counterparts. He attributed this to the stronger social bonds of Catholics that provided them with a sense of attachment to the community and to God. He noticed, however, that suicide increased among Catholics if they lived in parts of France dominated by Protestants. Eventually, he concluded that suicide was more influenced by social structure than by religion. The importance of this study demonstrated the power of statistical analysis of **structural effects**. In other words, variations in human behavior could be linked to the larger social structure and were not always simply a matter of individual differences.

Durkheim was also instrumental in the development of the concept of **social solidarity**—the bonds that unite society. In his classical work, *The Division of Labor in Society* (1964; orig. 1883), Durkheim described the importance of shared beliefs to the harmonious operation of society. In smaller societies, he maintained, this was accomplished through **collective conscience** in which the group shared common values, outlooks, interpretations of events, languages and dialects, and in general, identical ways of thinking that characterized pre-industrial societies. This he termed **mechanical solidarity**, defined as strong social ties and shared values that are based in common beliefs. Of course, in modern, more complex societies this is not possible. Yet modern societies do hold together and function somewhat smoothly. What holds these societies together? According to Durkheim it is a commonly held universal that survival depends upon cooperation.

With modern society came the division of labor where each member of the society performed a specialized task; no one was self-sufficient. As such, cooperation was necessary for the good of society. This he defined as **organic solidarity**—social ties based on a functional interdependence of the members of society. Durkheim recognized division of labor as a unifying force for society and regarded organic solidarity as less desirable than mechanical solidarity. He believed that organic solidarity was less personal and could in extreme cases, lead to a condition he termed **anomie**, a state of normlessness characterized by the loss of a sense of meaning and detachment from others in the society. Durkheim identified anomie as a major source of social unrest and pathological behavior.

Max Weber (1864-1920). Max Weber (pronounced "Vayber") is similar to Karl Marx in that his interests extended beyond the boundaries of sociology. Born and educated in Germany, he devoted his life to the academic world of ideas and writing.

Like Marx, he was interested in capitalism and government. However, he rejected the basic Marxist thesis that all social structure flowed from the economy. For Weber, cultural ideas and values were the driving force in shaping society, its institutions, and individual behavior. Central to this proposition was his work on religion. In his comparative study of world religions, Weber postulated that the ideas inherent to Christian thought in general, and to the Protestant in particular, were instrumental in the development and spread of capitalism in the West. This stands in direct contradiction to Marx's assertion that capitalism emerged solely from changes in the economy.

Likewise, while Marx stressed alienation, Weber emphasized **rationality**, a process whereby traditional thinking (craftsmanship) was replaced by thinking dominated by efficiency, self-control, and effectiveness in goal accomplishment. For Weber, this was an inevitable outcome of capitalism. He recognized that although the capitalistic mode of production certainly was a more efficient way to produce goods, it also had costs. For instance, with the development of capitalism came the expansive bureaucracies and bigger governments that tended to weaken traditional links between individuals and create more reliance on the state, a desirable goal for the bureaucracy but diminishing to the role of individuals.

George Simmel (1858-1918). George Simmel (pronounced ZIM-mel) was a German sociologist who lived and worked during the same time as Emile Durkheim. Simmel's main contribution to sociology was an examination and description of social interaction in groups. It was Simmel who first noted that patterned social interaction was very much influenced by the size of the group. The smallest group he termed a **dyad**—a group containing only two members. Social interaction changed significantly by adding another member. This, he termed a **triad**—a three member group. As the group continued to include more members, patterned social interaction changed.

In addition to his work on groups, Simmel was very much interested in the impact of industrialization and urbanization on social interaction. He noted that as industrialization increased, so did class conflict. Additionally, urbanization brought about more individualism at a cost to group cohesion.

In his important work, *The Philosophy of Money* (1890-1907), Simmel was the first to note the disruptive nature of consumerism. In industrialized societies, money became an end in itself. People became excessively indulgent to the point of losing sight of what really mattered. Everything and everyone had a price. This attitude resulted in the loosening of social bonds between individual members and between groups in society.

SOCIOLOGY IN THE UNITED STATES

Sociology spread from Europe to the United States in the 1890s. The first department of sociology was established at the University of Chicago. Later other departments of sociology would surface at other universities. Listed below are a few of the early American pioneers of sociology.

Robert E. Parks and Albion Small. Albion Small (1854-1926) founded the first department of sociology at the University of Chicago. Although he did his graduate work in Germany, he returned to the United States and became an influential force in American sociology with the publication of his book, *An Introduction to the Science of Sociology* in 1890. He also founded *The American Journal of Sociology* and edited it from 1895 to 1925. Robert E. Parks (1868-1963) was a member of the University of Chicago faculty, which created the American Sociological Society. Parks was primarily interested in the discord and disintegrating effect that urbanization had on social integration. He blamed urbanization for increasing crime rates, as well as racial and class strife, which in turn contributed to segregation and isolation of neighborhoods in the community.

Jane Addams (1860-1935). Best know for the founding of the Hull House, a settlement house for the poor, Jane Addams is the perhaps the best known early woman sociologist. In the course of her life, she authored eleven books and hundreds of articles, some of which were published in the American Journal of Sociology. Throughout her career, she was actively engaged in sociological endeavors. Her most scholarly work came with the publication of *Hull House Maps and Papers* (1893), an award winning publication that provided the framework for a methodological technique employed by sociologists for the next forty years. Despite all her accomplishments, she was never appointed to a permanent university teaching position even though the Hull House was extensively used by sociology professors for their work at the University of Chicago. For her work with the poor, Jane Addams was awarded the Nobel Peace Prize.

Jane Addams utilized her knowledge of society to help the poor. She also played a major role in the struggle for women's rights.

George Herbert Mead (1863-1931). Although he was a social psychologist, George Herbert Mead made important contributions to sociology, particularly in the area of socialization. Both of Mead's parents were academics. His mother served as president of Mount Holyoke College and his father taught at several colleges. At an early age Mead rebelled, rejecting his parents strong religious values. After completing college he traveled extensively throughout the Northwest while educating himself on a variety of subjects. He finally settled upon philosophy and enrolled in Harvard to complete his training. He accepted a teaching position first at the University of Michigan and later moved to the University of Chicago where he stayed until his death. Mead's most important contribution was to the body of knowledge regarding the development of self. Mead rejected the work of contemporary psychologists that emphasized the role of biology in personality formation. Instead, he centered his thinking on society, insisting that a concept of self develops only through social interaction. In turn, social interaction is made possible by our correct interpretation of symbols such as words, gestures, body language, and so forth (see Chapter Four). George Herbert Mead is considered the founder of the symbolic interaction perspective.

An interesting note on Mead that many students might identify with is that he detested writing. So, although he did publish some journal articles, he never authored a complete collection of his work. It was only after his death that his students, through his lecture notes and their own notes, published an extensive account of his work.

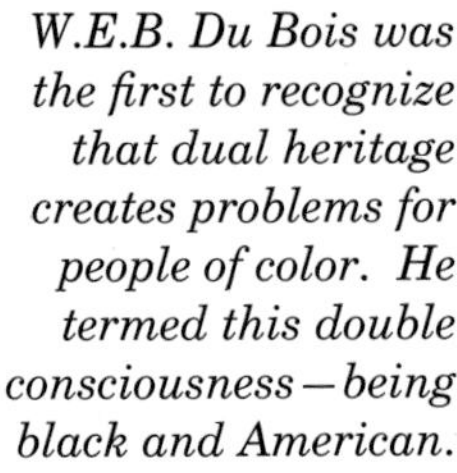

W.E.B. Du Bois was the first to recognize that dual heritage creates problems for people of color. He termed this double consciousness—being black and American.

W. E. B. Du Bois (1868-1963). W. E. B. Du Bois was the first African American to receive a Ph.D. from Harvard. Du Bois authored more than 20 books and more than a hundred scholarly articles. However, due to his race he was largely excluded from the inner circle of influential sociologists of his time. Even his most scholarly and important work, *The Philadelphia Negro* (1899), was ignored and not reviewed in the American Journal of Sociology. W. E. B. Du Bois is credited with establishing the second department of sociology in the U.S. at Atlanta University. From 1896 through 1914, Du Bois published one book based on his sociological research each year. He was one of the first to recognize the conflict that dual heritage creates for people of color. Early in his career, he espoused the virtues of scientific research and believed that through knowledge prejudice and discrimination would be eradicated. However, disillusioned with the pace of progress, he chose direct action and founded the National Association for the Advancement of Colored People (NAACP). By the time of the Civil Rights Movement, when race relations began to improve, Du Bois had immigrated to Ghana and committed his hopes for racial equality to Marxian movements.

Talcott Parsons and Robert Merton. Talcott Parsons (1902-1979) is regarded as one of the most influential contemporary structural functionalists. He perceived the family as being the most important institution required for the survival of society. Within the family he studied the usefulness of the division of labor between husband and wife. For Parsons, the husband performed the instrumental role of providing for the physical and economic needs, while the wife's main duty was that of taking the expressive role, of taking care of the home and family. According to Parsons, this division of labor was necessary for the smooth functioning of the family. The role of all other institutions, insisted Parsons, was to assist the family in carrying out its function.

Robert Merton (1910-2003) is another researcher identified with structural functionalism. His wide range of studies on voting behavior, public opinion, reference groups, deviance, and technology helped to substantiate the position of structural functionalism among American sociologists. Merton believes that all human action has two separate but equally important consequences. **Manifest consequences** are those intended to be produced by the initiator of the action. **Latent consequences** are those unintended, but equally important. He argued that not all action produces positive outcomes. In some cases, a **dysfunctional consequence** is produced that weakens social bonds and produces a negative societal effect.

C. Wright Mills was instrumental in developing contemporary social conflict theory.

C. Wright Mills (1916-1962). C. Wright Mills is commonly identified with the social conflict perspective. In characterizing himself, Mills stated that he was just "a plain Marxist." He is commonly identified with the concept of sociological imagination discussed later in this chapter. Mills chief concern was the injustice he saw in the American social and political system. Two of his most influential studies concerned a critical analysis of the "white collar" profession who Mills regarded as a new and powerful social class, and the "power elite" a small collection of powerful businessmen, politicians, and military leaders who he believed ran the country for their own self-interest. Because of his views, Mills was essentially an outcast of the profession for most of his career.

SOCIOLOGICAL PERSPECTIVES

Two major points are apparent from the above discussion. *First*, the study of sociology is not an easy undertaking. The questions asked and the data obtained are tangled, complex, and multidimensional (affected by many different variables). *Second*, once gathered, the data are open to interpretation. Therefore, it is easy to understand why sociologists often disagree. In order to provide some direction for their work, sociologists have constructed paradigms, or an overall view of their interpretation of how the world works. The paradigms then, become an umbrella under which a wide number of related theories could fit. However, rather than paradigms, we will use the word perspectives because it is more common in our everyday usage. Here we will discuss three overall perspectives: structural functional, social conflict, and symbolic interaction.

Before beginning, let's take a look at a couple of scenarios that may help us to visualize the differences between theories so that we can draw sharper comparisons.

Scenario One: Try to visualize a chemistry class you've taken in the past, perhaps high school. One day your instructor walks in with a set of tinker toys, the ones you used to play with as a child. His set contains a multitude of different colored balls and sticks to which the balls attach. Beginning to attach balls to sticks, he proceeds to explain how each color represents a different atom, and the combination of colored balls, a compound. Sound familiar? The next step, the most important in his discussion, is to explain how one atom is *bonded* to another. This, of course, has to do with neutrons, protons, and electrons. The relationship between each is the cohesive glue binding the molecule together.

Molecules then come together to form compounds that, in turn, make up the world. Interesting stuff, huh? Well sociologists have a parallel, but similar, interest. Society is made up of many different groups (like the multi-colored balls in the tinker toy set). As we already know, these groups form society. True, but what is the cohesive glue (sticks in the tinker toy set) that binds very different groups together?

Scenario Two: Let's use the example of a classroom altercation that a teacher once relayed to a number of his colleagues. At the beginning of class this particular professor held a pop quiz. Just love 'em, don't you? A few minutes after the quiz was over, a student walked in late. Having taken his seat, he discovered from another student that a quiz had been given. He raised his hand and asked to take the quiz. The professor refused, citing the student's tardiness. The student protested. In defense, the professor stated that it was a rule of the class that students who arrived late would not be given the quiz, and furthermore, it was important for the student to learn to be on time. Again, the student protested, only this time he accused the instructor of being heavy handed and a power-monger. Patiently, the professor pointed out that being on time was important for all the students so that the educational process wouldn't be interrupted. The student became belligerent. Challenging the professors' premise, the student stated that none of the students were in class because of education. They were only present because they were forced into the class so that they could get the degree that allowed them to get the job they wanted. On this note the professor instructed the student to leave class and return only when he could abide by the rules.

Now we are ready for our discussion.

Structural Functional Perspective

As we have just read, Comte and Durkheim were the first structural functionalists. Unlike smaller, homogeneous societies held together by a common belief system, modern industrial societies are larger and diverse. Many different groups coexist and although they may share some values, they find themselves distinguished from others in many different ways such as religion, ethnicity, race, gender, class, occupation, education, and geography. So what (as asked by scenario one) is the bond that holds the various groups together? The answer given by structural functionalists is the division of labor. In industrial society, work is specialized; no one individual is self-sufficient. To survive, one must rely upon others to perform specialized tasks needed by the society to survive. Cooperation is necessary for survival. Cooperation binds different groups together. Structural functionalists extend this line of reasoning to the institutions of society. Overall, certain functions must be performed if the society is to continue.

Each institution created by society is designed to carry out a specialized function. In turn, if society is to function properly, each institution must cooperate with others.

In our second scenario, structural functionalists would side with the professor. Again, go back to the division of labor. People are not born with knowledge they acquire it. Educational institutions are a means by which society meets its demand for a source of individuals with the knowledge and skill to perform a variety of needed functions. Without schools, do you think society could survive? So, although students rarely complain when the professor cancels class, they do recognize that it is important to receive an education so that they can obtain future work. On the other side of the coin, the professor recognizes that his future survival depends upon the students in his class obtaining the education they desire so that they may replace workers who retire or die. The process is mutually reciprocal. Thus, structural functionalists stress cooperation and harmony. The different parts of society are complementary and highly integrated. Thus, society is stable.

Several terms are associated with structural functionalism. The first is the **manifest consequences**. This is an *intended* consequence of an action. The opposite is a **dysfunction**. This action produces an unintended consequence. The last one is a **latent consequences**, also unintended, and rarely recognized or acknowledged by those subjected to it. To illustrate the three, let's return to our second scenario. When the professor kicked the student out of class, he did so with the intended goal of reforming the student. He hoped the student would think about his behavior, see the error of his way, return to class on time and be ready to work hard. This would be the manifest function. But let us say that instead, the student became angry, dropped out of school, couldn't find a job and ended up on welfare. Certainly this is not what was supposed to happen. As such, it would be unintended and an example of a dysfunctional consequence. Similarly, the latent function would apply to the other class members. Having witnessed the altercation and the action taken against the student, other members of the class are reaffirmed in their belief in the value of the prevailing social order. Although unintended, it is a powerful source of societal integration.

Critical Evaluation

Critics of the structural functionalist perspective maintain that it over-emphasizes the integrative role of human interaction. In its attempt to explain the cooperative relations between groups, critics claim that it fails to take into account divisions of social class, race, ethnicity and gender. The concept of stability is over-valued and the role of conflict is neglected. By embracing the concepts of stability and integration of group interactions, institutions, which often play a major role in influencing human behavior, are allowed off the hook of critical analysis. Consequently, this lends a conservative tone to interpretations of the social order.

Dressed in the garb of a previous generation of women, two sisters express their support for equality. From your reading, which perspective would you use to interpret their action?

Photo: baaker2009.

Social Conflict Perspective

While social conflict theorists can trace their roots back many centuries, Karl Marx is credited with attributing it to modern society. Later, other conflict theorists would deviate from the thinking of Marx to establish new branches of this perspective. Two such theorists were C. Wright Mills (1916-1962) and Ralf Dahrendorf (1929-2009).

Where structural functionalists argue for cooperation, harmony and integration, social conflict theorists maintain the opposite. Like structural functionalists they recognize the importance of the division of labor as well as the diversity of group membership in society. But this is where the similarity ends. In answer to the question poised in our first scenario, social conflict theorists would answer that the bond uniting the various groups in society is not cooperation, but **power**.

Different groups in society have conflicting interests. The conflict between groups is intensified as they compete for the scarce resources available to satisfy physical and human needs. In this competitive arena, some groups are able to gain power over other groups and place themselves in a better position to capture more of the resources. Once in a position of power, these groups attempt to consolidate power through structuring the institutions of society so as to maintain the **status quo**—the existing power structures. It is this struggle that ultimately produces the shape of society. Those without power find themselves capitulating to the demands of the powerful and that, in essence, is the bond holding the various groups together.

Turning to our second scenario, the social conflict theorists would more than likely side with the student. Schools, they maintain, like all of society's institutions are designed to perpetuate the advantage of the powerful. A strong correlation exists between occupational status and income. The higher the status of the occupation, the more likely it is to have high income. However, entry into higher status occupations requires baccalaureate and post-baccalaureate degrees. There is also evidence that attending a prestigious university increases one's chance to obtain and succeed in a higher status occupation. In other words, attending Harvard might reap more benefits than enrolling in the local four-year state university. One can now ask, who is most likely to attend college—children of the poor or of the affluent? Who is most likely to attend a prestigious college? As we shall see later in this text, the answer to the above questions lead one to conclude that for the affluent, education is a springboard to success. For the poor, it is a major obstacle in their path to upward social mobility. Finally, we ask the question—was the student in our example right when he stated that the other students were in class not because they were interested in learning, but rather, in getting a job? If you suddenly discovered that you were not getting academic credit for your sociology class, would you still come just to learn? Dare we ask?

Critical Evaluation

Critics of social conflict theory charge the perspective with being biased and lacking a scientific objectivity. In its quest to explain power struggles in society, theorists of this perspective immerse themselves in political contests to advocate policy decision. This leads to a natural bias of choosing sides.

A *second* criticism is that the social conflict theorist ignores the integrative nature of human interaction. Not all social interaction is a vicious struggle between groups. If so, society would not survive—but it does, with evidence of cooperation, integration, and unity.

A *third* criticism, leveled at both of the above perspectives, is that they center all attention on the broader aspects of social interaction such as group membership, interaction, and institutional structure. The role of the individual is never considered at its most basic, one-on-one interactive level. Do not these exchanges and outcomes affect the shape of society?

Symbolic Interaction Perspective

Whereas our two previous perspectives took a macro level view, the symbolic interaction perspective is micro level oriented. While the structural functionalists and conflict theorists ask questions about societies, institutions and the interactions of groups, a symbolic interactionalist focuses on the patterns of interactions of individuals in specific social situations.

The symbolic interaction perspective is rooted in the belief that both the individual and the entirety of society is the collective sum of human interaction based on language and other symbols. A **symbol** is defined here as something having cultural significance and thereby the capacity to elicit

A Cambodian boy gives the peace sign as he bikes home. Symbolic interactionalists insist that understanding symbols is the key to interpreting human behavior. To understand the larger society and its institutions, they maintain, you must first understand all symbols within the society.

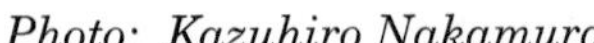

Photo: Kazuhiro Nakamura

a meaningful response. The range of symbols in human interaction runs the gamut from language (both verbal and nonverbal gestures) to physical objects.

Three important assumptions dominate symbolic interactionalist theory:

1. Individuals respond to "things" (actions, objects, other individuals, language, etc.) based upon the meaning they impart to it.

2. The meaning imparted to it is not inherent to the thing, but rather to the individual interpreting it.

3. The meaning of any one thing to an individual varies upon the time and the circumstance under which it is interpreted.

Seen in this light, to understand social interaction requires that the sociologist first understand how individuals interpret and define symbols and adjust their behavior accordingly. Understanding this is the key to understanding how millions of individuals weave their lives together and function as a society. To the symbolic interactionalist, understanding society begins with understanding individual interaction. The outcome of interaction is defined by the interpretation of the symbolic; and finally, the larger society and its institutions are the sum total of individual interactions.

An important distinction between this perspective and that of the previous two is that symbolic interactionalists tend to assign more freedom to individual acts. Unlike structural functionalists and conflict theorists who see the individual immersed and controlled by society, class, race, ethnicity, gender, institutional structure and culture, the advocates of this perspective stress that people are in a continual process of changing their social world. Another crucial difference is that symbolic interactionalists are as interested in what individuals think and feel as they are in how they behave.

Table 1.2		Sociological Perspectives	
Perspective	**Orientation**	**Assumptions**	**Societal View**
Structural Functional	**Macro-level**	**Social interaction is highly integrative. Cooperation and consensus form the bonds uniting diverse groups. Institutions exist to perform necessary tasks allowing society to function smoothly**	**Stable** **Social change is gradual and adjustive for the good of society**
Social Conflict	**Macro-level**	**Relations among groups are characterized by intense conflict and inequality. Institutions exist for the benefit of the powerful**	**Unstable** **Change is abrupt and often revolutionary**
Symbolic Interaction	**Micro-level**	**Humans define themselves through social interaction. The basis for interaction is the interpretation of symbols. The sum of human interaction defines society**	**Constantly changing** **The interpretation of symbols defines the outcome of human interaction which, in turn, determines change**

As we did with the two other perspectives, let's return to our two scenarios. In the first, symbolic interactionalists suggest that the bond that binds individuals into groups is a collection of symbols whose interpretative meaning is shared by members of the group. This allows the individuals to interact in a predictive and cooperative way. While it is true that we have many groups in society, it is equally true that there are symbols that are held in common by all groups. For example, the American flag, the national anthem, the language, the geographic outline of the country, a handshake, and so forth are such symbols and their interpretative value is what forms culture and provides the cohesive glue of society.

In our second scenario, symbolic interaction theorists would be particularly interested in the interchange between the student and the instructor. How does the student interpret the role of the instructor? How does the instructor interpret the behavior of the student? The conflict between the two is largely, for these theorists, the result of a disagreement on the purpose of education. Likewise, the student may feel that he is being treated unfairly, whereas the instructor believes that the student must adjust his behavior in order to learn and be successful. Again, the problem centers on a difference in interpretation of symbols. The symbolic interactionalist would also be interested in the outcome. Did the student readjust his behavior? What changes, if any, did the instructor make in his policies? Was the interaction between the two changed following the altercation? In conclusion, from this perspective, to understand society is to understand the interactions between people as well as the symbols that those interactions are a result of.

Critical Evaluation

Since the main function of society is to allow people to interact, the strength of the symbolic interaction perspective is its concentration on individual interactions. However, in its preoccupation with individual interactions, it ignores the important role culture and societal institutions have on social interaction. This is especially true of factors such as class, race, ethnicity and gender. In other words, social interaction is not a one-way process from the bottom up, it also is a top-to-bottom process.

Which Perspective?

By this time you've probably come to an initial conclusion regarding which perspective best fits your view of society and the interactions of those around you. Likewise, if you have carefully considered the assumptions of the other perspectives, you would have to admit that they too, have some merit. While this might be confusing, even disconcerting, it is precisely where you should be. In truth, all perspectives do have merit and no single perspective will answer all questions about society and human interaction. In some cases, the social conflict perspective best describes a particular situation. At other times, a structural functional approach is better suited. And then, in wholly different situations, symbolic interaction may reveal much about social interaction. So, all three perspectives can be complimentary. We therefore suggest a synthesis that combines the best of each perspective. Just as a worker would not carry one tool to a job, the toolbox of the sociologist must be appropriately equipped.

In the following chapters of this text, we have chosen to concentrate predominantly on two perspectives—structural functionalist and social conflict. We do so because these two perspectives, more so than symbolic interaction, dominate the views of sociology. However, upon occasion, we will reach into our toolbox and pull out symbolic interaction and use it where is appropriate.

SOCIOLOGICAL IMAGINATION

C. Wright Mills was the first to use the term **sociological imagination**. Mills described it as a way of thinking that provided individuals with an understanding of the societal forces that shape their lives. For Mills the problem was that we, as humans, tend to be so immersed in our own daily "personal orbits" that we lose track of what is happening in the broader society even though those forces have tremendous consequences in our lives.

According to Mills, by utilizing our sociological imagination we are able to answer the following important questions:

1. How is society presently structured?
2. In what way is society changing and what are the forces producing this change?
3. Where does our personal "biography" fit within the present structure and how will it be affected by the change?

Achieving this knowledge will allow individuals more control over their lives and the forces of society affecting them. In doing so, individuals are less likely to blame themselves for failures made inevitable by outside forces. Certainly this can contribute to our overall well being and healthy self-image. Likewise, the power of such knowledge provides the opportunity to play an important role in the collective effort to affect the direction of change away from the negative to the positive.

This is precisely what this course is about—achieving sociological imagination. However, before we begin, a couple of words of caution: if you take your studies seriously, this course *will* alter your life. Through the succeeding chapters you will learn that many things you thought were true, are either misrepresented or totally false. This may be good, but be aware that knowledge brings change and change can cause discomfort. An often-quoted adage is, "know the truth, and the truth will set you free." Although the truth might indeed set you free, you may have to spend some time "wandering around in the desert" (let's hope that it's not for forty years) before arriving home. The following case is an example:

> A female student, after studying bias and gender roles in a sociology class decided it was unfair that society dictated that the woman would surrender her last name in favor of her husband's. To her it represented one of many ways in which women in the society were disenfranchised, and the dominant patriarchal culture was maintained. Armed with this knowledge she confronted her fiancée. Any guesses as to the outcome? Eventually, the relationship broke up. However, some years later she did marry a man more sympathetic to her concerns and the issue was resolved through compromise (they created a new name for themselves by combining parts from both family names).

The above student also confessed that not only did what she learned in the sociology class affect her relationship with her fiancée; it also changed relationships with other friends, males and females alike. As she so aptly put it, "suddenly the world was different."

Secondly, during this course, you may learn things that will upset you. You will find that things you took for granted as fact, are fiction—and you are the one on the losing end—you are the victim. Another old adage is "ignorance is bliss." Keep in mind that it can also be deadly. This is exemplified in the case of the following student:

> At the age of eleven, the father of this particular student committed suicide. As a result, the student harbored a great deal of hostility toward his father, considering him a loser—a quitter. Through the course, the student began to understand some of the forces that shaped his father's decision: the periods of unemployment, bouts of depression and alcohol abuse. All were seen in a new light. Questions arose in the student's mind. Why couldn't his father find work? He was willing to work, but there were no jobs. Why couldn't he get the medical attention he needed? Certainly he lacked medical insurance (no job, remember), but where was the government he had helped to support with his tax dollars all the years he had worked? And what about the statistics that demonstrate a clear bias of better health services for the affluent? Why is it that people like his father struggle so hard for bare necessities while the rich keep getting richer through governmental subsidies, tax breaks and bloated contracts? Is this really the land of equal opportunity?

While the student was grateful to see his father in a new light, he was also angered and frustrated. His discovery led him to the conclusion that his father died needlessly, and not, figuratively speaking, by his own hand.

SUMMARY

Like the above two students, you will learn a great deal this semester. Likewise, by developing a sociological imagination you will gain a new appreciation of the role that society and its institutions play in your life. This is not to say that you will always like what you discover, but it is information you need for successful living. Now it is time for you to add your story to the tens of thousands of students who have passed through our course.

Terms You Should Know:

Sociology	Social Statics	Social Dynamics
Proletariat	Bourgeoisie	Alienation
Rationality	Social Solidarity	Anomie
Dyad	Triad	Power
Status Quo	symbol	Sociological Imagination

Can You Answer These Questions?

1. Briefly describe the contribution of Abdel Rahman Ibn-Khaldun to sociology.
2. Distinguish between micro and macro levels of sociology. Give an example of each.
3. What did Karl Marx mean by false consciousness?
4. How were Karl Marx and Max Weber similar in their thinking? How did they differ?
5. What is the central difference between structural functionalism and social conflict?
6. How does symbolic interaction differ from the above two theories?
7. According to George Herbert Mead, how do we develop a concept of our self?
8. To whom was C. Wright Mills referring to when he coined the term power elite? Did he believe this group was beneficial to society?

Critical Thinking Exercises:

1. Having read chapter one, would you be inclined to identify yourself more with structural functionalist or social conflict theory?
2. Can you identify some important symbols in our society and describe how they might have affected your life.
3. Using your sociological imagination, list some structural effects that have shaped, and/or continue to shape, your thinking and your life.
4. Why might studying sociology create some difficulties? Why might it beneficial to continue your study?
5. Thinking about how society is structured today, do you think it benefits or provides major barriers to your future? Explain.

Photo: Mike Martin Wong / flickr.com / photos / squeakymarmot

Everyday Sociology 7th Edition

Chapter 2

Social Research Methods

What do you think of the following statements?

> *Women are more likely to suffer from depression.*
>
> *Men are more likely to engage in antisocial behavior.*

Are they true? Are they statements of fact or opinion? How do you know? How did we come to know this information? If these statements are true, which they are, can one conclude that all women are depressed and that all men engage in antisocial behavior? The answer of course is negative, which suggests that the relationships between the variables involved have been tested through research and found that gender is correlated with depression for women and antisocial conduct for men. What do we mean by correlation? How does it differ from causality or causation?

Well, think of the following. You have, for sure, seen a number of infomercials on your television selling different products ranging from vitamins to exercise equipment. Their message is: should one use their product, the results will improve his/her life. The idea is to establish, in the mind of the customer, a link between the product and happy, healthy life. To convince the public, those same infomercials present testimonials and images of individuals for whom the products were supposedly effective. Are you convinced? Why? If not, what more information do you need to make an informed decision? How would you go about establishing a convincing relationship between the product and the result?

The purpose of this chapter is twofold. One is to introduce students to and prepare them for their research assignments throughout their academic journey and beyond. The second purpose is to equip the student with the tools necessary to examine and evaluate data and research findings that may come their way. Specifically, this chapter will:

1. Explain the scientific foundation of sociology.
2. Outline and explain the numerous research methods available to sociologists.
3. Explain the main concepts and terms in the field of social research.
4. Explain how sociologists conduct research and carry out projects that lead to valid and reliable findings.
5. Outline and explain the stages of the research process.
6. Outline and explain the structure and format of the research report.
7. Give a brief introduction to descriptive statistics and measures of central tendency.

By now you must be familiar with the fact that sociology refers to the scientific study of society. This definition raises a number of important questions which include: What is meant by science? How does science work? What is the scientific method and what are its strengths and limitations? What do sociologists study? How do sociologists study and examine events and reach their conclusions? Are the scientific methods used by sociologists any different from those used by other scientists such as psychologists, anthropologists, chemists, nuclear physicists, and the like? You may have your own questions to add to this list—think of your own questions about the meaning of science and social research methods.

Sociology may be perceived as the study of the familiar and the obvious. If it is only to study what we already know, the following question arises: what is the added value of sociology? What advantages does sociology provide us in our attempts to understand human behavior, human interaction, and the social environment? To answer this question, it is important to remember that sociology is a discipline, or a field of study that is based on scientific principles. It is generally accepted that **science**—a systematic method of investigation (research)—is the dominant method of knowledge acquisition that guides researchers from all disciplines and fields of study.

Humans acquire knowledge about their surroundings through their basic senses. Historically, a distinction was made between subjective and objective knowledge. While the distinction at times is difficult to make, it is generally accepted that **subjective knowledge** refers to the personal domain. It is based on personal opinion, experience and impressions. Subjective knowledge is usually limited to one's immediate environment and is the source of "common-sense" which could be biased and limited in its scope of applicability. **Objective knowledge**, on the other hand, refers to that type of information that is considered factual or non-biased. Objectivity, therefore, refers to suspension of bias. Emile Durkheim (1982) describes social facts as those, which can be examined and investigated. Objectivity is based on facts that are verifiable, observable, measurable and testable. Max Weber ([1904] 1973) reminded us to be cognizant of the distinction between the two types of knowledge by calling on sociologists to abide by the principle of value-free approach. According to him, sociologists ought to teach, not preach.

Given such arguments, it is important to note two significant points. First, philosophers and scientists are in agreement that scientific inquiry leads to a higher degree of objectivity; and second, while objectivity remains an ideal condition to achieve, social scientists have come to recognize the value and importance of the subjective dimension of human knowledge, which ought not to be ignored.

WHAT IS SCIENCE?

The term science is derived from the Latin word meaning knowledge, (*scientia, scire* to know). In general, the term science refers to any body of knowledge that is grounded in observations and is organized in a systematic manner. To further understand this notion, one must make a distinction between knowledge, opinion, and belief. While scientific knowledge is grounded in observable facts (evidence) that are capable of proof, opinion may or may not be grounded in scientific facts and is usually motivated by personal bias as well as political agenda. **Opinion** refers to a conclusion derived from a judgment of facts that may or may not be scientifically examined. **Beliefs** are not based on evidence but rather on the conviction of the mind. Therefore, beliefs may or may not be factual and are not capable of proof. These distinctions are extremely important in both the scientific and the legal realms as well as in our political and public discourse. For example, how should a jury convict the accused? What are they to rely on—evidence, opinion, or belief? How do governments articulate their policies in matters of importance to all? How about medical doctors and their diagnosis and prescriptions? Should they rely on evidence, opinion or belief? What do you think? Can anyone avoid blurring the lines between evidence, opinion and belief?

To further examine the unique contribution of science, it must be contrasted with **common sense.** Take a look at the following examples: (1) many Americans believe that the United States is a middle class nation, and (2) people believe that couples marry because of love. Scientific evidence points to the contrary and that those common-sense statements are incorrect – they are sentiments reflecting people's beliefs and wishes. Sociological research provides ample evidence that the American society is made of a number of unequal social classes, and that love in most parts of the world has nothing to do with marriage. Another example, a student argued that racism is no longer present in the American society because he was not racist nor were his friends. Again, the evidence points to the contrary. Although sentiments may sound appealing, they may not stand the test of science and verification. Common sense or sentimental propositions may or may not bring about a feel-good sensation but are not grounded in evidence.

The **scientific approach** is a vigorous, systematic method of observation and examination of the universe. Note that in this context the term universe can carry different meanings to different scientists. For the psychologist, the universe is the mind of the individual and its effect on behavior; for the sociologist, the universe is much broader and covers all forms of human behavior in different societies and under different social conditions. Stated differently, sociologists are interested in studying or observing and examining the "mind of society" (author's term) and its impact on behavior.

Scientific endeavors therefore are classified into two distinct categories; namely, the **natural sciences** and **social** or **behavioral sciences**. That is to say the universe is composed of two entities: the natural or the physical dimension. Some of the main disciplines included among the natural sciences are physics, chemistry, and biology. These are often considered the "hard" sciences that are interested in understanding the nature, structure and laws governing the composition and interactions in the physical universe. The second category of the universe refers to the social dimension. Here you will find disciplines such as sociology, psychology, anthropology, history and economics. These fields of study are focused on understanding human behavior and the interactions between humans at the individual, the group and the societal levels.

Science is important because it gives, not only answers to many questions and helps to solve many human problems, but also because it represents the most committed human effort to verify that the statements made about the world are true or not. This is done by observation and experimentation within the context of a theory. Science can only be applied to observable phenomena. Unobservable events, occurrences, or entities do not lend themselves to scientific examination. Scientific inquiry is **empirical**, that is to say, the unit under investigation must be observable, measurable, and testable. For example, scientists cannot study the existence of God and His qualities, but they can examine the beliefs and images that people have of God.

Furthermore, scientists are interested in identifying and explaining behavioral patterns and social trends. A **pattern** refers to a regular and systematic repetition of the same behavior that doesn't occur by chance. For example, you may have noticed that the traditional family pattern of patriarchy (male dominance) of the 1950s is giving way to a new **trend** of egalitarianism (a pattern in which both the male and the female have equal responsibility for family matters). Having a clear understanding of such patterns and trends and the forces that shape them is at the heart of the science of sociology.

The ultimate goal of any scientific activity is the betterment of the human condition. Specifically, the goals and objectives of any scientific activity include:

Description: Scientists are interested in describing the units under investigation. The act of description is intended to give a mental image and an accurate account of observable conditions, events, experiences or phenomena. Sociologists are very particular in their descriptive terminology and attempt to identify and provide full description and classification of concepts, events and phenomena such as society, culture, religion, crime, poverty, and groups, to name only a few. As an exercise, try to describe the characteristics of your campus, or the student body at your college. What is the racial/ethnic composition? What is the gender composition? What is the socioeconomic background or marital status of the student body? Now think about your family – describe its history, structure, size. Note that descriptions of this nature require clear, precise, detailed and accurate observations. To complete your task, you may have to both record those observations and use relevant terminology.

Exploration: Scientists examine and work on new areas of research. They study uncharted territories. The act of exploration refers to the process of searching for new information or frontiers. It is intended to bring about cutting or leading edge information and discoveries. Space research is an example of an exploratory research. Have you ever been to a new town or a new country? If the answer is yes, you might relate to the extent of effort you may have to put in exploring that new territory. While most tourists may keep a mental record of their observations, social scientists are expected to provide a systematic, written account of their observations. In his 2006 study, *Voices from the Camps: A People's History of Palestinian Refugees in Jordan*, Nabil Marshood described Palestinian refugee camps that were formed after Palestinians were forced out and removed from their homeland in 1948. He also explored life in those camps in Jordan and explained the impacts of forced removal, expulsion and dispossession on people's collective memory. He discovered that despite the traumatic personal, cultural and political experience, and notwithstanding their pain and alienation, Palestinians remain strongly attached to their homeland and stand waiting and ready to return to it.

Explanation: Scientists are particularly interested in explaining the phenomena under investigation, and seek valid and solid explanations for observable patterns. Sociologists are not only interested in describing crime and its types, but they also seek to understand the structural causes and context of crime. The act of an explanation is intended to answer why and how events or activities occur. To identify meaningful patterns, sociologists link social facts together. For example, crime and poverty, or population density and types of crime are frequently linked together. Examining the relationship between poverty and crime rates helps us understand criminal behavior and the conditions that might influence it. Keep in mind that sociologists don't accept the assumption that poverty leads to crime, but through the explanation process they are placed in a better position to shed some light on the differences in crime types and rates between poor and middle class communities.

Discovery and Invention: It is through scientific research that humans have established systematic methods that led the way in discovery and inventions. Medical and engineering discoveries have changed the way humans go about their daily activities. Life expectancy is much higher in scientifically advanced societies. The invention of the birth control methods and other related devices have changed the cultural norms pertaining to sexuality and liberated humans, particularly women from the shackles of patriarchy and sexual oppression. Moreover, the modern era, also known as the computer or information age, has drastically changed the ways of communicating, the meaning of communities and the dynamics of family life. While the term "community" used to be strongly associated with neighborhood and a specific physical location, community has taken on a different meaning. Through digital systems of social networks, humans have created digital communities that are not limited to any geographic space. Similarly, social research has contributed to our understanding of the human condition and has advanced our means of dealing with such reality. New ideas about race relations, gender and homosexuality are only three examples where social policy and our worldviews have also changed.

Challenges to Sociologists

The discussion thus far provides a window into the world of science and research of all disciplines. While objectivity is an ideal state that all scientists aspire to achieve, it is important to note that social scientists, in contrast with natural scientists, are faced with unique challenges:

1. The unit of observation resembles the observer. Social scientists are humans who set out to study humans, and by the nature of their humanness are subject to biases, attachments, and values. This, in turn, may have a direct and indirect impact on their scientific activity and its results.

2. Ethical considerations may limit experimentation. Studies on many topics, such as suicide or homicide for example, have always been done after the fact. It is, of course, inconceivable to ask individuals to commit suicide or homicide in order to study their motivation.

3. The observed subjects (humans) respond to and interact with the observer and are aware of the fact that they are being investigated. Some measures have been taken to address this particular issue of reactivity. These include, among others, utilizing unobtrusive techniques so that subjects are less aware that they are under investigation.

Although these challenges make social sciences in general and sociology in particular a unique science, they don't alter the fact that social research is based on scientific methodology that is adaptive to the complex nature of society, the individual and social interaction.

BUILDING BLOCKS OF SCIENCE

For any scientific activity to be considered effective and subject to evaluation by the public and other scientists, researchers establish a common language and conduct their research in accordance with set standards and guidelines. The main elements of scientific observation include concepts, variables, measurement, and the relationships between variables, hypothesis, and theory.

Concepts

A concept simply refers to a construct that describes a certain part of the unit of interest. It designates specific qualities, traits or attributes to that part. Jonathan Turner (1989) calls concepts, "the basic building blocks of theory." Philosophers sometimes disagree as to the meaning of this term and see it as the most ambiguous, and yet the most useful term. Concepts like personality, conformity, and national interest serve as good examples of abstract components representing categories of a given phenomenon. Once they are formed, concepts function as instruments in the service of observation, description, and explanation. According to Max Weber (1949; orig. 1904), concepts are useful for classification purposes, and should represent reality.

Variables

A variable is any item that can be measured and take on different values. A variable is subject to change. The term sex, for example, is a variable because it is made up of the attributes of being male or female. If you are to look around in your sociology class, you will find a group of students who vary from each other by many variables (attributes) including age, sex, grade point average, race, income, and ethnic background. All of these differences can be classified as variables. Variables refer to attributes of people or objects and are essential to any scientific activity. They help us focus, organize, classify, and provide a clear picture of the research project. They may be identified, measured and linked with each other in order to create concepts, hypotheses, models, and theories.

Measurement

Measurement is simply the act of assigning numbers to objects and is intended to determine the size or magnitude of a variable. If you wish to measure the length of your desk, for example, you are very likely to use a ruler. Once you complete your measurement, you'll end up with a number indicating the length of that desk. This number is unlikely to be disputed. Others who decide to measure your desk will obtain the same results. For scientists, measurement is acceptable only if certain basic criteria are met:

1. Measurement tools and instruments must be specific to the variables or type of variables being measured.
2. Measurement tools and instruments must receive a high degree of consensus; that is, repeating the measurement must consistently yield the same results.
3. Rules of measurement must be established, agreed upon, and applicable.

Having described the foundations of measurement, you might appreciate the challenges facing social scientists in general and sociologists in particular. Measuring the length of your desk is a simple task compared to measuring your emotions and your interactions. How would you go about measuring concepts such as love, hate, conformity, sexuality, crime, religiosity, poverty and the like? Stephanie Coontz (1996) in an attempt to gauge sexual behavior, noted, "Not that 19th century Americans were asexual: by mid-century, New York City had one prostitute for every 64 men; the mayor of Savannah estimated his city had one for every 39." Also, the research of the sociologists, David Harding and Christopher Jencks (2003), suggests that attitudes toward premarital sex had changed rapidly and that the percentage of Americans who believed that premarital sex was "not wrong" had doubled from 24 percent to 47 percent in four years between 1969 and 1973 and then skyrocketed in the seventies to 62 percent in 1982. These were attempts to measure the magnitude of sexuality on a large social scale. What do you think? Which of the two cities is more sexual? Does the number of prostitutes constitute a good measure of sexuality? What about the changing attitudes on premarital sex? Is that a good measure of sexuality? Do any of these measures preserve the meaning of sexuality? Would any of these two measures be equally applicable to other, more traditional communities?

Let's try measuring the term religiosity – that is the extent of one's religious beliefs. What indicators should be included in this act? Would affiliation with or belonging to a certain religion imply religiosity? Or, would believing in the doctrine of that religion make one religious? Or, reading their sacred book would perhaps make a person more religious than those who don't read. What do you think? Try with your classmates to determine a method for measuring religiosity. What would it be? And how would you determine if that method is in fact accurate and reliable, and indisputable.

The point is obvious! Social scientists are faced with major challenges. They are yet to come up with clear, accepted measures of human behavior. Critics argue that in contrast with the natural sciences, some segments of the social sciences can't be considered science. Yet, do you really want to reach a point where every aspect of human behavior, feeling and thought is measured scientifically in a very precise manner? The answer is very likely to be negative. Our challenge as social scientists, sociologists included, is to measure our personal and social reality within a framework of creativity. That is, social scientists are challenged to find creative ways of measurement that will allow objects to be counted without loss of meaning.

Measurement is a systematic method used by scientists to record their observations. In order for us to measure everything from the very specific to the very broad in human endeavors, scientists have identified four measurement scales.

Nominal Scales are used for measurement of variables with two or more categories that have no numeric attributes. This scale involves an operational definition that assigns observations to categories without ranking these categories. Marital status, for instance, is measured on this scale by categorizing individuals as married, single, divorced, and widowed. This scale identifies categories but makes no assumptions and sets no value or meaning to differences within each category.

Ordinal Scales are used to rank variables in numeric order. Ordinal scales are slightly more sophisticated than nominal scales because they involve quantitative (numerical) features. One example of an ordinal scale is the hotel rating system used by AAA (American Automobile Association). According to this rating system, a four-star hotel is considered to be of better quality than a three or two-star hotel. It is important to note that the intervals between the points on the scale are unequal. That is, the difference between a two-star hotel and a three-star hotel is not necessarily the same as the difference between a three and four-star hotel.

Interval Scales have the same qualities as the ordinal scale but the distance between points on the scale is equal. A unique characteristic of this scale is the absence of an absolute zero point. A thermometer used to measure temperature, for example, is an interval scale on which the difference between 20 and 30 degrees is equal to that between 60 and 70 degrees. The zero point on this scale doesn't mean lack of temperature. Actually the temperature could go below zero, which indicates that the zero is not an absolute point but a value on a continuum.

Ratio Scales have the characteristics of ordinal and interval scales. Additionally, they have an absolute, true zero point. Weight is an example of such a scale. In other words, objects that weigh zero or less do not exist. True zero is important for making sense of comparisons. If John weighs 200 pounds and Michelle weighs 100 pounds (ratio scale), then it is reasonable to conclude that John is twice as heavy as Michelle.

In order to obtain quality observation and measurement, researchers consider validity and reliability to be of special importance. **Validity** refers to the fact that the researcher is indeed measuring what he/she intends to measure. It refers to the accuracy of measurement. That is, the validity of a measure concerns the degree to which observed values successfully approximate the true score (value) of that variable. **Reliability** on the other hand refers to consistency. That is, for a measure to be reliable, it must be replicable. If an observation is not repeatable or consistent, its usefulness as scientific evidence is limited.

Relationships between Variables

Scientists of all disciplines are not only interested in describing each variable alone, but more importantly; they are interested in examining the relationship between two or more variables. For many, this emphasis on relationships between variables is the essence of any scientific endeavor.

At the heart of this activity stands a basic human tendency to describe and to explain behavior and the events around it. If, for example, you pass your class with a high grade, you are most likely to attribute your success to factors such as your effort, your intelligence, your liking of the course, your admiration of the instructor (or not!), and so on. The point is clear. You are trying to link your success with how you obtained it. By doing so, you have described, implicitly if not explicitly, each variable independently and have provided an explanation for your success. Success, as well as failure, does not happen independent of other forces. It is an outcome, a result of other variables. Scientists and philosophers have come to agree that relationships between variables can be established when one variable impacts another. That is to say, change in one variable affects change in another. The variable that causes the change is called the **independent variable**, while the one that is affected by it is called the **dependent variable**.

In a classical study in the field of socialization (Chapter 5), Melvin Kohn (1969) examined the impact of social class (independent variable) on parental values (dependent variable). To this end, the researcher compared middle class parental values with those parental values held by working class parents. Some of these results are reported in Table 2.1.

Examination of these data clearly demonstrates the existence of differences between working class parents and middle class parents as to their

Table 2.1: Social Class and Parental Values (Selected Variables)

	Middle Class Mothers	Working Class Mothers
Percentage who value that the child		
is happy	46	36
is considerate of others	39	27
obeys his/her parent	20	33
is clean and neat	11	20
is curious about things	18	6
has self control	22	13

Source: Kohn, Melvin L. 1969. *Class and Conformity: A Study of Values.* Homeword, IL: Dorsey

emphasis on those selected values. These differences were proven to be statistically significant at the $P<0.05$ level, which indicate that these differences represent systematic, non-random behavioral patterns. That is, children raised in middle class families are likely to encounter a different set of values than their peers of working class families. This conclusion suggests that a strong relationship, which we refer to as correlation, between social class and parental values does indeed exist.

Correlation refers to a relationship between two variables where change in one is associated with change in the other. It is important to note that the fact that two variables change together over time, or are otherwise statistically related doesn't prove that one is causing the other. That is to say, correlation is not causation. Studies, for example, have found a strong relationship between education attainment and the degree of prejudice. That is to say, people with higher levels of education are less likely to express racial prejudice. This however does not establish a causal relationship between the two variables (education and prejudice). In other words, it is possible for educated people to hold on to prejudice. Education does not eliminate prejudice, though it appears to make a contribution in that direction. Another example points out to the effect of family structure on children's success. Numerous studies (see chapter on Marriage and Family) point out that single-parent households place children at a higher risk of poor academic performance.

The purpose of doing correlations is to make a prediction about one variable based on what we know about another variable. Correlations take one of two directions. **Positive correlation** refers to change in both variables in the same direction. If X is positively correlated with Y, then an increase in X is related to an increase in Y. Diet and weight are positively correlated variables. Stated differently, the more food you eat the more likely you are to gain weight or the less food you eat the less likely you are to gain weight.

Negative correlation indicates an inverse relationship. That is, the more of X the less of Y. Our previous example on education and prejudice is a case in point (more education, less prejudice). A similar inverse relationship was observed by Durkheim in his study on suicide where social integration was found to be inversely related to suicide—the lower the rate of social integration the higher the rate of suicide.

Causation differs from correlation. It implies that a cause-and-effect relationship exists and allows us to make a clear, deterministic and precise prediction, while correlations provide us with probabilistic predictions. If you throw wood onto the fire, it will be consumed—this is certain to occur (determinism). On the other hand, if you claim a correlation between higher education and prejudice, your best conclusion would be that higher education is likely to reduce prejudice (a probabilistic position). In order for a relationship to qualify as causal, it must meet the following criteria:

1. The independent variable (the cause) precedes the dependent variable (the effect) in time.

2. There is an empirical (testable, measurable, observable) correlation between the two variables. While a correlation is required to claim causality, finding a correlation is not sufficient to prove causality.

3. Other independent variables must be ruled out. That is, a third variable must not be involved in the cause-effect relationship between two variables (X causes Y; Z is not involved).

Philosophers and scientists speak of causation as an outcome of two sets of conditions known as necessary and sufficient. To establish causation, one must ask the question whether X is a necessary and sufficient condition for Y. **Necessary cause** must be present for the effect to follow. In order for you to pass this course, for example, you must take the final exam. But this exam is not a sufficient condition for passing the course. You must pass the exam and successfully complete all other course requirements. A **sufficient condition** then, represents a condition that if it is present, will guarantee the effect to follow.

Hypothesis and Theory

Both theories and hypotheses are inseparable from science in that they simultaneously contribute to and are affected by research. A **theory** is one of the most important components in science. Some consider it as another word for explanation, and define it as a systematic explanation for observations that relate to a particular aspect of life such as poverty, crime, social class and the like. Most people think of theories as something abstract and removed from reality and the laws governing it. In fact, theories are systems of statements that entail interconnected laws designed to explain reality — they bring order to fragmented reality. The political theorist, Kenneth N. Waltz (1979) makes the point very clear. He states that a, "theory is a simple instrument which you hope to be able to use in order to understand and explain the real world. The emphasis is on explanation, not on prediction." Theories are a part of everyday life — our whole way of looking at the world depends on our theoretical view. Aristotle, the Greek Philosopher, eloquently articulated this point, "Men do not think they know a thing 'till they have grasped the 'why' of it."

Let's take a simple example. When we claim that success is a result of ability, we are in fact, stating a theoretical proposition. If we mean that ability is a concept composed of intelligence and effort, then our theory of success is a system that describes the relationships between intelligence, effort and success. Human behavior is rather complex, thereby requiring complex theories to explain. Our theory of success, for example, is simple but practical, yet it does not tell the whole story. A more complex model would include additional variables such as the difficulty of the subject matter, the motivation of the individual, the degree of support received from his/her immediate environment, including family and friends, and much more. In other words, a good theory of success must address all those matters. It must, in addition, make a clear distinction between various types of success, the multiple forms and patterns of success, and the differences between

Figure 2.1: Theory and Research: Interactive Model

Theory ⟷ Hypothesis ⟷ Observed Reality

successful and unsuccessful personalities. And a good theory of success must also address the social and environmental forces that contribute or hinder success such as, social class, social mobility, culture and much more. Moreover, a good theory of success must not be limited to an explanation of causes of success, it certainly must do more in terms of providing a profound understanding of this phenomenon and its ramifications. A theory then is a system of interrelated concepts that help explain, generalize and predict the event or the behavior at hand.

To establish a theory of success, researchers must clarify their observations, offer proof of the relationships between the various concepts in the system, and map out a clear path that will lead to success. Scientists are not satisfied by the claim that success is determined by, or is the result of, a number of factors. They attempt to further explain success by answering certain questions such as, how do these factors relate to each other? And, in what order must these factors appear to ensure success will follow?

The difference between theory and hypothesis is essential. Our discussion on theories highlights the challenges faced by scientists and the tension that appears, at least on the surface, between reality and theory. If reality and theory are treated as separate entities, then hypothesis should be treated as the bridge between the two. Figure 2.1 serves to illustrate this idea.

Hypothesis then is a statement of prediction that sets forth the basis for testing the relationship between variables in an attempt to link theory to reality. Said differently, a hypothesis is a tentative assumption made to draw out and test its logical or empirical consequences. A theory questioning the relationship between religion and society, for example, might contain the hypothesis that, "poor people are more likely to demonstrate a stronger degree of religiosity than the rich." Such a hypothesis could then be tested using the research tools that are available.

Why do we need theories and what are their functions? According to Dubin (1978), "The need for a theory lies in the human behavior of wanting to impose order on unordered experiences." Theories serve very important functions. They provide explanations; they make sense of observed facts; they establish rules of interactions; and they shape and direct research.

What constitutes a good theory? Scientists and philosophers argue, that a good theory is one that has the following characteristics:

1. A good theory can be tested and best fits the evidence;
2. A good theory has logical soundness, with consistent and rational relationships among the variables;

3. A good theory has the ability to make sense of the universe;

4. A good theory brings new information, new direction, new ideas or new approaches to research;

5. A good theory is popular and worthy of discussion among scientists and non-scientists.

To further understand the value of both hypotheses and theories and the relationship between them, consider the following hypothesis: Premarital cohabitation increases the chances for a long and happy marriage. Taken at face value, this sounds like a common sense argument. Many young couples believe that to be true. Living with your future spouse before making that important decision allows you to gain a better understanding of each other, thus strengthening the relationship and enhancing the chances for a successful marriage. Sounds like a good argument, right? Well, an examination of this hypothesis by social scientists has demonstrated the opposite result: Premarital cohabitation decreases the chances for marriage because cohabitation does not require the same level of commitment that is expected in a marital relationship.

This conclusion begs the following question: if this is the case, why do young couples end up in cohabiting relationships? The answer raises a number of possibilities, one of which is the exchange theory (Becker, 1991). This theory, based on the rational choice theory and grounded in economic theories, suggests that people are rational and calculated beings that make decisions about their relationships on the basis of cost-benefit analysis. According to the exchange theory, people decide whether to exchange goods and services by considering the benefits they might receive, and the costs they might incur if they chose an alternative course of action. That is to say, the benefits of cohabitation might outweigh the benefits of alternative arrangements. What do you think?

THE RESEARCH PROCESS

By now we have established that research is a logical and systematic activity that must follow specific steps and rules. The research system allows others, scientists in particular, to evaluate and critique the quality of the project at hand. Researchers usually follow the process as outlined below (see Figure 2.2) ensuring a standard system. Note that the cyclical form of the research process is of special importance. It points out that the study has produced new and valuable questions and hypotheses for future research. It also points out that research is an ongoing activity and that one research project is not sufficient to answer all the questions at hand.

Stage 1: Select Topic: Rationale and Purpose: Many avenues are available for researchers to select their topic of interest. Of course, the researchers' personal interest and areas of expertise have a great

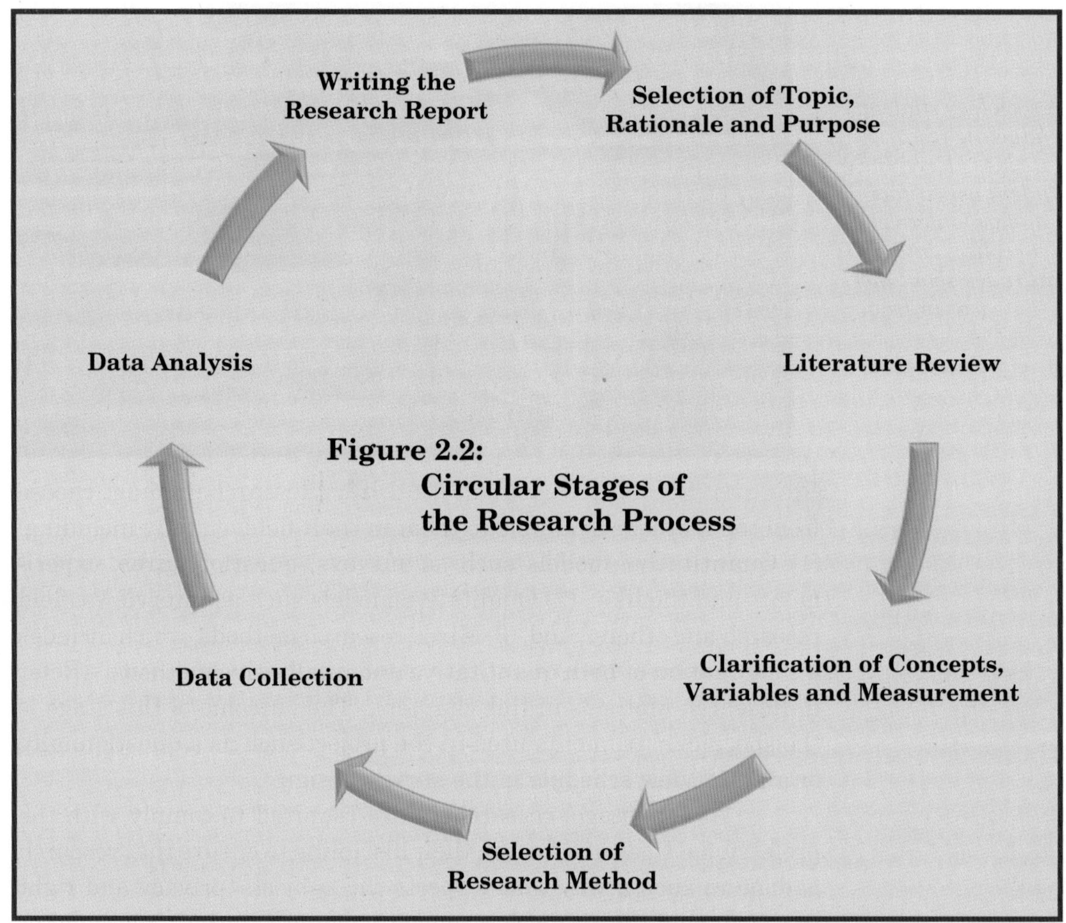

Figure 2.2: Circular Stages of the Research Process

impact on the choices they make. Other considerations may include availability of funding sources and popularity of the topic. Whatever the motives might be, it is important to write a clear statement of purpose for your research. Clarification of the research question or hypothesis, the research purpose as well as its rationale is an essential step that could set the project forward.

Stage 2: Review Literature: Researchers keep the central meaning of the topic in mind while examining the background literature, including qualitative and quantitative research and various theoretical models. At this stage, researchers gather existing information about the topic and provide a theoretical context to their research problem, hypothesis or question.

Stage 3: Clarify Concepts, Variables and Measurement: Precision in conceptualizing is critical in the social sciences. Concepts, even those that may appear familiar, must be defined precisely and in an appropriate method that makes their measurement possible. (Refer to measurement scales in this chapter).

A sociology student conducting research for class. Here, the student uses a"face-to-face" interview to collect data on attitudes about the war in Iraq.

Photo: SPP

Stage 4: Select a Research Method: Researchers must choose from the methods available to them in their field of study including: (1) Quantitative models such as surveys, questionnaires, experiments and the like. (2) Qualitative models such as interviews, field research and others. And, (3) Mixed research methods, which includes a combination of both quantitative and qualitative methods. (Refer to Research Methods in this chapter). The outcome of this stage is the specific instruments used in the project such as a questionnaire or an interview schedule in the survey design.

At this stage, researchers are required to comply with the professional Code of Ethics in their discipline to ensure that research is done in such a way that respects the subjects' privacy and right to refuse, and that it doesn't cause the subject harm—emotional or otherwise. For more information, visit the American Sociological Association web site and examine their code of ethics at http://www.asanet.org/images/asa/docs/pdf/CodeofEthics.pdf.

Stage 5: Collect Data: Once the research methods and designs are set, and once the research instruments established, and the study population and sample are well defined, researchers embark on a journey into the field to gather the needed data for their project. This is the stage where interviews are conducted, questionnaires are distributed, or experiments are administered.

Stage 6: Analyze Data and Results: Once the data are collected, they must be formatted to make analysis possible. Entering the data into a computer program is an example of this stage. This is also the stage in which data are analyzed using a variety of statistical methods that would produce the most important results of the study. Here data are tabulated and presented in a variety of formats including tables and graphs.

Stage 7: Write Research Report: The results must be written and presented to the public including interested scientists. Most research projects become the basis for articles, books, public policy

Figure 2.3: Format of the Research Report
1. Title Page 2. Abstract 3. Introduction 4. Literature Review 5. Methods 6. Results 7. Discussion and Analysis 8. Conclusion 9. References

reports and professional meetings. Details about the research report are listed below.

THE RESEARCH REPORT

Having completed your data analysis, you are ready to begin stage 7 above and write your research report, and share your results with others. Research reports have a very specific format that must be followed (see the Sociology Student Writer's Manual, 2010). Generally, research reports are organized under nine subtitles (see Figure 2.3).

Title Page: Finding a title for your research project could at times be challenging. It is advised to come up with a title after you have completed your project. Provide a title that is descriptive, meaningful, specific and attractive. Avoid general titles like "Domestic Violence," "Understanding Religion," or "Crime." The title page should also include the author's name. And if the project was part of your course requirements, you should also include the course title, the instructor's name and the date of submission.

Abstract: The abstract is a brief summary of the research problem, methods, results and conclusions. The purpose of the abstract is to provide potential readers with just enough information to allow them to decide if your research is relevant to their interests that they will read it in full.

Introduction: The introduction of the report should cover each of the following areas and explain the objectives, rationale and justification of the project:

1. Describe and define the research problem, hypothesis and the main guiding questions.
2. Explain the importance of the project and its rationale.
3. Highlight the goals and objectives of your research project.

Literature Review: Literature review is more than a simple summary. Researches must address related theories and empirical research available. The literature review should address a number of important questions including:

1. What is known about the topic at hand?
2. What is the nature of existing contradictions existing in the literature? Explain those contradictions and their importance for your research
3. What is missing from the literature that your research might advance? How? Discuss the potential contribution of your research to the existing body of knowledge. How could the existing literature advance your research? And what do you expect your research to add to it?
4. What is the researcher's assessment and critique of the existing research?
5. What ethical considerations ought to be addressed? Why? How?

Methods: The methods section should cover the following segments:

1. The design or the research method used in this project. Explain how the methods used in this project will help solve the research problem or advance the research topic.
2. The population and the sample;
3. The devices or instruments used to conduct the study;
4. Detailed explanation of the data collection procedure.

Results: Findings and analytical tools should be presented in this section including data and statistical methods. Presentation could be made in the form of figures, tables or graphs.

Discussion and Analysis: This section should bring the whole project together and tie the pieces into one comprehensive statement about the value of your project. More specifically, the purpose of the discussion is to:

1. Interpret the results;
2. Discuss the implications of the results;
3. Compare the results with previous research; and,
4. Make suggestions for future research.

Conclusion: In this section, researchers present their final concluding remarks and recommendations, and discuss the strengths and limitations of their research project.

References: All material cited in the research report must be included in this section. Citation rules must be followed properly and consistently. There is a number of writing styles that are available to researchers to choose from including the ASA (American Sociological Association) Writing Style, the Chicago Manual of Style, the MLA (Modern Language Association) Style, or the APA (American Psychological Association) Style. The choice is dependent on the nature of the document and publication requirements.

RESEARCH METHODS

Research methods, also referred to as research designs, are systematic ways for collecting data and information about the research topic. Over the years there has been a large amount of multifaceted discussion surrounding the topic of research methodology and the theory of how inquiry should proceed. Much of this debate has centered on the issue of qualitative versus quantitative inquiry. It is important to note that all methodologies have their specific strengths and weaknesses that the researcher should acknowledge and address.

Quantitative research methods refer to research designs that rely on numerical data (quantification of data). This method generates statistics through the use of large-scale survey research, using methods such as questionnaires or structured interviews. If a market researcher stopped to ask you questions about their products, or you have filled in a questionnaire, you have in effect participated in quantitative research. Quantitative research reaches many more people, but the contact with those people is much narrow and limited than it is in qualitative research.

Qualitative research methods refer to such designs that seek to describe and/or analyze individuals, groups, organizations, agencies, communities or some patterns of social interaction. These are methods that allow the researcher to see the world from the perspective of those being studied. Qualitative research explores attitudes, behavior and experiences and attempts to get an in-depth opinion from participants. This method reaches fewer people but the contact with these people tends to last a lot longer. Methods used under the umbrella of qualitative research include field observation also known as ethnography, open-ended surveys, life histories, archival research and unstructured interviews.

While quantitative research is more likely to be structured, measured and directional, qualitative research tends to be more open, intuitive, subjective and exploratory. There are situations that require the application of both qualitative and quantitative methods—also known as mixed research methods—which researchers use to study complex and large scale phenomena.

This section will focus on the following methods: surveys, secondary analysis or archival research, experiments, and field research. But, before we look at each of these methods, some important terms need to be clarified.

In research, the word population refers to the people who are the central focus of the investigation. **Population** is the total collection of objects, media, or people to be studied and from which a sample is to be drawn. Let us assume that you want to study the effect of the school environment on student learning. Your population would be the entire student body—but what student body? You are required to decide on the boundaries of the population you are interested in—grammar school or high school, private or public, national, state or local, which is it? Once your decisions are made, the population is defined and you may move to the next step: Sampling.

Sampling is a critical stage in all research. It is the process of obtaining representative selection and/or measurements of a subset of your target population. The quality of the sample determines the quality of the research and whether or not the readers could trust your study and its findings. A sample refers to a selected group of people (specimen) whose characteristics represent those found in the population. There are many sampling techniques available, but researchers are most often interested in those that closely approximate the sample to the population. To achieve this degree of similarity, researchers must concern themselves with two factors: the size of the sample and its degree of representativeness. Sample size is critical in that the closer the sample size is to the population size, the more reliable that sample will be. Large samples are therefore more likely to be trustworthy. Census data, for example, are considered reliable because census officials study every household in the U.S. Stated differently, for them, the sample is the population. In this case, the degree of representativeness is very high because the people in the sample not only very closely resemble the people in the population; they are the people in the population.

Researchers are not required to study such large samples. The availability of advanced statistical techniques and the quality of sampling selection techniques minimize sampling errors and make it possible for researchers to generalize and infer their findings from relatively smaller sample sizes to the population. Political polls serve as a good example in which a small fraction of the voting population is selected and surveyed. Pollsters have consistently predicted results of national election on the basis of samples that range in size from 1,500 to 2,000 voters.

Beyond size, the quality of the sample also depends largely on the method of selection. Generally speaking, there are two methods of sample selection: random and non-random. A random sample doesn't mean that you stand at the entrance of your school, for example, and ask every passerby to respond to your survey. On the contrary, a **random sample** refers to a systematic selection method that ensures an equal chance for every member in the population to be included into the study. **Non-random** samples, on the other hand, are non-representative.

Now we are ready to look at specific types of research methodology.

The Survey

Surveys allow for a systematic method of data collection needed for the purposes of describing and explaining events, attitudes, opinion and social phenomena. They are widely used by sociologists, and for many social scientists, the survey is the method of choice for gathering information. You are most likely to be familiar with political polls that measure and describe voters' opinions and attitudes. The Gallup organization, for example,—named after its founder, George Gallup, is an internationally well-recognized research establishment in the United States known for its extensive use of the survey.

Another well-known national survey you are likely to be familiar with is the Census, which is conducted once every ten years by the U.S. Bureau of the Census since 1790. A total of 3.9 million inhabitants were counted then in contrast with the current U.S. population size standing at approximately 310 million residents. The Census is designed to collect data about all of the households in the United States. Information gathered in the Census is widely used by social scientists, public and government officials, media personnel and many others. The Gallup Poll and the Census are examples of descriptive surveys, but some of their findings can also be explanatory. Sociologists have carried out many survey projects based on Census data that provided meaningful explanations and has had a significant impact on public policy-related matters. One such Census-based research-project in 1980 by James S. Coleman, "High School and Beyond", was a follow-up to the Coleman Report, a 1966 Congressionally mandated research project originally titled Equality of Educational Opportunity.

The main topic under investigation in "High School and Beyond" was whether public or private schools were better at educating high school students. The project began with the selection of a representative sample of high school sophomores and seniors in both public and private schools. To begin the selection process, a list of all high schools in the U.S. was required. This, as you can imagine, was not an easy task. Once the list was compiled, a sample pool of public and private schools, including some high performance institutions, was drawn. From this list of schools, a pool of students in the tenth and twelfth grades was produced. The final sample included more than 30,000 sophomores and 28,000 seniors (Coleman, et al., 1982).

What did all of this work produce? Well, the findings of this survey-based research project were of great significance. One of the discoveries was that, "achievement differences between students from advantaged backgrounds and those from disadvantaged backgrounds are considerably less in Catholic schools than they are in public schools" (Coleman, et al., 1982). This finding held true regardless of race or level of parental education. In the course of explaining these significant differences, Coleman and his associates demonstrated that private school students are more engaged in their education (do more homework assignments) and the behavioral climate in private schools was less conducive to fights and other disruptive activities that negatively impact learning.

Another and more recent study was done by Betty Hart and Todd Risley, *Meaningful Differences in the Everyday Experience of Young American Children* (1995), had focused on the achievement gap between students from advantaged and educated families on one hand, and students from disadvantaged families on the other. Through meticulous data collection and recording of communication between parents and children, they found significant gaps between the vocabularies of children from educated, advantaged families and children from families of low socioeconomic status. They also found that this gap translates into widely different academic and intellectual performances as the children grow.

Survey-based research requires researchers to adequately define the target population and the general makeup of the sample so that the questions included in the survey are asked in an appropriate and clear style. In a survey, the manner in which questions are presented, ordered, formatted and asked is critical to the outcome.

A widely used survey technique is the questionnaire, which is a series of well defined questions that is forwarded to all subjects in the sample. The quality of the questionnaire depends on the wording of the questions and its unbiased, non-judgmental approach. Researchers can choose between closed-ended and open-ended questions, or a combination of the two. A closed-ended format allows subjects to select a response from several choices provided by the researcher. This technique restricts the choice to a preset number of possibilities which are exhaustive and mutually exclusive. Its main advantage is to facilitate the task of data analysis. Open-ended questions, on the other hand, allow the subjects to respond freely and to express their opinion. This makes the tasks of data analysis more difficult but may provide insights that are not available with a closed-ended format.

Overall, the survey is a very effective and inexpensive method for gathering large amounts of data on a variety of topics. It helps to describe the conditions existing at the time the survey was conducted and it has the potential, if structured accordingly, to explain and test out hypotheses.

The Experiment

Experimentation is the classic research method that allows the researcher to control the variables being investigated and as a result, prove a causal relationship between them. The experiment permits the researcher to test a hypothesis by manipulating (controlling) the independent variable and measuring the impact of this manipulation on the dependent variable.

Figure 2.4: Experimental Design

Random selection of subjects to the research project
↓
Random assignment to experimental and control groups
↓
Pre-treatment test both groups
↓
Administer (treatment) independent variable to experimental group
↓
Give placebo or no treatment to control group
↓
Post treatment test of both groups
↓
Assess the difference between both groups

In the following simple example, you are encouraged to identify the independent and dependent variables. As an eighth grade mathematics teacher, you are interested in testing the effectiveness of a new method of teaching mathematics to your students. First, you randomly select a group of your students. To one half of them—the **experimental group**—you will teach the proposed new teaching method, while the other half, the **control group**, continues with the usual math instruction. Both groups are tested at the beginning and at the end of the school year. Comparison of the two groups will yield information about the differences in mathematical skills. Those results will provide evidence that the new method either works or does not work. In other words, observed success or failure is, in fact, an outcome of the new teaching method (see Figure 2.4).

If you deduced that the independent variable is the teaching methods and the dependent variable is the level of mathematical skills achieved at the end of the experiment, you are correct. Next, you may also ask why two groups, rather than just one, were chosen. The answer is that the experimental group alone doesn't really prove anything. We cannot be certain that our new teaching method did, in fact, do a better job than the old method when we have nothing to compare it to. However, by choosing a control group that received the original teaching method, we are able to compare the two group outcomes and find out whether a difference occurred and whether that difference is significant.

As you can imagine, experimentation is more common in the natural sciences because it is more likely to occur in a laboratory setting. Although the above example would work well and produce the desired results, laboratory centered experiments are generally not as conducive to the social sciences because, by definition, the study of people and groups generally occurs in a natural, uncontrolled setting. However, many classical social science experiments have been conducted and are still often discussed by sociologists. Examples include Stanley Milgram's experiment on obedience to authority, Philip Zimbardo's experiment on the pathology of imprisonment and role acquisition, and Solomon Asch's research on conformity and peer pressure (see chapter four).

The strengths of this method are embodied in its structure. Experiments allow the researcher to have full control over the independent variable while the progress of the research project in a laboratory setting ensures meaningful findings and provides significant evidence of causal relationships. On the other hand, experiments are often criticized because the laboratory environment may not be representative of real life situations. To counter this criticism, researchers have conducted natural (field) experiments, set not in the laboratory, but in natural settings during the natural course of events. While an appealing alternative, this format may reduce control over the variables being tested and therefore the outcomes may be in question. Another critical look at experiments suggests that, if experiments are not designed carefully, they might infringe on ethical and moral considerations.

Secondary Analysis

Catherine Hakim (1982) defines secondary analysis, also called archival research, as "any further analysis of an existing data set which presents interpretations, conclusions, or knowledge additional to, or different from, those presented in the first report." As such, secondary analysis is not considered a pure research method. Instead, it utilizes existing data to study problems different from those discussed by the original researcher(s).

Data collected by others is available for further analysis. Historical analysis, for example, must rely on existing data. Those interested in studying the American Civil War, for example, must resort to governmental and other original documents from that era. Sociologists often use this method where data collected by the U.S. Census Bureau on the entire U.S. popu-

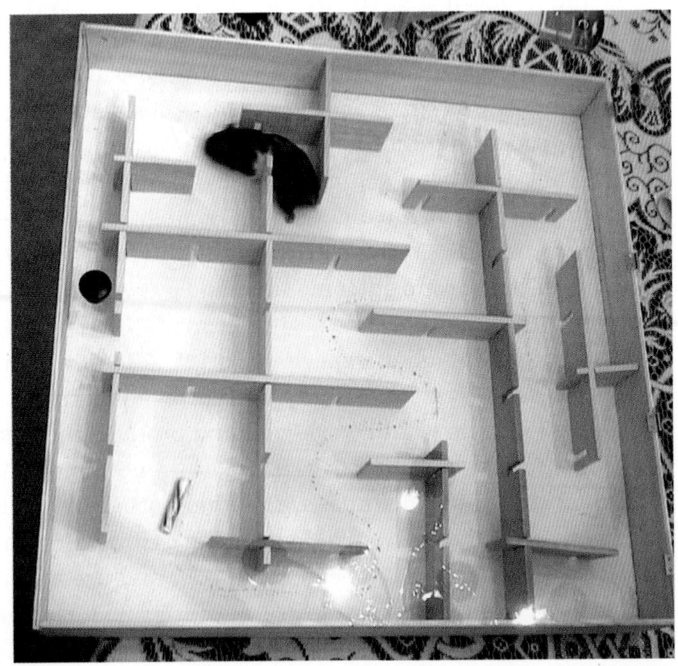

A rat finds its way through a maze. Social scientists have used such experiments to study a variety of traits including learning and memory. The findings often can provide clues to human behavior.

Photo: Mike Klein.

lation is cited. Also, records, documents and other empirical reports of the United Nations and the World Bank are available for sociological analysis. Besides availability of data, savings in terms of time and money are an advantage. Emile Durkheim's study on suicide is an excellent example of this methodology. It demonstrates that certain conditions cannot be studied or investigated by other methods. Surveys and experiments, for example, cannot be employed to study those who committed successful acts of suicide. By reviewing historical data, Durkheim was able to link suicide to several factors, including religion and social integration.

In addition to being readily available and inexpensive, secondary analysis has the advantage of being unobtrusive. However, secondary analysis presents limitations and raises questions as well. It is obvious that available data may not be suitable for the requirements of new studies. Additionally, concern about the accuracy of existing records is inevitable, as well as questions about generalizing to the population.

Field or Observational Research

Field research is also known as observational or ethnographic research. They are also referred to as field research. While other research methods (surveys and experiments) produce quantitative data appropriate for numerical and statistical analysis, field research generates qualitative data, which serve to describe why things happen the way they do.

To obtain this type of data, researchers do not rely only on what people say but rather on observation of the actual behavior. This requires that the researcher be present and, in some cases, be an active participant in the environment under investigation. There are any number of situations that lend themselves specifically to this method. John Lofland (1984) identified several "thinking units" where field research can uncover purpose and intent that would otherwise go unobserved in other research methods. These include:

1. Meanings: to cover culture, norms, world-view and the like;
2. Practices: the various types of behavior;
3. Encounters: two or more people meeting and interacting in immediate proximity with one another;
4. Episodes: divorce, marriage, death, crime, illness and the like;
5. Roles and the analysis of status: positions that people hold and the roles and behavior associated with these positions-ethnic groups, family roles, gender roles and occupation are some examples;
6. Relationships: friendship, marriage, father-daughter, mother-son, father-son, mother-daughter, etc.
7. Groups: families, work groups, athletic teams and gangs, among others;

8. Organizations: schools, hospitals, places of worship, governments, prisons, other formal organizations, and many more; and,

9. Settlements: small villages, towns, communities, tribes and others.

The social scientist, Elliott Liebow, spent his professional career conducting field research that was intended to highlight and empower groups and communities that he studied. His book, *Tally's Corner: A Study of Negro Street Corner Men* (1967 [2003]), was an example of a classic field research in which the researcher was active participant and observant of those men and their interactions on the street. This study illuminated the reality of urban poverty in the 60s and those men that one encountered at the corner could be getting home from work, or going to work, or actually working. This was a classic response to the argument made by the theory on "culture of poverty" (Lewis, 1959). According to this theory the poor remain in their poverty cycle because they are less likely to take on the values and norms found in the mainstream. Liebow's study on homeless women, *Tell Them Who I am: The lives of Homeless Women* (1993), is another such example. In this research, Liebow examines, describes and explores the challenges homeless women face and their daily struggles for survival. Here again, he breaks down stereotypes and images that are held against homeless women, and that their humanity and experiences are not any different from the rest.

These are also examples that point out that field research requires the researcher to be present and involved in varying degrees in the affairs of those being studied. Field research generates a huge amount of in-depth information, but it may be subject to the biases of the researcher(s). To avoid this problem and to minimize its effects, researchers organize their observations in a systematic manner and record them as soon as they occur. Today's technology of audio-video recording, for example, makes it possible to achieve a high level of accuracy. However, it may place researchers in a suspicious position where they could be perceived as outsiders who exhibit exotic but not genuine interest in the research subjects. They might even be confused with spies.

STATISTICAL TOOLS

Simply stated, **statistics** is a mathematical system used to classify numerical data. It is a discipline used to collect, analyze and interpret numerical data. Sociologists depend heavily on statistics to interpret and understand their data and to share their findings with others. In sociology and other social sciences, researchers often use statistical tables and other forms of data presentation because they convey a large amount of information in a relatively small space in a clear and concise way. In this section you will be introduced to the meanings of several commonly used statistical terms.

Statisticians make a distinction between descriptive and inferential statistics. **Descriptive statistics** provide us with measures or ways of describing the average and the typical in a population. **Inferential statis-**

Table 2.2: Frequency Distribution of Weekly Income	
Student #	**Income in U.S. Dollars**
1	$350
2	$1000
3	$115
4	$50
5	$800
6	$1500
7	$50
8	$100
9	$80
10	$215
11	$265

tics refer to a much more advanced and sophisticated branch of statistics that can be used to help scientists not only describe the differences between groups, but mainly to determine whether those differences are significant. **Statistical significance** is defined as a difference between groups that is likely to occur regularly and not by chance. As such, inferential statistics are often used to make inferences (generalizations) from the sample to the larger population, and to measure in a precise manner the interaction (relationship) between the variables under investigation as well as the strength of that relationship. In this section, you will be introduced to the main descriptive statistical measures known as measures of **central tendency**—the mean, the median, and the mode.

Let us assume that you wish to describe the weekly earnings of eleven students in your sociology class. In this case you may want to present information on each individual student as it appears in Table 2.2.

Presenting data in a frequency distribution allows us to see a complete list of all subjects included in the study and the variable—in this case the weekly income that each has received. As you can imagine, presentations of this type may be rather lengthy, depending on the size of the research group, and may not provide us with a meaningful picture of the group.

To make the data in the **frequency distribution** more meaningful, measures of central tendency are frequently used. The simplest measure is the **mode**, defined as the most common value—that value which occurs most often in the frequency distribution. In our example, the mode is $50 since that value occurs twice while each of the others occurs only once. Some distributions may have no mode and others may have more than one. Despite its simplicity, or perhaps because of it, sociologists tend not to use the mode because it provides information only about some, not all, of the values.

The **median** value is the middle case or that value which occurs midway in the frequency distribution when arranged in order of magnitude.

The median is positioned exactly in the middle of the distribution dividing it into two equal parts where fifty percent of the cases are above it and the other fifty percent fall bellow it. The median amount in our example is $215, since five incomes are higher and five are lower (note that generally the values must be listed in ascending or descending order before you can figure out the median). In the case of an even distribution, that is the number of items in the frequency distribution is even, not odd, the median is halfway between the two middle cases. You will notice that the median is not affected by extremes, which makes it attractive to use in certain situations. The U.S. Government uses the median income to determine wealth and poverty rates so that the income of the handful of multi-millionaires does not affect earning rates. To illustrate, the Census data point to the fact that the median income for all U.S. households of all races in 2000 stood at about $40,000 and at about 50,000 in 2007. Explain these figures and discuss their implications.

The most common statistical measure of central tendency is the **mean**, more commonly known as the **average**. The mean is calculated according to the following formula: $\mu = \sum x/n$. This translates to: the mean (μ) is calculated by adding ($\sum$) all of the values (X) in the frequency distribution and then dividing (÷) this sum by (n), the total number of research subjects. In our example, ($\sum$x) or the sum of the eleven incomes is $4525. When we divide this total by eleven (n), we get (X) or the mean income of $411.36.

What these values mean is that each measure gives us a picture of the "average" income, or the central tendency of this group. The fact that the mode stands at $50 points out that there are a number of individuals at the lower end of the distribution, but the mean ($411.36) demonstrates that there are few (three to be exact whose income is the highest) individuals who can actually influence the central tendency upward making the group look richer than what it is. The median ($215) divides the distribution in half and points out that the income of fifty percent of this group is much lower than the average. In addition, since the median is not influenced by extreme values on either end, it seems to be closer to the reality of the group's income.

CONCLUSION

It has become rather obvious that science is an intricate activity in which both scientists and philosophers engage in the pursuit of "truth". Socrates eloquently said, "We are not simply contending in order that my view or yours may prevail, but I presume that we, both of us, ought to be fighting for the truth." This chapter suggests that the business of scientific inquiry begins with questions and may end with questions. It also captures, in a simple form, the essence of scientific activity and offers its readers the tools and fundamental principals that can prepare them for the long journey of scientific inquiry.

Consistent with Emile Durkheim's assertion that social science can provide us with rules of action for the future; this chapter has established that the body of knowledge obtained by objective, logical, and systematic methods of research is the foundation of social science. Consequently it equips those who dare to take their first steps in this direction to start their journey of exploration, description, explanation, invention and discovery for the betterment of humankind.

Terms You Should Know:

Causality/causation	Concept	Content analysis
Correlation	Empirical evidence	Ethnography
Experiment	Generalization	Mode
Median	Mean	Measurement
Objective knowledge	Observation	Patterns
Population	Reliability	Sample
Statistics	Science	Survey
Trends	Validity	Variable

Can You Answer These Questions?

1. Explain the value of scientific research. Why should we trust scientific research over common sense?
2. List and explain the purpose of scientific research and give examples.
3. Distinguish between validity and reliability and give examples.
4. Distinguish between correlation and causality and give examples.
5. List and explain the strengths and weaknesses of quantitative research methods.
6. List and explain the strengths and weaknesses of qualitative research methods.
7. Define and explain the term "theory" and highlight the characteristics of a good theory.
8. Compare and contrast the survey research method with field research.
9. Explain the meaning of sampling and its importance.
10. Record the income of your family members or friends (a minimum of 20 persons) and calculate the average (mean), mode and median. What is the significance of such statistics? What is your conclusion?

Critical Thinking Exercises:

1. What research method is likely to examine cause-and-effect relationship? Why?
2. Follow the guidelines of the survey method and design your own survey. You could study as an example the opinion of students on your campus about same-sex marriage. Compare the answers along the lines of racial groups and gender.
3. Design and conduct an experiment on your campus. Walk into an elevator with your friend and begin dancing and partying. Observe and record the reactions of other people on that elevator.
4. Conduct systematic observations of a specific public area (train station, mall, and park). Focus on specific events or interactions: race, gender, social class, age. Record your observations and identify patterns that are unique to that area. How similar or different those patterns from the larger American society? Why?

Part Two

Foundations of Society

Chapter Three: *Culture and Social Structure*
Chapter Four: *Social Interaction, Organization & Groups*
Chapter Five: *Personal Development and Socialization*
Chapter Six: *Deviance*

It is not uncommon for those of us who teach sociology to hear students who have traveled to distant countries speak of the strange and wondrous experiences they've encountered. The world we live in is extremely diverse. Practices and beliefs we take for truth and as a matter of common sense are perceived by those from other cultures to be bizarre, even humorous. What is truly amazing is that while there is much difference between cultures, there is also tremendous similarity. For example, all cultures have developed rules and behaviors for social interaction. All societies have developed family systems for reproduction and the socialization of the young. All societies have built government institutions to provide leadership. All societies have developed religions to explain creation and death. We could go on, but we think you get the point. The bottom line is that while outcomes may differ, there is similarity to be found in the process.

In this section we explore the foundations of sociology. In Chapter Three we will address the concepts of culture and social structure. It is here we will learn of cultural universals (such as those mentioned above) and the diversity of beliefs. Additionally, we will explore norms and folkways and patterns of social interaction. In Chapter Four we will focus more closely on social interaction. We will discover why people behave differently in different social situations. From here we will discuss the importance of belonging to a group and the effect group membership has on our behavior. In Chapter Five we will look at the "nature versus nurture" issue. In other words, is your personality a matter of genetics or the way you were socialized? Or, do genetics and society wash together (blend) to produce personality? And, in the last chapter in this section, Six, we discuss deviance. We will learn that from a sociological viewpoint, deviance is not always bad or criminal. We will consider the question of what is deviant and who determines what qualifies as deviance. Too, we will see that what might be considered deviant in this culture may well be considered honorable in another.

As you can see, we have much to learn in this section. However, with your new found understanding comes the ability to see our world in a way that has escaped millions of others. Perhaps the best analogy we can offer is the difference between watching a movie in "black and white" or "technicolor." The spectrum of colors and lights are dazzling. And so is life.

Photo: flickr.com / photos / rudiroels.

Chapter 3

Society, Culture, and Social Structures

Envision the following scenario. It's late at night. You are alone with your "significant other." The lights are low and soft romantic music is playing in the background. Suddenly you both turn toward each other and your eyes meet. You move closer and closer. Inside, you feel the hormones rushing through your veins. Your head tilts slightly to the right, your eyes close, and then it happens—your lips touch.

It all seems so simple, right? Well, not exactly. In fact, sociologists who have studied kissing can testify that it's a rather complicated business. Let's take a closer look.

Although one might think that kissing has always been part of the human experience, it is a relatively recent phenomenon. Anthropologists, who have scoured clay tablets, cave paintings, and written records dating back thousands of years, have concluded that the first erotic kiss was delivered in about 1500 BCE in India. Up until this time a number of cultures rubbed noses and faces in an expression of erotic passion. Prior to this time, no illustration in art or literature was found referring to kissing. This is not so surprising, since the notion of romantic love was first introduced to Western culture sometime in the Middle Ages.

It was the Romans who first popularized kissing as we know it today. In fact, so enamored did the Romans become with kissing that they were soon puckering up for everything. Friends greeted one another with kisses on the cheek. To signify respect, statues of gods were kissed. People of higher status had their rings kissed in a demonstration of submission. Prior to Senate meetings, senators engaged in a sort of "kissing fest" in hopes of a peaceful and productive session. With so many different types of kisses, categories became necessary. First came the *osculum*, a friendship kiss. Second, was the *basium*, which was the passionate kiss. And then there was the variation on what is now known as the red-hot French kiss called the *savium*.

As the Romans pressed forward in refining the art of kissing, they were suddenly upstaged by the land that first invented kissing—India. In about 300 CE a book about erotic love, *The Kamasutra*, appeared. Here, author Vatsyayana, in graphic illustrations, detailed a variety of lovemaking positions complete with suggestions on "where" and "how" to plant a kiss on a variety of body parts. As one might guess, the concept of kissing was spreading faster than a Kansas prairie fire in the middle of August.

It was the Christians (oh, what a surprise) that first tried to put the kibosh on the practice. In 1311-1312, at the Council of Cinna, the Catholic Church passed laws against "whoopee kissing." A simple erotic kiss, according to church officials, constituted a "venial" sin (bad, but not so bad than one would have to spend eternity in hell). However, if one entertained thoughts about the "big, nasty deed" while kissing, it would qualify as a "mortal" sin (a fast ride on the down elevator, with no up button). Realizing the weakness of the flesh, the church invented the *osculatorium*, to help their members deal with temptation. This metal disk with pictures of the saints painted onto it was passed around at church services. The faithful would plant their kisses on the osculatorium, rather than each other (Chicago Tribune, 1998). In this way, they could leave their lust at church rather than taking it outside. Fortunately, this practice enjoyed only momentary popularity. Soon it was back to lip locking.

Of course, the story does not end here. Sociologists who have studied the phenomenon of kissing have discovered wide variations in the practice of kissing. First, not all cultures kiss, or do so in a manner that we in the West would classify as a kiss. The most well known "non-kiss" is that of nose rubbing by Eskimos. Here two lovers begin by embracing. Simultaneously they bring their faces closer while aiming their noses slightly to the side of each other's. When the noses make contact, they slide along the sides until they reach the tips. At this point each partner breathes in to savor each other's fragrance. Finally, while lowering the eyelids, a soft smack of the lips is given without touching the cheek or nose of the other. Noses are then slid up and down while occasionally bumping the tips of the noses. This non-kiss is popular among a number of cultures—the Maoris of New Zealand, the Society and Sandwich Islanders, the Tongans, most of the Malayan races, and in some cultures in Africa and Asia.

Lest you think nose rubbing is off the beaten path, consider the practice of the natives of the Trobriand Islands located approximately 1,800 miles north of Sydney, Australia. The inhabitants of these islands consider the Western form of kissing dull and unimaginative. Like the Eskimos, they rub noses. But this is just the beginning. As passion rises they begin to rub cheeks with their mouths without kissing. Next they proceed to suck and roll tongues (French style). At the high point of passion they suck and bite each other's lip until bleeding occurs. And, in a most unusual practice (for Westerners) they bite off each other's eyelashes in the final orgasmic stage of sex. In addition they exchange saliva from mouth to mouth and bite each other's cheeks and nose. Hair pulling is also very common at intense moments. At times the pulling of hair is so forceful that large clumps are pulled from the head (Crane, 1995). Yikes!

Even for those who practice what might be termed a Western style of kissing, there is much variation. For example, the Japanese are very shy about kissing. Within their culture it is considered a breach of decency to kiss publicly. The delivery of a kiss in Japan reflects this shyness. To kiss, one stands away from his/her partner without embracing or touching with the hands. The face is brought forward, eyes closed, and contact is made. The kiss is held without reaction for a brief moment before breaking off. It is customary to act shy and above all one must be discreet and say nothing about the kiss. Kissing is considered risqué and many Japanese, particularly the older generations, do not practice kissing at all. While some have criticized their kiss as sexless, the Japanese feel that it is the most erotic kiss in the world. The element of holding back (Taoist simplicity) preserves the excitement.

So now you might ask, what has all of this to do with sociology? In part, sociology is the study of culture. Each society builds a culture within which its members can live harmoniously. Cultures vary, beliefs vary, actions vary, and that is what this chapter is all about—the study of culture and society. So let's begin.

SOCIETY

Human beings are not solitary creatures. We are social. What this implies is that we live our lives in the presence of other humans. Underlying this assumption are three basic facts. The *first* is that when we come into the world, we are dependent upon others for survival. Without someone to care for it, the life of a baby would be measured in hours. Furthermore, years of care are required until a child reaches an age of independence, more so than any other animal on earth. *Second*, humans have always found it to their advantage to cooperate with others in order to obtain protection and the necessities of life. Although it would be possible after a period of time to exist alone, chances are that at some point the help of another human being would be required in order to sustain one's own life. *Finally*, there is something in the human spirit that seeks out others. Our capacity to laugh, to love, to feel isolation and loneliness are all pre-programmed emotions driving us to find and interact with others like ourselves.

For all of the above reasons humans gravitate toward one another. With this in mind, it is also important to understand one additional quality of human existence, that of predictability. Although we are naturally curious and can become bored without change, it is also true that we need to have some certainty in our lives. Consider for a moment what your life would be like if everything was in a constant state of change, if every act, every event, every response from others was totally unpredictable. Within a very short time the resulting stress would probably cause a nervous breakdown. We as humans must have some predictability in our lives. In order to attain this, we surround ourselves with familiarity—people we know, places we are comfortable in, objects we understand, and so forth. This, of course, leads us to our definition of **society**. A society is a relatively self-contained group of humans who share a common territory, and have organized themselves for the purposes of survival and perpetuation of a certain way of life. As we move through this chapter, not only will our definition of society become clearer, but also, you will come to understand the powerful influence it has upon your life. However, for now, let's turn to an examination of the two major components of society—culture and social structure.

CULTURE

Perhaps at some time you have heard someone remark that a particular individual lacks culture. The connotation in everyday language is that the person is crude. This, of course, is not a sociological interpretation. For the sociologist, everyone has culture. In fact, it would be impossible to live in society and not possess culture. A sociological definition of **culture** refers to all the shared knowledge, values, rules of behavior, and the objects that makeup a people's way of life. For the purposes of clarity, sociologists generally divide the study of culture into two parts—material culture and nonmaterial culture.

Material Culture

Material culture is comprised of all the things that people make and use. Included would be: the chair you are sitting in, the automobile you drove or the bus you took to school, the shoes on your feet, the jewelry you wear, the house in which you live, and the television you watch (*after* you do your homework, of course). The list is almost endless. The importance of material culture is that it shapes how we interact with the world around us. In primitive societies, tools were simple and directed people toward hunting and gathering. In complex society the tools are complex and sophisticated and our lives reflect a similar degree of complexity and sophistication.

An important aspect of the material culture is **technology**, the utilization of tools and machines to achieve greater practical uses of knowledge to increase power and conserve human energy. Anthropologists who study ancient civilizations and societies have noted the importance of technology for survival. Societies that developed technology leading to advanced weaponry had a superior advantage over those lagging behind. Even in modern society this is true. As such, America continues to develop war technology—Stealth Bombers, "smart" missiles, nuclear submarines, spy satellites, etc., in a continuing effort to protect our country and our national interest.

Nonmaterial Culture

Nonmaterial culture refers to all the non-physical aspects of human interaction. This includes symbols, language, values, and the rules of behavior. It is the non material culture that guides the entirety of our behavior. We move though our day interacting with others in a thousand (maybe tens of thousands) different ways each day. Rarely do we stop to think about how we should behave or what the meaning of an interaction is. How is this possible? Largely because our culture provides us with ready-made answers. Without these answers stress and indecision would immobilize us. Life would not be possible. Let's take a moment to examine some aspects of non material culture.

Symbols

Some sociologists, particularly the symbolic interactionalists (see chapter one), consider this the most important aspect of human interaction. A **symbol** is defined as anything that invokes within a human being a response. If you were suddenly asked by your instructor to identify a number of common symbols in your everyday life you might have to stop and think. Some students find this a particularly difficult task when actually the list is endless. Think about your trip to school today. Undoubtedly you were annoyed when you were unable to make a traffic light—a symbol. It tells you when to stop, when to go, and when to use caution. As you traveled along you might have passed a postal office with an American flag—a symbol of the nation. Cars on the road all exhibited emblems of their makers—symbols. You pass a church with a cross—a symbol of Christianity. A crossing guard moves into the street with a sign and places a hand up—symbols. Across the street, gang graffiti litters the outside wall of a building—a symbol. The light changes and you begin across the street only to be cut off by someone trying to make a quick left hand turn. To demonstrate your disgust, you "flip-the-bird"—an easily recognized symbol by just about everyone in the culture. After parking your car you walk into the building and as you enter a friend smiles and winks—symbols of friendship.

Get the picture? Our lives are filled with an endless array of symbols. The fact is that without them it would be impossible for us to function. And what is truly amazing about all of this is that millions of people live in the same country and all recognize and, to some extent, have a similar understanding of an endless number of society's symbols.

Curiously, symbols may have different meanings in varying situations. For example, in our discussion of kissing, it is well understood that a kiss

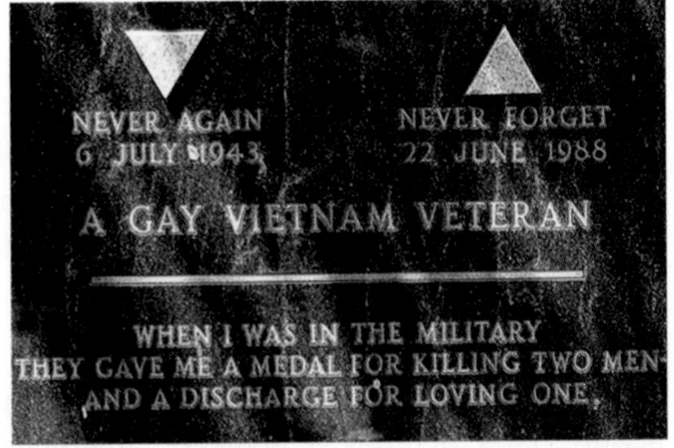

The headstone with the epitaph for Sgt. Leonard Matlovic. After three tours of duty where he received the Bronze Star, a Purple Heart, and an Air Force Meritorious Service Medal, he was discharged from the military for being gay. Matlovic was the first to challenge the military's exclusion of gays and lesbians. He later died of AIDS at the age of 45.
Photo: David B. King.

delivered to the cheek of a child is very different than one given to a lover. A wink by a member of the opposite sex is considered a show of attraction. A wink given to a member of an opposing team in the heat of competition could imply an insult. In the same fashion, a gentle pat to the gluteus maximus (butt) of a teammate is different than one delivered to the hind end of one's latest attraction. One can only imagine the confusion of visiting foreigners not familiar with the subtle nuances of this practice.

Then, of course, depending on one's views, a different interpretation of symbols can be held. Again, on your way to school, you pass a "street person" pushing a grocery cart down the side of the street. What do you see? For some this is a symbol of the decline of society, the inability, or unwillingness of society to care for those less fortunate. For others, it symbolizes a lack of self-respect, laziness, and disregard for societal values. In the same vein, one person could look at short skirts as symbolizing a lack of values while another could see it as stylish. This is true also for the uniform of a police officer. One person sees it as respectful and friendly; others view it as a symbol of oppression.

Symbols can also hold very different meanings for members of different cultures. Remember our example of the crossing guard holding a hand up to halt traffic? In West Africa this would be considered disrespectful, as it is akin to calling one a bastard (you have five fathers). In our country it is a sign of affection and admiration to pat a child on the head. In Japan it is an insult. Likewise, a dog to us is a symbol of our best friend. In many Asian countries, a dog symbolizes little more than a tasty dinner.

Language

A powerful form of symbolization is that of language. **Language** is a shared system of symbols used in verbal and written communication. It is estimated that spoken language developed among humans over 40,000 years ago. All cultures have developed some form of verbal language. The development of written language, where humans began to assign symbols to sounds in order to codify thoughts through language, began approximately 4,000 years ago. Although most cultures have created a written language to accompany the verbal, some have existed without it. An example here are the Yanomamo, an isolated tribe of South America, who up until their recent discovery have lived the same way as their ancestors for thousands of years. For them written language was not necessary, all their beliefs and knowledge about the world was passed from one generation to another verbally. However, the absence of a written language is found only in very simple societies. Without a written language it is not possible to develop complex thoughts and therefore advanced societies require written language to survive.

Language is important for three basic reasons. *First*, language provides humans with the ability to transmit culture through successive generations. Without this there would be no permanence to culture and all aspects of life would be in a state of perpetual change. *Second*, language allows humans to build upon existing knowledge. Without language, particularly written language, it would impossible to accumulate and store knowledge for the next generation. As such, each new generation would be in the position of having, so to speak, to "reinvent-the-wheel." Today, it is estimated that human knowledge doubles every ten years. Again, without language this would not be possible. And *finally*, language provides us with what one researcher has termed "semantic universality" (Greenberg, 1968). Simply stated, it gives humans the capacity to transcend time and place so that we may speak about other people and cultures in the past, present and future.

While it is easy to see how language has the ability to expand our world, most people are less aware of how it can limit our world. In the 1930s Edward Sapir, a linguistic anthropologist and his student, Benjamin Lee Whorf, proposed what is now termed the **Linguistic Relativity Hypothesis**. The central proposition here is that language acts as a mental filter, shaping the way we see the world. Through language, cultures attach certain meanings to different objects and events. Once defined, it is difficult to see the object or event in any way other than how it has been defined. Thus, the same object may have totally different meanings to people from different cultures because of the way it is defined in their language.

One example of this can be seen in the way people in the United States view the colors black and white. Black is generally associated with something dark and evil. Hence, in our language we have sayings like "black cat," "black magic," "black sheep," "black heart," "black market," "black mark," etc. Literally, there are hundreds of such terms. On the flip side, white is used to describe all that is good—"white knight," "white Christmas," "white lie," "White House," "white hat," "white horse," etc. The perceptions and associations related to these colors are so powerful that they can influence actions. A bride wears a white dress to symbolize purity and a black suit is worn to a funeral to symbolize our feelings about death. In movies and stories, the villain dresses in black, while the hero wears white. It has been suggested that the constraints imposed upon us by language are, at least in part, to blame for racial problems in this country because the emotional values instilled in our perceptions of color limits society's ability to see dark skinned people as equals.

Language is also important in that it is a mechanism of **social control** in society. A father who is fearful that his boy is acting too effeminate may try to alter the child's behavior by calling him a "sissy." Former president

George H. Bush, in the 1992 presidential election, deliberately altered his campaign style and positions on issues to reflect a tougher image when it was suggested that he was a "wimp." Likewise, have you ever wondered why we have different titles by which to address women—Miss and Mrs., and only one for men—Mr.? Why is it important to be able to designate the marital status of women, but not of men? In protest, some women who understand the issue use the term Ms. Also, language is used to control the sexual behavior of women. Consider the number of terms used to describe sexually active women in our culture—slut, nymphomaniac, whore, tramp, trash, floozy, easy, promiscuous, etc. Actually we could list many more, but we're too embarrassed. How many can you think of for men? What does this tell you about language and social control?

Values

Another common component of non material culture is values. Simply defined, **values** refer to a common set of beliefs about what is right and what is wrong. In our definition, we use the term "common" to indicate that there is widespread agreement by society's members on the value system. While this is true it should be noted that the agreement is not absolute. Let's examine two questions currently being debated in the larger society.

Question One: Should individuals be allowed to sell their organs?

Yes. Advocates base their arguments on several points. First, they believe that organs belong to individuals, and as such, individuals should be the sole judge of what to do with them. Supporting this argument is the rationale that we currently allow individuals to sell blood, sperm, and eggs. So, why prohibit the sale of organs such as kidneys, livers, hearts, etc.? The second reason advocates site is that despite all humanitarian efforts, the supply of organs needed for transplant falls seriously short of demand. According to recent statistics, of the 110,000 patients waiting for organs, less than 25 percent will receive an organ before their need results in death (Organdonor.gov, 2010). Advocates maintain that creating a legalized international market, monitored for abuses, would greatly increase the availability of organs and save countless lives. To do otherwise, they suggest, would be morally and ethically irresponsible. Finally, those advocating for the legal and regulated sale of organs point to the fact that a thriving black market in organ sales already exists. Creating a regulated international market would save lives by protecting donors from unsafe and unsanitary extraction, as well as insuring fair and equal compensation to all.

No. Opponents counter the above arguments on two major points. The first centers on the question of ownership. Just because an organ lies in the body of the person willing to sell it does not mean he/she has the legal right to market it to the highest bidder. For example, individuals cannot legally sell themselves into slavery or prostitution. Likewise, there are restrictions on how one can sell their labor, as with minimum age and wage laws. So, they argue, merely owning something, like one's body, does not confer the right to transfer it to someone else. The second argument, maintain opponents, is that the creation of a system where one can sell organs would be greatly exploitative of the poor and disenfranchised for the benefit of the rich and powerful. Those having the funds, political clout, and power would be allowed to prey upon the less fortunate of society who in desperation would have few options other than to sell their organs. As for the poor in need of transplants, they would be shoved to the back of the waiting line since they did not have the resources to purchase organs they need. Finally, opponents point out that women and children in third world countries would be the first victims of organ-for-sale schemes since husbands, fathers and brothers have power over them and they have no legal or social protection. What do you think?

Question Two: Should gay and lesbian couples be allowed the legal right to marry?

Yes. On the affirmative side of this issue, advocates argue that not allowing gay and lesbian marriages is simply a matter of sexual discrimination in which the majority (heterosexuals) enforces upon others (homosexuals) their view of morality. In the process, homosexuals have been stigmatized and subjected to oppressive and often violent acts. For many gays and lesbians, homosexuality is not a matter of choice, but biological orientation. Adopting a heterosexual lifestyle is not possible and thus they should not be denied access to legal marriage. In addition to the emotional commitment, marriage affords couples legal and property rights. Through marriage, a heterosexual couple can share medical and pension benefits. Likewise, in the event of a wrongful death, a spouse has legal standing to sue where a non-spouse does not. These are rights denied to gay and lesbian couples. Advocates also argue that allowing gays to marry would deepen their commitments and provide for better role models for children living with gay couples—a practice not outlawed by society. Presently, 36 percent of those surveyed believed gay and lesbians should be allowed to marry (The Pew Forum, 2008).

No. The most prevailing view supporting the ban against gay and lesbian marriage is that it violates God's law. To legalize such unions would be akin to informing God that He erred and we have the right to reverse His law by rewriting scripture. For others less religiously inclined, legalizing gay and lesbian marriages would serve to destabilize heterosexual marriages by allowing for people to choose which lifestyle they prefer (Pew Research Center, 2003). Others believe that allowing such marriages would send a message that homosexuality is as natural as heterosexuality. This would result in more children experimenting with and potentially adopting a homosexual lifestyle. Similarly, if gay and lesbian marriages are legalized, what is to prevent them from adopting children? Is it possible to deny a gay or lesbian couple the same rights of adoption as that afforded to heterosexual couples? In essence, the legal rights of the couple would take precedent over that of the children, as is the case of disputed custody between biological and adoptive parents. According to a recent poll, 55 percent of Americans oppose homosexual marriages (The Pew Forum, 2008). Where do you stand?

The preceding examples illustrate how divided our society can be on the question of values. Why is this so? A number of reasons can explain value conflict. First, we live in a period of rapid change. As mentioned previously, human knowledge doubles every ten years. Undoubtedly, as we move forward, the speed of change will become even more rapid. This produces what is generally referred to as **cultural lag**, a condition created when changes in the material culture occur at a faster pace than the nonmaterial culture. The ability to adjust to change varies from one person to another, hence differences occur between those that accept change quickly and those who prefer to hang on to cherished beliefs and ways of life. Also, conflict occurs because cultural patterns vary according to age, sex, ethnicity, race, religion, and social class. And finally, we tend to interpret values according to our own self-interest or advantage. An example here is how one might view affirmative action. Members of minority groups tend to support its continuation; more whites than non-whites tend to favor abolishing it.

Having said all this, it is important to note that while disagreement on values exists, there is also tremendous agreement on a wide number of values. We will explore these later in this chapter. For now, suffice it to say that without value agreement, society could not exist.

While others in society race to adopt and adjust to changes, others prefer to hold on to traditional values and beliefs. Here an Amish couple return home with their children in a mode of transportation from another era.

Photo: Debi Warson.

Norms

Just as there must be some common agreement on the values of society, it is equally important for society to have a set of rules of conduct. Sociologists use the term norms in describing these rules. **Norms** are the rules of society that prescribe how the members are to behave in given situations. Almost from the moment of birth, society begins to instruct us on proper behavior. Virtually everything that we think or do is governed by norms. One social observer, Marshall Clinard (1974), noted that the norms of society are so well instilled in us that we arbitrarily walk through our lives following them without even thinking about them. Think about the classroom. Students enter the room and take seats facing the front of the class at the appropriate time. The professor enters and moves to the front desk. Attendance is taken. Students respond without question. The professor proceeds to instruct. Students listen and take notes, occasionally speaking when called upon. When the allotted time for class is over everyone leaves and a whole new set of norms comes into play. Everything goes along without a hitch.

Simple, isn't it?

The answer is yes and no. It all appears to be very simple on the surface. However, this is only true because everyone knows what is expected and complies. Reflectively thinking, there is a positive and a negative side to norms. On the positive side, norms give us the freedom to act without thinking about everything we do. Life would be sheer chaos if we had to think about every decision or action we undertook. Not only would there not be enough time to do this, but we would lose our ability to predict the actions of others—again, chaos. On the negative side, norms limit our choices and ability to think about life in different ways. We dutifully follow prescribed patterns of behavior with a sense that this is the way life ought to work. In doing so, we close the door to creative ways of thinking that could provide better alternatives to life.

Also, norms can lead to discriminative behavior. For example, norms exist that tell us how men and women should behave. However, these norms sometimes provide men with advantages over women, as in the case of career selections. Likewise, women sometimes have advantages over men, as in the case of draft laws. Individuals who move out of these prescribed patterns of behavior are often subject to discriminative sanctions.

Table 3.1: FOLKWAYS
• picking your nose in public • answering your cellphone while in a theater • wearing a tank top to church • using foul language in the classroom • loudly belching in a restaurant • treating your parents with disrespect • throwing your cigarette butts on the ground • coughing up phlegm and spitting on the sidewalk

Table 3.2	LAWS
• **driving while under the influence of alcohol** • **murder** • **theft** • **embezzlement** • **arson** • **copyright infringement** • **counterfeiting**	

Generally speaking, two levels of norms exist. The first is that of **folkways**. These norms constitute the customary patterns of our lives. Members of society through both verbal and nonverbal reprimands discourage them (see Table 3.1).

While some of these things might be disgusting, they will not land you in jail or result in a serious penalty. At the most, someone may express to you that you are indeed crude and vulgar and the people of the community would be better off if you left town.

Norms considered to be more serious are termed **mores** (pronounced mo-rays). These are strongly held beliefs about acceptable behavior. Either rightfully or wrongfully, members of the society believe that the very stability of the community depends on these rules being followed. As such, violations are not tolerated. Mores can take one of two forms—laws and taboos. **Laws** are codified norms or rules of behavior that have been legally sanctioned by government. In order to enforce laws, the state establishes various institutions to deal with violators—police, courts, and prisons. Like norms, not all laws carry the same weight. A law against spitting on the sidewalk is not as serious as one against armed robbery. Here, the amount of enforcement as well as the severity of the sanction varies. While spitting on the sidewalk might be against the law, it is rarely enforced or punished. On the other hand, armed robbery is never overlooked; to do so would jeopardize the stability of society (see Table 3.2).

Taboos are also a classification of mores. Like laws, **taboos** are also strongly enforced by the state but they differ in that they delve into the area of the forbidden. Taboos violate our sense of humanness. They are highly offensive acts that most members of society consider to be unthinkable (see Table 3.3).

As with values, norms vary from place to place and from one period of time to another. At one time it was taboo to marry outside of one's own race. In fact, laws prohibiting such marriages existed in some places in the United States until the mid 1950s. This is no longer true. Disagreements over mores can occur. At one time in this country, nearly all members of society considered homosexuality taboo. Today, many people, while not advocating its practice, have developed more tolerant views about homosexuality.

Table 3.3	TABOOS
• incest • cannibalism • necrophilia • animal torture • desecration of a place of worship	

Culture—Ideal and Real

Within all cultures there is a tendency for a gap to develop between what we value and what we practice. What we *believe* is referred to as the **ideal culture**. What we *practice* is termed the **real culture**. What is truly interesting is that on the whole, we are mostly unaware of the discrepancy. For example, in the United States, premarital sex is discouraged and chastity is valued, particularly for women. Parents attempt to instill these values in their children, and church doctrine is still strongly opposed to sex prior to marriage. However, the actual practice of society is very different. The first major study of the sexual practices of Americans in the 1940s and 1950s found that 84 percent of the population had premarital sexual experiences (Kinsey, 1948; 1953).

Another example of a difference between what we value and what we practice is the conflict between our religious beliefs and our economic practices. One of the major tenets of Christianity is a belief in generosity and non materialism. The Bible states that it will be easier for a camel to pass through the eye of a needle than for a rich man to enter the kingdom of God. Is this what we practice in our everyday lives? Our economic system of capitalism glorifies greed and materialism. Ask yourself, do you think most of the students in your sociology class enrolled because of their unquenchable thirst for knowledge or for the prestige and economic rewards that a college degree can bestow upon them? Do you play the state lottery so that if you win you can practice your religion by improving the lives of the poor, or so that you can buy all the things that you always wanted?

ASPECTS OF CULTURE

Cultural Universals

When we speak of **cultural universals** we refer to social structures and events that seem to be shared across cultures. George Murdock (1956) identified over sixty cultural universals. Included were food preparation, feasting, story telling, death rites, music, and sex.

The existence of cultural universals is grounded in the fact that biologically we are all alike. This may seem obvious but because we all have the same physical needs, we are channeled into similar patterns designed for existence and the continuation of our species. We all must eat, find shelter,

A group of village children break into song and dance. Both signing and dancing are examples of cultural universals; can you identify some cultural universals in your society?

Photo: Neils Photography

procreate, care for our children, provide for our elders and the sick, and make arrangements for when we die.

A *second* reason for universals is that we must all contend with the unknown and try to find answers to questions that lie outside of the boundaries of science to explain, for example, who we are, where we came from, and what happens to us after death. These are universal questions. To disregard them is humanly not possible. And while it is true that we may come to different conclusions, it is equally true that we must have answers.

Third, since we all inhabit the same planet, we must contend with the same physical limitations and the availability of resources. It is for this reason that all societies have discovered and used fire and learned how to cultivate crops and domesticate animals. The wheel also is common to all societies. Why? Because it works better than something square.

Finally, as societies advance, all have had to find ways to deal with the complexity of social interactions. This means that rules regarding property, marriage, norm violations, education, financial exchange, and so forth, need to be developed. All of the above represent cultural universals that can be found in all societies.

Cultural Diversity

Having discussed cultural universals, we now address *differences* between and within cultures. We refer to these as **cultural diversity**. In some cultures, like those of Japan and Sweden, there is very little diversity. We refer to these as *homogeneous societies*, meaning that they are highly similar in their social, religious, racial and ethnical makeup. Other nations, such as the United States are *heterogeneous societies*. This means we are highly diversified in our social, religious, racial and ethnic background. One of the main factors leading to a heterogeneous society is **immigration**. This is particularly true of the United States who prides itself on being a "nation of immigrants." In our society a variety of cultural differences can be found. Walk down the street of a busy metropolitan city and you will notice people dressed differently and speaking languages other than English. Due to the size of our country, we also find regional differences. For example, a Texan speaks with a southern drawl and a New Yorker tends to have a more nasal speech.

Cultural diversity is also found between cultures. In our country we are somewhat modest and dress accordingly. In the Yanomami culture, clothing is not an issue because of the hot and humid climate. In the U.S. we practice monogamy but in primitive or aboriginal societies it is understandable that polygamy might be preferred. Death and warfare easily depopulate the number of eligible males as mates. Under such circumstances, it would be foolhardy to adopt monogamy; the tribe simply could not survive. The culture of a society has a ripple effect on all aspects of life for its members. For example, if a society's principle means to achieve food is limited to hunting, then it is likely that many aspects of their culture—family arrangements, religion, ruling structure—will be influenced by what hunting entails.

Finally, while understanding cultural diversity is useful, sociologists recognize that cultural practices vary greatly *within* cultures depending on religion, gender, wealth, and other variables of individual members. An example would be the eating of pork. While it is generally true that Americans eat pork, not all Americans do so. Some religious sects have strict prohibitions regarding the eating of pork.

Ethnocentrism

Ethnocentrism is a word used to describe our feeling that our own culture is superior to that of others. As young children we were all taught to take pride in our country. We were taught to recite the pledge of allegiance, sing the national anthem and other songs that glorify our nation and our way of life. We continue to do these things as adults. The good side of this is that it allows for a more harmonious society. Our loyalty and commitment to the society is bolstered. Unfortunately, as we learn what is good and right about our own society, we also have a tendency to develop an attitude that our way of life is "right" or superior to that of others. Let's consider a couple of examples.

First, consider for a moment that you are on a commuter train. You look across the aisle and someone is staring at you. Your eyes meet. You look away so as not to stare. However, when you look back, the person's eyes are still fixed on you. You look away again. In a second you glance up and still the person is staring. How do you feel—irritated, frustrated, angry, uncomfortable? Undoubtedly, all the above could describe your feelings. Why do you feel this way? The reason is because in this country we value space. In elevators and trains we avoid eye contact with others. If we do glance at them, it is only for a fleeting moment until their eyes meet ours, then we look away. To do otherwise would be considered rude and in some cases, could produce an aggressive and violent response from the person being stared at. However, in other parts of the world such as Latin

America and the Middle East, personal space is not highly valued. In fact, the opposite is true. When an American and, let's say, an Arab speak, it can turn into a dance where the American is continually backing away with the Arab pursuing. Each is attempting to do what is *natural*.

In another example, let us say that you are an anthropologist who has just entered the country with a member of the Yanomano tribe, who is entering civilization for the first time. It has been arranged for him to stay at your house with an interpreter to avoid the culture shock of a hotel. Within moments of entering your house you see the Yanomano sizing-up your wife. All at once he becomes very animated. You ask what is being said and the interpreter informs you that he has requested to have sexual intercourse with your wife. What would be your reply? Of course you would refuse. But don't be surprised to find that you have just insulted your house guest. In the Yanomano culture, it is considered a gesture of friendship and generosity to sexually share wives. In the best case scenario you are, in his eyes, rude and selfish. The worst case scenario is that you have greatly insulted him and he's going to haul out his blow gun to restore his honor. By the way, just in case you think this practice is an aberration, it has been practiced in many cultures at one time or another throughout history.

Cultural Relativity

Again, we have been trained to think of the way that we do things as natural. In fact, our ways seem so natural that we are truly surprised and shocked to find others behaving differently. A strategy employed by sociologists is to try to see our own culture through the eyes of an outsider. For instance, try to imagine how ridiculous a person from an Asian country might find our treatment of dogs. We write laws to protect them; we spend billions of dollars at the pet stores pampering them. Endless amounts of dollars go for medical care at the veterinarian (including things like hip and joint replacements, chemotherapy, insulin, etc.). We coo and baby talk to them. Cemeteries are built for them and people have gone so far as to will millions of dollars to them after they pass on. In many cases, our pets receive more attention than our children do. To many Asians all this fuss is laughable if not down right stupid. To them, dogs are nothing more than a tasty dinner entree. Similarly, an American traveling in India might experience the same feelings upon seeing people starving to death in the streets of New Delhi, when there's "meat-on-the-hoof" roaming around free, since in Indian culture the cow is sacred. To us, it may seem stupid not to eat the cow, but this is only part of the story. Not only is the cow sacred, it is vital to the economy as its waste is used for fuel, fertilizer, house flooring, and it provides farm labor, and of course, milk. To eat the cow in hard times would impair the society's ability to economically recover in the future (Harris, 1975).

The above is an exercise in what is termed by sociologists as **cultural relativism,** the practice of judging the culture of others by *their* standards and not your own. The importance of this practice will be even more apparent later in this chapter when we discuss how technology and the global economy is increasing the necessity to become more tolerant of the customs and beliefs of other cultures.

Subculture

Within large countries it is very common to have groups that, while identifying with a substantial portion of the dominant culture, hold values, beliefs, traits and customs that are distinct and separate from the rest of society. Sociologists term these **subcultures**. The origins for subcultures come primarily from two sources—immigration and annexation of lands. For the United States, the former explains most examples of subcultures. As we have seen, we are a nation of immigrants. With the exception of American-Indians, people came to America seeking their fortune or to escape religious, ethnic, or political persecution. While accepting much of the dominant culture, it was only natural for them to continue many traditions from their own culture. Over time, many of these differences disappeared or became accepted as a part of the dominant culture. In other cases, differences between groups were maintained and exist today in society as subcultures. Two such examples can be seen with the Amish and Hasidic Jews. Both groups immigrated to the United States to escape religious persecution. The cultural values of both groups are very different from those of the dominant culture. Yet, over generations these two groups have been able to resist assimilation into the dominant culture and the dominant culture has not adopted the values of the subculture.

In other nations, the annexation of territories is usually what explains the existence of subcultures. This is particularly true of Africa and Europe, where territorial lines were drawn more for political reasons than for cultural ones. In some cases subcultural differences between groups are not peaceful. Current examples can be seen with the Serbs and Muslims in the former republic of Yugoslavia and with the Hindus and Muslims in India and Pakistan. In both cases, territorial divisions were needed to provide some measure (though not entirely successful) of peace.

In the United States, subcultural differences originating from annexation of territories can be seen with Native American and Mexican American populations. Much of the land that now comprises our nation was forcibly taken from various American Indian tribes and Mexico.

In addition to origins, sociologists are interested in other aspects of subcultures. They ask, why are some cultural values more easily assimilated while others are not. How tolerant is the dominant culture to the existence of subcultures? What roles do subculture traits play in the stratification structure? What mechanisms do subcultures employ to protect their customs from being assimilated? Is it possible to maintain subcultural values indefinitely, or is assimilation inevitable?

Counterculture

Another common occurrence within society is the formation of counterculture groups. **Counterculture** is defined as a culture that is created in opposition

More characteristic of larger, modern society, countercultures deviate from what is perceived to be the norm for acceptable behavior. Some sociologists are quick to point out that what is normal or not normal is determined by the powerful majority at the expense of those without power in society.

Photo: Chris Brown

to the existing culture. Perhaps the best example of a counterculture group is the "hippies" of the 1960s. Rejecting society's culture as meaningless, materialist, repressive, and corrupt, they openly "dropped-out" to follow a lifestyle based on love, communal living, inner peace, and non materialism—values directly counter to that of the rest of capitalist society. Another example can be seen in the Hells Angels, a motorcycle gang formed in the 1950s.

Sociologists have noted that members of counterculture groups tend to be young (Roszak, 1969; Spates, 1976). It is a natural tendency of the young to experiment and look for alternative pathways to life before entering adulthood. It is for this reason that countercultures tend to be short-lived. As group members assume adult responsibilities there is a tendency to abandon counterculture customs upon entering the institutions of work, marriage, and family—bills have to be paid and children must be raised.

Having noted this, it is interesting to consider the development of countercultures on the flip side of work and marriage and family. Having met many of the responsibilities of adulthood, some people abandon dominant cultural values later in life. How many "old guys" have you seen on motorcycles running the streets and highways these days? Certainly these are not aging Hell's Angels. Rather, gray-beards on bikes represent many aspects identified with counterculture—a rejection of traditional values, the search for something new, and the development of **cultural values** (dress, language, values, mannerisms, etc.) deliberately distinct and separate from existing cultural expectations.

Many students have a difficult time understanding the difference between subculture and counterculture. Generally speaking, the difference is that counterculture arises in opposition to dominant cultural values, whereas,

Table 3.4: MAJOR U.S. CULTURAL VALUES

CLUSTER ONE	CLUSTER TWO
Freedom	Hard Work
Individualism	Success
Equality	Achievement
Patriotism	Materialism
CLUSTER THREE	**CLUSTER FOUR**
Progress	Religiousity
Efficiency	Humanitarianism
Practicality	Romantic Love
Technology	Sexual Restriction

Source: Robin M. Williams, 1970

subcultures predate dominant cultural values because they existed prior to immigrating to or being annexed into a new country. Another distinction between the two is that countercultures have a desire to instill change in the dominant culture so it more closely resembles its own value system. Subcultures, on the other hand, have no interest in changing the dominant culture. In fact, they voluntarily accept much of dominant cultural values. With this in mind let's consider a tricky question. How would you classify street gangs—as being a subculture or a counterculture? If your answer is subculture, you are right. This is true because while street gangs are different from the rest of the dominant culture, they have no desire to have the whole society become a delinquent gang. Likewise, street gangs accept many of the dominant cultural values, such as materialism, group loyalty, status symbols (cars, jewelry, fashion, etc.) and power.

CULTURAL VALUES IN THE UNITED STATES

Previously it was mentioned that every society needs a core set of beliefs and values. The belief and value system is the cohesive glue that holds society together and forms the foundation upon which harmonious relationships can be built. In investigating the major values of our society, sociologist Robin M. Williams (1970) was able to identify sixteen major values clustered around four major categories (see Table 3.4.)

Freedom, Individualism, Equality, and Patriotism

Perhaps the most important of all values held by Americans is that of **freedom**. In the very beginning, it was this impetus that drove people to risk all and migrate to this land. Likewise, it was the driving force behind the

Revolutionary War in which the American colonies freed themselves from British rule. For Americans, freedom is not confined to the political realm; it also extends to the personal. We demand to be free from the pressures to conform to the expectations of others. How many times have you said or heard someone else declare, "hey, it's a free country!"

An outgrowth of freedom is our belief in **individualism**. No nation on the face of the earth believes more in the rights and responsibilities of individuals than Americans. We pride ourselves, even boast about, how ruggedly individualistic we are as a people. Underpinning this value is the belief that we, as individuals, are responsible for our own lives. Whether we succeed or fail is dependent upon our own efforts. As individuals we assume either the credit or the blame. To a large extent our belief in individualism is at the root of the criticism directed at welfare recipients.

Equality is the third value in this cluster of beliefs. When Americans speak of equality, it is not in the context of egalitarianism or the belief that material goods should be equally shared. Equality as we see it implies a belief that everyone should be afforded "equal opportunity." As such, success or failure is determined upon merit or one's ability and efforts.

Finally, **patriotism** runs very strong among Americans. The bumper sticker "Love It or Leave It" is an expression of how strongly Americans believe in their country and their way of life. We are the best—politically, economically, and militarily. Rallying around the flag, as any politician can tell you, is a favorite past time of Americans.

Hard Work, Success, Achievement, and Materialism

As discussed in Chapter Fourteen, **hard work** has not always been valued. However, Americans deeply believe in the value of work. There probably isn't a teenager alive in this country who at one time or another has not had to endure the lecture from his parents on how hard they worked growing up and how this made them the person they are today, right? Although we might laugh about it, Americans do value hard work. Work is not just something we do to earn a living, it defines who we are and provides for our psychological needs of self esteem and dignity. Even more, hard work was necessary for the creation and expansion of this nation. Likewise, for the early Puritans it was tied to God's grace and eternal salvation.

Connected to hard work are the corollaries of success, achievement and materialism. The purpose of work is to succeed. Americans, perhaps more than any other nation of people, value **success**. Social mobility is highly desirable. We are not content to remain stuck in the position to which we were born. We revere and celebrate the lives of those who have started out at the bottom and were able to climb their way to the top—they are our heroes, our role models.

In the same vein, success is measured by **achievement**. As parents it is important to communicate to our children the necessity of establishing and achieving our goals. And finally, the outcome of hard work, success, and achievement is **materialism**. In our minds we believe that all of these bring an inherent right to material rewards. In many ways this is the cornerstone of our economic system—capitalism. We are a nation of consumers. It is our right to buy and possess. Others in the society may live in ghettos, the homeless may walk our streets, children may lack for food and clothes, but if one has the money and wants to buy his/her twelfth sixty-thousand dollar automobile, it is their "right" to do so.

Progress, Efficiency, Practicality, and Technology

A common expression among Americans is "that's progress." What we mean is that change is inevitable and somehow it will be for the best. There are probably no other people in the world that so firmly hold to **progress** or change. To some extent this is a result of the way the nation was founded. People who came to America expected change and wanted change. One positive outcome of this belief is that it allows the nation to escape the struggles, even wars, which have torn other nations apart when traditional values are replaced by new ones. Rather than fighting or resisting change we accept it, all in the name of progress.

Once Americans accept change, a second value of **efficiency** kicks in. We want to accomplish the task in the shortest time and the most convenient manner possible. To do otherwise would seem wasteful. This is not how others in the world always perceive matters. For other cultures doing things in a traditional manner is valued, even if it takes more time and energy. Religious protocol, tribal customs, governmental bureaucracy, and cultural traditions must be strictly adhered to for change or progress to occur. For Americans the battle cries of progress are "cut the red tape" and "onward and upward."

Efficiency is closely linked to the third value in this cluster, **practicality**. We tend to look for practical solutions: if it works, then it is desirable and acceptable. At one time in this nation it was customary for shops and businesses to close down on Sunday as a day of worship. Also, businesses generally closed their doors around 5 PM so people could spend time with their families. As the national economy changed, and the family system along with it, the old schedule was no longer practical. So we changed. Now it is possible to shop for anything at almost any time—practical.

Sliding neatly within this set of values is our belief in **technology**. Problem solving through science and technology is highly prized. Americans believe that future success and national survival are tied to science. When the Soviets launched Sputnik, the first satellite, into space in 1956, it caused such a furor in America that the national government devoted billions of dollars to scientific education and research. Similarly, when a great scientific or technological discovery occurs in another country, we feel somehow lessened by the fact it was not an American discovery. This, of course, leads to a new resolve and recommitment to science and technology.

Religiosity, Humanitarianism, Romantic Love, and Sexual Restriction

Studies of **religiosity**, or how religiously inclined people are, demonstrate that among industrial societies, Americans are the most religious (Woodward, 1992). References to God are found in our creed, pledge of allegiance, national anthem, and governmental documents such as the Declaration of Independence and the Constitution. Politicians frequently invoke the name of God and our laws are influenced by our religious concepts of what is right or wrong.

Despite our sense of individualism described in our first cluster, Americans do value **humanitarianism**. It was this belief that led to the creation of the Peace Corps and Vista (programs to help the poor abroad and at home). Likewise, programs such as Save the Children have always enjoyed widespread support. And too, songs like "We Are the World" play heavily into this theme.

In the popular musical *Fiddler on the Roof*, the unmarried daughter sings a song calling on the Matchmaker to make her a perfect match for marriage. In pre-industrial society arranged marriages were common. Financial and family ties were the basis for marital union, with romantic encounters being reserved for non marital affairs (Parker, 1990). **Romantic love**, *or* the belief that one has a right to select his or her own partner on the basis of love, is deeply rooted in our culture. Some sociologists have noted that in countries where arranged marriages are the norm, there is less divorce and discontent than in countries in which romantic love is the model (Giddens, 1992). While marriages are still arranged in many countries throughout the world, it most definitely is not the norm in America. However, given the possibility of less divorce and discontentment, maybe you should consider giving mom and dad a chance to set you up with the ideal marriage partner. What do you think?

Finally, despite the fact that we are preoccupied with sex—in fashion, print, movies, television, and the workplace—America is one of the most **sexually restrictive** industrial (and many non-industrial) countries in the world. Think back to the section about the differences between cultural ideals and realities. When we deviate from the cultural ideals of chastity and monogamy and sexual discretion, we have the tendency to lapse into self-deprivation and guilt (Christensen, 1960).

MULTICULTURALISM

In addition to the 16 central values that we discussed above, we must add that there is a rich diversity of cultural values in the United States. Although diversity has always been a part of our tradition it was, for the most part, down-played early in our history. Those who immigrated from abroad, with the exception of African slaves who were forcibly brought here, came primarily from England and other European countries. Certainly diversity was present, but those who came had the intention to assimilate into the dominant culture. For them, assimilation was a way to further their economic prospects and prepare their children for a new and better life. Names were shortened or changed to sound more American and old cultural traditions were abandoned in favor of those practiced or celebrated here. In less than a generation the children of immigrants were transformed. America was the "**melting pot**" of the world and proud of it. So proud were we (and still are to this day) that on every coin minted is stamped the Latin slogan *E Pluribus Unum*, which translated means, "out of many, one."

How effective were we at assimilating the many into one? In part we were very effective. In less than a generation, nations of immigrants were magically transformed into "hot dog, apple pie, and Chevrolet" versions of Americans. For those who supported assimilation, this was not only desirable, but also necessary, if we were to find the common ground necessary to promote harmonious and stable relations among so many different people. On the other hand, for those opposed to the process, assimilation represented little more than subjugation of all non-English populations to **Anglicanization**, a process whereby everyone had to accept English social, political, and institutional patterns of life. Likewise, this provided enormous advantages to those from an English heritage in the developing class system.

As the nation began to mature, Anglicanization was replaced with **Eurocentrism**, a dominance of European cultural patterns. Eurocentrism occurred as waves of immigrants from European countries (Germany, Ireland, Italy, Poland, etc.) began to arrive in the U.S. Not only did the sheer numbers necessitate a shift in ethnic emphasis, but also European immigrants were seen, with the arrival of increasing numbers of people of non-European lands, as more desirable than the multicultural alternative.

Today, **multiculturalism** is a social issue. Unlike those from the past, today's immigrants are less willing to forgo their own cultural traditions. Increasing demands are being made for all institutions of society to recognize and accept the customs of others from distant lands that immigrate to our nation. In some instances our society has made adjustments, such as offering bilingual education and pressure on educational institutions to offer material and courses in multiculturalism. However, in other cases, resistance to multiculturalism is very strong. One example is the religious practice of Muslim women wearing the head covering called a hijab. A recent study found that of Muslim women who wear head-scarves, 69 percent reported instances of discrimination compared to 29 percent of those who did not (Ripley & Newman, 2008).

Critics of multiculturalism maintain that it promotes confusion, delays assimilation that impedes entry into the economic mainstream, hinders the people it is supposed to help integrate into society, and promotes division and disunity. In the years to come, the issue of multiculturalism will surely become more controversial. This will be especially true, as we shall see later in this book, when people of color constitute the numerical majority in the U.S.

SOCIOLOGICAL PERSPECTIVES

Structural Functional

Recall our earlier discussion of the structural functionalist perspective in Chapter One. Structural functionalists are primarily interested in the bonds uniting society, or what allows it to work as a cohesive and harmonious unit. For advocates of this perspective, the core values discussed in this chapter are essential to maintaining society. These values encompass all of the cultural beliefs of society. They promote cooperation and solidarity, two essential ingredients of a successful society. Likewise, without culture and the expectations flowing from it, human interaction would be impossible. Think of your average day and how it would be impossible to function if everything you had to do, every decision you had to make, you had to weigh alternatives and try to figure out your every move. On a psychological level, our culture provides us with sense of origin and future. It answers the grand questions of where we come from, why we are here, and what happens to us after we die. Without such answers and assurances it is doubtful, maintain structural functionalists, that society could survive.

On a societal level, structural functionalists recognize that there is no universal acceptance of culture. Differences do exist. This is only to be expected since societies are not static. Societies become larger or smaller through wars and annexations and migration from one country to another. However, through assimilation, core values are established and eventually accepted. Structural functionalists consider assimilation a valuable and necessary tool for solidarity and social cohesion.

One key question we might pose to structural functionalists is, why is there so much variation in culture throughout the world? In other words, why hasn't there been more gravitation toward similarity in culture? Structural functionalists answer this question by directing us toward environmental differences in which societies live. Each society has access to different resources, different climates, different technologies, and different terrain. No two societies are alike. Hence, cultural differences are to be expected. It is also true that conditions change over time. As conditions change, so does culture. However, such changes are slow and adaptive, with each change, in some way or another contributing to increased stability and harmony.

Social Conflict

Advocates of this perspective would not deny the necessity or importance of culture. Again, in the absence of culture chaos would reign. Rather, conflict theorists are concerned with how culture is formed and for whose benefit. Karl Marx was first to provide insights into these questions. Rather than culture originating from a process of cooperation and mutual consent, Marx believed that it flowed from the economy. He stated that,

> It is not the consciousness of men that determines their existence.... It is their social existence that determines their consciousness (Marx, 1977; orig. 1859).

In this perspective, it is the economy that ultimately determines the shape of the value system. Where groups compete for power and material advantage, the value system of the winner will become dominant and all others will be subjugated. In the process of subjugation, those adhering to different cultural values are relegated to lower rungs on the stratification system ladder. Moreover, the dominant culture is constructed to perpetuate the advantage of the powerful and the affluent. For example, children of the upper classes look right, dress right, speak right, act right, go the right schools, and overall "fit better" into corporate and professional structures that are dominated and controlled by members of their own class. Conversely, kids from the "wrong side of the tracks"—minorities and those from lower classes—soon discover that their cultural values are major obstacles to social mobility.

From the conflict perspective, the core values of the United States such as hard work, individualism, achievement, and materialism are all an outgrowth of our economic system of capitalism. Inherent within this value system is a tendency to blame victims for their failures. Proof is found in a recent national poll demonstrating that fully one-half of Americans rejected the idea that our society is divided into the "Haves" and "Have Nots" (Pew, 2007). And among those who do not recognize class polarization, the largest group expresses a belief that a "lack of effort is more often to blame than individual circumstances if a person is poor" (NPR, 2010). Hence, a self-perpetuating mechanism is established, one that has the support and allegiance of the very people it victimizes. This is what Marx refers to as "false consciousness." It is for this reason that conflict theorists' stress that the first step in building a cultural system founded on equality is a recognition and understanding of class consciousness.

SUMMARY

In this chapter we have explored the meaning and diverse nature of culture. Before leaving this topic it is noteworthy to examine the impact of culture in relationship to the issue of freedom. Does culture promote greater freedom in our lives or does it limit our freedom? As you might already suspect, the answer is not simply a "yes" or "no." In reality it does both. On the one hand, culture supplies us with a foundation upon which to interact and build. It is this foundation upon which we construct institutions and expected patterns of behavior. These patterns provide freedom in that we do not have to think about everything we do, and they give us assurances that others will behave in a predictable and acceptable manner. This frees us to invest our time in exploring our world and creating. This is, in essence, why our species has elevated itself above all other creatures.

On the other hand, it must be recognized that culture also limits freedom. First, we are not free to select our culture. By birth our culture is pre-selected and to a large extent, so are the possibilities that are presented to us. For example, a woman born in a Middle Eastern culture will experience different constraints than one born in the United States. The same is true for a black child. Being born in the United States will have different consequences than being born in an African nation. In both cases, and others similar to it, culture will greatly influence and shape their lives.

Also, since we acquire culture at an age in which we lack the ability to think critically, we have a tendency to accept rather than to evaluate. In this way culture becomes a part of our "psychic self." We develop a sense of "ought-ness" about the way we think and act. In essence, we are in a cultural rut and unable to see things about ourselves that are contradictory or unfair. In this way, culture limits our ability to think about ourselves and others in an unbiased manner.

What does all of this mean, especially when one accepts that culture is inevitable and necessary? To see the world and ourselves more clearly, we must recognize the impact of culture on our lives and try, as we stated in Chapter One, to "think sociologically." Then, and only then, can we experience the richness that all cultures offer.

Terms You Should Know:

Society	Culture	Technology
Language	Social Control	Values
Cultural Lag	Norms	Cultural Universals
Cultural Diversity	Ethnocentrism	Cultural Relativity
Cultural Relativism	Eurocentrism	Multiculturalism

Can You Answer These Questions?

1. Provide some examples of material and nonmaterial culture.

2. List the three reasons why language is important.

3. Describe the Linguistic Relativity Hypothesis.

4. What are the three types of norms? Give an example for each not already listed in the text.

5. What are the two classifications of norms? To which do taboos belong?

6. Distinguish between subcultures and countercultures.

7. Give a few examples of cultural universals not provided by your text.

8. Why do sociologists believe that culture is a liberating force in our lives? How might it restrict our freedom?

Critical Thinking Exercises:

1. Think about the society in which you live. Can you provide some of examples of words that have shaped your view of the world or people in it?

2. Can you provide a current example of cultural lag in today's society? Do you think your parents experience more instances of cultural lag than you? Is this normal?

3. If the United States is so sexually restrictive, why do so many advertisements use sexually suggestive material in their ads?

4. Do you believe that there is more resistance to multiculturalism today than in years past? If so, why?

Photo: U.S. Army in Iraq.

Everyday Sociology 7th Edition

Chapter 4

Social Interactions, Organizations & Groups

On September 21, 2010 four female students at Dougherty High School in Albany, Georgia, cornered a fifteen year-old sophomore in the girl's bathroom. In a flurry of violence, the girls, one seventeen year-old and three sixteen year-old's, proceeded to punch, claw, and scratch the victim, causing numerous physical injuries. A number of other students, who did not participate in the beating, videotaped the act and then distributed it to others at the school. School administrators, who were alerted to the video by other students, turned the tape over to the police.

Upon investigation, the police learned that the incident was an initiation rite commonly termed a "beat-down" in which a new member is inducted into a gang. In this case, the instigators of the "beat-down" were members of the Savage Diamond gang that operated out of the school. The district attorney charged the three sixteen year-old's as juveniles and the seventeen year-old as an adult. The fifteen year-old victim was also charged with gang participation since she voluntary submitted to the initiation rite. Since gang violence had greatly escalated in the community, the district attorney publicly announced that he would seek jail time for the adult and time in a juvenile facility for the rest of the girls (Wallace, 2010).

Citizens of the community and school officials were shocked by the incident. Many expressed confusion and dismay over the fact that a gang was operating inside their school. Why was it, they asked, that these girls felt the need to form a gang?

Sociologists are also interested in gangs. However, unlike the layperson who is baffled by such activity, the sociologist considers the formation and existence of gangs as normal—they represent just one of many types of groups formed in the natural order of human interaction. Sociologists are less interested in passing judgment on gangs than in investigating the societal conditions that lead to gang formation, gang leadership, gang culture, connections between gangs and the existing social order, recruitment techniques, and patterns of gang order that perpetuate their existence. Researchers who have studied gangs intensively have found many similarities between them and any other group in society—Knights of Columbus, the Masons, American Legion, Junior Chamber of Commerce, and the Boy Scouts of America just to name a few. Although this may come as a surprise to you, it will be clearer after you have completed this chapter where we will explore four main topics. *First*, we investigate the various types of groups in society. *Second*, we explore the social attributes of group behavior. *Third*, we examine organizations and how they relate to social structure. And *finally*, we investigate how groups contribute to social control.

SOCIAL STRUCTURE

In earlier chapters we learned that humans need structure in their lives. It would be impossible to live without some connection to other humans or to exist in a society that is in constant chaos. As humans we need guidelines, parameters, and a sense of predictability as we interact with others. Indeed, from the very moment that we are born we need the presence of others to sustain our lives. As we grow, we need the guidance and experience of family to show us how to interact with others. Still later, we need the help of friends and teachers to grow into adulthood and assume responsible roles in society. And it does not end there; each new stage of life presents different challenges. To be successful, we must continually learn from others.

All of this does not occur in a haphazard fashion. In order to be successful, to function smoothly and harmoniously, society develops a **social structure**, or expected behavior patterns to guide social interaction. These expected behavior patterns are encoded in the values, norms, and beliefs of society and are transmitted by the institutions of society—family, religion, schools, media, government, etc. These institutions allow for a continuation or perpetuation of society's belief system to generations of new members. As a result, a reciprocal relationship is established between society and the individual. We as individuals need society to survive, and society needs us to learn and accept its belief systems. We turn now to a discussion of social structure and its functions.

SOCIAL AND INFORMAL GROUPS

The foundation of social structure is composed of groups. A **social group** is defined as a collection of people who interact with each other on a regular basis. The size of a group can vary from two people (you and your significant other) to any number in the millions (the population of the United States). Common to all groups is a perceived sense of identity with other group members. For example, the people of a country are considered a group. The common sense of identity is our citizenship and acceptance of a common belief system, as discussed in Chapter Three. Sociologists term this an **in-group** or one to which we give a strong attachment and loyalty. Conversely, we perceive that others are different in some way from members of our group. The perceived difference could be minimal, as with groups within a high school, or substantial, as would be the case with people from diverse cultures. But, in each case the individuals within the group clearly understand who belongs and who doesn't. In some cases there is strong resentment, even hatred, toward other groups. These groups would be **out-groups**. An example here would be racist skinheads who hate racial minorities and consider them to be out-groups.

As we associate with others in society we become members of many different groups. The number of groups we join depends on how interactive we are. Think about your own life. How many groups do you belong to? First, you have membership in your family. As we shall see later, this is a very important group. Also, you might be affiliated with a church, hence you have a religious group. As a student, you will probably meet people at school that you hang around with in the cafeteria, halls, gym, or in the library. Perhaps you have formed a study group with other class members. While this group is limited in time and by purpose, it nevertheless constitutes a group. At work you might belong to a union. After school or work you have friends that you meet for entertainment. All of these are examples of groups. Some group memberships are maintained over a lifetime. In some cases we leave one group to become a member of another. The point is that we all belong to groups and as we move through life, group membership varies.

The value of group membership is that it provides us with a sense of identity and security. As we mentioned previously, we are social animals. We *need* to belong. It provides meaning to our existence. Evidence of this is found in Durkheim's (1951; orig. 1897) classic study where he found a correlation between lack of social integration (group membership) and suicide. The more a member of society feels detached from others, the more likely he/she is to take their own life. In group membership we find security. By security we refer not only to protection from some of life's nastier creatures, but also that our basic physical and psychological needs are met. Collectively, we have assurance that we will have a roof over our heads, food on the table, clothes on our back, and the comfort of others when we

Of all primary relationships, the family is the most important. It is in the family where we first learn about relationships. Beyond all other institutions in society, the family provides us with the foundation for the development of our personality and perceptions of the world.

Photo: Michael Witzel.

are in need. Finally, as we shall discuss later in this chapter, groups are an important source of social control. Not only are they a powerful source of socialization, they exert enormous control over our lives. The desire to belong and to fit in is a basic human need. Individuals who fail to live up to group expectations often find themselves ostracized and alone. To avoid this, individuals go to extraordinary lengths to conform.

Before moving on we should mention that not all groups are social in nature. At some time or another, nearly everyone has had the pleasure of using public transportation. Let's say that it's time for spring vacation and you have planned to meet some friends at a warm ocean destination hundreds of miles from your home. A plane ride is the logical choice. You travel to the airport and as you wait for the plane to board, find yourself surrounded by other passengers. Is this a social group? The answer is no. Sociologists term this a **social aggregate**, or a collection of people who find themselves gathered together at a particular time and location, but do not interact or share a common sense of identity.

Social categories are another classification commonly used but different from social groups. A **social category** is a collection of people who share something in common but who do not interact with each other. As a student you would constitute a social category with all other individuals who also happen to be students. Other examples of social categories would include those based on age, income, race, religion, ethnic background, occupation, and the like. While sociologists might find social categories fascinating topics for research, few people spend much time thinking about their social category relationships.

Types of Groups

Richness and variation in life gives rise to many different groups. Although it would not be possible to offer a full description of all types of groups, useful classifications have been formulated in an attempt to provide some insights into group affiliations. Charles Horton Cooley (1909) was the first sociologist to draw a distinction between primary and secondary groups. Later, two additional classifications—reference groups and social networks—were contrived.

Primary Groups. The most important of our group memberships is that of the primary group. In describing primary groups, Cooley penned the following words:

> By primary groups I mean those characterized by intimate face-to-face association and cooperation. They are primary in several senses, but chiefly in that they are fundamental in forming the social nature and ideas of the individual.

Primary groups are those that are instrumental in the formation of our identity. They are the groups in which we develop our most basic perceptions of the world and understand the meaning of existence. The lessons we learn here are those that follow us for a lifetime. The most important of all primary groups is the family. Later, other primary relationships develop as we move though life. These will be the marriages we enter, the children we create, and the lifelong friendships we acquire. The importance of these relationships is the intimacy that flows from them. Within these groups we feel the comfort of emotional commitments and genuine concern for our well-being. Likewise, it is within these groups that we experience the joy of reciprocal sharing. Cooley was concerned that membership in primary groups would be weakened by the rise of large and expansive bureaucratic organizations in modern society. This he predicted would limit our ability to form close and intimate contact, a condition that could hinder our capacity to lead fulfilling lives. Still, other sociologists have suggested that the outcome might be more freedom. Primary relationships such as the family can be comforting but can also be repressive, controlling, and suffocating. Less influence by primary groups can allow the individual to seek new experiences and achieve interpersonal growth (Durkheim, 1964; Simmel, 1955).

Secondary Groups. Although Cooley himself did not specifically use the term secondary groups, he implied it when defining primary groups. Secondary groups are large, less personal, and more formal. In contrast to primary groups where people seek intimacy, secondary groups are those we join to accomplish a goal such as obtaining a college degree, seeking to improve the environment, running for public office, or sharing recreational adventures. Our behavior is very different in secondary groups. In primary groups we tend to be more open and honest, less guarded. In secondary groups our guard is up. We feel the need to perform or play a role. We feel a sense of being evaluated and judged, so we are less likely to allow our "true self" to appear. Additionally, secondary group membership is less enduring. We tend to fall in and out of various secondary groups or relationships as our needs and interests change or the reason for belonging ceases to exist.

Reference Groups. It was the happiest day in Singh Lee's life. Well maybe not *the* happiest, but certainly one of the happiest. Finally, Tim, the man of her dreams, had asked her out. They worked together for over a year in different divisions of the same company. Occasionally their paths would cross and when they did Singh could see a spark of interest when their eyes met. He seemed perfect. Through friends she learned that they shared similar interests, enjoyed the same activities, and on the surface appeared to have compatible personalities. Then, when she least expected, he walked up, introduced himself, and asked her out. She immediately accepted. Arrangements were quickly made. He would pick her up at her home on Saturday night. They would catch a movie and dine later. Although she felt somewhat sophomoric, she immediately phoned her friends to share the good news. Everyone was happy. It was perfect, just perfect—or was it? Suddenly, doubt hit her. Tim was to pick her up at her home. What would her parents think? He was German. She was Chinese. Her parents would have a fit. Her mother dreamed openly of the day when Chinese grandchildren were running around the house. And it wasn't only her mother, her father was proud of his heritage and suspicious of outsiders. Furthermore, she and her family were Catholic, Tim was Jewish. Monsignor Herman would die. Maybe she should just forget about it; but then, what would her friends think?

The above scenario provides an example of reference groups. A reference group can be your family (primary group) or your work colleagues (secondary group). The importance of reference groups is that we use them as a yardstick to measure our attitudes and behavior. As we shall see in the chapter on socialization, we define ourselves through others. We are not born with any predetermined notions about ourselves. Rather, we take cues from other individuals and groups about whom we are or would like to become. As you can see, we look for direction and guidance from our reference groups.

Consider for a moment the way you dress or wear you hair. If you see yourself as an up-and-coming corporate executive, you will probably cut your hair short and wear fashionable clothing, perhaps a suit and tie. On the other hand, if you aspire to be a singer in a rock band you'll probably grow your hair long, hang some metal around your neck, and engage in a little body piercing. Reference groups greatly influence our actions.

A problem occurs when conflicts develop between your reference groups. For example, you see yourself as the next Bill Gates, making millions of dollars, but your garage-band buddies keep reminding you that you could be the next Mick Jagger. Take a moment to think of the reference groups you belong to. Are there any conflicts you can identify?

Social Networks. Inevitably, in large groups there are some people with whom we get along better than others. In meetings of the group we tend to gravitate toward these individuals. We joke with them, we take our breaks with them, and we sit at the same table during lunch. Sound familiar? Of course, this is what we commonly refer to as a *clique*. In high school cliques were very evident in the social structure of who was "in" and "out." But just as cliques form so do links between and among cliques. The links between individuals, families, cliques, and other groups are referred to as **social networks.** Anyone who's ever looked for a job knows about "the old boys network." If you're tied into this network good jobs are easily obtainable. However, for those on the outside, securing the right job can be a frustrating endeavor. This has given rise to the cliché, "It's not what you know, but who you know." Sociologists who actively track career paths have demonstrated that there is truth behind this statement (Knoke, 1990; Marsden and Lin, 1982; Wellman, Carrington, and Hall, 1988).

Because belonging to the right network can be crucial to career advancement, some people go to extreme lengths to gain acceptance into its membership. They change religion, change political allegiance, join country clubs, and even learn to play golf. However, all of this does not guarantee admittance into the network or access to the advantages it affords. It is for this reason that many groups have become more active in developing their own networks. For example, successful women have developed their own network and actively engage in what is termed "gender networking." Many religious groups and racial minorities have followed suit. Unfortunately, these networks, while being beneficial, lack the power and influence of those of upper class white males (Marsden, 1987). A lack of social networking continues to be a major source of social and economic inequality.

THE INDIVIDUAL IN SOCIETY

We have seen the importance of groups and formal organizations within the social structure. Now we turn to a discussion of how individual behavior is shaped by these two components of society. Within the context of social structure flow two important concepts of human behavior: social status and roles.

Social Status

Status is a commonly used term in everyday conversation. Generally, when one speaks of an individual's status they are making reference to how much money, power, or prestige they have. Sociologists define status differently. To the sociologist **status** refers to the position that one occupies in a group or organization. For example, in this class your status is that of a student. After school you go to a job where your status is that of an employee. In your family, your status may be that of a son or daughter, or perhaps you may be the parent. As you can see, you occupy a multitude of statuses. Some

In society, we all carry a master status. This is the status that others are most likely to attach to us. Here we have an African American female police officer. What would her master status be in society? Think about your own master status. What would it be?

Photo: Mike Schinkel

statuses change frequently while others remain constant throughout life. Illustrative of this is that you will, assuming you have children, be a parent far longer than you might be a professional hockey player.

In studying status, sociologists have noted the difference between **ascribed status**, those that come to us either by birth or through some condition over which we have no control, and **achieved status**, that which we gain through our own efforts. Examples of ascribed status are one's sex, race, class, religion, and nationality. Achieved status might be student, professional, father, carpenter, president. In some cases, ascribed status can be changed. An example might be religion. Religion is considered an ascribed status. After all, being born into a Christian family coupled with the fact that one acquires their religious orientation at a very young age allows for little choice. Later, however, an individual as an adult may well decide to become a Buddhist. At this point religion would be an achieved status. Likewise, the status of being disabled may be an ascribed or an achieved status depending upon if one is born with the disability or achieved later in life.

Not all statuses are equal, some are more important than others. When we say more important, we mean that other members of the society attach more significance to some statuses than others. Race in the United States qualifies as a **master status**. Black professionals often complain of being treated differently both outside and inside their organizations due to their race. On the other hand, for white females, master status would not be race, but gender. As a result of being female, opportunities might be limited by other members of society because their perceptions of women are limited to traditional gender roles. Some master statuses are ascribed and some are achieved. A woman who is born with beautiful physical features (according to dominant cultural beliefs of ideal beauty) will have more opportunities than another who is less fortunate and prone to obesity. This would be an example of ascribed master status. On the other hand, let's say you decide to break with convention, grow your hair long, get a few tattoos, wear torn jeans, and join a commune. To be sure, your master status will change and you will notice a marked difference in the way others treat you. This is an example of a master status that is achieved.

From the above discussion, it is apparent that master statuses have the capacity to greatly limit or expand one's life chances. Furthermore, it is the majority and power elites who will determine what is normal, what is beautiful, what is desirable, what should be rewarded, and what should be punished. Unfortunately, since in many cases it is not possible to change a master status, many in society find themselves unable to escape unjust treatment. In some cases, the meaning attached by the powerful to a master status, changes over time as a result of power struggles between groups. This is certainly true of race, gender, and sexual orientation. Although all of these groups still experience discrimination, changes in the political structure have afforded some measure of protection through the legal system if rights are violated.

Roles

Now that we have a clearer sense of what status is, let's consider the subject of roles. Attached to each status is a **role**, or a set of expected behaviors. Each expected behavior is a **norm** and around each role is clustered a set of norms. In sum, this cluster of norms constitutes a role. Let's take you as a student. Being a student is a status position you occupy in society. The way people expect you to behave, as a student, is what makes for a role. Therefore, as you enter class you take your seat and wait for the professor to arrive. As she begins to lecture you are expected to listen, ask questions when appropriate, and take notes. You are expected to do your assignments and hand them in on time (this is a very important norm). Similarly, your professor has a status. Attached to her status is a role different from yours. And, just as is true of your role, her role is surrounded and defined by a different cluster of norms. The obvious benefit of all of this is that each of you, the student and the professor, has an understanding of each other's roles. It is this common understanding of what behavior is expected and provided that allows for smooth and harmonious social interaction.

This brings us to an interesting point. If roles prescribe how a person should behave in certain situations, why is there so much variation in behavior of people occupying the same role? Lots of people occupy the student role yet there is a huge variation in how individuals fulfill their roles as students. Some get straight A's while others fail; some graduate with honors, others dropout. In another example, let's take the case of your professors. Certainly there is some similarity in the way professors behave—they show up for class, present material, give exams, and issue grades. This is all true, but there is great variation from one professor to another, a fact you have undoubtedly already discovered. Of course, this is true not only of your professors, but of everyone.

We can offer three basic reasons why the behavior of people occupying the same role varies. *First*, as people go about the business of fulfilling the roles they occupy, they encounter situations sociologists refer to as **role strain**. Role strain results when it is not possible to successfully fulfill all the expectations of a role because of contradictory demands within an existing role. As a teacher it is expected that your professor be friendly, nurturing, and supportive of your educational plans. On the other hand, your professor must also evaluate your progress and issue a final grade. What happens if your performance is not good and the professor is faced with issuing a failing grade, knowing that this might result in you dropping out of school? This is an example of role strain, and how professors' handle it varies from individual to individual. One might issue the failing grade, not liking it, but believing it to be the only fair way to handle the situation. Another might assign extra-credit work in order to makeup a failing assignment and thereby allowing you to pass by the "skin-of-your-teeth." Still another will issue a passing grade on your existing work in order to make an allowance for personal difficulties you encountered during the semester.

Second, role conflict also accounts for varying behavior of people in the same role. **Role conflict** is present when two or more roles you occupy are in conflict. The opportunity for roles to conflict is great because we all occupy a number of roles at the same time. Let's use you as an example. Right now you are fulfilling your role as a student by reading this textbook. However, this is not your only role. You probably hold a job. You are also a member of a family, perhaps even a parent. You have friends that depend upon your companionship. The potential for role conflict is enormous. Let's say today your professor has a great idea for a class project and assigns a paper for the next class. Exactly what you needed, right? But, it's okay because you are motivated and want to do well. Mentally, you prepared yourself for the work ahead of you tonight. But first, you have to go to work.

Although you don't know this yet, a crisis is unfolding at work. Two workers for the next shift have called in sick. Your boss is frantic and demands that you work late. Just then your beeper goes off. It's your daughter. You quickly return the call to find that she has just broken up with her long-standing boyfriend. She's crying and wants you to come home. She needs to talk to you. Before hanging up she tells you that your good friend Eva called to remind you that this is the opening night of her art exhibit. This is her first show and she is counting on you for emotional support. By now you should be getting the idea of what we mean by role conflict. Obviously you want to meet all of your obligations, but often it is just not possible. How people handle role conflict varies and this results in differences among individuals and how they handle the same role.

Finally, we all bring to a role our different personalities. Some of us are outgoing. Some are more reserved. Some of us approach life with a grand sense of humor. Some are more serious about life. Some of us are right brained. Some of us are left brained. These are just a few of the individual differences we bring to our roles. These differences interact with the role we are in to produce different behavior. Let's return to our example of your professors. One professor might like a more orderly classroom. In line with this, open discussion without the raising of hands is discouraged. Likewise, this individual may like to stick to the course syllabus so that all material is covered during the semester. Another professor might enjoy a more open and lively environment. Students may be encouraged to talk whenever the opportunity presents itself. To this professor, spontaneous learning is valued over regimentation. Thus, differences in personality will greatly affect each individual's performance of the same role.

Role Distancing and Role Exit

Sociologists note that when individuals find themselves in roles they dislike or that are stressful they have a tendency to consciously and openly portray an attitude of disinterest or non-commitment to that role (Goffman, 1961b). This is termed **role distancing**. For example, a student working at a job he considers demeaning but needed for educational expenses at the counter of a fast-food restaurant might deliberately go out of his way to communicate to certain customers that, although he is working there, he really is a "college student" and this situation is just temporary. At work, he simply goes through the motions, doing only what is minimally required, and openly taking little pride in job performance. This is the image he wants to project.

A final related concept is that of **role exit**. Here an individual voluntarily chooses to exit a role from which he/she has become disillusioned. According to Helen Rose Fuchs Ebaugh (1988), the process occurs in a four steps.

1. The individual experiences doubt or burnout in the role.
2. The individual searches for an alternative and plans to exit the role.
3. In a crisis, the individual finally makes the decision.
4. The individual assumes a new identity.

A minister, who no longer feels the religious commit to his/her faith and leaves to enter the business world, is one example. Another is a spouse who finally calls it quits and divorces.

FORMAL ORGANIZATIONS

With the development of the modern state came an increasing reliance on formal organizations. An **organization** is defined as a group with an identifiable membership that engages in concerted collective action to achieve a common purpose (Aldrich and Marsden, 1988). The development and proliferation of organizations have their roots in secondary group membership and industrialization. Prior to industrialization, few secondary groups existed. The primary group was the dominant form of membership. This is understandable since most people earned their living in agriculture. Social interaction was limited by distance and lack of transportation. With industrialization this all changed. People moved to the city where interaction among people increased greatly. The location of work changed from home to factory. Both forces lead to the development of organizations. As people began to interact with greater frequency, secondary groups increased in number. As work was taken out of the home and the division of labor established, organizations formed to direct economic activity.

Another reason for the rise of formal organizations was the dramatic transformation of society from traditional authority and customs to rationality. In traditional authority, it was assumed that past custom and tradition was the best guide for future action. This was believed to be true since it was "time tested" and it worked. Traditional authority viewed change as unnecessary and, in most cases, undesirable. Those in power fought against change because they feared that their position in society would be negatively affected. Since industrialization required rapid and continuous change, traditional authority resisted its implementation. However, over time industrialization won out and with it came rational authority, or the acceptance that human affairs should be governed by rules, efficiency, and practical and measurable results.

Sociologists offer differing views as to why rationality won out over traditional authority. Max Weber offers the Protestant Reformation as a key turning point. Unlike Roman Catholics of the time who were heavily invested in the power of the clergy and resisted change, the newly formed protestant groups embraced change. Likewise, their religious beliefs, particularly the Calvinists who believed in predestination (see Chapter Twelve), were impressed with productivity and believed it to be a sign from God that (those who produced and were therefore well-off) they were destined to enter the kingdom of heaven. It is for this reason that capitalism and formal organizations flourished in the predominately protestant countries, in comparison to those where Roman Catholics were the majority. On the other hand, Karl Marx offers a different explanation. For Marx it was capitalism itself that ended traditional authority. Once people realized capitalism's capacity to increase wealth and goods, their views changed.

Categories of Formal Organizations

In order to gain a better understanding of formal organizations, sociologists have attempted to develop classification schemes to categorize them for study. One of the more useful classification systems was presented by Amatai Etzioni (1975) who categorized organizations on the basis of why people join them. Three categories were established.

Utilitarian organizations. These organizations are primarily those established for economic gain. People who work for the organization do so voluntarily in order to earn a living or accumulate wealth. Your college or university would be included in this category. Although we like to think that people attend college for the lofty goal of learning for its intrinsic value, we fully understand that it is usually to obtain a degree for the purpose of entering a career.

Commitment to the organization is moderate to weak depending upon how members perceive the organization's rewards. The higher up one is in the organization, the more likely he/she is committed to the goals of the organization. Conversely, at lower levels, commitment to organizational goals is almost nonexistent. For these individuals their association with the organization is simply an exchange relationship of work for money.

Normative Organizations. People who join normative organizations do so simply to pursue what they believe to be worthy. There is no pay or material rewards offered and none is expected. The only reward one expects is altruistic, or one that is believed to help society or further a just cause. Examples include churches, the Salvation Army, the Peace Corps, Greenpeace, the Girl Scouts of America, and the Anticruelty Society. Association is, as expected, voluntary and those who join have a high commitment to the goals of the organization.

Coercive Organizations. Membership in these organizations is not voluntary. As implied by its name, those who join have little choice. Likewise, there is no identification with organizational goals. Examples would include prisons, mental hospitals, and the military. Characteristics of these institutions include strict rules and codes of conduct. Those who do not comply are subjected to forceful and often painful methods to induce compliance. These institutions are what one researcher classifies as "total institutions" (Goffman, 1961).

Mixed Organizations. Before leaving this topic it is noteworthy to mention that in practice, pure forms of the above organizations are difficult to find. Even in our last category, prisons typically rely upon aspects of normative organizations to achieve their goals. Hence, prisoners are counseled, education is provided, early release incentives are offered, and other programs to help inmates voluntarily cooperate exist. In the same fashion, the military may utilize coercive means to punish violators, but within each soldier they attempt to instill a sense of pride and commitment to organizational goals. It is this identification with the normative side of military life that allows for the performance of duties in highly dangerous and life threatening situations. Many soldiers have willingly given their lives to save others in their group. Similarly, utilitarian organizations employ coercive means to ensure compliance with company policy. Researchers are required to sign documents protecting company secrets. When broken, the organization can seek legal redress.

Bureaucracy and Organizations

Organizations arrange themselves for maximum efficiency and productivity. It was Max Weber (1919) who first recognized and detailed this process. According to Weber, as modern society became more complex and the division of labor more specialized, there was a natural tendency for organizations to develop highly patterned rules and authoritative administrative structures. Without such rules and structures it would be impossible for large and highly specialized organizations to coordinate the activities of personnel and production. The process is one that is now referred to as bureaucracy and is present in both business and government organizations.

Although bureaucracy does not have a positive connotation, Weber saw it as the instrument for successful administration in modern society. From it flows the perfect ordering of labor, capital, and tools for the production of goods and services. In order to better describe this arrangement, Weber suggested an "ideal" version of bureaucracy. While he would admit that no single organization possessed all traits, it nevertheless served as a model upon which an organization's performance could be measured. The following is a description of the traits of an ideal bureaucracy.

1. ***Written Rules***. In order to be as efficient as possible, organizations must have written rules for all to follow. The larger and more diverse the organization, the more extensive its rules must be. As little as possible is left to individual discretion. All members of the organization must have a clear understanding of the rules and an expectation that they will be followed. In this way, the organization gains a measure of control over both employees, production, and distribution of services.

2. ***Division of Labor***. The purpose of the organization, be it the production of an economic good or the distribution of a service, must be broken down into a series of tasks that allow for maximum efficiency. Each worker in the organization is assigned a specialized task. Workers do only their task. Through order and training workers are able to master their tasks and thereby increase production and efficiency.

3. ***A hierarchy of authority with upward and downward accountability***. The organization is divided into specified levels with clear-cut responsibilities and obligations. Upper levels are responsible for providing direction to lower levels and lower levels are accountable to upper levels for fulfilling assignments.

4. ***Written records***. All employees are required to provide written documentation of their activities. The importance of these records is not only to track goods and services (a difficult task in large organizations) but also to evaluate the performance of employees and provide information that the organization can use to further increase efficiency.

5. ***Separation of organizational life and personal life***. Individuals are expected to separate their personal lives from their organizational lives. Clearly this implies that one works in a *position* and not for an individual who may later be replaced. In organizational life, individuals are expected to put their personal feelings aside and do what is good for the organization. It is for this reason that many organizations have rules prohibiting office romances. Likewise, one's own personal life is considered secondary to the good of the organization. Good employees are those who put in long hours at the expense of family life and will accept transfers out of their communities when their expertise is needed elsewhere.

As societies have become more complex, the bureaucratic organization has gained increasing prominence. Likewise, in a global marketplace where competition is fierce, the efficiency of bureaucracy can be a deciding element of an organization's ability to survive.

Problems with Bureaucracy

So you ask, if bureaucracy is so great, why don't I feel like jumping around and shouting with joy having read the above? Well, the truth is that a whole lot of people are not very happy about bureaucratic organizations. Nearly everyone has had the unpleasant opportunity of encountering some bureaucratic drone that thrives on making our lives miserable. This is where we come in with the old phrase "welcome to the real world." What this means, in terms of bureaucracies, is that there is the "ideal" version and then there is the "real" one. In the ideal version, the purpose of the organization is to produce and distribute goods and services in the most efficient and cost effective manner possible. Unfortunately, in the real one, the rules and regulations themselves become more important than the original purpose of the organization. When this occurs, bureaucracy can no longer function effectively. Bureaucrats become fixated on the rules rather than on what they are supposed to accomplish. Anyone who has ever applied for a driver's license has had the distinct pleasure of interacting with bureaucrats more concerned about rules than service. In one encounter a young man approached a window when no other customer was present and was sternly reminded that he had to stand behind the red line before being called—that was the rule. The young man walked back behind the line and waited a full minute before the bureaucrat called him forward.

Another troublesome feature of bureaucracy is the tendency to perpetuate its existence at all costs. Once an organization is established, let's say a governmental agency, and it becomes a part of the power structure, the people who run it will do anything and everything to maintain its existence, even when the need for it has ceased to exist. Rules are created, alliances are established, and systems are developed that make its elimination impossible. All of this is done not to improve production and delivery of goods and services, but rather to guard against any attempt to eliminate it. In this way bureaucracies become ever expanding.

A good example of this is the National Foundation for the March of Dimes. Originally, the purpose of the organization was to raise funds for the elimination of polio. Because this horrific and crippling disease struck small children without warning, people across the nation rallied to the cause. The organization was a grand success. Then, in the 1950s, Dr. Jonas Salk conquered the disease when he was able to develop a vaccine from an altered version of bacteria. Almost overnight, the disease was wiped-out. It was a perfect ending for everyone, except the March of Dimes. Now that the disease was gone, there was no longer a need for its services. The organization was doomed—or was it? Faced with the loss of jobs and power, the organization quickly shifted its focus to birth defects. Now it would live forever. The perfect ending!

A final problem associated with bureaucracy is what has been labeled "trained incapacity." Thorstein Veblen (1899), a contemporary of Weber's, first used this term that implies that individuals within organizations are trained to follow rules and regulations to the degree that they become incapable or afraid of exercising independent thought. They become obsessed with the rule book. Thus, when they encounter a situation that is not covered by the rules, which invariably will happen in life, they attempt to find a remotely related rule to cover the situation even when that particular rule cannot resolve the problem. The fact that a reasonable solution is not applied is less important than the fact that a rule from "the book" was used.

GROUP DYNAMICS

In studying group behavior sociologists have noted that all groups display a number of operational characteristics. We refer to these as group dynamics, or the way groups work. The following is a description of some of the more common characteristics.

Group Size

George Simmel (1858-1918), a German sociologist, was first to trigger an interest in group dynamics with his research on two and three-person social groups. Of interest to Simmel was the relationship of size to social interaction and group solidarity.

A two-person group is termed a **dyad**. It constitutes the most basic and intimate bond between individuals. Since the individuals are involved with only one other person, emotional dependencies as well as self-identities are tied to the dyad. You and your significant other are a good example of a dyad. The dyad also is the most fragile of social groups because if one individual leaves, the relationship is ended. As you might have surmised, the end of a dyad is particularly "gut-wrenching" because of the emotional weight placed on the bond between the individuals.

As the size of the group increases, so does the complexity of the relationships. A three person group is termed a **triad**. While this may not seem to be a significant increase in size, it changes the dynamic within the group greatly.

Of all relationships, a dyad is the least complicated. Here, two boys show their friendship. Even adding one additional boy to the group would change and complicate the dynamics of the group.

Photo: Brittany Culver.

Adding a third person gives rise to the possibility of coalition formation. Let's take the example of a single father with only one of his two children living with him. Here the communication is relatively straightforward with each individual dealing directly with the other. Now, his other child comes to live with them. We now can expect that the two children may form a coalition in order to extract concessions from the father. Or, one of the children may align with the father in opposition to the other child. Likewise, coalitions constantly shift between individuals with the odd-person-out becoming the target of group pressure. As we will see later, polygamous marriages are particularly vulnerable to inter-group coalitions.

In terms of size, sociologists have attempted to define what differentiates a small group from a large group. Is it strictly a matter of numbers? Or are other factors involved? Although numbers are important, sociologists generally agree that the critical factor is whether members within the group are allowed to interact informally and on an individual basis, as opposed to having to conform to group standards. Investigators have found that once a group reaches approximately twelve people, personal interaction is difficult to maintain and cliques within the larger group begin to develop.

Group Cohesion

Take a moment to think back on your high school graduation. Like most graduating students, you probably got together with your friends to celebrate your leap from high school to the *real* world. And somewhere amidst all of the hoopla and hollering, there were pledges exchanged between you and your friends that the group would remain tight forever. Sound familiar? Now ask yourself, what happened? If you are like most people you very quickly found the group members drifting apart. At first, there might have been an attempt to maintain contact, but as time went on so did the distance between group members. Although this is not what we envision when we make "the pledge," in the real world this is how it most often happens. Why?

In their investigation sociologists have found a number of factors affecting group cohesion. *First*, when we use the term **group cohesion** we refer to the strength of the bond uniting group members. You and your friends might have used the word "tight." One of the factors affecting group cohesion is the frequency of interaction. The more that members of the group interact, the more attractive group membership is. Likewise, the more attractive group membership is, the more members want to interact. In this way a circular relationship develops. This takes us back to why you and your old high school friends drifted apart. The less that your old group is able to get together (college, jobs, military, and new commitments) the less attractive membership in the group becomes. Eventually, other groups fill the void, contrary to the old expression that, "Distance makes the heart grow fonder."

A *second* factor affecting group cohesion is how the group perceives other members. If members believe that others regard them with esteem, membership becomes more important. Group cohesion will be strong. Previously we mentioned high school cliques. These cliques arranged in hierarchical fashion with regard to popularity. Many students spend considerable time and effort attempting to get into the right cliques. This is also true of many adults who often spend beyond their means in order to get into the right group at the right country club. And they say kids are immature and foolish! Conversely, if the members of a group feel that others in society have little regard for their group, then in all probability, cohesion will be weak.

It is possible that hostility or threats to the group can increase group cohesion. For example, motorcycle gangs certainly understand that the rest of society does not regard them highly, yet this has not had a negative affect on cohesion in the group—rather, it has strengthened their bonds. This is typical of subculture and counterculture groups. Nations also are affected by this phenomenon. Nothing pulls a nation together more than a threat from an outside enemy. It is for this reason that many experts believe Israel is headed for trouble once the Palestine issue is resolved. Without a clearly defined outside threat, it will be harder for such a diverse population to resolve internal issues.

Finally, new members can affect the cohesion of the group. Many times the members of a group become so comfortable with each other they resist the entry of new members. Then, when it becomes apparent that membership must grow or the group cannot survive, new members are accepted. These new members bring with them new ideas and attitudes that have a tendency to weaken the established bonds. It is for this reason that the best advice to groups is to maintain a steady and controlled flow of new members into the organization, so as to ease integration problems.

Groupthink

Let's use an example of groupthink that many of us can relate to as either individuals or as parents.

> It's late at night. You and your friends decide to go to a party being given by a friend whose parents are out of town (sound familiar?). It's a large party and you circulate, getting to know other people. A couple of hours later, one of the kids you came with yells across the room that it's time to leave. You make your way to the door. Everyone is in the car waiting. You jog over to the car and yank open the door. As you get in, you can't help but notice that the car reeks of alcohol. The moment of truth has arrived.
>
> "Hey, Jim," you inquire. "You been drinking?"
>
> Jim turns around and smiles. "A couple," he replies with a slight slur. "Nothing to worry about, pal."
>
> "I could drive," you quickly offer.
>
> Jim is still smiling. "Relax, will ya? A couple of beers ain't gonna hurt anyone driving, right guys?" he asks, looking at the others in the car. Without hesitation, they all back Jim.

As humans we have the need to fit into a group and be well-thought of. Often this leads individuals to behave differently in a group than when they are alone. Too, in groupthink, it is often the leader that determines the behavior of others. Recently, bullying has become a major concern in schools, especially with the advent of cellphones and other social media such as Youtube. Is this just another form of groupthink?

Photo: Bill Peterson.

> "So whatcha say, man?" he asks you. "We ready to roll? Or you gonna wait for your mommy to come pick you up?" Everyone laughs.

This situation exemplifies **groupthink**, the process whereby a group arrives at a decision that they privately know is wrong, but feel that they cannot, as individuals, challenge. In all probability, others in the car were uncomfortable with Jim driving after drinking. However, because Jim is the undisputed leader of the group, the others are unwilling to challenge his decision for fear of ridicule by the others or because they want to preserve the cohesiveness of the group.

Groupthink is present in every aspect of our daily lives and we are constantly confronted with decisions to either fall in line or challenge. In most cases individuals find it very difficult to challenge group decisions. Hence, groupthink plays an important role in everyday decision-making.

Potentially, groupthink is a major problem for institutions of power, businesses, and government. Often, disastrous decisions are made because no one is willing to challenge the thinking of the leader. Two political examples of groupthink are the 1962 Bay of Pigs Invasion and the Vietnam War. During the Bay of Pigs invasion President Kennedy made the decision to invade Cuba. Although many in his administration felt the decision was a poor one, they remained silent to gain Kennedy's approval. The same thing happened when President Johnson decided to escalate the war in Vietnam rather than seek resolution through peaceful negotiation. Although many citizens took to the streets to oppose the decision, no one in Johnson's administration and few in Congress would speak against the futility of the war, for fear of destroying group consensus. As a result, many Americans died in combat for a lost cause. In similar ways, many businesses have failed due to groupthink.

Group Polarization

A closely related occurrence is group polarization. Here, a group moves to an extreme position, one arrived at in a group situation, that few individuals would favor apart from the group. A number of researchers have termed this action *the risky shift* (Stoner, 1961; Wallach, Kogan, and Bem, 1962).

The following is a common example of the risky shift.

Tina, Erin, and Jill were at the very same party as you and your friends. Jim had promised them a ride home but had forgotten and taken off. You knew nothing about the promise to the girls.

Standing outside, the girls considered their options. Billy could give them a ride, but they wouldn't be caught dead riding with that geek. Instead they decided to walk the couple of miles to Erin's and get a ride from one of her parents. The street was a main thoroughfare and well lit. It was safe. Along the way they discussed the party and the behavior of the boys. For the life of them they just couldn't figure out why the guys always had to act so cocky. Why couldn't they be themselves?

They had walked about eight blocks when Jill commented. "There is one good thing about guys though."

"What, the sex thing?" replied Erin. With that both Erin and Tina laughed.

"No, seriously," replied Jill. "If we were guys we wouldn't be walking a mile out of our way just to get home. We'd take the shortcut through the rail yard.

"That creepy place," shuttered Erin. "It's so dark and isolated."

"But that's what I mean," countered Jill. "We always have to take the long way. We always have to play it safe."

"Yeah," drawled Tina. "My brother always cuts through the rail yard.

"Mine too," joined Erin.

"Hey," Tina said. "Maybe it's time we stopped being afraid of everything. How are we ever gonna compete with the guys in life if we always play it safe like nice little girls should?"

"I agree," said Erin sternly. "There are three of us. We can take care of ourselves."

"Yeah," said Jill. "Let's go!"

The above example illustrates how the risky shift works. At first the girls were playing it safe. Then, suddenly the conversation turned to equality. Angered at their position, they made an emotional decision on a treacherous course of action, the decision to cut through the rail yard. It was a decision that none of them actually welcomed or would have decided upon alone.

Group polarization does not necessarily mean selecting a riskier position. It can also take the form of an overly conservative approach. This occurs especially in organizations in which the membership engages in a lot of "finger-pointing." Not wanting to be placed in a position of blame, members adopt overly conservative positions. While this may seem safe in the short run, the competition ultimately ends up miles ahead.

GROUP LEADERSHIP

In order to accomplish its goals, all groups must have a leader or leaders. A **leader** is someone who exercises formal or informal influence over those within the group. Sociologists have identified three basic styles of leadership: authoritative, democratic, and laissez-faire.

Authoritative leadership is generally found in formal organizations that have a top to bottom flow of power and communication. Each individual has a clearly defined role in the organization and a specific amount of formal power to exercise. Orders originate at the top and flow down to the bottom through successive layers. Failure to comply and carry out one's duties results in sanctions that are clearly spelled out in organizational manuals. Authoritative leadership is not confined solely to formal organizations. This form of leadership may be present in informal groups. Let us say that your neighborhood suddenly begins to experience a rash of home burglaries. After much discussion a meeting is planned at one neighbor's home. At first, there is open discussion, until it becomes known that one member of the group, Tina, is a police officer in an adjoining community. Recognizing her expertise, the group selects her as the unofficial leader. Tina then rolls into action by assigning a number of different tasks to specific people and setting deadlines. While it is true that Tina has no formal power, she clearly utilizes an authoritative style by deciding what needs to be done and assigning duties. The group, for its part, complies because they recognize her expertise. The advantage of authoritative leadership lies in efficiency and goal completion.

Democratic leadership. This is the reverse of authoritative leadership. Here the power flows from the bottom-up. Rather than assigning tasks, the leader initiates discussion and encourages members to volunteer. This leadership style usually occurs in informal groups. An example would be a church organization whose goal is to help needy families. For the organization to function, the leader must establish consensus among members as to who is in need of aid and what aid should be provided. A failure to establish consensus would result in the breakdown of the group. One weakness of democratic leadership is that it requires an inordinate amount of time for consensus building. An advantage of democratic leadership is that group members have strong commitment to organizational goals because they set the goals.

Laissez-faire leadership. This type of leader is one who might well be described as "laid-back." Of all three styles, the laissez-faire leader exercises the least amount of control and direction. Rather, this leader encourages the group to clarify its goals and then volunteer for leadership positions. Laissez-faire leaders rarely assume responsibility for the group's success or failure. If the group fails, it's their fault; if the group succeeds, it's their success. Good examples of laissez-faire leaders are consultants paid by companies to help resolve problems. In providing leadership the consultant helps the group identify the problems, develop solutions, and establish time lines for completion of tasks. However, from the beginning, it is understood that the consultant will not be a part of the team resolving the problems. This will be the group's responsibility. Laissez-faire leadership is the least commonly exercised of the three leadership styles.

No style of leadership is the *best*. What works in one group may not work in another. In formal organizations where decisions need to be made quickly and efficiently, the authoritative style is best. Likewise, in prisons or mental institutions, democratic or laissez-faire leadership would be ridiculous. On the flip side, in professional organizations, where individuals are similar in training and rank, democratic leadership is best. And finally, though rare, laissez-faire leadership works in situations where authoritative or democratic styles would surely fail.

There are cultural differences in preferences for leadership styles. Americans generally are more comfortable with a democratic leadership style, due to our political and cultural values. On the other hand, a more authoritative style might work better in a country such as China that has a cultural history of unquestioned rule by leaders. This is not a matter of right or wrong, but simply of what works.

Drift Toward Oligarchy

Political sociologist, Robert Michels (1967) proposed what he termed, "the iron law of oligarchy." According to Michels, while most organizations publicly identify themselves as democratic, few if any, actually practice democracy. In fact, he states that the natural tendency is for the leadership to control and run almost all aspects of the organization. In this way it is more accurate to identify most organizations as oligarchies rather than democracies.

Michels listed several reasons why organizations that start out as being committed to democracy drift into oligarchy. The *first* is that the leadership is in charge of the day-to-day running of the organization's business. This places it in the position of having access to more information than the membership. As anyone who has ever worked for a large organization knows, information is power and competing powers tend to withhold information in order to gain the upper hand. *Second*, most people who belong to an organization do not have the time needed to keep track of organizational affairs. Life is complex; we belong to many organizations; often, there aren't enough hours in the day to take care of the things we are responsible for. Heaven forbid we challenge the leadership and end up with the job ourselves. As such we are indebted to the leadership. And *third*, there is a natural tendency for leadership to want to entrench itself in power. Few leaders, even in organizations committed to change, want change. As long as the status quo is maintained, the power of the leaders is secure. As discussed earlier, this is a characteristic of bureaucracies as well as organizations.

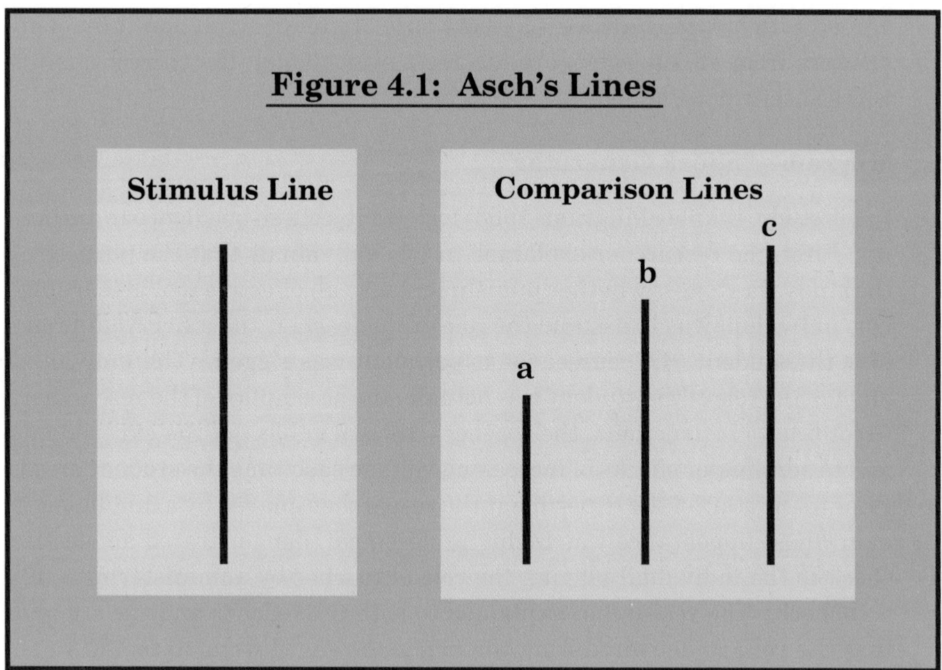

Figure 4.1: Asch's Lines

GROUP CONFORMITY

Few of us like to think of ourselves as followers. Instead we like to picture ourselves as individuals who weigh facts and make-up our own minds. While this may be true some of the time, often we unknowingly follow the lead of the group. This speaks to our need to "fit in" by conforming to expected behavior. Two classic studies demonstrate the power of group conformity (Asch) and obedience to authority (Milgram).

Asch's Lines

In his research on group conformity, Solomon Asch (1952) brought together a group of people to view a series of lines and compare them to a stimulus line. The stimulus line was placed in close proximity to a series of three lines as depicted in Figure 4.1.

The respondents were asked to identify which of the three lines matched the stimulus one. As you can see, the task is not difficult. The respondents were asked to make twelve sets of judgments. However, in the experiment, only one individual was really being studied and the rest were all accomplices of the researcher with instructions on how to answer. All answers were given aloud, with the individual being studied placed in the last or next-to-last position. In the first six rounds all the respondents answered correctly. Then in the following six rounds the accomplices all chose incorrect answers. The point of the experiment was to determine what effect this would have on the subject. Originally Asch assumed that since the correct answer was so obvious, subjects would not conform to the group by giving incorrect answers. Asch was wrong. Over 75 percent of the subjects studied agreed with incorrect answers at least once. In total, about one-third of all answers from all subjects were incorrect even though the correct answer was so easily determined.

Milgram's "Shock Generator"

In his study, Stanley Milgram (1963) tested subjects on obedience to authority. First, the researcher explained to two individuals that the purpose of the study was to test whether punishment was an effective tool in learning. One individual was to assume the role of the teacher, the other would role-play the student. Of course, the experiment was rigged. The individual playing the role of the student was actually the accomplice of the researcher. According to instructions, the teacher (the real subject of the experiment) was to administer shocks of increasing voltage each time the student erred. Prior to the start of the experiment the researcher (played by a middle-aged man whose appearance was highly professional) demonstrated an electric shock to the individual playing the role of teacher by administering a 40-volt shock. The researcher explained to both the teacher and the student that the voltage delivered from the machine ranged from 40 to 450 volts, with increments labeled progressively from "slight shock" to "danger, severe shock" and alarmingly, to "XXX". The accomplice (person playing the role of the student) then expressed concern because he suffered from a heart condition. The researcher informed him, in front of the teacher, that the experiment was perfectly safe. The experiment then began. The student was strapped into a chair and electrodes were attached.

The central question was how much shock was the teacher willing to administer before refusing to continue? The teacher was paid in advance and informed that he could keep the money regardless of the outcome of the experiment. The script was carefully arranged. The student responded correctly for a period of time and everything was pleasant. The student made an error and the teacher administered a 15-volt shock that made the student flinch. Actually, no shock was delivered. The student only pretended to feel the shock. Suddenly the errors accumulated and the student was forced to move the dial from "slight" to "moderate" to "intense." With each increase the discomfort of the learner was more pronounced. At 75 volts he groaned loudly. At 150 volts he requested to be released from the experiment. At 180 he yelled and jerked the chair he was strapped to. At 270 he was screaming in agony, demanding to stop and saying that his heart was bothering him. At some point all teachers attempted to stop the experiment. In their initial attempt to stop they were told, "Please continue." If they persisted, the researcher responded, "Go on," or "The experiment requires you to continue." In cases where the teacher was adamant in his wish to stop, the researcher sternly replied, "You have no other choice—you must go on!"

Astonishingly, 65 percent of the participants (twenty-six of forty) continued to administer shocks all the way to the end of the shock series. This was true even after the learner had ceased to scream after the 330 plus level.

The subjects chosen for the study constituted a cross-section of the American population. They ranged from twenty to fifty years-of-age. Twenty percent were professionals, forty percent were employed in white-collar jobs, and 40 percent were unskilled laborers. When the study was repeated with women in the role of teacher, almost identical results were discovered.

The importance of the above studies is that they demonstrate how powerful the group is in shaping our opinions and behavior, and how strong our allegiance is to authority. We may not believe that we would follow the lead of the group and answer obvious questions incorrectly, as did the subjects in Asch's experiment, but we have all, at some time, "caved-in" to group pressure. Think back to when someone in your group at a social function tells a particularly offensive joke that is ethnic, racial, or sexist in nature. How many times have you just let it slide, thereby giving tacit approval when you know that really, you disapprove?

And while we might have contempt for the individual administering the shock in Milgram's experiment, we all at some time in our lives blindly "do what we're told." We can use Milgram's work to try to understand a recently discovered atrocity in Afghanistan where members of the Stryker Combat Brigade formed a "kill-team" to murder innocent Afghan civilians. The ringleader, Staff Sergeant Calvin R. Gibbs, told his team- mates that he had gotten away with similar "stuff" in Iraq. The first attack occurred one wintery day when a solitary Afghan man approached the team. A fragmentary grenade was tossed on the ground by one of the men creating the illusion that the soldiers were under fire. The members of the "kill team" where then ordered to open fire on the man, killing him. All members of the squad participated in the murder with the exception of one soldier who claims to have fired high. This became the prototype for a months-long shooting spree that resulted in countless deaths of innocents. Members of the squad have been charged with additional counts of dismembering and photographing corpses, as well as hoarding a human skull and other bones (Whitlock, 2010).

SUMMARY

The future of social groups and bureaucratic organizations is inextricably tied to the expected pace of change in the future. Prior to industrialization, the small social group provided for our need of human interaction and structure. With industrialization old patterns gave way to new ones. One of the most significant changes that occurred during this period of time was the rise of bureaucratic organizations. Work was taken out of the home and small agricultural communities and moved to the larger, more impersonal urban settings of factories. With this move, old patterns of social interaction, primarily the informal reliance upon small groups, gave way to more complex, formal, and less permanent relationships. An example of this is visible in the geographic mobility of the population. At one time, generation after generation of family members resided in the same location. With industrialization, we suddenly became a nation on the move. Millions of people were in a constant state of relocation, ending old relationships and beginning new ones.

What does this tell of our future? If the past is a judge of the future, and many scholars believe that it is, we are about to take another turn. The pace of change is increasing, bringing with it dramatic transformations for social groups and human interaction. Corporations are presently in an unprecedented period of change brought about by technological advances in computers, telecommunications, and transportation. Globalization, downsizing, and the virtual workplace (the ability to perform work from any location in the world via computers and telecommunications) will alter the way we work and live. More and more workers will be moved out of formal business organizations and shifted to workstations either at home or in far-away places as companies restructure to meet competition from abroad. Undoubtedly, this downsizing and streamlining will mean less bureaucracy, but it will also bring more uncertainty and more relocation. While this might well result in more efficiency (as bureaucracy previously brought to formal organizations), it will also place more stress on existing group memberships such as family, friends, church, and community.

Terms You Should Know:

Social Structure	Social Group	Status
Role	Role Strain	Role Conflict
Bureaucracy	Dyad	Triad
Group Cohesion	Groupthink	Group Polarization

Can You Answer These Questions?

1. Name several in-groups to which you belong. List some out-groups presently in your life?
2. What is the difference between a social aggregate and a social category?
3. List and define the three types of groups discussed in the text.
4. Describe the difference between ascribed and achieved status.
5. Can you remember a time in your life when you experienced role distancing? Role exit?
6. Name and briefly describe the four categories of formal organizations.
7. Why does Max Weber believe bureaucracy is so important in modern societies? Do you agree?
8. List the factors affecting group cohesion?
9. What was the major finding of Solomon Asch's experiment? Of Stanley Milgram's work?

Critical Thinking Exercises:

1. Do social networks expand or limit your freedom? How important have they been in your life?
2. What would you identify as your present master status? Has this helped or hindered your social advancement?
3. In your opinion what is the best type of leadership that should be utilized in your future occupation? Why might the others not be better suited?
4. Are there certain professions that might be more susceptible to obey authorities than others? If so, why?
5. Is bullying just another form of groupthink? What suggestion do you have that might alleviate the problem.

Photo: Christine Sommer

Chapter 5

Personal Development and Socialization

In the year 1798 in Aveyron, France, hunters captured a naked boy running on all fours. He was four and a half feet tall and appeared to be about twelve years old. Although he was obviously a human male, he behaved like a wild animal, walked on all fours, and did not speak. He ate only potatoes, acorns, and chestnuts. Victor, as he was later named, was eventually put into the care of Dr. Jean-Marc Itard who tried unsuccessfully to teach him to behave like a human being. Victor did learn to walk upright and to speak a few one-syllable words. However, by the time he died in 1826, he was not much different than when he was discovered by the hunters in the woods of Aveyron (Itard, 1962). Over the centuries, a number of children have suffered similar fates. Abandoned or lost by their parents these children are referred to as **feral** (wild) **children**.

Different from feral children are isolated ones, those discovered locked away and denied access to other humans. One such child, Anna, was born to an unwed mother. Her grandfather was so outraged that he locked Anna away in the attic. She had little contact with other humans and was given only small amounts of exercise, just enough to sustain her physical life. At the time of her discovery she was six and a half years-of-age. She possessed no language skills and was incapable of feeding or dressing herself, keeping herself clean, or interacting with others. In essence, Anna was stuck in an infantile stage of development. After her discovery, various experts worked diligently to remediate her. However, only minimal progress was made. By the time Anna died at the age of ten from a rare blood disease, she had failed to master the skills necessary to function in her new world (Davis, 1947).

In another well-documented case, Genie, a thirteen-year old girl, was discovered locked in a small closet. According to evidence gathered by authorities, she had been put into the closet when she was eighteen months old and not allowed to leave. For days at a time she was strapped to a potty-chair. When not forced to sit in the chair, she was imprisoned in the windowless room and forced to lie in a crib. Her blind mother was allowed to feed Genie, but was under orders from her father and brother not to talk to her. At times, the mother's father and brother would take turns barking at Genie to torment and frighten her into submission. As in the case of Anna, at the time of her discovery Genie could not speak or care for herself. Years later and after much rehabilitation, Genie still could not speak in complete sentences, or socially interact with others as we do (Pines, 1981).

BEING HUMAN: NATURE AND NURTURE

What do the above three cases teach us? For one, they certainly present a different picture than Hollywood brought to us in the classic film, "Tarzan." Supposedly, Tarzan, lost in the jungle, was befriended and raised by all of the *nice* animals. In the movie, we see a fully developed human being with the capacity of language and the ability to interact with others. Nice story, but a far cry from reality. What we have learned from feral and isolated children is that socialization is a vital ingredient in becoming, in a cultural sense, human. Moreover, if this socialization is not provided sequentially at specific ages, permanent damage can occur. This leads us to ask, exactly what is the relationship between nature and nurture? By **nature**, we mean that which we bring into the world at birth. **Nurture**, on the other hand, refers to what we learn or gain via our interactions with others in our group and the world in general.

As we know, most animals possess an array of skills at birth. We refer to these skills as **instincts**. Instinct allows animals to function in the absence of learning. Anyone who has ever owned a pet has had occasion to marvel at patterned behaviors that just seem to pop-up from nowhere. For centuries, humans have taken advantage of animal instincts by using breeding techniques to obtain the right combination of desirable traits. Since human beings are also animals, how do we fit into this model?

At some time or another you have heard someone say, "Well, that's *human nature*." What this means is that there is an underlying instinctual quality, something inborn, related to the observed behavior being commented on. Following Darwin's line of thinking, a number of social scientists have utilized human nature to explain everything from personality to economic systems. For example, in our chapter on deviance, you see that many social scientists (most notably early sociological thinkers) believed that criminals were born to be criminals. In other words, something in their genetic code prevented them from adhering to acceptable customs and practices. Therefore, it was believed that whole groups of people were biologically flawed or predisposed toward criminal behavior. Noting the differences in normative practices around the world, these researchers provided a biological explanation—people behaved differently because they were biologically different. This line of reasoning has even been used to justify our economic system. Have you ever heard someone express the belief that people are basically greedy? Such a belief validates our notion that our nature is essentially competitive and materialistic. Therefore, capitalism is seen as logical and necessary while socialism, which is based on cooperation and sharing, can't possibly work.

As the social sciences matured, we began to discover many things that challenged naturalistic or biologically determined theories of behavior. Psychologist John B. Watson (1878-1958) advanced an opposing view known as **behaviorism**. He argued that patterned behavior is not biologically determined, but *learned*. At the core of Watson's theory was the belief that all humankind consisted of one biological species. Since we share a single, common genetic background, cultural differences were seen as the result of factors other than biology. For example, we know that the culture of Eskimos is different from the culture of Aborigines. This is a difference we would expect, due to geography and climate, and not because one is more evolved than the other. Watson suggested that another misinterpretation of the naturalistic position was its attempt to explain why Western Europe was more advanced in science and technology than many African countries. The assumption naturalists made was that the people of Western Europe were more evolved than those in African countries and this accounted for their cultural differences. Sociologists debunked this theory by comparing cultural differences between societies with similar levels of technological advancement. For example, China and the United States have radically different cultures. Does this mean that one is more evolved than the other? If so, how would you account for similar levels of science and technology? We now recognize that many of these early explanations were based on ethnocentric thinking.

Although most social scientists have moved away from naturalistic thinking, it does occasionally reappear. Recent examples can be found in the works of Arthur Jensen (1980), Richard Herrnstein (1994), and Charles Murray (1994), who suggest the possibility of intelligence differences between whites and blacks.

Sociobiology

Even though most social scientists have moved away from the naturalistic position few, if any, would say that nature plays no role in human development. Instead, human development is attributed to both, usually with a heavier emphasis on nurturing. In opposition to this thinking, a new position arose in the mid to late 1970s. **Sociobiology** assigns a much greater role to nature in explaining personality and behavior than the majority of other social sciences. To support their position, sociobiologists point to the fact that only one percent of our genetic material differs from that of apes, an animal that relies heavily on instinct. In humans, they maintain, lies genetic material that contains information that ultimately shapes our behavior in ways that we are not consciously aware of. Let's look at an example.

In the animal world, the need to propagate the species is encoded in sexual behavior. More specifically, animals seek out mates to perpetuate their own genetic material. Males compete or battle for the rights of reproduction with the most genetically superior females. In this sense, males are the aggressors. A male lion that enters a new pride and replaces (through battle) the old leader will often kill all the young cubs. This is done (instinctively) to destroy the genetic material of the previous male leader and in order to gain sexual access to females who are constrained by nursing. All new offspring of the pride will carry the new leader's genetic material.

Interesting, you say, but what does it have to do with humans? Sociobiologists would point out that in the human species, it is the male who pursues the female and like the lion above, is more aggressive in his behavior and tends to be more promiscuous, looking to mate with as many females as possible.

Most other social scientists offer a different explanation of sexual behavior and aggression. They contend that gender differences are due to socialization (nurture). In other words, we're back to that "boys will be boys" thing. Males act out sexually and aggressively because we allow and expect them to. On the flip side, society has stricter standards for girls and neither expects or allows them to act out aggressively or sexually. Sociobiologists would, of course, disagree and argue that what is actually attributed to learning (socialization) is behavior encoded in our genes.

Consider a human mother who runs into a burning building to save her child. We attribute her heroic action to altruism (love), an emotion acquired through socialization. Sociobiologists would disagree and point to animals in the wild willing to fight against overwhelming odds, even to the point of baring their throats to an aggressor, to save their young. This they contend, is not something learned, it's instinctual. Sociobiologists would argue that instinct was largely responsible for both the human and animal mother's sacrifice, because both are attempting to preserve their own gene pool through the lives of their children and their future offspring.

As a relatively new field, sociobiology has few proponents. Opponents criticize sociobiologists for their lack of scientific research (experimental results capable of being replicated). Critics maintain that sociobiology is rooted in inference and speculation. Likewise, of all the genes scientists have isolated, not one related to instinct has ever been found. Proponents of sociobiology remain undaunted, maintaining that because of ethical research issues many experiments, like those associated with human breeding, cannot be conducted. Likewise, they point out that science has yet to discover the necessary technology to fully explore our nature. As technology and science advance, proponents are confident that the instinctive origins of our behavior will be discovered.

Nature versus Nurture: A Summary

If the above discussion has left you hanging, academically speaking, don't feel that you are alone. You are, in fact, in good company. Presently, the best minds in the world have pondered the nature/nurture question and have come away scratching their heads. In light of this, we offer the following explanation.

It is obvious that we inherit physical traits. Some of us are tall, some are short. Some people are thin, some are heavier. Some people have light skin color, some have darker skin. This is a given that we all recognize. However, these physical traits are not culturally neutral. In other words, some traits are judged by others to be more desirable. It is at this point, the intersection of the physical with the cultural, that we as individuals, including our personality and our behavior, are shaped. Again, an example is in order.

Have you ever noticed that good looking people seem to get all the breaks in life? Studies of attractiveness seem to lend credence to this notion. In an analysis of seventy-six major attraction studies, researchers found that attractive people, according to culturally defined standards of beauty, were perceived by others to have better personalities and were seen as more likely to succeed in life. Both women and men equated beauty with goodness, and this relationship was believed to be true at all ages, even as early as infancy (Eagley, Ashmoe, Makhijani, and Longo, 1991). Moreover, studies also demonstrated that since we expect beautiful people to be sociable, kind, competent, etc., we treat these individuals in ways that confirm our expectation and thus *cause* the beautiful person to be highly sociable, kind, competent, and so forth (Snyder, Tanke, and Berscheid, 1977, Feng, 2002). Finally, recent studies demonstrate that perceptions of beauty extend to the labor market where those judged to have good looks earned significantly more than their less attractive counterparts (Hamermesh, 2006 & 2007).

In some individuals nature plays a stronger role, although not completely independent from nurturing. In regard to personality, social scientists suggest that we inherit temperament. By temperament we mean a tendency or predisposition to act in a certain way. Some people, as you have already noticed, seem to be calm and laid-back; others are fidgety and hyper. Think about your own family, in particular your siblings. Do you all have the same temperament? If you are a parent, think about your children. Are they different? Most parents confess that each of their children were different at birth, while one might have been quiet and pleasantly content, the other was much more vocal and demanding. Of course, as children grow up they *acquire* personalities and refine traits. Over time, siblings that started out different as night and day may actually begin to be more and more alike. Conversely, siblings that started out as very similar may become rather different. In either case, we can see the role of nature and nurture. At birth we have certain traits, temperament being one. After birth, the forces of society shape temperament to ultimately determine whom we become. Let's look at one more example before leaving this topic. Social scientists have spent much time investigating intelligence and aptitude as they relate to the nature versus nurture issue. In their jargon, **intelligence** is our inherent ability to understand and comprehend concepts, and **aptitude** is our potential to develop or maximize skills, such as athleticism or linguistics. Although disagreement exists, most social scientists would agree that nature sets limits both for our intelligence and our aptitude. However, our environment determines the extent to which we reach our limits. For instance, one might have the potential (capacity) to master complex mathematics, but whether one does is a matter of training and nurturing. Likewise, one might possess the ability to become the world's best boomerang thrower, but unless introduced to a boomerang, it is highly unlikely that he/she will master the skill. Plus, it is far more likely that this skill would be mastered in an Aboriginal society than in the contemporary United States. This, of course, is the role of nurture.

THEORIES OF PERSONAL DEVELOPMENT

Although one might think that personality and its development is a matter for psychologists, sociologists have long noted the importance of society and its institutions in personality formation. Who we are, what we become, how we think, and how we see ourselves are all influenced by human interaction. In this section we will discuss four different theories of personality. Like many of the concepts we have discussed in this text, considerable disagreement exists on how our personality develops.

Charles Horton Cooley: The Looking-Glass Self

The ability to think of ourselves as individuals apart from others is generally referred to as an understanding of existence. "I am" is an attempt to capture this image of self. Charles Horton Cooley (1864-1929) was one of the first theorists to tackle the question of how we develop personality and view ourselves. For Cooley, the single most important determinant in personality formation was how we interpret other people's perceptions of how we look and act. It was for this reason that Cooley referred to his theory as the "looking-glass self" (Cooley, 1902). He used the following couplet to summarize his view:

> *Each to each a looking-glass*
> *Reflects the other that doth pass.*

The formation of self takes place in a three-step progression.

1. First we consider how we believe other people see us. In other words, we may think that others see us as smart and witty, or conversely, as rather dull and humorless.
2. As we interact with others we interpret how others treat us. Do they treat us as smart and witty or as dull and humorless?

3. Based on our interpretation of others reactions to us, we develop an image of ourselves. We conclude that we are smart, dull, witty, or humorless.

Two aspects of Cooley's theory are important to remember. *First*, in developing our self-image not all "others" are of equal importance. Those we identify as "significant others" are more important than those we see as either causal observers or people that we do not respect. Certainly this is not difficult to comprehend. As adults we look into the mirror (the eyes of others) to find ourselves. But not all people's evaluations carry the same weight. For example, if I meet an individual who is a member of a hate group, I could care less about how he/she perceives me. In fact, I might welcome a negative reaction. On the other hand, there are other people who are very important to me, like my spouse, friends, teachers (some), siblings, and parents. In developing our personalities, Cooley suggested that our concept of self develops most fully within primary groups. The most important is the family. Psychologist Urie Bonfenbrenner (1992) captured this essence with this comment: "Kids need people who are crazy about them." We first catch a glimpse of who and what we are by paying attention to each gesture, word, and sound that our parents make, and with this information we form the foundation upon which we build our image of self. If we have intelligent and loving parents, chances are that we will grow into secure adults. If not, the images we form of ourselves may be laden with doubts and insecurities.

Secondly, Cooley's idea is not only of a one-way mirror in which our image of self is determined by others. Remember that the process outlined by Cooley is that we first form images of how we think people see us. Then, through social interaction we attempt to interpret their reaction to us based on these preconceived images. What happens if our interpretations are incorrect? What happens if we believe that others see us as dull even though we really are rather bright? The answer is that our incorrect interpretation becomes reality. So, even though we are capable of being very bright, our belief that we are dull makes us so. An example of this can be seen in anorexia. Anorexics develop a perceived notion that they are fat. As they meet others they attempt to interpret the actions of others against their preconceived image of being fat. Others might gasp in disbelief at how emaciated the anorexic is, but to the anorexic the reaction is interpreted as others being repulsed because they are too fat. As a result, the anorexic attempts to lose even more weight.

George Herbert Mead: The Role-Taking Process

Like Cooley, George Herbert Mead (1863-1931) was a symbolic interactionalist interested in the question of personality formation. Agreeing with Cooley, Mead believed that personality development and self-image was a product of social interaction. However, he disagreed with Cooley's "looking-glass" process. Instead, Mead believed that children learn who they are by taking on the roles of others in **play**.

Herbert Mead believed that personality was developed through role-playing. Here a child role-plays as he pretends to drive the a tractor. This play will become an important building block in developing his personality.

Photo: moyerphotos.

Mead divided the process leading to self-image and personality into three stages—imitation, play, and game.

Imitation stage. For the first two years, a child simply imitates gestures and sounds he observes others producing. As the child grows, imitation becomes more complex. For instance, an infant in her crib may simply reproduce sounds that she hears others make. But later, when she observes her father mowing the grass, she may use a miniature plastic mover and push it across the lawn while making mower noises. A little boy may see his mother cooking and proceed to play with pots and pans in imitation of her. Although the child is mimicking the behavior of parents, he/she has no concept of the work they are doing or why it is being done. The importance of this play is that it prepares the child for the next, more complicated stage.

Play stage. In this stage, the child begins to assume the roles of others. Dressing up in a costume, the child assumes a role and pretends he/she is that person. While pretending to be another person—a mommy, daddy, or a superhero—they act as if they have the abilities that person possesses and thereby see the world through their eyes. In this stage, the child will assume the role of a *significant* other, generally a parent, but cannot understand what the *role* of being a parent is all about. From this perspective, they come to see themselves as this significant other sees them. Likewise, this is a period in which children internalize the values and attitudes of those closest to them. By playing a role, they learn what is and is not acceptable behavior.

After children mature and gain more experience, they begin to assume the roles of individuals less important in their lives. However, they still do not understand the significance of those roles. It does not occur to them that people act in a particular way because of the role they occupy. Put differently, the child plays the part of the individual, not the role. This period lasts from approximately two to six years-of-age.

Game stage. In the final stage, children move from playing the person to playing the *role*. The importance here is that this moves the child to a different level of recognition and maturity. Here they learn that people behave the way they do because they play a role in society. Furthermore, all people in the same role act, more or less, in the same way. At this stage children also learn that not all roles are equal. People in different roles interact differently with people in other roles.

The ability to understand roles is crucial to human interaction because human interaction is built upon these roles. Each person assumes many roles. As we have seen, attached to each role is a set of expected behaviors. Mead characterized this final stage as the game stage because through games, children come to understand organized activity. Additionally, in the game stage the child learns that people occupy different roles at different times.

For Mead, personality and self-esteem are direct results of role-playing. Children play at many roles. They are good at some and in others they fail. Through this gradual process, children develop an image of who they are, what they are capable of, and how they fit into society. Under ideal conditions, the experiences of children in role-playing situations are positive and contribute to their self-esteem. Unfortunately, this is not always the case. Failures can lead to a negative self-image and lays the foundation for a lifetime of personality and esteem problems.

Sigmund Freud: The Role of the Unconscious

As we have seen, Cooley and Mead emphasize the importance of social interaction in the development of self and personality. **Socialization** is a process by which we learn to fit into society and thereby achieve harmony. Sigmund Freud departed from this line of thought and instead, pointed to the role of biological forces, instincts and physical needs in the socialization process. While Cooley and Mead stressed harmony in the relationship between self and society, Freud believed that harmony was not possible because of an inherent and unavoidable conflict between the needs of the individual and the needs of society. This situation produced a perpetual state of conflict in which the individual was doomed to live life in a state of disharmony. At one point Freud remarked, "The more civilized we become, the more unhappy we must be," (Freud, 1962 orig. 1930).

Freud conceived the mind as being divided into three distinct parts: the id, the ego, and the superego. All operate, for the most part, in the unconscious. The **id** represents the basic, innate natural drives that all humans are born with. Included in these would be the tendency for aggression and the desire for physical pleasure, especially sexual pleasure. The id wants what it wants and it wants it now, no delayed gratification, no patience! For the most part, we are unaware in our everyday behavior of the demands of the id. Indeed, the id is the source of the infamous "Freudian slip." While we all have the desire for aggression and pleasure, it is inappropriate in civilized society for us to allow them free reign. Chaos would ensue and

Sigmund Freud greatly influenced our thinking about human behavior. He believed much of our needs and desires were hidden in our unconscious.

Photo: Max Halberstadt, 1921.

societal breakdown would result. You may wish to think of the id as your "evil twin".

In order to tame the wild id, we as a society have established rules for behavior that lead to order and stability. We teach people what is right and what is wrong. This is part of the process of becoming civilized. Sociologists, of course, refer to this as the socialization process. Freud suggested that all of this "teaching" and socialization was contained in our **superego**, a stern parent or policeman-like entity in your personality that insists that you follow the rules and suppress the "dangerous" demands of the id. As you can see, the id and the superego are the source of conflict within us that leaves us, as Freud believed, in constant conflict, caught between the opposing demands of the id and the superego.

How then are these conflicting needs balanced? Freud believed that this function belonged to the third aspect of our mind, the **ego**, whose role is to balance (think of a referee) the id's need for the immediate gratification of uncivilized wants with the requirements of society for order, civility, and stability. According to Freud, the work of the ego is hidden from view because it, like the id and the superego, occurs mainly in our subconscious. Picture an iceberg, only a small part of it (your conscious mind) is visible. Hidden from view, lurking beneath the cold, dark water, is most of the iceberg's mass. It is here, concealed from easy access, that the subconscious and unconscious lie with the subconscious being closer to the water's surface and therefore more easily accessible. Meanwhile the unconscious lies far beneath the water and is difficult to access.

To understand Freud, consider a common student experience: You have just worked a long and tiring shift. In fact, you've put in a couple of extra hours for overtime pay. The bills are mounting and you're falling behind. Your significant other just gave you a piece of his/her mind because you're not spending enough time together. Your friend and companion of the last fourteen years, Fido, died yesterday morning. In spite of all of this you are determined to get a degree and move forward with your life. You drive to school. You're nervous because the paper you were supposed to hand in is not quite completed. You'll have to ask for an extension. After class you approach your professor, Dr. Headstrong. You ask for a delay. But before you can explain, she sternly replies that the paper was due today and will not be accepted late. "Furthermore," she quips, "if you're not interested in school, you should drop out and save yourself the time and money you're wasting." Your first impulse is to take your sociology text book and smack her upside the head. This is your id talking. However, the policeman in your head, your superego, is urgently reminding you that this is not the way a civilized person acts. "After all, you can't just go around smacking everyone you get mad at. What would happen to society if everyone used violence to solve problems?" On the other hand, your id is telling you how good it would feel just to give her one little whack. At this point your ego kicks in to try to squash some of the noise by making you realize that smacking her is going to cause you a lot of trouble—expulsion from school, police, court, fines, and the possibility of jail. In the end you bite your tongue, try to work out a compromise, and on the way out of her office, when she isn't looking, "accidentally" knock the cup of coffee off her desk.

In the context of his concepts of development and personality, Freud's id, ego, and superego must be in balance if the individual is to avoid personality disorders. In a well-adjusted person, the ego is successful in balancing the opposing needs of the id and the superego. Freud believed that if conflicts between the id and the superego were not resolved in childhood, personality disorders were inevitable, but the source of these problems would be hidden from the conscious mind.

Jean Piaget: The Development of Thinking

Jean Piaget (1896-1980) extended the work of Cooley and Mead on personality by delving into the thinking process. His primary research concerned the thinking process development in children. In the developmental stage, Piaget (1956) noticed that younger children consistently gave incorrect answers when taking intelligence tests. This was not true of older children who more often responded with the correct answer. Piaget reasoned that this was indicative of the thought (cognitive) development process.

Piaget tested his cognitive process ideas on various age groups. From his studies he concluded that, as a child's mind matures, it passes through four stages. In each of these stages, a new mode of reasoning replaces a less mature process. The ages associated with each of the following stages are approximate and some variation is not uncommon.

Sensorimotor stage (Birth to two years). In this stage, the infant has not yet developed a sense of self. For the infant there is no recognition that their bodies are separate from anything else in the environment. Too, the infant has no sense of "cause and effect," or the ability to connect an action with an outcome. For example, while parents might believe that children cry in order to be fed, babies actually cry because of *discomfort*.

An important aspect of this stage identified by Piaget is **object permanence**, usually attained by approximately ten months of age. Early on, infants lack the ability to be aware of objects that are not in sight. Try this with a youngster under ten months: In play, roll a brightly colored toy within reach of the child and watch as he/she attempts to touch, grasp and put the toy in her mouth. Then, in plain view, cover the toy with a blanket. A child who has not achieved object permanence can watch you cover the toy and may cry because it is gone, but will make no move to uncover the toy because for him, the toy has ceased to exist. Consider the important ramifications this may have for infants in day-care.

Preoperational stage (Ages 2 to 7). The most significant accomplishment of this stage is the ability to use symbols. However, using symbols and understanding what they mean are two different things, and while children at this stage may be able to count, they may not actually know what the meaning behind the numbers are. Many children develop the ability to count at an early age (perhaps by watching, "The Count" on Sesame Street) but lack the ability to conceptualize what the numbers mean. This was demonstrated in an experiment (Phillips, 1969) where children were presented with two piles of objects, pennies and flowers. When counting, the children were able to correctly count each group as containing six items. However, when the researcher then neatly stacked the pennies and spread out the flowers, the children consistently identified the flowers as having the greater number of items (even though they had previously counted each pile as containing six items). When the researcher reversed the process so that the flowers were piled closely together and the pennies were spread out, the children told him that there were now more pennies.

At this stage of development, children, while able to play-act at being others, are unable to understand the *role* those others play, an important stage previously identified by Mead. They may well be able to play a role, but are unable to grasp the significance of that role. They are unable to see the world through someone else's eyes. Instead, they are only capable of seeing things from their own perspective.

Concrete operations stage (Ages 7 to 12). The reasoning ability of children begins to develop at this stage. Here, the child still sees objects and events in concrete circumstances but now has the ability to understand the concepts behind numbers, speed, weight, size, and volume. For example, the child will recognize that if you take a regular glass of water and pour it's contents into a long slender tube, the amount of water stays the same even if it *looks* like the long tube contains more. Piaget called this the **law of conservation**. Try that with a younger child who has not yet reached this stage and you will get a very different answer.

It is at the concrete operations stage that children begin to understand the *roles of* the others and are able to see the world not only from their own stage, but also from the perspective of others who share their world. Finally, it is here that children begin to understand "cause and effect" relationships.

Formal operations stage (Ages 12 and over). The single most significant aspect of this stage is the ability to reason and think about objects and events in an abstract context. This includes not only single abstract concepts, but also combinations of them.

For example, we can ponder the relationship between wealth and happiness and other philosophical questions such as the existence and nature of God and the universe, and complex issues such as death, love, and altruism.

It is also at this level that personality may change and self-concepts can be altered. To some extent, our views about ourselves are shaped by society. Society tells us what is good and what is bad, what is beautiful and what is not. Armed with the ability to think abstractly about society's biases, it is possible to see ourselves in a new light, with perhaps a greater sense of appreciation. Suddenly, we can recognize that even though we are not wealthy, we still have worth. Also, we realize that we don't have to make the cover of *Glamour* to live a happy life. In fact, we may realize that we can be even happier if we're not rich or beautiful.

Within each of the above stages there are a multitude of levels, and not everyone will obtain the fourth level (Kohlberg and Gilligan, 1971). For some it may be more a matter of nature, not having been born with the cognitive ability to achieve higher levels of abstract thought. For others, society may have limited the ability to develop abstract thinking. Being born into a family with the financial means to foster abstract and creative goals can greatly affect one's ability to achieve higher levels of cognitive ability. On the flip side, it's tough to concentrate on the beauty of the pond when you're up to your neck in alligators.

AGENTS OF SOCIALIZATION

In the previous chapter we learned about the importance of social structure, the expected behavior patterns that guide social interaction. We also learned that society constructs institutions to teach new individuals what is expected and how to interact with others. The process by which the individual learns how to interact socially with others is termed socialization.

At this point we turn to a discussion of the various agents of socialization. While some may be more crucial than others, all play an important role in the process of developing the individual into a full-fledged, participating member of society.

The Family

Singularly, the family is the most important of all socializing agents. It is the family that provides our first socializing experiences and influences us when we are most vulnerable, in infancy and early childhood. It is with our family that we first learn about the world in which we live. Our core values, beliefs, and attitudes are forged early within the context of family. Research has established that if we are raised in a warm, loving, and moderately restrictive family, chances are that we will become productive and well-adjusted individuals. On the other hand, research suggests that if we are raised in cold, hostile, and authoritative family, we are destined to find much unhappiness in our lives (Corsaro and Eder, 1995; Gecas, 1981).

Viewed in the context of society, the family is ideally suited for what is termed **primary socialization**, because it occurs in a small primary group allowing for face-to-face interaction, an opportunity to closely monitor behavior, and an appropriate and comfortable place to experience success and failure. In other words, under the best possible conditions, family is the best possible place to develop a positive-self image and a positive set of beliefs, attitudes and values. On the negative side, under bad family conditions, the exact opposite is true. For example, children who receive their initial socialization experiences in intolerant and racist homes generally acquire the same attitudes. While it is possible, through positive social experiences and re-socialization, to overcome early prejudices and other negative socialization, it is a long and arduous process that often does not lead to rehabilitation.

The family is also important in setting the stage for our position in the hierarchical class system. In our chapter on class and stratification, we see that money, occupation, gender, power, race, religion, and culture differentiate individuals. Our initial position in the class system is obtained from our parents. If one is born into a working class family, his/her experiences will differ considerably from someone born into a professional family. Likewise, life chances will differ as well and although there is some movement up and down the hierarchical class scale, most people are destined to remain in the class to which they were born.

Sociologists have predicted a changing role for the family in advanced industrialized countries. In pre-industrial societies the impact of the family on individuals was greater both in terms of influence and number of years spent closely tied to it. This is still true today in traditional societies, but in modern postindustrial societies such as the United States, the role of the family has been somewhat diminished. This is the result of a number of factors. *First*, dual wage-earner families have become common, leaving less time for child rearing. *Second*, there has been an increase in the number of children living in single parent families. Again, this presents in most cases, a strain between the need to earn a living and the time required raising a child. With more parents working, child rearing activities are increasingly relegated to others outside of the family—friends, relatives, day-care and pre-school providers. *Third*, technology has impacted the role of the family. Today, children are bombarded with an endless array of multi-media messages about the world in which they live. The development of the Internet allows children to communicate globally. Advances in telecommunications allow children instant access to peers and the worldwide web. Compared to traditional agricultural societies where families were isolated by distance and lack of technology, and where days could pass before children came into contact with others, it is easy to recognize that the influence of the family has greatly decreased.

Although many sociologists condemn these changes and blame the erosion of influence exerted by the family on them, others disagree. While the influence of the family has changed, they suggest that family is still the primary source of socialization for the child because it exerts influence at our most vulnerable time in life. An example of this is that many people, as they grow older, express surprise at how much like their own parents they have become. A good exercise would be for you to talk to your own parents about this to see if they agree or disagree.

A Hamer woman with her child agrees to be photographed. The Hamer live among the bush covered hills of southern Ethiopia. Their basic livelihood is provided by herding goats and cattle. They move often in search of grazing land. Children of the Hamer are closely watched and learn the ways of the tribe from parents and elders. The Hamer have greater control over their children than parents in modern industrial nations.

Photo: Dietmar Temps.

School

As we just mentioned, changes in the economy altered the role of family in the socialization process. This is also true for schools (formal institutions of learning). In traditional society, the role of schools was minimal. Children attended school (some never attended) only for a brief period, to learn to read and write. With industrialization came a crucial need to educate those in the workplace. This was the beginning of mass education where school attendance became mandatory. In post-industrial society, it is almost impossible for individuals to survive without a formal education. This is true because schools today have a dual role—one is to provide education, the other is to issue degrees which certify who is qualified to perform specific types of work. It is this certification process that has given new power to schools and added years—on both ends of our lives from pre-school to graduate school—to the schooling process.

For the individual, entry into the formal education process marks a new phase in the socialization experience. Whereas the home was personalized and emotionally centered on the child, school is not. For the first time, the child is expected to interact with others in a more systematic and depersonalized way. Also, whereas in the family the child was taught to obey parents out of love and recognition of dependency, school demands obedience for the sake of order and productivity. Seen in this way, the family fosters diversity while school encourages and rewards conformity. Finally, it is in school that the child encounters "grading," a process in which progress is evaluated and students are compared against their peers. As such, children catch a first glimpse of their true abilities.

In addition to their manifest function (chapter one) of providing the individual with the knowledge and skill to become a productive member of society, schools also perform several latent socializing functions. *First*, it is in school that the child is exposed to new sets of values that create the foundation for group solidarity, a necessary ingredient of a stable society.

Second, the child learns how to function in an organized society. They begin to understand roles, expectations, and how to become part of a group working together for a common purpose. And *third*, schools instill within the child a sense of societal identity. For most students, the day begins with the pledge of allegiance to the flag. Then, they are taught the history of the nation and sing songs and read poems and stories that glorify their country. Through this process, children become citizens.

Peer Groups

A peer or peer group refers to individuals who are similar in either age or social position. Hence, your peer can be someone of your own age or someone of a different age but in a similar social rank. Look around your class. Odds are that there are people who are much younger or older than yourself—still, they are your peers.

A significant difference between the peer group and the family or the school is that of power. Whereas the family and the school exercise formal power over individuals, in peer groups there is a sense of equality. It is this single aspect of peer relationships that sets it apart from all other socializing agents. Within peer groups the adolescent is able to escape the bombardment of parental expectations and school demands. Likewise, it is where teens learn to set their own limits and experiment with society's taboos—drinking, smoking, premarital sex, body art and piercing. Within the peer group the adolescent finds acceptance and support for the often traumatic passage into adulthood. While adolescents find freedom within peer groups, they also experience great pressure to conform to the group's attitudes, beliefs and values. In our last chapter, we learned the power of peer group conformity as it relates to "groupthink," "group polarization," and "group cohesion."

Even for those of us who have already made the great leap into adulthood, peer groups are still important. Throughout life we pass through

Three young women pass time with each other. It is within peer groups that adolescents attempt to develop a sense of individuality. It is also within such groups that they experiment with society's taboos.

Photo: miss pupik

many stages—aging, marriage, parenthood, occupations, and social relationships—and as we pass through, we find ourselves constantly challenged by new peer groups. And, while we are more likely to resist the pressure to conform, we still find comfort in the acceptance of those we identify as peers. Hence, some measure of conformity and readjustment to our beliefs, attitudes, and value system is inevitable. Why? Because we are social creatures and as such desire and need the company and approval of others.

Church

Like the family, the role of the church as a socializing agent has undergone dramatic changes within the last half-century. In traditional societies, the church exercised great influence. This is still true in many countries where the role of government and religion are intertwined. But in modern postindustrial societies secularization of government has dramatically reduced the influence of organized religion. This is true of the United States. In spite of the fact that most Americans identify with a religious group, fewer than 22 percent attend church on a regular basis and an even smaller number of children and teens do so (Hadaway and Long, 2005). Critics who bemoan the declining influence of religion use this to explain the increase of everything from teen pregnancies to gang murders.

While overall church attendance has declined, religion remains an important source of socialization for many in our society. This is especially true of those immersed in the fundamentalist Christian movement and others such as Orthodox Jews, Mormons, the Amish, and others that might commonly be labeled as cults. Here, religion exercises an almost absolute role. It defines what is right and what is wrong, it tells its members how to live their lives, how to raise their children, and what they may and may not believe.

Even for those who do not attend church on a regular basis, religion can still exercise an indirect influence through normative and belief systems. Much of what we consider to be right or wrong is grounded in religious doctrine. Hence, we do not steal or kill simply because it is against the law. We obey the law because it is the “right” thing to do.

Media

While the influence of family and church has declined in the last half century, the power of media as an agent of socialization has skyrocketed. Today the average child in the United States spends more time watching television than they do directly interacting with their parents. Television and video recorders are tools used by parents to assist with childcare. Young children, often under the age of two years, are told to sit quietly and watch their favorite show or movie while parents complete household, work or school tasks. This is time passively spent watching, listening, and absorbing messages and information that once belonged to the family. Media time far exceeds the time that parents are fully engaged with their children. In fact, so dominant has television become that by the time that children graduate from high school they will have spent more time in front of the TV than at

Religious institutions are instrumental in defining moral values. Here a young boy holds a sign in a protest sponsored by the Reverend Fred Phelps, a well-known anti-gay activist. Recently, Phelps and his followers have targeted military funerals of soldiers killed in action. Phelps believes that dead soldiers are a punishment from God for homosexuality. Attempts to curtail Phelps' protests fell short when the Supreme Court upheld his right to protest as a protection of free speech in March 2011.

Photo: Rob Ward.

school—20,000 hours of television watching (Barwise and Ehrenberg, 1988). In addition to television viewing time, one must also take into account the time spent with other media socialization tools: books, magazines, radio, electronic media, and movies.

One great impact of media on socialization is its ability to transcend time, geography, and culture. In short, everyone in the world has access to the same information, regardless of location or social standing. The effect is twofold. *First*, information has created a foundation for a common culture. By watching television or communicating with virtually anyone in the world (Internet), we have the ability to listen to and communicate ideas. This two-way flow of information provides for assimilation of ideas and values. Some sociologists have predicted that mass communication will result in a global culture. A *second* effect is a further weakening of the influence of institutions: the family, school, church, and government. Is this good or bad? The answer, of course, is a mixed bag. In cases where children come from deprived and intolerant environments the media can play a positive role. Through mass media values that contribute to cooperation, cohesiveness, and understanding can be conveyed. Children have the opportunity to learn that differences among people can be positive; that there is no need to fear or hate others who differ in skin color, language, social class, and ethnicity. On the other hand, depending upon the material presented, media may have a negative impact. Recently, much attention has been devoted to the negative side of mass media, particularly television, as socializing agent.

Media Violence and Aggression. Violence in mass media has caught the eye of social researchers and they're concerned by the tremendous flow of brutal acts and sexually explicit material being presented to children of all ages. By the time that a child reaches age 18, he/she will have seen approximately 18,000 people either kill, raped, stabbed, beaten unconscious, or robbed. Even more startling is the fact that in a great number of murders and assault, it is the "good guy" administering the punishment to the "bad guy" in retribution for some wrongdoing. In essence, the message given that "scores" need to be settled and violence is an acceptable means by which to achieve this end. The next time you attend an "action" movie or sit with friends to watch television at home, watch their reactions when the hero finally has the opportunity to slowly and painfully squeeze the life out of the villain. Do they turn away in disgust, or do they hoot, holler, jump around, and squeal with delight? Chances are the reaction of your friends will be the latter. Is this the way we should behave or feel? Does it really matter? After all, it's only make-believe.

Attempts to measure the effects of television violence and aggressive or violent behavior in life sought to correlate the violence of shows people watched, and level of aggressive behavior exhibited. The result of some research involving children and their response to violent shows indicated a positive correlation between violent shows and aggressive behavior (Huesmann, 1982). An inherent problem that researchers encountered however was whether violent shows *cause* violence. Perhaps the subject was predisposed toward violent behavior prior to watching violent shows. In an attempt to answer these questions, Eron and his colleagues (Eron, Huesmann, Lefkowitz, and Walder, 1972) used longitudinal data to show a causal link between media violence and later aggression. In their study, third-grade boys' preferences for violent or nonviolent TV programs were measured and comparisons were made for aggressive acts reported by parents and teachers. Ten years after initial contact with the boys, Eron, et al. revisited the same participants and found a significant correlation between violent TV preferences in third-grade and later aggression. In their follow-up of this group of boys, the researchers discovered that a preference for television violence, as measured when they were only eight years old, was positively correlated with criminal behavior twenty-two years later.

In another study on aggression and media, Josephson (1987) found that those most affected by media violence were predisposed toward violence. In this study, two action films were shown to second and third-grade boys. One film was of a bicycle race containing no violence. The other film was a story of police officers violently avenging the death of a fellow officer. After the film, the boys engaged in a game of floor hockey where violent behavior (kicking, elbowing, hitting with the stick, etc.) was measured. For those children who were identified by their teachers as non aggressive, the violent film had little impact. However, for those boys identified as aggressive, viewing the violent film had a dramatic impact. Watching the violent film significantly increased the number of aggressive acts.

In an extensive review of the data, Jonathon Freedman (2003), maintained that the overall evidence is weak or at best inconclusive. He cites inconsistency in methodology, flawed research designs, and overreach in drawing conclusions from the data. Likewise, he maintained that other social and psychological factors such as culture and family structure had not been properly taken into account. As a result, he suggested that it is impossible to accurately determine the effect of media violence on aggression. Conversely, in a more recent study, Paul Boxer (2009) refutes these claims in his work by demonstrating that when additional factors of academic skills, community violence, and emotional problems were taken into account, violent media contributed significantly to aggressive behavior.

Investigators who attempted to replicate the experiment using girls as participants failed. Although mixed, no clear-cut patterns emerged. On the other hand, studies on a possible link between TV violence and adult aggression also showed a positive relationship (Linz & Donnerstein, 1989). The explanation may be that the socialization process for females in our culture is quite different than for males. Generally, it is not culturally acceptable for girls to display aggression. Boys, on the other hand, are socialized and rewarded for their aggressive play. As gender barriers erode, it may be that this finding will reverse.

Finally, it has been suggested that the relationship between media and violence is culturally based. The implication is that the relationship between media violence and aggression is uniquely American; there is a long history of violence in our culture. The culturally based hypothesis did not stand in cross-cultural research in Australia, Finland, Israel, and Poland. The conclusions we can draw from the above studies suggest that violent TV can predict subsequent aggression (Huesmann and Eron, 1986).

Media Violence and Sex. Sexual crimes and violence against women are major social problems in our society. As such, researchers have attempted to identify potential causes and contributors in efforts to reduce the violence and criminal behavior. Early studies demonstrated that non-aggressive erotic material had no affect on sexual violence against women (Donnerstein & Barrett, 1978). However, when erotic violence was introduced, the findings were dramatically different. In one of many studies, Donnerstein, Linz, and Penrod (1987) found that in films showing women as victims of violent sex acts, males became desensitized to the inhumanity of the brutality being inflicted upon the victim.

More dramatic were the findings that the level of aggression increased when men had been angered by a woman prior to viewing a sexually violent film (Donnerstein and Berkowitz, 1981). In this study, male participants were deliberately angered by either by a man or a woman just prior to viewing an erotic film laced with violent sex acts. After viewing the film, males were given an opportunity to retaliate against the person who had angered them. The results indicated that males who were angered by a woman were much more likely to retaliate than those angered by a man even when retaliation carried no sanctions. The conclusion that Donnerstein presented was:

> These findings . . . suggest that the aggressive responses elicited by the film were heightened by the arousal in the film itself. In addition, the disinhibitory cues present in the film (e.g. aggression is OK) acted to potentially reduce any aggressive inhibitions on the part of male subjects (Donnerstein, 1983).

More recent studies demonstrate mixed findings. Catherine Itzin (1993), in a comprehensive review of the literature, argued that pornography had a profound harmful effect on both men and women. Her conclusion was supported in a 1998 study of U.S. women which found that viewing pornography is significantly related to violence between partners. However, a comprehensive study by Michael S. Kimmel and Annulla Linders failed to find any significant correlation between pornography use and attitudes toward rape. Furthermore, some feminist have argued against censorship maintaining that many women choose to use it for sexual freedom (Nadine Strossen, 2000).

While mixed, conclusions of the work on erotica and violence suggest a twofold impact of viewing sexually violent materials. *First*, it increases male aggression by heightening arousal; and *second*, it dehumanizes the victims and thereby lessens the moral consequence for the aggressor.

THE SOCIALIZATION PROCESS

Now that we have learned about socialization and socializing agents in our society, it is time to put it all together and discuss the process. How does it work? Social scientists who have researched this issue point to three identifiable processes working in concert: selective exposure and modeling, reward and punishment, and nurturance and identification.

Selective Exposure and Modeling

Through selective exposure we attempt to place children in situations where they will see and hear those things we consider desirable. Parents, for example, take children to the zoo to see and talk about the animals. We pre-select movies to ensure that the content is appropriate for children's age and moral development. In a similar vein, we attempt to shield them from some of the more undesirable facts of life. For example, one would not take a small child on a visit to a prison. Nor, would we expose a child to wanton acts of violence against others to teach them about aggression. The state is involved in this process. For example, most communities have laws against children being in bars. Likewise, we restrict children from certain films in movie theaters and we set age limits on when individuals can drive, drink, or smoke. All of this is an attempt to construct an environment that is mentally and physically healthy for children.

Studies have shown that children are great imitators of adult behavior. As such, we put on our best face, so to speak, for our children. This process is referred to as **modeling**. Albert Bandura's (1977) work on modeling demonstrates that it is a complex and progressive process. Children first watch the behavior of significant others and commit the behavior they witnessed to memory. After a period of time, children begin to imitate or recreate the behavior as they recall it from their memory. If rewarded for their imitation, they will repeat the behavior over and over until it becomes a matter of habit. Finally, as they mature, they will develop attitudes and beliefs to support the desirability of the behavior.

Selective exposure and modeling work in concert because it is impossible to imitate something that is not seen. It is for this reason that we attempt to protect children, for as long as possible, from life's potholes. However, as we have already noted in our discussion of mass media, this is not always possible. Let's take a little side trip and consider the following (parents and potential parents pay close attention). What happens to children when they hear adults say one thing and do exactly the opposite? Do they model what they are told or what they see? If you answered—what they see—you're right. Research demonstrates that when it comes down to "do as I say, not as I do," the child will consistently model the behavior (Rushton, 1975).

Reward and Punishment

Reward and punishment work hand in hand with selective exposure and modeling. After imitating a behavior, the child will look for feedback—approval or disapproval. Behavior that we approve will be rewarded. The reward can be as simple as a smile, a nod of the head, verbal praise, or it can take the form of presenting the child with something concrete—a piece of candy or a gift. In any form, the child recognizes approval and understands that if she/he continues to imitate the behavior, good results will follow. On the other, if the behavior is judged to be bad or inappropriate, the child will be confronted with disapproval. In most cases, disapproval will be a mild reprimand, such as, "No, Johnny, good boys don't do that." If Johnny repeats the behavior, a stronger reprimand will be given, perhaps Johnny will be sent to his room for a period of time. Johnny soon discovers that as he continues to repeat the behavior, the punishment grows in severity. At some point, we hope, Johnny abandons the behavior and conforms to our expectations. As simple as this might seem on the surface, rewards and punishments are powerful tools in the socializing process. Likewise, they can be a source of mental illness. If messages children receive are not clear or, even worse, contradictory, the child will be confused, in a constant state of uncertainty, and the results may manifest in psychological illnesses of all kinds.

Nurturance and Identification

The influence of both processes—selective exposure and modeling and reward and punishment—are enhanced a third process—nurturance and identification. That is, children look to significant others for approval and generally, first in line, are parents, followed closely by older siblings. Since it is parents, and to some degree older siblings, who nurture, strong bonds are forged between the child and his nurturers. Sociologists have long pointed to a reciprocal relationship between child and parent: the child depends upon the parent for every need, physical and emotional, and in turn, the child senses an obligation to the parent to cooperate and obey. Again, these three processes of socialization are intertwined, each supporting the other.

RESOCIALIZATION

The life cycle represents a continual and gradual process of socialization. As mentioned previously, we pass through many stages of life with each presenting new expectations and adjustments. For most of us, we make adjustments without ever being really aware of the process. It just sort of happens as we go about our lives. However, in some cases, a process of resocialization is required. **Resocialization** is the process of stripping away old values and behavior patterns so those new ones may be introduced. A few examples of individuals undergoing resocialization are prisoners, new military personnel, mental patients, cult members, and prisoners-of-war.

In most cases, individuals who undergo resocialization do so in what Erving Goffman (1961) termed, "the total institution." The label of **total institution** applies to any organization or institution—the military, prisons, monasteries, mental hospitals, prison-of-war camps and cults—in which the individual is completely controlled for the purpose of erasing previous socialization and substituting new values and behavior patterns. Although total institutions vary by size and purpose, they employ essentially the same process to accomplish their task.

The process can be broken down into two distinct phases. In the *first* phase, individuals are stripped of their old identity. Upon entering, the individual must surrender their clothes and all personal items that connect them to their past lives. Most institutions, prisons, the military, and prison-of-war camps, perform this in a similar ritualistic fashion. All individuals are herded into a common hall where they must remove all clothing and walk naked to the next location where uniformed personnel issue new clothing. As one might imagine to stand and walk naked in front of others is degrading and depersonalizing. Of course, this is the desired effect, a situation that breaks the human spirit so that the individual is at the mercy of the institution. Also, in the total institution, personal names are used as little as possible. In prison, the inmates are referred to by number. In the military, the term "soldier" or "sailor" is substituted for the name of the individual. Little, if any, contact is allowed from the outside so as not to remind individuals of previous lives. In an attempt to weaken their resistance to change, long hours of physical labor are often required with little time to rest or sleep. As they weaken, their old identities begin to slip away.

Prisons are an example of total institutions where individuals are stripped of their present values and are introduced to new values and behaviors. In some institutions, like prisons, old values are often replaced with new ones that are even more destructive.

Photo: Digital Stock.

In the *second* phase, the stripped down personality is reconstructed; one that conforms to the wishes and needs of the total institution. New values and attitudes are substituted for those washed away in phase one. As with children, a system of reward and punishment is used to effectively weld these new values and attitudes to the reconstructed individual. And, just as in the case of a child, the expected outcome is that individuals will develop a belief system to justify their new values and behaviors.

Using Goffman's theory, it is easier to understand why the military and monasteries are successful examples of resocialization and prisons have failed miserably. One might suggest that the main reason lies with the fact that individuals are imprisoned against their will while those in monasteries are willing participants of the process of resocialization. However, in times of the draft, the military's resocialization efforts were just as effective with draftees as with those who voluntarily enlisted. The main reason for the ineffectiveness of prisons lies in the fact that while they break individuals down, little effort is made to provide new models for acceptable behavior. Taking a lesson from the military, many states have created boot camps for juvenile delinquents. A major feature of these programs is to offer positive role models in much the same way as the military. The net result has been a notable rate of successful rehabilitation.

SOCIOLOGICAL PERSPECTIVES

Throughout this chapter we have attempted to illustrate the power of socialization. Understandably, this could be the source of some consternation. Exactly how free are we? Social scientists have debated this question, as well as the role of socialization, at length. Again, as always many different views have emerged. Here, we present the counter views of our two theoretical perspectives regarding the role of socialization as well as the question of individual freedom.

Structural Functional

Structural Functionalists stress the positive side of socialization. Individuals live in societies. In order to function, societies must have some common agreement on values, attitudes, and behaviors. These are passed to individuals through the socialization process that, in turn, allows the individual to become a productive member of society. Not only is this desirable for the society, it also benefits the individual in two ways. *First,* it provides for the satisfaction of human needs—love, friendship, identity, and esteem. As we saw earlier, providing for these needs are as necessary as satisfying our physical needs for food, clothing, and shelter. The inability to satisfy human needs leads to mental and physical illnesses and, in some cases, suicide.

Second, social interaction would not be possible without socialization. Humans are not born with a set of instincts that tell them how to interact with others. These must be learned. Is it even conceivable that 250 million Americans could function without common values and expectations? For structural functionalists, the answer is obviously, no. History, they point out, is replete with examples of nations where the institutions of socialization failed. In all such cases, the collapse of the society followed on the coattails of war and mass destruction. As such, socialization benefits the individual in that it provides a secure and safe environment in which to live life.

In terms of freedom, structural functionalists maintain that while socialization does push us toward common agreement, we are by no means robots or victims in a great scheme to depersonalize the human spirit. As powerful as socialization is, we have a "self." Formed early in our childhood, it is dynamic and changes throughout our lives. We are intelligent and thinking creatures with the power to change our lives and the environment in which we live. So, while it is true that through socialization we receive a core set of values and attitudes, it is also true that each individual, depending upon their biological heredity and the environment in which they exist, will build a unique self.

Social Conflict

The concern of social conflict theorists is not with the basic concept or need for socialization, certainly they recognize that society must socialize its members. The concern of social conflict theorists rests with how the wealthy and the influential use the process as a tool to perpetuate their own power and wealth. Individuals are taught not to question the legitimacy of the system. Instead, they are provided with a false set of beliefs that attempt to make them believe that all people are equal, that everyone in America can be successful. And furthermore, those who fail do so because of their own shortcomings or lack of effort. Those who challenge the system are quickly labeled as malcontents, deviants, or anarchists. An expression of this attitude is seen in the infamous bumper stickers that many Americans stuck to their cars during the war and civil rights protests in 1960s: "America: Love It or Leave It!" More recently, those who questioned the War in Iraq at the early stage of the invasion were accused of being disloyal to the country and not supporting our troops.

A second concern of social conflict theorists is what two social researchers identified as **social channeling** (Bowles and Gintis, 1976). The process of social channeling prepares children of the upper class for lives of wealth and power. Through their socialization process, they are taught upper class values and attitudes needed for the time when they will assume the role of parents in society. Similarly, the children of the poor are taught the values and attitudes reflected by poverty which essentially trap them into a powerless position. A more complete discussion will be presented in succeeding chapters on stratification, class, race, and gender.

Finally, in terms of freedom, for the social conflict theorist the central question is not whether we are all stamped copies of each other, but whether we have the freedom to develop our talents to the fullest. In society, some people are freer than others, they would argue. In this sense, socialization is a hindrance to freedom.

SUMMARY – SOCIALIZATION AND FREEDOM

In this chapter we have seen how society and its agents of socialization are powerful forces in shaping how we think and act. Likewise, we have considered how changes in the economic structure brought about changes in the socialization process, which in turn, has altered the beliefs and normative systems in society. Also, we have discussed how mass media and telecommunication is moving the world toward the development of a common cultural experience. All of this talk regarding socialization leads us to question how much freedom and individuality make up who we are. Given time, will we all be exactly alike? Or will humans always differ?

If you think hard about some of the information presented in this chapter you will probably come to the conclusion that there is no clear answer to these questions. Undoubtedly, there are forces in the world that are moving us toward a common cultural experience. Today, ordinary people from all over the world communicate with each other on a daily basis through the Internet and telecommunication devices. Hundreds of millions of people across the globe tune into the same television programs. People move across the earth, from one corner to another, in a matter of hours. As we have seen, when different cultures meet, there is a natural tendency toward assimilation. In the future we can then expect to see an emerging common culture. This may not happen tomorrow, but over decades, over centuries, and over millennia there will, without doubt, be a funneling effect toward this end.

This does not mean that individual differences will disappear. Writing on this point, Dennis Wrong (1961) suggested a number of reasons why differences among humans will always exist. *First*, as humans we are as much a product of biology as society. No two humans (with the exception of identical twins) are exactly alike. We have different biological urges and drives that interact with society to produce real variety among us. *Second*, as we saw earlier, the socialization process is laden with "role conflicts" and "role strains." As humans attempt to resolve these dilemmas, differences in behavior emerges. *Third*, history is replete with individuals who have deviated from expected behavior. In some cases, this deviance produces a criminal, in others, a genius. There is little reason to expect that deviance will disappear from human nature. And *finally*, as Freud (as well as others) pointed out, the more civilized we become the unhappier we become. There is something intrinsic in the human spirit that yearns for individuality. It is our best guess that this quality cannot and will not be erased.

Terms You Should Know:

Nature	Nurture	Instincts
Socialization	Id	Ego
Superego	Object Permanence	Primary Socialization
Modeling	Resocialization	Social Channeling

Can You Answer These Questions?

1. How are the theories of behaviorism and sociobiology different?
2. According to Charles Horton Cooley, where does our concept of self develop most fully? Do you agree?
3. List the three stages of play that George Herbert Mead considered important for the development of personality.
4. According to your text, which socializing agent is most important?
5. How do schools contribute to social solidarity?
6. How do structural functionalist and social conflict theorists differ over the value of socialization?

Critical Thinking Exercises:

1. Think about your own family. Are you similar or dissimilar to your siblings? To your parents? Do you think this is a result of biology or socialization?
2. In thinking abut your own life, who do you think influenced you the most?
3. Do you believe that parents today have more or less control over the development of their children's personality? Why?
4. In your own view, do you believe that media violence increases crime in our society?
5. Do you believe that the world will eventually amalgamate into one culture? If so, do you believe that this would be good or bad?

Photo: Thomas Hawk

Everyday Sociology 7th Edition

Chapter 6

Deviance and Crime

Beginning in childhood and continuing throughout our lives, we are faced with social constraints. Our earliest socialization involves learning what is acceptable behavior and what is socially unacceptable. On the one hand, most people feel a need to be as independent as possible, to make their own rules, to push against the boundaries that have been set for us. We try to convince those who are in control that we are old enough or wise enough to enjoy greater freedom with more privileges; that we are mature enough to resist the pressure of peers. But then, we argue that we will be social outcasts if we are not allowed the freedom to do some particular thing. We are expressing contradictory needs: to be free to behave as we choose, while at the same time expressing a need to conform to the values and norms of our peer group.

As we mature and our involvements become more complicated, our social rules become more complex and explicit. At times we may feel that our freedom has been limited. But, as members of social groups we realize that without some common set of values and limits to behavior there would be chaos. We are also aware that failure to follow the norms of behavior, whether within our own small group or in the larger society, usually results in some type of sanction. **Sanctions** are positive or negative responses to an action. Those sanctions may be as simple as a frown and a temporary dismissal from our group, or as formal as a legal sanction, perhaps even incarceration in the criminal justice system.

In this chapter we will explore some of the terms associated with deviance and attempt to understand how group affiliation and deviance interact. We will see how social groups redefine what is and is not deviant, as well as other ways in which societal norms are changed, clarified, and redefined by deviant behaviors. We will look at deviance from various theoretical perspectives. Finally, we will monitor some trends in criminal behavior and explore deviance among women and juveniles.

DEFINING DEVIANCE

Deviance is defined in the dictionary as behavior or characteristics that violate important social norms and consequently result in societal sanctions. While this seems straightforward and simple, the sociological definition is somewhat more complicated and **situational**–relative to particular settings–as well as dependent upon whom is doing the defining.

Amelie Bloomer broke all the rules when she advocated for women's rights. Rosa Parks broke the law when she refused to move to the back of the bus. Strong women, strong action, strong sanctions: Deviance redefined.

CHOOSING GROUP MEMBERSHIP

Although most of us would like to believe that we are individualists and can function and exist just fine by ourselves, the truth is that we are social beings and have a powerful need for affiliation. As such, in order to create a stable environment for ourselves, we look for a group that seems to have the stability we need. At best, we choose groups that reflect who we are—our values, beliefs and moral attitudes—and uphold our political outlook, social consciousness, and religious convictions. However, when we are in a state of confusion or **anomie**, a feeling of confusion and loss of direction which is often the result of rapid change and the breakdown of social norms and values, we may choose a group that has altered values and is operating in a manner that society deems deviant (Durkheim, 1895).

If the values of this group are contrary to the values that we previously held, the process of **resocialization,** a changing of values and behaviors, occurs. Resocialization may include adopting a particular dress code or hairstyle. We may have to learn a new language or ***argot*** (slang) in order to set ourselves apart from those outside of the group; we may even have to go through some type of initiation ritual in order to prove both our worth to the group and our discarding of previously held values and old group ties.

If membership in this particular group is important to us, however, we may allow the group to pressure us into pushing our own values aside and rationalize or ignore our feelings. This process is known as **groupthink** (Janis, 1983). If these alternate values are too different from our previous belief system, we may choose to leave the group and seek one more in line with our thinking resulting in a **risky shift**. A risky shift requires that a group member make a difficult choice: leave the group and lose the group's protection or stay and risk harsh social sanctions.

Resocialization does not always result in negative deviance. It is just as possible for someone from a deviant group (street gang) to adopt more normative behavior by joining a socially acceptable group (church youth group). Additionally, sometimes, deviant behavior is the result of society's reevaluation of the current norms to determine whether or not there is a need for change. It is the majority, those who hold the political and economic power, who are most likely to determine what is deviant.

Finally, the term **resocialization** can be used in connection with the criminal justice system. When we attempt to correct deviant behavior by incarceration, we are actually attempting to resocialize someone who is exhibiting deviant behavior. We hope that by imposing a very stiff sanction (prison) on what society views as deviant behavior, we are sending the message that in order to avoid future sanctions, behavior must change and comply with societal norms

Who Defines Deviance?

An example of deviance at the macro level would be the efforts of black South Africans to gain the majority position in their country. Majority position refers to political and economic power. Black South Africans were a majority of the population but held the minority political position. The ruling or majority group of white South Africans perceived the movement to end apartheid as deviant; however, the perceived deviant behavior of the black population resulted in support from all over the world, forcing Apartheid laws to be removed from the books, and a more tolerant and just social order to be put into place.

On the micro level, there is the case of the six year-old boy who was charged with sexual harassment for kissing a classmate. At one time, this behavior might have been considered cute, "Oh well, boys will be boys." However, various groups, especially those associated with women's rights issues, have redefined what is and what is not acceptable behavior, even for six year olds.

Moral Panics

Moral panics are "responses to exaggerated fears and concerns of a particular group in society created when the social system fails to respond positively to the group's belief in the need for change" (Goode, et al., 1994). In the past, *moral crusades* were thought to be the result of the need for change motivated by moral interests, while *moral panics* are thought to represent more irrational and protective interests guarding the social structure as a whole not just the moral values. Goode captured the essence of moral panics by stating:

> During the moral panic, the behavior of some of the members of a society is thought to be so problematic to others, the evil they do, or are

> thought to do, is felt to be so wounding to the substance and fabric of the (society), that serious steps must be taken to control the behavior, punish the perpetrators and repair the damage. (Goode, et al., 1994)

Goode suggests that there are at least five criteria needed for a movement to be termed a moral panic. The *first* is that moral panic movements are volatile; they erupt quickly and may just as quickly subside. *Second*, there is a heightened level of concern regarding the behavior in question and its consequences for the rest of society. *Third*, society will define the group engaging in the deviant behavior as the enemy and exhibit an increased level of hostility toward them. *Fourth*, there must be widespread consensus that the threat is real; and *fifth*, there is the perception that a disproportionate number of people are engaged in the behavior and a large number of innocent members of society are being harmed by the behavior in question.

Stanley Cohen (1972) sees moral panics as being the result of the participation of a number of groups reacting in concert to a perceived threat. For example, the media may present the problem to the public in order to gain consensus, sometimes distorting or stereotyping the information. The police and courts then respond to demands by the public for protection from the perceived danger, adding to the sense of legitimacy. Politicians respond to the threat perceived by their constituents. If the threat continues, action groups may form, advising the public of impending disaster and the need for preparation for the worst possible outcome.

Young (1971) gave an example of how these forces work together to legitimize a social problem. The "moral panic over drug-taking results in the setting-up of drug squads." This in turn, "results in an increase in drug arrests." The reporting of an increase of arrests by the media confirms the drug "problem" which allows action groups to increase their financial and community support for it's eradication. Other examples include Megan's Law which set up the monitoring system for sex offenders and the Patriot Act which contained over a thousand pages of law and was passed 72 hours after 9/11.

UNDERSTANDING DEVIANCE

Erich Goode (1990) explains that we make rules for behavior because we are "evaluative creatures," always comparing our behavior to that of others. We tend to divide the world into two parts, the good and the bad. When we form these evaluations we are most likely to shape them from one of three perspectives: the absolutist perspective, the normative perspective, and the reactive perspective.

From the **absolutist perspective**, "deviance resides in the very nature of the act itself" (Goode, 1990). Therefore, it is wrong at all times—past, present, and future—and in every situation. The absolutist is likely to be a strongly religious person with unyielding views, and who sees aberrant behavior as a sin against God. From this perspective, laws set forth by God supersede laws made by man.

The **normative perspective,** advocated by many sociologists, is one of relativity. What is deviant in one place, at one particular time, may not be deviant in another place and time. The use of drugs, opium in particular, was not only condoned during the 1800s but doctors encouraged its use in their female patients to keep them "calm and more ladylike." Also, killing during a war or in self-defense is not considered deviant, but necessary. The extent of acceptance or non-acceptance of an act depends on how society views the situation in which the act occurs and whether or not the act protects the social order.

Drug use in our society has caused a moral panic. Is it justified? Some people feel that drugs should be legalized. Where do you stand?

Photo: Copyright UN Office on Drugs and Crime.

The **reactive perspective** holds that something is not deviant until it is defined as deviant by society and sanctions are set in place. In the past, truancy was considered to be deviant behavior and truant officers were on the streets every day hunting down the student who skipped school. Today, truancy is at an all time high but few school districts employ officers to search for missing students. While society appears to be concerned about the rising tide of juvenile delinquency, the act of truancy has become a lesser evil than drugs, or weapons on campus, and therefore, until the truant commits a "real" crime, he is virtually ignored.

Both the normative and reactive perspectives may reflect a "grassroots" approach to deviance where norms are an "expression of the right and wrong held by the majority and are a barometer of the moral and social thinking of the society" (Friedmann, 1964). New norms and sanctions may evolve in relation to a problem that has been ignored until concern is created by the media or an activist group with a particular agenda. Conversely, the level of perceived deviance may lessen over time when the act is repeated often enough to create a feeling of normalcy. A minor example might be clothing or hair fashion that appears outrageous at first, but after a time becomes more accepted and less scandalous. Likewise, marijuana use in the 1960s and early 1970s was considered a serious offense punishable by years in prison. With repeated and widespread use, states began to reclassify personal use as a misdemeanor rather than a felony. Additionally, in the general population there is considerable support to legalize it altogether.

The Relativity of Deviance

As mentioned earlier in this chapter, defining deviance and interpreting the degree of deviance can be approached from different positions. Statistics can be used to determine an average or norm behavior and comparisons can be made to determine any degree of deviation from the norm. Religious groups, for example, often judge social conduct in terms of absolutes, judging behavior against some predetermined and unconditional standard set forth by some divine revelation.

Sociologists, in order to explain the enormous variations in people's behavior, tend to define deviance from a *relative* viewpoint. For example, in the Japanese culture it is disrespectful to look someone in the eyes as you talk. In the United States, we believe that an inability to look at someone when you speak denotes dishonesty.

Deviance from customs and norms not only occur across cultures but also occur between cultures and subcultures within a society. The Amish believe that the use of modern tools and conveniences contradicts their core religious philosophy. Other people living in the same area often find that Amish lifestyle interferes with the normal activities of daily living, such as when Amish buggies block normal traffic or when metal buggy wheels result in constant road repairs.

Even within a group there can be variations of behavior where certain activities would be acceptable at one time or place and considered deviant in another. Rowdy behavior at a ball game is considered appropriate, whereas the same behavior at a funeral would be seen as deviant. We accept these variants of behavior because we have been socialized to understand which behavior is appropriate relative to a particular situation.

The theory of primary and secondary deviance (Lemert, 1972) assumes that all of us are likely to, at some point in our lives, engage in some form of deviant behavior. If we are not caught and labeled, or if our behavior is excused and we are not sanctioned for our primary deviance, we may or may not engage in deviant behavior again. As long as the deviant behavior does not become a normal part of our repertoire of behaviors, it remains primary deviance.

If, however, we integrate the deviant behavior into our lifestyle because it has achieved a desired response from others, a more aggressive act may follow and we are then in a stage of secondary deviance and at risk for social or legal sanctions. Secondary deviance is ongoing and may become more offensive to society as time goes on. Once we define ourselves by the label placed on us we have moved to the tertiary, or third, stage of deviance.

THEORIES OF DEVIANT BEHAVIOR

Sociologists and other social scientists have spent considerable time investigating deviance. As one might suspect, a number of different explanations have arisen in an attempt to understand deviance. Although these theories differ, it is possible to place them into one of two broad categories—individual blame and system blame.

Individual blame theory falls into the functionalist perspective supporting the premise that the normative social belief systems of society are functionally correct and contribute to a smooth and harmonious society. The problem lies in the inability of individuals or groups to either understand or follow what is acceptable. The solution is for the individual to change.

System blame, on the other hand, falls more easily into the premise of social conflict theory. Advocates of this theory view deviant behavior as either a manifestation of inequality, or the attempts of the powerful to force their views of right and wrong on those with different views who are powerless to resist. Deviance, then, is the symptom and not the disease. Advocates of this theory believe that the solution to the problem lies in changing society.

Biological Theories (Individual Blame)

Some of the earliest theories of deviance focused on biological explanations. One study that gained notoriety was that of Caesare Lombroso (1835-1909). In a comparison of criminals to law-abiding citizens, Lombroso pointed to physiological differences. The criminal was described as being unusually hairy, having long arms, protruding ears, and a low, sloping forehead. This was supposedly a result of their failure to evolve. Before you begin looking around at fellow classmates (or your professor), it should be noted that this theory and others like it have long since fallen by the wayside.

Until recently, few additional biological explanations of deviance were offered. Now with the remarkable progress in biological and genetic research, new theories are emerging. We now know for example, that many learning disabilities are not the result of laziness, rebellion, or retardation, as previously assumed. The diagnosis and treatment of Dyslexia and Attention Deficit Disorders has made a huge difference in the lives of thousands of children (and adults). Likewise, conditions such as schizophrenia, phobias, and anxiety are medically treated allowing sufferers to lead normal lives. Also, new research in addictive behavior suggests that some individuals may possess a genetic susceptibility toward alcoholism, drug addiction, and eating disorders. Recent information on homosexuality, long considered by the majority to be deviant behavior, suggests that it has a biological origin. Gays and lesbians have long maintained this view, namely that homosexuality is a matter of orientation (biology) and not preference (choice).

Without question, as we learn more about our genetic make-up and how our bodies work, more explanations about human behavior will surely be discovered. However, it is important to keep in mind that social structure and social interaction play a profound role in shaping outcomes. For example, the fact that one has a genetic predisposition toward alcoholism does not mean that alcoholism is inevitable. Under the right social conditions, with the support of family and friends, the disease can be avoided; on the other hand, if the wrong social forces interact with a genetically predisposed individual, it is likely that the outcome will be addiction.

Psychological Theories (Individual Blame)

Psychological explanations of deviant behavior are rooted in personality disorders. One of the earliest theorists offering a psychological explanation of deviance was Sigmund Freud. According to Freud, deviant behavior is the result of an underdeveloped ego. Without a strong ego, the individual is unable to control the impulses of the id (the pleasure seeking aspect of our personality). Another Freudian explanation of deviant behavior suggests an over developed superego where individuals are so repulsed by their own fantasies or feelings that they commit deviant acts so as to be arrested and punished. Only through punishment do they find relief from their psychological conflict.

Other psychological theories posit that deviant behavior results from a number of interpersonal conflicts with intimates, such as parents, siblings, and peers. For example, parents who are too strict, too lenient, not loving enough, etc. produce offspring with a tendency for pathological behavior. The profile of a serial killer, for instance, often has an aspect that suggests trauma by either parent(s), other family members, or significant others in childhood and during adolescence.

One of the criticisms leveled at such theories is that they ultimately are a manifestation of conditions occurring in the larger society. In other words, while these theories may be helpful in treating individual disorders, it is the societal problems within the social system that produce conditions leading to the deviant behavior. It is these problems that interest sociologists.

Sociological Theories

***Differential Association Theory* (individual blame).** Edwin Sutherland developed the **Differential Association Theory** in the 1920s and 1930s. Sutherland believed that "deviant behavior is learned in interaction with other people, for the most part within intimate primary groups such as families and peer groups" (Sutherland and Cressey, 1978) where individuals are socialized to engage in deviant activities. We observe significant others engaging in a deviant manner; we attempt the activity ourselves and receive feedback; we ask for clarification and then try again. If the feedback is positive, we learn to value the deviant behavior more than non-deviant behavior.

An example of this theory would be inner-city gang activity. The intersection of segregation and poverty produces large numbers of poor kids who find themselves to be in continual association with gang members. The gang members encourage kids to join their ranks and reward deviant behavior. Having been rewarded, the child embarks on a criminal path.

Although presented more formally here, this is a theory that just about every kid has heard from his or her parents. Shaking a finger in your face, the parent yells, "You hang around with that crowd and you're gonna be just like them." This statement embodies the essence of differential association theory.

***Opportunity Structure Theory* (Individual Blame).** Merton (1957) assumes that all Americans value achievement leading to material success and that they **conform** to the societal norms of education, employment, and investing (or saving for) the future, to reach their goal of economic independence. Those people in society who have less access to education and employment but believe in the idea of material success will either: 1) adjust their goals downward; 2) extend the length of time needed to reach their goal; or, 3) find ways outside the norm to achieve their goal. Merton refers to these options as **innovations**.

Gang membership is on the increase in our society. Sociological explanations include breakdown of families, peer associations, and problems in the economy.

Photo: Digital Stock.

Merton suggests that some people believe in the values of society and conscientiously follow the means for achievement even when there is no hope that success will follow. He labels this action as **ritualism**. **Retreatists**, on the other hand, refuse to follow the socially approved means for reaching their economic goals because they do not accept the prevailing societal values and/or feel they have no chance to achieve them. They may have tried and failed in the past using legitimized norms and now see no point in trying. Instead, they now choose to retreat from society, perhaps through drug or alcohol use.

Finally, Merton suggests that the **rebel** rejects both the values of society and the norms for achieving those values and strives to destroy the system and to replace it with one he/she believes to be better. Rosa Parks, a young African American woman who refused to sit in a section at the back of a public bus designated for blacks, is a case in point. Legally, segregation was sanctioned by law. But believing the law to be immoral, she chose to disobey it. Her action, along with thousands of other civil rights activists, eventually led to the end of segregation.

***Culture of Poverty* (Individual Blame).** The culture of poverty theory is an extremely controversial theory introduced by Edward Banfield (1974). This theory proposes the idea that lower socioeconomic groups in society develop a different value system from the dominant culture because their experiences are different from working class and wealthier members of society. The theory puts forth the idea that poor people have different educational and lifestyle experiences and associations that create a different sense of morality. Morality for these groups is not necessarily what is right (by definition of the dominant culture) but what works and what one can get away with.

Banfield argues that the underprivileged personality is one weak in ego, with a present-time orientation, an inclination for risk-taking behavior, and a lack of empathy for the pain of others. This theory suggests that members of the lower classes have a higher propensity toward criminal behavior and has been used to explain everything from teen pregnancy to murder.

Critics argue that first of all, *if* a different value system does indeed exist, this value system is *imposed* on the poor due to lack of opportunity and money. Others argue that the poor do not have a *different* value system, but one that is based on adaptation or probability. In other words, people in lower socioeconomic groups want the same things that working people want - a safe place to live and raise their children, the opportunity to improve their lives or at least their children's lives, and security in their old age. If the opportunity to achieve this is less likely, then they either innovate, as Merton suggests, or lower their expectations.

For example, one of the problems faced by administrators of public assistance programs is that middle class, college educated people who have never lived with the sense of immediacy that the poor often have to deal with, design most of the social welfare programs. A mother feeds her child the last of the food and sends that child off to school not knowing where she will find food for the evening meal. Her day is spent doing whatever is necessary to find food for the next meal. This kind of pressure makes it almost impossible to think in terms of employment that requires you to work a week without pay. Where does the daily food come from until the first paycheck? Where do you get the money to get to work? Do you take food money to buy work clothes at the expense of your child? These are issues that program developers seldom consider. And, they are the most likely reasons for failure—not laziness or lack of desire but basic everyday needs.

Labeling **(System Blame).** Labeling theory suggests that people are more likely to become deviant when social groups label them as such. Think of your junior high school experience–the more your teacher labeled Johnny as the class clown, the more he acted the part; and the more you and your friends labeled Michael as the class nerd, the nerdier he got.

Our self-concept is developed early in life and is usually the result of trusting others' evaluations of our behavior. If our behavior is viewed as conforming and is rewarded, we will usually continue along the same path. If we are told that we are deviant and receive attention for that behavior, we are most likely to continue the non-conforming behavior for a variety of reasons, including getting attention.

Society may also label or stereotype people as deviant based on some generalized idea about the group to which they belong and not on personal behavior traits. Think about labels attached to minorities or ethnic populations. These labels can limit interaction with positive role models and move individuals toward interaction with deviants who are more likely to accept them as part of their group, while at the same time reinforcing the label they have been given.

Political Economy **(System Blame).** In the Marxist social conflict perspective, norms of behavior are usually defined and enforced by the influential or powerful members of a group (or society) in order to maintain their own power and protect the status quo. Deviance is seen as a natural result of capitalist ideology. Social conflict theorists argue that violations of the law (crime) are a result of the unrestrained competition for monetary gain in capitalist society (Blau and Blau, 1982).

In a capitalist society, a few wealthy owners privately control natural resources and the means of production with free competition between producers, with profit as the primary motive guiding people's behavior. It is these few wealthy and powerful owners of the means of production that also dictate social norms that will protect their own interests.

Marxist theory proclaims that the capitalist system forces individuals and groups in the least powerful economic positions to achieve their goals for monetary gain, power, and status outside of the system. No job prospects? Deal drugs or steal cars! Their actions are often labeled deviant and legal sanctions are imposed on their activities and behaviors because they do not follow the prescribed social norms.

Political economy theorists argue that by adopting a more socialist system where the natural resources and the means of production are owned collectively by the group, and not by a few wealthy owners, goods and services would be equally distributed and there would be little or no need for deviant or criminal behavior.

SOCIETY AND SOCIAL DEVIANCE

While we generally view deviance as a negative societal force, it actually serves several important positive functions in society as well. In this section we explore both the positive and negative consequences of deviance.

Positive Consequences

Self-Evaluation and Change. A group or society defines itself by the ideals and norms it has agreed upon. It defines how its members are supposed to behave and creates a level of measurement by which members can judge how far they or others have deviated from this norm. This implies that not all members of the group adhere to norms at all times. When a group is open to self-evaluation and is concerned with meeting the needs of all of its members, a certain degree of deviant behavior is acceptable. When rules are broken it forces the group to reevaluate the rules, determine if they are as clearly defined as they need to be and decide if the rules or norms need to be amended.

Clarification and Change. Norms that are clearly defined allow an individual to more easily determine whether or not they are willing to accept the sanctions for non-compliance. When we break a moral or ethical law, we are labeled as immoral or unethical; when we break a statutory law, we are defined as criminals. Each of these instances can carry strong, but very different types of sanctions. Sometimes, we as individuals must take a stand against a norm that we disagree with. Knowing what the consequences of deviation are allows us to decide whether we are willing to accept those consequences. For instance, a student may feel it is morally or

Deviance can bring together different groups for a common cause. Here a demonstrator joins others from different socioeconomic groups to protest government action.

Photo: Gay Liberation Network.

ethically wrong to dissect a frog in biology class. Failure to comply with the school's curriculum, on the other hand, may result in a failing grade or dismissal from the class. A student willing to face those sanctions (especially if joined by other students and parents) may effect a change in the curriculum that allows them to perform a substitute task or even change the teaching method to something that does not require the use of animals.

Group Cohesion. A third function of deviance is that its presence can encourage members of diverse groups to come together for a common cause. When criminal activity becomes threatening to a neighborhood, people come together to protect their community. If they are unable to effect a change on their own, they may go out into the larger society to garner support. Representatives from differing socioeconomic, racial, and ethnic groups that have previously remained apart from each other may now come together in common cause. For instance, the appearance of gangs in certain neighborhoods across America has united people from different racial background in a common goal to save their communities and children. Although the primary goal is to eliminate gang activity, an additional goal is also achieved, that of reducing racial tensions.

Pressure Valve. Deviance also gives us a way to measure our own behavior against that of others and to set a limit of tolerance for deviant behavior. Many sociologists believe that deviance protects society by allowing a person who feels abused by the system to perform an objectionable act rather than to directly attack the social structure itself. For instance, screaming at or making obscene gestures toward someone who cuts us off on the highway is less destructive than shooting the driver. The negative effect of "pressure value" deviance is that when deviant behavior becomes more acceptable, some people will move on the to the next level of deviance. For example, some studies show that viewing pornographic material satisfies the sexual fantasies of viewers. Other studies, however, have shown that reading or watching pornographic material will cause some viewers to progress to violent pornography and then to violent sexual behavior.

Employment. The last positive effect of deviance is that it provides many jobs for those who are responsible for maintaining social order. These jobs range from personnel in the corrections system, to the providing of food and shelter to the homeless, to the treatment of the physically and mentally ill.

Negative Consequences

The negative impacts of deviance are often more obvious than the positive ones. Widespread and persistent deviance disrupts the social order, causing people to believe that those responsible for social control are not concerned or are ineffective. Group members may even believe that controlling forces are allowing the disorder to continue for some personal gain. When society perceives that a particular racial or ethnic group is engaging in unacceptable behavior, the level of trust between members decreases, encouraging violent or racist responses. Last of all, attempts to control widespread deviance are costly.

After consulting economists and numerous individuals in the criminal justice system, David Anderson reports in the *Journal of Law and Economics* that the cost of crime has risen to more than one trillion dollars. This comes to $4,118 per U.S. citizen.

From a structural functional perspective of society and deviance, the values of the population evolve to accommodate a changing world. By 2011, six states have enacted laws allowing civil unions for gay couples. In February, 2011, president Obama stated publicly that he believed DOMA, the Defense of Marriage Act, was unconstitutional. This act declared that marriage can only exist between a man and a woman.

From a social conflict perspective, those in opposition to gay marriage have resisted change through peaceful resistance with demonstrations, sit-ins, and courtroom challenges. Their failures have led them to engage in the creation of a moral panic creating political action groups, using the media to promote their cause and engaging in inflammatory rhetoric.

MEASURING TRENDS OF DEVIANCE

Sociologists are less interested in isolated incidents than they are in *trends*. Although there was much public interest in the Oklahoma City bombing, it was that event combined with other terrorist activities that caught the attention of sociologists. They began to observe a pattern, or trend, of increased terrorism in the United States. While the events of September 11, 2001 were beyond anything that we as citizens could have imagined, the idea that such an act could take place had been predicted by the abundance of collected evidence of terrorist activities against the U.S.

Collecting data regarding criminal activity allows us to compare the types of crimes committed, the age, gender, and race or ethnicity of the perpetrators, and time and place. We are able to track the rise and fall of illegal activity and to predict, to some extent, the probability of criminal activity in the future. One available means for determining the level of criminal activity is the Uniform Crime Report (UCR). The UCR consists of detailed information supplied by approximately 15,000 law enforcement agencies throughout the United States. The FBI compiles this information into four categories of violent crimes—murder, rape, robbery and aggravated assault,

Figure 6.1

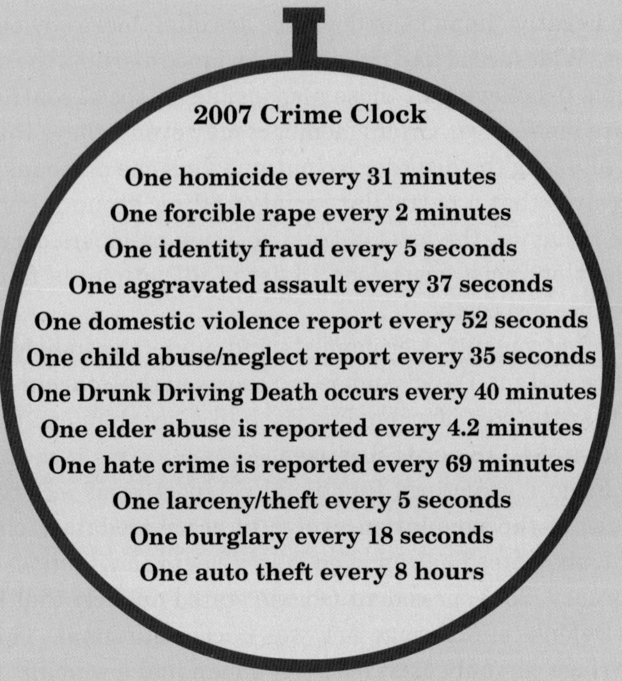

The Crime Clock, based on 2009 crime data collected by the FBI. Calculations were made by the National Center for Victims of Crime. Visit the website wheelgun.blogspot.com/2009/07/2009-fbi-crime-clock.html

and three types of property crimes-burglary, larceny and motor vehicle theft. These statistics are often referred to as **index crimes**. The **crime rate** is reported as the number of crimes committed per 100,000 people in an area. The UCR may not truly reflect the actual crime rate because it is believed that only about fifty percent of crimes are actually reported to the police. There are several possible reasons for this.

A more reliable source of information is the National Crime Victimization Survey (NCVS). The NCVS was created in 1973 and provides an anonymous means of reporting victimization. Statistics from the NCVS as well as the UCR demonstrate a correlation between race and one's chances of being a victim of a serious crime.

Criminal Behavior

The study of criminal behavior has an interesting and often amusing history. For example, earlier in the chapter we discussed the theory that body shape and bumps on the skull were predictors of criminal behavior. Early twentieth century sociologists argued that certain groups, such as females and African Americans, were less evolved than white males because they were created after Adam (whom they assumed to be white) and therefore, had not *existed* as long as white males. Because of this, they were considered to respond to problems on a more emotional and primitive level. As researchers find continuing evidence that Adam may have been dark skinned rather than white, we have to wonder where that leaves the theories regarding behavior.

For example, lower class people in general, regardless of color, are more likely to commit murders on the weekend, usually Saturday night (Levin

Table 6.1: Possible Reasons for Inaccuracies in Reporting Crime

- **Crime is recorded by police and reported by victim.**
- **Crime is recorded by police but not reported by victim.**
- **Crime is reported by victim but not recorded by police.**
- **Crime happens but is neither reported or recorded.**
- **Crime is reported that did not take place (i.e. fraud or revenge).**
- **Crime recorded by police that did not occur (i.e. for bigger budget).**

Source: United Nations Office on Drugs and Crime 2011.

and Fox, 2001; Parker, 1989). These homicides are most likely to be the result of alcohol induced arguments with acquaintances and are one-on-one assaults. On the other hand, most serial killers and mass murderers are white, middle-class males who carefully plan their crime and then carry it out.

It is also interesting to note that we are inundated with warnings regarding crime in the inner city school system where poverty and race are key issues. Criminal activity does take place in inner-city schools, but again it is almost always one-on-one. The Columbine massacre and other mass shootings at high schools were committed by young white males who carefully planned and carried out the assaults. It is important that we understand that social researchers are often college educated, middle class people who are less likely to study their own groups. In order to get a clear picture of crime, we must be willing to look at all groups and compare honestly and without prejudice the why, who and how of criminal behavior.

Gender Based Crimes

Using the same theory of evolution, women deviants were seen as more susceptible to primitive urges (sexual/prostitution) and emotional instability (mental illness, drug and alcohol abuse). Because of their lower evolutionary status, they were less creative (unable to think out a criminal act) and more passive. Pollack, in 1950, elaborated on these ideas by theorizing that

Table 6.2: Trends in Violent Victimization by Race, 1973-2005

- **per every 1,000 persons, 27 blacks, 20 whites and 14 persons of other race sustained a violent crime**
- **black & white persons experienced similar rates of simple assault**
- **black, white, and other races experienced about the same rates of rape/sexual assault**
- **about 49 percent of murder victims were white, 49 percent were black, & 3 percent were Asians, Pacific Islander, or Native Americans**
- **American Indians experienced violence at a rate more than twice that of blacks, 2 1/2 times that of whites, and more than 5 times that of Asians**
- **between 1993 and 2005, the rate of victimization against Hispanics fell 55 percent to 25 victimizations per 1,000 persons**

women were naturally more manipulative and were the instigators behind many of the crimes men committed. He believed that the social protection of chivalry toward women protected them from blame and prosecution. It is amazing that this idea continued until the sixties when the Supreme Court declared that a woman was not the property of her husband.

In a complete theoretical reversal, Eleanor Miller (1986) argued that it is males who instigate and manipulate women to engage in criminal activity, knowing that a woman, if caught and charged, is less likely to receive as harsh a punishment as a man. Nancy Lee (Freund, Leonard and Lee, 1989) also observed this type of manipulation in her study of street prostitutes. She found that men or boyfriends encouraged their women to engage in all types of criminal activity in order to insure enough income to provide an adequate drug supply and cover living expenses. The offenses, such as prostitution, shoplifting and street scams, that these women engaged in were less likely to draw harsh sentences. On the other hand, for the men to make the same amount of money, they would have to commit burglary or felony crimes that carry more stringent sentences. When women were arrested, the men would quickly find other women to take on the role of provider.

Even though the crime rate among women is increasing, it is more likely to be the traditional types of crime mentioned above, or white collar crime. When a woman does commit a violent crime, it tends to be extreme. This extreme behavior can be the result of pent up anger or fear such as seen in "battered wife syndrome," or the need to prove their worth in comparison to men. Terrorist experts say that the female member of a terrorist group is likely to be more violent than the men because she must justify her place in the group.

Rape

Rape is a crime that seems straightforward: someone is forced to engage in sex against his or her will. However, it is not as straightforward as it appears because it is socially intertwined with three basic attitudes toward women.

The *first* is the traditional attitude that women are the property of men. We are incredulous when we hear that women in other countries are not allowed to speak to any male outside of their family. We are horrified when we read that a woman has been stoned to death because she was raped, or was sexually mutilated so that sex would be so painful as to be avoided except at her husband's will. And yet, it wasn't until the 1960s that the U.S. Supreme Court declared that a woman was not the property of her husband. In many states if a man's job requires him to move and his wife refuses to go with him, he can sue for desertion. If her job requires that she move, he does not have to go if he doesn't want to go and he can still sue for desertion.

This attitude impacts on the issue of rape, especially in the area of marital or date rape, where a man may feel that he can do anything he wants with "his woman." Unfortunately, this attitude has impacted on women's views, as well. One study of eight to ten year-old girls showed that the majority of the girls interviewed felt that if a boy took you to a movie and out to eat, he had a right to expect sex.

A *second* attitude is that women are trophies to be won in some kind of male status game. "Have you scored this week?" Guys hear this all the time and are ridiculed by their peers if the answer is no. Add to this the idea promoted through advertising that if you have the right car, the right toothpaste, the right beer in your hand, you will attract the opposite sex and live happily ever after—or at least until the next partner comes along. Reports are increasing that girls as young as nine and ten years old are engaging in oral sex in school lavatories using the excuse that this keeps the boys happy and ensures that the girl will still be popular without having to engage in intercourse.

A woman joins a protest against domestic violence. According to U.S. Department of Justice statistics, one-third of all women in the United States report being abused by a spouse or intimate partner. And, of all female victims of violent crimes, two-thirds were related to or knew their attackers.

Photo: Women's eNews.

This leads to the *third* attitude, that women really want "it" no matter what they say; that women want to be raped. This attitude is a throwback to the old idea that women were not supposed to enjoy sex and that any woman who did was loose, or a whore. A good woman's husband would be appalled if his wife initiated sex or appeared to enjoy it. But if she were *forced* to engage in intercourse, no one could hold her responsible. This type of thinking also allows us to blame the victim because she dressed a certain way or was out too late. She should have known better.

Of course, there are other cases of rape where men rape men, or women rape men or women. These also carry the stigma of blaming the victim. Gay men are either rapists or deserve to be raped; any man who would *let* a woman rape him is no real man. These attitudes totally deny the reality of rape; that it is a crime of violence not sex. It is a crime of degradation and humiliation and force against another person.

Juvenile Crime

The misconduct of juveniles has concerned every generation since the ancient Greeks and Romans. In the 1800s, reporters warned the citizens of San Francisco that it was unsafe to walk the streets because of young hoodlums (Parrillo, et al, 1996). Until the 1900s, children were treated like little adults and expected to behave in an adult manner. With the advent of compulsory education the idea that childhood was a special period evolved, along with the idea that children should not be held to adult standards. This led to a separate criminal division for juveniles. Certain juvenile activities such as truancy, running away, and disobeying parents were deemed important enough to require court intervention. These activities were labeled **status offenses** and applied only to juveniles under the age of sixteen.

More serious offenses are considered on an individual basis. Depending on a variety of factors including demographic location, a person under the age of eighteen may be tried as a juvenile or as an adult. In making a determination, the court considers recommendations by teachers and family along with investigation of past criminal involvement and the likelihood of behavior change. In determining the ability to reform, the most important considerations are whether the juvenile understands the seriousness of the act, whether the crime was planned or premeditated, and the level of remorse demonstrated.

The juvenile justice system is concerned with rehabilitation and whether a child can be resocialized and returned to society as a responsible adult. Early juvenile detention facilities were actually called reform schools.

While all states have provisions for prosecuting children as young as fourteen as adults, the youngest child to be sentenced as an adult is a twelve year old Michigan boy (Kellerman, 1998). Kellerman has studied the cause of delinquent juvenile behavior and believes that the majority of these children are victims of neurological damage due to prenatal exposure to alcohol (fetal alcohol syndrome). "There is a sixty percent risk of (an FAS child) being charged or convicted of a crime" (Kellerman, 1998 and Streissguth, 1998).

Younger children are being arrested for increasingly violent crimes and the criminal justice system is sentencing more of them to adult facilities. Society appears to have taken a "zero tolerance" attitude toward youthful offenders.

Princeton professor Alfred Blumstein (1995) attributed the dramatic change in juvenile behavior to the introduction of crack cocaine in 1985. Blumstein predicted that the population of juvenile males between the ages of fifteen and nineteen would increase by approximately 30 percent between 1995 and 2010 and that many of these young men were growing up "fatherless, godless and in poverty." He feared that we would see a tremendous growth in crime among this group and that their coming of age will be devastating to society and the social order.

During the 1970s and 1980s society attempted to relate social circumstances to criminal behavior and leniency in sentencing, introducing alternatives to incarceration, especially for juveniles and first time offenders. In the 1990s however, our move toward a zero tolerance attitude resulted in more juvenile offenders being sentenced to adult facilities, and in more stringent sanctions for less violent offenses. Many states are also passing laws that make parents liable for the misconduct of their children. In some cases, this results in parents being fined or held financially responsible for damages.

Adult Systems

Adult prisons, on the other hand, while concerned to some degree with rehabilitation, are set up for containment and carrying out the sentences imposed by the court system. Indications are that little rehabilitation occurs. Instead, the rate of **recidivism**—the probability that those incarcerated are likely to return to prison after they are released for new crimes committed—is very high.

A 1999 study by the University of Delaware found that approximately 70 percent of drug involved inmates return to prison within three years of release if they get no treatment. The rate drops dramatically to 31 percent for those who receive drug treatment while incarcerated and follow-up care after release.

White Collar and Corporate Crime

While we hear about violent crimes more often, white collar crimes are actually most prevalent. Again, statistics show that men are more likely than women to commit white collar crimes, but the reason for this may be that men own more businesses than women and hold positions where the opportunity for committing a crime is more likely.

Edwin H. Sutherland introduced the concept of white collar crime in 1939. He defined it as a "violation of the criminal law by a person of the upper socioeconomic class, committed in the course of his occupational activities" (Parrillo, Stimson, and Stimson, 1996). He pointed out that crime often occurred in situations where prevailing theories of individual pathology did not exist. "General Motors does not have an inferiority complex. U.S. Steel does not suffer from an unresolved Oedipus problem, and the DuPonts do not desire to return to the womb" (Gilbert and Geis, 1977).

We are no longer surprised to discover that major corporations have engaged in activities that are criminal at worst, and at best, immoral or unethical. Major tobacco companies have been charged with withholding information from the public regarding the addictive nature of nicotine and increasing the amount of nicotine in cigarettes in order to increase the desire to smoke. The National Cancer Society estimates that almost 90 percent of cancer is caused by environmental factors–tobacco, illegal dumping of toxic wastes, oil spills, the release of toxic chemicals into the air, as well as unsafe products. These factors cause more deaths and waste more taxpayer dollars than the sum total of violent crime costs.

The use of defective or unsafe materials in products, cause hundreds of deaths each year. Companies often make false claims that jeopardize users' health or even their lives. In Japan, a corporation found guilty of producing a product that caused harm pays a monetary sum to consumers and the president and vice-president of the company got on their knees in front of the jury and begged the injured parties for forgiveness. Corporations in the United States rarely face criminal charges when they commit crimes. More often, they make a monetary settlement that usually includes a secrecy clause that binds the recipient of the settlement to non-disclosure regarding the details of the settlement. To the public, the amount of the award may seem large but when compared to the profit incurred by the company, the awards have little or no impact on the corporation.

Table 6.3 Percentage of Arrests for White-Collar Crimes, by Sex

	1981		2002		2007	
	Male	Female	Male	Female	Male	Female
Embezzlement	70	30	50	50	48	51
Fraud	58	42	55	45	56	44
Forgery/Counterfeiting	68	32	60	40	62	38
Fencing stolen property	88	12	82	18	80	20
Totals	71	29	61	39	61	39

Source: FBI Uniform Crime Reports, 2007: Table 42.

Employee crime, another type of white collar crime, is a crime committed by an employee against an employer. Almost everyone has taken something from their place of work: from pencils to paper clips, or too many breaks, or long distance calls on the company phone. We justify our behavior by rationalizing that, "They can afford it," or, "We're not paid enough or appreciated enough," or that, "Everybody does it." The fact is that the sum of these "minor" offenses results in millions of dollars of losses to companies each year, causing the company to increase the price of their product, which means that in the end, you as the consumer pay for others theft.

While technology has benefited society in many ways, it has also created a whole new type of crime. Skilled techno-criminals can shift money into non-existent accounts, and with the use of sophisticated electronic equipment, the theft of information can result in major financial losses. Computer hackers use telecommunication equipment to create computer havoc by planting viruses that cause irreplaceable loss of information that companies may depend on to survive, or cost millions of dollars to replace. Simply being able to use someone else's phone number in order to make long-distance telephone calls—a simple cloning activity—can cost unsuspecting individuals huge amounts of dollars and identity theft can cause irreparable harm to an individual's credit and their reputation.

Government Crime

We do not like to think of our government as engaging in criminal behavior, yet on the other hand, we often refer to government officials as politically corrupt, immoral, and thieves. The government is composed of individuals just like those in the rest of society, so it is logical to assume that a certain percentage of those in politics will commit criminal acts. When official representatives do engage in deviant acts they are more likely than the average person to receive national attention. It may also be that the old saying, "Power corrupts and absolute power corrupts absolutely" is true. It is very difficult for a person to have power and not use it inappropriately at times. Think about the parents who has absolute power over their child. They may try to parent in a manner that allows their child to participate in decision making, but from time to time, circumstances push them to say, "I'm the parent, that's why!"

Our government has been asked to justify its behavior in several instances. In the 1930s and continuing into the 1960s, the government participated in a highly unethical longitudinal study involving the effects of syphilis on uninformed indigent African American subjects. Even after a cure (penicillin) was found, researchers denied these subjects treatment. After conducting a congressional hearing, the government admitted liability and apologized to the families of those who died during the study and to the few remaining participants.

The above example is by no means an unusual one. Rather, there seems to be a governmental scandal every time we open a newspaper or turn on the TV. For instance, the government conducted LSD experiments in the 1960s using military personnel without their consent. In 1974, Richard M. Nixon resigned from the office of President of the United States to avoid impeachment proceedings for his part in Watergate, a political scandal involving an illegal break-in of the Democratic Headquarters by members of the Republican re-election Committee.

Former president Bill Clinton served under a cloud of accusations of illegal, unethical, and immoral activity during both terms of his presidency. In spite of the accusations, the people re-elected Clinton to a second term. Many sociologists are asking why. In the past, politicians tangled in ethical, moral, or legal issues, even as mild as a divorce proceeding, were quickly cut from the party platform and never heard from again. What has changed?

There may be several explanations as to why the voters would re-elect a president whose activities were under congressional investigation. Some propose that the continued attacks against Clinton, with no clear-cut evidence of wrongdoing, drew the support of the people in his favor. There appeared to be resentment regarding the millions of taxpayer dollars spent without any illegal activity proven. One major reason may have been an empathetic response by members of the baby boom generation who can, perhaps, identify with Clinton and see themselves in a similar position. President G. W. Bush's tenure was riddled with scandal and accusations. This time, however, it is the people who are pointing fingers and feel that Congress has not acted to protect the people. A recent Gallup poll showed that only 12 percent of those polled said they have a "great deal" or "quite a lot" of trust in the legislative branch (Cohen, 2008).

Mental Illness

Social pressures and medical advances determine the definition of mentally aberrant behavior. It is the medical community that usually defines mental illness. The **medicalization** of deviance leads us to the concept that a person who engages in abnormal behavior may be "mentally ill." The medical model tells us that a person who is recognized as being ill is not expected to engage in the regular activities of daily living–we have the flu, therefore we are not expected to go to work. Rather, if you are ill, you are expected to seek treatment and follow doctors orders to "get well." Who decides whether a person is "different", deviant, criminal or insane? Is a person responsible for his behavior or is society to blame?

Until 1980, the American Medical Association defined homosexuality as a mental disorder. Premenstrual Syndrome (PMS), a condition many women suffer from prior to or during their menstrual period, was listed in the *DSM III* as a mental disorder, removed when women fought to have it recognized as a medical condition, and added again to the *DSM* in 1996. Schizophrenics, labeled as mentally ill, often hear voices that tell them what to do. Yet millions of people go to psychics or mediums who speak to unseen entities and we label this activity as an amusement.

Differentiating mental deviance from social deviance becomes especially important when we are determining how to prosecute a crime. A person charged with a crime must:

1. Be able to understand the charges which have been brought against him and;
2. Understand the difference between right and wrong.

If either of these criteria is not met the person is deemed incompetent to stand trial and placed in a psychiatric setting.

A person may also have committed a crime while *temporarily* unable to distinguish between right and wrong for a variety of reasons. In this case the person may be deemed "temporarily insane" and either be excused for committing the crime, or face a lesser charge. As we move toward a zero tolerance policy of deviant behavior, we see very few cases of temporary insanity.

A third defense for deviant behavior is a type of post traumatic stress disorder called "**battered wife syndrome**." In this situation, a person defends their assault or murder of another by attempting to prove long-term battery, rape, or assault on the part of their victim. Although the accused was not necessarily being battered at the time of the crime, they appear to be responding to the perceived threat of future battering. The condition is also a defense for children who assault their parent after years of abuse. On the basis of this condition being identified as a mental illness, several women convicted of murdering their abusive partners were granted a new trail and released from prison.

CRIMINAL JUSTICE SYSTEM

The criminal justice system is responsible for providing a means of enforcing existing laws, providing a forum for defense against arrest, and for providing protection from convicted criminals. Laws are created to protect individuals and the social structures that are essential to survival. For example, laws against incest protect the family structure by protecting its most vulnerable members.

In Western culture, we use primary and secondary socialization to encourage **internalization of values**. Internalizing prevailing values results in voluntary obedience to laws protecting those values. For example, we learn that stealing is wrong, that there are laws against stealing, and that if we break those laws we may be arrested. Internalizing this and agreeing to follow the rules reduces the need for the creation of a police state.

Police in the United States are given discretionary powers regarding the response to a situation. This is referred to as **street level justice**. If a situation does not appear serious and the participants are cooperative, the officer is more likely to forego an arrest. However, if the people involved have a history of arrest, refuse to obey the officer, or if the victim insists, the officer is more likely to make an arrest.

The Court System

After an arrest, the court determines the guilt or innocence of the alleged suspect. The majority of court cases are settled outside of court by lawyers acting as officers of the court. In criminal cases, these settlements are called **plea bargains**. Guilty verdicts from the court are open to an appeal process if circumstances warrant. Cases settled outside of court are not open to appeal.

Prison System

Juvenile detention centers see rehabilitation as a priority. The adult prison system, however, rarely addresses rehabilitation. Instead, it focuses on retribution and deterrence. **Retribution** is moral vengeance by which a society inflicts suffering on the offender comparable to that caused by the offense. The death penalty is the ultimate form of retribution and is most

Table 6.4: Prevalence of Imprisonment in the United States

- In 2005, there were 2.2 million inmates in the nation's prisons and jails.
- The U.S. ranks first among all nations in the incarceration of it own citizens with 737 prisoners per 100,000 of the population. Russia is number two with an incarceration rate of 611 per 100,000 population.
- The proportion of persons held in jail awaiting trial has risen from 51 percent in 1990 to 62 percent in 2005.
- The prevalence of imprisonment has had a dramatic impact on racial minorities:
  —black males are incarcerated at more than six times the rate of white males and Hispanic males more than double the rate
  —one out of every eight black males age 25-29 is incarcerated on any given day
  —black females are incarcerated at four times the rate of white females and Hispanic females at nearly double the rate of white females.
- Despite falling crime rates, the rate of incarceration has increased by more than 50 percent between 1991 and 2005 due to changes in sentencing policy and practice.

Source: The Sentencing Project, 2006.

often used in first degree murder convictions. Some states also allow the death penalty for kidnapping a child.

Incarceration is also used to deter further criminal activity. **Specific deterrence** occurs when the individual who committed a crime is unable to commit further crimes due to their incarceration. **General deterrence** occurs when the punishment acts as a deterrent to others. Specific deterrence appears to have a short term effect since the majority of inmates have served at least one other prison term.

As a society, we are concerned that enforcement agencies do not abuse their powers. There have been nationally reported instances of police brutality, racial profiling, and criminal behavior by police officers. These incidents represent the actions of a minority of officers. The majority of officers are dedicated to their jobs, their community, and to preserving order.

Police officers face a variety of difficulties in their jobs. Annually, more than 230,000 police officers become victims of non fatal violent crime while on duty. Between 1997 and 2006, 562 police officers were killed in the line of duty (FBI, 2007). Nationally, police departments are working to reestablish mutual respect and cooperation between citizens and officers. Community policing, increased foot patrols, and school programs are some of the strategies being used to re-establishing trust.

Police are not the only ones who may abuse their power. In February, 2011, a juvenile judge in Pennsylvania was convicted of receiving kickbacks from private juvenile detention centers in exchange for placing juvenile defendants at those facilities. Children were sentenced by the judge at a rate two to three times higher than other courts and with harsher sentences (abc.com).

Terrorism

By its very definition, **terrorism** is an act of violence committed against an unsuspecting group of people. Terrorists may use weapons of mass destruction, such as bombs or chemicals, or they might hijack airplanes or other types of public transportation. The United States has experienced only a few acts of terrorism when compared to many other countries. The most recent terrorist act was the destruction of the Twin Towers in New York City on September 11, 2001. Close to 3,000 people died in that event. This attack was carried out by foreign terrorists. However, domestic terrorists have also caused death and destruction in America. One example of this was the Oklahoma City bombing where both adults and children where killed. America has responded to acts of terrorism by forming a new government agency, Homeland Security, and by passing the Patriot Act which gives the government extended powers to investigate and protect against future acts of terrorism. The creation of this agency and the passing of the Patriot Act have profoundly influenced the lives and freedom of Americans. Undoubtedly most Americans experience this directly with Homeland Security and new rule for boarding airplanes and traveling abroad. Less noticeable, however, is the Patriot Act that grants the government new powers over the individual liberties of citizens.

Additionally, terrorism has seriously damaged the American economy. It is estimated that the bombing of the Twin Towers cost America 95 billion dollars. This included the cost of the building and planes. However, the real costs go far beyond this figure. Since the attack, America has engaged in two wars and now spends 500 billion dollars or 20 percent of the U.S. federal budget in combating and prevent terrorism (Zalman, 2011). Certainly, one can understand the necessity of defense, but it does come with opportunity cost. The additional money spent now on terrorism, is money that is drained away from needed infrastructural improvements as well as spending on education, health and the welfare of the poor.

Israeli fathers teach their children how to use automatic weapons. Although, it is a commonly held belief that only the Palestinians teach their children violence, this photo seems to suggest otherwise.

Photo: Birdeye.

Although most Americans identify terrorism with international extremists, domestic terrorists have been a constant threat to the nation throughout our history. Perhaps the first terrorist organizations operating openly and at times freely are the Ku Klux Klan and White Citizens Council. These two organization instigated and carried out acts of violence and murder to achieve their personal, economic, and political agendas. Although marginalized, both organizations still operate in American Society, along with the Aryan Nation. Additionally, there are a large number of right wing militia groups opposed to national government policies and taxation. These groups have been linked to numerous bombing plots, conspiracies, and serious violations of law. Right wing extremists were responsible for the Oklahoma City bombing that claimed 168 lives, including 6 children, and injured 680 people. On the other side of the political spectrum, there is the Earth Liberation Front and the New Black Panther Party. In between exist numerous organizations that have occasionally resorted to unlawful practices to influence social and political policy.

The statutory definition of domestic terrorism has changed many times over the course of our history. Recently, the government sought to clarify its definition of domestic terrorism in the USA Patriot Act. The law states that acts of domestic terrorism are those which:

> (A) involve acts dangerous to human life that are a violation of the criminal laws of the United States or any State; (B) appear to be intended—(i) to intimidate or coerce a civilian population; (ii) to influence the policy of a government by intimidation or coercion; or (iii) to affect the conduct of a government by mass destruction, assassination, or kidnapping; and (C) occur primarily within the territorial jurisdiction of the United States (USA Patriot Act, 2001).

The intent of the act is to give the government enhanced powers to investigate various organizations that pose a threat to the security of the nation. However, critics maintain that the scope of governmental powers far exceeds the needs for security. Under this new interpretation, a wide variety of organizations have suddenly found themselves the focus of government investigations. Among them are Greenpeace, Operation Rescue, WTO protestors, Jewish Defense League, and the Environmental Liberation Front, just to name a few.

SOCIOLOGICAL PERSPECTIVES

Structural Functional

Structural functionalists focus on the individual, and are very much aligned with "individual blame." Likewise, structural functionalists are concerned with adherence to a normative belief system that fosters the smooth and harmonious functioning of society. In this light, they see deviance as disruptive to the system. For the structural functionalist, deviant behavior is the result of inadequate socialization. This can occur for a number of reasons. Sometimes it is the result of a breakdown in the socializing institutions of society, such as the family, schools, and religious institutions. Other times, it occurs because the individual was raised in a deviant subculture. Or perhaps, it might lie in a physical abnormality. Whatever the cause, it is the individual that must be rehabilitated. In cases where rehabilitation is not possible the individual must be isolated from the rest of society.

Social Conflict

This position advocates a system blame approach. For the social conflict theorist, deviant behavior is only the symptom of the disease. The problems of crime, teen pregnancy, drug addiction, embezzlement, school dropouts, welfare dependency, high abortion rates, juvenile delinquency, prostitution, and others are rooted deep within the institutions and normative structures of society. For advocates of this perspective, to resolve the above problems, it is necessary to change society. The political, economic, and social institutions of society must be altered to provide equality and opportunity to all. In particular, this includes a more equitable distribution of wealth and power. Then and only then, will deviance be eliminated.

WHAT'S AHEAD?

The United States has some of the highest crime rates in the industrialized world, with more murders, rapes, and more persons incarcerated. Does this mean that we are a nation of criminals? Is our country no longer safe for the average citizen? These are questions that are debated daily by groups interested in the future of our country. The fact is that with the freedoms granted us by our Constitution comes the misuse of those freedoms. The right to bear arms makes guns more readily available than in other countries; the freedom to speak freely sometimes leads to violent protests.

America has always had a violent streak. Think about the words we use in an every day sports conversation; it sounds like we are involved in a war, not a national past time. Think about a conversation concerning education, with the "war" on student literacy; how we have to "fight" drugs in our schools and "attack" gang involvement with our school children. This does not even address the 10,000 murders that the average ten year-old sees on TV every year, or the violent movies we allow our children to attend.

But for Americans, violence is not a 20th or 21st Century phenomenon. During the restrictive Puritan days, public displays of affection between married couples–such as holding hands while walking down the street–were punished violently. Offenders were placed in the stocks, manacled and out in the open, while citizens were free to curse them, spit on them, or throw rocks or garbage at them. In the Wild West disputes were settled with guns in the streets. In the roaring 1920s mobsters shot it out in restaurants, alleyways and out on the street in broad daylight.

Despite our levels of violence and crime, the majority of citizens remain stable and law-abiding, internalizing the norms and values they are learn early in their lives. Those same law-abiding citizens are the ones who, when society appears to be moving towards instability, react by instituting more restrictive laws and increased sanctions until the crisis is past. The 1990s saw a strong movement towards more moral and ethical behavior, the strengthening of families, a return to the idea of individual responsibility, and reduced tolerance for aberrant behavior.

There are several areas of concern, however, that sociologists and other social scientists will be investigating. These include the increased use of intravenous drugs, particularly among women, the increasing number of violent crimes committed by juveniles, the growing number of international gangs, and the threat of both national and international terrorists. As such, it appears that much of future research will be focused on these forms of deviance. It is important that we determine which of these acts threaten the stability of our society, which, if any, are moral panics created by the media and other groups in pursuit of their own agenda and which acts must be addressed or seen as normal adjustments to society.

Terms You Should Know:

Anomie	Resocialization	Groupthink
Deviance	Ritualism	Group Cohesion
Index Crimes	Crime Rate	Status Offenses
Recidivism	Medicalization	Retribution
Battered Wife Syndrome	Street Level Justice	Terrorism

Can You Answer These Questions?

1. Why do sociologists believe that deviance is situational? Do you think the general public thinks this way?
2. Discuss the difference between "individual" versus "system" blame theories of deviance.
3. List and be familiar with the sociological theories of deviance presented in your textbook.
4. Identify Robert Merton's three types of innovation.
5. In general, deviance is considered as detrimental to society. However, some sociologists believe that there is a positive side to deviance. How is this possible?
6. What attitudes held by some men lead them to commit rape?
7. What is the main difference between white collar crime and violent crime? Which is more prevalent?
8. How does the internalization of values prevent crime?
9. How does terrorism differ from other crimes?
10. Define the difference between "specific" and "general" deterrence.
11. What is the cost of terrorism to this country?
12. How do structural functionalist and social conflict theorists differ over deviance in our society?

Critical Thinking Questions:

1. Do you believe that criminal behavior is more of a biological or a social condition?
2. Insisting that the "War on Drugs" has be a colossal failure, there are those that suggest we should legalize or decriminalize the use of drugs in this country? Do you think drug use would increase? Would this be a good policy?
3. Statistically, racial minorities are overrepresented in U.S. prisons in comparison to whites. Is this evidence that our society is racist?
4. There are those that believe our problem with terrorism is created by our foreign policy of meddling in other countries affairs. In your opinion is this true?

Part Three

Social Divisions

In our last section we discussed diversity. We have seen that human diversity is not something to fear, but rather a reality filled with richness and value. As a nation of immigrants it is only understandable that we continue to celebrate diversity through our core values of individualism and liberty. However, diversity can also be the root of division in society, division not only in cultural values, but also in how wealth and power are distributed.

In this section we examine the divisions that exist in our society. In Chapter Seven we define the concepts of class and stratification and how both relate to the separation and classification of individuals. We will see that within all societies, even our own, a hierarchical scale exists that defines where and how we fit. We will learn that where one falls on the scale has profound effects on our life chances. In Chapter Eight we will see the impact of race and ethnicity on social stratification. We will learn that although we proudly celebrate diversity, there are dark consequences for members of minority groups. We will learn about prejudice and discrimination. Likewise, we will examine why some minority groups have been more successful than others. And last, in Chapter Nine, we consider women as a minority group even though they outnumber men in our society. We will learn that minority status is not simply a matter of numbers, but rather one measured in dollars and power. We will see how the institutions of society treat women and how the powerful effects of socialization perpetuate gender discrimination.

Finally, within each chapter in this section we examine why it is that some individuals and groups are more successful than others. Again, you will find that there is considerable disagreement among experts as to why some individuals and groups are more successful than others. We will present the theories, and as always, *you* must decide what the best answer may be.

Photo: Kurt Hammond

Photo: James Thompson

Everyday Sociology 7th Edition

Chapter 7

Class and Stratification

Figure 7.1 Titanic Survival Rate by Class of Ticket

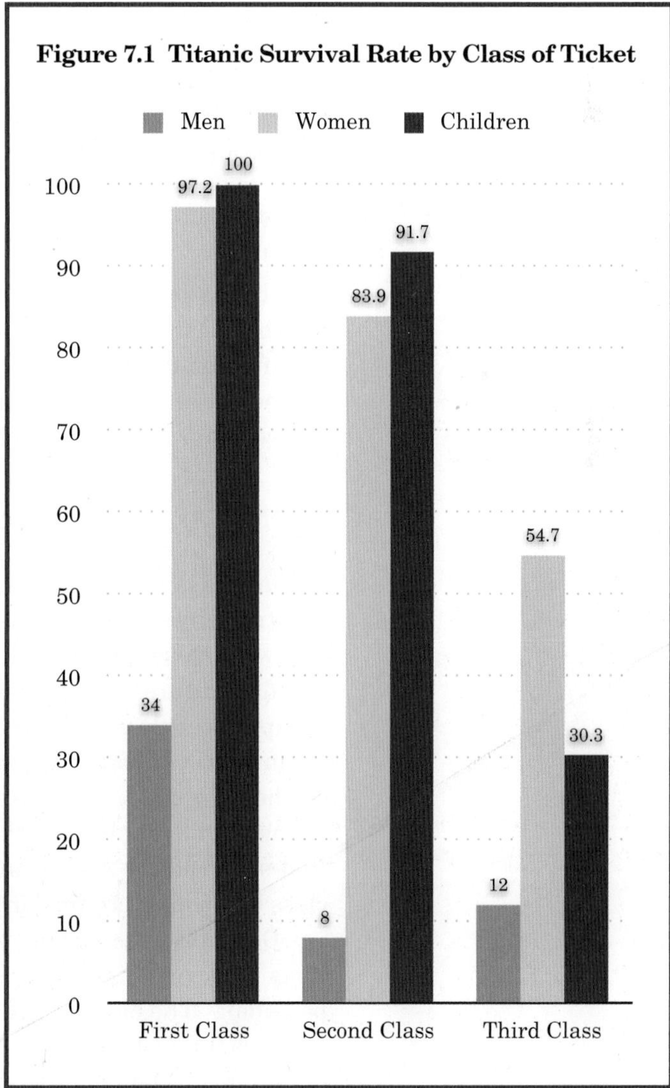

Source: Russell, 1995

Do you remember the **Titanic**? I know that most of us were not around when the "unsinkable" ship set out on the fatal voyage. But the mega hit, romantic movie is an example of the value of how social class can be used as a critical analytical tool. Our **ideal culture** values "women and children first." This should have trumped social class privileges on the doomed ocean liner. As the chart on the first page of this chapter graphically confirms, the influence of class cannot be denied. Men with first-class tickets had a higher survival rate than did the children who were in third class.

Why and how did the Titanic tragedy occur? It is a complex story with many puzzle-pieces fitting together that allowed for the chain of events that led to the demise of the "unsinkable" ship. One piece of the story that you should contemplate is that in order to allow first-class passengers enough room to walk the deck, the number of lifeboats on the ship was reduced. This decision resulted in fewer seats on lifeboats than there were passengers and crew on board. Additionally, lifeboats were kept on the deck, close to the cabins of the first class passengers, allowing them greater access to the means of survival. As you read this chapter, ask yourself if the social class structure conditions found on the Titanic are similar to class structure found in capitalist societies today. Keep this thought in mind as we explore social class.

What impact does your social class have on your life chances? Are some social classes key groups in capitalist society while others are not? Is our social class structure grounded in merit or in injustice? What is the relationship between social class, race and gender? What is your social class? Do you live in a community consisting of diverse social classes or in one dominated by one class? These are some of the questions we hope you will be able to answer after reading this chapter.

WELCOME TO SOCIAL CLASS

Social class is a core principle of sociology and as the story of the Titanic illustrates, we can apply a social class analysis to many societal spheres. The word class is commonly used in everyday conversation, the media, and popular culture, and its range of use makes it difficult to apply correctly to groups of people in society. The word class is derived from the 16th Century Latin word *classis*. It meant a division into groups of the people of Rome on the basis of property. Its modern day meaning is rooted in the economic changes brought about by the Industrial Revolution and the political conflicts that spawned the American and French Revolutions. During this time, the class divisions were first introduced.

Describing these changes, historian E. P. Thompson (1963) wrote, "Relations between employer and laborer were becoming both harsher and less personal." The emerging class relations in England, the country where the Industrial Revolution began, transformed interpersonal ties and the values of the older order began to erode. The new order valued the free market and maximizing profits.

At the root of the sociological use of the word **class** is the division of people into large groups having similar economic assets. These available resources affect life chances and according to sociologist Anthony Giddens (1991), "Ownership of wealth, together with occupation, are the chief basis of class differences."

For Michael Zweig class is best understood as a power relationship. He identifies four major classes:

> The **working class** consists of people with little personal control over the pace or content of their work and without supervisory control over the work lives of others. There are nearly 90 million working class people in the US.
>
> The **capitalist class** includes the corporate elite, senior executives, and directors of large corporations whose job it is to give strategic direction to the company, who interact with government agencies and other corporate executives.
>
> The **ruling class** has as its members those who give strategic direction to the country as a whole, extending beyond their own business or institution. The entire U.S. ruling class could fit into the seats at Yankee Stadium (capacity 54,000).
>
> The **middle class** is comprised of professionals, small business owners, and the managerial and supervisory employees (Yates, 2007).

Newman and Chen (2007) have called attention to the **missing class**. They are about one-sixth of the U.S. population who live just above the poverty line. Their income is far below the middle class. The missing class is typically forgotten. Since the missing class earnings are not completely secure and have incomes that are too high to qualify for government benefits. When the economy is down, they are "very vulnerable." Most of them are service-sector workers who are the first to suffer the consequences of unemployment. Twenty percent of the children in the U.S. are part of the missing class. As we will see, belonging to a social class is more complicated than belonging to a cluster of people who share the same economic rung of society.

Social stratification is common to all societies. "Every society has a system of ranking. Some strata rank higher; some lower. Their sum constitutes the stratification system of that particular society" (Berger, 1963). In stratified societies, social groups are classified based on how much **power**, **prestige**, and **wealth** their members hold. It is considered *social* because individual members share a similar life style and, typically, have an awareness of collective interests, as well as a collective identity. Also, people who occupy a common class tend to create their own subculture. This consists of definite norms, attitudes, and values that are peculiar to them as a social group. This is not to say that people who occupy a particular class do not share common norms, attitudes, and values with others in different classes.

Sociologists adapted stratification from geology. In his critique of social stratification Aronowitz states that substituting "class with strata deny that society is propelled by social struggles; for the stratification theorists, people are arranged along a social grid by occupation or income." For him, it emphasizes the description of status and differences in opportunity at the expense of "how social structure or history is" created (Aronowitz, 2003).

The idea of **life chances**, introduced by political sociologist Ralf Dahrendorf, offers a useful framework that further aids our understanding of social class. Life chances are the opportunities and choices made available by society to people in a particular social position. Each social class has access to a different quality and quantity of goods and services. The lower the social class, the greater the challenges one encounters in acquiring the necessities of life and societal rewards (Dahrendorf, 1979).

After studying the social causes of disease, Sir Michael Marmot found a strong link between social class and health. He concluded that the poor, compared to other classes, suffer with inferior health. For the working and middle classes, inequality and societal factors such as the safety of our communities, the quality of our work, and job security adversely affects health.

> If you get on the Metro in Washington DC and travel about 12 miles out to Montgomery County, Maryland, life expectancy has risen about a year and a half for each mile traveled. There's a 20-year gap in life expectancy between the low rate of about 57 for men in Washington DC, and 77 for men in Montgomery County, Maryland (Marmot, 2006).

In his comprehensive review of *The Impact of Inequality*, Wilkinson documents how in more prosperous societies like the U.S. class inequality contributes to inferior health.

> As infectious diseases declined, many of the so-called diseases of affluence reversed their social class distribution to become more common among the poor in affluent societies. For example, heart disease, which had been a rich man's disease more common in the upper classes, became a disease of the poor in affluent countries. The same thing happened with a number of other conditions, including stroke and lung cancer. Most indicative of all perhaps is the reversal in the social distribution of obesity (Wilkinson, 2005).

In order for us to understand this link let us look at the life experiences of a working class woman. Rachel is a twenty-eight-year-old single mother of two. She works at a fast-food restaurant and is a full-time student at a community college. The food-stamps Rachel receives only cover about one-half her monthly food budget. Purchasing food for her family is very stressful. Rachel experiences persistent role strain and role conflict.

Stress is a normal human experience that triggers a biological response that mobilizes a chemical reaction that causes us to be more alert, increases our reaction times, strength and ability to run fast. This human evolutionary response helps "prepare us for fight or flight." The other bodily reaction that stresses triggers is the suppression of "tissue maintenance and repair, immunity, growth, digestion, and reproductive processes" (Wilkinson, 2005).

In the distant past we would endure emergencies for very brief periods of time. Today, the working classes, middle class and the poor can experience stress for very long periods. The prolonged periods of stress that Rachel is exposed to have a high probability of weakening her immune system. This in turn can shorten her life and increase her likelihood of becoming sick or contracting serious illnesses.

As you read this chapter and ponder social class, assess what you are presented in terms of the idea of life chances. The community or place one lives is strongly influenced by social class. Rural and inner city communities have a higher incident of poverty than suburban communities. Cushing and Bishop have found that in the Iraq war U.S. soldiers from "small rural counties have a death rate nearly twice that of counties that have the same population but happen to be part of metropolitan areas." Why? Military studies consistently find that a poor economy is a boon to recruiting. The higher rate of deaths from rural counties likely reflects sparse opportunities for young people in those places (Cushing & Bishop).

Race, ethnicity, and gender also have a special relationship with social class. Unmarried women with children, and some racial and ethnic groups, have lower incomes. These factors impact the health hazards one encounters at work, the quality of health care, the quality of the education, etc.

CLASSICAL SOCIOLOGICAL ROOTS OF SOCIAL CLASS

Sociologists have documented that social class exists and also how factors, such as wealth, occupation and education, create unequal access to social goods through income and power. Studies by sociologists and economists clearly establish that inequalities in income exist and that these inequalities have consequences for the quality of life of people. Nevertheless, sociologists are interested in going beyond the facts to understand why inequalities exist and why inequalities become structured into societies. Some focus on the consequences of inequality. Sociological theories are means by which sociologists explore the reasons behind the facts of social class.

Karl Marx

Social class was a core theme in the writings of Karl Marx (1815-1883). The challenge in interpreting his theory is that he did not furnish us with a detailed explanation of his ideas. This leaves his work open to interpretation and has led to disputes within Marxist circles and between Marxists and non-Marxist theorists. Most sociologists would agree that for Marx, class refers to all members of a group who share the same ties to the **means of production**, or the way we create goods and services. For Marx, there were two primary classes: the **capitalists** (or **bourgeoisie**) who own and direct the means of production and accumulate profits, and the **working class** (or **proletariat**) who make their livelihood by selling their labor to the capitalists.

The relationship between the workers and the owners is grounded in their dependence on one another and **class conflict**. Class conflict is by nature social, political, and economic. **Capitalism** is an economic system that concentrates ownership of the means of production in the hands of the few and is coupled with a network of wage labor provided by the many. The capitalist invests money in the production of goods and services to generate private profit. The application of labor power on raw materials, through the use of machines, achieves this end. Commodities and services are created and sold for a price that is greater than the sum cost of labor, machinery, and raw materials. Marx called this **surplus value**, which is the source of the exploitation of the working class by the capitalist elite.

Surplus value is in part at the root of the exploitation of the working class by the capitalist or ruling class. "The directing motive, the end and aim of capitalist production, is to extract the greatest possible amount of surplus-value, and consequently to exploit labor-power to the greatest possible extent (Marx, 1976)." **Labor power** is the total "mental and physical capabilities existing in a human being, which he exercises whenever he produces," a good or service (Marx, 1976). Labor is transformed into a commodity. The capitalist attempts to increase or maintain profits by reducing labor costs and/or increasing productivity or decreasing wages. The tendency is to treat workers like raw materials or machinery, as a tool for the extraction of surplus value. What did Marx mean when he said, "The material expression of this use is money which represents the value of all things, people, and social relations (Marx and Engles, 1964)?"

This mode of creating goods and services is rooted in cooperation between the capitalist and worker in combination with the exploitation of the worker by the capitalist. In other words, capitalists cannot generate surplus value without the worker and workers and their families require employment to provide the necessities for survival and more. The drive to increase profits repeatedly leads the capitalist to adopt cost cutting measures. Today, this is embodied in corporate downsizing and relocation. Corporate executives may subject themselves to much anguish over the decision to downsize, but this has not inhibited them from moving production to regions inside and out of the country in an effort to lower the cost of labor. The capitalist is driven to make his decision in response to the impersonal bottom line.

Capitalists frequently use their class position to amass greater wealth and power. Their power flows from owning and dominating the forces of production. During the 19th Century, powerful businessmen like J. P. Morgan, the son of a banker who, during the Civil War, bought 5,000 rifles from the Army for $3.50 each and then sold them to a general in the field for $22 each, personified the capitalist class. Unfortunately, the rifles Morgan sold were defective and frequently blew off the thumbs of the soldiers. Interestingly enough, Morgan and other members of the capitalist class, like J.D. Rockefeller and Andrew Carnegie, avoided serving in the Civil War by acquiring a military substitute for a mere three hundred dollars (Zinn, 1995). (What kind of life chances did they have compared to those from the rural, high poverty areas who are dying today in disproportionate numbers in Iraq?) Even more ironic, when the U.S. government needed to raise money for the war effort, instead of selling the $260 million in bonds itself, it awarded the contract to the Drexel, Morgan and Company who made a $5 million commission at the expense of tax payers.

Union workers strike for a fair contract. The development of labor unions was not anticipated by Karl Marx. However, labor unions have seriously declined in the last three decades leading to lower wages and less rights for workers.

Photo: Michael Whitney

But beyond banks, investment houses, and insurance companies, Morgan and other capitalists like him, were able to manipulate the means of production to form monopolies and extract revenues from the people of the U.S. while putting the work force at risk. The Interstate Commerce Commission records show that 22,000 railroad workers were killed or injured during the construction of major railroad systems in the U.S. (Zinn, 1995).

Class conflict between workers and capitalists is a historic reality for Marx and those who subscribe to his theories. Can you provide examples of class conflict, initiated by workers or capitalists?

Although Marx expressed that an appreciation for the relationship between the two primary classes was vital to the understanding of capitalism, he did not ignore the role of other classes. He considered small businesses, farmers, professionals (doctors, lawyers etc.) among other noteworthy classes. Marx acknowledged the divisions within classes and how the interests of small and large businesses come into frequent conflict. There may be a division within the financial sectors of the **ruling class**. One set of institutions may desire to invest in businesses that create local jobs. Others are attracted to more profitable investment opportunities. "Why invest in low-profit production when you can borrow in Japan at a zero rate of interest and invest in London at 7 percent" (Harvey, 2010). Finally, the working class can be divided along the lines of the skilled, semiskilled and those chronically out of work.

While Marx was highly critical of class relations and exploitation under capitalism, he also had high praise for it. He considered capitalism a progressive and historical step. "It has been the first to show what man's activity can bring about. It has accomplished wonders far surpassing Egyptian pyramids, Roman aqueducts, and Gothic cathedrals; it has conducted expeditions that put in the shade all former exoduses of nations and crusades (Marx and Engles, 1964)."

Marx died before the huge increase in middle-class membership and the massive growth in the size of governments but contemporary Marxists extended Marx's theory to include both of these circumstances.

Max Weber

Like Marx, Max Weber's (1864-1920) theory of social class was grounded in society's economic arrangements. For Weber, class was defined as belonging to a group where people share similar life position and acquire similar economic rewards. Class, or **class status**, is "dependent on the kind and extent of control or lack of it which the individual has over goods or services and existing possibilities of their exploitation for the attainment of income or receipts within a given economic order (Weber, 1947)." Weber, like Marx, believed that major class divisions were rooted in who owned the means of production.

Weber differed from Marx in that he recognized important differences in the status and power within the propertyless classes. He believed that individuals were assigned different market values for the skills they possess and the services that they can provide. This accounted for the different strata within the larger class.

For Weber being a member of what he called the "positively privileged property class" enhanced life chances. This class "monopolize the purchase of high-priced consumer goods, monopolize opportunities for the accumulation of property, monopolize control over executive positions in business and they may monopolize the privileges of socially advantageous kinds of education so far as these involve expenditures (Weber, 1947)."

At the bottom of Weber's class structure are those he termed, "negatively privileged with respect to property." They are members of this class because they are, "objects of ownership," "outcasts," "debtor classes and the poor" (Weber, 1947). The middle classes existed between the "negatively privileged" and "positively privileged" property classes and consisted of those who "have all sorts of property, or of marketable abilities through training, who are in a position to draw their support from these sources (Weber, 1947)." Small business owners, white collar and blue collar workers, are members of the middle classes.

Several other factors distinguish Weber from Marx. *First*, for Weber, variables other than ownership or non-ownership determine class membership. For instance, the value assigned by the market to the skill of the propertyless can define class position. *Secondly*, Weber recognized that the management of a country or corporation demands a bureaucracy who demands skilled workers that in turn, contributes to the growth of the middle classes. *Lastly*, Weber acknowledged that there are non-economic sources of power such as **status**.

Weber's inclusion of **power**, as well as ownership of property, into the class equation opened an important door for those studying class relations. "Power is the probability that one actor within a social relationship will be in a position to carry out his own will despite resistance, regardless of the basis on which this probability rests (Weber, 1947)." This suggests that while economic position is a strong factor in determining class membership, another, sometimes independent factor, is status. Status can originate in property or in the prestige associated with a life-position achieved by heredity (birth) or by political position.

For Weber, class was assigned objectively. It arose from earnings and property. Status, on the other hand, was based on the subjective opinion in a given society. Consider then, that Weber and Marx might say that the CEO of Microsoft, Bill Gates, is a member of the "positively privileged property class" because he is an owner of the means of production. Additionally, Weber might add that the nine justices on the United States Supreme Court have high prestige and power (status) because of their powerful position which places them in a situation that is independent of the amount of property they own. So for Weber, their status gives them an equivalent power to that of Bill Gates. Based on this description, what categories of people or groups, from your community, can you place into Weber's stratification system?

Emile Durkheim

A third important classical sociologist was Emile Durkheim. He was interested in the function, or purpose, of social class and its hand in the preservation and well-being of society. Durkheim believed that, "the division of labor is, therefore, the result of the struggle for existence, a natural phenomenon (K. Thompson, 1985)." He viewed social class as a product of the division of labor.

> A function can only become specialized if this specialization corresponds to some social need. But each new specialization has the result of increasing and improving production. If this advantage is not the reason for the division of labor, it is its necessary consequence (K. Thompson, 1985).

For Durkheim, the division of labor is common to all organizations and exists because it is required for a smooth operation. If labor is divided into specific categories, you will as a result, have classes associated with those categories. For Durkheim, the division of labor (and as a result, class) was a necessary and important aspect of survival for all members of society and it evolved naturally to fill societal needs. Additionally, it produced social solidarity, an interdependence of all members of the society on each other. For Durkheim, forms of solidarity were key elements in understanding the survival of societies.

MODERN SOCIAL CLASS PERSPECTIVES

Structural Functionalism

Durkheim's writings provided the foundation for structural functionalists. They believe that systems of stratification are equitable, justified, and ethical because they are fundamentally an indication of common values. Additionally, the blend of the various divisions within society is critical to its smooth functioning. Finally, social stratification is inescapable since it originates in the shared values that are a required ingredient of all social systems.

Davis and Moore (1985) give us an excellent illustration of the structural functionalist perspective of stratification. For them, stratification satisfies a basic societal need to slot individuals into various positions for the division of labor. It motivates them to accomplish their goals. In other words, stratification matches the most competent people with the most important tasks. This is achieved via the greater payoffs tied to these tasks. The desire to attain these payoffs produces competition and normally, talent wins out. For structural functionalists, status and high economic position are achieved through merit.

Inequality, they argue, is a natural outcome of the competitive process. Rewards must be distributed unequally because all jobs in society are not equally pleasant or equally important. For example, why would an individual devote years to educating themselves to become a physician and assume the stress and risk that comes with treating patients, if the compensation received would be no more than a clerk in a store earns. It would be economically foolish to invest the time and energy. Likewise, individuals vary in their willingness to work and the energy they put forth on the job. If one individual works harder, shows more initiative, and works longer hours, is it not fair to reward him/her more than someone with less ambition? This, of course, results in stratification, but overall it assures that the important societal functions are fulfilled. Likewise, by fulfilling these functions all members of society benefit.

Structural functionalists are not so naive as to assume the absence of inequality. Instead, they argue that inequality does exist and is caused by the inappropriate implementation of theory. Structural functionalists assume that society, through a gradual, self-adjusting process moves to resolve its problems. At its core, structural functionalist theory is conservative. This is demonstrated in its reluctance to engage in social dissent or criticism. Moreover, its approach to the resolution of social problems always occurs within the *existing* institutions of society and the status quo (Gouldner, 1970).

Social Conflict

Social conflict theorists take a wholly different view of stratification. To them, conflict is unavoidable because in all societies there is scarcity or unequal distribution of valued goods and services. Likewise, in all societies some classes and groups accumulate more power and control over these resources than others do. These elite classes have access to wealth and status. For conflict theorists, power has become concentrated in the hands of the few and has been consolidated at the expense of those who are not members of the elite classes.

In his critique of Davis and Moore, Tumin asserts that functionalists have glossed-over the impact of power on the uneven distribution of rewards:

Figure 7.2: Dollars of Wealth Held by the Top One Percent for Every Dollar held by Median Households
Source: U.S. Census Bureau & Economic Policy Institute

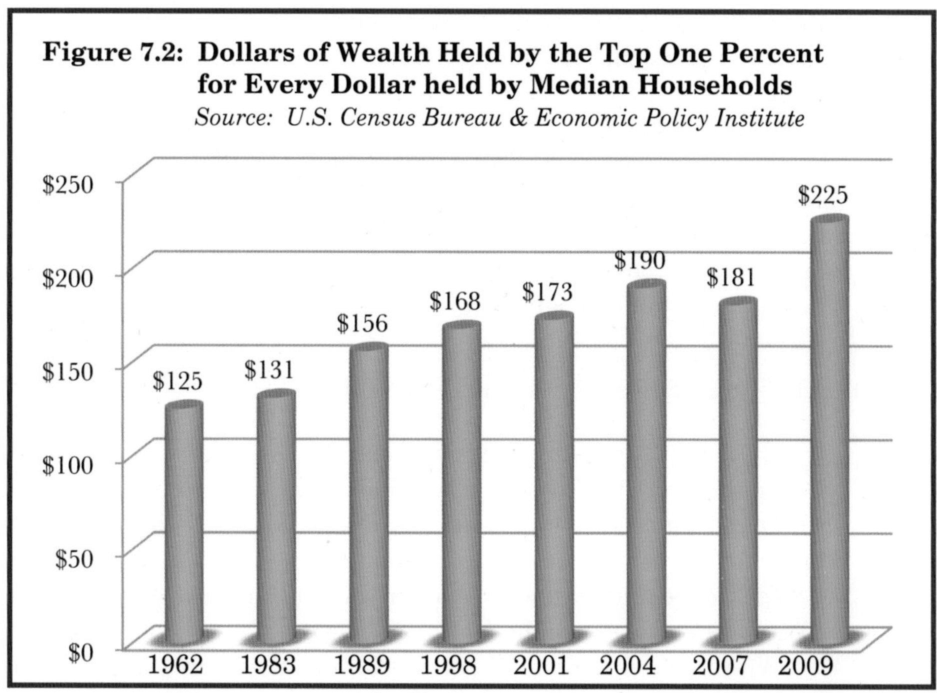

> It is only when there is genuinely equal access to recruitment and training for all potentially talented persons that differential rewards can conceivably be justified as functional. And stratification systems are apparently inherently antagonistic to the development of such full equality of opportunity (Tumin, 1953).

This thinking demonstrates what lies at the heart of the different beliefs of social conflict and structural functionalist theorists. Structural functionalists believe that stratification and the resulting social inequality unconsciously and naturally evolves within society (Davis and Moore, 1998). Social conflict theorists, on the other hand, believe that stratification perpetuates class inequalities and advances the interest of the elite.

Two other means that sociologists' employ to understand the depth of class and inequality are income and wealth. **Income** is what a person or family earns. It can include salary, wages, interest generated from savings, and stock dividends. The total income of the top 20 percent of U.S. households is slightly more than the total income of the rest of the population. In fact the top 5 percent of households have 1.8 times the income than the bottom 40 percent. "The adjusted gross income of the country's top 400 taxpayers totaled almost $70 billion in 2000, according to the IRS, for an average of $173.9 million." They "paid 22.3 percent of their income to federal income taxes, down from 26.4 percent in 1992. (Los Angles Times, 2003)." Is there a connection between their class status and the decrease in their tax rate?

Wealth is what a person, household or family owns minus debt. For most of us, our wealth includes our home, vehicle, and savings while shares of stock in corporations, and land are the sources of wealth for a minority of the population. Wealth is much more unevenly distributed than income. The top 10 percent of wealth holders have almost 2.5 times net worth than those of us in the bottom 90 percent. Does this mean that we are just one paycheck from the poorhouse? How does wealth inequality impact life chances?

What does it mean to those of us who are trying to understand why there are so many have-nots? Is their condition of poverty a result of the systematic withholding of wealth, opportunity, and power as conflict theorists believe? Or is it the result of a natural evolution of society where a natural adjustment will occur when having poor groups no longer serves the function of the society as functionalists believe?

OTHER THEORIES OF STRATIFICATION

Is our system of stratification based on merit, inequality, or some combination of the two? We know that within society some groups, the poor, non-white and women are systematically disadvantaged. This brings us back to the nature of stratification in contemporary society and why it occurs in a disproportionate manner. Another way to frame the question is to ask, "What are the causes of inequality and poverty?"

Within the discipline of sociology, two dominant explanations have emerged to answer this question. The *first* is that the poor themselves are to blame either because they are biologically flawed or because their culture promotes a climate of failure. The *second* explanation shifts the blame to society and its institutions. We now turn to a detailed discussion of these two explanations for individual success and failure. These theories attribute life chances to genetics, culture, society or some combination.

As you might already have guessed, each explanation can be linked to the perspectives we just considered. As you read, see if you can identify which perspective best fits the explanation: structural functionalism or social conflict theory.

Biological Deficiency

Biological Deficiency theories have gone in and out of popular acceptance. Herbert Spencer is generally recognized as the founder of **Social Darwinism.** Arriving in America in 1882, Spencer believed that people were poor because they were biologically unfit. Darwin documented the evolutionary tendency of nature is toward natural selection in which the "fittest" survive and the weak die off. Overall, this promotes a healthier species that increases its probability of survival through time. Spencer applied the same concept to people by suggesting that not all individuals are born alike; some are healthier and more intelligent. It is for this reason that some individuals end up with more than others, simply because they are superior human beings. Likewise, Spencer maintained that governments or private charities should not assist the poor because it only serves to interfere with the natural evolutionary process, and in the long run, serves to weaken the species by polluting the human gene pool with inferior beings.

Although the views of Herbert Spencer caused quite a stir, they have over the years been adopted by others. (Researching the eugenics movement will illustrate one of the more sinister consequences of Social Darwinism.) Until recently, the scientific community generally has not supported Spencer's theory, but his beliefs now appear in the writings of three contemporary theorists.

In the late 1960s, Arthur Jensen, a professor of educational psychology, strongly suggested a link between IQ scores and innate intelligence. According to his estimates, approximately 80 percent of intelligence is inherited while 20 percent are the result of environmental influence.

Jensen's views were advanced in the work of Richard Herrnstein, a professor of psychology at Harvard University. While agreeing that intelligence is largely the result of genetics, Herrnstein presented a model of how it worked along with social interaction to perpetuate a **hereditary caste system**. According to Herrnstein's model, intelligence is inherited. Since success in our society is based on merit, those with lower intelligence will naturally fall behind those of higher intelligence. Additionally, in our society success is used to determine one's social class. Since people generally interact with those from their own social class it is reasonable, he maintains, that they will marry someone similar to themselves and reproduce. In reproduction, the parents pass on their genes to their child, which perpetuates the hereditary caste system.

In 1994, Richard Herrnstein and Charles Murray collaborated to produce *The Bell Curve*, an 845-page book with a heavy statistical emphasis. The appearance of this book reignited the debate over the causal link between intelligence and class structure. Included is a cryptic explanation for poverty stricken women. They determined that:

> Generally these results provide evidence for those who argue that a culture of poverty transmits chronic welfare dependency from one generation to the next. Our analysis adds that women who are susceptible to this culture are likely to have low intelligence in the first place (Herrnstein and Murray, 1994).

Continuing, Herrnstein and Murray state that admission to the ranks of the poor is virtually assured to a person with a lack of innate intelligence via an immersion into a culture of poverty. They illustrate their analysis with blunt and controversial conclusions. "Going on welfare really is a dumb idea, and that is why women who are low in cognitive ability end up there (Herrnstein and Murray, 1994)."

The socio-historical presentation in *The Bell Curve* identifies a transformation in the general characteristics of the poor during the post WWII era in the United States:

> As late as the 1940s, so many people were poor in economic terms that to be poor did not necessarily mean to be distinguishable from the rest of the population in any other way... As affluence spread, people who escaped from poverty were not a random sample of the population. When a group shrinks from over 50 percent of the population to less than 15 percent that has prevailed since the late 1960s, the people who are left behind are likely to be disproportionately those who suffer not only bad luck but also a lack of energy, thrift, farsightedness, determination and brains (Herrnstein and Murray, 1994).

Culture of Poverty

In 1959, Oscar Lewis in his book, *Five Families: Mexican Case Studies in the Culture of Poverty*, popularized the concept of a **culture of poverty.** Lewis claimed:

> The culture of poverty is both an adaptation and a reaction of the poor to their marginal position in a class-stratified, highly individuated, capitalistic society. It represents an effort to cope with feelings of hopelessness and despair, which develop from the realization of the improbability of achieving success . . .
>
> Once it comes into existence, it tends to perpetuate itself from generation to generation because of its effect on the children. By the time slum children are six or seven years old, they usually have absorbed the basic values and attitudes of their subculture and are not psychologically geared to take full advantage of changing conditions or increased opportunities which may occur in their lifetime (Lewis, 1970).

For Lewis, some poor, through their efforts to adjust, adopt a lifestyle that clearly differs from that of other members of society. While aware of "middle-class values," people within a **culture of poverty** do not live by these values. He presents four distinct points where the culture of poverty interacts with success or failure.

1. At the level of society, Lewis finds an absence of a meaningful presence and assimilation of the poor in major institutions.
2. In the community, he finds inferior organization beyond the family.
3. Within the family, Lewis identifies a range of traits. These include the lack of a childhood and the abandonment of women and children.
4. On a personal level, individuals exhibit a strong sense of "marginality, helplessness, dependence and inferiority."

Edward Banfield, an advisor to several Republican presidents saw a difference between the cultural values of the poor and those of the non poor. The poor have a present-time orientation. They tend to live for the moment, the hour, the day. On the other hand, the non poor tend to put off gratification of immediate needs or desire for future gain (Banfield, 1974). For example, the culture of poverty hypothesis could be used to explain why the poor have little success in school in comparison to the non poor. The non poor are more willing to invest time, energy, and money in obtaining degrees that lead to occupational success. On the other hand, the poor, because of cultural values are more likely to spend their time, energy, and money satisfying immediate wants and desires. Instead of studying, they hang out with friends; instead of buying books, they spend money on MP3 players and cell phones.

Others have also questioned the underlying assumptions of the culture of poverty thesis:

> In the first place it is not clear of what culture these families and their children can be deprived, since no group can be deprived of its own

A man on the street begs for spare change. In the late 1970's, the deinstitutionalization of patients from mental hospitals dramatically increased the number of street people. Also, the recent recession has served to add more homeless to American communities. Approximately 1.6 million Americans seek relief in a warming or homeless shelter each year. Many are children.

Photo: Mo Woods.

> culture. It appears therefore that the term becomes a euphemism for saying that working class and ethnic groups have cultures which (are) inferior to, the 'mainstream' culture of the society at large (Keddie, 1973).

Are the poor isolated from the mainstream values, or do they share those values? Elliot Liebow, in his classic study of lower class African American men found that the poor have not abandoned the dominant values of society. They retain them while simultaneously holding an alternative set that they have adopted for survival in a hostile environment. As stated by Liebow:

> From this perspective, the street corner man does not appear as a carrier of an independent cultural tradition. His behavior appears not so much as a way of realizing the distinctive goals and values of his own subculture, or of conforming to its models, but rather as his way of trying to achieve many of the goals and values of the larger society, of failing to do this and of concealing his failure from others and from himself as best he can (Liebow, 1967).

Opportunity Theory

Sociologist William Julius Wilson presents an alternative to genetic theories and the culture of poverty. Like Herrnstein and Murray, Wilson focuses on how changes in the post WWII period affected the underclass. He emphasizes the impact of the **structural changes** on the deterioration of the quality of life for inner city African Americans:

> This growing social and spatial concentration of poverty creates a formidable and unprecedented set of obstacles for ghetto blacks (and) the social structure of today's inner city has been radically altered by the mass exodus of jobs and working families and by the rapid deterioration of housing, schools, businesses, recreational facilities, and other community organizations, further exacerbated by government policies of industrial and urban laissez-faire that has channeled a disproportionate share of federal, state, and municipal resources to the more affluent. The economic and social buffer provided by a stable black working class and a visible, if small, black middle class that cushioned the impact of downswings in the economy and tied ghetto residents to work has all but disappeared. Moreover, the social networks of parents, friends, and associates, as well as the nexus of local institutions, have seen their resources for economic stability progressively depleted. In sum, today's ghetto residents face a closed opportunity structure (Wilson, 1978).

At the core of Wilson's thesis is the isolation of the African American underclass from the opportunity structure created by the economic and social networks of the working and middle class. He also identifies the abandonment of the inner city by corporations, the government and schools as restricting the opportunity structure. The structural changes in the economy marginalized the inner city African American. For Wilson, "Class has become a more important factor than race in determining job placement for blacks (Wilson, 1978)."

Opportunity theory focuses on the gap between universal goals for success and the unequal means of realizing them. Cloward and Ohlin (1960) examined access and opportunity for the working class in the inner city. They analyzed how limited opportunity restricts individual choice. MacLeod's first person study, *Aspirations and Attainment in a Low-Income Neighborhood,* documents the experiences of Wilson's underclass. One resident, Slick, expresses the discouraging effect of class inequalities:

> Tell a person like that to come on down. I'll let 'em stay at my mother's house. The rich people you're talking about. Let 'em stay there with the cockroaches and the junkies shooting up outside and see how they react to it. Without their little Porsches and their little Saabs. Y'know, let 'em survive for a little while (MacLeod, 1995).

Slick, while acknowledging the curbs on his capacity to lift himself out of the inner city, feels responsible for his plight:

> I personally should've finished high school, then went on to some sort of college, any kinda college. Then looked over my options and planned on what I was doing. Planned on having children. Planned on my career. Instead of things just happening (MacLeod, 1995).

Opportunity theory weds individual, cultural and structural elements with a class perspective:

> . . .The individual, the cultural, and the structural play their part in the reproduction of social inequality. Had Slick been born into a middle-class family, he probably would be sitting in an office with a suit and tie on. Had his peer group been into Shakespeare and square roots rather than beer balls and bong hits, Slick might not be so blistered and dirty. Finally, Slick would be in better shape had he made different choices himself. Although all three levels have explanatory power, the structural one is primary because it reaches down into culture and individual agency. The culture of Clarendon Heights with its violence, racism, and other self-destructive features (as well as its resilience, vitality, and informal networks of mutual support) is largely a response to class exploitation in a highly stratified society. Similarly, Slick's individual strategies have developed not in a social vacuum, but in the contests of chronic social immobility and persistent poverty. To be sure individual agency is important. Causality runs in both directions in a reflective relationship between structure and agency. Structure constraints on opportunity lead to leveled aspirations, and leveled aspirations, in turn affect job prospects. Contrary to popular belief, structure is still the source of inequality (MacLeod, 1995).

Institutional Discrimination

Michael Harrington's book, *The Other America* was a chief intellectual stimulus to the policy initiatives of President Kennedy's, "War on Poverty." Harrington claimed, "the contemporary poor in the United States are those who, for reasons beyond their control cannot help themselves. They are victims whose lives are endlessly blown round and round the other America (Harrington, 1963)." The culture of the poor made them, "an internal alien," with, "a culture that is radically different from the one that dominates the society (Harrington, 1963)." He suggests that, "The real explanation of why the poor are where they are is that they made the mistake of being born to the wrong parents, in the wrong section of the country, in the wrong industry, or in the wrong racial or ethnic group (Harrington, 1963)."

Ryan asserts that the influence of the culture of poverty on poverty is, "...relatively small. The simplest and at the same time, the most significant proposition in understanding poverty is that it is caused by lack of money (Ryan, 1971)." In other words, the role of culture is not as important an influence on determining if one is poor, as are **situational constraints**.

In sum, **institutional discrimination** occurs when the accepted ways of doing things work to the disadvantage of the poor and to the advantage of the non poor. We can see examples of this in virtually every institution of society. Bruce Springsteen, a rock n' roll star with working class roots, describes his experiences:

> I grew up in this house where there was never any books or I guess anything that was considered art or anything. And I remember when I was in school, at the time, the things that they were trying to teach me and the things that later on, when I got older, I missed not knowing . . .

> when I was fifteen or sixteen, either (there was a problem with) the way that they were tryin' to teach it or I just wasn't interested. But when I got older I looked back and I saw that my father, he quit high school and went in the Army and he got married real young and picked up jobs where he could, workin' in a factory, driving a truck. And I look back at my grandfather and he worked at a rug mill in the town that I grew up in. And it seemed like we all had one thing in common and that was that we didn't know enough, we didn't know enough about what was happening to us (Marsh, 1987).

Most children of the working class will not achieve the level of success of Bruce Springsteen. For instance, to get ahead one needs to have an education. To succeed in education one needs parents with the experience and expertise to guide their children through the vast educational network and to have high expectations for them. Parents from the upper sectors of the economy are better prepared to accomplish this task than poor parents are. Likewise, most jobs leading to social mobility require a college education. Often, the poor, because of low expectations of teachers, poor quality of schools, and lack of support services, are ill prepared for college. Likewise, most poor students are unable to afford the ever-increasing cost of tuition. In total, all of this serves to promote a self-fullfilling prophecy of failure. But discrimination against the poor does not stop here. Other societal barriers serve to discourage the poor. Endless studies have demonstrated that due to ever present stress, improper diet and lack of preventative health care the poor get sick more often and miss more days of work. Unlike workers in higher status jobs, the poor do not have sick leave and hence forgo wages when they are unable to work. This serves to further intensify problems with diet and health.

Class Matters: Power, Privilege, and Inequality

In this last section of this chapter we will illustrate the connection between class power, privilege, inequality & poverty. Marx by implication and Weber directly documented the importance of power to our understanding of class. It is through the lens of power that we will attempt to better understand the complex relationship between class, race and gender.

Table 7.1: Income Limits for Each Fifth and Top Five Percent of All U.S. Households in 2009

Upper Limit of Each Fifth in Dollars:				Lower Limit of Top Five Percent
Lowest	Second	Third	Fourth	
$20,453	$38,550	$61,801	$100,000	$180,001.

Source: U.S. Census.
http://www.census.gov/hhes/www/income/data/historical/inequality/H01AR2009.xls

Table 7.2: The Distribution of Income for Each Fifth and Top 5 percent in U.S. 1970-2009

Year	Lowest Fifth	Second Fifth	Third Fifth	Fourth Fifth	Highest Fifth	Top 5%
2009	3.4%	8.6%	14.6%	23.2%	50.3%	21.7%
2007	3.4%	8.7%	14.8%	23.4%	49.7%	21.2%
2005	4.0%	9.6%	15.3%	22.9%	48.1%	21.1%
2000	4.3%	9.8%	15.4%	22.7%	47.7%	21.1%
1995	4.4%	10.1%	15.8%	23.2%	46.5%	20.0%
1990	4.6%	10.8%	16.6%	23/8%	44.3%	17.4%
1980	5.3%	11.6%	17.6%	24.4%	41.1%	14.6%
1970	5.4%	12.2%	17.6%	23.8%	40.9%	15.6%

Source: U.S. Census Bureau.

Many opinion polls indicate that a majority believe that they are middle class. Of course, most of us cannot be middle-income. As Table 7.1 demonstrates, in 2009 three-fifths of U.S. households have a yearly income of less than $62,000. Tables 7.2 and 7.3 provide us with a statistical picture of income and wealth inequality. Over the last 40-plus years the United States has experienced increased inequality. The top ten percent of income earners have the largest share of income since 1923 (Saez, 2008). Why? What are the causes? What are the consequences?

In 1983, according to the Bureau of Labor Statistics, men 45 to 54 years old kept their jobs for about 12.8 years. By 2004, these same men held their jobs for 9.7 years. Both white-collar and blue-collar workers experience job insecurity. Many layoffs occur in large corporations that are more likely to offer better pay and offer benefits. In the 1980s, "13 percent of Americans between 40 and 50 years of age spent at least one year living in poverty, but by the 1990s, 36 percent did (Tabb, 2007).

Table 7.3: Distribution of Wealth Each Fifth and Top 10% in U.S. 1962-2007

Year	Bottom 40%	Third 20%	Fourth 20%	Bottom 80%	Top 20%	Top 10%
1962	0.3%	5.4%	13.4%	19.1%	81.0%	67.0%
1983	0.9%	5.2%	12.6%	18.7%	81.3%	68.2%
1989	-0.7%	4.8%	12.3%	16.5%	83.5%	70.6%
1998	0.2%	4.5%	11.9%	16.6%	83.4%	70.9%
2001	0.3%	3.9%	11.3%	15.6%	84.4%	71.5%
2004	0.2%	3.8%	11.3%	15.3%	84.7%	71.2%
2007	0.2%	4.0%	10.9%	15.0%	85.0%	73.9%

Source: Wolff, 2010.

The great gap is between the top one percent or the top one-tenth of a percent and the rest of the country. The myth of the United States as a middle-class nation with endless prospects for upward mobility is increasingly contradicted by the evidence. Those at the top are a ruling elite and are concentrating more income and wealth into their own hands. The top 10 percent of wealth holders own 85 percent of the value of taxable stocks and mutual funds, the top one percent own about half. The share of pretax income going to the top one percent of Americans doubled between 1980 and 2004. The last time the top one percent had such a large share of the total was in 1937. What about after-tax income?

In a May 2006 statement advocating the continuation of his huge tax cut going overwhelmingly to the wealthiest Americans, President Bush asserted that the failure to extend the tax cut would be "disastrous" for "all working Americans." As experts from mainstream think tanks, the Brookings Institution, the Urban Institute, and the Center on Budget and Policy Priorities said in response, "The president's claim is implausible in light of the distribution of the reconciliation bill's benefits. Some 68 percent of all American households will receive no tax cut at all from the legislation...." They noted that an even larger fallacy was the assumption that the tax cut should be seen as a cost-less gift from a beneficent government since the tax cut was being paid for with borrowed money. It turns out that 99 percent of Americans are net losers under this tax cut—for every dollar they received they also got a bill of $3.74 in the form of a larger national debt for which they will be paying interest (Tabb, 2007).

Who are the wealthy? In 2006, the wealthiest one percent, those with family incomes of more than $1.25 million received an average tax break of $84,482 per family member. Welfare is generally linked with government subsidies to low income households. Most people do not tie welfare to corporations. This is called **Corporate Welfare**, and it occurs when a government gives grants, or special treatment and/or tax breaks to one or more corporations. Typically, corporate welfare and bail-outs result in increased expenses to the citizens and other corporations.

According to the libertarian CATO Institute the federal government distributed almost $97 billion in corporate welfare in 2006 (Slivinski, 2007). Others estimate that "each year, U.S. taxpayers subsidize U.S. businesses to the tune of almost $125 billion, the equivalent of all the income tax paid by 60 million individuals and families" (Public Citizen, 2003).

What is your favorite professional sports team? Do they have a new stadium or arena? Who paid for the construction or renovation?

The system of subsidies that has emerged has created what economist Robert A. Baade calls the "reverse Robin Hood effect"—taking from the poor, the near-poor, the working class, and middle class, and giving to the rich. When stadiums are built and paid for by taxpayers, there is a clear transfer of wealth from those taxpayers to owners and players. Urban scholar Mark Rosentraub says, "that sales taxes paid by lower-income people produce excess profits that are divided between players and owners, all of whom enjoy salaries about which the taxpayers can only dream" (Eitzen, 2000).

A stadium subsidy, in addition to defraying the owners' construction or renovation costs, also increases the value of a team, so that when it is sold, the owner reaps higher capital gains. In 1993, for example, baseball's Cleveland Indians had a market value of $81 million. The next year, with the opening of their new Jacobs Field facility, the team's value immediately jumped to $100 million, then to $125 million by 1996; the team sold for $320 million—a return of 295 percent in the three years following the new stadium's debut.

Transfer of wealth also takes place when luxury suites and club level seats are built, and the additional revenues they generate go to the owners. It's estimated that Abe Pollin, owner of the Washington Wizards (basketball) and Washington Capitals (hockey), will receive about $28 million a year from the luxury boxes and club level seating provided in the new arena built for him in Washington, D.C. (Eitzen, 2000).

According to Pulitzer Prize winning journalist, David Cay Johnston, the owner of the New York Yankees and the owners of the New York Mets each received over $600 million from the City of New York. "In fact, the City of New York gave them money to lobby against the taxpayers to get more money."

The Washington Nationals baseball team was bought for $450 million. Johnston documents how the owners of the team were given a new stadium worth $611 million:

> Now, in this country right now, we are spending $2 billion a year subsidizing the big four sports: baseball, basketball, football and hockey. It accounts for all of the profits of that industry and more. Now, there may be individual teams that make money, but the industry as a whole is not profitable. And that's astonishing because the big four leagues are exempt from the laws of competition. By the way, irony is not dead, because here are people who are in the business of competition on the field who are exempted by law from the rules of economic competition (Democracy Now, 2008).

INEQUALITY AND POVERTY

In this section we consider three issues. *First*, we attempt to define poverty. As we will see, this is no easy task. *Second*, we will present an overall picture of the poor in America. And *third*, we will briefly examine how class and income intersect with race, gender, and children.

Defining Poverty

Starting with the Great Depression of the 1930s, through the War on Poverty programs of 1960s, and continuing with "Welfare Reform" in the 1990s, poverty in the United States has been at the center of federal government policy debates. The federal government did not adopt an official definition of poverty until the mid 1950s:

> At the root of this definition of poverty was the **economy food plan**, the least costly of four nutritionally adequate food plans designed by the Department of Agriculture. It was determined from the Department of Ag-

> riculture's 1955 *Household Food Consumption Survey* that families of three or more persons spent approximately one-third of their after-tax money income on food; accordingly, poverty thresholds for families of three or more persons were set at three times the cost of the economy food plan (Fisher, 1992).

Although some adjustments have been made to this original definition, its essence continues to form the foundation of our understanding of poverty in the United States. Today, it is called "the definition of **relative poverty**."

How does a definition of poverty come to exist at the government level? As in the 1950s example, people in power calculate the relative poverty of a given society based on what they assume to be a fair and agreeable standard of living and lifestyle. They adapt it to the perceived customs and overall economy of the day and, as customs and the economy fluctuate, the definition changes.

In 2010, a single mother and her two children were considered poor if their income was below $17,607. According to the U.S. formula, at this income level the family should have a nutritionally adequate food plan by spending $5,896. per year on food (or $1.79 per person, per meal). For much of the recent history of the U.S., one out of seven people have subsisted on that $1.79 per person, per meal; could you? In fact, you should remember that the above figures represent poverty ceilings and many poor people fall well below that threshold.

Who are the poor? In 2009, 14.3 percent of the population were poor; almost one-in-five under the age of 18 were poor. A plurality, 43.5 percent were white, however African Americans and Hispanics were disproportionately represented in the ranks of the poor.

Poverty also has a geographic dimension. Residents of the South and West have a higher incidence of poverty than do those in the Midwest and the Northeast. It should be noted that the South has made some economic gains. However, experts suggest that this gain could have been greater if the South had not been as hostile to the effort to organize workers (labor unions). Many businesses have chosen to relocate to the South for this very reason. As noted by one expert, the South, because of past poverty, has been unable to shed its belief that *any job is a good job* (Cobb, 1984). Inner cities and rural communities also have a higher incidence of poverty. Accounting for this fact is the high concentration of racial minorities in inner cities and the movement of industry to the suburbs and other locations.

Finally, a frequently overlooked group is the working poor. While definitions vary, the Bureau of Labor Statistics defines those who worked during twenty-seven weeks of the year, and whose families exist below the poverty line, as the **working poor**. Almost eight percent of the poor live in households with one or more workers.

Why does poverty exist? Some argue that it is inevitable. This is especially true in capitalistic societies. However, others insist that it depends on the maldistribution of income and wealth in society. Of all wealth in the U.S., 73.9 percent is owned by the top 10 percent of the population. That leaves about 28 percent for the rest of us to share. Likewise, of income, the

A group of street ministers pause for a moment of prayer with some homeless people. With the recession of 2008 came large deficits at the national, state, and local levels. This, in turn, triggered massive cuts to social programs serving the needs of our poorest citizens. With the crisis in government budgets, more cuts are probable in the near future.

Photo: David Haley.

top 20 percent of the population earns more than 50 percent of all income. Worldwide, income and wealth are much more unequally distributed. According to the United Nations, the richest fifth of the world's population consumes 86 percent of all goods and services while the poorest fifth consumes 1.3 percent. In 2002 the world's 225 richest individuals, of whom sixty are from the US, had a combined wealth of over one trillion dollars, equal to the annual income of the poorest 47 percent of the world's population (Fletcher, 2003).

Welfare "Reform" in the United States

In 1996 President Clinton signed "The Personal Responsibility and Work Opportunity Reconciliation Act." This new welfare law eliminated Aid to Families with Dependent Children (**AFDC**) and replaced it with Temporary Assistance for Needy Families (**TANF**). Focus shifted to forcing those on public assistance into the labor market. The Social Security Act of 1935 established Aid to Dependent Children (ADC). This New Deal program was enacted, in part, as a response to the economic and social hardships of the Great Depression. While ADC originally limited assistance to the children of single mothers, it was extended in 1950 to include financial support for the caretaker or mother of the child. This created a right to aid based on need. By 1962, the program was called AFDC and it became an important part of "The War on Poverty."

The passing of Roosevelt's New Deal welfare programs in the 1930s came more than thirty years after similar programs were enacted in other countries, including England. It was not until the 1960s that welfare "as we know it" came into being. In 1960, total social welfare spending was $52,293,000 or 10.3 percent of the gross domestic product (GDP). By 1975, disbursements reached $289,174,000 or 18.2 percent of the GDP. Federal social welfare expenditures include social insurance, public aid, health and medical programs, veterans' programs, education, housing, and other programs. Public aid itself represents only a small part (16 percent) of all social welfare payments.

The increase in welfare spending did affect the number and percent of those considered poor. In 1975, there were 13.6 million fewer poor people and their population percentage was reduced to 12.3. Today, welfare programs are still playing a significant role in helping to move people out of poverty.

In 1996, some 57.5 million Americans (21.6 percent) would have been classified as poor if government benefits were not counted as part of their income. Instead, this figure is cut nearly in half to 30.5 million Americans (11.5 percent). These figures imply that in 1996 government benefits helped to lift 27 million people out of poverty (Porter, et al., 1998).

TANF imposes severe limitations on the right to assistance. Each family can receive benefits for a maximum of 60 months. It requires all able-bodied adults to work a minimum of twenty hours per week to maintain their benefits. Some states end all assistance after two years. By 1999, 90 percent of two parent families were expected to work. The number and quality of jobs produced by the economy shapes the successful transition from welfare to work. For the welfare recipient, the quality of job training, job placement services, and the availability of childcare are additional factors that will impact success.

The number receiving public assistance declined after TANF was enacted. However,

> *well over half* of the decline in caseloads since the mid-1990s was not due to a decline in the number of very poor families with children that qualified for assistance, but rather a decline in the *share* of such families that actually receive income support from TANF programs. A recent report by the U.S. Department of Health and Human Services showed that in 2005 state TANF programs provided cash assistance to just 40 percent of families who are poor enough to qualify for TANF cash assistance and who meet the other eligibility requirements for these programs (Schott, 2009).

Under AFDC almost two-thirds of children living in households with incomes less than one-half of the poverty line had their incomes lifted above 50 percent of the poverty line. By 2005, TANF elevated less than 25 percent. An additional issue, childcare, relates to the complications associated with poor working mothers. A typical single mother today would either have to reduce hours worked per week or pay up to $3,000 per year for childcare. Either way, she is forced to take a reduction in gross income that places her family well below the poverty line (Children Defense Fund, 2005).

Class Inequality: Poverty, Race, Gender, and Children

Although poverty touches every segment of our population, it is particularly concentrated in three groups—racial minorities, women, and children of the poor.

Race. The synthesis of class and race has been difficult, with one frequently ignoring the other and attempts to analyze their complex relationship few and far between. In the United States, "Races and classes interpenetrate one another (Blauner, 1972)."

Figures 7.3 and 7.4 highlight the complex relationship between class and race. Those with lower income have a greater chance of living near a toxic waste facility. However, when we look at this through the lens of class and race it is clear that if you are non-white you have an even greater chance of living next to a facility that can adversely impact health.

One indicator of class-race inequality relates to the disproportionate number of non-whites among the ranks of the poor. While most of the poor are white, African-American median per capita income is 58 percent of median white income, while Hispanic income is 50.6 percent of white income (DeNavas-Walt, 2007). At the rate that the income gap between African-Americans and White Americans is closing we will have parity in the year 2445.

Oliver and Shapiro criticize the reliance on income when determining racial inequality. "... A change in focus from income to wealth ... reveals deep patterns of racial imbalance not visible when viewed only through the lens of income" (Oliver and Shapiro, 1995). In 2004, non-white wealth was 27.3 percent of white wealth. For African-Americans, their median household wealth was 14.6 percent of median white wealth, while Hispanic wealth was 13.2 percent (White, 2006 & Kennickell, 2006).

> ... the class perspective emphasizes the relative positions of blacks and whites with respect to the ownership and control of the means of

Figure 7.3: Median Yearly Income of People Living Near Hazardous Waste Facilities

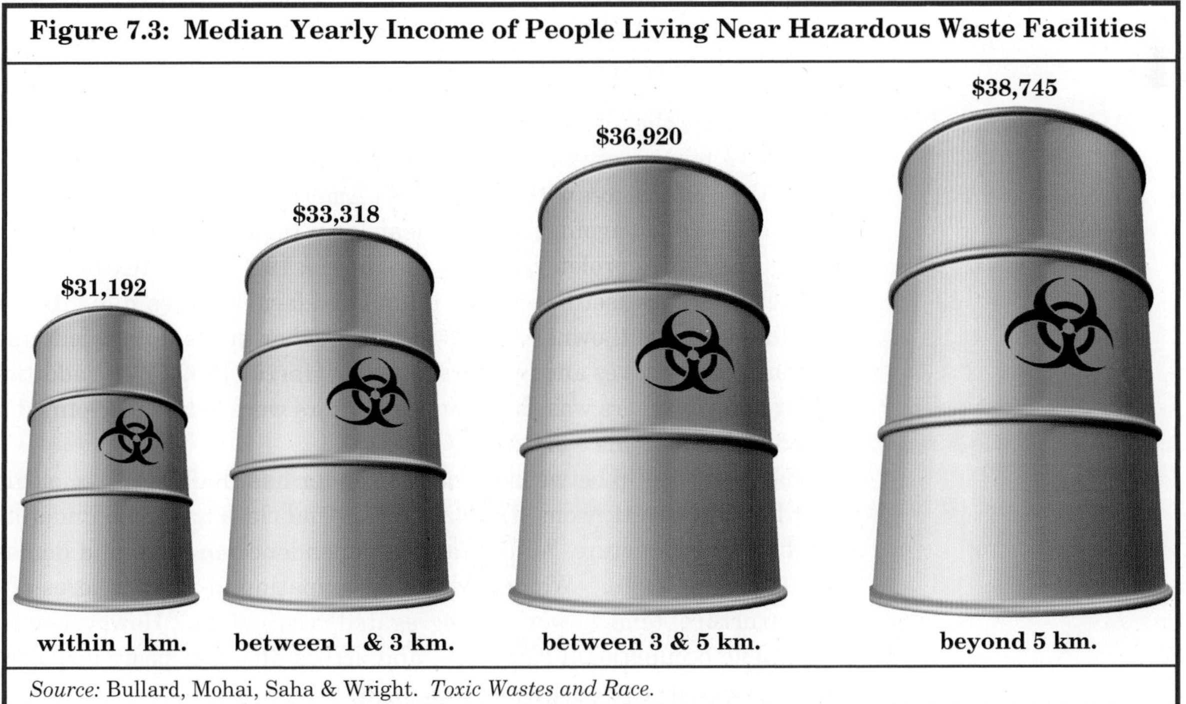

Source: Bullard, Mohai, Saha & Wright. *Toxic Wastes and Race.*

Figure 7.4: Percent of Non-Whites Living Near Hazardous Waste Facilities

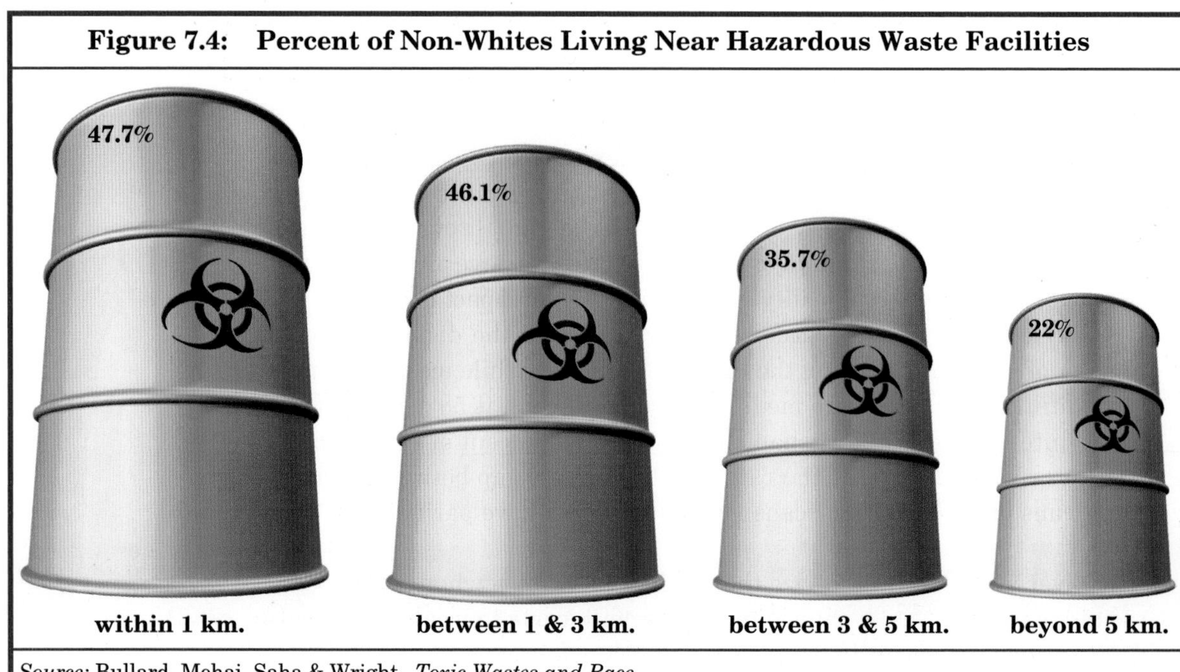

Source: Bullard, Mohai, Saha & Wright. *Toxic Wastes and Race.*

production and to access to valued occupational niches, both historically and contemporaneously. Because blacks have traditionally had access to few of these types of valued resources, they share an interest with the other have-nots. 'Ownership carries with it domination; its absence leads to subordination.' The subordinated and unequal status of African Americans, in the class perspective, grows out of the structured class divisions between blacks and a small minority of resource-rich and powerful whites (Oliver and Shapiro, 1995).

Women. From the colonial period of U.S. history to the present, women have been active participants in the class structure. "Home and family were to remain the centerpieces of their lives. Yet America's lack of an adequate supply of workers and ongoing need for cheap labor required that women become the first industrial proletariat (Kessler-Harris, 1982)." The textile factories of Lowell, Massachusetts recruited unmarried farm families' daughters and according to the mill owners, "a few years of labor in the mills would make them into better wives and mothers (Kessler-Harris, 1982)." The additional benefit to mill owners was that women workers were better disciplined and earned less than male workers.

The relationship between class and gender has challenged sociologists. According to Barrett, women's relation to social class has to be understood in light of the structure, "of the family, dependence on men, and domestic labor (Barrett, 1980)." Women, while participating in most spheres of the class structure, tend to work in segregated occupations. However, within comparable occupational categories and across different positions, women receive unequal compensation (Sydie, 1987)."

Table 7.4: Racial and Ethnic Profile of the Poor: 2009

	White Non-Hispanic	African-American	Asian-American	Hispanic-American*
% of Population	**79.6%**	**12.9%**	**4.6%**	**15.8%**
% of the Poor	**9.4%**	**25.8%**	**12.5%**	**25.3%**

Source: U.S. Census Bureau. (*Hispanics may be of any race.)

With respect to income and occupation, women occupy a unique position in the class structure because we can tie their household income to a husband, if one is present. In 2009, the typical family in the U.S. had an annual income of $60,088. Families headed by women with no man present had a median income of $29,770., while those headed by men with no women present had average incomes of $41,501. (U.S. Bureau of the Census, 2009). Most of the poor are women and their dependent children.

What is most revealing about the class position of women is that more than one-fourth of all households headed by a woman live below the poverty line. Between 1959 and the present, the percent of poor female headed households more than doubled. In 1959, 23 percent of all poor families were headed by a woman; today, that number is over 50 percent (U.S. Bureau of the Census, 2004). Most of the poor are women and their dependent children.

Children. There is a big difference between being born into a household in the lowest 20 percent of mean income or into one that is in the top 20 percent. Although one might argue, that poverty is largely a result of genetics or lack of trying, it is more difficult to make the same case for children. Poverty comes to children through their parents and unfortunately the number of children slipping below the poverty line has increased. In the U.S. today, one in five children and nearly half of all African American children are trapped in poverty. Despite these numbers, one-third of all poor families do not get food stamps and three-fourths receive no housing assistance. As a result, approximately 1.5 million children today are without a permanent roof over their heads. Of these children, well over one-third eat only one meal per day or less, while only a fourth receive three meals a day. In 2009 the U.S. Department of Agriculture documented that more than 21 percent of households with children under eighteen experienced food insecurity. "At times during the year, these households were uncertain of having, or unable to acquire, enough food to meet the needs of all their members because they had insufficient money or other resources for food" (U.S. Dept. of Agriculture, 2009).

Even when poor families can scrape together enough money for housing, their life chances improve only slightly. What occurs is commonly called **the grim rule of three**. Overall, poor children are three times more likely to live in substandard housing than children of the non poor. They are three times more likely to go without heat or electricity. As a result, they are three times more likely to be exposed to damp, moldy housing which, in turn, leads to higher rates of asthma and other respiratory illnesses. The children of the poor are three times more likely to live with cockroaches and mice, exposing them to allergies and contagion from bites and animal wastes. Children of the poor are three times more likely to be exposed to overcrowding and lead poisoning from peeling paint. Finally, they are three times more likely than children of the non poor to live in mobile homes where they are three times more likely to die from home fires (Sherman, 1994).

In sum, a total of ten thousand children in the United States die each year from poverty-related causes. In the early 1960s, President Johnson launched, "The war on poverty." And while some progress has been achieved in the last four decades, it is painfully clear that we are still in jeopardy of losing that war.

CONCLUSION

Throughout this chapter we have tried to clarify the meaning of stratification and class. Likewise, we have attempted to show the diversity of thinking and the effects of class on individual lives and our society. In doing so, it is our hope that we have shown the complexity of these two concepts and the role that they play in our lives. While most sociologists would agree that some stratification of society is inevitable, they question how much is necessary. Or, more appropriately, at what point does stratification and class work to the disinterest and division of society? Another way to ask this question is to see it in concrete terms of everyday life. At what point does this profit become too great or exploitative in the sense that it leaves too little for others? Does one person amassing a huge fortune create the condition of poverty for countless others? If so, should the government regulate profit taking? If it does, how much profit should be allowed? Is the government able to decide in a way that promotes more equality, but does not hamper ambition and work to the disinterest of society as a whole? And too, is equality an achievable goal? If it is, at what cost, and who will pay the price? These, of course, are just a few of the many questions we can ask ourselves when discussing stratification and class.

In summary, let's ask one more question. Return to our opening discussion of the Titanic for a moment. We've heard that you and your friends are booking a winter cruise. If you had a choice, which level of the ship would you prefer to stay on?

Terms You Should Know:

Social Class	Working Class	Capitalist Class
Ruling Class	Middle Class	Missing Class
Social Stratification	Life Chances	Class Conflict
Surplus Value	Class Status	Wealth
Income	Corporate Welfare	Poverty
New Deal	AFDC	TANF

Can You Answer These Questions?

1. What is the connection between social class, life chances, and health?
2. J.P. Morgan's 19th century civil war experiences and the death rate of rural soldiers in the 21st century can be explained by social class. How?
3. What did Karl Marx mean by class conflict? Can you provide current examples of class conflict?
4. What were the similarities and differences between Karl Marx's and Max Weber's views on social class?
5. What are the core differences between structural functionalist and social conflict theories of social class?
6. How has the biological deficiency theory of social class been put into practice since the late 1800s?
7. According to the culture of poverty theory, what is the cause of poverty?
8. How does MacLeod's "Slick" illustrate the core elements of opportunity theory?
9. What has happened to the distribution of income and wealth in the U.S. during the past 40 to 50 years?
10. What is corporate welfare? How is the construction of public stadiums and arenas an example of corporate welfare?
11. What were the major differences between AFDC and TANF? How have these changes impacted the poor?
12. Explain the connection between poverty, race, gender, and children.
13. How do structural functional and social conflict theorist explain stratification in America?

Critical Thinking Exercises:

1. Which theory of social class matches your perspective?
2. Can you provide some examples of life chances?
3. In your opinion, is the government doing enough to help the poor in this country?
4. Some argue that the bail-outs of Wall Street during the Great Recession were examples of socialized risk and privatized profit. They claim it was corporate welfare because middle and working class taxpayers subsidized big-business. Do you agree?
5. Do you believe that you, personally, have as much opportunity to succeed as previous generations of Americans?

Photo: Morton Hatlevik

Photo: flickr.com/photos/rudiroels

Photo: Francois Bester

Photo: Jason Hickey

Photo: Sukanto Debnath

Photo: babasteve

Chapter 8

Race and Ethnicity

In 1901, President Theodore Roosevelt extended an invitation to Booker T. Washington to dine at the White House. At the time, this simple act provoked outrage among many citizens of this nation. Now, a century later, with the election of Barack Obama as the forty-fourth president of the United States, the nation has moved beyond another major milestone in attempting to resolve its racial problems.

In capturing the presidency, Barack Obama relied on a heavy turnout among minority voters. According to election returns, he received 95 percent of all votes cast by blacks and 66 percent of Hispanic votes. Among whites voters, he captured just over 45 percent of votes. In addition, he was able to capture three southern states, Virginia, North Carolina, and Florida; an accomplishment no other Democratic candidate has achieved since the 1976 election of southerner Jimmy Carter.

But does this tell the whole story? In the aftermath of the election, there were over 200 separate racial incidents from cross burning to race-tinged graffiti sprayed on public walls. The White National Movement has ramped up their recruiting efforts believing that the election of an African-American to the presidency will increase membership.

While the above racially inspired incidents represent only a tiny minority of Americans, there is little doubt that the issue of race in this country remains a serious problem. In fact, no single issue has preoccupied the American conscience and torn at our social fabric as much as race. But what is race? Ask, and you will find that your family and friends all have different ideas as to what constitutes race. Unfortunately, most of these definitions are wrong.

President Obama speaks to a crowd of supporters. His election to the presidency of the United States gives hope to people of color in their quest to achieve full equality.

Photo: Violentz

In this chapter we will explore what constitutes race, the difference between race and ethnicity, current problems associated with race in our society, how sociologists differ over their views of the role of race and, finally we conclude with what lies on the horizon with regard to race relations for our nation.

SOCIOLOGICAL CONCEPTS

The Meaning of Race

A Biological Perspective. Historically, the task of defining race has fallen to physical anthropologists and biologists. Given the nature of their science and the tools at their disposal, they measured skulls, bone lengths and facial features, categorized skin colors and classified hair texture. These measurements led early scientists to the development of three separate racial groups: Caucasoid, Mongoloid, and Negroid.

Soon after groups were created, problems began to arise. First, as scientists came into contact with more of the world, they found that not all people fit neatly into one of the established groups. For example, dark skinned Polynesians with Caucasian features and Australian Aborigines with dark skin and blond hair presented categorizing problems. This led to the creation of new groups—thirty at one point. Additionally, as people moved around, interracial reproduction produced wide variations within groups. This can clearly be seen today. Look around your classroom, your campus, or your community and you will discover people who are classified as white but have darker skin than some African Americans. Likewise, if you examine facial features and hair color and texture, you will find more variation within racial groups than between races. To deal with these confusing matters, and in an attempt to place these variations on a continuum, some societies created terms such as mulatto or moreno. However, these attempts are outdated and were doomed to fail as people moved about the world in record numbers.

With this blurring of human physical characteristics, and the discovery by anthropologists that all human life began in Africa hundreds of thousands of years ago, scientists have abandoned classifying racial groups as a biological concept. In other words, there is no such thing as a pure racial type or a biological definition of race.

A Sociological Perspective. Sociologists have stepped in to fill the void left behind by biologists and anthropologists. Certainly, sociologists do not counter the claim that there are no pure racial types, or that race has much physiological meaning. Instead, they concentrate on the social meaning of race.

Sociologists distinguish between a legal and a social definition. Legally, race is incorporated into the laws of our nation. Some states defined being black as anyone who possesses "one-eighth of Negro blood." Others allow those with "any ascertainable trace of Negro blood" to identify themselves as black. The government has constructed similar classifications for other racial groups. These classifications have been useful in affirmative action programs and in tracking the economic and social progress of racial groups in society. Currently, the federal government identifies up to ten racial classifications including: African American, Asian American, Hispanic, Native American and white American. Socially, race in our society rests upon how others view us and how we view ourselves. **Race** then, is more cultural, being defined as belonging to a group of people who others *believe* to be physically and genetically unique. Likewise, we confer status upon ourselves when we identify ourselves as a member of a particular racial group. If I identify myself as being African American, Asian American or white, I tend to take on the *perceived* attributes of that particular racial group and behave accordingly. So, even though race has little or no biological consequence for humans, it is, as we shall see in this chapter, a wellspring for stereotyping, prejudice, and discrimination.

The Meaning of Ethnicity

As with race, most Americans hold strong opinions about ethnicity and can easily identify their own ethnic background. As with race, the concept of ethnicity is laden with much confusion and misrepresentation.

Ethnicity is attributed to groups of people who share a common cultural heritage such as language, geographical origins, religion, values, food and dress. Think about your own ethnic background. Can you identify it? If so, there are probably some traits you share with other people who classify themselves likewise. The internalization of these traits, whatever they might be, is the first step in the establishing an **ethnic identity**—a process that begins very early in life and leads to the acceptance of certain images and roles.

Although people in the United States commonly associate their ethnic background with a particular geographic location, this distinction is not an absolute. For example, Jews are generally considered an ethnic group. However, people of Jewish heritage do not share a common geographic location, but rather are spread out across the world. In terms of racial origins, Jews differ considerably. Those who trace their origins to the Middle East may be olive-skinned, while those from Europe tend to be light-skinned. Even in terms of religious practice, there is considerable variation with some professing a belief in atheism yet identifying as part of the Jewish heritage. The Swiss are another example. Although Switzerland is a recognized nation, it is impossible to identify a Swiss ethnic group. Instead, the nation is composed of three distinct ethnic populations: German, Italian and French. These groups maintain their own separate identities, recognizing the others as different.

It is also true that race and ethnicity can overlap with confusing results. Chinese Americans are considered to be both a racial and ethnic group. This is also true for people from Africa and Japan, as well as those from other regions of the world. Confusion results when the classification scheme of one ethnic group overlaps with that of a more dominant culture. Caribbean Hispanics who live in the United States serve as an example. In the Caribbean, race is measured on a continuum with various classifications for darkness. In the United States, racial division is basically black and white. Caribbeans who are mulatto in their native land suddenly find themselves grouped with African Americans when they migrate to the United States. Similarly, they are accepted in white Hispanic communities based on their ethnic heritage, but rejected by whites on the basis of their race.

Despite the confusion, two important points emerge. *First*, as with race, ethnicity is a matter of self-identification and the recognition by others that important cultural differences exist between themselves and other ethnic groups. *Second*, once identified and categorized, ethnicity can become a powerful force for role acceptance and the singling out by others for preferential or discriminatory treatment.

Table 8.1: Projected Population of the U.S by Race and Hispanic Origin: 2000 to 2050

Percent of Population	2000	2010	2020	2030	2040	2050
White Alone, Not Hispanic	69.4	65.1	61.3	57.5	53.7	50.1
Black Alone	12.7	13.1	13.5	13.9	14.3	14.6
Hispanic (of any race)	12.6	15.5	17.8	20.1	22.3	24.4
Asian Alone	3.8	4.6	5.4	6.2	7.1	8.0
All Other Races 1/	2.5	3.0	3.5	4.1	4.7	5.3

1/ Includes American Indian, Alaska Native, Native Hawaiian

Source: U.S. Census, 2004 & 2008, "U.S. Interim Projections by Age, Sex, Race, and Hispanic Origin."

Assimilation and Acculturation

Prior to the 1990s, the United States prided itself on being the "melting pot" of the world. Everyone has heard this expression, but what does it mean? To sociologists, it means a process of **assimilation** or absorption into the dominant culture of recent immigrants. For some, particularly those of Western European descent, this was generally accomplished through **acculturation** or the voluntary adoption of the norms, values and lifestyles of the dominant culture. Immigrants perceived it as a way to speed their acceptance and economic progress. It should be noted, however, that the process of assimilation is not a one-way street. Generally, an **amalgamation** occurs with the dominant culture picking-up some elements—food, clothing, language, and music—from the immigrating group's culture.

For other groups, the process of assimilation was little more than cultural annihilation of their own heritage. Robert Blauner (1972) terms the process **internal colonialism**. Using the analogy of international colonization, Blauner describes a similar process occurring within a society where people are forcibly required to surrender their own culture for that of the dominant culture. The culture of the African slaves and Native Americans serve as examples, both cultures being virtually obliterated by force. Still, other groups have managed to maintain their cultural heritage after immigration. The Amish and Hassidic Jews are two commonly cited examples. Both groups resist intermarriage, live in communities apart or segregated from the influence of the larger community, dress differently and attempt to instill the values of their own heritage in their children.

Minority Groups and Discrimination

In society there is an infinite possibility for group membership based on hair color, weight, height, blood type, skin color, sexual orientation, gender, etc. Not all of these characteristics would qualify the possessor as belonging to a **minority group**. Such status is reserved for those groups singled out by the dominant or more powerful members of society for differential treatment. Thus, minority groups tend to have less power, lower status and little access to economic resources. As such, racial minorities, homosexuals, and the physically challenged would qualify as minorities; red hair or blue eyed individuals would not. Minority group membership also implies more than numerical distinction. Women outnumber men in our society but are still considered by sociologists to be a minority group due mainly to their lack of status and economic power.

The persistence of minority groups in our society can be explained by the forces of prejudice and discrimination. **Prejudice** refers to unfounded or biased attitudes held by one group toward another. These attitudes are rigid and unchanging even when strong conflicting evidence is presented. Neo-Nazis around the world are persistent in their belief that the Holocaust never occurred. Holding firmly to this belief, even in the face of unquestionable documentation—books, films, first hand accounts, etc.—they main-

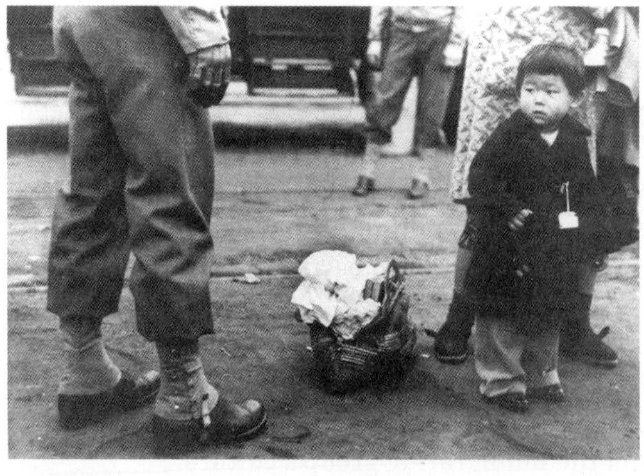

During WWII, many Japanese Americans were confined to concentration camp-like facilities regardless of how long they had been in the U.S. Here, a young Japanese child waits, tagged and packed.

tain that it is a Jewish plot to gain power and special economic treatment. Likewise, some Americans still hold strongly to the notion that racial minorities are genetically inferior to whites.

Problems develop for society when individuals turn their prejudices into actions. This process, termed **discrimination**, results in unfavorable treatment that reinforces minority group status. The processes of discrimination are maintained through a system of **stereotyping**. Here, a particular trait, usually negative, is generalized to all members of a particular group. It reinforces the original prejudice that, in turn, justifies the discriminatory behavior. The process becomes self-perpetuating. For example, the belief in the stereotype that African Americans are lazy and incompetent might keep employers from hiring them. The resulting higher unemployment and welfare rates then confirm the original prejudice of white employers, thus setting the stage for a new round of discriminatory behavior.

Racism describes a particular type of prejudice and discrimination where individuals believe that people are divided into distinct groups based upon heredity. Furthermore, racism upholds that these groups possess innately different mental and physical capabilities allowing them to be ranked on a hierarchical scale.

In general prejudice and discrimination go hand-in-hand, but not always. Robert Merton (1949) attempted to clarify racism by placing people into one of four categories

1. ***Unprejudiced nondiscriminator*** or all-weather liberal, is a confirmed and consistent liberal; is not prejudiced; doesn't discriminate; and believes in the American creed of justice, freedom, equality of opportunity, and dignity of the individual.

2. ***Unprejudiced discriminator*** or fair-weather liberal, thinks in terms of expediency; is not prejudiced but keeps quiet when bigots are about; will discriminate for fear that to do otherwise would hurt business; and makes concessions to the intolerant.

3. ***Prejudiced nondiscriminator*** or timid bigot, doesn't believe in the American creed but conforms to it when the slightest pressure is applied; hates minorities but hires them to obey the law.

TABLE 8.2 Comparative Economic and Social Standing of African Americans in 2008 & 2009

	African Americans	White Americans
median household income	$39,879	$52,115
percent of persons in poverty	24.7	8.2
percent with high school degree	75.4	82.8
percent with four/more years of college	19.3	26.0

Source: U.S. Census Bureau, 2010.

4. ***Prejudiced discriminator*** or all-weather bigot, is a bigot, pure and unashamed; doesn't believe in the American creed and doesn't hesitate to tell others; and believes it is right and proper to discriminate and does so.

RACIAL MINORITIES IN THE UNITED STATES

Present-day barriers to social mobility faced by racial and ethnic minorities have roots embedded deep in history. Only by examining prejudice and discrimination in a historical context can we begin to understand the magnitude of the problem and what is required to resolve it.

African Americans

Unlike all other immigrant groups, African Americans were forcefully brought to this country. By the time of the American Revolution, nearly four million slaves populated the South. Any hope for freedom after the revolution soon evaporated with the writing of the Constitution in 1787, when it became clear that the nation's future rested with the continuation of slavery.

Opposition to slavery came from all quarters. Many who recognized slavery as an economic necessity also recognized it as an evil practice. Slaves themselves opposed their captivity and physical punishment was necessary to force many of them to work. Those who resisted were routinely tortured or killed. Those who attempted to escape were shackled, branded and even castrated. Periodically, slave rebellions occurred—a total of more than 250 before the Civil War, the most famous of which was that led by Nat Turner in 1831. Turner, an African slave, nearly captured Richmond, Virginia, the state capitol. A more subtle form of resistance occurred on a cultural level, with Africans refusing to abandon their own heritage. The development of ragtime, jazz, and blues music serve as an example of the cultural blending that occurred.

With the victory of the North in the Civil War, the practice of slavery was officially abolished in 1865. Moral indignation over slavery was, however, confined primarily to an educated elite and newly freed slaves encountered much hostility in both the North and the South.

Economically, the end of slavery brought little improvement to the lives of African Americans. Needing a continual supply of cheap labor, plantation owners replaced slave labor with a system of share cropping. Here, former slaves continued to work the land in return for a small share of the profits. This practice replaced the type of slavery that was built upon human ownership with one founded on political, economic, and social domination.

With the passage of the 14th and 15th Amendments, guaranteeing respectively, citizenship and the right to vote, African Americans attempted to improve their lot politically. Initially, gains were achieved. A number of African Americans were elected to Congress and many to state offices. This progress alarmed many whites and soon a series of **Jim Crow laws** were enacted to curb the rising tide of black political power and, also, to physically segregate racial minorities from the white population. Also as a result of the Jim Crow laws, voter registration among African Americans declined dramatically, as did representation in political office. In one commonly cited example, black registration to vote in the state of Louisiana fell from slightly over 130,000 to 1,342 in a mere eight years.

Prior to 1900, more than 90 percent of African Americans lived in the South. But disillusioned by prospects, they began migrating to the North in large numbers. Although prejudice and discrimination were encountered there as well, a more industrialized economy offered the promise of better paying jobs. This migration began in the 1920s and continued prior to and after World War II. During this period, over six million African Americans left the South in search of a better life in the North. Today, many have returned and just over half of all African Americans live in the South.

In 1954, nearly ninety years after the end of slavery, the Supreme Court, in the case of *Brown v. Board of Education, Topeka, Kansas*, declared that, "separate educational facilities are inherently unequal." Less than one week after this historical ruling, Brown was being applied to cases involving public

TABLE 8.3 Comparative Economic and Social Standing of Native Americans in 2009

	Native Americans	White Americans
median household income	$33,132	$51,224
percent of persons in poverty	23.6	9.8
percent with high school degree	80.0	85.0
percent with baccalaureate degree	16.0	26.0

Source: American Indian Report, 2010.

beaches, golf courses, buses, dining counters, and more. Although the quest for compliance with Brown proved to be a long and arduous road, and the death of Jim Crow laws did not bring with it the dream of equality, Brown had a huge impact on the lives of African Americans.

Yet, while we no longer have legally sanctioned segregation, **de facto segregation** is a cold, hard fact. Here, races are separated not by law (**de jure segregation**) but by residential patterns. Think about your own neighborhood and consider its racial and ethnic composition. Is it mixed or made-up of people pretty much like yourself? Demographic studies clearly demonstrate that as a nation, we live in communities divided along racial lines. Ironically, the data proves that nowhere is this division more apparent than in northern cities, the very place where African Americans fled with hopes of a better life (U.S. Census, 2000).

Native Americans

In 1969, seventy-eight Indians, mostly college students outraged over the disregard of federal treaties, invaded Alcatraz Island and occupied the abandoned prison for sixteen months. In an attempt to dramatize their case, they offered to purchase the island for $24 in glass beads and red cloth. Furthermore, to demonstrate their honorable intentions, they promised to set aside a portion of the island where Caucasians could live under the protection of the "Bureau of Caucasian Affairs." Although many Americans found the incident humorous, it clearly illustrates the anger and hostilities felt by Native Americans for their position in American society.

Native Americans are perhaps the most overlooked minority in our society. Although it is impossible to know exactly, scholars estimate that there were approximately five hundred separate tribes in North America, with a total population of forty million, by the time the Europeans arrived. By the middle of the nineteenth century that number fell due to a combination of warfare, European diseases, genocide, relocation and poverty, to about 250,000.

Within the last fifty years the number of Native Americans has increased. According to current figures, if one includes Eskimos and Aleuts, the population of Native Americans is about 4.9 million. Forty percent of Native Americans live on reservations and land trusts (American Indian Census Fact, 2008). Also, since the oil embargo of 1973, and the subsequent energy crisis that brought some tribes large sums of money, many Americans have developed a stereotype of affluent reservation life with wealth-laden Native Americans driving Cadillacs. This stereotype is far from reality for the vast majority of Native Americans. The per capita income for Native Americans residing on reservations is nearly one-half of those living in the general population. Furthermore, only half of all Native Americans on reservations have benefited from mineral wealth. For most Native Americans, life remains a precarious and daily struggle for existence (Paisano, 2003).

The current problems of Native Americans are rooted in the nation's history of exploitation. From the beginning, with the arrival of the first whites,

Indians were unable to resist encroachment upon their land. Organized into scattered bands, lacking a common language, and divided by cultural differences, Native Americans were unable to pool their resources and mobilize their power to resist the highly centralized and political military might of the Europeans. At best, their attempts to protect their land amounted to little more than sporadic retaliation. In the end, their story would be one of complete and total victimization. With the conclusion of the Indian Wars in 1880, the fate of Native Americans was exclusively in the hands of the federal government. Under federal control, they were lied to, cheated, robbed, and herded like cattle onto barren reservations far from their homelands. Even then, defeated and humiliated, their subjugation was not complete.

In 1887, Congress, in an attempt to destroy Indian culture, passed the General Allotment Act and with it **Indigenismo**, the singular goal of which was total assimilation of Native Americans into white culture. Under this policy, Indian children were forcibly removed from their homes and taken to government boarding houses, where they were educated and socialized to fit into white industrial society. Perceived correctly as cultural genocide (elimination of a way of life), Native Americans bitterly resisted the program until finally, it was abandoned in 1934 by the Indian Reorganization Act. Today, the thirty-four years of Indigenismo remains a bitter memory for Native Americans.

In the wake of the Civil Rights Movement, Native Americans joined other minorities in expressing their frustration over the procrastination of the federal government in addressing their grievances. In addition to the previously mentioned incident at Alcatraz, others occurred. Perhaps the most dramatic was in late February 1973 when a small band of militant Oglala Sioux led by A.I.M. (American Indian Movement) leaders, occupied the hamlet at Wounded Knee, South Dakota. Historically significant, Wounded Knee was the site of the infamous and senseless slaughter of more than three hundred Sioux, mostly women and children. Wounded Knee marked the end of Indian resistance to white domination in 1890. With the national press looking on, the small band of Indians held authorities at bay for seventy days. Two people were killed and several injured before the occupation ended. Although all that participated were indicted, few were convicted due to legal irregularities in their prosecution.

Police make an arrest during a protest over government immigration policies. Currently, there are some 12 million illegal immigrants in the U.S. constituting 4 percent of the population. Children of immigrants account for approximately 7 percent of the enrollment in elementary and secondary school. Although there is much criticism of illegal immigrants, some economists maintain that the nation could not survive without their labor.

Photo: Nevele Otseog.

Internal disagreements within A.I.M. leadership have led to splits in the organization that, in turn, have severely hindered achievement of gains through political action.

Hispanic Americans

Hispanics or Latinos are comprised of a number of different cultures sharing Spanish or Latin American ancestry and language. Included in this group are Mexican Americans, Puerto Ricans, Cubans, and others. According to U.S. census data, the Hispanic population increased 28 percent, from 35 million in 2000 to over 48.4 million in 2009. With this enormous increase, Hispanics have replaced African Americans as the largest minority population in the United States today, and, according to demographic analysis, this trend will continue. Today, of all children living in the United States, 26 percent are of Hispanic origin. Given these statistics, Hispanics are projected to constitute 30 percent of the nation's population by 2050 (U.S. Census Bureau, 2009).

According to new census data, nearly three-quarters of Hispanics lived in the West or South. Nearly half live in two states: California and Texas. Other states with high Hispanic populations include New York, Florida, Illinois, Arizona, and New Jersey (U.S. Census Bureau, 2009).

Mexican Americans. The disenfranchisement of Mexican Americans closely resembles that of Native Americans. Most Mexicans were initially incorporated into the United States by expansionist military conquest beginning in 1819, when Mexico granted permission to southern Anglo immigrants to settle in its northern region, now Texas. By 1845, Mexico was forced to concede over half of its country to the United States in the Treaty of Guadalupe Hidalgo. Thus, with the stroke of a pen, the United States acquired what is now Arizona, California, Colorado, New Mexico, Texas, Nevada, and Utah, in addition to portions of Kansas, Oklahoma, and Wyoming. Mexican citizens living within the territories were given one year to decide whether to relocate south of the new border or become U.S. citizens. Those who elected to stay were guaranteed full citizenship rights, including the protection of their property and religious rights.

TABLE 8.4 Comparative Economic and Social Standing of Hispanics in 2008 & 2009

	Hispanics	White Americans
median household income	$38,679	$52,115
percent of persons in poverty	24.3	8.2
percent with high school degree	68.1	82.8
percent baccalaureate degree	13.0	26.0

U.S. Census Bureau, 2010.

In June of each year, Puerto Ricans gather for an annual parade to celebrate the culture and heritage of their island. Puerto Ricans now constitute the second largest Hispanic population in the U.S. According to estimates, there are more Puerto Ricans living stateside than on the island itself.

Photo: Oquendo.

In spite of these federal treaties and guarantees, Mexicans soon became the victims of violence, tax schemes, and border disputes. It is generally estimated that four-fifths of Mexican land holdings were transferred into the hands of Anglos. By the end of the century, dispossessed of their land and victimized by prejudice and discrimination, most Mexican Americans would become a poverty-stricken, mobile labor force serving the interests of their Anglo conquerors.

In the decades following, Mexicans crossed the border into the United States in record numbers. For the most part, their presence was a matter of active recruitment by agricultural and mining interests who organized barrio programs that assisted in their migration. Mexicans represented a cheap and exploitable source of labor and possessed a willingness to perform demeaning and dangerous work refused by other ethnic groups.

To date, the conditions of Mexican Americans are unavoidably tied to their past. Over-represented in agriculture, they constitute the second lowest-paid Hispanic sub-group and lag behind most Americans in health, education, employment, and occupational status.

Puerto Ricans. Puerto Rico is a territory of the United States, and its people are American citizens. Therefore, they face no barrier to immigration. The first great wave of Puerto Ricans migrating to the mainland, termed *La Migracion*, occurred after World War II. Most possessed little education, were unskilled agricultural workers and settled in New York City and a handful of other northern industrial cities. Facing language and cultural barriers as well as ethnic prejudice, most have not fared well on the mainland. Yet each year approximately 30,000 more islanders choose to come to the United States. In fact, by the mid 1980s, nearly one-third of the entire population of Puerto Rico has migrated to the U.S. mainland. Over half of all Puerto Ricans living in the United States reside in New York City. Why do Puerto Ricans

Figure 8.1: Composition of the Asian American Population in the U.S.

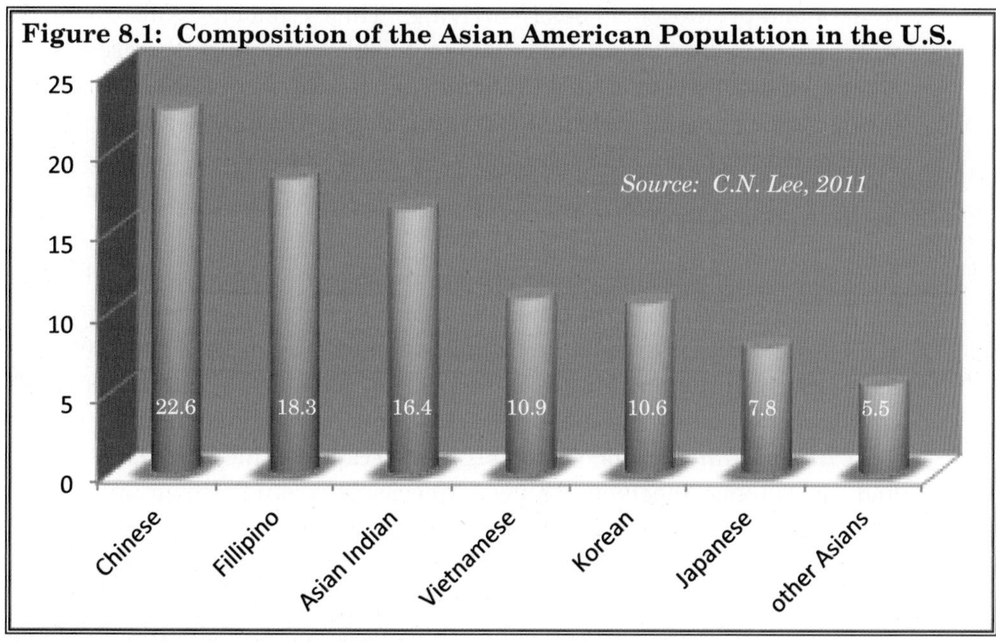

come to America? They migrate mainly for economic reasons. Typically, with an unemployment rate of over 16 percent (Bureau of Labor Statistics, 2011) and median family income of $18,318 per year, Puerto Rico holds little promise for those seeking a better life (U.S. Census Bureau, 2009).

Due to their substantial African ancestry some Puerto Ricans have faced double discrimination—as African Americans and as Hispanics. Of all Hispanic groups, Puerto Ricans are the poorest, with 44 percent living below the poverty line (U.S. Census Bureau, 2008).

Cubans. Historically Cuba and the United States have always had close ties until 1959 when Fidel Castro took control of political power by force and declared Cuba a communist country. The ensuing oppressive ideological and economic State resulted in large numbers of Cubans immigrating to the United States. Although some sought political asylum, most were members of the middle class fleeing economic policies that favored the poor at their expense. The last major migration of Cubans in 1990 saw over 125,000 leave the island. Allowed by Castro to leave and termed *Mariel* immigrants, named after the port from which they departed, the media mistakenly characterized them as refugees from the jails and mental wards. Subsequent information revealed, however, that they were very similar to the first wave of middle class Cuban immigrants.

Most Cubans settled in Miami. On the whole they have fared better than all other Hispanic groups. Due to anti-communistic sentiments in the United States, the government moved quickly to help move these immigrants into the economic mainstream. Nearly three-fourths of all Cubans who immigrated prior to 1974 received some form of government assistance. The real success of Cuban Americans, however, is more a function of their educational and economic status prior to immigration. Many were business leaders and professionals before arriving. Their economic skills combined with political expertise allowed them to quickly reestablish themselves. It should be noted though, that economic figures can be misleading. While faring better than other Hispanics, most Cubans are employed as clerical or semiskilled workers. Likewise, many fall below the poverty line.

Asian Americans

Next to Hispanics, Asian Americans are the fastest growing ethnic group in the United States. Prior to 1990, Asians accounted for less than 1.5 percent of all people immigrating to the United States. Between 1990 and 2000, this figure rose to an astonishing 31 percent. How have Asian Americans fared? In this section we examine a number of ethnic Asian Americans.

Chinese Americans. Attempting to escape famine, the Opium Wars and the Taiping Rebellion, Chinese Americans began arriving in the mid-nineteenth century as a work force for the Transcontinental Railroad and the boom days of the California Gold Rush. Although valued for their work ethic, they faced discrimination similar to that of African Americans after the Civil War. In 1845, the presiding chief justice of the California Supreme Court denied them the right to testify against whites in a court of law. In his ruling he declared the Chinese, "a race of people whom nature has marked as inferior...incapable of progress or intellectual development beyond a certain point."

In 1882, Chinese immigration all but came to a screeching halt with the passage of the first Chinese Exclusion Act. It was not until recently that changes in immigration laws again opened the doors of the United States to the Chinese. As a result, the population of people of Chinese Americans nearly doubled from 1990 to 2004 (Teitelbaum, 2004).

Japanese Americans. The plight of Japanese Americans was only slightly better than their Chinese counterparts. Japan, a world power, was in a better position than China to protect its immigrants from outright discrimination and exploitation. However, during sporadic outbreaks of *yellow phobia*, Japanese immigrants suffered greatly. Perhaps the most tragic incident occurred during World War II, when President Franklin D. Roosevelt signed Executive Order 9066 that stipulated that virtually all Japanese Americans were stripped of citizenship rights and interned in relocation camps. Not only degrading and humiliating, the incident resulted in a substantial loss of property. Although our country was also at war with both Germany and Italy, Americans of neither heritage suffered a similar fate. In December 1944, the Supreme Court ruled that such activity was illegal and abolished the camps. The damage, however, was already done. In being forcefully relocated, Japanese Americans had to sell businesses, homes, furniture and other possessions for pennies on the dollar. Those who attempted to maintain their property while in internment found themselves the victims of politically connected bank foreclosures and shady real estate dealers. In the end, many lost everything. Recognizing the injustice to Japanese Americans, Congress in 1988 provided funds in the amount of $1.2 billion for the 65,000 survivors of the relocation camps.

Despite the many obstacles to success, Japanese Americans have, on the whole, fared better than other racial minorities. In immigrating to the United States, the Japanese were more familiar with the American way of life than their Chinese counterparts. Likewise, strong traditional family ties with close supervision of children resulted in low delinquency rates and a commitment to upward social mobility through hard work and education paid-off. As a result, third and fourth-generation Japanese Americans have had more success assimilating into the dominant culture. Few live in Japanese enclaves and many marry non Japanese Americans. Despite their success,, the Japanese American population has decreased relative to other Asian American groups in the United States.

Even more so than Chinese Americans, Japanese Americans have fared very well economically. On the average both groups have an income twenty to thirty percent above the median income of all American families. These statistics have provided ammunition to some researchers and politicians who argue against providing special consideration or preferential treatment for racial minorities in general. Does such an argument have merit? Not if one examines the data more carefully. Most comparative income studies fail to adjust for the fact that Asian Americans are more highly educated and bring to the labor market a greater sophistication in technical training than the average worker. Adjusting for these differences, we find that in terms of income, Asian Americans fare less favorably than whites with similar qualifications.

New Asian Americans

The most recent census data estimates the Korean population of the U.S. to be about 1.5 million. Of this figure, approximately two-thirds were foreign born (U.S. Census, 2007). Koreans first began coming to the United States in substantial numbers between the mid-1960s and 1970s. Most were well educated and many occupied professional positions such as mathematicians, scientists and doctors in their native land. The early arrivals, facing language barriers and discrimination, were prevented from assuming comparable employment in the United States and were forced into manual labor. After the 1950s, however, a substantial number of Koreans began establishing small businesses and slowly their economic status began to improve. Today, over forty percent of Korean American males are employed in middle and upper level white-collar jobs.

Following the fall of South Vietnam, the United States opened its gates to Vietnamese refuges that sought political asylum. Today there are close to 650,000 Vietnamese Americans. Due to the unique political nature of their entry into the country, the government initially provided support, housing them in special camps and then seeking sponsors to integrate them into jobs and new communities. Although an attempt was made to disperse them, most ended up in California. In addition to the Vietnamese, many Cambodians and Laotians were included in this program. Unlike other Asian immigrants, these groups have not fared well economically. Their lack of success may be attributed to the lack of an established ethnic community to assist them, extreme cultural differences, language barriers and the existence of a weak economy at the time of their arrival. Today many still exist below the poverty line and encounter difficulties obtaining work commensurate with their previous training and educational levels.

Two other immigrant groups that have fared considerably better are Indian and Filipino Americans. Filipino Americans began their exodus from their homeland to the United States in the 1920s when they were recruited to work the sugar plantations in Hawaii. Working twelve-to-fourteen hour days, these immigrants received little more than minimum wage. Despite harsh working conditions, a flow of Filipinos into the United States continued until restrictive immigration laws were passed in 1934. After World War II, a new exodus occurred with many of the arrivals possessing business and professional credentials. Today, Filipino Americans have the second highest income level of all Asian Americans (Le, 2011).

Immigrants from India have also done very well in the United States. Known as Asian Indians (avoiding confusion with American Indians), this group has also encountered discrimination. Fear of cultural differences led to a ban on immigration from India in 1917. However, with passage of the 1965 Immigration Act, over one million Asian Indians have arrived in the United States. As a group they are exceedingly well-educated with nearly sixty-five percent having earned a college degree and twelve percent possessing advanced degrees (Le, 2011).

White Ethnic Americans

The term **white ethnic** refers to those who identify their background as being from nations predominately populated with white people. According to current U.S. Census data, this includes sixty million Germans, thirty-nine million Irish, twelve million Italians, and nine million Poles. Also included are smaller numbers of Greeks, Russians, Slavs, Scandinavians, and others.

Due to the similarity of their culture and race, they assimilated with less difficulty than others. As noted previously, most immigrants from these countries welcomed assimilation. They learned the language, encouraged their children to embrace American culture and, in many cases, changed or shortened their names to more easily fit in. Although they were willing, assimilation was not instantly attained. Early on, religious, economic, and other forms of discrimination led to the development of ethnic enclaves for security and camaraderie. To this date, one can still identify Italian, Irish, Polish, and other white ethnic neighborhoods in major cities.

RACIAL DISCRIMINATION IN THE UNITED STATES

Sociologists have long noted a disparity among races along the important dimensions of income, employment, education, housing, and health. Listed below is a brief summary of how different racial and ethnic groups fare.

Income, Poverty, and Wealth

The most visible measure of status in the United States is income. It is the most widely talked about and easily understood comparison. How do various racial groups stack up? Surprising to many, Asian Americans have the highest family income of all racial groups. In 2008, the average family income for Asian Americans was $64,238 (Le, C.N., 2008). However, this figure is misleading. First, Asian Americans, as a group, are better educated and work more hours. Additionally, they tend to live in extended families and have more family members employed which boosts their family income. Also, the median household income differed greatly by Asian group. For example, the median income of Asian Indians in 2006 was $69,470; for Vietnamese-Americans, it was $45,980. (U.S. Census Bureau, 2006). Among Asians the percentage with at least a high school diploma ranged from 47.3 percent for Hmongs to 91 percent for Japanese. And the percentage of Asians with at least a bachelor's degree varied from 9.2 percent or less for Cambodians, Laotians, and Hmongs to 64.4 percent for Asian Indians (Le, 2011).

Comparisons of white, African American, and Hispanic family income levels demonstrate a clear advantage for whites. In 2008, the average family income for whites was $52,115 while for African Americans and Hispanics it was $39,878 and $40,446 respectively. In other words, white family income was more than 75 percent more than that of African Americans and Hispanics (U.S. Census, 2009).

In terms of poverty levels, all racial minority groups exceed that of whites. Again, the figures can be misleading since the majority of people living below the poverty line are white. Minorities however, are over-represented in poverty statistics in relationship to their percentage of the population. In fact, minorities are nearly two and a half times more likely to live in poverty. Government statistics for 2008 reveal that 8.2 percent of whites live below the poverty line. For African Americans and Hispanics it is 24.7, and 23.2, respectively (U.S. Census, 2009). Of all groups, Native Americans are the poorest ethnic group in the United States. Overall, their poverty rate is 23.8 percent, and for those living on reservations, the rate exceeds fifty percent (American Indian Report, 2010). According to the most recent statistics, 43 percent of Native Americans under the age of five live in poverty (U.S. Census Bureau, 2001 and U.S. Bureau of the Census, 2006).

Another interesting comparison of economic discrimination is wealth. Perhaps of all measures it is the most devastating. **Wealth** refers not to income (although income can be used to acquire wealth), but to what one owns (property and capital). It would be difficult, if not impossible, to draw an exact comparison within the limits of this text. However, an interesting comparison may be made in terms of a dollar—for every dollar of average net worth (wealth) held by a white household, African American and Hispanic households own a little over seven cents (Domhoff, 2010). This astounding difference amplifies the reason racial minorities are particularly hard hit by economic recessions since they do not have the cushion of wealth to fall back on and tide them over until better times. Likewise, differences in wealth can be a hindrance to upward social mobility. As stated by one author, "wealth begets wealth. When you do not have it, you cannot play the game (Braun, 1997)."

Education

For those without access to inherited wealth, the route to upward social mobility in the United States has historically been education. Certainly this is not the only means to achieve economic success, but the correlation between educational attainment and income is very strong. It is precisely for this reason that sociologists are interested in educational inequality or differing educational opportunities presented to different groups in our society. Prior to *Brown v. Board of Education*, racial minorities were denied access to quality education by means of **de jure segregation**. With the elimination of de jure (legal) segregation and the Civil Rights Movement of the 1960s, racial minorities were able to make some gains. However, the disparity of educational opportunities between whites and racial minorities continues to be substantial.

According to current educational data, the high school dropout rate for Hispanics between 16 and 24 years-of-age is four times higher than for white students. For Native American students the rate is three times higher and for African Americans it is twice that of their white counterparts (U.S. Department of Education, 2010).

Additionally, for all Hispanics ages 20 and older in the U.S., 41 percent do not have a regular high school diploma, versus 23 percent for comparable aged blacks and 14 percent of whites (Fry, 2010).

College attendance statistics reveal an interesting pattern. According to the most recent data, the racial gap among high school graduates enrolling in higher education has narrowed dramatically. For whites the enrollment rate was 69.2 percent. For blacks and Hispanics it was 68.7 and 59.3 percent respectively (U.S. Department of Labor, 2010). However, when looking at the statistics for college graduation, the racial gap reappears. 29.9 percent of whites graduated while blacks and Hispanics graduated at 19.3 and 13.2 percent respectively (U.S. Census, 2010).

The primary cause of this disparity is a result of inferior K-12 preparation and an absence of family college tradition. However, economics also plays a major role. Of students who dropped out, 69 percent of blacks listed concern over high loan debt in comparison to 43 percent of white students (The Journal of Blacks in Higher Education, 2011). Additionally, other factors contribute to the problem including: lower per-pupil expenditures, language barriers, nutritional deficiencies, teen pregnancy, lack of tutoring

Table 8.5 Occupations with the Highest Concentration by Race/Ethnicity/Sex

African American Women	Social workers, postal clerks, dietitians, child-careworkers and teacher's aides, private household cooks and cleaners, nursing aides and orderlies
African American Men	Vehicle washers and equipment cleaners, bus drivers, concrete workers, guards, sheriffs, bailiffs, and other law enforcement positions
Hispanic Women	Private household cleaners and servants, child-care workers, janitors and cleaners, health service occupations, sewing machine operators
Hispanic Men	Janitors and cleaners, construction trades, machine operators, cooks, drivers, laborers and helpers, roofers, groundskeepers, gardeners, farm and agricultural workers
White Women	Physical therapists, dental hygienists, secretaries, bookkeepers, accounting and auditing clerks
White Men	Marketing, advertising, public relations managers, engineers, architects, surveyors, dentists, firefighters, construction supervisors, tool-and-die makers
Asian Women	Marine-life workers, electrical assemblers, dressmakers, laundresses
Asian Men	Physicians, engineers, professors, technicians, cooks, laundry workers, longshore equipment operators
Native American Women	Welfare aides, child-care workers, teacher's aide, forestry workers (except logging)
Native American Men	Marine-life workers, hunters, forestry workers (except logging), fishing

Source: Household Data Annual Averages Table 11, employment by industry, sex, race, and occupation, 2009.

and other support facilities, necessity of working outside of school and many more. All of these, of course, relate to existing patterns of discrimination in society for students from families of lower socioeconomic status.

As we have already indicated, the link between educational attainment and income is strong. When race and gender intersect, gender adds an additional dimension. Among those holding a bachelor's degree, white women earned 67 percent of what white men earned while African American and

Hispanic women were 75 percent and 62 percent respectively (U.S. Census Bureau, 2006). Some researchers explain the disparity by pointing out that women select lower status jobs and work fewer hours than men. Others maintain that socialization and gender bias prevents women from entering jobs and professions dominated by men. Also, the amount of time a woman can devote to her job is limited by childrearing responsibilities. And finally, as we shall see in the next section on employment, African Americans and Hispanics with college degrees have higher rates of unemployment than do whites holding the same credentials.

Employment

The two factors that must be considered under this heading are unemployment and type of employment. Unemployment rates vary according to the economy. However, for African Americans and Hispanics, unemployment is always higher than it is for whites. In 2010, white unemployment was 8.8 percent while unemployment among African Americans was 16.5 percent and that for Hispanics it was 12.6 percent. This statistic held true even for minorities with college degrees (Rosenberg, 2010). And, as one might suspect, the unemployment rate for minority youth was even greater. The percentage of white youth unemployed was 16.2 percent compared to 33.4 percent for African American youths and 22.1 for Hispanic youths (Bureau of Labor Statistics, 2010).

The simple fact of having a job does not tell the entire story of discrimination in employment. One must also examine the types of jobs different groups are capable of securing. On this point, study after study has demonstrated that racial minorities, more so than whites, find themselves channeled into dead-end jobs with no prospect for advancement. This is particularly true with the recent change from a manufacturing-based economy to one based on service. As such, today one-fourth of all African American and Latino workers find themselves chained to the lower rungs of the occupational ladder. Consider the following data: Approximately ten percent of the work force in the United States is African American. However, African Americans comprise 31 percent of nursing aides and orderlies, 25 percent of all taxi drivers, 25 percent of hotel maids, and 22 percent of all janitors. On the flip side, they are seriously under represented in more prestigious fields, for example: only 3.2 percent in law, three percent in medicine and 3.2 percent in engineering. The picture for Latinos parallels that of African Americans (U.S. Bureau of the Census, 2002). The importance of employment is underscored by its relationship to issues we have discussed. The inability to obtain employment beyond a subsistence level forecloses on one's ability to secure housing in a decent neighborhood. This in turn affects the quality of education one can provide their children, which in turn affects the ability of their children to obtain meaningful employment in the future. It is, as one can easily see, a vicious cycle. Additionally, nutritional and health benefits are negatively affected by poor employment, which in turn, reinforces the above pattern.

Health

In a capitalistic economy such as ours, health care is operated on a for-profit basis. This is true of health care providers, hospitals, pharmaceutical companies and other ancillary businesses associated with health care supplies and services. It then comes as no surprise to find that the distribution of health care in the United States is skewed in favor of the financially well-to-do. The consequence is that on every possible measure, a direct relationship is found between health and poverty. Furthermore, since race and poverty intersect, racial minorities are less likely than whites to receive treatment for serious illnesses. One study found that white patients were more likely to receive bypass surgery than either African American or Latino patients. Similarly, in treatment following a heart attack, white patients were more likely to be given cardiac catheterization (a test to determine the extent of blood vessel blockage) than black patients (JAMA, 2007).

This lack of treatment is further seen in a number of comparisons between African Americans and whites. First, the average life expectancy for white men is 73.6 years—for African American men it is 66.1 years. A similar comparison between women reveals that white women live an average of four years longer than African American women do (AOA, 2010). The rate of African American infant mortality is 2.5 times that of white babies. In part, this is accounted for by low birth-weight due to poor nutrition and lack of prenatal care (National Center for Health Statistics, 2007).

Finally, studies reveal that minority children are less likely to receive routine medical attention. Since early detection is crucial to avoiding long term illness, this only serves to explain earlier death rates among minorities (U.S. National Center for Health Statistics, 2001).

SOCIOLOGICAL THEORIES ON RACIAL INEQUALITY

Sociologists have attempted to explain why racial inequality exists. Three basic theories have emerged for our consideration.

Deficiency Theories

The basic foundation of deficiency theories lies in genetics. Early theories postulated that whites were mentally superior to other racial groups and therefore their achievements and dominance were simply a matter of natural selection (Social Darwinism: Herbert Spencer). Again, as the science of sociology developed, these early theories were dismissed. However, the basic tenets of this theory have resurfaced in the works of Arthur Jensen (1969) and Richard Herrnstein (1973). Focusing on data from standardized IQ tests, Jensen speculates that approximately eighty percent of intelligence is inherited while twenty percent is a result of life experience. Because African Americans consistently score lower on IQ tests, Jensen suggests the possibility of genetic differences in intelligence between the two racial groups.

Figure 8.2: Myrdal's Principle of Cumulation

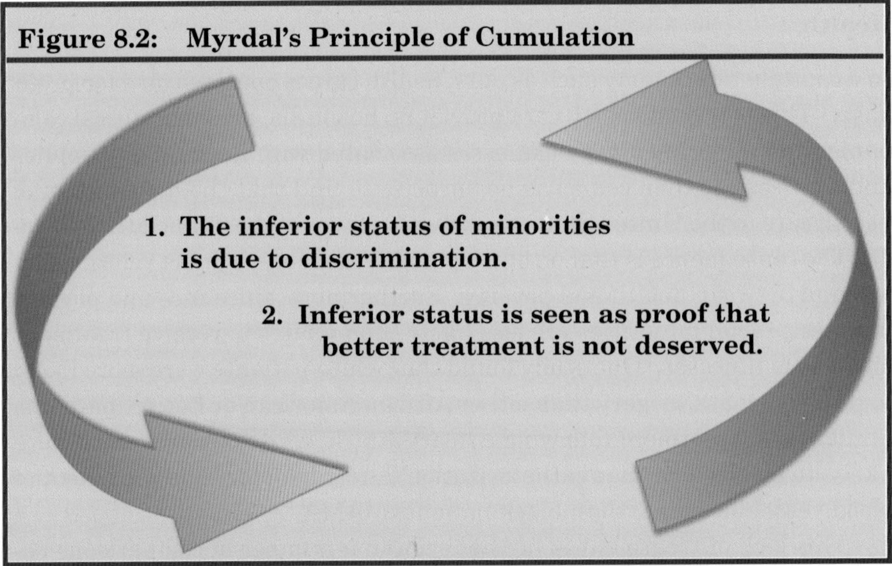

With the support of this data, Herrnstein carries his hypothesis one step further by suggesting that stratification is maintained through the self-selecting process in courtship and marriage. Members of a group tend to select marriage partners from within their own group—**endogamy**. If one subscribes to the theory that most of intelligence is inherited and that African Americans are intellectually inferior to whites, then through endogamy, the inferior status of African Americans is destined to be passed on to succeeding generations.

Few scientists today accept these theories. IQ tests are a suspect tool because they do not necessarily measure what is important to succeed, for example, motivation, work ethic, creativity, etc. Also, all tests, including IQ, are culturally biased in that they use language and experiences more familiar to the dominant social group and as such, disadvantage minorities.

Bias Theories

A leading proponent of the bias theory was Gunnar Myrdal (1944). In his classic work, *An American Dilemma*, Myrdal carefully investigated racism in the United States and concluded that it was the result of prejudiced attitudes held by the white majority. According to Myrdal, prejudices are transformed into discrimination via stereotyping. Members of the minority group are denied access to the same opportunities in education, housing, employment, political office and health care, unlike those in the dominant culture. This leads to failure that further reinforces the belief that racial minorities are inferior. Thus a new round of discrimination is set into motion. Myrdal termed this the **principle of cumulation**. Figure 8.2 presents a graphic illustration of this concept.

Structural Theories

Proponents of structural theories maintain that the focus of bias theories is too narrow and fails to explain the behavior of many whites that are not overtly prejudiced against minorities, but still defend a system that negatively affects the welfare of racial minorities. To understand the structural theory of discrimination, one must first distinguish between individual and institutional racism. **Individual racism** is overt and direct. Here individuals hold extreme prejudices and act in discriminatory ways. An example of individual racism would be the stoning of the home of an African American family who has moved into an all-white neighborhood. The use of racial slurs and denying an individual employment due to his/her race would be further examples. Individual racism, generally associated with lower class, uneducated whites is declining and viewed by most Americans as unacceptable.

Interestingly enough even though individual racism is on the decline the position of racial minorities shows little improvement. Why? Structural theorists maintain that the answers lie in the effects of institutional racism, a form of racism more injurious to racial groups than that which is directed by individuals. **Institutional racism** is deeply embedded in the customs and operational practices of society and prevents racial minorities from moving out of their subordinate positions and into the economic and social mainstream. Likewise, those who practice institutional racism generally don't resort to individual acts of racism and would abhor those who do. But in supporting the present institutions of society and their customs and operational practices these individuals, while not recognizing it, play a major role in the perpetuation of racism. The following are just a few examples of institutional racism.

1. ***The use of IQ or standardized testing in the selection of job applicants***. As we have seen, standardized tests contain bias—bias that favors the selection of members of the dominant group. This is true because such tests contain language and cultural experience that favors the dominant cultural group. Likewise, many employers utilize tests that have little or no connection to the job the applicant will be required to do. For example, relying on a written test to select police officers. Who is most likely to score higher as a group—whites or racial minorities? Does scoring higher on a test guarantee that one will be a better police officer than the other? Or are other skills, such as honesty, courage, commitment, etc., more critical to the performance of the job?

2. ***The use of seniority systems in the promotion and firing of employees***. The use of seniority, or the number of years one has worked at his or her job, is pervasive in both the private and public sector of our economy. On the surface it appears unbiased and most

Americans would readily support it as a fair means to either promote or terminate employees during periods of personnel reduction. However, racial minorities are most likely to suffer when seniority is utilized. Due to discrimination they are generally the ones with the least seniority, and as such, are the last to be promoted and the first to be terminated.

3. ***Recruiting job applicants from selective colleges and universities.*** Companies and recruiting officials compete yearly for the best graduates. In many cases, the recruiting effort is restricted to highly regarded universities and colleges with name recognition. The assumption is that students from these institutions are superior in both intellect and training. Needing qualified employees, few personnel officials would consider this discriminatory. After all, talent is needed for the company to survive in global markets. But who normally attends such institutions? With a disproportionate percent of their population below the poverty line, few racial minorities have the opportunity to study at a prestigious institution.

4. ***Support for a fragmented educational system.*** Ultimately, the state is legally responsible for education. To fulfill this responsibility, the state has created school districts and then, passed funding responsibility on to those districts. Districts in turn tax citizens of their district (generally in the form of property taxes) to support the school system. It is at this point that race and class overlap to create rich and poor schools. White middle and upper class students receive a disproportionate share of educational resources at the expense of working and lower class children. Since education is a major component in future success, the quality of education dramatically affects economic and social mobility. Attempts to alter the pattern by changing district boundary lines, busing or more progressive taxing systems have encountered strong resistance. The general reply is, "Why do we have to have *these* kids in our schools," or "Why do we have to pay for *their* kids education?"

5. ***Giving preferential treatment to job applicants with advanced or baccalaureate degrees.*** Given the current financial situation of many minorities, their limited access to good elementary and secondary schools, and the statistics that confirm that far fewer minorities attempt, as well as finish, advanced degrees, it should be fairly obvious that awarding preferential treatment for job applicants with advanced degrees only further promotes members of the dominant culture and hinders minority access to mainstream economic and social mobility.

SOCIOLOGICAL PERSPECTIVES

Structural Functional

For structural functionalists, stratification between minorities and whites is simply a matter of assimilation. They anchor their argument in the experiences of immigrating white ethnics. These groups came to the United States and blended into the great melting pot making a life for themselves and their children by adopting the values of the dominant society. Most arriving immigrants began working at undesirable jobs—those with poor working conditions and low pay. Such jobs have always existed and will, quite naturally, be performed by the least fortunate—those with little education, language and job skills. It was only natural that new immigrants would fit this bill. However, over time, through hard work and education, white ethnics moved up the social ladder to assume better jobs with more prestige and money.

Structural functionalists argue that the inability of certain racial groups to assimilate is due to their different cultural values. They propose that once these groups adopt the prevailing values of the dominant culture, they, like white ethnics, will assimilate. To support their position, they point to certain Asian American groups (Japanese, Korean, Chinese, etc.) who occupy positions of prestige and power in American society. Furthermore, they point out, not all members of any racial group are economically disadvantaged. Those who have chosen to adopt dominant values have found economic and social success.

Finally, structural functionalists point out that the process of assimilation is of value to society. The stability of society rests upon the development and acceptance of a common culture. It allows society to function smoothly because its members share common ideas, values, and beliefs. Structural functionalists are also quick to point out that the process is not a one-way street where new members must totally submit to the values of the dominant culture. Rather, through the process of amalgamation subculture traits are blended with the dominant culture. Likewise, while assimilation and amalgamation occur, there is still room for an appreciation and an acceptance of cultural diversity where distinct subculture traits of ethnic and racial groups are tolerated as long as differences do not prove dysfunctional.

Social Conflict

Social conflict theorists would agree with structural functionalists that undesirable jobs are a necessary reality of society. Likewise, they would agree that the less educated and unskilled perform these jobs. However, they depart from the structural functionalist explanation of racial inequality.

Social conflict theory suggests that it is not so much a matter of assimilation, but rather, one of power and subordination. Whites have positions of power and seek to maintain their positions by subordinating members of racial groups. The subordinated groups are denied access to quality

A Hispanic youth is lead away by police. Today, 68 percent of the U.S. prison population is comprised of racial or ethnic minorities. A wide variety of factors account for this; one being a discriminatory system. Studies show minorities are five times more likely to be incarcerated and receive longer sentences than whites for the same crime.

Photo: Chris Yarzab.

education, housing, job advancement and health care, all of which create a perpetuating cycle of poverty. This cycle ensures that those in power and their children will maintain their advantage in society. The claims of structural functionalists that certain racial groups or members have assimilated are dismissed by social conflict theorists who argue that these groups or individuals are, in reality, paid less, work harder and occupy less prestigious positions than whites possessing similar qualifications.

The bottom line for social conflict theorists is that racial minorities were never meant to assimilate. Historically, they were brought to the United States to perform undesirable jobs and have been kept in a subordinate position by racial prejudice and discrimination. Evidence of this institutionalized pattern of prejudice and discrimination is seen in studies demonstrating a higher degree of prejudice between various ethnic groups (U.S. Bureau of the Census, 1992) and lower income whites in comparison to middle and upper class whites (McDermott, 2006). Social conflict theorists argue that this tension serves to maintain the status quo by focusing attention away from the real problem of inequality: the system. As long as various groups continue to fight amongst themselves, usually for "table scraps", the powerful have little to fear (Hamilton, 1995).

SUMMARY: THE COST OF DISCRIMINATION

The costs of discrimination are many. On an individual level it has physical and psychological costs. The desire to lead a productive and comfortable life is germane to all, regardless of our racial or ethnic background. To accomplish this we must compete against others for scarce resources. This is the nature of capitalism, an economic arrangement that this nation advocates as the best of all possible alternatives. Capitalism is in essence a commanding ideological principle of this society. While this may not be the easiest system, we are guaranteed that the process will be fair, allowing each of us to compete on equal footing. Are we not the land of equal opportunity?

Unfortunately, the practices of the society do not live up to its ideals. For some, the competition is not fair. Picture for a moment a foot race. All contestants are lined-up on the track in a position that puts them at an equal distance from the finish line. For a brief time all is equal. Suddenly, a man carrying a twenty-five pound weight appears. He moves to one of the contestants and straps it to their back. The gun sounds; the race begins. Who is most likely not to win? For many of our citizens, those of color, this is precisely what competition in the United States is like. For them, race is the invisible weight they must carry through life as they attempt to compete for the financial resources to provide adequate housing, education, medical care and other services for themselves and their families. As such, for many in our society, there is little hope that their efforts will be rewarded in the same manner as others.

Also, for the victims of racism, there are psychological costs. Each and every one of us wants the respect of others. Everyone needs to feel the warm comfort of self-worth. This is a human need and as real as the physical needs for food, clothing and shelter. Think back on our discussions of personality development. Without question, socialization plays a major role. Hence, the images society presents to us from birth on are powerful forces that shape our view of ourselves. Is it possible for members of the minority to develop positive self-images when members of the majority label them as inferior? Is it not understandable when many of those who have been thus labeled, quit trying? The answer to this question is yes, it is understandable. For, if one understands the process of socialization, then one also understands its effects.

It would be erroneous to believe that the cost of racism is confined to its victims. Society also bears a substantial cost. First, racism is a major barrier to inter group communication and cooperation. As we have seen, society is a collection of many diverse groups who cooperate with each other despite cultural differences. As we have also seen, for society to function smoothly, the various members of society must share a common belief system founded upon an acceptable ideology. When the belief system begins to break down, social conflict is inevitable. For example, the 1991 riot sparked by the beating of Rodney King resulted in the deaths of 54 persons, caused more than 10,000 injuries, destroyed over 1,000 buildings and cost one billion tax-payer dollars (Time, 2008). And this is only one of scores of riots experienced in the United States. Added to this is the enormous cost of crime; murders, thefts and assaults. Additionally, society bears the cost of individual problems—drug abuse, alcoholism, medical costs for the poor, child neglect, etc. The roots of most of these problems can be traced to poverty. In turn, racism is clearly the gateway to poverty. Take for example the startling fact that while African Americans comprise only about 13 percent of the population, they account for nearly half of all prisoners. Viewed another way, on any given day in America, 1 out of 8 African American men between the age of 18 to 34 are in jail or prison (Butterfield, 2003). Today, there are more African American men incarcerated in penal institutions than colleges and universities. The cost of keeping one man in prison is approximately $40,000 per year. This cost, as well as all of the above, are borne by society as a whole. Is racism really worth the cost?

Finally, there is the compelling issue of self-interest to end racism. No longer can a nation stand alone. It is a global world and a global economy. To survive we need the talents of all of our citizens. Consider the talent squandered in the ghetto. When children become gang members and welfare recipients instead of doctors, engineers, architects, painters, teachers, computer operators, medical technicians, etc., we all lose.

According to demographic experts, by the year 2050, the United States will become a nation of color. Whites will no longer represent a numerical majority. Although no one can foresee the future, it is clear that there is a fork in the road ahead—one leading to harmony and success, the other to disintegration and failure.

Terms You Should Know:

Race
Assimilation
Amalgamation
Discrimination
Indigenismo
Ethnicity
Mariel Immigrants
Internal Colonialism
Prejudice
Endogamy
Ethnic Identity
Wealth
Minority Group
Stereotyping
White Ethnic

Can You Answer These Questions?

1. Why do social scientists claim that race is a cultural construct?
2. What is the difference between the terms race and ethnicity?
3. According to your text, what is the difference between prejudice and discrimination?
4. On what basis do we differentiate between "dejure" and "defacto" discrimination?
5. Of all the minority groups in the United States, which is the poorest?
6. According to current statistics, what is the largest racial minority in the United States?
7. What is the distinguishing factor differentiating between assimilation and internal colonialism?
8. Of Asian immigrants, which ethnic group is the fastest growing population in the United States?
9. List figures comparing minority groups to whites for income, poverty, education, and health.
10. What is the basic premise of the following theories: deficiency, bias, structural?
11. How does individual racism differ from institutional racism? Give examples.
12. Structural functionalist and social conflict theorists acknowledge that racial stratification is a reality in society. How do they account for it?

Critical Thinking Exercises:

1. Why might some consider "defacto" discrimination more destructive than "dejure" discrimination?
2. There are some in our society that believe that promoting racial and ethnic diversity is divisive and harmful for society. Instead, they suggest we should encourage minorities and new immigrants to embrace the dominant culture. What do you think?
3. How harmful are racial or ethnic jokes in our society? If you were in the presence of someone telling a racial joke, what do you think would be an appropriate response?
4. Considering Robert Merton's four classifications of racism, where would you place most people in the United States?
5. Do you believe that eventually the world will evolve into one race?

Photo: Anja Disseldorp

Everyday Sociology 7th Edition

Chapter 9

Unraveling Sex and Gender

Someone once said (source unknown) that learning from the past provides hope for the future. Suffragist leader Susan B. Anthony (1820-1806) once proclaimed of the U.S., "This government is not a democracy...it is an odious aristocracy." Anthony, a Quaker, not only dedicated her life to fighting for women's voting rights, which became known as "The Cause," but also rallied sentiments condemning slavery in the U.S. Her early accomplishments paved the way for the eventual passage of the 19th amendment in 1920, fourteen years after her death.

Among the others who joined Anthony, who was later dubbed the Napoleon of the Women's Movement, was Elizabeth Caddy Stanton (1815-1902) the first president of the National Women's Suffrage Association. Stanton, according to reports, was long occupied with the legal relations between men and women and when she married abolitionist Henry Brewster Stanton in 1840, she insisted that the word "obey" be dropped from the vows the couple exchanged. Another early crusader, Lucretia Mott (1793-1880), was born into a Quaker family in Massachusetts. In her own words, she was "thoroughly imbued in women's rights" from an early age. By 1818, she was serving as a Quaker minister, accompanied by her husband who supported her activism, and organizing women's abolitionist societies. Often, the Mott's offered shelter to runaway slaves in their own home.

In the realm of American political life, it has become clear that women have steadily been stepping out of traditional roles and attempting to shatter the vaulted glass-ceiling of America's elite politi-

Hillary Clinton lost her bid to become the Democratic presidential nominee in 2008. Afterwards, she was appointed Secretary of State in President Obama's cabinet.

Photo: Clinton Campaign, 2008.

cal power structure. Moving to the front of the line, more and more women are offering their names as candidates for elected office and succeeding. No better example of this can be seen than Hillary Clinton's attempt to capture her party's nomination for President of the United States. Although falling short of her quest, she captured over 17 million votes and narrowly lost to the eventual winner, Barack Obama. She is now Secretary of State. Another example of women attempting to step up to our highest governmental offices is seen in Sarah Palin's vice presidential bid. In accepting the party's nomination, she became only the second woman in history to run for the office of Vice President of the United States (Garaldine Ferraro lost her bid in 1984).

On January 1, 2007, Nancy Pelosi became the first woman to assume the powerful position of Speaker of the House, second in line for presidential succession. In other top elected governmental positions for the 112th Congress, six women are serving as governors of their state, 17 women serve as senators in the U.S. Senate, and 74 women occupy seats in the U.S. House of Representatives. Another example, at the state level, and one lost in all of the excitement of the 2008 presidential race, was the historical election in New Hampshire which became the first state to elect a female majority to their legislature with 13 of its 24 senate seats being occupied by women.

Women are also being appointed to the highest positions in presidential cabinets. Madeleine Albright was appointed by President Clinton in 1996 as the first female Secretary of State, perhaps the most prestigious position in the presidential cabinet. Condelessa Rice followed with her appointment by George W. Bush as the first African American female Secretary of State in 2005. And most recently, after being bitter rivals in the Democratic primary, Barack Obama selected Hillary Clinton to serve as his Secretary of State,

In spite of these accomplishments, women are still woefully underrepresented in government. Evidence of this is that while constituting over 50 percent of our population, women today occupy only 16 percent of the nations top elected positions.

In business, more and more women are moving up the corporate ladder. But here again, the story is similar to that in the political arena; the progress is painfully slow. In fact, progress here looks to be even slower. As of 2008, only eight women were listed as CEOs of Fortune 500 companies. Even more startling is the prediction by several of the nation's top researchers that the number of women who will rise to top corporate positions in America will increase by only five to six percent by the year 2016 (New York Times, 2008). While the saying goes "You've come a long way, baby," it is clear that the real saying should be, "Baby, the road ahead is very, very long."

This chapter will explore the sociology of sex and gender. Together we will explore questions pertaining to sex and gender issues that impact current everyday life in politics, sports, entertainment, and the corporate world, as well as others. Consider this question—have recent changes in attitude, and treatment of individuals based on gender, improved relations in the workforce? The same question can be asked regarding sports, medicine and other sciences, the business world, home life, dating, marriage and family, and religion.

Evolution of Change

The winds of the 1960s brought with them some radical changes and new traditions. While there were fence-straddlers and middle-of-the-roaders that could be characterized as taking the path of least resistance and sticking to tradition because it was a more comfortable blanket, many people welcomed the winds of change and adapted to a new attitude in the post 50s, 60s, and 70s.

As a result of civil action brought on by the Women's, Civil Rights, and Gay and Lesbian Movements, Americans today continue to challenge the patriarchs. Many view our patriarchal society as a phenomenon whose time has come and gone. And yet, so many questions still remain:

Should the opposite sex be allowed to work in institutions such as all male or female prisons—or allowed to coach opposite sex athletic activities? Is gender equity a valid concern? Haven't women always been subordinate in status? Why were many of the contributions of females such as noted anthropologist Margaret Mead, Susan B. Anthony, Jane Adams, Elizabeth Cady Stanton, Lucretia Mott, Sojourner Truth, and others ignored for so long? How are gender roles reflected in the values and economics of our society? How many of you male students feel that you can compete with professional women athletes? Is America the only country grappling with sex and gender and age and race and other diversity issues? How many male students enroll in a course on Women's studies or Women's literature? Better yet, how many educational institutions offer courses in Women's U.S. History?

Overview

Sex and gender conjure up different images and meanings across cultures and also within cultures. Today, the boundaries between what is considered to be "normal" sex and what is deviant or kinky, are much fuzzier than they were during the tranquil decades of the 1950s and 60s. Recently, the way that determines how individuals think of themselves as male or female, in accordance with the cultural norms associated with those roles, has raised new and perhaps troubling questions as we begin a new century where demographics change daily. The traditional view that the major breadwinners and ultimate decision-makers are male is being challenged in all arenas as we carve new definitions and boundaries that guide everyday living in the 21st century. Working outside of the home allowed women to keep their children fed and clothed and the nation was able to continue to function.

It was tradition for the husband/father to identify with his job while a wife's identity was established via her husband and the children she produced. The wife/mother inherited the responsibility to fulfill the role expectations of motherhood, associated with and primarily responsible for the rearing of children. Society then reinforced and encouraged the images of wife as the happy homemaker and husband as the breadwinner through its socializing agents. Still other questions remain. How would you account for the change in sex and gender roles? Is it the result of legislation, moral conscience, movements, or attitude adjustments?

Media, education, politics, and economics, family, religion, and peers influence how we view ourselves and others in terms of expectations associated with gender roles. How we see ourselves has a profound impact on women's status and the dominance of males in most industrialized societies. All societies adopt certain expectations for men and women, just as they do for children and adults. Traditionally, American society did indeed expect father to know best. Tradition posited that it was normal for men to view and possess women for their beauty rather than their intelligence, talents, professional qualities and accomplishments, all of which were considered to be of secondary importance.

Traditionally, war was the domain of men. Women did not participate in any direct way in militias. They had no role in the decision-making that involved us in war or kept us out of the same. They served in supportive roles only. But in the last 20 years, starting with the Gulf War, women have taken a more direct role in serving our country. Most recently, in Iraq, over 100 women have lost their lives and many more have been injured (icasualties.org 2008).

However unfortunate, privileges in most societies are tilted in favor of adult males. In most western industrialized societies the laws, ordinances, and sanctions protecting these privileges are governed by the white Anglo-Saxon protestant males. It is this same WASPM group that made, enforced and continued to produce the laws, ordinances, and sanctions that keep them in their positions of power and wealth, usually at the expense of others in society. Other nonindustrialized, third world, and Asian nations are not exempt from patriarchal dominance. In reviewing our history, one cannot help but question how far we've actually come and wonder how much further we have to go in our quest for equality.

In classroom polling during the last edition of this textbook, both men and women remain unclear on what constitutes sexual harassment and see it as vague and complicated. Some men don't see what the big deal is, and a considerable number of women are still angry because, "some men (and some women) just don't get it."

It is not that simple. Sexual harassment is a highly complex issue mired in socialization issues on both sides. Adherence to traditional or nontraditional values, gender roles, and also, sexuality, all play a part in what we see, or don't see, as sexual harassment. As many would admit, there was a time when *no* didn't always mean no. Instead, it was often left open to interpretation and perceived to mean, "I don't know if I really want to." When it came to sex, women were taught to say no; only bad girls said yes! Today, we want no to mean no. But for some men, the question still exists: is it really no? Advocates against date rape and other acts of sexual violence want people to understand that today, "No, really does mean NO!"

The scope of sexuality, however, is much broader than sexual harassment. Other facets related to the concept of sexuality (often forms of sexual deviance), can include sexual orientation, date rape, sexual predators, pedophiles and serial rapists, spouse and child abuse, "sexploitation," pornography and other types of prostitution.

This chapter is divided into four major sections. Section one will focus on the biological, psychological, and sociological perspectives with regard to sexuality and gender roles. The second section will explore the impact that socializing agents have on gender and gender roles in our society, and how they contribute to sexism, sexual harassment, and gender differences. In section three we will explore sexuality and deviance with specific focus on the issues of sexual orientation and domestic violence. The fourth section will explore sexual harassment. A slightly different approach to the usual bars, graphs, and statistics is presented in narrative form in the summary of this chapter to present progress made in the last several years.

BIOLOGICAL AND PSYCHOLOGICAL PERSPECTIVES

Biological Explanation

The biological perspective has its roots in physiology, instinctive behavior, and the natural order of things. Scientists who espouse this explanation of male-and-femaleness believe that behavior may be programmed through our genetic makeup and passed down from one generation to the next via heredity. Additionally, they uphold that body and brain chemistry may help define our sex and gender roles.

Conversely, a number of us use words like sex and gender synonymously or interchangeably. Despite parallels having been drawn between them, sex is not the same as gender.

Is sex biologically or sociologically based? What about gender? What is it that fascinates people and researchers about sex and sexuality? Why do other cultures hold varying views on sexuality and issues such as nudity, prostitution, and extramarital sex? Are there really sexual differences between males and females?

What is Sex?

Sex is the *biological* distinction of being male or female that develops before birth. It is our physiology. In addition to the birthing staff, those of us who are parents (especially fathers) initially identify the newborn by his or her genitals, and in some respects, immediately place social significance to the sex of the newborn child. Biologically, sex distinguishes us in other ways, including the physiological functions of our bodies. Sex differences also occur years later when we reach puberty and our reproductive systems become physiologically matured. During puberty, which is a biological function, females develop a wider pelvis, breasts and soft, fatty tissue, all of which serve to facilitate and accommodate pregnancy. Males develop more muscles in the upper body, deeper voices and extensive body hair. While some females with a higher testosterone (male hormone) level may have a heavier or more muscular build, deeper voice tones and more body hair, some males who have less testosterone or a higher estrogen (female hormone) level, tend to have sparse body hair, speak in a higher tone and have smaller frames. In rare cases, a hormone imbalance before birth produces a **hermaphrodite**–a person with a combination of male and female internal and external genitalia.

As an act of intimacy, sex can be stimulated physiologically, with erotic physical contact and/or orgasm. Or, it can be stimulated psychologically with the cognitive process of fantasy and desire. Generally, a combination of the physical and psychological is involved. In most western industrialized societies, sex is psychologically related to physical attraction and beauty. Sex is also influenced and reflected by other factors including race, social class and gender. Some of these factors such as sexual stereotypes, are based on myth: "hot-blooded" Latinas (female) and Latinos (male) make better lovers, African American women are promiscuous nymphomaniacs, African American males are sexually potent and, of course, blondes do have more fun.

These myths vary according to the cultural and global context and are socially constructed. From the social class context, sex as a trait of attractiveness is evident in most beauty pageants. For the longest time, Miss America was tall, slender, beautiful, blond, white and from someplace in Texas or another southern state. Additionally, she came from a middle or upper class background. Part of her status was based on biological attributes: blond (if it was natural), white, and tall. Other aspects of her status were social, and she was considered highly attractive, knowledgeable, and affluent. Even later, as minorities began to be considered for the Miss America Pageant, they too came from more affluent family backgrounds.

Sexual attraction is a complex experience and it is safe to conclude that people in America view sex differently than in most other countries. Magazines, store windows, bumper stickers, the success of Victoria's Secret, MTV, The Bachelorette, The Bachelor, Joe Millionaire, and other reality shows, tend to support this statement. This will be explored in the section "Psychological Explanation" of sex.

Finally, as a basic human (biological) drive, sex is experienced for its physiological experience and related to its reproductive capacity. This biological experience often creates emotional ties and results from social intimacy between people. Sex is not only physically gratifying but it also reinforces social meaning. Therefore, our attitudes and enjoyment of sex is shaped as much by cultural (arousal) influences as it is by biological chemicals (hormones).

What is Gender?

While it may be argued that sexuality is a mix of biology and society, can the same be argued for gender? Scholars are still debating this question. While sex carries little argument for either application, gender entails a much broader perspective and has wider applications. It is difficult to understand gender without understanding its historical development. It is the contention of some social scientists that gender has not always been a component of society and that, at most, it played a minimal role in terms of attitude and the division of labor.

Gender can be defined as the socially constructed attitudes, meanings, beliefs, and behaviors associated with the sex differences of being born male or female, and learned through the process of socialization. Some social scientists have argued that biological factors have programmed males and females with different motives, talents, and behaviors. Most would argue however, that gender, more than sex, is a mental and social construct, not a biological one. One can then define gender roles as the attitude and activities that a culture links to being male or female and learned through the process of socialization. From our previous discussion, we have discerned that despite the mystery and questions that may exist regarding male and female differences, there are certain things we do know: only women can naturally bear children, and men typically excel in physical strength. Despite these biological differences, understanding the distinctions is usually dictated by how society interprets them. It might even be argued that God's gender is a social construct. Patriarchy has been in power since before the advent of modern religions. Of course we see God as male! Before modern religions, when men and women were more equal, there was a common belief in both gods and goddesses. Among the most powerful was the Earth Mother, known as the giver of life and fertility.

A key element in gender stratification is power. Certain religions support the belief that Eve was created to serve as a loyal and nurturing companion to her husband and their offspring, and to bear the seeds for future generations. This is the premise most religions use in banning women from positions of leadership. It can be otherwise argued that Adam and Eve were created as equals, both subservient to a higher deity and asked to govern all that was placed on earth, thus substantiating other denominations that have women in leadership positions. Of course, there are also those who have offered the suggestion that the creator was female and not male, suggesting female superiority.

Current defense policy prohibits women from serving in direct combat roles. In January 2011, a special military commission recommended that this policy be terminated to allow all qualified service members, including women, to serve in units directly involved in combat.

Photo: Expertinfantry.

Gender is determined by society based on its perception of male and female qualities and communicated through the dominant ideology. **Gender roles** are learned and reinforced through associated behaviors and attitudes with the help of socializing agents such as the family, schools, peers, the media, politics, and religion. They are the result of society's expectations regarding the proper behavior, attitudes, and activities associated with being male or female. Studies have shown that although attempts have been made over the last century to establish a gender-neutral language and equal rights and opportunities for males and females, attitudes still persist that suggest women's natural instincts for nurturing inhibits their ability in leadership roles and positions of authority.

Linguist Deborah Tanner, in an interview on NBC Today (Oct. 22, 1997), suggested that men and women communicate differently. Is that a result of our socialization or our biology? According to Tanner, boys and girls learn to communicate differently and this transfers to the workforce when we become adults. For example, Tanner believes that, "Boys learn that they have to be better than other boys, sort of a one-upmanship. Girls on the other hand, don't call attention to themselves, and instead focus on equalizing situations and being a cooperative spirit." Men are hired based on demonstrated or expected performance, while women are still being hired, to some degree, based on physical attractiveness and convenience. This is not to say that some men are not hired based on similar attributes. Tanner also suggests that, "Some women feel that men like to brag about their achievements. (But) men simply feel that they are just realistically letting people know what they are doing. In the workplace, women (including those in supervisory positions) look for more common ground." There is an unspoken belief among many males and some women that a woman's natural disposition for calmness, her emphasis on quality, and eagerness to please are her most desirable traits. But are these the traits needed for leadership and positions of power?

Educational psychologist Carol Gilligan, in 1990, studied personality development in young girls and her findings seemed to confirm Tanner's conclusions. Investigating attitudes, self-concepts, and self-esteem in a sample of over two thousand girls ranging from 6 to 18 years-of-age, she found that gender roles for both males and females are learned during early childhood and reinforced through other socializing agents. Moreover, she demonstrated that female self-concept—understanding what being female means—is stronger at a younger age than male awareness. One interview question asked girls how often they felt happy that they were girls. Sixty percent of the younger girls and only 29 percent of older (high school) girls replied "always." When boys were asked the same question, 67 percent and 46 percent responded respectively. Gilligan attributes this and other similar findings to age. As girls grow older, more of their teachers and authority figures are males (and some females) who still view submissiveness, dependency, emotionality, timidity, and being passive, receptive, and cooperative to be among the acceptable female traits. These are opposed to the more valued male traits of being intelligent, dominant, rational, assertive, strong, active, and ambitious. Differential treatment by these authority figures inevitably has an effect on self-esteem and self-concept. Additionally, the expectations that authority figures held demanded that girls conform to the ideal of being female which, in the long run, turned out to be the very traits that society does not value as much.

At its inception, the relatively new concept of androgyny was used to describe a compassionate, discerning, receptive, cooperative and understanding male who was in touch with his feminine side. Sociologically, **androgyny** incorporates the social and personality characteristics associated with being both male and female. From this definition, androgyny can also refer to women. There are women who possess traits that have been traditionally attributed to males—they are strong, logical, dominant, independent, rational, ambitious, and competitive, etc. The fact that gender roles vary across cultures and change over time is supported by the study conducted by anthropologist Margaret Mead (1963; orig. 1935).

Among the New Guineans, Mead found that the characteristics defined as feminine in Western culture were not necessarily universal. Among the Tchambuli tribes, the personalities of males and females were not only different, but opposite to western conceptions of masculine and feminine traits. Among Tchambuli women, dominant traits were business shrewdness or savvy, logic, common sense, and the major economic role. The men, on the other hand, were more interested in aesthetics and included gossiping, decorating, and adorning themselves in makeup and jewelry. Mead was able to show that the whole concept of gender behaviors, emotions, and interests are patterned by culture.

In more contemporary western cultures, individuals who possess a combination of male and female traits are considered to be gender neutral or androgynous. In most societies, organization, division of labor, access to education, health, economic and social privileges, and gender roles are based on a system of **patriarchy**, which literally translated means, "the rule of the fathers." All stratification systems favor men, to varying degrees. Male dominance is more pronounced in societies where men have more power and control over economic resources. Conversely, male dominance is less pronounced in societies where women have higher degrees of control over economic and political resources.

Historically, gender inequality was minimal in the early hunting and gathering societies, where tribal chiefs or *shamans* were virtually all male and the population consisted of small bands of nomadic tribes, and all activities were based on food production for survival. The social organization of less advanced technological societies was simple, and division of labor was based primarily on sex and age. Women gathered, men hunted; the elderly and the young did what they could to contribute to survival and food production. It is plausible that, despite the patriarchal organization of hunting and gathering societies, women were more important to the survival of the tribe since vegetation was the most reliable food source. As a result, in these types of societies a more collective conscience governed ownership of property and tools. Ironically, in more technologically advanced societies where there exists a surplus of goods and services, social organization and division of labor is more complex and competition for resources is more pronounced (Lenski, 1982), aspects that detract from women's social status.

As seen in the historical perspective of women's roles in the United States in the last one-hundred years and in the tribal studies of Margaret Mead, conceptions of gender roles vary from culture to culture and change over time. In addition to Gerhard Lenski and Jean Lenski, and Talcott Parsons (1942) see structural functionalist perspective theorists Jessie Bernard (1981), Elise Boulding (1976), Ralph Linton (1990) and George Murdock (1937); all offer separate but somewhat parallel studies on the various roles between males and females and their impact on society. But the fact remains that gender roles are learned through interaction and reinforced by various environmental and socializing agents which include: the family, peers, religion, government, the workplace, and in advanced societies, school and mass media.

Psychological Explanation

The psychological perspective focuses on explaining gender differences by understanding individual perceptions and behaviors associated with gender roles and sexual identity. Initial research regarding gender related attitudes and sexual behavior was conducted by psychologists and only later gradually drifted into the realm of other social scientists, including sociologists.

Although considered ancient history by some, perhaps no body of work is more prolific and influential than the studies, theories and myths postulated by Sigmund Freud (1856-1939). Freud shocked the academic world when he introduced sex into scholarly studies, so much so, that some of his closest colleagues and apprenticed students left his tutelage for fear of reprisal from the Victorian Austrian and British public that were their contemporaries. There are those that believe Freud was misunderstood and misinterpreted and a genius; that the historical time period and setting in which he lived and worked is in part the explanation for how his research was directed, accepted or rejected, and therefore can be explained and adapted to our own times. Whatever the case may be, Freud's theories and his psychoanalytic school of thought have influenced generations and are still believed and widely practiced today.

Freud postulated that sexual identity begins in early childhood and continues to develop well into adulthood. Freud theorized that sexual energy or *libido* was one of the major instincts or driving forces that defined human beings. He further theorized that the two basic drives behind our human personalities are *Eros,* derived from the name for the Greek god of love and *Thanatos*, also from the Greek meaning death or aggressive instincts. Freud regarded these as not only our basic instincts but also as the most powerful of our human drives or life forces. As you might expect, men and women, according to Freud, have varying degrees of these two life forces and, of course, utilize them quite differently.

Certain critics have denounced Freud's work as androcentric in approaching an issue from the male perspective. Further criticism includes that most of Freud's research participants were male and most, including the few women he worked with, were suffering from some mild to acute form of mental disorder. However, the bottom line for Freud and many other prominent psychologists is that men and women are radically different, each with their own strengths and weaknesses, their own problems and issues, and unique way of dealing with the world.

One bothersome aspect for psychologists is that, paradoxically speaking and as we saw in Chapter Three, there is a difference between real and ideal culture. Another confusing aspect that diminishes our understanding of ourselves as gendered and sexual beings, and sometimes results in psychological symptoms, is that in our society we are both sexually permissive and repressive at the same time. One can argue that Freud's psychosexual description of various Western European cultures is embedded in a constant battle between real and ideal notions about sexual behaviors, taboos, nudity and appropriateness. Sex isn't shrouded in mystery but Westerners are viewed as both repressive, and liberal or permissive, in our sexual behaviors. This conflicting notion is analogous to what health professionals faced when working with people who were once labeled as "manic-depressive." They questioned how one could be excited or anxious (manic) and in a dark state of feeling (depression) at the same time. To resolve their concerns, a new name, bipolar, was introduced. Similarly, how is the libido satisfied if society dictates behavior and sends mixed messages about sexuality?

While all churches and most parents denounce premarital sex, the media portrays the glories of sex and being sexually attractive on a daily basis in movies, magazines, and TV, so much so, that there are few people getting married today who are sexually inexperienced. While the sexual revolution ushered in widespread changes in male and female sexual roles, and more public acceptance of sexuality, it did little to help us understand how and why our sex, gender and sexuality are inexorably intertwined. While both attitudes and sexual behavior have changed as a result of the movements of the 1960s and 70s, we are still, to some extent, tied to our physiological and psychological makeup. Fewer women are virgins at marriage today, more people are having sex at a younger age, and despite the HIV scare, women are having sex with multiple partners, a behavior that was traditionally expected from and reserved for males. Yet, although things have changed, most people continue to perceive sex and sexuality as being synonymous and heavily overshadowed by our specific gender and the roles attached to that gender by our society.

Psychological research has shown gender differences in many aspects of daily life: how we handle stress, emotional and interpersonal problems, how we communicate with each other; what we value and believe in as well as what our attitudes are. Pop psychologist Dr. Joel Grey even suggests that the differences between men and women is so great that *Women are from Venus; Men are from Mars* (book title). The good news is that he believes that if we can only learn to understand our differences and allow each other the freedom to be different, we can get along just fine. Sound too simple? Maybe, but in fact, the key to many things is to understand them in the first place.

SOCIOLOGICAL PERSPECTIVES

Sociological perspectives focus on how and why social distinctions between males and females are established, perpetuated and maintained. One view shared with psychologists is that gender roles are learned and reinforced through behaviors and attitudes via modeling and the various agents of socialization.

Structural Functional

From this perspective, society is viewed as a system of complex parts working together to promote the whole, thereby maintaining equilibrium and stability. This approach posits that every social structure and institution contributes to the overall operation of society. Although Talcott Parsons (1942) and other structural functionalists did not specifically endorse the gendered division of labor, they perceived it as natural, inevitable and necessary. If one subscribes to this view, traditional gender roles are important not only for individuals, but also for the economic and social order of society. If an aspect of society ceases to contribute to the overall operation, or is deemed dysfunctional, it is not carried to the next generation. For structural functionalist theorists, rapid change is neither necessarily nor eagerly desired, for them the natural order of things results from slow and gradual change. From a structural functionalist viewpoint, the counter culture movements of the 1960s—Hippie, Civil Rights, Women's, and Students for a Democratic Society—put a strain on society because of the rapid changes that occurred in a span of less than 15 years.

As discussed earlier, gender roles are socially defined activities, behaviors, and attitudes deemed appropriate for each sex, and learned through the process of socialization. These roles play an integral part in choosing a mate, courtship, marriage and family, transition from childhood and adolescence to adulthood, and the division of labor. From a structural functionalist point of view, society would be a better place in which to live and work if these systems remained stable and people were integrated into the dominant ideology. Structural functionalists would say that if a society is to survive, it must reproduce itself and train its offspring to perform functions vital to the operation of society; how a society defines and socializes its members into gender roles will determine the type of family structure, child-care, division of labor and impacts the social, economic, and political systems.

According to Parsons, gender forms a complimentary set of roles that link males and females together into family units that fulfill the various functions necessary for the operation of society, with women being largely responsible for the caring and nurturing of children and overall management of the household, while men connect the family to the larger society through their participation in the workforce. Parsons (1942) argues that this division of labor contributes to the socialization process by teaching young boys and girls appropriate gender identity and gender related skills that will be needed later in adult life.

Recent achievements by women have certainly challenged some of the traditional notions and attitudes regarding the contributions of women to overall society. For example, according to the 2005 Forbes 400 Richest in America list, Oprah Winfrey, a television talk-show host, and the woman mentioned earlier as one of the two who opened and closed the 20th century, is listed as the richest woman celebrity in America and the 280th richest woman in the world with a current net worth of 900 million dollars (http://www.forbes.com/celebrities/). According to Forbes, the most influential women in the world include Condelessa Rice, Sandra Day O'Connor, Wu Yi, Ruth Bader Ginsburg, Sonia Gandhi, Megawati Sukarnoputri, Laura Bush, Gloria Arroyo, Hillary Rodham Clinton, and Carleton Fiorina.

Among the early 20th century pioneering women, Madame C.J. Walker (1867-1919) was born Sarah Breedlove and was America's first black millionaire businesswoman. She achieved her success by inventing a new hair care process and marketing a line of cosmetics for black women. In 1905, Walker invented and patented a straightening comb which, when heated and used with her patented pomade, transformed women's hair into a shining, smooth mane. In 1906, she married Charles J. Walker, and was known thereafter as Madame C.J. Walker. She dubbed her hair straightening process the "Walker Method." The popularity of her products grew so rapidly that she soon established a manufacturing company that occupied an entire Denver city block. Madame Walker's company employed more than 3,000 people. Before the advent of the Avon Lady and Mary Kay representatives, she trained young women to sell her products door-to-door. Her agents were required to sign contracts binding them to a strict hygienic regimen; later, these standards would be incorporated into Colorado's state cosmetology laws.

Recent years have seen changes in the way modern industrialized societies address gender roles through improved communication, and the civil and equal rights movements. Regardless, Parson's statements are still reflected in the way our society continues to teach males to be rational, self-assured, strong, and competitive–traits that he classified as *instrumental* qualities. Additionally, society still socializes females into what he called *expressive* qualities–child rearing, nurturing, sensitivity, and emotionality.

Parsons' view that society promotes gender roles through various schemes has recently come under critical evaluation. For example, he excludes the fact that poor women and single mothers, through necessity, have always worked outside of the home and increasing numbers of wives successfully juggle the dual status of motherhood and career. Parson also fails to include the numbers of feminists who defy the traditional gender roles orchestrated by a male dominated society and pursue non-traditional life-styles and careers.

Social Conflict

Traditional Marxist perspective—the basis of social conflict theory—argues that gender stratification results from the private monopoly of the ownership of the means of production. Men not only have a monopoly over property and distribution of goods and services, but also gain power over women through marriage. According to Marx/Engles doctrine, marriage serves to reinforce the system of patriarchy, a form of socialization where men are socially, politically, culturally and economically dominant over females. Wealthy men created the institution of marriage so that they could be certain of the paternity of their offspring, particularly sons, who would inherit their wealth and keep the patriarchal lineage alive.

From the social conflict perspective, the gendered division of labor within families and in the workplace results from male control and dominance over women and valued resources. Men and women differ in their access to power, privilege, prestige and resources, with the axis tilted in favor of males. Traditional social conflict theorists would argue that the creation of socially distinct institutions is an example of the rich and powerful flexing muscles under the guise of genuine concern for the welfare of less fortunate citizens. The struggle for equality continues to be an uphill battle in most of the industrialized nations throughout Western Europe, Canada, Japan, and the United States. Karl Marx's criticism of capitalism included the economic struggles and conflicts between males and females over valued resources. Although women are making gains in the world of work, their status and pay is still not on par with those of men. The technological contributions of women still go largely unnoticed. Men still have social, political, and economic power over women. In a comparison of all occupations, the average women's earnings were 76.5 percent that of men's. Women in executive and professional full-time occupations, average about 73 cents to every one dollar of men's salary (Current Population Survey, 2008).

The social conflict approach may help to unravel the mystery of award money for top athletes in their respective sports. While there have been recent controversies and political debates over Title IX, which federal law intended to prevent discrimination based on sex regarding student activities on college campuses (particularly in sports), it can be argued that recent shattering of world records by women may not have been achieved without such legislation. We saw how "effective" other legislative acts regarding civil rights impacted the lives of African Americans and other minorities.

A young ballerina accepts flowers after a performance. Although our society is moving toward a more progressive notion of gender roles, there are many more girls than boys that dream of dancing in a Ballet.

Photo: James Emery.

Forbes statistics clearly reflect that there is great disparity in the pay that male athletes receive when compared to female athletes. While Tiger Woods, Michael Jordan, Shaquille O'Neal, Andre Aggassi, David Beckham, and Lance Armstrong have been among the top earning athletes, Serena and Venus Williams, Annika Sorenstam, Lindsey Davenport and any other female athlete you can think of come in a far second to even third-rate male athletes.

Despite some breakthroughs, we still are a nation where some people are more equal than others and where some, for example African American and Hispanic women, face double-jeopardy (of being female and a minority) when it comes to sexism and discrimination.

Feminist

The feminist movement has aligned with the basic tenets of Karl Marx's Social Conflict perspective. From this perspective, the social, economic and political powers in the United States and other western industrialized nations are dictated by males. **Feminists** advocate social and economic equality for women in opposition to the male dominated system of patriarchy. Most people associate the feminist movement with the sixties and seventies and remember outspoken women such as Betty Friedan and Gloria Steinem. But the drive for gender equality in America has been constant and enduring in some form for over 150 years.

It is interesting to note that feminist theorists have sought to explain male dominance and gender stratification utilizing the writings of Marx and Engels. Research reveals that there have been very few systems of **matriarchy**, a hierarchical system of organization in which the cultural, political, social, and economic structures are controlled by women, usually the eldest female family member. Of those few that did or do exist, most are in third world or underdeveloped countries of Africa, South America, and a few other small countries.

While the women's movement of the 1960s and 70s was aligned with the Civil Rights Movement, the first feminist movement drew parallels to the abolitionists, led by women who were opposed to slavery. One of the first men to speak out for gender equality was John Stuart Mill (1806-1873). In his book *On Liberty*, he argued for, "absolute freedom of opinion and sentiments on all subjects." He was an enthusiastic supporter of women's rights and fought for women's suffrage in 1867, a cause that, at that time, failed. His contention was that legal subordination of one sex by the other was morally wrong (Spielvogel, 1997).

The turning point for women in the United States came with the first women's convention held at the Wesleyan Chapel in Seneca Falls, New York, in 1848 attended by pioneer Lucretia Mott, a mentor of Elizabeth Cady Stanton, who was a primary coordinator for the convention. Some years later, Stanton met Susan B. Anthony who had been arrested for attempting to vote in the 1872 election. Nearly fifty years later, Anthony's continuing effort led to the passage of the nineteenth amendment to the constitution affording women the right to vote in all national elections. Obviously, women have made much progress in the political arena.

Although there are variations within the feminist movement, most agree that gender stratification must be eliminated. Another point that most feminists agree upon is the promotion of sexual autonomy, particularly in the area of women having the right to determine what can be done to their bodies and their right to make decisions to control reproduction. Yet, there remains some dissension within the ranks because the definition of the pursuit of sexual equality varies among parties and group goals remain ambiguous and sometimes conflicting.

Liberal feminists, for instance, want the same rights, privileges and protection afforded to African—and other minority—Americans under the Civil Rights Act by the passage of an Equal Rights Act. They support the family as an institution with the understanding that ambitions of both males and females must be accommodated. Their focus is on personal and individual liberation.

In contrast, **Socialist feminists** support the philosophy of Marx and Engels. They consider housework drudgery and view stay-at-home wives as domestic slaves. Current domestic conditions, they assert, are fostered by capitalism and keeps women working without wages and economically dependent on their husbands. For this group, gender equality will only come with drastic changes in the economic structure.

Radical feminists are more aggressive in their drive for liberation and consider men as, "necessary evils" and traditional concepts of parenthood and family as obsolete (Bernard, 1971). The agenda of radical feminists is to wipe out gender roles and gender inequality. They insist this can only be accomplished through extreme means. Such means would include requiring children to dress in non-gender clothing, cut their hair in a non gender style, and be given non gender names. Similarly, radical feminist insist that before equality between the sexes can occur gender identification in all institutions of society must be outlawed and legally enforced by the government. However, since most members of society would find the above remedies abhorrent, it is highly unlikely that this group will achieve its goals.

Even though divided, action by the above feminist groups has resulted in positive strides in the pursuit of sexual equality. Sexual harassment complaints are being vigorously pursued in the workplace and more women are assuming positions of power. One issue that continues to plague women however, despite all of the strides made, is domestic violence, discussed in section three of this chapter.

SOCIALIZING AGENTS

Helen Keller was once asked if there was anything worse than blindness. She responded, "Yes, to have sight but no vision." To have a genuine understanding of sex and gender in everyday life, it is important to have some knowledge of the agents of socialization and their impact on gender roles. Gender roles don't just happen; we are socialized to fit into those molds through various agents. Here, we will look at seven major socializing agents: family, school, peers, workplace, media, religion, and politics.

Family

The first and most important agent in the socialization process is the family. Parents are our initial *significant others*. It is through the family that we inherit our identity and sense of self, which includes our self-esteem. It begins the moment we are born and introduced to our home. Families socialize children through deliberate and intentional means by instilling values requiring obedience to norms and teaching them the rules of society. It is through the family that we learn our heritage, ethnicity, race, and of course, gender. As we increase our interactions outside of the family we accept, confirm, or deny these identities. Gender identity then, just like race and ethnic identity, is confirmed as we experience everyday life situations.

Gender socialization begins as soon as the sex of the child is identified. From the decor of the hospital nursery to the nursery at home, the clothing, blankets, and baby kits are gender specific. Once at home the bassinets, crib, toys, and clothes are all gender specific (blue for boys, pink for girls) while yellow or white are considered neutral colors. Dress your new baby boy in pink? No way! In stores, we find diaper labels that instruct us as to which are constructed to fit the anatomy of boys and which are designed for girls.

Humans are naturally inquisitive and sexual creatures. We learn at an early age that there are physical differences between males and females. Sociologists Bernard (1981) and Bonner (1984) conducted research that illustrates how parents convey gender messages to children by the way they act and even unconsciously handle their daughters and sons. Most often this is accomplished through **modeling**. Our parents model various appropriate roles for us—mom cooking, cleaning, sewing, adorning herself with makeup and jewelry, while dad mows the lawn, fixes the plumbing, washes and waxes the car, tinkers with gadgets, shaves, and exhibits strength in disciplining us.

Whether our parents exhibit affection and intimacy for one another in our presence is a good indicator of how we will manage our affections towards siblings and mates as we grow. In essence, we learn from our parents the expectations and appropriateness of male and female behaviors. Also, we learn via our parent's model, how to parent, resolve conflict, manage time, the values of ownership and occupation status, and the importance or non-importance, of education. Finally, our parent's attitudes, beliefs, and values make an impression on our attitudes toward gender roles. If we see both parents participating equally in decision making, it is probable that we will model the same behavior with our mates. If, on the other hand, we see one parent dominating the relationship, making all of the decisions, and even abusing the other, then we may be predisposed to continuing the cycle with our mates. Sometimes parental teaching is unintentional as they model behaviors that are not intended for children to emulate. Children learning to drink, smoke, curse, and lie are examples of behaviors that most parents don't want for their children. Nevertheless, parents teach these behaviors through modeling.

Equally important to our socialization is being allowed as children to be a part of planning and decision making. If parents are gender neutral and impartial, we can reasonably expect children to follow that example. If mom tinkers with cars, mows the lawn, and dad cooks, does laundry, and parents share chores that are traditionally other-sex oriented, children will consider this to be normal family behavior. It is interesting to note that it is not atypical for males raised in female single-parent families to be somewhat more androgynous than those raised in traditional two-parent families. Generally, these males will not be consumed with resentment if a female spouse earns more or is better educated. It is incumbent upon parents and caregivers to raise (socialize) children to be productive and responsible adults able to function in an evolving society.

School

The second major socializing agent is school. Schooling is a very important aspect of the socializing process because it reinforces what is taught in the family by encouraging or discouraging those values. Unfortunately, throughout our history schooling has perpetuated gender inequality in academics, sports, and related activities. Plus, as children grow older and venture farther away from the immediate control of parents, teachers and others in the educational process become significant role models. Their teaching is most often deliberate and intentional in that the education system generally has the intention of providing children with the knowledge and tools necessary to sustain and strengthen an industrialized nation. That is to say, in order for a nation to sustain itself, it requires a well-trained and educated labor force. This often means protecting and reinforcing the status quo, often a deterrent to the advancement of women.

When education became a formal institution and necessary to sustain and improve existing technology, the life span consisted of childhood and adulthood. The requirement for formal education produced a new cycle in the life span that we call adolescence. Prior to industrialization, most males went to work on their families' farms and females were expected to marry and bear children, usually well before their 18th birthday. As such, there was little need for formal education. Additionally, in the early years, formal education was restricted to wealthy, white, Anglo Saxon males. Ironically, for the 19th and most of the 20th century, almost all elementary and secondary education teachers were female. Post-secondary education centered on majors in medicine, theology, philosophy, and law and, as may be expected, most professors were male.

Until recent years, and yet to some degree even today, males were directed into fields which focused on the sciences, mathematics, medicine and engineering, while females were directed toward more domestic and less technical fields like subordinate health professions, social service oriented careers, and of course, teaching. The irony is that if it were not for teachers (even today the majority of secondary teachers are female)—doctors wouldn't be doctors, engineers—engineers, or teachers—teachers.

The news is that we are now seeing a reverse trend, especially in post-secondary education, where more women are making inroads every day. And while more women are becoming physicians, architects, and engineers, there is also some evidence of a trend reversal with males venturing into fields that were previously dominated by females, such as nursing and secondary education. An interesting point to ponder, and a trend that some experts forecast, is that as a larger number of women enter the previously male-dominated professions such as medicine, higher education, and law, a decrease in status and pay may be inevitable.

Table 9.1: Gender Ratios at Sample Universities

	Percent Male	Percent Female
U. North Carolina, CH	44	56
U. Wisconsin, Madison	46	54
U. Texas, Austin	47	53
Rutgers University	36	64
U. Iowa	46	54
U. Virginia	43	57
Michigan State U.	47	53
U. Wisconsin, Madison	47	53
U. California, Berkley	44	56

Source: University of Missouri Columbia. Table PA1-C:AAU Public Universities enrollment by gender, Fall 2007.

Since 1980, women have been attending and graduating from college in record numbers. The overall number of women enrolled in postsecondary institutions grew by 136 percent, while enrollment in professional school grew by a whopping 853 percent. This growth, combined with the relative stagnation in the rates of enrollment for men, has led to imbalances in college gender ratios across the nation.

Early studies suggested that both male and female teachers are patronizing to female students (Gilligan, 1982). Although there has been an attempt to eliminate this practice, it still persist in many educational institutions. Nowhere is this bias more evident than in the field of higher education where women comprise only 19 percent of the tenure-track professorships in math, 11 percent in physics, and 10 percent in electrical engineering. And, according to leading experts, looking down the pipeline, future gains do not look promising. Why so? One of the real problems is that women tend to self-select careers in education, English, psychology, biology and art history. Men tend to be drawn to mathematics, engineering, and computer science. Much of this, according to researcher Virginia Valiam, is that our male dominated society constructs and enforces gender schemes in which boys and girls are raised differently. The gender scheme for boys includes being independent, assertive, competitive, and being task-oriented. On the other hand, schemes for girls includes being nurturing, expressive, communicative, and having concern for others. Valiam sees the only solution to end these schemes is to raise children in an egalitarian environment where both boys and girls are taught to play with dolls and trucks (Valiam, 2008).

Years ago, books, stories, and games typically made males the focus of attention (Weitzman, 1972). Females, less mentioned in book titles–were usually depicted as damsels in distress, living in a shoe with a house full of kids, losing their slippers, kissing a frog in an effort to turn it into a handsome prince, or being frightened away by a spider. Males were typically mentioned in book titles (Gullivers Travels, Paul Bunyon, Huck Finn, Oliver Twist, etc.) and were depicted as being engaged in interesting activities. Girls were submissive and attractive; males were dominant knights in shining armor. Today, because of increased awareness of the inequalities associated with gender roles, many books, movies, and professions attempt to portray males and females in more balanced roles.

Peers

Peers, our contemporaries with whom we identify, see as friends, or just want to be like, are the third major socializing agents. Despite concerted efforts of modern parents emphasizing gender neutrality, peers often make these efforts more difficult for parents. Male peer groups place more emphasis and pressure on other males to act, dress, and speak in a masculine way. Females place less emphasis on being feminine than their male counterparts do. For example, while it is okay for girls to wear jeans, skateboard, play soccer and softball, a male is generally ridiculed by both sexes if he engages in playing hopscotch, wears a dress, or plays with Barbie dolls. Pressure to adhere to traditional gender traits increases during adolescence, especially among boys. This is especially true of male bonding exercises that involve ridiculing girls and other males who don't conform to traditional standards of appearance and do not engage in gender related activities. For example, boys will bully other boys who play a violin rather than a more traditionally male instrument such as a tuba, and boys who are studious bookworms, rather than athletic jocks. Girls who are overweight, dress unfashionably, or who are tomboyish or athletic, may also experience ridicule.

As males and females reach college age or young adulthood, they are bombarded with many gender-related messages. Peer pressure plays an important part in choosing mates, intimate relationships, and career aspirations. Studies of college females reveal that many women who initially pursue careers in engineering and the sciences are derailed by peer pressure, inadequate counseling, pregnancy or other relationship issues. Some of these young women marry and their husbands continue their pursuit of academic study while they do not, others divorce and eventually settle into more traditional, female dominated fields such as nursing or teaching (Sommers, 2008).

The Workplace

Gender socialization continues after males and females complete their training and education and enter the workforce. For those who work full-time (generally 35 or more hours per week), the workplace, the fourth socializing agent, is where we spend most of our waking hours. Therefore, it plays an integral and logical part in socializing gender roles and perpetuating the belief that certain jobs are endemic to being male or female. This is evident in areas of salary, promotions, and benefits such as vacation, family and medical leave, and tasks assigned. According to the 1963 Council of Economic Advisors the salary for women was 58 cents for every dollar earned by men. Today, while still unequal, the salary for women is 76 cents to the dollar for men with equal education, seniority, and job skill level (Current Population Survey, 2008). Society is still not comfortable affording women the social status accorded to men in professional fields. The glass-ceiling—that imaginary place so difficult to transcend unless you are a WASPM—is firmly in place but beginning to show a few cracks.

Media

If the family is the earliest and most important agent in the socialization process, the fifth socializing agent, the media, is the most influential. Television, movies, newspapers, magazines, and radio all mirror and reinforce society's attitudes regarding gender. Women in the media are still depicted and exploited as sex objects and admired for their overall looks. Even when cast in leading roles, women are often depicted as the femme fatale, a romantic interest central to the plot but not necessarily a character that can stand alone. Instead, women tend to be cast in light of their traditional traits, where the character portrayed is cooperative, sensitive, vulnerable, peaceful, useful, sociable, and of course, attractive. Rarely do we see women portrayed as action figures who are capable of getting themselves in-and-out of trouble without the aid and assistance of a man—usually one that is stronger, smarter, and sometimes even better-looking than they are. Males are more likely to be cast in serious roles, his character strong, logical, rational, and independent. Males are more likely to be cast as villains or other characters that initiate violence where women are usually the victims. When women are cast as villains, they are more likely to get away with violence. Additionally, it is worth noting that women are increasingly depicted in more positive roles. But for every positive role, there are numerous other shows that portray women as sexual objects, sidekicks, or helpless victims.

If you watch TV closely, you will notice that most advertising is sexist in its portrayal of women. Everything, from automobile commercials to beer and tobacco ads, from laundry to baby products, reflects sexist attitudes. More often than not, the sexism in advertising is very subtle, reinforcing gender stereotypes. A woman is taller than a man only when the man is her social inferior; women usually are dressed in provocative apparel, women's hands are always holding or caressing—never grasping, manipulating, or shaping as men's hands are portrayed; men are always instructing women; and when advertising requires someone to sit or lie on a bed or a floor, that someone is almost always a woman or a child, rather than a man.

Advertisers of household cleaning agents and feminine hygiene products generally depict women neatly dressed, including high heels and makeup, as they mop or wax the kitchen floors. Even in the shower, they are portrayed with glamorous makeup on; not a hair out of place as they awake from a nights sleep. Anyone over thirty who has ever awakened next to a significant other after a night's sleep can seriously question the reality of someone who looks as good as they do in the Oil of Olay and Victoria's Secret commercials.

Religion and Politics

Religion and politics, the sixth and seventh socializing agents, reflect society's attitudes regarding gender in similar ways. Both institutions have a common history of limiting the participation of women in leadership positions. While there are few religious denominations that place no restrictions on women, there have been some recent rumblings for more modern thinking. Undoubtedly, the catalyst for change is the decreasing participation in many religious denominations. As such, many churches are revisiting the question of women in leadership roles. Too, the question of homosexuality has surfaced as a key issue in church membership and leadership. The Evangelical Lutheran Church of America, one of the largest Lutheran denominations, debated the issue of ordaining gay and lesbian ministers and blessing same-sex marriages at its 2005 Conference of Bishops. In the end, however, the bishops rejected both issues by a two-to-one margin. Change? Well, maybe not just yet.

While women have made some headway in the political arena, they still lag behind in representation and power. One hundred and nine individuals have served on the U.S. Supreme Court, only two were women. In 1981, Sandra Day O'Connor became the first woman ever appointed to the Supreme Court and served until she resigned in 2005. In 1993, Ruth Bader Ginsberg became the second woman appointed and still sits on the Court. By the end of 2010, there had been only four female Supreme Court Justices, two of whom–Sonia Sotomayor and Elena Kagan–were appointed by President Obama.

Chosen as John McCain's running mate, Sarah Palin is only the second woman to run for Vice President of the United States. After losing, she did not discount a future run for national office.

Photo: McCain / Palin Campaign, 2008.

From a global perspective, Margaret Thatcher, former Prime Minister of England, and Golda Meier, former Prime Minister of Israel, are often cited as evidence that women can fulfill the expectations and obligations that have been traditionally reserved for men. But despite these women's excellence in their respective capacities, women the world over are rarely in positions of real political power. In the United States, no woman has ever served as President or Vice President (except on television). No woman has ever been nominated by a major party to run for president. Only two women were nominated as Vice Presidential candidates. Geraldine Ferraro was chosen by Walter Mondale as his vice-presidential running mate in 1984 and Sarah Palin was selected by John McCain as his running mate in 2008. Both lost their bids for election

Finally, research on the traditional institution of marriage dispels some commonly held myths concerning male attitudes of marriage. Although it is believed that men resist marriage more than women, current research demonstrates that while men are marrying later in life, most express a desire to marry. Only two out of ten hold negative attitudes toward marrying and these men are most likely to come from nontraditional and nonreligious families (Popenoe and Whitehead, 2004). Research also demonstrates that men derive the major benefits from committed relationships in terms of longevity, physical and mental health, and reported life satisfaction when compared to men who are single (Nauert, 2008). For women, the health benefits of being married are more complex. Studies indicate that women obtain the same health benefits as their husbands but in order to do so, they must perceive the marriage to a happy one (DeNoon, 2008).

As we have seen in this chapter, gender based roles serve to maintain a certain equilibrium in society. Achieving gender neutrality is a major obstacle to be overcome in order to achieve gender equality. A person who practices gender neutrality, like one who is color blind when it comes to racism and prejudice, is mutually inclusive rather than exclusive of other people's needs and is attuned to the concept that each individual has self-worth, dignity, something to contribute to the common good, and is worthy of respect. One safe conclusion we can reach is that America is still largely a male dominated society in which males are favored over females in everything from education to the job market, to health care, and certainly, to economic resources.

SEXUALITY AND DEVIANCE

Together, society and biology create wholly different social experiences for men and women, and as a result, there are as many variances in attitudes, beliefs, and values among the sexes as there are between the sexes with most variations contingent on family structure, occupational status, cultural taboos, and environment. The result is a blurred range of what is considered normal and that, which falls under the umbrella of what we choose to label deviant. In other words, what some consider normal may well be labeled as deviant by others. For this reason, there should probably be a question mark directly attached to anything labeled as deviant because deviance, as well as normalcy, is an idea that changes over time, geography, culture, setting, as well as in each individual's own mind. A case in point: In 1992, The Minneapolis Star Tribune became the first newspaper to list gay domestic partnerships on the wedding page, thereby adding a little normalcy to what was still considered by many as deviant.

Sexuality refers to how society views sex and how we feel about ourselves as sexual beings. Much of sexuality is about appropriate and inappropriate behaviors, of what is right or wrong. Labels have been fixed to identify differences in sexuality. Some labels have negative connotations, as well as consequences, for the members in our society that wear them. The competition, struggles, and conflicts between heterosexuals and homosexuals are illustrative of past and present attitudes regarding sexuality. In addition, topics related to sexuality may include hermaphrodites, bisexuals, transsexuals, asexuality, transvestism, androcentrism, and an increasingly more accepted identity among males—androgyny.

Sexual Orientation

All societies throughout history have embraced **heterosexuality**, which refers to being emotionally and/or sexually attracted to another of the opposite sex. For reproduction and the continuation of the species, this is a good thing! Although there is no known society where homosexuality was the norm, anthropologists suggest that homosexuality has always been a subculture throughout the history of humankind, even though instances of hate crimes committed against homosexuals were not unusual and the consequences for identifying as a homosexual included ridicule, banishment, torture and even death. Ironically, even though all societies endorse heterosexuality, some ancient cultures celebrated homosexuality. Among the ancient Greeks, homosexual men—often elite members of the society—dismissed women as inferior creatures whose worth was primarily for procreation.

More and more, gay couples have chosen to openly display their affection for each other. As such, the institutions of society are increasingly challenged to confront discrimination against gays.

Photo: Gary Simpson.

Today, while homosexuals are moderately represented in middle-class America in white-collar occupations and other professions, the majority of them prefer to remain, "in the closet," keeping their sexual orientation confidential. Regardless of social class, the struggle they face to be recognized as normal human beings, deserving the same participation and protection under the laws, has been awesome. Our society is not the least bit hesitant to label nontraditional preferences as deviant, and non-traditional sexual difference is no exception.

From a sociological perspective deviance is in the mind of the beholder. For most intents and purposes, **deviance** can be defined as any behavior, attitude, belief, or condition that violates tradition and/or cultural norms. Based on this definition, ambiguity and conflict exist between and among both heterosexuals and homosexuals. Research continues to show that there is as much variance in attitudes and behavior in homosexuals as there is among heterosexuals. For example, many people consider themselves to be heterosexual but do not participate in sexual behavior, while others, who participate in same-sex activities, may not consider themselves to be homosexual. Additionally, in the homosexual community some men, as well as some women, label themselves as gay, while other women utilize the label lesbian. The term **gay** comes from the homosexual movement of the sixties and seventies and is meant to convey satisfaction with a homosexual orientation.

Prior to any discussion, it is important to have a working definition of the word homosexual and an understanding that there is a difference between a homosexual identity and homosexual behavior. In our case, the word **homosexual** refers to being sexually and or emotionally attracted to a member of the same sex. **Homosexual identity** refers to an individual's willingness to wear the label of being homosexual. In order to claim your homosexual identity, you must to some degree accept your sexual orientation. Homosexual behavior refers to sexual relations between people of the same sex. This behavior varies throughout the world and has held differing status in societies throughout history. For example, in the Keraki culture of New Guinea, boys are initiated into sodomy during puberty rites and for the next year play a passive role in sexual activity with a same sex partner. Until he marries, he is expected to participate in like activities with younger boys (Ford and Beach, 1972).

Rules and attitudes regarding homosexuality are culturally and socially constructed. Today, homosexuality is met with more tolerance and several states are in the process of acknowledging this alternative lifestyle by allowing domestic partners the same rights and privileges as heterosexual married partners. The Federal Hate Crimes Statistics Act of 1990 directed the Department of Justice to gather data on crimes against individuals motivated by a person's race, ethnic origin, religion, or sexual orientation. Despite this ground breaking legislation, in 2007 more than 1460 criminal acts related to **homophobia**, the irrational fear of homosexuals, were reported (Gier, 2008).

Many researchers consider accurate reporting of the numbers of homosexuals in the population as an impossibility as long as prevailing attitudes force individuals to respond less than honestly when surveyed regarding their sexual orientation. Alfred Kinsey (1948), head of the Indiana University Institute for Sex Research, was commissioned by the Federal government to conduct a study on sexual behavior in America. He estimated that while only four percent of males and two percent of females have an exclusively homosexual orientation, about one third of men and one eighth of women had at least one homosexual encounter resulting in orgasm. Since Kinsey's original report, data dependent on any number of factors indicates that the numbers more realistically range between six and twenty percent of the population, with a larger number of homosexuals being males.

Other sexual orientations that have been labeled as deviant include **transvestism**, which refers to the practice of wearing clothing appropriate to the opposite sex, and is often, although not necessarily, a manifestation of homosexuality. **Transsexuals** are people who feel they are one sex, even though biologically they are the other. This suggests that the sexual physiology you were born with is not always psychologically, sociologically, or biologically etched in stone. Some transsexuals elect to have surgery and hormone injections to alter their sex in an effort to alleviate the emotional confusion of being trapped in the wrong body. Research reported in the July 1998 issue of *Pediatrics* indicates that there is a "window of time" after birth when babies identify as boys or as girls dependent on what they are told they are and treated as. Finally, there are rare cases of hermaphrodites, individuals who have some combination of both internal and external male and female genitalia.

It helps to remember that sexual orientation is not determined in the same way for everyone. Viewed from a sociological perspective, sexual orientation is merely a construct, much like gender, determined by the dominant ideology of the society.

The definition of domestic violence varies from one country to another depending on cultural norms and laws. Based upon reported cases, statistics by the Center for Disease Control shows that 10 percent of women in the U.S. have been victims of domestic violence. Also by their estimates, only one-third of abuse is reported to authorities.

Photo: Lesisha Jones.

Domestic Violence

While there are those who still categorize homosexuality as deviant behavior, they do not necessarily classify homosexuality as tragic. Abuse of spouse, children and other household members, however, is seen as violent, deviant, and tragic by all members of society. Domestic violence has many faces and its definition is dependent on who is doing the defining. One definition—attempting to cause physical, mental or emotional harm to a spouse, children, or others in the household—sums it up, but does not address all of the forms that it takes, such as sexual coercion by force, threats, duress or by placing a family member in fear of imminent physical, psychological or emotional harm, or the intentional isolation of the abused spouse from family, friends, neighbors, and agencies that might provide help.

Most forms of domestic abuse involve a male inflicting physical harm through beating or sexual abuse on a woman and/or child. However, recent studies suggest that up to fifty percent of physically abused women in turn abuse their children. More than three million children witness ongoing acts of violence each year and seventy percent of batterers abuse their children as well as their spouses. With over four million women being beaten by their male partners every year, it is awesome to consider that there are three times more animal shelters in the United States than there are shelters for victims of domestic violence.

Even when a shelter is available, space is usually severely limited and the length of stay is often temporary and of short duration. Women who elect to leave their homes and seek a shelter are often risking poverty, homelessness and even loss of custody rights. Needless to say, the picture painted by domestic violence suggests that many women today are still virtually powerless economically, politically, and socially in the pursuits of their right to life, liberty, and happiness.

Studies reveal that between 1998 and 2002, almost 3.5 million violent crimes against family members were reported to authorities. Of these, 84 percent were against female spouses and 86 percent were against dating females. Statistics also demonstrate that of all domestic violence cases ending in death, 81 percent were wives murdered by their husbands. And, of male offenders in prison for domestic violence, 50 percent had killed their victims (U.S. Department of Justice, 2005).

Domestic violence is not only costly in terms of lives. The economic impact on society through loss of contributing, productive members and the societal costs to taxpayers is immense. In an average year, domestic violence costs the nation 5.8 billion dollars . Of this total, nearly 4.1 billion dollars is for direct medical and mental health care. Lost productivity and earnings due to domestic violence totals over 4 billion dollars (American Institute on Domestic Violence, 2001).

Finally, consider the 50,000 U.S. soldiers killed in the Viet Nam War from 1960 to 1972. Yes, we said soldiers; people fighting a war with guns, tanks, and bombs. Now, consider that in the same amount of time, between 1984 and 1995, the same number of women died at the hands of their abusers (Chicago Tribune, 1998).

Why do women put up with it? The answer is complex and lies buried in layers of multifaceted, socially constructed reasons. Due to religion, culture, and socially learned beliefs, women stay with their abusers out of a sense of duty, obligation, or the need to keep their marriages together. Often, abused women are financially dependent on their mates and face serious economic hardships for themselves and their children if they choose to leave. Additionally, fear of more abuse, even death, is a common reason for staying in abusive situations.

SEXUAL HARASSMENT

In 1900, there were 4.8 million women working, representing about 18 percent of the total workforce (U.S. Bureau of the Census, 1975). By 1970, 43 percent of women 16 and older worked. This number rose steadily until 1999 and has remained constant since then. Today, over 60 percent of all women work outside the home (U.S. Department of Labor, 2005).

There is no question that sexual harassment is discrimination which violates Title VII of the Civil Rights Act, affording employees the right to work in a hostile-free environment, free from discriminatory ridicule, hostility, insult, or intimidation. The Equal Employment and Opportunity Commission (EEOC) was established by the Civil Rights Act of 1964 as the agency responsible for enforcing Title VII. The EEOC defines **sexual harassment** as: unwelcome sexual advances, requests for favors, and other verbal or physical conduct of a sexual nature. The EEOC recognizes two non-mutually exclusive categories of sexual harassment: **quid pro quo** and **hostile work environment**. Quid pro quo is defined as a situation where a supervisor who has the power to hire, fire, or promote makes employment conditions dependent upon the sexual favors of the employee. A hostile work environment is one in which unwelcomed behavior(s) of a sexual nature by anyone in the workplace creates a hostile, abusive, or intimidating environment or reasonably interferes with an individual's work performance. Both of these categories manifest themselves in a variety of ways and produce a variety of reactions that may be psychological, physical or both. Additionally, individuals may suffer economic consequences.

The Civil Rights Act was amended in 1991 to include more issues, such as same sex harassment, sexual preference discrimination, liability to former employees for references, harassment by non-employees, and employer liability for harassment perceived by an employee that was not acted upon promptly, effectively and with remedial action.

Understandably, complaints filed with the EEOC have risen sharply. In one year, after Anita Hill testified against Clarence Thomas at his Supreme Court confirmation hearings, the EEOC received nearly 10,000 sexual harassment claims. In fiscal year 1996, they received over 15,000 sexual harassment charges. The Merit Systems Protection Board (MSFB) estimated that between April 1992 and April 1994, sexual harassment cases cost the Federal Government $327 million dollars. It should be clear that besides the enormous economic cost, sex discrimination is costly in terms of productivity loss, sick leave, and job turnover, not to mention that it violates the dignity and self worth of individuals.

There is no shortage of sexual harassment suits and with the above figures in mind, chances are that there will not be a shortage of sexual harassment lawsuits any time soon. Sexual harassment suits have been filed, almost exclusively by women, from boardrooms to assembly lines, by military personnel and white house aides, as well as factory workers, office clerks and students. Sexual harassment charges have been leveled at Supreme Court judges, military officers, senators, and even the President of the United States. Testimony given by former president Clinton's sexual harassment accuser Paula Jones, along with other information supplied by additional Clinton accusers, has prompted some detractors to name his administration *Zippergate*. Meanwhile, the Tailhook and Citadel incidents have brought national attention to the sexist treatment of women in the U.S. military, while the Mitsubishi case squarely placed the blame for factory women's harassment on management. Anita Hill and Clarence Thomas are old news. They may have started the sexual harassment ball rolling, but if there is one thing that we can be sure of it's that every day when we pick up the daily paper, there will be yet another new case to capture our attention.

Obviously, there are some burning questions that people are asking themselves regarding sexual harassment. Where to draw the line is a question often asked by both men and women. Is it wrong to recognize and/or compliment beauty, or to voice attraction to another person? Does a consensual office relationship always suggest sexual harassment? For as long as there have been men and women in the workplace, has there always been an undercurrent of attraction among coworkers? Who is to tell adults with whom they can or cannot have relationships?

Sexual harassment is not only risky but costly. In Fiscal Year 2008, EEOC received 13,867 charges of sexual harassment. 15.9 percent of those charges were filed by males. EEOC resolved 11,731 sexual harassment charges in 2008 and recovered $47.4 million in monetary benefits for charging parties and other aggrieved individuals (not including monetary benefits obtained through litigation). Imagine if this amount of money were spent on programs for education, research and development, salaries, bonuses and promotions. Now think about how much consumers have to pay in order for corporations to recoup the litigation funds disbursed because of alleged or litigated behavior.

Perhaps **risky behavior**, which can be defined as actions that may seem sincere and seemingly innocent but sends signals that may be interpreted by others as having sexual overtones, is what sometimes places individuals in precarious situations. Hugging a fellow employee, whether male or female; displaying a revealing photo on one's desk, maybe of a wife or girlfriend in a bikini; sexually oriented magazines, even closed, on your desk; and having a secret affair with someone in the workplace who is neither a subordinate or supervisor, are all risky behaviors.

Experts suggest that sometimes a workplace can become too friendly. Sometimes we can cross a line without being aware of it. When does a comment, joke, gesture, or touch cease to be innocent? Perhaps the more thought provoking question is when does sexual harassment begin, and humor, attraction, and hopes of attracting another end? The best position, according to New York attorney Chris Reynolds from the law firm of Morgan, Lewis, and Bacchus, is to avoid risky behavior and thereby avoid sexual harassment situations. Reynolds suggests that we can be engaging and supportive of a fellow co-worker without physical contact. Additionally, he recommends, we should take the stance that no means no. Behaviors that are unwanted by the recipient are generally considered grounds for harassment. The key is that the recipient must either verbalize, or in some other fashion make it known to others that he/she is not receptive to these behaviors.

From a structural functionalist perspective, sexual harassment is viewed as disruptive to the institutions of society. In general, they see it as a matter of individual deviance and one that requires a change in the behavior of the individual. Social conflict theorists would suggest that it goes beyond the individual and is rooted in the norms and institutions of society. They point to the fact that women are often hired for their attractiveness and are usually in a subordinate position to the men who make advances toward them. Often, women in subordinate positions lack the resources to ward off such advances and fear reprisals that could result in loss of a job or promotion, and capitulate to the demands placed on them. For social conflict theorists, sexual harassment is once again proof that subordinate workers are vulnerable and exploited to the benefit of the more powerful and wealthier citizens of our society.

FUTURE OUTLOOK

Until 5,000 years ago, women held equal status with men, especially when it came to food production as a means of survival. In technologically simple societies, the division of labor was based only on sex and age; men did the hunting and women and children did the gathering of vegetables and fruits. Even though meat was a commodity and highly valued, vegetables and other edible plants were a more reliable source of food. Based on this reliability factor, one might appropriately question whether the status of women in hunting and gathering societies was underrated. According to Elise Boulding (1976), technological breakthroughs propelled men into positions of dominance. When technology increased in agrarian societies, the status of women was reduced because technology allowed for a food surplus, which negatively impacted women's importance to their communities. To this day, women are engaged in a struggle to regain equal status.

The recent debate over proposed amendments to Title IX is a challenge being faced by today's women. In the recent past, Title IX provided a more level playing field, particularly in our colleges and universities. Statistics have improved slightly for minority access to higher education though it is too early to predict other trends resulting from the end of the Civil Rights era and how it impacts women.

Tolerance of homosexuality, as well as other behaviors previously labeled deviant, is on the rise, homophobia is on the decline, and laws have been implemented to protect gays from hate crimes and job discrimination. Before the close of the 20th century a violent and dreadful hate crime caught the attention of millions of Americans. Matthew Shepherd, a young, gay, college student was lured by two men from a Laramie Wyoming bar to a deserted open field. The two men tied Matthew to a fence and viciously beat him unconscious and then left him for dead in near freezing temperatures. Eighteen hours later he was discovered by two motorcyclists. He was flown to a Colorado hospital where he lay in a coma until his death six days later. The only motive for the attack—Matthew Shepherd was gay. The death of Matthew stirred the national conscience and resulted in a resounding call for tolerance in the treatment of people with different sexual orientations.

The Connecticut Supreme Court ruled in October of 2008 that gay and lesbian couples have the right to get married. This allows domestic partnerships to be recognized as legitimate families and extends to them the right to jointly purchase homes, qualify for partners insurance, access banking and borrowing opportunities jointly, and qualify for protection under the Family Leave and Medical Act. In the future, the trend may well be acceptance of homosexual relationships rather than mere tolerance for them.

For years, advocates have tried to repeal the Armed Forces "don't ask, don't tell" policy that allowed gays to serve in the military only if they neither were open about their homosexuality nor if someone found out that they were gay and reported them. If found out, they were dismissed from service. On December 22, 2010, "don't ask, don't tell" was repealed allowing openly gay people to serve in the Armed Forces.

The effects of racism and sexism are the same. The only difference is that one refers to discrimination based on gender, the other on race and ethnicity. Both are based on prejudices and stereotypes. Both groups are denied equal and full access to opportunities for employment, promotion, education, housing, purchasing power, and status in the political, social, and economic structures of society. And, as stated earlier, even though we still occasionally hear the phrase, "You've come a long way, baby," after reading this chapter, you know that the reply should be, "but we still have a long way to go."

SUMMARY

Progress was slow and unsteady during the twentieth century. Notable pioneers included such pathfinders as Harriet Martineau, Ida B. Wells, Jane Addams, Anna Freud, C.J. Walker and Mary Cover-Jones. Perhaps the most noted anthropologist of this century—Margaret Mead—had her contributions not only initially ignored, but had her classic study of the environmental effects on Samoan women replicated in an attempt to disprove her theory. According to the article: *It's Time for Working Women to Earn Equal Pay,* even though equal pay has been the law for over 41 years women still only earn 76 cents for every dollar that their male counterparts earn. But the news is not all bad, because even though progress is slow, it is steady.

We end this chapter the same way we began, with noting some of the progress that women, individually and as a group, have made. You've heard some variation of the saying, "it's difficult to know where you're going, if you don't know where you've been." Well, here are some of the places we've been.

Utah and Wyoming were the first states to allow women to vote. That was in 1870, 51 years before the 19th amendment gave all women in the United States that right (1921). Women actually ran for and were elected to office before the amendment was passed. Jeannette Rankin of Montana was elected to the House of Representatives in 1917. The first woman to run for the presidency was Victoria Woodhull (Equal Rights Party) in 1872. It took another 112 years before another woman, Geraldine Ferraro (Democrat) was successfully nominated for the vice-presidency (1984), In 1972, Congresswoman Shirley Chisholm became the first African American woman to have her name placed as a nominee for her party's (Democrat) presidential candidate. In the first eight years of the 21st Century, we have had 17 women governors. In 2008, 16 women served in the Senate and 75 in the House of Representatives

1992 was officially billed as "the Year of the Woman" by the Center of American Women and Politics because a record number of women were either appointed or elected to major political offices. But in spite of these accomplishments, and from a macro-level perspective, most women still find themselves marginalized by their gender and relegated to second-class status. Will this change in the foreseeable future? One can always hope. If America is to overcome its current economic crisis and compete successfully in the global marketplace it will need the talent and creativity of all of its citizens. As a nation, we can no longer turn a blind eye to the existing cultural bias against over half of our population.

Terms You Should Know:

Androgyny	Feminist	Gay
Gender	Hermaphrodite	Matriarchy
Modeling	Patriarchy	Sex
Sexuality	Sexual Harassment	Shaman
Significant Other	Transvestism	Transsexual

Can You Answer These Questions?

1. What is the difference between sex and gender?
2. How does the thinking of Margaret Mead and Talcott Parsons differ on gender roles?
3. According to Sigmund Freud, how is sexual identity formed?
4. List the three types of feminists and describe each. Which do you think is more relevant today?
5. Which institution in society is most important in determining our gender identity? Can you think of some socializing instances in your life?
6. How have women traditionally been treated in religion? Is this changing?
7. How has society treated homosexuality in the past? Are norms regarding homosexuality changing?
8. How prevalent is domestic violence in America?
9. What is the difference between "quid pro quo" and "hostile work environment"?
10. How do structural functionalist, social conflict theorists, and feminists view gender roles?

Critical Thinking Exercises:

1. Do you believe that society can ever achieve an androgynist society? Do you think it would be desirable even if we could? Why?
2. In your view, is homosexuality an "orientation," or a "preference"? Should we grant homosexuals the same rights, including marriage and adoption, as heterosexuals?
3. Some say that we have gone too far in attempting to define sexual harassment? Do you agree or disagree?
4. Women constitute over half of the voting population in the U.S. Given this fact, why haven't they done more to assert their rights?
5. Given the degree of domestic violence in our society, do you think the government has done enough to prevent it? If not, why?

Part Four

Social Institutions

In primitive societies the values and customs of the band or tribe are passed along informally. Generally, the family, and in some cases designated members of the tribe, assumes responsibility to ensure that all new members are properly instructed as to what is important and how to survive. In small communities, such methods are relatively effective. After all, the very fact that humans are here today is testimony to the success of this method. However, as humans flourished and their communities increased in size, it became apparent that the old methods were not going to work. This point marked the beginning of the development of formal social institutions. Let's be clear on this: social institutions have always existed—family, religion, tribal authority, etc. The point here is that as societies became increasingly more complicated, so did their social institutions.

In this section we study institutions—the structures designed to teach and promote the values and customs of society as well as carry out the necessary functions for survival. In Chapter Ten we examine the oldest and perhaps most important institution, that of family. As we are already aware, it is within the family that our first socializing experience takes place. We will learn that although we have a stereotypical view of family structure, there is much variation to be found in modern families. We also spend time examining divorce, remarriage, and children within stepfamilies. In Chapter Eleven we discuss education. Here we consider the forces that fostered mass education in society and their ties to the stratification system. A major question considered in this chapter is why some members of our society do better than others in our educational institutions. As always, many different views will emerge. Chapter Twelve is reserved for religion. As sophisticated as science may be, there are still unanswered questions—who are we, how did we come to be here, what happens to us after death. Although unanswerable, these are the most important of all questions for humans—hence religion.

In Chapter Thirteen, we discuss government and the economy. All societies wrestle with questions of authority and legitimacy. How societies answer these questions very much effects the arrangement of their government and the lives of their citizens. In this chapter we also discuss economic systems, their variations, advantages and disadvantages, and their relationship to the stratification system. In our final chapter in this section, Fourteen, we look closely at work. We will see how the lives of individuals and institutions are very much affected by the economic system. We see how social theorists are divided in their view of work and the economy. And, in conclusion, we look at the challenges of work in a new and ever changing economy.

John Coburn Photography

Chapter 10

Marriage and the Family

Consider these groups who live together in shared households. Which would *you* consider to be a family?

- Mary and John have been married for ten years. They have two children, Sally age eight and Tommy age six.
- Ruth is divorced. She lives with her son Andy, age 15.
- Jane was 18 and unmarried when she had a daughter, Chrissy. Chrissy is now 16 and has just had a baby boy. The three of them live together.
- George and Mark are a gay couple, who together have been raising George's son from an earlier heterosexual relationship.
- Patty and Arthur have never married, but have been living together as a couple for twenty years. They have bought a house and plan to grow old together.
- Betty never married, but she wished to be a mother. She adopted Susie at age four; Susie is now ten.

Many college students in the United States consider only some of these groups to really be families. Others feel that they are all families even if they do not entirely approve of the relationships.

WHAT IS A FAMILY?

The question, "what is a family?" is controversial. This question is the focus of debate among politicians and policy makers as well as sociologists. How one answers it, has important consequences for social policy. Legislation on welfare, health care, child-care, sexual discrimination in the workplace, taxation, abortion, family leave, family violence, and other issues frequently hinges on the legal definition of family. Those who define family only as a married couple with their own biological children often oppose health care, child care, welfare, and family leave legislation that would also be helpful to single parents (divorced and unwed), cohabiting partners and remarried couples (Coontz, 1997).

Sociologists agree that the family is a primary social group based on kinship. **Kinship** includes socially recognized relationships of **conjugality** (sexual relations), **consanguinity** (blood relations) and adoption. In this context adoption means social conventions that create recognized kin-like relationships between individuals not already blood related. This includes not only parent-child relationships but also sibling relationships, and many societies have conventions for creating kin-like relationships among adults.

Humans attach meaning to the world, to their own actions, and to the actions of others. It is the social recognition of relationships and attaching expectations and responsibilities to those relationships that creates kinship and the family. Around the world cultures vary considerably in which conjugal or sexual relationships are recognized as forming kinship or family. Cultures also vary in which consanguine or blood relationships are recognized as kinship or family. Thus, although family is always a primary social group based on kinship, there are substantial differences between cultures and over time over precisely who is counted as kin and family,and how those family members are supposed to relate to one another,

Family is also feelings and ideas, attitudes, and sentiments, mutual awareness and a sense of belonging together. Among humans, family is a relationship of some permanence and endurance over time. Humans create and maintain relationships that extend longer than simple physical dependency requires. Family relationships extend over most of our lifetime. Moreover, humans expect family relationships to be qualitatively different from other relationships. Family members have responsibilities toward one another. The exact nature of those responsibilities varies from culture to culture, and over time within a culture, but they tend to include responsibilities for raising children and providing economic and emotional support for members. The emotional quality of family relationships is different, more intense, and more multidimensional than other human relationships.

Sociologists who study family in the United States often must rely on data that is collected by government agencies, especially the Census Bureau, to gain insights into the change in family over time. One problem with this is that the definitions of family used by the Census Bureau do not always line up well with the sociological definition of family. The Census Bureau is constitutionally charged with enumerating the population of the United States, and determined more than two hundred years ago that the best way to accomplish this charge was to identify "households" which are groups of people living together within a single housing unit. The Census Bureau distinguishes between "family" and "non-family" households. A "family household" is one in which the head of the household is related by blood, adoption or legal marriage to at least one other person in the household. This would include married couples (with and without children), single parents with children, siblings sharing a single housing unit.

The focus of the Census Bureau on "family households" misses the reality of actual families in several ways. One of these is that a person who is living alone (such as a young person or an elderly person) is classified by the Census Bureau as a "non-family household" suggesting that these are people without family, when most people living alone are in fact active members of families, as sons and daughters, parents and grandparents, brothers and sisters, aunts and uncles, and so forth. There is substantial research (such as that by Carol Stack discussed later in this chapter) that indicates that families extend beyond the boundaries of a single household. This is particularly true among working class and lower class families in both rural and urban America, but can be observed among middle class families as well in older suburban areas where multiple generations live near each other and share family responsibilities on a daily or weekly basis.

FAMILY AND CULTURE

In this section we will examine some of the ways in which the ideas of who is part of a family and what family relationships should be like (social institution) vary from one culture to another and over time.

Families as Institutions and Social Groups

Every human society has its own culturally shared ideas of the right and moral patterns of sexual mating and biological descent. The **family** as a social institution includes: beliefs about what a family is, values about what family ought to be, norms about how its members should act, and statuses and roles that specify who in the family holds what responsibilities. Actual collections of individuals who call themselves families are what sociologists call social groups. It is the social institution that influences which groups of people may claim the title family. The social institution also influences individual behavior in families and sets the standard by which this behavior is measured. Both individuals and groups within a society can deviate from cultural ideas about family. Both the social institution and families as social groups vary across societies and over time.

Change in the life experience of people may or may not result in changed ideas about family. When a husband loses his job and his wife becomes the family breadwinner, their ideas about the appropriate roles of husband and wife may or may not change. Also changes in cultural ideas may or may not result in changes in the life experience. Today, most young parents value shared parenting as an ideal, but studies show that childrearing responsi-

Geisha entertainers wait for clients in front of a geisha house called a hanamachi. The geisha tradition of caring for the pleasure of men has long been an accepted custom in Japanese culture. Modern day geishas are among the most successful business enterprises in the society and are strictly matriarchal. Men play only limited roles such as hair stylists, dressers, and accountants.

Photo: Conveyor Belt Sushi.

bilities still fall overwhelmingly to mothers. Gaps between family ideals (social institutions) and the real-life experiences of families (social groups) often occur in times of rapid social change and are a source of stress and conflict for individuals and families.

Marriage and Other Socially Approved Sexual Relationships

Every society has shared ideas about which sexual relationships are and are not acceptable and appropriate.

Marriage Sociologists use the term **marriage** for one type of sexual relationship that a culture socially recognizes and formally sanctions. Most societies have some form of ritual to initiate or mark the beginning of a marriage. Many societies also have an economic contract between the parties or their families as an important part of the ritual process. These vary from "bride service" and "bride price" where the husband-to-be or his family provides economic service or payment to the family of the wife-to-be, to various forms of dowry, where the family of the wife-to-be makes provides material goods or payment to the husband-to-be.

Marriage comes in a variety of forms around the world. In the United States and Europe, **monogamy**, the marriage of one man and one woman, is the only accepted form of marriage. A large number of Asian, African, Pacific Islander and Middle Eastern societies, however, legally allow **polygyny**, where one man is married to two or more women at one time. One country that allows legal polygyny is Kazakhstan in central Asia. In other central Asian nations, such as Uzbekistan and Tajikistan, polygyny is illegal but widely practiced and political movements to legalize polygyny exist. The loss of men to civil war, wide spread poverty and few opportunities for women to support themselves outside of marriage, have contributed to the appeal of polygyny more so than the regions Islamic traditions (Eshanova, 2002). Another, much rarer form of polygamy (the general term for multiple marriage partners) is **polyandry**, where a woman may have more than one husband. Most of the societies that historically practiced polyandry were found in the Himalayan region (Nepal, Tibet, Northern India). Today, despite its illegality, polyandry is still practiced in Tibet. One news report from the 1990s described Tibetan villages where about seven percent of the adult population was involved in polyandrous, illegal (but locally accepted) marriages (Macartney, 1994).

Socially Approved Sexual Relations. Many cultures have established patterns for sex outside of marriage. One such institutionalized form of extramarital sex is called concubinage. Societies that accept sexual relationships in addition to marriage generally do not accord the same legal rights and recognition to either the extramarital sexual partner or the biological offspring of that mating. **Concubinage** was a common practice among the more affluent Chinese until the twentieth century. In China, concubines and their children usually didn't inherit property. However, if a man's wife had no male children, it was common practice for the male child of a concubine to be considered the offspring of the wife rather than the concubine, thereby allowing for a legitimate heir (Queen, Habenstein, and Quadagno, 1985).

A variety of cultures have accepted **homosexual** relationships. Some cultures allowed homosexuality for all men at one life stage, such as at adolescence, because the expectation was that most would move into heterosexual marriages later. Elsewhere, homosexuality was accepted as an adjunct to heterosexual marriage. In ancient China married men were allowed to take male lovers as well as female concubines. Finally, homosexuality has been approved as a lifelong option for certain individuals, while most people engage only in heterosexual relationships (Adam, 1986; Coontz, 2005).

Institutionalized or socially approved sexual relationships vary considerably across cultures and some members of all societies engage in sexual relationships that are not socially approved. Cultures also vary in the degree to which they tolerate violations of sexual norms.

Biological Descent: Parents and Children

As self-aware, cultural beings, humans pay close attention to some biological relationships and ignore others. We also create relationships that we treat the same as our biological kin. One common form of this is **adoption**.

Biological and **social parenthood** can be quite different. Social parents are the persons whom society recognizes as a child's parents. They are held responsible for socially defined parenting duties and hold the rights and privileges accorded to parents. The Chinese example above demonstrates separation between the biological mother and the social mother. When the concubine's son is treated as that of the wife, he has the same legal rights as the wife's biological children, the right to inherit his father's property. The separation of biological and social motherhood, however, is much less common than the separation of biological and social fatherhood. Early humans did not understand the connection between sex and pregnancy. They, therefore, didn't have the ability to identify biological fathers. Fatherhood was a social relationship based upon the acceptance of responsibility for children and their upbringing. Even when people understood the biological role of the male in pregnancy, biological fatherhood may have been less important than social fatherhood. Among the Tibetans that practice polyandry, husbands take turns sleeping with their common wife, and the children all call the eldest husband "father" and the other husbands (usually brothers of the oldest) "uncle," regardless of who was the biological father (Macartney, 1994).

In some societies, biological fathers may be known and acknowledged but less important in their children's lives than other relatives such as the mother's brothers (uncles). The Hopi and other Native American groups practice this pattern. Hopi boys often have close, affectionate relationships with their biological fathers but their maternal uncle is the primary disciplinarian. The boy's uncle is consulted in choosing a marriage partner. He is considered the male representative of the boy's family (Queen, Habenstein, and Quadagno, 1985).

In the U.S., it is not uncommon for individuals to be raised by someone other than their biological parents. Adoption, divorce, death, remarriage, or other circumstances may result in a child's viewing someone other than a biological parent as their mother or father. We generally consider those adults who took responsibility for us, nurtured and taught us, as our parents, regardless of their biological relationship to us. In most societies it is acting like a parent that creates a parent. As with sexual relationships, the parenting behavior of individuals may diverge from cultural ideas. Regardless of their biological relationship to a child, we may deny the rights of parenthood to mothers and fathers who do not "act like parents."

SOCIOLOGICAL PERSPECTIVES

All sociological theories of family do two things: *First*, they direct our attention, telling us what things to look for in our observations of the real world; and *second*, they provide us with a framework that can help explain why the things we observe are happening and what their consequences are likely to be. When we examine the world through the lens of structural functional theory we are encouraged to notice the ways in which families serve the needs of society as a whole and not just their individual members. On the other hand, the lens of social conflict theory draws our attention to the inequities that exist between and within families.

Structural Functional

Structural functional theory dominated sociological understanding of the family as a social institution in the mid-twentieth century. It continues to exert an influence on thinking about the family. Structural functional theorists view the family as an extremely important element of society because it fills some of society's most basic needs or functions. These functions, in turn, determine the family's *structure*. Those who use this theoretical perspective also consider any deviation from this functionally determined structure to be dysfunctional or harmful to society.

Functions. Several structural functional theorists (Parsons and Bales, 1955; Etzioni, 1983; Popenoe, 1996) have listed **five** functions that families serve in society. The two most central, related functions of the family from this theoretical perspective are: *first*, procreation or childbearing; and *second*, the socialization of children. To survive, societies need new members. A society acquires most of its new members by giving birth to them, or procreation. That society must teach its new members the cultural knowledge required to be participating members, a process called **socialization**. For structural functional theory, the institution of the family best provides for these two societal needs. Moreover, this theory argues for the family to successfully fill these social needs, it requires a structure with two parents (Etzioni, 1983), preferably the biological father and mother (Popenoe, 1996).

A *third* function of the family, related to procreation, is the regulation of sexual behavior. Structural functionalism suggests that primary socially approved sexual relationships are those occurring within the family in the form of marriage. Family also restricts sexual access through the **incest taboo**. All societies forbid sex among certain family members. This is based on rules of social relationship rather than biological kinship–societies forbid adoptive parents and stepparents, as well as biological parents, to have sex with their children.

Fourth, structural functionalism notes that the family provides for the material or economic needs of its members. The precise nature of this family function varies considerably from society to society and consequently, the structure of family varies also.

In pre-industrial societies family served the economic function by organizing production. All family members, males and females, young and old, engaged in activities such as gathering, hunting, planting, tool making, and other activities necessary to meet the basic needs of the family. The function of economic production in industrial societies is transferred to business organizations, but the family still serves the economic function of organizing consumption. Society expects the family to collect the wages earned by its members and use them to purchase things they need.

Parsons and Bales argued that modern industrial society required a **nuclear family** structure: only two generations–parents and children. According to Parsons, the nuclear family was isolated from extended kinship networks and more mobile than the **extended family**, with three or more generations (grandparents, parents and children) which he assumed was the dominant family form in pre-industrial societies. Parsons and Bales also believed the best way to meet the economic function in industrial society was for men to specialize in earning wages while women specialized in overseeing the family's consumption of goods and services.

The *fifth* function of the family is to provide emotional support (Parsons and Bales, 1955; Etzioni, 1983). In structural functional theory the primary responsibility for this falls to the wife, who fills the role of **expressive leader**, nurturing the children and her husband and maintaining the families emotional health as a homemaker.

Dysfunctional Family Structure. When there is disparity between the cultural ideas of the social institution and the real behavior of family members, structural functionalists consider the deviations to be **dysfunctional**. In structural functional theory the label dysfunctional has little to do with psychological harm to individuals (such as that which occurs to victims of family violence and incest). Instead, it refers to a presumed failure of families to meet the functional needs of society as a whole. According to structural functional theory, single-parent families, regardless of the parenting skills of the individuals within them, are by definition dysfunctional and unable to meet the procreation and socialization needs of society. Although a society may be able to tolerate a small number of families that deviate from the social and institutional structure, an increasing number of such families may result in major societal needs not being met.

Critiques of Structural Functionalism

As African Americans, women, and other minorities became social scientists in greater numbers in the 1970s, they widened the scope of research on the family. New empirical data on the history and present conditions of family challenged the assumptions of structural functional theory.

New research provided evidence that, contrary to structural-functional theory, three generational extended families were rare prior to industrialization and that most present-day families, while nuclear, are not isolated, but are firmly embedded in networks of extended kin.

Demographers and family historians documented that before the twentieth century the combination of significantly shorter life spans and later marriages resulted in few people living long enough to know their grandchildren, much less live in an extended family with them (Uhlenberg, 1989). Moreover, numerous studies of poor and working class families in both urban and rural settings (Stack, 1974; Beaver, 1986) provide clear evidence of present-day multi-generational families caring for children, sharing financial resources, and cooperating in economic activity as well as emotional support. In short, the primary criticism of structural functional theory is that the nuclear family existed long before industrialization and that the extended family is more common, rather than less so in the twentieth century.

Social Conflict

Social conflict theories, such as the Neo-Marxist and Feminist theories brought the issue of power and its unequal distribution in society into the picture to help us understand variation and change in the family. Where structural functionalism assumes that the family performs functions for the benefit of society as a whole, social conflict theories assume that the social institution of family provides benefits for society's most powerful groups.

Randall Collins (Collins and Coltrane, 1990) argues that a family's position in the stratification system is the single most important factor in determining the characteristics of the family, such as family structure. Family forms held up as the ideal in the media are consistent with the practices of powerful societal groups. Less powerful groups may be prevented from attaining that idea by discrimination or lack of resources. Nonetheless, less powerful groups are often judged against the cultural ideals that favor the powerful.

Neo-Marxist theories of family. Neo-Marxist theories of family draw upon Marx's idea that the mode of production—how goods are produced–is the primary determinant of societal structure and therefore family structure. Each society has a characteristic mode of production with a particular pattern of ownership of the means of production. Societies are divided between the owners and the non-owners of the means of production. Ownership of the means of production is the source of power. Therefore, owners have greater power to determine their own family structures and to dictate the family structures of the non-owners. Marxists believe that owners will force non-owners into family structures that benefit owners by providing them with cheap and plentiful labor, often detrimental to the health and well being of the non-owners. For example, the families of slaveholders prior to the Civil War were maintained through the subjugation of slave families. Laws forbade legal marriage among slaves. Slaveholders often separated family members (partners, parents and children, siblings) through sale and relocations (Queen, Habenstein, and Quadagno, 1985).

When the mode of production changes, especially when patterns of ownership of the means of production change, then the structure of the family must also change. In the pre-industrial economy of the United States, small independent family farmers owned most of the means of production (land and the resources for farming the land). When the mode of production changed from farming to manufacturing, the ownership of the means of production changed hands from family owned farms to the few wealthy business owners of the factories, etc. This economic transformation changed family life to the new breadwinner/homemaker family of the small affluent class and the wage earning family of the working class. Maintaining the upper class family depended on the existence of the labor of poor families (Lerner, 1979). Consider how low factory wages made possible the profits that paid for the services of poor women and children for domestic services to maintain the large households of the wealthy.

The importance of Neo-Marxist theories is that they allow us to understand the connection between families and their relationship to the ownership of the means of production. Stack (1974) found that poor African Americans (non-owners) who were denied entry into higher wage positions developed creative family structures to meet the needs of their members. Families in this study created flexible networks of kin that extended beyond the boundaries of a single household. These networks shared responsibility for the care and nurturing of children. The extension of the kin network assured that someone would have access to resources, through employment and welfare to provide food, housing and clothing for children and other family members. While powerful groups have labeled the family structure of poor African Americans as fragmented, broken and pathological (Moynihan, 1965), Stack argued that poor African American children often lived within a flexible, stable supportive family network incorporating several physical households. Other researchers have found similar family networks sharing resources and parenting responsibilities among white working class families, in both rural (Beaver, 1986) and urban areas (Darling and Greer, 1986; Harvey, 1993).

Feminist Theories of the Family. There is no single "feminist theory." American feminism embraces a wide range of theoretical viewpoints. However, all feminists share the view that men and women have unequal resources for power and that conflict and power-plays between the genders exist within the family (Bokemeir, 1997).

The shape the family takes at any point in history or in any society reflects the social, political, and economic power of the genders. The structure of the family is the outcome of a power struggle. It meets the needs of those family members, primarily men, with the most power. Changes in the power relationships between the genders will result in changes in family structure.

Feminist theories have drawn attention to many problems involving the abuse of power that exist within families such as: spousal violence, marital rape, incest, and child sexual abuse.

To some extent child abuse has been a subject of public concern and sociological study since the late 1800s. But, neither the public nor social scientists were aware of the extent of spousal violence in American families until the 1970s. When violence did come to the public's attention it was assumed to be the result of the deviance of individuals from cultural norms. Feminist theory, on the other hand, proposed that wife abuse was a normal, expected outcome of family norms that placed men at the head of the family (Gelles, 1994). Men's position and authority in the home was reinforced, feminists argued, by society's legal, educational and economic systems. Women's dependence on men made escape from an abusive situation more difficult (Straus, Gelles, and Steinmetz, 1980). A higher risk of spousal violence was associated with lower educational attainment for women, lower family incomes (U.S. Department of Justice, 1994), and male unemployment (Gelles, 1994). Such empirical data led some feminists to theorize that husbands are most likely to engage in violence when they feel least secure in their position as head of the family.

Critiques of Social Conflict Theory

Unlike structural functional theory, social conflict theories are well grounded in empirical reality. However, the strength of these theories is also their weakness: Neo-Marxist and Feminist work on the family rarely rises above an empirical description. Both theoretical schools have failed to articulate coherent, unified theories of "the family" as a distinct social entity (Winton, 1995).

Critics from the fields of Family Therapy have suggested that Neo-Marxists are losing sight of the role of human intention and action in their focus on the broad forces of the economy, politics and inequality. Family therapists note that wealthy families are not without their troubles and that many poor and working class families have happy and satisfying family lives (Day, 1995).

Others have criticized Feminist theorists as being too optimistic in their view of unwed motherhood, divorce, single parenting, and the increased participation of mothers in the labor force (Coontz, 1997). Numerous studies suggest that many Americans, women as well as men, do not find these trends as "liberating" as Feminist theories would predict. An intact, two-parent family continues to be the American ideal, even for those for whom it is not realistically attainable.

THE AMERICAN FAMILY IN TRANSITION

The American family is undeniably changing. Most Americans see some changes in family as positive. Other changes are seen by most as negative. Still others are the focus of heated controversy and debate. Some concerns about family changes spring from a lack of knowledge and distorted information in the popular media.

This section reviews some of the vast array of research on the American family. One must remember that family sociology is a field of ongoing inquiry. Some of the trends examined here are well documented and difficult to dispute. Among these are family trends tracked by the U.S. Census Bureau. But some "trends" are really mathematical projections into the future; they require making assumptions about what will happen. Such assumptions do not always turn out to be correct. Also, researchers debate the causes of trends, what they mean, what their consequences are for individuals or for particular families, for "the family" as a social institution, or for society as a whole. At the end of this section we will examine how sociologists with different theoretical perspectives view changes in the family.

There are many opportunities for sociologists of the future to make meaningful discoveries and expand on our understanding of the family and how it is changing. Many questions have yet to be asked and even more have been asked but have no definitive answers.

To Marry or Not to Marry?

There is widespread anxiety about the state of marriage in America, which is based more on conservative ideology than it is on scientific fact (Coltrane and Adams, 2003). A recently released (November 2010) Pew Research survey done in conjunction with *TIME* carried the provocative title: "The Decline of Marriage and the Rise of New Families." However, the title refers to attitudes about marriage, not actual trends. These attitudes about the obsolescence of marriage and anxiety about marriage are often based on misperceptions and misunderstandings of trends in cohabitation, unwed childbearing, and especially of divorce. The divorce rate has been declining steadily for the past thirty years. The Pew study (2010) showed that only five percent of all the people polled were aware that divorce was declining; most believed that divorce was increasing.

There are also substantial misunderstandings, by both the general public and social scientists, of the crude marriage rate which compares the number of marriages in one year to the total population in that year and is highly sensitive to changes in the age composition of society, and changes in the age at which people marry. The crude marriage rate fluctuated substantially over the past 70 years (see Figure 10.1 with both marriage and divorce rates shown), going down in the 1950s and 1960s, up again in the 1970s and 1980s and tracking back down again since 1990. The crude marriage rate goes down when the size of the cohort of young people approaching marriageable age (their twenties) declines in size compared to the rest of the population, and is also strongly affected by delays in the age at which most couples marry. A more accurate measure of the popularity of marriage is to track the marital experience of people in specific age cohorts over time. The Census Bureau examines the marital experience of people in five and ten year age cohorts. Examining people 40 to 44 years old, we find that in 2009 only 13 percent had never been married, meaning that 87 percent had married at least once. This is only a small reduction in marriage since 2000 when 89 percent of 40 to 44 year-old's had married, and a slightly greater change compared to 1970 when 94 percent of 40 to 44 year-old's had married. Overall, the vast majority of people still marry, and declines in likelihood of marriage by age 44 are slight (U.S. Census Bureau, 2011).

Tables like 10.1, which take a one time snapshot of marital status, exaggerate changes in marital status because young people are waiting longer to marry, thereby swelling the ranks of the never married. The most significant marital trend has been the rise in age at first marriage. In 2010 the median age of men marrying for the first time was just over 28 years old, while the median age for women marrying for the first time was 26 years old.

This represents a substantial increase in age compared to the 1950s, and is a return to the pattern of the 19th century. Contrary to popular belief, less than 75 percent of the population married in the second half of the nineteenth century (Coontz, 2005). Yet, no one accuses our great, grandparents' generation of lacking a commitment to the institution of marriage despite their lower incidence of marriage. Some of the changes in marriage are the result of changed economic and social circumstances and some are the result of changed attitudes about marriage and singlehood. Nonetheless, marriage is hardly about to disappear as the choice of the majority of Americans.

Sex Outside of Marriage. Sex before marriage isn't new. Studies of marriage and birth records in the U.S. colonial period, such as Carr and Walsh's (1977) study of the Maryland colony, suggest that perhaps one third of all brides were pregnant at marriage. The premarital pregnancy rate declined in the 18th century to just over ten percent (Degler, 1980), but it is clear that some premarital sexual relations still existed. There is little evidence indicating any differential treatment of pregnant and nonpregnant brides. Carr and Walsh (1977) suggest that premarital sex was within social norms, so long as a wedding took place prior to the birth of a child.

Table 10.1: Marital Status of People Fifteen Years and Over, 2010.

Marital Status:	Married	Widowed	Divorced	Separated	Never Married
Percent of population over age 15	51.3	5.9	9.8	2.3	30.7

Source: **U.S. Census Bureau, 2011. Table A-1. Origin, 2010. http://www.census.gov/population/socdemo/hh-fam/cps2010/tabA1-all.xls Access March 8, 2011.**

Still, there is no question that there is far more sexual experience outside of marriage today than fifty years ago, but there has been some slight reversal in trends in the past two decades. In recent decades the sexual experience of young men and women has converged, becoming more similar. The Centers for Disease Control regularly survey American high school students concerning a variety of risk behaviors (the National Youth Risk Behaviors Survey—YRBS), including sex. In 2005, the CDC survey found that 45.7 percent of females and 47.9 percent of males reported having at least one experience of sexual intercourse. This was down slightly from a high of 50.8 percent of females and 57.4 percent of males in the 1991 survey (Centers for Disease Control and Protection, 2006). The recent declines in teenage sexual activity is reflected in declines in teenage pregnancy rates, teenage abortion rates and teenage birthrates (Ventura, Abma, Mosher, and Henshaw, 2009).

Does the change in behavior represent a change in our cultural ideas about sex outside of marriage? The Pew Research Center found that sixty percent of American adults, in their 2010 survey, viewed pre-marital sex as "not wrong", a substantial shift from 1970, when only twenty-one percent considered it "not wrong" (Pew Research Center, 2010.

Cohabitation. Heterosexual couples living together without legal marriage—cohabitation—is another indicator of changes in attitudes about sex outside of marriage in America. However, it is not an indicator of widespread abandonment of marriage. In 2010, the Census Bureau Current Population Survey found 58.4 million households headed by married couples and only 7.5 million headed by opposite sex unmarried couples. While unmarried couples have increased at a faster rate than married couples, married couples still account for 89 percent of all opposite sex couples (U.S. Census Bureau, 2010). In addition to making up only a small proportion of opposite sex couples, cohabitation is not a long term alternative to marriage for most people. Nearly fifty percent of cohabiting relationships end within five years (National Center for Health Statistics, 2002). Moreover, a large proportion of terminated cohabitations result in a marriage. Studies such as London's (1991), show that slightly over half of all cohabiters eventually marry each other.

People enter cohabiting relationships for many reasons. Some view it as an alternative to marriage. This attitude is especially common among previously married individuals who fear going through another divorce. Others view it as a "trial marriage" period to test compatibility before making a final commitment. Often, it is a choice motivated by financial, logistical or practical considerations among couples that may or may not intend to marry. Several studies find that male unemployment is higher among cohabiters than among married couples. In our society most people still think of husbands as the primary breadwinner and head of the household. The economic differences between cohabiting and married couples suggest that some couples may delay marriage until the man can fulfill societal norms. The Pew survey found that sixty-nine percent of respondents in an unmarried partnership wished to marry their partner (Pew Research Center, 2010).

Most studies find little difference in the marital adjustment, marital happiness, or the length of marriage among those who cohabit before marriage and those who do not. The exception to this is the higher risk of divorce among individuals who have had a series of cohabiting relationships with other individuals before marrying (Lamanna and Reidmann, 2003).

Cohabitation has become a stage of courtship before marriage rather than a replacement for marriage, a trend that is accepted by most Americans. The Pew Research Center's 2010 survey found that more than half of those under age 50 had cohabited at least once, and that 55 percent of all respondents viewed this trend of increased cohabitation as either a positive thing or as neutral (neither positive nor negative) for society (Pew Research Center, 2010).

Homosexual Relationships. For the first time, in 2000, the Census Bureau made it possible for an unmarried head of household to indicate another adult in the household as their "unmarried partner" and 594,400 adults identified a same sex adult as their "unmarried partners." About fifty-five percent of those households involved two male partners and forty-five percent were two female partners. The Census Bureau draws no conclusions about the sexual orientation of respondents, but it is reasonable to assume that these same sex partners represent homosexual relationships.

In the United States homosexuals have gradually earned public acceptance and legal rights since the 1970s. These changes have not been accepted by all Americans and have created significant political opposition from some groups. Homosexuals in long-term committed relationships have been seeking rights to be treated as next-of-kin for medical and legal issues and property rights. Some homosexuals have argued for the opportunity to have civil unions or domestic partnerships that are legally recognized, others have expressed the desire to have the legal right to marry.

The issue of rights for same sex partners has been highly contentious in the United States in the 21st century but attitudes about homosexuality and same sex marriage have gradually liberalized. Between 1996 and 2010 opposition to same sex marriage dropped from 65 percent of the population to 48 percent while support grew from 27 percent to 42 percent. Among the youngest adults support is over fifty percent. Support for domestic partnerships, or civil unions, is much higher than support for legal marriage for same sex partners (Pew Research Center 2010).

The split in attitudes is reflected in the legal status of same sex couples across the country. Six U.S. states have granted same-sex couples the right to legal marriage: Vermont, New Hampshire, Maine, Massachusetts, Connecticut and Iowa. Same sex marriage is also legal in Washington, D.C. As of March 2011, the state senate in Maryland had passed a bill legalizing same sex marriage which was to be taken up by the lower house of the Maryland legislature later in March 2011; if passed, Maryland would become the seventh state to legalized same sex marriage (Breitenbach and Newman, 2011). Another six states have allow same sex couples to register domestic partnerships to obtains some of the legal rights accorded married couples: New Jersey, Washington, Oregon, California, Nevada and Hawaii. On the other hand, thirty states have constitutional amendments to their state constitutions that prohibit marriage by same sex couples (including some of the states such as California and Oregon that allow domestic partnerships) and thirty-six states have statutes that prohibit same sex marriage (there is overlap with twenty-five states having both statutes and constitutional amendments) (Vestal, 2009).

Changing Circumstances, Changing Structure and Changing Norms. The path that most people take to marriage today is longer, more varied, and less certain than it was fifty years ago. Our ideas about acceptable sexual behavior have also changed. For most, sex is no longer necessarily tied to marriage but Americans are not unanimous in their views. There is more conflict than consensus over sexual norms.

Most Americans value marriage. Young people still plan to marry and most still do. When we marry, we continue to profess vows to love and honor, to remain constant through good and bad times, to cherish and remain faithful. Moreover, we generally promise to do these things for life. This promise is harder to keep today, than it was a hundred years ago. Yet, surprisingly, Americans remain married longer than ever before. We hear so much about divorce, which has actually been on the decline since 1980, that we forget that increases in life span outweigh the increases in divorce (Uhlenberg, 1989). In 1800, life expectancy was only about 35 years. It reached 47 years in 1900, jumped to 68 years in 1950, and steadily rose to 77.2 years in 2001 (U.S. Census Bureau, 1997; World Almanac, 2005). Between longer lives and declining divorce rates, the chances for celebrating a fortieth wedding anniversary are greater than ever (Coontz, 1997).

Recent comparative research supports the view that marriage continues to be a viable, rewarding institution for most Americans, but there are some changes in how married people relate. Amato, Booth, Johnson and Rogers (2007) identified five dimensions of marital quality (based on the reports of subjects): marital happiness, marital interaction, marital conflict, marital problems, and "divorce proneness" (meaning how often the individual thought about or talked to others—including spouse—about the possibility of divorce, etc.). Using two national studies in 1980 and 2000, the researchers found that: 1) reported levels of marital happiness and "divorce proneness"

A young mother takes time from her work schedule to interact with her child. Today, over 50 percent of all children during any given year will have a working mother. Economic conditions necessitating two incomes to make ends meet along with changing attitudes of women wanting to pursue careers have accounted for the rise of the "working mom."

Photo: ep.Sos.de.

An only child? More than likely in Japanese society which has the lowest birthrate among industrialized nations. In fact, the rate is so low that a new term has surfaced in the culture—shoshika, meaning a country without children. If current trends continue, the population of Japan will shrink by 20 percent by the middle of this century leading to serious economic problems. To counter falling birthrates, the Japanese government has adopted the "Plus-One-Proposal" which offers financial incentives for women to have an additional child.

Photo: Masayuki Takau.

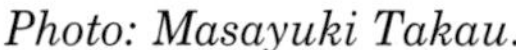

had not changed; 2) on the positive side, reported levels of marital conflict and marital problems declined moderately; and 3) overall levels of marital interaction declined. So, on two of the five measures marital quality stayed the same for 20 years, on two measures marital quality improved, and on one measure, "interaction," there was a decline. Overall, the way in which husbands and wives interact, the amount of time they spend in joint activities, has changed, but satisfaction with marriage, feelings of love for ones spouse, have remained the same or improved and levels of conflict in marriage have declined.

Having Children

A key element of family is the relationship of biological descent, especially between parent and child. Like marriage, childbearing has undergone significant change both in terms of our behavior and our ideas about children.

Birthrates. Americans, like people in most industrial nations, are choosing to have smaller families. The number of children born to U.S. women has been declining for more than 200 years. Fertility rates declined steadily from 1800 until 1946. There was a temporary reversal during the "Baby Boom" years (1946-1964) and then a return to the long term declining trend. Currently, the fertility rate is 66.7 births per 1,000 women age 15 to 44, which has been steadily falling since the mid-1960s (National Vital Statistics Report, 2010). There has been substantial downsizing in what Americans consider the desirable number of children. In the 1940s, four or more children was considered the most desirable family size; today, the most desired number of children is two (Pew Research, 2010a). Exactly why parents began limiting births is a matter of debate among social scientists. The usual explanation is that the progressive shift from a rural agricultural economy to an urban industrial one changed the meaning of children in people's lives. Children are important economic producers in an agricultural economy and the care of infants and toddlers can easily be integrated with mothers' and fathers' economic activities. The shift to a factory-based economy both lessened the

Table 10.2: Birth Rates for Teens and Young Women (number of births per 1,000 women)

Age	1960	1970	1980	1990	2009
10-14			1.1	1.4	0.5
15-19	89.1	68.3	53.0	59.9	39.1
20-24	258.1	167.8	115.1	116.7	96.3
25-29	197.4	145.1	112.9	120.2	110.5

Source: U.S. Census Bureau, Statistical Abstracts for 1985 and 1990 and National Vital Statistics Reports, 2002 volume 50, no.4 and 5; and 2010 volume 59, no. 3.

opportunities for children to contribute to economic production and placed limits on the ways in which mothers could participate in the paid economy. The decline in birthrates involved conscious decision-making by married couples to have fewer children. This took planning because the two primary methods for limiting conception prior to the late 19th century were abstinence and *coitus interruptus* or withdrawal (LeVine and White, 1987). Barrier methods of contraception did not become widely available in the United States until the 1920s.

Developments such as the birth control pill introduced to the public in 1962, and the legalization of abortion in 1972, have made it easier for women to limit their childbearing, but the patterns of childbearing depend more on economic and social changes, such as increased education and participation of women in the paid workforce.

Delayed Child Bearing and Childlessness. There has been a substantial shift in the timing of childbearing, especially birth of the first child. While childbearing rates have been declining overall, they have declined more slowly for older women than for younger women, so that by 1990 the birthrates for women 25 and older are greater than the birthrates of women under age 25 (see Table 10.2). In recent years, the rate of childbearing has actually gone up slightly for women 40-44 and women over 50. The percentage of babies born to mothers over 35 has gone up 64 percent from 1990 to 2009 (National Vital Statistics, 2010).

In addition to smaller family sizes and delayed childbearing, the proportion of American women who have remained childless has also increased in the past two decades, but has not risen to the level of childlessness during the Great Depression and World War II. Among American women born in 1911, twenty-two percent had no live births by age 50. By comparison, for women born in 1941 only eight percent had no live births by age 50 (the lowest recorded). For women born in 1951 fifteen percent had no live births by age 50. Early indications are that the next cohort of women born in 1961 will reach age 50 with approximately sixteen to seventeen percent of their cohort having had no live births (Hamilton and Cosgrove, 2010).

Several researchers have recently argued that much of the recent increase in childlessness was not a conscious choice, but rather the unforeseen consequence of delaying childbearing until one could become established in a career (Hewlett, 2002; Crittenden, 2001), There has been steady increase in the birthrates of women over 35 (and a corresponding decrease in the birthrates of women under 25) over the past two decades (Ventura, Hamilton and Sutton, 2003). However, a significant number of women who wish to begin childbearing after age 35 are unable to do so due to decreased fertility, and other considerations (Hewlett, 2002).

Unwed childbearing. One of the most significant trends of the past thirty years has been the rise in childbearing outside of marriage. Currently, 41 percent of children in the United States are born to an unmarried mother. However, only ten percent of children in 2010 actually lived in a single parent household headed by an unwed mother (National Vital Statistics Report, 2010). Most children born out of wedlock spend a significant portion of their childhood in a two parent home. A large percentage of unwed births occur to mothers who are cohabiting with their children's biological father; another significant proportion of unwed mothers marry while their children are small. When most people think of unwed mothers, they think of teenagers. In the 1960s, more than 80 percent of teenage mothers were married at the time they gave birth. Many teenage births in the 1960s were the planned and desired outcome of young marriages. Unplanned, premarital pregnancies almost always resulted in marriage prior to the arrival of the child. The overall rise in marriage age and decreasing stigma of unwed childbearing has resulted in 87 percent of teen births to now occur outside of marriage. It is this high proportion of unwed childbearing that causes people to focus on teenagers. However, teenagers account for a declining share of all births and increasingly for a declining share of unwed births as well—only one-fourth of the unwed childbearing in the U.S. today, compared to fifty percent in 1970 (U.S. Health and Human Services, 2004). As the overall birth rate has declined faster than the decline of unwed births, unwed childbearing has become a larger percentage of all births for women of all ages (National Vital Statistics Report, 2010).

Commonsense observation suggests that the stigma attached to unwed childbearing has significantly decreased in the past 50 years. For example, families almost never attempt to conceal an unwed pregnancy by sending a daughter out of town. Unwed mothers are nearly as likely to enjoy baby showers and baby gifts, and even small town newspapers display birth announcements for single mothers and unwed couples along side those of married couples.

On the other hand, in recent surveys sixty-five percent of Americans consider the rise in unwed childbearing to be a "bad" thing for American society, and only four percent view it as a "good" thing (Pew Research, 2010a).

Some concern seems reasonable. Households headed by single women have higher rates of poverty (28.3 percent in 2006) than married couple households do (4.9 percent in 2006). However, concerns about unwed childbearing are probably driven more by moral concerns than by rational ones. Consider the debates over welfare reform in 1996. Much of the debate centered on unwed teenage pregnancy even though teenagers (both wed and unwed) accounted for less than six percent of all AFDC families in 1994 (U.S. Department of Health and Human Services, 1994).

Sociologists' views of the impact of unwed childbearing on the family as a social institution vary. Popenoe (1996) argues that being fatherless is inherently problematic for both children and society. Other social scientists, such as Cherlin (1981) and Crittenden (2001) argue that the problems female headed families experience are not due to their family structure but to the lack of economic equality for women and to the lack of societal supports such as health care and childcare.

The Place of Children in the Family and Society. Changes have occurred in our cultural ideas about children and their place in the family. Before the twentieth century, people viewed children primarily as economic assets. Today we view children as emotional assets (Zelizer, 1985). To become parents, infertile couples are willing to pay for expensive medical procedures, private adoptions or even surrogate mothers. Children may be more precious to parents for emotional reasons but some feminists have noted that children are less supported (Coontz, 1997; Crittenden, 2003; Hewlett, 2002) by U.S. society as a whole. These observers argue that many Americans view children as "consumer goods": only those who can afford the full costs should be allowed to have them (Hewlett, 1986). We are less willing to pay for public education, health care, and especially for welfare, which primarily goes to support poor children. What was once viewed as an entitlement of poor children to basic economic support is today seen as an undeserved handout to lazy and irresponsible parents. Politicians want to cut or eliminate existing programs and they show little sign of supporting desperately needed new programs to provide broader health coverage and child care for working parents. The costs of childrearing are becoming more privatized just when families' resources are declining.

Family Roles

Roles are important for any social institution. Family roles include the allocation of responsibility for tasks related to economic survival, childrearing, and maintaining the family household. These roles are changing, but not for the first time.

Breadwinning. Prior to the 1880s in America the majority of families lived and worked on family farms, where husbands, wives and children were work partners in "breadwinning." Even in urban communities many families engaged in small businesses that required work by all family members. It was not until the industrial revolution that a separation between "breadwinning" and "homemaking" became widespread. From the end of the 19th century through the 1970s, the division of responsibility between a male breadwinner and a female homemaker/childrearer—what most people call traditional—was well understood, but not actually attained by the majority of families until after World War II. Women entered the paid workforce slowly in the 1920s and 1930s. There was a significant jump during WWII and a slight decline in the years immediately following the war. The rate at which women have entered the paid labor force accelerated in the 1970s. By 2004, 60 percent of women age 16 and older participated in the paid labor force compared to only 38 percent in 1960 (Bureau of Labor Statistics, 2005b;

Smith and Bachu, 1999). The greatest increase has been among women with children under the age of six. Sixty-two percent of married mothers with children under age six participated in the labor force in 2004. Only 19 percent did so in 1960 (U.S. Census Bureau, 1997b). Even among mothers with children under three years old, 57.3 percent were in the labor force in 2004 (Bureau of Labor Statistics, 2005b). According to the Bureau of Labor Statistics (2008) in families where both husband and wife work, one-fifth of wives earn more than their husbands.

Why is this happening? Researchers offer several explanations based on trends and events that have paralleled women's entrance into the labor force. Women's wages increased significantly over the past 30 years, while real wages for men (adjusted for inflation) stagnated and declined. For families to maintain or increase their standard of living, additional workers are needed to enter the job market (Bergman, 1986).

Another explanation focuses on changing cultural ideas that the feminist movement heralded. Feminist ideas encouraged women, even without financial necessity, to pursue a career for personal fulfillment. Attitudes about working mothers of young children are shifting in America. The Pew Research survey (2010) found that thirty-eight percent of Americans felt that mothers working had a neutral (neither positive nor negative) impact on society and twenty-one percent felt that mothers working had a positive impact or benefit to society. The Pew (2010) survey shows that Americans hold contradictory values around family; on the one hand seventy-one percent of Americans describe themselves has having "old-fashioned" family values, but seventy-five percent of the same people also say that they do **not** think that women should return to "traditional" female roles. There exists in the United States, in the twenty-first century a type of schizophrenia on the subject of mothers working outside of the home. The Personal Responsibility and Work Reconciliation Act of 1996 (the "welfare reform" act) made it absolutely clear that mothers of small children who turn to the government for assistance in providing for their family through welfare must leave their children with other caretakers and enter the workforce. Welfare recipients with small children are required to begin working (at least twenty hours a week) after two years of receiving benefits (and even earlier in some states). The

Throughout the world, childrearing responsibilities still fall primarily to women and girls.

Photo: Anonymous

exact same lawmakers who created welfare reform have also worked to create tax laws that would encourage married mothers with affluent husbands to remain out of the labor market.

Welfare reform has sent the message to poor, young women who are pregnant or have children that they must remain in school (until age 18) and must expect to work outside the home to qualify for government assistance in supporting their child; assistance that will end after five years. At the same time more affluent, bright young women contemplating graduate programs and fast track careers are sometimes warned to delay their career goals, marry and have their children early to avoid ending up childless (Hewlett, 2002). Dangerous advice, as we will see when we discuss the consequences of divorce later in the chapter, because choosing to be a full-time mother and depending upon a husband for support, may well land young women in poverty if divorce results (Crittenden, 2001).

Other industrialized nations do a better job of providing support (paid maternity leave, subsidized childcare, universal health care, and even cash payments) to mothers, which makes it easier for women to combine paid employment and children (Crittenden, 2001).

Childrearing. As more married mothers work, ideas about childrearing responsibilities change. The Pew Research survey (2010) shows that today sixty-two percent of Americans feel that husbands and wives should both have jobs and both take care of the house and children; a significant increase over the forty-eight percent who held that view in 1977. But the reality often falls short of the ideal. In *The Second Shift*, Hoschild (Hoschild and Machung, 1989) shows that even when fathers spend the same amount of time in childrearing activities, they do different–and usually more enjoyable–things than mothers do. Fathers spend far more of their childrearing time playing (Popenoe, 1996), while mothers do more rigorous maintenance activities. The research provides no definitive answer about why fathers continue to have both a lesser and a different role in childrearing. One structural functionalist (Popenoe, 1996) suggests that men and women are "naturally" different in their childrearing behavior. Most studies however, look to social factors either in the socialization experiences of men and women or in the differing opportunities and demands of the paid workplace for men and women (Hoschild and Machung, 1989). One thing that is certain, fathers, especially younger fathers, are spending more time interacting with, and caring for, their children, including being the primary caretaker during the mothers hours of employment outside the home.

Working Parents and Childcare. With the rise in two job couples and single parent families we clearly need new childcare arrangements. The United States lags behind most industrialized nations in providing and financially supporting childcare facilities. The Census Bureau periodically gathers information on the childcare arrangements for children under age 5. In 2006, the top childcare arrangements made by families of small children were organized facilities (such as Head Start, pre-schools), grandparents, the "other parent" (other than the primary caregiver), and daycare centers. A significant group of families indicate that they used multiple arrangements, and by far the largest group of families (including families with mothers working outside the home) indicated that they had no regular arrangement for childcare (U.S. Census Bureau, 2006. For a great many people, childcare is unreliable and is constantly renegotiated as family work schedules change.

Many studies have examined the impact of mothers' employment and of different types of childcare on children's emotional and social well-being. The results of studies have been contradictory. Psychologist Elizabeth Harvey of the University of Massachusetts at Amherst reviewed six studies with conflicting findings, all of which were based on the same National Longitudinal Survey of Youth (NLSY). She found that many of the conflicting results were due to methodological differences such as, the ages of the children selected, the measures of child behaviors used and the way in which mothers' employment was defined. Harvey then engaged in her own study using a much larger sample from the NLSY than any previous study had. She included more than 6,000 children of all races. Harvey explored not only mothers' employment in the first three years, but also the timing of that employment and its duration and continuity. Harvey's analysis found very few effects of mothers' employment by itself on the development and adjustment of children. The effects she did find were small and generally disappeared, as children grew older (Harvey, 1999). The general consensus is that children over six months old placed in high quality childcare settings suffer few adverse effects and may enjoy some advantages in social and intellectual development. But these findings do not apply to the majority of children whose childcare arrangements are ad hoc, unpredictable, and vary frequently.

Housework. Despite the past century's enormous technological changes, the amount of time full-time homemakers devote to housework has changed very little. In the 1970s, technological change meant raised standards not less work (Vanek, 1979), but more research suggests that by the 1990s women and their families were lowering expectations about housekeeping standards (Hoschild and Machung, 1989). Women carry the primary responsibility for housework even when they work in the labor market. Our ideas about housework responsibilities have become significantly more egalitarian. In a review of surveys that have tracked changes in American attitudes from the 1960s through the 1990s, Thorton and Young-DeMarco (2001) found that women were more than twice as likely today compared to the 1960s to expect husbands to assist with housework. The Pew Research survey (2010), as previously mentioned, found that sixty-two percent of American adults believed that both husband and wife should be responsible for housework (as well as income earning and child care), but that willingness to do housework was not a particularly important characteristic of a good mate (male or female).

Amato, Johnson, Booth and Rogers (2003) compared two national surveys of married couples on in 1980 and the other in 2000, and found both significant increases in the wife's contribution to family income and the husband's share of family housework. Nonetheless, men are not increasing their participation in housework as much as women are increasing their participation in the paid labor force. Working women still put in twice as much time as their husbands on housework and childcare, while their husbands claim 40 more minutes of leisure time a day (Bureau of Labor Statistics, 2005a).

Hoschild (Hoschild and Machung, 1989) coined the term **the second shift** for the hours of household labor that must be done in addition to paid employment. Hoschild found that women bear the brunt of the responsibility for the second shift. Some studies find that lack of sharing in household tasks may contribute to wives' increased thoughts about divorce (Hoschild and Machung, 1989). But it is unclear to what extent conflicts over housework actually contribute to the decision to divorce (see the next section on reasons for divorce). Wallerstein and Blakeslee (1995) interviewed a number of two career couples with self-described happy marriages. These marriages had a higher level of shared housework and childcare than did the traditional marriages in the study but the women in two career couples still shouldered more of the home responsibilities than did their husbands without significant loss of marital satisfaction.

Clearly, both our ideas about and our actual allocation of responsibilities for breadwinning, childrearing, and housework are changing. How much change, the reasons for the change, and what consequences the changes will bring are still areas for investigation.

Divorce, Remarriage, and the Stepfamily

Significant changes have occurred in American's experience of divorce. Not all of these changes are what one might expect. For example, one of the best kept secrets is that the rate of divorce has been declining for thirty years. The Pew Research Survey (2010) found that only 5 percent of American adults knew that divorce was declining; two thirds of Americans believe that divorce is increasing, not declining.

There are many widely recognized problems associated with divorce. One of those is the higher rate of poverty experienced by families headed by women as single parents. Since divorce produces single parent families, at least briefly, often women and children experience poverty after divorce. Some sociologists place the blame for this problem and others on the divorce action itself. Consequently, they are concerned with reducing the divorce rate. Other sociologists blame post-divorce poverty on women's unequal economic opportunities and the lack of societal supports for families such as childcare and health care. They focus on economic and political changes that would increase the resources available to all families.

Declining Divorce Rates. Anyone who watches the news or talk shows or any television program probably has the impression that divorce is at an all time high in the United States and getting worse. Nothing could be further from the truth. Examination of the National Center for Health Statistics reports shows a clear downward trend in divorce rates over the past thirty years. Thirty years is long enough to conclude that this is not a fluke. Divorce trends are shown quite clearly in Figure 10.1 (along with marriage rate trends).

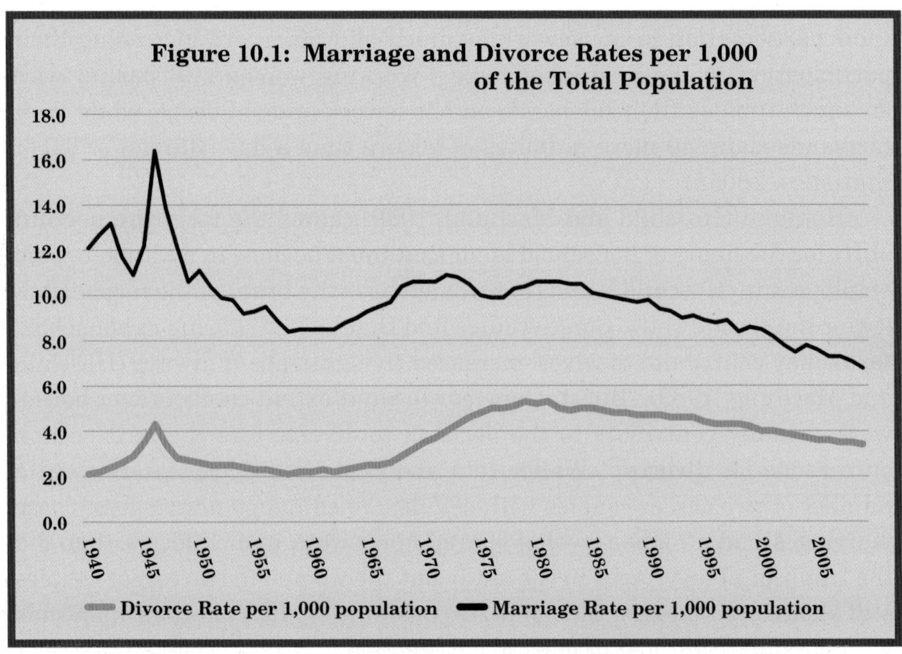

The decline in divorce shows up no matter what method is used to measure the prevalence of divorce (Pew Research Center, 2010). One common method used to measure divorce is the ratio between the number of marriages and the number of divorces in one year. This can be a deceptive measure, however, because the pool of individuals who could divorce (married people) is not the same as the pool of individuals who could marry (single people above age 15). Changes in the relative sizes of these two pools can result in changes in the divorce/marriage ratio, even without change in the actual likelihood of divorce. This comparison between marriages and divorces has contributed to a mistaken idea that many people have that half of all marriages end in divorce—a figure that is simply not true.

The most commonly used measure of divorce (the one most often reported in the news and the one used in Figure 10.1) is the ***crude divorce rate,*** the number of divorces per 1,000 of the total population, the standard for reporting divorce for many decades. The 2010 crude divorce rate was 3.4 divorces per 1000 of the population, much lower than the 5.3 peak rate noted in the next paragraph (National Vital Statistics Reports 2010).

As is clear from Figure 10.1, the crude divorce rate has changed dramatically over the past eighty years. A dramatic rise at the end of World War II was followed by return to nearly pre-war levels. Then, beginning in the 1960s, the divorce rates began to rise rapidly. They reached a peak at a 5.3 crude divorce rate between 1979 and 1981 (U.S. National Center for Health Statistics, 1995). It was this rapid increase, and unprecedented high rate that alarmed many people.

Contributing to the public concern about divorce was the publication in 1980 of a report "National Estimates of Marriage Dissolution and Survivorship" by James A. Weed, a demographer employed in the Division of Vital Statistics. Very few Americans read Weed's highly technical article. Instead, most were only exposed to the distorted reports about the results in newspapers and popular magazines. Weed tracked the actual divorce experience of couples married from 1950 to 1975 up through the year 1977. Using their experiences as a guideline, he used a variety of statistical techniques to estimate what might happen to couples married in 1976 and 1977. Weed concluded that *if* the divorce rate of 1976 and 1977 (which was 5.0 crude divorce rate) was to continue at the same level for the next 40 years, at the end of those forty years (by 2017) approximately 49 percent of those married in 1976 and 1977 would have divorced. The popular press grabbed this finding and produced screaming headlines that fifty percent or half of all marriages end in divorce. However, by the time Weed's research was published the divorce rates were already beginning to decline, so his predictions were incorrect before the public ever heard about them.

Thirty years later we realize that divorce rates have declined steadily, further invalidating Weed's prediction. Despite significant declines in divorce, politicians, religious leaders and the media continue to draw public attention to the "divorce problem" as a means of promoting conservative family values (Coltrane and Adams, 2003).

Why did divorce rise so greatly in the 1970s? Why has it declined? What causes divorce? Who is at greatest risk for divorce? And, what are the real consequences of divorce for individuals, families and society?

Causes of Divorce? One type of sociological research on the causes of divorce looks for statistical correlations between divorce and various social, economic, and demographic characteristics of persons. Another examines the correlation between divorce rates and broad social, historical, economic and political trends in society. A statistical correlation suggests a connection between two phenomena and may suggest a possible causal connection, but does not automatically prove that one thing causes the other.

The correlation between age at marriage and divorce is very well documented. Bramlett and Mosher (2001) found that women who first married in their teens were twice as likely to divorce within the first ten years of marriage than women who married after the age of 25. This may be because young age is associated with other factors that have also been found to correlate with a higher chance of divorce: lower educational attainment, lower income, higher rates of unemployment, and higher likelihood of premarital pregnancy. However, at least one study has found that when these other factors are held constant, younger couples still have a higher rate of divorce suggesting that simple maturity is an important factor in developing a flexible and durable marriage relationship (Lamanna and Riedmann, 2003). This association of age with divorce may help to explain both the rise of divorce in the 1960s and 1970s, and the subsequent decline of divorce in the past twenty years. Age at marriage reached its lowest point ever during the 1950s and early 1960s. This may have contributed a decade later to the surge in divorces. The rising marriage age in recent decades has contributed to the stabilization and decline of divorce rates (Amato, Booth, Johnson, Rogers 2007).

Lower educational attainment is correlated with a higher chance of divorce. Education contributes to the development of flexibility in attitudes, tolerance, willingness to try new things, and communication skills all of which might contribute to more durable marriage relationships. This would lead one to expect that divorce rates would have declined during the 1970s, as rates of attending college and graduate school, especially for women, increased. However, for one generation of women, those of the Baby Boom, post-baccalaureate degrees attainment correlated with higher likelihood of divorce. This association of graduate education and divorce does not hold true for recent generations of women, but only for Baby Boom generation women. The continuing rise of educational level is a significant contribution to the decline in divorce. One explanation for the different experience of the Baby Boom generation is that men and women of that generation faced significant changes in female and male roles in the workplace and marriage; changes that are now taken-for-granted by younger couples.

Family income and employment and unemployment also correlates with the risk of divorce. The lower the family income and the presence of unemployment, the higher the risk of divorce, but the gap between poor and more affluent families in the divorce rate declined slightly during the 1980s (Raschke, 1987). It would appear that economic factors, differences between families, and changes in the economy over time are important contributors to divorce. The importance of economic factors may account at least in part for racial differences in divorce. The divorce rate for African Americans is higher than for whites. In addition to ethnic differences in income and employment history, there are also differences in premarital childbearing and women's employment that may contribute to higher rates of divorce (U.S. Department of Health and Human Services, 2004).

One discredited explanation of the rise in divorce during the 1970s was the passage of "no-fault" divorce laws, which made divorce simpler and less expensive to obtain. However, the rise in divorce began before no-fault laws were passed and divorce rates rose at the same rate in states that did not adopt no-fault laws (Peters, 1986).

To what extent does the changing divorce rate reflect cultural change? Are we more individualistic and less committed to marriage as some claim? It is not easy to measure changes in individualism. Surveys of people's attitudes show no change in recent decades in Americans' desire for a lifelong marriage and happy family life (Orthner, 1995). One suggestion is that we place greater value on the emotional quality or happiness of our marriages than in the past, but historians note that the shift in emphasis to emotional rewards over practical rewards occurred in the 19th century, well before the rise in divorce rates (Coontz, 2005; Degler, 1980). Divorced individuals are clearly more accepted in our society today than in the past. But the role that such acceptance plays in the prevalence of divorce is still subject to study.

Some Consequences of Divorce. Despite significant decline, the divorce rate in the U.S. is still high compared to most industrialized nations (Pew Research Center, 2010). Divorce affects millions of adults and children. Many people, including sociologists of the structural functionalist school, are concerned about divorce simply because they fear that its prevalence undermines the institutions of marriage and the family. They worry that this jeopardizes the basic structure of society. Other sociologists are more concerned with the specific outcomes–psychological, social, and economic–of divorce. Some sociologists argue that the problem is less with the divorce rate than it is with our society's failure to meet the needs of adults and children after divorce.

One major consequence of divorce is its contribution to creating single parent families, primarily headed by women. In the 1970s when divorce rates were higher and out-of-wedlock pregnancies a smaller percentage of births, most single parent households were the result of divorce. Today, the largest contributor to single parent households is unwed parenting. In 2010, sixty-nine percent of all children under 18 lived with both biological parents, twenty-three percent lived with only their divorced, widowed, or never married mother, four percent lived with only their divorced, widowed or never married father, and four percent lived without either mother or father present (Census Bureau, 2010).

One must remember that a hundred years ago children had a 25 percent chance of losing at least one parent to death prior to age 15. Moreover, the economic and social conditions of that time made single parenting a nearly insurmountable task. Consequently, many children with only one living parent were placed in orphanages or adopted out to relatives or neighbors (Zelizer, 1985). Indeed, it was not uncommon for families facing financial difficulties (even with both biological parents living) to place their children in the care of others for extended periods of time. As a result, a child of a hundred years ago had a much higher likelihood of growing up in a home without either biological parent (Uhlenberg, 1989). Currently, only four percent of children live in a household without either biological parent (U.S. Census Bureau, 2004).

There is still reason for concern about the rise of female-headed single-parent families. These families have higher rates of poverty than married couple families. About forty percent of divorced women fall into poverty at the time of divorce, and many turn to welfare for support (Crittenden, 2001). A review of national studies estimated that women's standard of living declined between 13 and 35 percent in the first year following divorce. Men on the other hand, experience about an 11 to 13 percent rise in their standard of living (Peterson, 1996a). This period of poverty for white women from previously affluent marriages is generally ended within a couple of years by remarriage (Bane, 1986). Although fairly short in duration, such poverty can result in severe dislocations. Often, women need to find a less expensive residence in a different school district. This increases the level of disruption that children experience following divorce (Crittenden, 2001).

The rates of poverty are even higher for single parent families headed by African American women, but the divorce itself is less likely to be the precipitating factor in poverty. African American women are more likely to have been part of a two parent family that was below the poverty line before the divorce occurred (Bane, 1986). The poverty of African American female-headed families is likely to last longer. African American women have fewer opportunities to marry a man with adequate income to raise the family out of poverty than do white women (Katz, 1989).

The poverty of women and their children after divorce is largely due to the economic price women pay for having children (Crittenden, 2001). Numerous studies have demonstrated that women suffer losses in income and career development as a result of having children, even when they do not take any extended time out of the labor market (Hewlett, 2002). If they do leave the labor market to become full-time caregivers, they are almost never able to return to the career and income level they had before child-rearing (Crittenden, 2001). Men on the other hand suffer no such career disadvantages from having children. When divorce occurs, men take their earning power with them. Today, alimony or support payments to wives are granted in only about 9 percent of divorces (Crittenden, 2001). Child support payments, although mandated in a larger percentage of cases, are rarely large enough for the children and their mother to maintain a standard of living near that they had before the divorce. Ironically, college educated women who had full-time, high paying careers and gave them up to become full-time mothers are the least likely to get alimony, and may have child support payments severely reduced on the (demonstratively false) assumption that they can quickly and easily return to the same career and earnings they had prior to child-rearing (Crittenden, 2001).

How does divorce affect children? Two starkly different views can be found in the literature. Mavis Heatherton studied 1400 families and their 2500 children over 30 years. Her conclusion, supported by extensive statistical data, was that although divorce was neither painless nor pleasant, over the long haul most children were resilient in coping with the challenges and ended up happy and competent (Coltrane and Adams, 2003) Judith Wallerstein studied only 60 families with 131 children over the same 30 year period. Her conclusion, based on largely anecdotal evidence, was that divorce was a disaster from which most children do not rebound (Coltrane and Adams, 2003). Sociologists view Heatherton's research as more scientifically valid, but Wallerstein's conclusions have gained more popular attention from the media.

There are several possible explanations for the negative effects observed in children. They may be affected by the impact of the divorce itself, by the conflict in the family prior to the divorce, the loss of one parent from the home, inadequate parenting after the divorce or by the economic hardship experienced by most women and children after divorce.

Some structural functionalists (Popenoe, 1996) argue that single parent families cannot adequately meet the function of socialization. They argue that social problems such as juvenile delinquency, drug use, school failure, teen pregnancy etc., are the consequences of rising divorce rates and unwed childbearing. Conflict sociologists (Cherlin, 1986) tend to stress the impact of economic hardship as the primary contributing factor. In this view, single parent families can provide a good environment for children if they have adequate income and access to childcare, health care and other services.

Remarriage and Stepfamilies. Sociologists have recently coined the term **serial monogamy** for individuals who marry more than one person in the course of their lifetime. The practice of serial monogamy however, is not new. Well before the twentieth century the death of one partner generally led to remarriage and the creation of a stepfamily. Today, divorce is more likely to end a marriage before the fortieth anniversary than is death, but remarriage is still very common. In 2001, among women age 50-59, fifty-nine percent of those who divorced had remarried, and among men of the same age, fifty-seven percent remarried (U.S. Census Bureau, 2005). Nearly half of all marriages by the 1990s involve at least one previously married and divorced partner (Clarke, 1995).

The likelihood of remarriage varies with age. The older one is at the time of divorce, the less likely one is to remarry (Clarke, 1995). Children from the first marriage, especially when one has physical custody of them, also deter remarriage. Some of the differences between men and women's remarriage rates are due to the fact that most children are in the physical custody of mothers.

Some of the problems that today's stepfamily faces are similar to problems of last century's stepfamilies; other problems are unique to today's stepfamilies. Family therapists (Wallerstein and Blakeslee, 1995) and sociologists (Ahrons and Rodger, 1994) have observed that one ingredient in a successful marital relationship is for a couple to have the space and time to develop and explore their new relationship. They need to establish their own patterns of interaction and develop a sense of themselves as a couple. Children, especially those physically residing in the same household, compete for the attention of the partners and make adequate private time highly problematic (Wallerstein and Blakeslee, 1995; Ahrons and Rodgers, 1994).

Intact nuclear families have relatively impermeable boundaries. The parents in the nuclear family have complete authority over family finances, residence, time, children's discipline and education. When a divorced individual with children remarries, the resulting family must have permeable boundaries. The former partner continues to have a legitimate and often legal interest in many family decisions (Ahrons and Rodgers, 1994). This is most often true when the remarried couple has physical custody of the children.

As a society, we have no established norms to provide guidance for the allocation of roles among biological and stepparents (Ahrons and Rodgers, 1994). Each family must negotiate its own expectations. This is enormously stressful. Remarriages fail at a higher rate than first marriages, although there is some disagreement as to how much higher the re-divorce rate is. Moreover, there is some evidence that after five years remarriages may be more stable than first marriages (Wallerstein and Blakeslee, 1995).

A century ago when widowed parents remarried they also faced the problems of privacy in their new marriage. Conflicts existed between stepchildren and stepparents. What is unique about remarriage after divorce is that the family expands to include both biological parents, stepparents, step- and half-siblings. We have not yet developed a new cultural institution to provide a shared way of organizing all these new relationships.

TRENDS IN THE AMERICAN FAMILY

What do these trends we have discussed mean? Why are they occurring? Sociologists' theoretical perspectives influence how they view change in the family.

Structural functional theorists generally believe that the two parent nuclear family structure is essential for the family to meet the functional needs of society. Individual theorists vary in their views about women's employment but most agree that one parent must focus their efforts on childrearing to be effective in socializing children. To structural functionalists the rise in divorce and unwed childbearing is a serious problem representing a "breakdown" of the family. Structural functionalists locate the cause of this breakdown in inadequate transmission of cultural values and norms. They blame the family itself for failing in the socialization of children. They also fix blame on schools, media and government for undermining traditional family norms and rewarding single parent families (with programs such as welfare).

Social conflict theorists take a more positive view of the changing family. Feminists view the male-headed nuclear family as repressive to women. In traditional families women's educational and career development is subordinate to the interests of her husband. The rise in female-headed families is seen as an unavoidable consequence of women's emancipation. Feminists are primarily concerned with the barriers women face to equal employment opportunities and equal pay. Feminists champion legal changes that would promote even greater freedom for women (and potentially greater family change) such as better access to birth control, abortion and marriage, and parental rights for lesbians and gays.

Neo-Marxists view family changes as a consequence of changing economic structure. The concentration of capital into large corporations, the rise of conglomerates and multinational corporations has changed the market for labor with negative consequences for the family. Declining real wages for men have prompted more women to enter the labor market. Economic stresses on the family have contributed to the rise of divorce. High unemployment rates among men, especially minority men, have made marriage less attractive and increase unwed childbearing. Neo-Marxists tend to consider these changes as negative, not because they view single parent families as inherently bad, but because the changes are forced upon people due to their powerlessness in the economy. Neo-Marxists argue for better wages, benefits, and social services (such as child care, parental leave, health care, housing, and so forth) for all workers, male and female. The aim of Neo-Marxists is for all individuals to be empowered to choose the life that they desire. The particular family structure that results is less important than the fact that it is chosen freely, rather than a consequence of economic pressures and powerlessness.

Terms You Should Know:

Birthrates	Comcubinage	Conjugality
Consanguinity	Family	Kinship
Marriage	Monogamy	Polyandry
Polygamy	Polygyny	Social Parenthood

Can You Answer These Questions?

1. What are some of the ways in which families vary around the world?
2. What functions do structural-functionalist view families as providing for society?
3. What does social conflict theory tell us about the impact of the economy and inequality on families?
4. What are the trends in marriage been over the past fifty or sixty years in the United States?
5. How is having children different today than it was fifty or sixty years ago?
6. How are family roles (income earning, housework, and child care) changing?
7. What factors might have contributed to both the rise (until 1980) of divorce, and explain the decline of divorce since 1980?

Critical Thinking Exercises:

1. After reading this chapter and learning what the actual trends in marriage, cohabitation, having children and divorce are, do you feel pessimistic or optimistic about the future of marriage? Of the family?
2. Most Americans today have a more rigid, narrow definition of "marriage" than they do of "family." That is, even people who disapprove of homosexuality and divorce, still recognize gay parents and their children, or divorced parents and their children as "families." Why do you think this difference exists?
3. Attitudes about income earning, housework and child care have become more egalitarian and most adults say that men and women should share these tasks. But the reality is that women still do more housework and spend more time and energy on child care. Why do you think that behavior has changed more slowly than attitudes?
4. Did you know that divorce was declining before you read this chapter? Why do you think that so many people are unaware of the decline in divorce rates? Who might benefit by keeping people believing that divorce is getting worse when it really is not?

Photo: Lee Shaver.

Chapter 11

Education

"Educational institutions like any other segment of American institutional life, must embrace diversity. Why? Because it is the rational, logical and intellectual thing to do given the changes in our society. To do otherwise is to continue to insulate ourselves from the very society we are charged with serving." Mariopa Community College

Try to visualize the following scene. It's Monday morning. The time is approximately 7:45 a.m. as you pull into the college parking lot. The sky is clear and a slight warm breeze greets you as you step from your car. The weather report promises more of the same. As you walk to your class you think ahead to your week. School and work fill your days. Arriving at your class, you take your usual seat in the front. It's now two minutes before class and the room is filled almost to capacity. Eight in the morning is a popular time. The door opens and your sociology professor enters. It will be almost two hours until the end of class, as it meets on Mondays and Wednesdays only. However, the material is interesting and the professor is enthusiastic and presents the material in a comfortable and enjoyable manner. You ease back in your chair and wait.

Putting her briefcase on the desk, she removes her class roster and notes for the day. It takes several minutes to run through the names of those present and absent. It's now time to get down to business. Looking up, she smiles and announces that a problem has come up. She has agreed to deliver a speech before her professional association on Wednesday. A substitute teacher was scheduled to take the class in her absence. Unfortunately, that individual has fallen ill and will be unable to handle the class. Although she has searched for another substitute, none can be found. Apologizing, she announces that the class will have to be canceled.

A young student in the middle of the room raises his hand. His name is John and from a brief conversation with him last week you know he is serious about his education. The professor recognizes him and he begins to speak. He expresses concern that there is no substitute for the Wednesday class. Again, the professor apologizes indicating that she had tried very hard without success and that there is no alternative but to cancel the class. It is college policy that classes cannot meet without a certified instructor. It has something to do with legal liability. John indicates he understands this. However, he is upset. He feels class is important and although he understands the situation he also feels that he is entitled to the class. After all, he explains, he paid for a full semester of classes and feels that the college is obligated to each and every class within the semester. The professor states she understands, but does not know what to do. John thinks for a moment and then offers a solution—extend the semester by one day. As the professor considers the suggestion, you look around the room and wonder what the response of the other students will be to John's suggestion. Will they support John or reject his solution?

Interestingly enough, this scenario was presented informally to a number of students at one institution. For the vast majority of students the response was to reject John's solution. In fact, most students welcomed the cancellation of the class. This is a puzzling situation. How is it possible that people are willing to pay for something that, if not delivered, they are happy? Why do they pay? Why do they attend? What is it that makes students pay for and attend classes that they really don't appear to appreciate or want to attend, but are willing to spend hard-earned dollars and precious time on?

In this section we take up the subject of education. We begin with a brief history of education, and then look at some sociological aspects of education as they relate to the needs of society and the individual. We consider how education affects stratification in society as well as in work. We then turn to a structural functional and social conflict analysis of education and finally conclude with some thoughts for the future.

SOCIOLOGICAL LANGUAGE

Individuals are not born with knowledge; they acquire it through a process of life experiences. This process of acquiring knowledge about the world and society is referred to as **learning**. As we will soon see, society, if it is to be successful, cannot leave the process of learning to chance. All societies, traditional as well as modern, have developed systematic processes and institutions to accomplish this task. **Education** is the term used to describe the processes as well as the formal institutions designed to accomplish this task. The educational process can be carried out by a wide number of institutions: a parent who teaches a child how to tie shoes, a church which instructs individuals on what is right and what is wrong, a politician who espouses political values, the media passing information on a wide variety of topics, and so on. However, specific institutions expressly designed to teach individuals through professional instruction are termed **schools**.

Although schools vary greatly, we can distinguish between secular schools and non-secular schools. **Secular schools,** commonly called public schools, are those where there is an attempt to separate religion from the formal educational process. In the United States, the First Amendment to the Constitution dictates that there will be a separation of church and state. Historically this was meant to prohibit the establishment of a state religion, but it has been extended to include schools. The reasoning, of course, is that public education is supported by tax dollars, and since we all contribute, it would be unfair to use tax money in the propagation of a particular religion or religion in general. Needless to say, this has been quite controversial. **Non secular schools**, on the other hand, are private. They are supported through private sources and hence can incorporate religious teaching into the curriculum.

Another term used by sociologists and other social scientists is **mass education**. This refers to the widespread expansion of formal education in the larger society. This process is accomplished through compulsory education laws in which children are required by state decree to receive formal education for a number of years. The development of mass education gave rise to **credentialism**, the process of certifying that individuals possess the knowledge or skills to qualify for a particular job. For example, upon successfully completing a course of study a student is awarded a degree that, in turn, allows that individual to enter a certain profession. In essence, schools have become society's filter in the workplace. Simply possessing knowledge does not qualify one to be a teacher, physician, architect, nurse, or engineer. The individual must have a degree from a qualified institution (school) in order to participate in their field. Employers use the degree as a means to screen candidates for positions, even in areas that do not require certification. For example, a business may require all of its salespeople to have college degrees. A hospital may hire only high school graduates to be custodians. As a result, certification is a major determinant of income, job status, and social class.

A BRIEF HISTORY OF EDUCATION

The importance of education can be understood by the fact that no society can survive without it. Each new generation must learn and master the knowledge of the generation before it. Likewise, each new generation builds upon the knowledge of the previous generation and then assumes responsibility for passing it along to a new generation.

In traditional societies information was passed along informally. Families and religious institutions were the primary sources of this vital function. Within the family, children were taught various skills needed for survival while outside of the family, religious leaders conveyed messages about the spiritual world. Only a few ancient societies deviated from this pattern by establishing formal schools—the Greek, Roman, and Arabic civilizations. In traditional societies, the movement toward mass education was encouraged by major social changes in society such as the following:

Protestant Reformation. Prior to the Protestant Reformation the position of the Roman Catholic Church was that only the clergy possessed the ability to interpret the Bible. Hence, there was no need for individuals to read. The road to salvation was to be found in the words of the clergy. Martin Luther rejected this idea. For him, every Christian had a right, even an obligation, to read the Bible and construct his/her own interpretation. Of course to do so required the ability to read. So mass education became imperative. The need to learn to read was soon widespread among most Christian sects of the time.

Democratic Revolutions. Both the American and French revolutions rejected the traditional notion that people were not capable of governing themselves. Certainly self-interest was a powerful force but it was countered by an equally powerful desire for order and stability. Thus, at times, people were able to put aside self-interest for the good of the larger society that, of course, was in their own best interest. However, for democracy to work citizens needed to be informed voters. Again, mass education comes into play. Throughout the world this pattern emerges over and over—the demands for democracy and the need for mass education.

With the Industrial Revolution came mass education. As depicted in this drawing, children were subjected to heavy doses of corporal punishment.

Industrial Revolution. Before industrialization, 80 percent of the population was engaged in farming. The work of farming did not require literacy. However, with industrialization the need arose for an educated workforce. While this need was not so apparent in the early stages of industrialization, it would become crucial in the latter period. It did not take industrialists long to recognize the quality link between education and production. Today, the very economic survival of a nation rests upon its ability to provide it citizens with the skills necessary to compete in a global economy. The real wars of the future will be on the economic battleground and the winners will be those nations with superior educational systems. Carrying this theme one step further, sociologists have noted the link between industrialization, education, and democracy. To survive economically, a nation must industrialize; to industrialize, a nation needs educated workers. As citizens become more educated there is an increased demand for democracy and freedom.

Equal Opportunity & Right to Social Mobility. Along with the political revolutions came new thinking that all people should have the right to advance. Unlike traditional society that was rigid and locked individuals into social stratum based upon birthrights, the new democratic societies sought equality. In the United States this did not equate to material egalitarianism (all individuals would obtain equal wealth), but rather to the *opportunity* to use their intellect, skills, and hard work to achieve material wealth. This was very much in line with capitalistic thinking. In fact, if capitalism was to succeed, individuals must be allowed to achieve wealth on merit. Otherwise, there would be little incentive to work hard and invest in the future.

As society became more advanced and the skills necessary to compete increased, equal opportunity was linked to educational opportunity. No other country in the world has a more open and extensive educational system than the United States. According to 2009 U.S. Department of Labor data, over 70 percent of high school graduates were enrolled in some form of college, representing a growth rate of 26 percent in less than a decade (U.S. Department of Labor, 2010). And, according to leading educational experts, more increases are expected in the foreseeable decades (AASCU, 2006).

Clearly the right to attend school is deeply embedded in the value structure of the country. For the most part, the community college system, with its open enrollment policy, emerged from this cherished belief.

EDUCATION AND SOCIAL MOBILITY

As mentioned previously, Americans place a high value on education. It is not so much that we have an extraordinary love of learning, but rather that we perceive it as a necessity tool for social mobility. Indeed, studies of income and prestige establish that a correlation exists between education and success.

Stratification and Education

Americans take two facts as a matter of faith. The *first* is that "getting ahead" includes making money. The *second* is that to get ahead one needs to stay in school. It is these two beliefs that underpin the movement toward mass education in the United States. However, believing something doesn't necessary make it true. Therefore, sociologists have spent considerable time investigating the relationship between education and income. The results indicated that there is a substantial difference between the best-educated and the least-educated people. As indicated in Figure 11.1, an individual who has a Master's Degree earns 3.4 times the income of someone who did not finish elementary school. Comparisons between a college graduate and a high school graduate reveal that the former earns 170 percent of the income of the latter. Computed over a lifetime, such earning differentials lead to substantial variations in wealth accumulation.

The above statistics indicate that education and income are highly correlated. However, this is only part of the picture. For sociologists concerned with the issue of education and income, two additional questions are crucial:

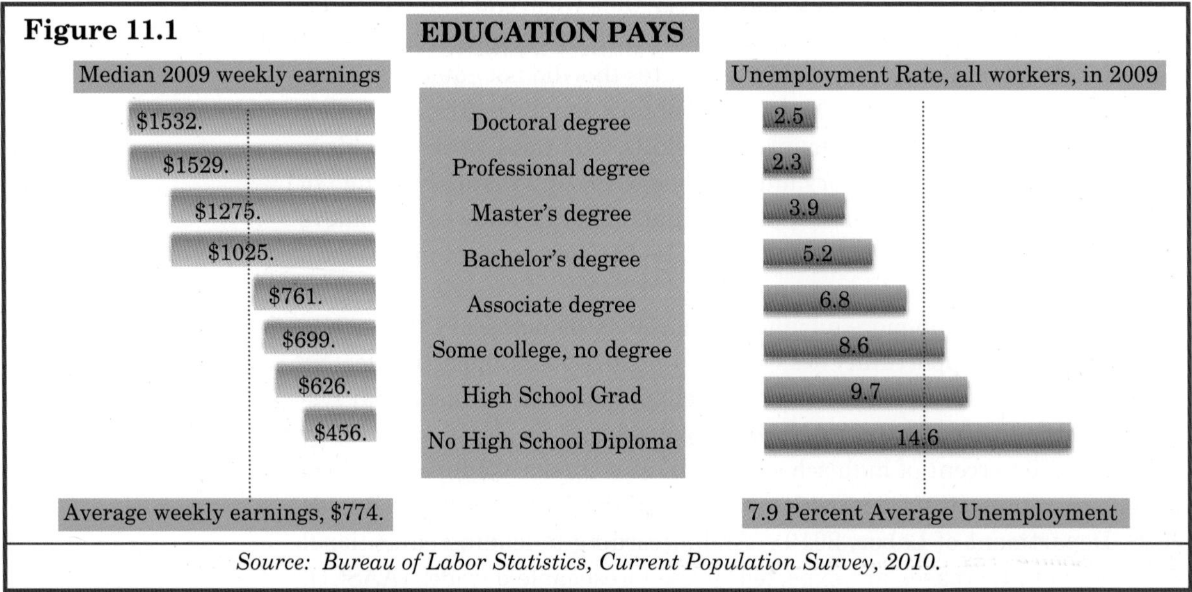

Source: Bureau of Labor Statistics, Current Population Survey, 2010.

1) Why is it that some individuals end-up with more education than others?

2) Having obtained the same educational credentials, is there any variation in income between individuals?

Educational Attainment

Sociologists categorize the amount of formal education a person has achieved by the term **educational attainment**. Anyone who has ever attended a high school class reunion ten years after graduation can attest to the fact that considerable variation can be found in levels of education. Some of the kids you knew dropped-out of high school (perhaps elementary school). Some finished high school and went into the labor market while others enrolled in college. Of these, some dropped-out and others finished. Of those finishing college, some went on to take jobs and others continued on in graduate or professional schools. In other words, as you walk around the room and talk to people you will find differences. Intuitively you probably could have guessed beforehand which individuals would have ended-up with the most education. And with few exceptions, you were probably right. Think about it for a moment. What factors did you, or would you, use in forming your guesses. Let's see if you're right—here is what sociological research has proven.

Status. One of the first factors you might have selected was the family backgrounds of your classmates. In other words, those kids from affluent backgrounds *generally* ended up doing well in classes and went on to college. Research, both historical and present-day, indicates that this is, in fact, true. In an early study, Bowles and Gintis (1976) compared student

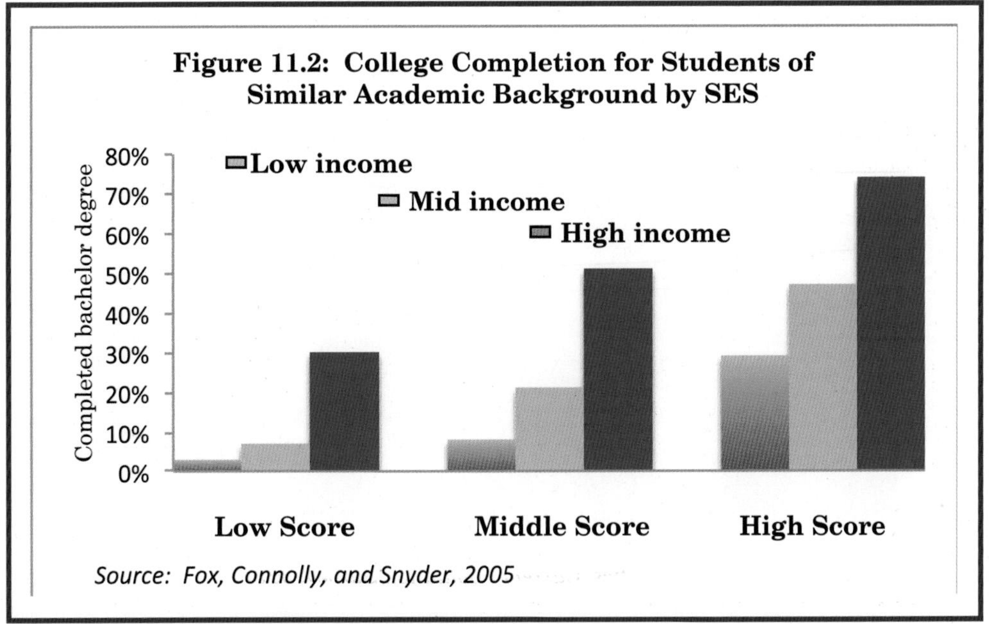

Source: Fox, Connolly, and Snyder, 2005

IQ and family background as it relates to educational attainment. The data showed that those from the lowest ten percent of socioeconomic background with identical IQ scores as those from the upper ten percent of socioeconomic background attain almost five years less education. In 1994, a Carnegie Task Force (a highly respected and very prestigious American think-tank) revisited the issue and described the disparity as "the quiet crisis." Finally, a more recent study compared the baccalaureate success rates of students of equal academic ability but from different socioeconomic backgrounds. The data, as seen in Figure 11.2, clearly demonstrate an disproportionate advantage for students from higher socioeconomic backgrounds (Fox, Connolly, & Snyder, 2005).

Similar data are found when examining college attendance. Overall, the cost of attending college has quadrupled the rate of inflation since the mid 1980's. (Wadsworth, 2010). One result is that the rate of attendance by low income students has dropped dramatically due to declining availability of scholarship money. Many low income students who attend college are forced to work long hours to support their education. This is one reason that only 26 percent succeed in obtaining any type or degree or certificate (The Educational Trust, 2009). On the other hand, students from affluent families work fewer hours and have less trouble affording the steep tuition fees at selective public or private universities. And, even more alarming is current research documenting the fact that selective public universities are providing millions of dollars to students from affluent families while seriously underfunding low income and minority students (The Educational Trust, 2010). Furthermore, even when low income students graduate, they find themselves at a disadvantage when compared to their more affluent peers. Studies consistently demonstrate that students who graduate from more

Figure 11.3: 2007 HS Freshmen Who Graduated On Time

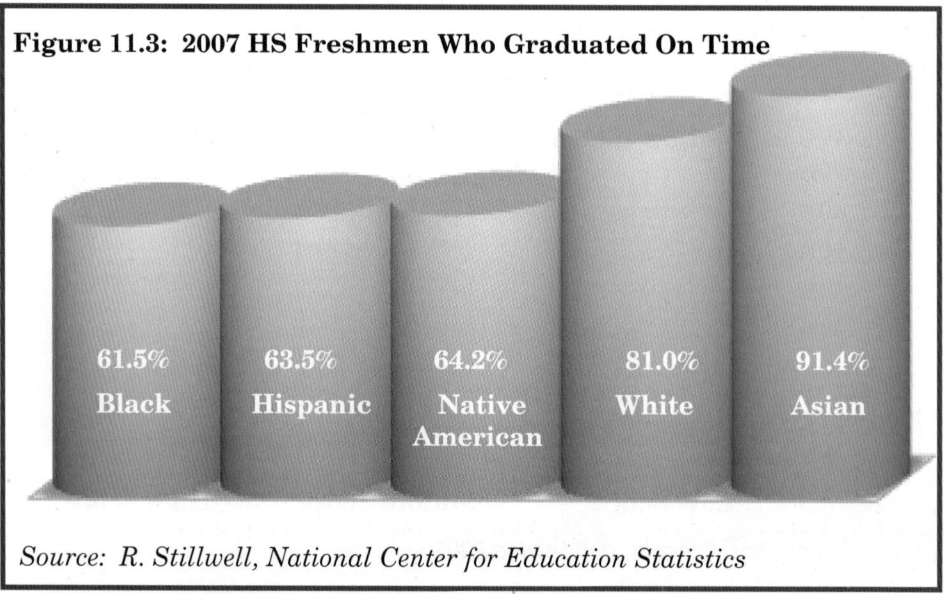

Source: R. Stillwell, National Center for Education Statistics

selective schools have a better chance of obtaining employment in prestigious firms where, not only is their initial salary higher, but they stand a better chance of being promoted into management and executive positions (Gilbert, 1998; Bridgeland and Dilulio, 2007). While a college education continues to be an important stepping stone to upward social mobility for talented low income students, there is little question that education also is a powerful force in maintaining the present class-stratified system in the United States.

Race. The first major contemporary study of education and race was completed by sociologist James Coleman in 1966. Encompassed in his study were over 4000 public schools and 650,000 students. The conclusions clearly demonstrated a relationship between race and education. Here it was demonstrated that students predominately attended racially segregated schools. Furthermore, on almost all measures of success, white students out-performed minority students (Coleman, et al., 1976). Although attempts have been made to desegregate schools and reduce the disparity in educational resources provided to all students, serious gaps remain. With the lone exception of Asian Americans, all other minority groups clearly lag behind whites in graduating from high school on time. While 81.0 percent of all whites completed high school on time, the numbers decrease to 61.5 percent for black students, 63.5 percent for Hispanics, and 64.2 percent for Native American students. For Asian American students, the on-time graduation rate was 91.4 percent, the highest of all groups (see Figure 11.3).

The data for college attendance and completion is even more skewed in favor of whites. According to 2008 data, 71.7 percent of white high school graduates age 16 to 24 enrolled in college. In comparison, 55.7 percent of blacks and 63.9 percent of Hispanics enroll in college (U.S. Census, 2011). College completion rates show a similar trend with 26 percent of whites earning a bachelor's degree in comparison to 19.3 blacks and 13 percent Hispanics (U.S. Census, 2010).

Gender. Historically, women have been treated as second class citizens by the educational system. In the past, society seemed more interested in training women for the home than for the workforce. Consequently, women have lagged behind men in obtaining formal education, particularly baccalaureate and professional degrees. As such upward mobility for women in our society was achieved largely through the accomplishment of their husbands. In 1950, women earned less than 25 percent of college degrees. After 1950 the pattern of male dominance in education began to shift more favorably toward women entering and finishing college. A number of progressive movements accounted for this change. The first and probably most important was a shift in the economy from an industrial base to one centered on service. Not only was this change more conducive to positive changes in career patterns of women (a shift from manual labor to technology), but also suddenly there was a need for a larger number of workers with technical skills. Likewise, as we have seen in previous chapters, the shift in the economy along with global competition resulted in declining per capita incomes in the United States. As family incomes began to slip, more women entered the workforce out of necessity. These two factors alone resulted in significant alteration of attitudes toward working women in our society. As the number of women in the workforce grew, so did their strength. Suddenly the ranks of organizations devoted to gender issues began to swell and with it, the political power of women. Building on this new-found political strength, women were able to make demands upon the

Figure 11.4: Percent of Baccalaureate Degrees Earned by Females and Males in 2008

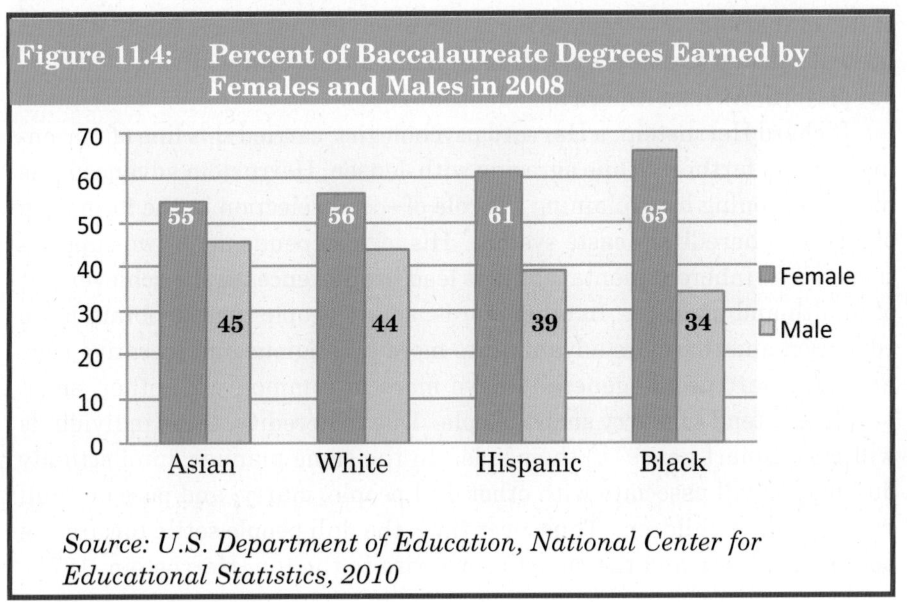

Source: U.S. Department of Education, National Center for Educational Statistics, 2010

educational system to alter its traditional view of women. In response, schools began to promote nonsexist attitudes and adopt texts, films, and other educational materials to reflect a more gender-neutral curriculum. Colleges responded by creating programs in women's studies and women's support groups. For its part, Congress passed Title IX, mandating that every school receiving federal aid had to provide equal opportunity for women. These changes have produced dramatic results. Today, women earn the majority of baccalaureate degrees. Figure 11.4 clearly demonstrates this dominance occurs across racial lines.

EDUCATIONAL ATTAINMENT THEORIES

Inherent Deficiency

As seen previously, the roots of this theory are embedded in the original work of Herbert Spencer and his theories of **Social Darwinism**. Here the focus is on innate inferiority. Individuals are born with different abilities—some lead to success, others lead to failure. For Spencer, some individuals are destined to fail due to their genetic make-up. They simply do not measure up intellectually to the successful. Spencer would argue that since failure is a matter of inferior genetics, the state should not assist individuals, because to do so is simply a waste of time and money and interferes with the natural law of "survival of the fittest," which is detrimental to the society as a whole.

More recently, a contemporary version of Spencer's work is found in the writings of Arthur Jensen, Richard Herrnstein, and Charles Murray. Jensen, an educational psychologist at the University of California, advanced the idea that African Americans are not as gifted intellectually as whites. Jensen's conclusions are based upon his study of IQ tests and overall school performance. According to Jensen, approximately 80 percent of IQ is inherited. The remainder is due to environmental factors. With so little attributed to environment, Jensen maintains that whites will always out perform African Americans (Jensen, 1969).

Richard Herrnstein, a Harvard psychologist, carried this line of reasoning one step farther. While agreeing with Jensen, Herrnstein advanced this line of reasoning by explaining the role of social selection in the formation of a type of hereditary caste system. His logic depends upon two suppositions. *First*, inherent mental abilities lead to differences in the achievement of wealth and prestige. In other words, smart people tend to obtain more education and therefore advance into more prestigious and lucrative jobs. *Second*, smart people generally have more in common with other smart people and tend to marry smart people. Due to heredity, these individuals will pass "smart genes" to their kids. In the same manner, intellectually dull people will associate with other dull people, marry, and pass on "dull genes" to their children. Thus, over time, the dull people settle toward the bottom of society and the smart people rise to the top (Herrnstein, 1971).

However, recent work by Robert Plomin and John C. DeFries (1998) included a review of several decades of studies in addition to their own work. They concluded that genetic inheritance is linked to about half of the difference in individual intelligence.

Herrnstein, in conjunction with Charles Murray (1994), extended this line of reasoning with the publication of *The Bell Curve: Intelligence and Class Structure in American Life*. They asserted that the innate difference between white and African American IQ scores was 15 points, and posited that as time progresses, this difference would become increasingly more polarized.

Criticism. It would be difficult to find a scientist that would deny the importance of biology in the determination of intelligence. While we cannot *see* the work of biology in intelligence, we see it in all other aspects of human differences. Parents who are tall are most likely to have children who grow to an above average height. Two people with blue eyes are more likely to produce children with blue eyes than a brown-eyed couple. Likewise, one can see the work of biology in traits such as aptitudes for music, art, language, athletics, etc. However, few scientists would carry this argument to include intelligence as far as the above theorists. This is true for a number of reasons. *First*, and most important, is the inherent assumption that IQ tests are a measure of innate intelligence. This is simply not true. IQ tests are a measure of acquired knowledge at a certain period of time, as measured against a similar group of people. While it might be possible to infer some association between IQ tests and innate intelligence, it is highly unlikely that it is to the extent that researchers indicate (80 percent). To a large degree, IQ tests have inherent biases favoring middle-and upper-class environments and experiences. The language that is used, the experiences utilized in testing, even the manner in which instructions for the test are given, are laden with the assumption that all people are alike. This is simply not true.

Second, the Jensen-Herrnstein-Murray argument assumes that an innate racial difference exists between white Americans and African Americans. This assumption is based on IQ score differences. Again, as in the case of race, biases exist. Just as people from different classes have different language patterns and experiences, so do people of color. Research has demonstrated that rewriting tests in the language and experience common to the culture of the people taking the exams dramatically affects scores. Individuals are born with different potential for areas like mathematics, language, reasoning, art, etc. The extent to which they achieve their potential depends on life opportunities and experiences. One only has to look at the world in which we live to see that individuals are afforded different opportunities.

Finally, it would be erroneous to assume that a perfect relationship exists between IQ and school achievement. School achievement is a complex process involving any number of motivational and social factors. Simply

Few parents object to busing. In fact, they view it as a convenience. However, when forced busing was instituted by the courts as a means to desegregate schools in the early 1970's, a protest rose up across the U.S. An unintended consequence of forced busing was white flight as many families relocated to avoid the issue. Others simply enrolled their children in private schools. Since, the 1990's, most schools have been released from court ordered busing. Recent evidence indicates that there is now resegregation in American schools.

Photo: woodleywonderworks.

being intelligent does not guarantee success, just as the lack of a high IQ score does not doom one to failure. Motivation, self-esteem, parental expectation, need for achievement, etc. are all factors that affect whether one is successful at school or not. The real problem with IQ scores, as we shall see later, is that they tend to become labels that impact chances of future success.

Culture of Poverty

Like inherent deficiency, this theory belongs to the victim-blame approach in that it holds those in poverty responsible for their own plight. Originally, the **culture of poverty** theory was advanced by Oscar Lewis, an anthropologist who examined poverty in a number of countries throughout the world. According to Lewis, the mental attitude of poverty is fixed within the minds of individuals after extended periods of poverty. Lewis (1971) describes these attitudes and values in the following manner:

> The individual who grows up in this culture has a strong feeling of fatalism, helplessness, dependence, and inferiority, a strong present-time orientation with relatively little disposition to defer gratification and plan for the future, and a high tolerance for psychological pathology of all kinds.

Lewis also pointed out that while the origin of the culture of poverty arose in the down periods of capitalistic society where little work was available for poor, unskilled workers, the attitude remained even when conditions improved and work was available. In essence, the newly acquired attitudes and values limited future opportunities to escape poverty. Another key element of this theory is that poverty tends to isolate the poor from the rest of society. This encourages the poor to develop hostile attitudes toward social service and educational institutions, the very institutions that provide an avenue of escape. Finally, once developed, the culture of poverty attitude is passed through successive generations, creating a permanent underclass.

A more contemporary theorist holding to the culture of poverty theory is Edward Banfield. Noting the differences in the cultural values of the poor in comparison to the middle and upper class, Banfield (1974) maintains that little can be done about the situation. Middle and upper class values stress hard work, ambition, and deferred gratification. Here, an individual invests time, energy, and money in education for future rewards. The poor on the other hand, prefer immediate gratification. Rather than investing in education, they tend to spend their time, energy, and money on satisfying their immediate needs for pleasure. Hence, they make poor students and eventually drop out due to self-defeating culture traits.

Criticism. Needless to say, this theory has received much criticism. The principle argument is that it misplaces the blame of being poor on the victim and not the causes of poverty. Eleanor Leacock (1971) makes the argument that while it might be true that the poor lack the value of deferred gratification, it is a rational response to being in the condition that they are in. For example, does it make sense to defer today's pleasure for tomorrow's gains if one truly believes that there are no gains to be had? Will minimum wage jobs produce a meaningful and worthwhile future? Certainly, if these jobs were entry level positions leading to higher paying future jobs then it would make sense to defer present gratification. But as seen previously, most minimum wage jobs are dead-end positions leading nowhere but to future poverty. Seen in this light, it is understandable that the poor have abandoned middle and upper class standards simply because they are irrelevant to their lives.

Even more adamant in his objection to the culture of poverty theory is William Ryan. For him the theory is a convenient excuse for abandoning programs designed to assist people out of poverty. Not only does this excuse the very system that produces the situation, it allows the middle and upper classes to solidify their position and that of their children in the class structure. Current examples of this can be seen in the movement to abandon affirmative action programs and remedial education in higher education.

Structural Disadvantage

The term **structurally disadvantaged** is used here to describe the way in which certain students are denied access to quality education due to institutional processes. Unlike the above two theories, this approach centers the blame for failure not on the individual, but rather on the system.

In the United States, race and class highly influence the quality of the education one receives. In our federal system of government each state is responsible for providing educational opportunities to citizens. However, states vary in resources available to them. States with high per capita income, elevated property values, and lots of industry have the ability to raise

Table 11.1 Per Pupil Expenditure by Selected States

New Jersey	**$17,620**	**Tennessee**	**$7,820**
New York	**$16,794**	**N. Carolina**	**$7,798**
Washington D.C.	**$16,353**	**Arizona**	**$7,727**
Alaska	**$14,641**	**Oklahoma**	**$7,683**
Connecticut	**$14,610**	**Idaho**	**$6,951**
Rhode Island	**$14,459**	**Utah**	**$5,978**

Source: New American Foundation, 2008

substantial sums of money for education. Conversely, in those states with low per capita income, devalued property values, and little industry there is limited ability to raise revenues to support education. Hence, *where* a child is born greatly affects the type of education he/she will receive. An example of this can be seen in Table 11.1, comparing the per-pupil expenditures of the top six wealthiest states and the six poorest states.

The importance of the above disparity is demonstrated in the statistics showing a high correlation between education, occupational prestige, and income. Likewise, all three of the above are correlated strongly to life chances. Hence, simply being born in the right state dramatically affects your chances of living a longer and healthier life. It is for this reason that the federal government has attempted to reduce disparity through a process of equalization. Here, more federal education dollars go to poorer states rather than to wealthier states. However, this program has done little to help matters for two reasons. First, the overall contribution to public education by the federal government is only six percent. Thus, federal impact on achieving equality is very small. Second, the very nature of federalism does not allow for equality. To achieve total equality would mean that the richer states would have to contribute even more to the federal government than they presently do. This money would then be sent to poorer states. Understanding the political consequences of such a plan, politicians from richer states routinely block efforts to achieve full equalization.

A greater disparity between per-pupil expenditures can be seen *within* states. Recent data indicates that affluent school districts can spend more than four times as much as poorer districts in educating their children (National Center for Education Statistics (NCES) and Census, 2005). Why is this true? The basic underlying cause of this is that although the state is responsible for providing educational opportunities, they farm out this task to local districts. Districts then tax their citizens to raise the necessary revenues. With few exceptions local school districts rely upon real estate taxes to finance the bulk of their educational expenses. Since real estate taxes are dependent upon property values, it is only natural that wealthier districts will be able to raise more money than poorer districts. This is true even though poorer districts, because of lower property values, tax at a higher rate than wealthier districts (Liu, Wiener, and Pristoop, 2006).

The use of real estate taxes to finance education compounds the problem for people of color, particularly African Americans. Since a greater portion of minorities live below the poverty line, they are more likely to live in communities where property values are the lowest (Mckinsey, 2009). Due to past discrimination, the educational needs of the children of the poor are greater than those from affluent backgrounds. This produces an inverse relationship between need and funding. Namely, those most in need of educational funds are the ones least likely to receive funds while those who have the least need receive the lion's share of tax dollars. Not only does this exacerbate the problems of the poor, it ensures that those born into poverty will remain in poverty.

Criticism. Although one might assume that there is a fairly straightforward relationship between the amount of dollars spent on a child's education and outcomes, many theorists claim that this is not true. Returning to the previously cited study by James Coleman, he found little correlation between educational success and the quality of the school, per-pupil expenditure, or teacher quality and school performance. The single most important predictor of academic success was family background. This would suggest that what occurs within the family is more important to academic success than what occurs within the classroom. Shortly after Coleman's study was released, Christopher Jencks, along with others, reported similar findings (Jencks, et al., 1973). A more recent comprehensive study confirms not only the importance of socioeconomic background in student achievement, but also, race. Among students of similar socioeconomic background attending the same school district, white students outperformed black and Hispanic students on standardized tests measuring cognitive skills (Mckinsey, 2009).

However, as one might expect, the results are still in dispute. A different study in which classroom observations and questionnaires were combined with traditional statistical methods over a four year period found that the quality of student-interaction, the types of course materials, and the commitment level of teachers made a significant difference in educational outcomes. Moreover, it was predominately within poor schools that these factors were lacking (Hedges, Laine, and Greenwald, 1994). In support of these researchers, another recent study demonstrates that even if equal funding were achieved it would not be enough to counter the disadvantages of poor students. Hence, they recommend greater funding for schools in poverty-stricken communities (Wilson, Lambert, and Smeeding, 2004).

Tracking

In chapter six the concept of labeling was discussed at length. There we defined **labeling** as the process of assigning a negative status to an individual, which ultimately defines their identity and comes to dominate their behavior. To a large extent, tracking parallels labeling in form and consequence. Sometimes defined as "ability grouping," **tracking** is the process of placing students into various categories based upon their perceived or assumed academic ability. It is estimated that at least three out of every four schools use some form of tracking.

Critics of tracking have objected to the process for a number of reasons. First, tracking is just another means by which the powerful can perpetuate their privileged position. To bolster this claim, critics point to research which demonstrates that social background more than personal traits influence which group a student will be placed into (U.S. Department of Education, 1990). Likewise, students from affluent backgrounds generally perform better on standardized tests because of previous advantages. Once in upper track positions, these students are slotted into college-bound tracks while those from lower tracks are assigned to the technical trades.

Research also demonstrates that schools have a tendency to assign their best teachers to students in upper tracks. These teachers in turn work harder, have higher expectations for their students, and treat them with greater respect. Conversely, lower track students are subjected to teachers who emphasize memorization, drill and practice, and a culturally deficient curriculum (Rachlin, 1989).

Also, students in lower tracks are stigmatized and because of their assignment to lower tracks, develop a feeling of inferiority that in turn leads to a self-fulfilling prophecy of failure. On the other hand, students in the upper tracks feel superior to those in lower tracks, which reinforces the stratification systems. In other words, these students believe they are destined to achieve and justly deserve an elevated position in society due to their intellectual prowess.

In a major research study of elementary and middle-schools, Johns Hopkins University compared differences in performance between students in upper tracks to those in classes where student abilities varied. Their findings showed no difference in performance of the upper track students. Hence, there was no major advantage in separating students. However, students of lower ability performed better in classes that were not tracked than compared to those who were tracked (Rachlin, 1989). As a result of this study and others, the Carnegie Corporation recommends that for middle schools tracking be abolished, because "it discriminates against minorities, psychologically wounds those labeled slow, and doesn't work (Rachlin, 1989). Finally, a recent cross-country study clearly demonstrated a correlation between social class and tracking. Here, lower class students, regardless of their academic ability, were more likely to be shuffled into lower tracks. (Schnepf, 2003). Moreover, an examination of data suggests that the earlier students are tracked the greater the inequality is magnified. And, furthermore, separating high and low performing students produces negligible benefits to those in higher tracks. (Hanushek & Woessman, 2005).

In conclusion, critics stress that tracking stigmatizes students, instills attitudes of failure among lower tracked students, and perpetuates unjust stratification. Hence, it should be abolished.

Criticism. Supporters, on the other hand, maintain that tracking produces more benefits than harm. Grouping students by ability allows for a better fit between educational needs and resources. Those students in the upper track are not held back by inordinate amounts of teaching time trying to remediate lower ability students. As such, intellectually gifted children are able to move at their own pace rather than being bogged down and bored with a non-challenging curriculum. Not only does this benefit the gifted students but the nation is also a benefactor as it can take advantage at their increased skill development. Proponents of tracking maintain that lower track students also benefit. Curriculums can be designed to concentrate on specific problem areas and thus achieve quicker remediation. Also, when separated from high achievers, lower tracked students tend to be more comfortable speaking out and thus develop more positive self-images. When combined with students of higher ability levels they tend to develop a negative self-image as they are unable to compete effectively.

Summary

In this section we have provided four major explanations concerning educational attainment. Undoubtedly, there is a measure of truth as well as some fallacy in each. The only absolute is that this subject will continue to be a hotbed of sociological investigation as researchers attempt to unravel the many factors associated with educational success and failure.

SOCIOLOGICAL PERSPECTIVES

Structural Functional

Building on the work of Robert Merton, modern-day structural functionalists distinguish between the *manifest* and *latent* functions of education. The manifest functions of education are intended and latent functions are unintended. Several manifest functions are apparent.

Manifest Functions. *First*, technologically advanced societies demand a highly trained workforce. At the turn of the twentieth century, when slightly more than 80 percent of the population was engaged in farming, it was possible to earn a living without knowing how to read or write. A strong back, desire to succeed, and some luck with the weather was all that was required. No longer is this possible. Even the simplest task requires sophisticated levels of education. Just going to the supermarket or managing household finances requires reading, writing and math skills. Similarly, as the pace of technology accelerates, the need for highly trained individuals possessing sophisticated scientific and mathematical skills increases. Without such people, the society will not be able to progress or maintain its current standard of living. Viewed in this way, people are considered human resources and it is the responsibility of the educational institutions to continually develop what is now termed the **human capital** of society.

A *second* manifest function of education is the process of matching the right person to the right job. Basically this is a threefold process. First, the right individual with the right talents must be identified. Once this has occurred, that individual must be trained. And finally, once trained, the individual must be allocated to the correct position in society. Educational institutions fulfill these three processes. It is the responsibility of the schools to select students and then guide them into the right career paths. By law, compulsory education legally dictates that all children must attend school. Once in schools, a sorting process takes place. Examinations are given and grades are assigned. Through this process students begin to receive clues as to their abilities and limitations. Likewise, national exams are given. Included are the ACT or SAT tests that you took while in high school. Based upon your performance, grades, and national examinations, options become available. Some students will select a career path; others will continue their education. For those continuing, their grades and national test scores will be used to determine which curriculums they enter and which institutions they may attend. Once there, a similar process of learning and testing will occur. At the conclusion of this process a degree is issued, which will be used by employers along with performance records, to match the appropriate individual to the correct job.

A *third* manifest consequence is that of developing an informed citizenry. Democracy is one of the most difficult governments to maintain. It requires literacy and an informed public. Likewise, the members of society need a basic understanding of how their government operates. Without such training citizens can easily be manipulated by those in power. It is for this reason that at some time in your formal education you were required to take a civics course. Studies that have investigated the correlation of political participation and education clearly demonstrate a positive relationship. The more education one has, the more likely he/she is to vote and engage in other forms of political participation.

Latent Functions. Emile Durkheim pioneered work in this area. For Durkheim the central role of education was to facilitate the creation of a sense of social solidarity in society. Traditional society was more homogeneous and as such there was great agreement on values (high social solidarity). As societies became more heterogeneous and specialized, there was a natural tendency for common bonds to weaken (low social solidarity). Carried to its extreme, this condition could result in the breakdown of social order. If society is to survive, a means must be found to re-establish the bonds necessary for harmony and order.

It is "bonding" that Durkheim perceived as a major function of education. The diverse masses could be socialized to accept what he termed the **moral order** or the norms necessary for the smooth functioning of society. While there are objections to the term "moral order" as value laden and inherently authoritarian, structural functionalists point out that all societies must reach agreement on societal values and transmit these values to members of society. Without a "moral order" society would inevitably fall into social chaos.

How do schools accomplish the teaching of moral order? An obvious example can be seen in the Pledge of Allegiance which is recited tens of thousands of times daily in schools across the country. This simple, but powerful act instills feelings of patriotism and respect for the political and social system. It provides a common ground of unity in a society with diverse racial, ethnic, and religious groups. Again, study after study points to the fact that educated people are less likely to be racist and ethnocentric than those with lower levels of education. Likewise, schools promote a sense of cooperation and teamwork through a variety of activities—sports, plays, academic competitions, etc. Students begin to develop a sense of tolerance and respect. These attitudes become important to society once students leave the schools and take their place in the larger society of work and community.

A primary function of any government is the education of its citizens. Without education, the society is unable to develop the skills and talents necessary to survive and prosper, especially in a highly technological world.

Photo: SC Cunningham

A final, rarely mentioned latent function of school is that of custodial care. Here schools provide structure and care to the lives of children. Some have gone as far as to claim that schools perform a "baby-sitting" function for those families in which one of the parents is not able to remain at home as a full-time caregiver. With the number of single parent and double income families growing, the schools have become a critical institution in which to place children with idle time on their hands.

In conclusion, structural functionalists maintain that education is a positive force for order and harmony in society. Not only does it provide society with the skilled workers necessary to maintain society, but it also performs a crucial integrative role in uniting a diverse and segmented population.

Social Conflict

Like structural functionalists, social conflict theorists agree with the principle that one should receive rewards commensurate with talent and effort. This is the basis of **meritocracy**, a cherished belief in our society. However, advocates of the social conflict perspective believe that advancement on the basis of merit is not what occurs in larger society. Rewards are distributed not on merit, but according to a system where the established elite exploits those without power. Furthermore, they believe education is an effective instrument utilized by those in power to maintain the status quo.

The beliefs of social conflict theorists are buttressed by research demonstrating that the education system is biased against the poor and the working class. As we have already seen, not all children in the United States have access to the same educational resources. Since a large portion of school funding comes from local communities, those in poorer neighborhoods will be unable to fund their schools at the same level as the affluent. As a result, students from affluent homes are six times more likely to attend and graduate from college than lower class students (Sewell and Hauser, 1980). Evidence also demonstrates that those attending selective colleges and universities are more likely to experience occupational success than those graduating from lower status institutions. Due to early educational and social experiences, students from upper class homes tend to score better on national entrance exams and therefore constitute the bulk of enrollment at elite institutions. Even when lower class students have the talent to overcome the inherent disadvantages of an unequal educational system, they often find themselves unable to enroll in elite universities due to the high cost of tuition. The importance of a degree from an elite state university is demonstrated by the fact that such graduates have lifetime earnings that are 28 percent higher than graduates from less prestigious institutions (Hoekstra, 2009). And finally, comparing graduates of elite universities, it has been clearly demonstrated that it is those graduates from upper class backgrounds that receive the bulk of prestigious job offers. Hence, social background appears to be more important than academic ability after graduation. This, according to social conflict theorists, is further proof of how the educational system functions to the advantage of elites in our society.

Social conflict theorists also disagree with the structural functional argument that education prepares members of society for jobs in the workforce. Here, they argue that the tremendous expansion of mass education, in reality, reflects an attempt to reinforce the political and economic ideology of equal opportunity. It is for this reason that when pressed to provide educational opportunities the system responded with the community college system, which is identified by advocates of this perspective as a "revolving door" to placate the poor. Viewed in this light, community colleges are the barriers protecting the elite university from the onslaught of the disadvantaged.

Contrary to structural functionalists who see education as a means to prepare skilled workers for society's workforce, social conflict theorists see it as yet another barrier thrown against the poors' door of opportunity. Credentialism, as seen by social conflict advocates, arose not to train workers but rather to solidify the class system. Those most able to gain entrance to degree-granting institutions and complete a course of study leading to advanced certificates are those from the higher ranks of the class system. Thus, it is not surpassing to find that the majority of successful applicants to schools of medicine, law, engineering, etc. are from affluent backgrounds. Furthermore, in most fields it is questionable whether a degree or advanced degree is even necessary. Lester Thurow (1980) believes that 60 percent of U.S. employees derive all their work skills on the job. As such, certification becomes little more than a screening process favoring those higher up in the class system.

Finally, whereas structural functionalists see mass education as a means to achieve social solidarity through assimilation, social conflict theorists perceive it as a means through which the powerful majority can subvert the cultural beliefs of the minority. Historically, this can be seen in the early cultural exploitation of the Native Americans and African slaves. From the very outset, educational institutions took an active role in the battle to force Anglo-Saxon values upon people. Treatment of minority culture was openly hostile. People and customs of other lands were stereotyped as being shiftless, humorous, and ignorant, while those of Western Europe were lauded in textbooks as inherently superior. Children were encouraged to abandon the traditions of their parents and adopt the "American way"—that of the dominate culture.

All minority cultures have received similar treatment throughout history. Today, this same battle is manifested in the current controversy over bilingual education. Critics of bilingual education maintain that such an approach deters assimilation and thus becomes an obstacle to upward social mobility. However, social conflict theorists disagree, citing evidence that even when people of color do adopt the values of the dominant culture, they still face serious roadblocks to social and economic advancement (see chapter eight).

ACHIEVING EQUALITY

Despite all the disagreement on education in America, there are two areas where total agreement can be found. *First*, that education remains an important avenue to upward social mobility in the United States. And *second*, that equal opportunity cannot be achieved without equal access to education. Therefore, much discussion has been addressed to the areas of equal access to education.

Integration and Busing

In spite of all efforts to eliminate segregation in schools, it remains a reality today. Current statistics reveal that two-thirds of all African American students and three-fourths of all Latino students attend a school where the vast majority of students are minorities. When one looks at urban areas alone, the results are even more dramatic. Today, fifteen out of sixteen African American and Latino students attend schools that have few whites ("New Era of Segregation," 1993).

How did this happen? For the most part it is the result of custom and law. During the period of slavery in the United States it was illegal to teach slaves how to read and write. After slavery was abolished, Jim Crow laws took effect to segregate the races. Segregation was based upon laws that were upheld by the Supreme Court (Plessy v. Ferguson, 1896); this type of segregation was termed **de jure**. In 1954, the Court reversed itself in Brown v. The Board of Education of Topeka, Kansas. Hence, segregation of schools was outlawed.

However, this did not end segregated schools. In its place a system of **de facto** segregation evolved. Rather than law, this pattern of segregation is maintained by residential patterns. Since schools are broken down into unit districts based upon residence, and since most people are racially and ethnically segregated, the schools, for the most part, remained segregated. To break the hammerlock of de facto segregation, the Court began to order predominantly segregated districts to transport, or **bus** their students to other area schools in order to achieve a racial balance. Studies by a number of researchers indicate that both African Americans and Hispanics scored higher in predominantly white or integrated schools than in segregated schools (Wortman and Bryant, 1985; Entwisle and Alexander, 1992).

Conversely, other researchers have indicated that busing actually hurts integration by causing **white flight**, the migration of whites out of communities to escape the forced integration (Wilson, 1985). Likewise, due in part to the ensuing hostilities, other researchers have reported mixed results of improved performance by minority students (Rist, 1978). In many cases, once in their new school, minority students were again segregated by tracking. Finally, a number of recent court cases have taken serious tolls on the ability to use school busing as a means to achieve racial equality (Orfield and Montfort, 1993). To this day, busing remains a controversial means to achieve equality, since often all parties oppose it.

Privatization of Schools

At present, 11 percent of all students enrolled in elementary and secondary education attend some form of private school. Catholic schools account for slightly more than half of the private school enrollment. The rest are comprised of Protestant church schools, particularly Lutheran and some non-profit institutions. Although the majority of children attend public schools, their parents are split on the value of private education. Approximately 49 percent believe sending their children to a private school would improve their performance, whereas, 46 percent are opposed to sending their children to such a school (CAPE, 2008).

Sociologists have examined the question of whether private schools offer a better opportunity for children than public schools. Again, as one might guess, the results are split. James Coleman, in a study for the National Center for Education Statistics, researched the question with a sample of nearly 60,000 students enrolled in 1,015 public and private schools. His results demonstrated a positive value of private over public education (Coleman and Hoffer, 1987). The following are the major factors Coleman presents in favor of private schools:

1. Test scores reveal that students enrolled in private schools do better on reading, writing, and arithmetic, as well as in science, civics, and vocabulary.

2. Private schools had lower teacher/student ratios.

3. Private schools had fewer discipline problems.

4. Private schools offered greater academic challenges.
5. Private schools had lower dropout rates.
6. Private schools, though smaller, had less racial segregation.

Following the release of this report, supporters of public education roundly criticized Coleman and Hoffer. Comparison between public and private schools were unfair since those attending private school normally came from more privileged backgrounds, had more parental support, and were predominately composed of children destined to enter colleges and universities. If private schools were forced to accept all students from all socioeconomic, racial, and ethnic backgrounds, their success would be considerably less. Likewise, many criticized the achievement tests selected by Coleman for his study, maintaining that there were culturally and racially biased.

In recent years there has been a movement toward achieving equality through "schooling for profit." Advocates of this concept maintain that schools can be better run by private enterprise. Unitizing marketplace economics and efficiency, privately owned educational corporations would be more adept at producing results while avoiding the bureaucratic bloat and entanglements of public education. Here, schools would compete against each other for students. Through competition, the consumer (the student) would receive the best education for the least amount of money. Many educators object on the grounds that the humanitarian goals of education do not translate well to the "dog-eat-dog" world of commercial marketplace capitalism. Others believe that while the principle seems great on paper, in the day-to-day world of mass education it would be an unworkable concept.

"No Child Left Behind"

On January 8, 2002, President Bush signed the "No Child Left Behind Act." The intent of this legislative act was to attempt to close the achievement gap by offering more flexibility to states and granting more options to parents in choice of schools. In turn, states are required to describe to the federal government how they plan to close the gap, provide annual state and school district report cards informing parents and communities of their progress, and provide remedial tutoring for students in need. Schools that do not meet minimum standards are placed on a "needing improvement" list and corrective actions are initiated. If no progress occurs within a five-year period, the school must be restructured along with replacing most of the staff or turning over operation of the school to the state or a private company with a demonstrated record of effectiveness.

Although many hail the plan as a step forward, critics contend that the plan is doomed to fail due to inadequate funding. Under the act, states are mandated to measure gaps in achievement, but the federal government provides no funding to correct problems. Hence, cash-strapped states find themselves unable to remediate problems. Additionally, another feature

Here, students from a private school make their way home. As taxpayers become frustrated with public education, more and more parents enroll their children in private or charter schools. Approximately 10 percent of all school children attend private schools.

Photo: David Lisbona.

of the plan would allow students in schools that fail an option to transfer to better schools in the district. However, in many cases, though the option exists on paper, transfer is impossible. Parents who would like to transfer their children find that neighboring schools are no better their own or that too few seats are available in more desirable schools.

Charter Schools

Another plan that attempts to bridge the quality and educational inequality gap is the formation of **charter schools**; public schools that operate under a contract or "charter." While held to the same standard of academic accountability as a traditional public schools, they have greater autonomy and control over educational decisions to facilitate educational reform. Additionally, on the average, charter schools have a smaller teacher/student ratio, hire more experienced teachers, and compensate their staff better than teachers from traditional public schools.

As most Americans are aware from the blockbuster movie, "Waiting for Superman," enrollment in charter schools is awarded on the basis of a lottery system. In many communities the competition for available seats is fierce. A recent study showed a waiting list of more than 200 students in over 60 percent of such schools (Center for Educational Reform, 2008).

Embedded within the philosophy of charter schools is the goal of serving diverse populations. To this end, the data appears to shows success. The overall national composition of charter schools boasts enrollment rates of 38 percent for blacks, 37 percent for whites, and 19 percent for Hispanics (U.S. Department of Education, 2004).

Of course, the final question is how well have charter schools performed in comparison to traditional public schools. In the most comprehensive analysis of data to date, the conclusion is not favorable. Academic success, as measured by standardized tests, showed no significant difference in student learning between charter and traditional public schools (U.S. Department of Education, 2008). However, proponents of such schools point out that charter schools serve a wider and more disadvantaged population making comparisons between the two unfair. Regardless, with President Obama's new educational initiative, "Race to the Top," there is sure to be a renewed interest in alternative education strategies.

CONCLUSION

Although the controversy directed at education is endless, everyone agrees that educational changes must occur if America is to compete in the global economy. The development of our children is the key to the future. Human beings are resources. An examination of the most recent data clearly demonstrates the United States lags behind significantly other advanced nations in educational performance and is slipping further behind each year. Comparing the performance of U.S. children with that of their counterparts overseas, it was found that America ranked 25th of 30 nations in math and 24th of 30 in science (McKinsey & Company, 2009).

Additionally, within the United States, large gaps exist between racial and socioeconomic groups. Whites, as a group, out-performed racial minorities. Among what is now being referred to as the "top gap," less than 3 percent of black and Hispanic students are at the advanced level for their grade. By twelfth grade the percentage declines to less than one percent. Similar results are found when comparing students of different income groups. Impoverished students are roughly two years of learning behind the average better-off student of the same age (McKinsey & Company, 2009).

One might ask how the American economy emerged as one of the strongest in the world if we do a poor job educating our citizens. The answer is that we do a great job educating the top quarter of the class. In other words, those from higher socioeconomic backgrounds do, in fact, receive a superior education. And it is these students who upon graduation take their skills into the marketplace and do an excellent job. However, since the top quarter cannot possibly fill all the technical and scientific jobs, America simply fills in the rest by importing highly skilled immigrants wanting to come to this country with skills they have developed in their native lands.

The rest of Americans lacking the education and training necessary to compete effectively in the new global economy become the next generation of fast-food servers, back office clerks, janitors, gardeners, drivers, and housemaids. While this strategy has worked thus far, it is doubtful that it will continue to do so in the very near future. Relegated to dead end jobs, workers become alienated from work and society. Alienation leads to hopelessness and despair which in turn leads to a host of social ills—poverty, drug usage, domestic violence, theft, etc. On the economic side, workers without adequate pay can no longer purchase the goods produced by the marketplace. This leads to economic cutbacks, increased unemployment, and recession.

The reality is that we need to educate all of our citizens, not only to remain a healthy and vibrant nation economically, but out of concern for the kind of society we want our children and grandchildren to live in. Economists estimate that by narrowing the racial gap seen in education we could add 2 to 4 percent to the GPD (Gross Domestic Product) or $310 to $510 billion dollars. Closing the low income gap could add another $400 to $600 billion dollar or 3 to 5 percent to the GPD. Stated differently, maintaining these gaps in our educational system essentially imposes a permanent national recession on the economy (McKinsey & Company, 2009).

Closing both the racial and socioeconomic education gaps will require both a commitment of moral and political will. Substantial resources will need redirection, and how we structure our schools and educate our children will have to change. However, if we as a nation are going to successfully compete in a global and increasingly technological world, we have little choice.

Terms You Should Know:

Learning	Education	Schools
Credentialism	Social Darwinism	Tracking
Human Capital	Compulsory Education	Meritocracy
Educational Attainment	White Flight	Charter Schools

Can You Answer These Questions?

1. What is the difference between secular and non-secular schools? Why don't we publicly support non-secular schools?
2. List the factors that lead to the development of formal institutions of education?
3. Of all the factors, which is most predictive of who ends up with the better education?
4. Historically, who has obtained the most education–men or women? Is this true today?
5. On what evidence do "Inherent Deficiency" theorists base their beliefs?
6. According to Oscar Lewis and Edward Banfield, why are members of the lower class unable to escape poverty?
7. How does the theory of "Structure Disadvantage" differ from "Inherent Deficiency" or "Culture of Poverty"? Which would you be more likely to support?
8. According to Emile Durkheim, modern society leads to a weakening of traditional values that provide for social solidarity. When this occurs, what is needed to replace it?
9. What is the difference between "de jure" and "de facto" segregation?
10. From what source do schools obtain they're financing? Why might this benefit a student from a more affluent family than one from an impoverished one?

Critical Thinking Exercises:

1. Today's labor market demands an ever-increasing amount of degree certification. Do you believe all of this formal education is necessary or are we just requiring people to obtain more education when it really doesn't affect their performance on the job?
2. From your experience in life and education, do you feel that innate intelligence or social factors play a larger part in educational attainment? Is this also true of occupational success?
3. The "No Child Left Behind" program requires more and earlier testing of students than ever before. Do you think this is good?
4. Do you feel that tracking of students on ability levels is beneficial or harmful to society?
5. Do you feel that every child growing up in the United States has an equal chance at success? On what do you base your belief?
6. What suggestions can you offer to close the "achievement gap" between racial minorities and whites in this country? Would this be the same set of suggestions for the difference between low income and more affluent students?
7. In your opinion, is equal opportunity a myth or reality in the United States?

Photo: Heidi Germann

Chapter 12

Religion and Society

From what we currently understand, humans are the only animals that have a foreknowledge of their own death. Likewise, our advanced intellect has allowed us to gaze at the heavens above and brood about our existence. Where did we come from? For what purpose did life evolve? What of time and space, are they endless? Is life endless? What happens to us when we die? It is these questions, and others like them, that both intrigue and plague us.

Over the ages, thousands of religions have suddenly appeared and then, just as suddenly, vanished. Others have metamorphosed into newer forms claiming converts from all over the globe. Still others have endured for centuries with few, if any real changes. Undoubtedly, many more religions will be founded before humankind ends its tenure on this rock. It is precisely this that underscores the need we have for religion in our lives and its importance to the development of the societies we build.

In this chapter we will examine religion from a sociological view. We will explore some of the major religions of the world. We will see how religion mirrors or contributes to social stratification and then see how structural functionalists and social conflict theorists differ on what role religion plays in our lives. Finally, we will offer some thoughts on the future of religion in our society.

SOCIOLOGICAL LANGUAGE

Defining Religion

All people have a common understanding of the concept of religion. However, attempts to find a concrete definition have produced considerable confusion. It is useful therefore, to begin with a common sociological understanding of what religion is and what it is not.

The best authority, at least one whose definition has found acceptance among sociologists, is Emile Durkheim. In his famous work, *The Elementary Forms of the Religious Life* (1915), Durkheim began his definition by first separating events of everyday life from those in the religious sphere. Events of everyday life are termed the **profane**. Derived from Latin the term profane means, "outside the temple." Examples would obviously include work, play, eating, child rearing, and so forth. For those events that pertain to the supernatural and the unexplained, inspiring a sense of awe, inspiration, or perhaps fear the term **sacred** is applied. Durkheim thus defined **religion** as:

> ...a unified system of beliefs, and practices relative to sacred things, that is to say, things set apart and forbidden—beliefs and practices which unite into one single moral community called a Church, all those who adhere to them (1915).

Elements of Religion

Ronald Johnstone (1995) lists five elements necessary to define a belief system as a religion. *First*, a religion must consist of a **group** of people who share a common belief system. Certainly it is possible for an individual to hold private beliefs (as many do), but the influence of those beliefs does not extend beyond the individual. Sociologists are concerned with religious movements affecting many individuals over an extended time period.

Second, religion focuses on what is considered **sacred** as opposed to the profane. What is considered sacred defines religions. For example, Hindus in India believe that the cow is sacred because it is linked to the god Vishnu. In the Christian religion, man was given dominion over animals and, as such, animals serve our physical needs for food and clothing.

Third, within a religion there is a **creed** to which all believers must subscribe. The creed defines the universe, existence, and life after death. For Christians, death brings about a final judgment in which one is accountable to God. For a Nichiren Buddhist, life and death is a continuous process of incarnations in which the soul grows toward perfection. In this belief system, an ant is as important as a human.

Fourth, incorporated into religion is a set of practices termed **rituals**. Durkheim defined rituals as the values that dictate how the members of the religion are expected to behave in the presence of the sacred. A critical distinction is that rituals do not have meaning in and of themselves. Rather, they take on religious significance when used in a particular manner to express a relationship with the sacred. An example would be holy water in the Roman Catholic Church. Once blessed, the water takes on a religious meaning as it is used in the signing of the cross or the baptism of a baby.

Fifth, all religions embody a set of **norms**, the purpose of which is to guide the religious membership in a way of life that is considered morally and spiritually right. The Ten Commandments are one such example, providing Christians with a clear and concise set of rules by which to live their lives. The difference between a creed and a set of norms is that the creed defines the relationship of the supernatural to the believer, while norms provide rules to guide everyday behavior.

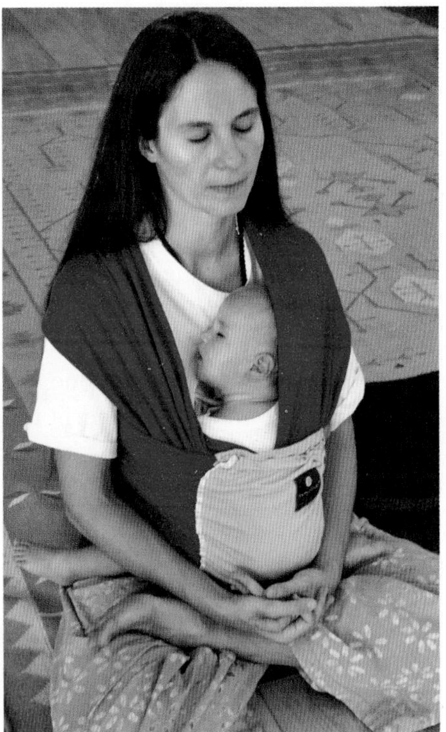

A young woman meditates with her child. Meditation is common among Eastern religions. Today, approximately 10 percent of the U.S. population engages in some form of meditative practice.

Photo: Pre Massagar Rose

Classification of Belief Systems

Distinction among religions can be made in terms of how a god or supernatural being is defined. **Monotheism** is a religion that believes in the existence of one god. Christianity, Judaism, and Islam are three well-known examples. In some religions, **polytheism**, the belief in many gods or goddesses, exists. The ancient religions of Rome and Greece had such beliefs. A modern example can be seen in Hinduism. Practiced mainly in India, each village has its own god along with specialized rituals and ceremonies. Gods of other villages may also be worshipped if they are perceived to be especially powerful or suited to a momentary need of an individual or village.

Less familiar to the west are the beliefs of Buddhism, Confucianism, Shintoism, and Taoism. These religions practice what is termed **transcendental idealism**. Rather than worshipping a god or supernatural being, these religions lay forth a set of moral, philosophical, or ethical teachings to be adhered to by their followers. A strict adherence to the teachings is required to achieve inner peace and enlightenment.

Many preliterate societies practiced a form of **totemism** in which an animal was seen as both a god and an ancestor. Almost always, the animal selected was central to the lives of the tribe either as a food source or dangerous predator. The rituals of the tribe revolved around celebrations in which tribal members dressed-up in costumes portraying the animal and mimicked its behavior in dance and vocalizations. Experts consider totemism humankind's first religion from which all others evolved. Totemism is still practiced by Aborigines in Australia and by some remote tribes of New Guinea.

Another disappearing religion is that of **animism**. People practicing animism believe that the supernatural being or beings, spirits, or deceased ancestors actively exist in the bodies of present-day people or in creatures or physical objects of the natural environment.

While not constituting a religion, **atheism** and **agnosticism** are belief systems held by many individuals in society today. Of the two, atheism is the more extreme exerting that a supernatural being or god does not exist. Likewise, atheists believe in a finality of life. With death, the human being ceases to exist; there is nothing beyond the here and now. Although atheists vary on how life came to exist, most tend to accept a more scientific explanation (this is not to imply that one has to be an atheist to believe in science). Occupying the middle ground is the agnostic. While not discounting the possibility of a Supreme Being, the agnostic simply states that the existence of god or a supernatural being is unknown or impossible to determine.

RELIGIONS OF THE WORLD

The economic and political interdependence of the world has brought together people from all corners of the earth. Increasingly, it is becoming more important to learn about the cultures of others and respect their differences if we are all going to get along on this planet. A failure to understand the religious beliefs of others can lead to disastrous consequences as demonstrated in the conflict of Bosnia-Hertzegovina among Croatian Catholics, Serbian Eastern Orthodoxy, and Bosnian Muslims.

A complete description of all existing religions is impossible—literally thousands exist. Therefore, we will confine our discussion to those major religions that account for approximately three billion believers.

Judaism

Although Judaism is one of the oldest modern-day religions, it is also the smallest. Only about 14 million, or one percent, of the world's population are Jews. Almost half of all Jews live in North America. Other large Jewish populations are found in Southeast Asia (four million), countries of the former Soviet Union (three million), and Israel (4.5 million). Israel, formerly Palestine, is the official state of Judaism.

The history of Judaism reaches back 4,000 years before the birth of Jesus Christ. Originating in the ancient culture of Mesopotamia, the original religious practice was animistic. However, this changed after Jacob, grandson of Abraham, moved his family to Egypt, where they were enslaved and remained so for hundreds of years. The end to their bondage came with the birth of Moses in the thirteenth century BCE. Adopted by an Egyptian princess, Moses was chosen by God to lead the Jews out of Egypt to find the chosen land. For forty years, the Jews wandered in the desert. It was during this time that a *covenant* between the Jews and God was established in which they became God's chosen people. It was also during this time that God revealed to Moses, at Mount Sinai, the Ten Commandments.

The Torah is a significant spiritual book for the Jews. Christians are familiar with the Torah, because it is contained in their Bible and called the Old Testament; including the first five books. Jews use the Torah as a guide to help them understand the will of God in all matters. The Jewish tradition reflects an image of a personal and loving God. Everything comes from and is dependent on Him. A covenant or agreement exists between God and the Jews, and mitvot are key parts of the agreement. Six-hundred and thirteen mitvot are found in the Torah. Strictly speaking, a mitzvah (singular of mitvot) means commandment, but the word is also used to mean good deed. In the broader sense, mitvot are actions a Jew is called to do to fulfill his part of the covenant with God and community. These are normative actions governing all realms of behavior. Some examples include loving and worshiping God, giving to the poor, not bearing a grudge, and not eating unclean animals. (Robinson, 2000).

Three major branches make-up Judaism today: Orthodox, Reform, and Conservative. Orthodox Jews are the most conservative. Strict adherence to Jewish custom is required. Historic dress, consumption of kosher foods, and separation of men and women in religious services are just a few of the practices that set them apart from other Jews. Orthodox Jews number about one million. Many early Jewish immigrants to the United States broke from traditional customs in order to assimilate into their new culture. This led to the formation of Reform Judaism and now has approximately 1.3 million members. The largest number of Jews, somewhere around two million, belong to the Conservative branch. The teachings and practices of these Jews lie between the Orthodox and Reform branch. It should be noted that many people who identify themselves as Jews do not attend **synagogue** (Jewish house of worship). In essence, being Jewish is as much a cultural heritage as it is a religious experience.

The history of the Jewish people is one of discrimination and persecution. The English term **ghetto** is derived from the Italian word *borghetto* that translates to "outside the city wall." Here, Jews were forced to live in poorly maintained and cramped neighborhoods due to **anti-Semitism** (prejudice against Jews). Anti-Semitism reached a peak with the holocaust of World War II, in which over 6 million Jews were exterminated in what Adolf Hitler termed, "The Final Solution." With the defeat of Nazi Germany, the intensity of the Jewish quest to establish a homeland in Palestine, identified by the Torah as the center of Judaism, greatly accelerated. This movement termed Zionism, achieved reality with the creation of the state of Israel. During this process many Arabs were displaced, creating political and military unrest in the region. Today, Israel and the PLO (Palestinian Liberation Organization) move in and out of attempts to reach some accord for peace.

Christianity

With approximately 2.1 billion members, Christianity is the world's largest religion. Although Christians can be found living almost anywhere in the world, the majority reside in Europe, North America, and South America.

The origin of Christianity is found in a small cult that arose from the older Judaism, a religion centered, as noted above, in the Middle East. Like most religions, Christianity arose from a charismatic figure, Jesus of Nazareth. Preaching a message of repentance, forgiveness, and eternal salvation, Jesus was proclaimed the Son of God and the long-awaited Messiah of the Jews. Although Jesus preached an apolitical message, the existing powers found cause to be alarmed by him and eventually Jesus was tried, convicted, and executed by means of crucifixion on a cross. The cross later became the symbol of Christianity. According to his followers, on the third day of his death, Jesus arose from the dead and subsequently ascended into Heaven. It is upon this claim that adherents to Christianity stake their claim to Jesus' divine nature. The apostles of Jesus fanned-out across the Mediterranean region to spread their beliefs. By the fourth century, Christianity was adopted by the Roman Empire as the official religion of the state. Later, the colonial empires of Europe would be responsible for its spread throughout much of the world.

Christianity is built on the Jewish faith, but its major spiritual beliefs and practices center on the life and teachings of Jesus Christ. Just as the Jews strive to live their commandments, Christians strive to live by the commandments Jesus left his followers. They are:

> "You shall love the Lord your God, with all your heart, with all your soul and with all your mind. This is the greatest and first commandment. The second is like it: You shall love your neighbor as yourself." (Matthew: 22; 37-40)

The concept of the Trinity in Christianity dramatically sets it apart from Islam and Judaism. The Trinity is an understanding of the nature of God as one, unified in three distinct persons (The Father, The Son and The Holy Spirit). Christians believe that Jesus Christ was the Son of God, and after his death and resurrection he is said to have given his followers the gift of the Spirit. The Spirit is seen as a living presence of God that moves in peoples lives as a source of holy strength and guidance. For a Christian, the idea that God manifests himself to the world in three forms does not detract from the unity and oneness of his being (Alexander, 1994).

Two major splits have occurred in Christianity. In the tenth century, the religion split into two churches: the Roman Catholic Church and the Orthodox Church, centered in what is now Istanbul, Turkey. The split was largely a result of power conflicts arising out of difference between eastern and western influence. The second major split occurred in the sixteenth century with the rebellion of Martin Luther, as well as other reformers, who established independent churches under the name of Protestantism

Even in the most difficult situations, Muslims pray. Prayer, or Salah, is performed five times daily and is obligatory. When praying, Muslims always face Mecca. The time of Salah is determined by the sun's movement.

photo: Ramy Raoof.

(from the root word protest). Throughout the centuries, many different denominations (churches) arose as conflict developed over doctrine.

Islam

Like its counterparts, Christianity and Judaism, Islam is also a monotheistic religion. Muslims believe in one God and trace the roots of their faith to Abraham. Some scholars refer to these three religions, which have had a major impact on world civilizations, as the three branches of the "Religion of Abraham." Today, Islam is one of the fastest growing religions in the world as well as in the United States and North America. Muslims account for more than 1.5 billion followers world wide, making Islam the second largest religion after Christianity. While most Muslims are not Arabs, the majority of Arabs are Muslims. One of the largest concentration of Muslims is found in Indonesia, Afghanistan, and Pakistan.

Muslims have been in America since the early days. Hudson and Corrigan (1999) state that early on in the Spanish exploration of the New World, "Isfan the Arab" accompanied Franciscans to Arizona and some Muslims settled in North America. In addition, some Muslims were brought here as slaves from North Africa. Today, Muslims in America represent three to four percent of the total population (6-8 million), and compose a wide mix of African Americans, Arabs, Asians, and whites (The Pew Forum, 2011).

Historically, Islam began in Mecca, Arabia, among peoples who claimed their descent from Abraham's son Ishmael. Islam dates from the seventh century CE when the series of revelations to Muslims was received from God (*Allah* in Arabic) through the prophet Muhammad (570 CE-632 CE) who received his first revelation in the year 610 CE. Within two generations of his death, these revelations were collected and compiled in one of the most important and sacred documents to Muslims, the Koran (Qura'n). The Koran is written in Arabic, and for Muslims it is the final and correct word of God to the human race. Muslims believe that God had in essence one message that was delivered in stages to the human race through a number of prophets, mainly Abraham, Moses, Jesus, and Muhammad, who is believed to be the last and final prophet or messenger of God. Accordingly, Islam acknowledges Christianity and Judaism as legitimate religions, regards their followers as true believers and considers them to be, "People of the Book."

Islam literally means submission—submission to the will of God. Islam considers its message universal and independent of its ethnic or geographic origins. The Islamic faith is grounded in what is known as the "Five Pillars of Islam." They are principles and acts that all Muslims are required to fulfill and can be carried out by any person. The Five Pillars are:

1. Shahada. Arabic for "witnessing." Shahada is the declaration that there is no god but God and that Muhammad is His messenger.

2. Prayer. Muslims must participate in five periods of prayer each day as an act of daily and routine purification and a sign of submission to the will of God.

3. Zakat. Arabic for the act of giving. Zakat means the giving of alms and contributions to charity and to the needy. It is an act of purification through giving.

4. Siam. Arabic for fasting. Muslims are required to fast during the daylight hours in the month of Ramadan. Exceptions are granted for medical reasons. Siam is an act of purification through fasting and abstaining from worldly, profane matters. Fasting is supposed to make the person humble and identify with the hungry, the poor, and the needy. Ramadan is considered a holy month in the Islamic calendar because it is believed that God's revelations to Muhammad had occurred during this month.

5. Hajj. Arabic for pilgrimage. Muslims, who are financially, physically, and mentally able must make a pilgrimage (Hajj) to Mecca, once during their lifetime.

Islam is considered a theology and a way of life. It derives its legal, theological and ethical principles from both the Koran as well as the Hadiths. The Hadiths are reports of what the prophet Muhammad said and did. Although the Islamic literature and scholars contribute to the interpretation of these sources, the ultimate act of interpretation and application of the meaning of these two sources is up to each individual Muslim and his/her cultural context. This fact explains the wide range of diverse ways in which Muslims practice their faith throughout the world. For political and theological reasons, Islam was divided into two major branches, Sunni, and Shi'a. There are more Sunnites worldwide and most of the Shi'ites are concentrated in Iran.

In modern times, Islam faces a number of challenges. The changing economic, political and social forces place traditional Islam, as is also the case in other traditional religions, under a significant pressure to change. As social institutions, religions are very slow, and in fact very resistant, to change. Islam, Judaism, and Christianity emerged in an agricultural society with a patriarchal social organization. Consequently, and judging by today's standards, their theologies regard women as second-class citizens and deprive them of many social, religious and political rights. A second and important challenge to Islam is its political position on a number of issues including the separation of church and state and the threat to Islam by secular and modern forces. The trend toward secularization and modernization, and in contrast the push for return to traditional Islamic fundamentals, will be discussed later in the chapter.

Hinduism

Hinduism has the distinction of being the world's oldest religion, dating back nearly six thousand years. It is the source from which Buddhism and Sikhism found their roots. Hindus number some 900 million principally located in India and Pakistan. Significant settlements of Hindus can also be found in southern Africa and Indonesia. Approximately one million Hindus reside in the United States.

Hinduism is a polytheistic religion that recognizes many gods, both male and female. The greatest god is Brahman, the creator of all, eternal, and as such, containing the spirits of all the lesser gods. Other principle gods are Vishnu, Rama, and Krishna. The major source of knowledge for Hinduism comes from sacred writings known as the *Vedas*. These writings, it is believed, were received from Brahman and passed from generation to generation. Although there is no formal organization, gurus (teachers) take on the responsibility of teaching the sacred writings to followers.

While the practice of Hinduism varies considerably from region to region, there are some beliefs common to all Hindus. One of the foremost is a belief in a moral force or *dharma* with which all Hindus must act in concert. The caste system is one such example. If one is born an untouchable (the lowest caste), it is their obligation to accept, according to dharma, their position. A second belief is *karma*, or the view that one's behavior or adherence to dharma, will affect one's position in the next life. This brings us to a third belief, that of reincarnation, which is a cycle of life, death, and rebirth. Unlike Christians, Jews, or Muslims who believe in the finality of death and judgment, Hindus believe that one's soul progresses to higher or lower stages within the caste system. Once one has achieved the highest state of spiritual perfection, termed *nirvana*, reincarnation ceases and one is spared rebirth. Although the caste system was officially abolished in 1949, it still remains an important part of Hindu life.

Hindus have many common practices governed by dharma that affect all stages of life including birth, puberty, marriage, work, and death. Ceremonies for all events are important. A particularly important ceremony is *Kumbh Mela*, the single largest religious ceremony in the world. Occurring every twelve years, over 20 million Hindus migrate to the Ganges River to bathe in its purifying waters.

A group of young monks relax in a courtyard. Monks practice a form of asceticism or avoidance of any worldly pleasures. This is done so the individual can concentrate on pursuing religious or spiritual goals without distraction.

Photo: Neils Photography.

Buddhism

As mentioned previously, Buddhism has its roots in Hinduism. However, many followers consider it more an ethical way of life rather than a religion. Originating in the sixth century BCE, its founder, Siddhartha Gautama, was a Hindu prince who gave-up his lofty position in search of enlightenment. Through a lifetime of travel, poverty, and spiritual searching, he became Buddha—the awakened or enlightened one.

Since Buddhism is more a way of life than a succinct doctrine or belief in a single god, it is hard to estimate the number of people practicing Buddhism. Estimates of actual followers vary from 300 to 500 million.

In some ways, Buddhism parallels Hinduism. One important difference is that Buddhists reject the caste system. The philosophy of Buddhism is embodied in the "Four Noble Truths":

1. All beings of life—gods included—are subject to the same hopeless cycle of pain, suffering, and rebirth (their *karma*).

2. Suffering is an extension or result of our attachment to worldly possessions and pleasures.

3. *Nirvana,* or the freedom from karma, is obtainable.

4. Attainment of *nirvana* lies in pursuing what Buddhist characterize as the Eightfold Path, which includes: the adoption of a simple life, strict adherence to the pursuit of ethical behavior, a rejection of material pleasures and possessions, and meditation.

The overall goal of the Buddhist is the attainment of nirvana—a blissful state of emptiness. Buddhism does not insist on any one exclusive religious view. In fact, many Buddhists, like their Hindu counterparts, profess belief in local deities and gods. The strongest Buddhist influence can be seen in the Far Eastern nations of Burma, China, Korea, Thailand, Sri Lanka, and Japan.

Confucianism

Confucius lived in the same century as Buddha. Like Buddha, Confucius was concerned with the suffering of existence. Unlike Buddha, who instructed his followers to withdraw from worldly pursuits, Confucius taught his disciples to engage the world, but in a highly moral and ethical way. The tenets of Confucianism are contained in the sayings and instructions of its master. These are recorded in the Analects. The most famous of all of Confucian's statements is one that is comparable to the much-quoted golden rule:

> Tzu asked, "Is there one word which may serve as a rule of practice for all one's life?"
>
> The Master said, "Is not reciprocity (*shu*) such a word? What you do not want done to yourself, do not do to others." (Noss, 1980)

The above is embodied within *jen*, a central concept of Confucianism, which teaches total subordination of self-interest to the moral life. Beginning in the family, one must practice loyalty. In the same manner, members of the family must always be mindful of their obligations to their community. As such, one layer builds upon the other, integrating the entirety of society.

From about 200 BC until the beginning of the nineteenth century, Confucianism was the official religion of China. Almost all followers of Confucius live in China. The spread of Confucianism to other countries has been slight, occurring mainly through immigration. It is estimated that about 100,000 followers live in United States.

Shintoism

The word Shinto was coined to distinguish itself from Buddhism. Practiced largely in Japan, it was once the official state religion and a significant force in the modernization of Japan. Followers today number about 4 million worldwide. Shinto has no formal congregational worship and very little theology. Instead, it is a complex set of ethical and moral principles steeped in ancient folk beliefs and rituals, specifically practiced to bring honor and glory to one's ancestors. In many ways it can be viewed as a nationalistic cult, even today, with the new Japanese constitution proclaiming a separation of church and state. Shinto philosophies are recorded in two books: Kojiki (712 CE) and Nihongi (720 CE).

CULTS

The contemporary connotation of the word cult implies a sense of deviance to the lay person. Undoubtedly, this is the result of the media's portrayal of recent cult disasters such as the Heaven's Gate suicides, the Jonestown suicide/massacre (People's Temple, founded by Jim Jones), and the Branch Davidians shoot-out. Likewise, the everyday activities of the Unification Church of Sun Myung Moon (Moonies), the Hare Krishna, Satanic Worshippers, and others, reinforce unsavory and stereotypical images.

Sociologists do not share the above views. For sociologists, **cults** and cult activities are significant social movements arising out of disruptions in the social fabric of society. Their importance is not due to what they believe, but rather, the origins and the conditions within a culture that gave rise to their existence.

In attempting to arrive at a definition of a cult, it is important to understand the difference between cults and sects. A **sect** is generally an off-shoot of a major, well-established religion. In many ways, sects typically incorporate a substantial portion of the doctrine of the religion from which they originate. Like cults, sects most frequently arise at a period of social instability or when the belief systems of a society break down. So, what is the difference between cults and sects?

1. Unlike sects, cults arise outside of well-established religions, are not to be considered an off-shoot or branch of established religions, and as such, are a new source of religious beliefs.
2. Cults are centered on a charismatic figure who is all-important to the survival of the religious movement.
3. Cults, as opposed to sects, are more at odds with the existing culture, due to their radical ideas.
4. Cults are, more often than not, short-lived because they are less likely to fit into the prevailing culture of the society.

Two additional points should be made before leaving this topic. First, while cults have a bad reputation, it should be remembered that all major religions, at some point in their origins, were considered cults. For example, Christianity traces its roots back to ancient Jerusalem where both Jews and Romans considered it a dangerous cult. Thus, its disciples and followers were widely persecuted. Second, what is considered a cult in one society can be regarded a well-established religion in another. Such might be the case when Evangelical Protestantism arrives in a distant eastern culture. Likewise, the *gurus* of India are typically cast in the images of cult leaders when they teach in the United States.

THE RELIGIOUS EXPERIENCE IN THE UNITED STATES

With all the media hype about the disappearance of religious values in America today, one might conclude that religion is on its deathbed. Is this true? The answer is not clear. Sociologists who investigate religious trends have found mixed results.

Religiosity is a sociological concept meaning the importance of religion to one's life. Religious (church) affiliation, attendance at worship services and practicing spiritual elements of a belief system; like prayer, are various measures that gauge the level of religiosity (Marshall, 1994).

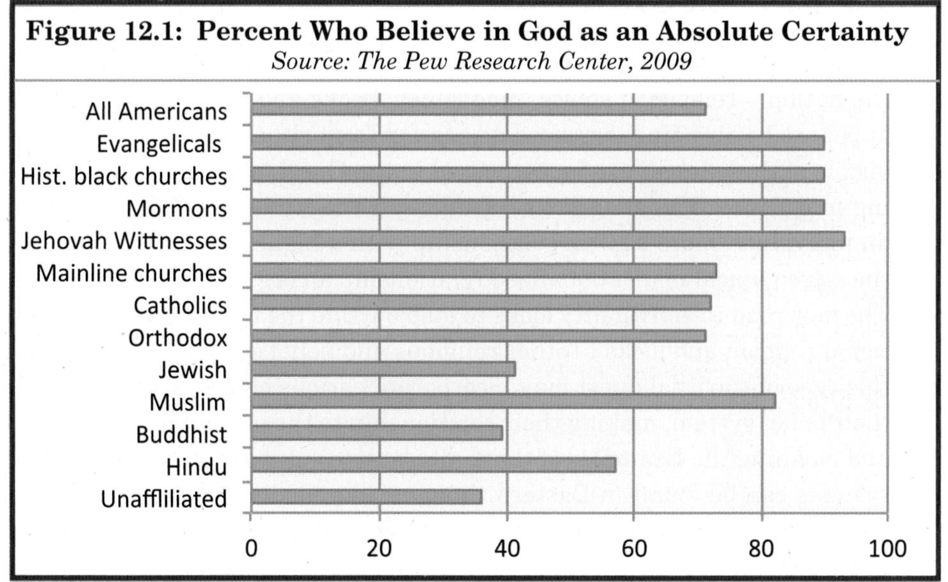

Figure 12.1: Percent Who Believe in God as an Absolute Certainty
Source: The Pew Research Center, 2009

At the time of the American Revolution, about one in six Americans was affiliated with a church. By the Civil War, the proportion had increased to two in six, and in the early 1900s it was roughly three in six. Today, this proportion appears to be holding strong along with 71 percent of Americans professing absolute certainty in the existence of God and 54 percent claiming religion to be an important factor in their day-to-day lives. Even among those who are unaffiliated with any church, 46 percent say religion is at least somewhat important in their lives (The Pew Forum, 2008). Looking at this information, it seems clear that Americans have been and continue to be very religious. In fact, Figure 12.1, along with other comparative data, indicates that America is one of the most religious countries in the world.

But do statements of belonging to a religious group, or feelings of the importance of religion, really indicate the strength and commitment to a faith system? The two additional measures in religiosity, attending worship services and spiritual practices, may give us a different picture of the American religious nature. Worship Service attendance is reported at its highest level since the 1960s. It is estimated that of those surveyed in a recent study, 39 percent of the respondents reported attending religious services at least once a week and another 27 percent stated they attend a few times a year (The Pew Form, 2008). In addition to making a time commitment, these worshipers appear to be making significant financial commitments as well with more than 100 billion dollars of annual voluntary donations to religious organizations reported (Hall, 2010). Spiritual practices seem to be holding firm with 58 percent of Americans indicating that prayer was an important part of their life and that they pray daily (The Pew Forum, 2009).

Religion versus Spirituality

In fact, there seems to be much attention given to the spiritual mindset of the nation. Television shows, magazines, books and other media sources appear to be directing increased discussion to spiritual wellness. The most visible of these forces can be witnessed in the Oprah show and corresponding magazine. The alleged new found spirituality is one that focuses on an individual, more flexible relationship with a higher power that opposes the stereotypical institutionalized relationship an organized religion holds. The new road to spirituality looks to step outside the boundaries of a traditional religion and looks to other religious and belief systems. A person on this type of spiritual quest may incorporate various elements of faiths into their belief system, making their relationship to the eternal more personal and meaningful. Examples of these alternative spiritual practices or belief systems can be found in Eastern thought; like mediation, yoga, etc. or in various new age methodologies involving crystals or practices from Native American faiths. In a recent study, 9.4 percent of Americans reported looking for a more personal experience of faith and that they participated in meditative practices (Barnes, et. al., 2007). Four out of five respondents stated they have personally experienced or felt the presence of a spiritual being or God, and almost half of these people say they have had this type of encounter multiple times (Sheler, 2002).

It appears that religion is still a major dynamic of American life, but is there a shift in attitudes about the face of religion? Are Americans moving away from institutional religions and focusing more on a less structured approach to faith; i.e., spirituality? There has been a dramatic increase in the last eight years in the number of Americans who state they have no religious preference. This figure has doubled, increasing from seven percent in 1991 to 16.1 percent in 2008. Even though this group has disavowed a specific religion, their unwavering belief in God has increased as well, moving from 13 percent in 1991 to 36 percent in 2008 (Pew Forum, 2008). This group not only believes in God, but they believe in spiritual phenomena like life after death and miracles (Cristol, 2002, The Pew Forum, 2009).

Discussing and viewing spirituality apart from religion appears to be the new trend. In a recent survey, Americans stated that "being spiritual" and "being religious" were different activities, however, they were definitely connected phenomena. Of those who participated in the survey, the majority stated they were religious and spiritual (Marler and Hadaway, 2002). One factor that might contribute to the desire to separate the two concepts could be the changing face of religious institutions in the United States.

Religious Affiliation in the United States

Generally speaking, in most countries of the world, the population is affiliated with a single religion. This is not true of the United States. In fact, it can be stated with authority that no other country in the world is more religiously diverse than the United States.

Table 12.1: Major Religious Traditions in the United States

Christian	78.4	Other Religions	4.7
Protestant		Jewish	1.7
Evangelical churches	26.3	Buddhist	0.7
Mainline churches	18.1	Muslim	0.6
Hist. black churches	6.9	Hindu	0.4
Catholic	23.9	Other Religions	1.5
Mormon	1.7		
Jehovah's Witness	0.7	Unaffiliated	16.1
Orthodox	0.6	Don't know/Refused	.8
Other Christian	0.3		

Source: The Pew Forum on Religion and Public Life, Report 1: Religious Affiliation, October, 2008.

In recent years there has been a rise in participation and interest in nontraditional worship systems such as, New Age approaches, nondenominational churches, Eastern faiths, cults, occult practices, and other sects (Marler and Hadaway, 2002). These belief structures are seen as nontraditional in America because historically, and still today, the United States is a Christian country. The 1965 Immigration Act opened immigration to America from countries that had historically had limited numbers of immigrants allowed to enter the United States. This Act not only changed the ethnic face of the United States, but also added variety to the religious arena. Muslims, Sikhs, Hindus and Buddhists along with many others have increased their presence in America. Even though the number of non Christian faiths is relatively small (4.7 percent of the population), they are growing. There are now more Buddhists in this country than Presbyterians and the number of Islamic people is coming close to that of the population of Jews, and with the current rate of growth could soon surpass it. Table 12.1 gives a detailed picture of religious affiliation in the United States.

RELIGIONS RESPONSE TO MODERNIZATION

We have been discussing at length the importance of religion and the viable existence of faith systems. One reason sociologists direct attention to religious trends is, in part, due to the structural and philosophical changes that a society undergoes in a modern, scientific, technological/industrial age. In the last century, there have been dramatic technological advances that have opened up political and cultural boundaries. Media sources and transportation advances are bringing different cultures together as never before. To accommodate this change, all social structures will ultimately change. Political, economic, education, family, and religious structures will have to respond and adapt for the society to continue to thrive within the new environment that change brings.

As C. Wright Mills once noted, rapid change often limits peoples' ability to cope, overwhelms them, isolates them, stops them in their tracks or turns them romantically towards the past. Although response styles may differ, on a very real level the globe is racing to respond to contemporary society's structural challenges. How religious institutions respond to this type of change is of major importance, especially since September 11th. Nine-Eleven was a tragically violent religious and political response to what some would call the increased secularization of the modern world.

Secularization

Secularization is one of the varied societal responses to increased diversity of belief systems. It institutes a policy of separation—often dramatic—between the sacred and the profane; between religion and other social structures such as education and political. Religion is pushed out of the public realm as some see it, and the influence and power of religious organizations is lessened. There is a distinct difference between church and state in a secular society, a concept Americans are quite familiar with due to our history. However, not all cultures, and even all Americans, appreciate this division.

Pluralism

Another response to modern plurality doesn't necessarily conflict with separatist secular attitudes, but looks to unify belief systems. Vocabulary like, pluralism, ecumenism, interfaith, and unitarian illustrate a movement that looks to in some way merge belief systems into a peaceful coexistence. Granted, the majority of these movements represent unification within the Christian faith. One interesting example of a faith that attempts to incorporate the main doctrines of various world religions is the Baha'I faith which is number thirteen of the top twenty faiths in the United States (NSRI & ARIS, 2001). In fact, in recent years the ecumenism movement is looking to unify and promote cooperation among faiths outside the Christian world. This phenomenon can be seen in the increasing number of prayer services that include Muslim, Jewish and Christian religious figures and scriptures. The spiritual responses to September 11th depict this attempt at unity despite the violent separatist, fundamentalist actions.

Fundamentalism

Fundamentalism is a third, very dramatic, response to the structural changes brought about by modernization. Again, **fundamentalism** is a term that was used to describe a trend within Christianity, but today is often used to describe conservative, traditional movements within Judaism and Islam.

> "Fundamentalism represents a kind of revolt or rebellion against the secular hegemony of the modern world. (A) fundamentalist typically wants to see God, or religion, reflected public life" (Armstrong, Heschel and Wallis, 2002).

Increased plurality of beliefs and values and scientific and technical advances are seen as an enemy that is eating away at the traditional values and sacred character of a culture and faith. In order to preserve their faith, fundamentalist groups tend to form isolated communities devoted to preserving "pure faith where they try to keep the godless world at bay..." (Armstrong, Heschel and Wallis, 2002). The dynamic of fundamentalism is one of an "us versus them" mentality, and as with many "us versus them" scenarios there are strong negative emotions directed towards the enemy or the "them." The "them" in the fundamentalist world is generally seen as those who align themselves with more open, secular/pluralistic beliefs. These beliefs are seen as the aggressor destroying their faith. The aggressor's face will change depending on the faith, but the aggressor's heart is always beating a secular rhythm.

For a fundamentalist Christian in America, the main enemy is a democratic secular humanist. Many American Christian Fundamentalists immerse themselves in political activity in an attempt to influence elections and public policy decisions against behavior or phenomena that illustrate the eroding effect of the liberal secular lifestyle. Examples of behaviors that a Christian fundamentalist would work to stop are homosexuality, pornography, abortion, drugs, and sex and violence on television. The Moral Majority is one group who participates in this area politically.

On the other hand, for some Islamic Fundamentalist groups, the face of the enemy takes the form of the Christian West. Reasons for Muslim anger and fear of the West—most specifically America—are numerous. United States policies and funding supporting Israel and other political activities in the Middle East is one reason for the animosity. Also, many Middle Eastern countries have historically adopted politically oppressive strategies toward conservative/traditional Islamic sects in the effort to modernize. For example, Iran and Egypt have killed and imprisoned citizens who opposed the regimes bringing in the secular/modern world while outlawing historic Muslim customs and traditions (Armstrong, Heschel and Wallis, 2002). Political parties advancing the cause of modernization are seen by some groups as having been corrupted ideologically and materialistically by the West. A third reason Islamic Fundamentalist groups oppose and demonize the Christian West is based on a strict or purist interpretations of perceived theological differences. For example, some interpretations of Islam teach defense and war (Jihad) against the infidel. Infidel is a term used to describe nonbelievers or believers in many gods. In a strict Islamic interpretation, Christianity and its belief in the Trinity represents a pagan faith, because God is depicted as three persons (Lippman, 1982).

Regardless of the faith, fundamentalist groups typically have a goal to "convert the mainstream society back to a more godly way of life" (Armstrong, Heschel and Wallis, 2002). Conversion is a theme in most religions, but the degree and intensity of working to convert varies. According to a recent survey, only 15 percent of Christian respondents who identified themselves as being highly religious stated that they felt it was a requirement of their faith to seek to convert others. (The Gallop Poll, 2007). The main point of being fundamentalist is to seek to change the "them" to the "us", and if this cannot be done or appears futile, some groups seek to destroy the outsiders/ unbelievers. Believer building techniques run the gamut. They include individual recruitment plans, political activity, media campaigns, financial incentives, and educational institutions, among others.

Fundamentalism today is often equated with radical and violent actions, but this violence is apart from mainstream traditionalist movements; in fact, those involved in violence are extreme fundamentalists and a small percentage of the fundamentalist population. We also seem to direct our attention to Islamic Fundamentalists, not the only faith that has been know to turn to violence. However, the number of fundamentalist believers in all faiths is growing. So chances are the number of extreme fundamentalists will grow as well. And the questions on most Americans minds are, "Why do these groups hate us?" and "What can we do to stop the cycle of hate and violence?"

One answer to both questions could be education. A rapidly growing educational trend in South Asia exists in increasing number of extremely traditional Islamic schools. The mission of these schools is to preserve and defend Islam from the corrupting forces of modernization. These schools are known as **madrassas**, and are seen by some as terrorist fundamentalist training camps. The student population of these schools consists of young Muslim boys. In the last decade, these types of schools have been the fastest growing educational system in the region with most of them formed in Pakistan where there were approximately 40,000 madrassas in 2008 as opposed to 10,000 in 2002 (Hyat, 2008). The most renowned madrass in Pakistan is know as Darul Uloom Haqqania (House of Knowledge of Haqqania). It was responsible for educating ninety percent of Afghanistan's Taliban movement (Lamb, 2002). It is not uncommon for a prestigious school to train political leaders, but one notable difference between most countries private religious schools and those of the madrassas, is the age and economic conditions of the children entering them along with the lessons on aggression. The majority of the children attending these schools are from the poorest of the poor. Most parents send their children to these schools for the offer of free room and board, and it is the only way they see survival and escape from poverty for their children. The pain of poverty and separation from family is one fueled and directed towards the enemy of Islam. The issue of poverty is very real, and may be a key reason why peaceful faiths and people turn to violence.

RELIGION AND STRATIFICATION

Class

One only has to look around at the cars in the parking lots of various denominations on Sunday to understand that religion is not untouched by class distinctions. Comparisons using income level, educational attainment, and occupational prestige reveal wide variations in class among different denominations. For the most part, Jews, Episcopalians, and Presbyterians are found in the upper strata of the population. Mostly, the members of these churches can trace their background to northern European countries and families who arrived in the United States at least two centuries ago. These groups encountered little discrimination and quickly attained affluence.

At the opposite end of the stratification system, one finds the members of the Southern Baptist, Nazarene, and Churches of God denominations. Members of these denominations generally are from the working and underprivileged classes. It is interesting to note that Catholics are among this group. The principle reason is due to the discrimination they faced upon arriving in the United States. Originally looked down upon, and very different from Protestants, they were denied the opportunity to assimilate fully into the economic structure. However, this has changed in the last half of the century. In 1960, John F. Kennedy was the first Catholic elected to the presidency. With the spread of religious tolerance (at least of white Catholics) many soon found themselves entering corporate leadership positions. As such, many Catholics have climbed the social ladder and now find themselves in the ranks of the upper class.

Another group who found their way to the upper class despite discrimination is the Jews. Although they encountered (and still do) anti-Semitism from a Christian majority, they have managed to overcome these obstacles. Some reasons for their success are strong family ties, good work ethic, and importance placed on achieving higher education.

Race

A much repeated adage is that the most segregated hour of the week in America is Sunday at 11:00 a.m. Even today, decades after *Brown v. Board of Education*, churches remain predominately segregated.

The segregation of American churches was not a coincidence. Africans were transported to America as slaves to toil in the fields. Forced to become Christians, they blended Christianity with their native religions. After emancipation, churches in the United States chose to either ignore segregation or actively support it. It was only later, in the twentieth century, that a few churches became concerned with race issues. Even then, a pattern of segregation was deeply woven into the fabric of American worship. Today, just two percent of members of historically black Protestant churches are white, the same percentage of members of mainline Protestant churches who are black (The Pew Forum, 2008). Racial attitudes, class barriers, residential patterns, and cultural practices ensure the continuation of this pattern.

For many African Americans, the church has been the center of their lives. It is, as one writer commented, the only institution in which they have been able to exercise control and in which they can act autonomously. Additionally, the church has been at the forefront of the political movement advancing the civil rights of African Americans.

A rare occurrence—a husband and wife both ordained clergy with their church. Historically, women have been in a subservient position in most world religions. Although attitudes are changing, most major religions still hold fast to the belief that only men can be ordained or serve as deacons.

photo: Julia Abebe.

A similar pattern exists for Mexican Americans in the Catholic Church. White Catholics attend predominately white Catholic churches while Mexican Americans worship in Catholic churches of their own. Although many point out that this pattern exists due to the preference of Mexican Americans, there is little doubt that it is a preference exercised due to intense racial tension and the inability to fully assimilate into American society.

Gender

The dominant religions of the United States—Christianity, Judaism, and Islam, are patriarchically oriented. In all three, God, and for the most part his prophets, are male or father figures. Likewise, within the religious organization, males dominate and have higher status and privileges than do females. The inferior status of women within Christianity has long been noted and recognized. The Bible instructs its followers:

> Let the wives be subject to their husbands as to the Lord; because a husband is head of the wife, just as Christ is head of the Church, being himself savior of the body. But just as the church is subject to Christ, so also let wives be to their husbands in all things (Ephesians 5:22-24).

One might reasonably argue that not all, current Christian denominations follow this teaching today, however, as we noted previously the fastest growing denomination of Christians are fundamentalists who practice a strict interpretation of the Bible. Returning to the Bible, the position of women is established early on. It was Adam who was created first and Eve, second. Additionally, it was the evil and weakness of Eve, a woman, who succumbed to the devil and successfully, tempted Adam and brought about the end of the Garden of Eden. As such, according to the Bible, Eve and all women thereafter were punished by having to bring forth their children in pain.

For Catholics, the secondary status of women can be seen in that only men are allowed to be priests. Although women are allowed to be nuns, they operate in a subservient role to the priest. After decades of debate, the Catholic Church is steadfast in its position prohibiting women from obtaining equal status with males in the clergy.

The practices of Judaism vary depending on the degree of conservatism. In the Orthodox Jewish tradition, men and women engage in communal worship. However, women must sit behind men while worshipping in the synagogue. In keeping with tradition, men engage in daily prayer and religious study while women are assigned the role of the religious training of the young as well as other domestic religious duties. In Orthodox Judaism, men can divorce women, but women are unable to divorce their husbands. Also, women are not allowed to bequeath property without their husband's consent. In conservative and reform Judaism, the practices are more egalitarian. This is especially true of reform Judaism, where women are allowed to serve as rabbis.

Islam is on the rise in the United States due to immigration. The roles of men and women are strictly delineated by the Koran. Men are the unquestioned head of the household and women are instructed to be obedient to the wishes of their husbands. Women and men do not pray together. In most areas, women are prohibited from entering a mosque (place of worship for Muslims). Women are expected to function entirely within the domestic role of being a wife and mother. Underpinning the dress code of women is the belief, in some Islamic societies, that women are so attractive to men that they must cover their face and body in acceptable clothing, so as not to attract unwanted attention. Likewise, they must be escorted by a male relative when traveling.

SOCIOLOGICAL PERSPECTIVES

Structural Functional

For structural functionalists, the all-important question is: how are the various parts of society held together? Another way of stating this is to ask what promotes stability and harmony? To answer this question, structural functionalists examine various institutions within society and attempt to understand how each function to contribute to social cohesion. In their investigations, structural functionalists have stated that religion contributes to stability in several fundamental ways. *First*, it provides society with a cohesive belief system from which the values and mores of society originate. This cohesive belief system binds various and potentially competing fractions of society together under a perceived system of shared beliefs. It is this system of shared beliefs that, in essence, is the cohesive glue allowing people to identify as one collective social group. This is central to Durkheim's concept of social solidarity. In fact, this was so important to him that he issued the claim that religion *was* society.

Secondly, Parsons (1966), another structural functionalist, stated that religion was important in that it answered the all-important questions: about our relationship to other members of society, the purpose of existence, the nature of happiness and suffering, and the presence of good and evil. Without answers to these questions, harmony, both at the individual level and societal level, was all but impossible. In agreement, Durkheim states that religion helps prevent people from withdrawing from life through suicide.

A *third* point made by structural functionalists is that religion promotes political stability by fusing the sacred cultural norms of society with the political state. Peter Berger (1967) terms this the "sacred canopy" as it shields and protects the government from continual upheaval.

Finally, religion can provide a legitimate avenue for social change. The most notable example of this in the United States was the civil rights movement under the national leadership of the Reverend Martin Luther King. Emanating from the churches of America, the insistence for social justice was enveloped in religious philosophy and thus provided a powerful impetus for change.

Social Conflict

The social conflict perspective of religion is similar to that of its view of other institutions of society. According to this perspective, religion, like government, education, and the media, exists to promote and perpetuate the advantages of the powerful.

Perhaps the most comprehensive explanation of this perspective comes from Karl Marx who wrote, "Religion is the sigh of the oppressed creature, the sentiment of a heartless world, and the soul of the soulless condition. It is the opiate of the masses." By this, Marx meant that religion is a means by which the rich and powerful members of society can focus the thoughts of the lower classes away from the harsh and unjust reality of their present existence to an after-life of eternal bliss. To achieve this after-life, all one needs is to follow the tenets of their religion. Of course, according to Marx, it was the rich and powerful that controlled religion and established its tenets for their own gain. An example of this can be seen in Christian scripture that instructs adherents to, "Render unto Caesar that which belongs to Caesar and unto God that which belongs to God." Likewise, one of the principal Commandments is, "thou shalt not steal." However, what stealing is and what it is not, is not so much a matter of inspired scripture, but instead, a political interpretation codified into law by the powerful.

A further example of this can be seen in the historical interpretation of the Bible by southern slave holders. Slaves were told that their entry into heaven was dependent upon being obedient to their masters, as instructed by God. Similarly, slave holders used the Bible to instruct slaves that they were the descendants of a people who had disobeyed God and so were relegated to an inferior status on earth. Likewise, the teachings of dharma in Hinduism dictate that one must accept their position in society as determined by their caste in order to achieve a higher status in the next life.

In addition to the above line of reasoning, other social conflict theorists have challenged the structural functional assertion that religion promotes stability. The very nature of religious belief invites intolerance toward competing religions. From the Crusades to the fighting in Northern Ireland, religion has played a major role in not uniting people but rather, in promoting hostility and violence.

THE FUTURE OF RELIGION

Inevitably, secularization of society will continue, and so too will the struggle to balance religious institutions' response to this change. As we have seen, secularization is not a process that is continuing. There are movements that resist this change just as there are those who attempt to adapt to it. Social and political upheavals will occur, and with them will come confusion and discontent. More than likely, renewed interest in organized religion will continue to grow, but the compelling force for the need for secularization will drive it forward. A number of factors lead us to this conclusion.

First, the growth of science and the answers it provides to a wide range of phenomena, such as creation and existence, has gained widespread acceptance. Since the dawn of time science and religion have been at odds. However, recently, the tide has greatly turned to science, and many contemporary religions have updated old theological teachings or adopted new ones to fit current scientific theory.

Second, government is increasingly moving away from theological ideologies where the clergy exercises tremendous power, and moving toward governments that are totally secularized. To some extent, this is a result of the growth of nation-states and the necessity to interact on a global scale where increasingly, secularization of laws and governmental policies are necessary.

Third, the triumph of capitalism in the world has led to greater secularization of economic systems. The bottom line of capitalism is profit. Theology is antithetical to the marketplace. More and more, religion must adjust its views to accommodate practical economic decision-making. Even traditional religious holidays such as Christmas and Easter have lost much of their religious significance as consumers rush from store to store to buy gifts and cards to express their love for one another.

Finally, the shrinking globe and immigration of people from one country to another has increased secularization. As people travel more and the population of nations becomes more diverse, the need for secularization with its accompanying religious tolerance becomes more important for societal stability.

Having stated the above reasons demonstrating why secularization will continue to grow, it is important to note a couple of qualifiers. First, the movement toward secularization will not progress in a linear fashion. Social and political upheavals will occur and with them will come confusion and discontent. More than likely, this will lead to a renewed interest in organized religion. Good examples of this can be seen in the rise of fundamentalism in the United States. The rise of conservative Islam in the Middle East is a further example. Although renewed interest will occur, more than likely the compelling force of the above factors for secularization will eventually surface. Our second qualifier is that while it is true that many people have turned away from formal religious organizations, this does not mean that there is a decrease in religiosity. Although science can tell us a lot about the world we live in, it has yet to answer the greater human questions of our purpose, the meaning of life, and what happens to us when, so to speak, "the light goes out." As such, religion, or what sociologists refer to as religiosity, will remain an important part of our lives.

Terms You Should Know:

Creed	Ritual	Sacred
Totemism	Animism	Transcendental Idealism
Atheism	Agnosticism	Synagogue
Ghetto	Anti-Semitism	Cult
Sect	Religiosity	Madrassas

Can You Answer These Questions?

1. According to Ronald Johnstone, what five elements are necessary to define a belief system as a religion? Can you identify each of these in your own religion?
2. Briefly describe the differences between monotheism and polytheism?
3. Which religions belong to the "Religion of Abraham"?
4. How do Eastern Religions differ from the major religions found in the Western world. How are they different from religions in Middle Eastern countries?
5. Are religion and spirituality the same? If not, how are they different?
6. According to C. Wright Mills, how has rapid change affected people's religious beliefs?
7. How are private religious schools in this country similar or different from madrassas in Islamic nations?
8. How do structural functionalism and social conflict theory differ over the role of religion in our society?

Critical Thinking Exercises:

1. Why is it that we call one group of believers a religion and another a cult? Is this fair, or simply the dominate group in society exercising power over the smaller one?
2. Increasingly, religious groups are entering the political arena attempting to influence public policy. Do you feel this is good or bad for the country?
3. List some of the reasons many Muslims are angry with the West? Do you believe this anger is justified? Can you offer ways in which we can reduce tensions?
4. According to recent statistics, American churches are still racially segregated. Doesn't this violate our moral and religious teachings? If so, why isn't more being done to integrate churches?
5. In your opinion, how much change has occurred within religious institutions to advance gender equality?

Photo: Alaska

Chapter 13

Politics and the State

On August 29, 2005, hurricane Katrina slammed into the coastline of Louisiana, Mississippi and Alabama. Hardest hit, with winds in excess of 140 mph and storm surges from 15 to 30 feet, were New Orleans and Biloxi, Mississippi. One day prior to the arrival of Katrina, Mayor C. Ray Nagin, ordered the first mandatory evacuation of New Orleans. Although nearly a million people in the metropolitan area complied, 150,000 thousand others were trapped due to the lack of transportation, either private or public, or illness. Most of those left behind were the poor blacks that comprise a substantial portion of the city's population. In an attempt to aid those left behind, Mayor Nagin opened the Superdome as a "refuge of last resort." Although designed to house no more than 9,000, the number quickly swelled to over 60,000. In the midst of Katrina, electricity and running water failed. Also, no provision was made for long term care of those within. Food and water were in short supply. Toilets plugged creating unsanitary condition and, without adequate security, mob violence spread quickly among the occupants. Media reports of suicides, rape, drug dealings, assaults, and murder were reported on national newscasts.

A body lays in the streets after water recedes. Others wait for government help to arrive days after Katrina's impact.

Photo: Student.

Elsewhere in the city, looting and fires broke out as angry mobs roamed the streets in search of water, food, and items of value. Others, trapped on expressways and on rooftops, waved signs desperately pleading for help. Many, the elderly and ill, simply died waiting for that help to arrive. In all, it is estimated that over a thousand died, the vast majority not from the storm itself but from the lack of governmental response.

Five years later, on April 20, 2010, another national disaster occurred with the massive explosion of the Deepwater Horizon oil platform forty miles off the coast of Louisiana. In the initial explosion, eleven workers were killed and seventeen injured. Not withstanding the loss of life, it soon became apparent that this would be the worst ecological disaster in the history of the United States. Before the well was finally sealed five months later, an estimated 5 million barrels of oil spewed into the Gulf, onto the beaches and into the marshy bays of Mississippi, Alabama and Florida. The economic impact of the disaster has been estimated into the tens of billions of dollars. Many of those whose livelihood depended on tourism and the fishing industry in the Gulf lost everything—businesses, homes, personal savings. Even more devastating and long-term was the damage to the ecosystem which some experts predict could take decades to repair. An independent government commission investigating the disaster (OSC) laid most of the blame on BP oil company and Halliburton for attempting to cut corners to maximize profits. However, the commission also reserved harsh criticism for the government for its lack of oversight of the oil industry, for it's failure to regulate it, and for early reports down playing the extent of the disaster. As such, the final report states: "the federal government created the impression that it was either not fully competent to handle the spill or not fully candid with the American people abut the scope of the problem (OSC, 2011).

In the days following both disasters, government officials attempted to defend their actions against reports of confusion, irresponsibility, political cronyism, and mismanagement. However, as electronic images streamed into the homes of Americans the failure of governmental efforts was irrefutable. Suddenly, the attempts by political officials to praise their initial response turned to finger-pointing and political damage control. In the end, the vast majority of Americans disapproved of the way the president and federal, state, and local officials performed (Gallup Poll, 2005 & 2010).

All of this points to the importance of government in our lives and what can happen when there is a breakdown in organized structures created to manage society and ensure its orderly and continual function. In this chapter, we examine the elements of government and types of leadership. Likewise, we look at the relationship between government and economy and how sociologists differ in their view of government. Finally, we turn to government in the United States. In doing so, we examine the principle upon which our government was founded, its structure, and how politics is practiced. In conclusion, two differing perspectives on our democratic charter are offered and concerns for the future are considered.

PEOPLE AND GOVERNMENT

For most of human presence on earth, governance was relatively simple and straightforward. Living in small nomadic tribes, members relied primarily upon kinship authority to settle disputes, reward behavior, punish offenders, and plan for the future. In turn kinship or clan leaders relied heavily upon consensus in order to accomplish tasks and enforce rules. Thus, power was diffused and shared in an informal manner. Certainly, some members of the tribe held more power or influence than others, but participation in governance was widespread.

SOCIOLOGICAL LANGUAGE

Power

Power is a concept central to all governments. In its simplest form, power is defined as the ability to exert one's will and thereby accomplish goals. In doing so, power can be exercised in four different ways. *First*, governments can choose to reward individuals for certain behavior it deems necessary for the common good. An example of this would be tax incentives offered to citizens who invest in public projects such as building a new school in the community. The government offers the bonds to raise the necessary capital to build the school, citizens buy the bonds, and in turn, the government does not tax the interest earned from the bonds. *Second*, governments can influence citizens by controlling the sources of public information. The decisions made by people are only as good as the information they have upon which to base their decisions. Hence, if the government is effective in manipulating and controlling information, it is likely that its citizens will voluntarily conform to the will of the government. This underscores the necessity of a free press to democratic governments and is also the reason many non-democratic governments are presently attempting to control use of the Internet within their country. *Third*, governments can rely upon the prevailing ideology to exercise power. All countries have a common ideology shared by its citizens. In politically stable countries, the belief in ideology is strong and citizens conform to certain behavior, not out of fear, but because they believe that such behavior is right. In America, for example, the division of resources is not equal but highly stratified. Although one might think this would produce civil unrest (revolution), it doesn't. Why? Because inherent in our culture is the acceptance of two ideological beliefs—capitalism and equal opportunity. As an economic system, capitalism essentially dictates an unequal division of resources. This does not pose a problem as long as the members of society feel that they have the same chance to compete fairly for the goods of society (equal opportunity). In conjunction with each other, the twin ideologies of equal opportunity and capitalism promote tranquility and stability. And *fourth*, if all the previous three methods fail, governments can rely upon force to enact its will. Force is simply the use of physical coercion to ensure that citizens conform to the behavior desired by those in power. It is generally the function of the military and secret police to serve the government in this capacity. Keep in mind that only about one-fourth of the world functions under true democratic rule. Although all governments use force to some extent, including our own, its use is more common in countries with authoritative governments.

Authority

The question of authority is one of who has the right to exercise power. In essence, this is a matter of domination or the likelihood that people will obey orders. Max Weber divided domination into two forms: raw coercion and legitimate authority. Raw coercion relies upon force. Legitimate authority is more complicated and was further divided by Weber into three types: traditional, legal-rational, and charismatic (Weber, 1947).

The root of **traditional authority** is to be found in the historical beliefs and practices of a particular society. An individual (or group) rule is legitimized by birthright or because the religion of the society has conferred upon the leader a divine right. While it might not be uncommon to question a particular ruling by the leader, it would be considered sacrilege to question the leader's right to rule. Grave harm would undoubtedly come to an individual who dared to dissent. Although societies that rely on traditional authority have declined in the twentieth century, examples can still be found. Prior to World War II, the people of Japan considered their leader divine—a god. In defeat, the emperor was forced to renounce his divinity. His position in the society then took on the more common role of a figurehead much like that of the Queen of England. A current practicing example of traditional authority can be seen in the Pope of the Roman Catholic Church whose rule is considered to be of divine origin and hence infallible.

Legal-rational authority is derived from the members of a society who create positions of authority and rules that limit the scope of power of those occupying the positions. A critical distinction between this type of authority and the one previously discussed is that in this case it is the position that is important, not the person who occupies the position. This can be seen in the presidency of the United States. One respects the president, not because of who he/she happens to be, but because they hold the office of president. Likewise, the president must exercise power within the parameters set forth in the laws and constitution or else he/she would be subject to being removed from office. As we shall see later, democratic governments rely upon this form of authority.

Charismatic authority derives its source of power from the magnetic personality of the leader. The members of the society attribute unique, almost godlike characteristics to the leader. The end result is an unquestioning devotion to the leader and his or her political agenda. Religious leaders are well known for charismatic authority; an obvious example would be Jesus Christ. Weber notes that, although powerful, charismatic leadership is very unstable in the long run. Since authority is dependent on charismatic personality, once the leader dies, a power vacuum is created and the movement is left in chaos. If the movement is to survive, it must revert to a different base of authority, either traditional or legal-rational. This can be seen in our example of Jesus Christ. Once Jesus died, it was necessary for a transformation to traditional authority, and along with that the doctrine of the Bible and the Catholic Church.

The State

Weber defines the **state** as "a political apparatus possessing the legitimate monopoly over the use of force within its territory." (Weber, 1946) Central to this definition is Weber's use of the term *legitimate,* which he implies is a recognition by people of the state's rightful use of force to execute its edicts and laws. The development of the modern state has its roots in the city-states, which developed around 3000 BCE and extended to the end of the Middle Ages (1500 CE). As trade, industry, and knowledge increased during this time, a number of wars were fought for exclusive rights over territory. This led to the consolidation of land, which began the movement toward the modern nation-state. In contrast to the city-state, the **nation-state** established geographic boundaries, communication networks, and the means to defend the newly incorporated territories. Another distinguishing point, as noted by Weber, was the development of citizenship and specific legal obligations and rights.

There are several other important characteristics that distinguish the modern nation-state from earlier forms. The *first* is that of **sovereignty**. In claiming sovereignty, the government of a nation declares to the world, not only its territory, the sole right to exercise authority over the people of its territory. Sovereignty is a key concept in global politics. Although we might not agree with the way a particular government treats its people, if we recognize the country as a legitimate nation-state, we have no right to interfere.

A young man confronts Egyptian police. In December 2010, a young street vendor's desperate act of protest sparked an uprising in Tunisia that ended with the forced resignation of the country's longtime leader. The successful revolution inspired uprisings across the Middle East and North Africa against authoritative regimes. Hosni Mubarak of Egypt was soon toppled. At least a half dozen other regimes, including Muammar Gaddafi in Libya, are under siege. In March, 2011, a United Nation's coalition force launched air strikes in support of the rebels.

Photo: Gaelic Neilson.

The recognition of sovereignty is crucial to world peace. Without it, there would be continuous war between nations as they interfered in each other's internal affairs.

A *second* concept is that of law. **Law** is defined as a binding custom or practice of society that is codified (written down) and enforced by legitimate governmental authority. Prior to the development of law, disputes were handled on an informal basis. Grievances were presented and an elder or specifically designated person of the tribe or clan would listen and then attempt to devise a mutually agreeable solution. Compromise was important since it restored the harmony necessary for clan or tribal members to cooperate for survival. With the emergence of the nation-state, as societies became larger and more diverse, compromise was not always possible. Therefore, the state suddenly realized that the survival of the nation depended upon compliance with the laws. Hence grievances were no longer between individuals, but between state and individual. This necessitated the development of laws.

A *third* distinction of modern states is the extension of rights to citizens. The rights of citizens encompass three broad areas. The *first* is **civil rights**. These rights are defined as those that ensure that citizens are protected from harm by other citizens of the state and from the government itself. In the preamble of the Constitution of the United States we term these inalienable rights—the right to life, liberty and the pursuit of happiness. The *second* area of rights is termed **social rights**. These rights include a broad range of social and economic programs such as social security, welfare, medical care, etc. The *third* area is **political rights**. These rights underpin the philosophy that one has a right to participate in the political process. Prior to the development of the nation-state, the thought that people had the ability or right to rule themselves would have been considered ridiculous. In today's modern nation-states, even the most dictatorial governments extend political rights in some form or another to their citizens. This does not mean that they abide by their own laws guaranteeing participation, but the fact that they attempt to demonstrate such rights is testimony to the acceptance of political rights in modern society.

Another distinction of modern states is a sense of **nationalism**. As indicated, the modern states can encompass large geographic areas, such as the United States, Canada, India, China, Russia, etc. Living within a territory are diverse people in terms of race, religion, and ethnicity, but despite an understanding of these differences, all people have a shared sense of identification that comes from a commitment to a common ideology and shared values. It is this sense of nationalism that is the cohesive glue that binds people together in a nation-state. Without this sense of nationalism, it is highly unlikely that the nation-state could survive.

CLASSIFICATION OF WORLD GOVERNMENTS

If you listen to people discussing politics you are likely to hear them use the terms *state* and *government* interchangeably. Although few of us have difficulty understanding what is meant by the words, sociologists clearly delineate between the two. The state is the highest authority in a specific geographic area whereas government refers to those who direct the power of the state.

All governments must exercise power in order to perform the tasks necessary for the continuation of the state. However, governments do not exercise power in the same way. Sociologists have divided governments into two broad categories: authoritative and democratic. In authoritative government, people are denied rights of participation. In democratic government, people are not only allowed to participate, but also encouraged to become actively involved in governing themselves. Authoritative and democratic governments can take several forms.

Authoritative Governments

Monarchy is the oldest form of government. In monarchy, power is passed down from generation to generation on the basis of family lineage. The leader of the society is all-powerful. Any rights granted to citizens are the sole discretion of the leader. Historically, many monarchs have also claimed the right to be the spiritual leader of the country. The coupling of political and religious authority serves to strengthen the power of the monarch.

Monarchy was more common to agricultural and feudal societies of the past (Skocpol, 1979). However, some have survived modern times. Examples of monarchy can be found in the Middle East: Jordan, Saudi Arabia, Kuwait and a number of other countries still practice this form of government. Modern industrial nations, such as England, Spain, and Japan, also have monarchs, but they are little more than figureheads in the government. In all probability, this form of government will cease to exist in the near future. As nations become more industrialized and more educated, their adherence to traditional values and norms decrease, as will their loyalty to monarchs.

Oligarchies. In this form of government, the exercise of power rests not with one individual but a small group. The former Soviet Union might serve as an example. After the death of Stalin, no other soviet leader was able to consolidate enough power to rule single-handedly. Instead, power was dispersed among a group of individuals in the *Politburo,* a collection of twelve of the highest communist party members. The leader of the country, the party chairman, headed the politburo, but could not rule without the support of the other members. Leadership was informal and the party chairman could be replaced on a moment's notice if he fell out of favor with the other members of the *Politburo*. The Soviet Union ceased to exist when Mikhail Gorbachev called for free elections and allowed for succession of its member states.

Oligarchies are usually found in countries dominated by a powerful clergy. Iran is a present-day example. Although there is a parliament and elections are held, the clergy is so powerful and integrated into the parliament, that it maintains a stranglehold on all decisions.

Dictatorships. Under a dictatorship, one individual exercises complete and absolute control. Any challenge to the leader is met with swift and lethal retaliation. Today, many dictatorships attempt to establish the appearance of democratic rule. Elections are held and candidates compete for positions in the government. However, behind the scenes the dictator carefully orchestrates the process with propaganda and violence. All in all, the election is little more than a stage show with a predetermined outcome. Saddam Hussein, former ruler of Iraq, is the most notorious present-day example.

Military Juntas. These governments fall somewhere between oligarchies and dictatorships in their true form. The distinguishing characteristic is that power is seized by the military in what is termed a **coup**. Unlike a revolution, the coup does not have the participation of the population nor does it occur over a span of time like the American Revolution. It is quick and decisive. For many countries a strong military is a double-edged sword. It guarantees protection against hostile neighbors, but poses an internal threat to the government in times of domestic crisis. Such was the concern of the fathers of our own government when they made the President of the United States, a civilian, the commander-in-chief of the military.

Totalitarian Governments. Of authoritative governments, totalitarian is the most extreme and repressive. Totalitarian governments are distinguished from other authoritative governments in that there is an attempt to control every aspect of people's lives. Often, millions of lives are lost in the attempt, as was the case under Stalin in the Soviet Union, Pol Pot in Cambodia, and Mao Tse Tung in China. Of course, the best example of totalitarian government is that of Germany under the leadership of Adolph Hitler. Here, millions of Jews, Gypsies and others deemed genetically inferior were exterminated in an attempt to maintain the purity of the Aryan race.

Democratic Governments

Direct Democracy. This is the purest form of a democratic government. It is a government in which all citizens participate in all governmental functions and decisions. The oldest example of direct democracy is the classical city-state of Athens. All decisions of the government were debated openly and voted upon. Direct democracy in Athens was feasible only because of its small size and the fact that women and slaves were excluded from the rights of citizenship. Another example of direct democracy can be found in some communities that hold what is referred to as "town meetings." However, the complexity and size of modern day societies far outstretch the ability of this form of government. People simply do not have the time or energy to accumulate the knowledge required to make informed decisions regarding the thousands upon thousands of complex issues facing the nation. This has given rise to our next form of government—representative democracy.

Representative Democracy. In representative democracies, citizens elect or appoint others to make decisions for them. These elected officials reside in executive, legislative and judicial offices. The theory behind representative government is that as long as the people have the right to replace leaders in periodically held elections, democracy is guaranteed.

Three principle types of representative democracies can be found. The *first* is a **constitutional monarchy** wherein a monarch may claim the throne through heredity, but whose role in the government is strictly limited to a ceremonial function. Real power is exercised by the popularly elected government officials. Again, England serves as an example. A *second* type of representative democracy is the **parliamentary system**. In this form of government, political parties are very important. Strong ideological differences can be found between parities and the allegiance by voters to a particular political party is very strong. Political parties select candidates to run under their banner and people vote for the political parties that espouse their ideologies rather than individual candidates. The leader of the winning political party becomes the Prime Minister, a position that is similar in power to that of being the President of the United States. Governments practicing this type of democracy generally have diverse ideological beliefs and many different political parties. In most cases, no one party has a majority of votes to rule, thus, necessitating the formation of **coalitions** where two or more political parties will join forces to form a majority, termed "the government." Most democracies in the world practice a parliamentary system. The United States provides an example of a *third* type of representative democracy—the **democratic republic**. Three features distinguish this form of government from a parliamentary system. *First*, and foremost, the chief executive officer of the government, usually termed a president, is elected separately by the people. This means that a party different from that of the president could control the legislative branch. *Second*, the loyalty to political parties does not seem to be as great. Citizens vote more for the candidate than for the political party. This makes the representative more responsive to the wishes of the people than the party. *Third*, countries that successfully practice this type of government seem to possess similar ideological beliefs. As such, political parties tend to agree on what is ideologically correct and disagree on ways to implement that ideology. The best example here can be seen with the Democratic and Republican parties in the United States. Both parties accept capitalism as a desirable economic system (ideological belief), but differ on the role of the government in regulating it.

POLITICAL ECONOMY

Unfortunately, we live in a world of scarce resources. It is impossible for everyone to have everything that he/she wants. One of the prime functions of government is to either decide or devise a system for the utilization and division of resources. Through its economic system, the society will answer three basic questions: "What is to be produced? How much?" And, "Who gets what?" In this section we discuss three economic systems employed by governments: capitalism, socialism, and communism.

Capitalism

Founded in 1776, by Adam Smith, a Scottish economist, this system extols the virtue of private property, profit, and competition. Private property means that all (or almost all) property, from land to the means of production (industry), is owned privately by the people. Under a perfect capitalistic system the government owns nothing. This is considered a desirable situation. Profit is the accumulation of wealth. This too is considered desirable. Finally, to ensure that the best product is produced at the cheapest price, competition must be present. Without competition the market place will not function efficiently and the system will fail.

For Adam Smith, capitalism was the answer to two great concerns of governments: societal cohesiveness and the regulation of greed. In terms of societal cohesiveness, one might expect that with the promotion of self-interest there would be less cooperation and thus eternal conflict. He maintained that the exact opposite was true because the laws of the marketplace demanded cooperation. In order to make a profit, one must be willing to produce what people want. As such, the people of the state, not the government, determine what is to be produced. How is this accomplished? Every time you pull out your billfold and purchase a product you are sending a signal to the marketplace of what is demanded. If entrepreneurs (producers of goods) find a high demand for a product, they will produce more in order to gain a higher profit. If suddenly, people stop buying a particular product, then entrepreneurs will produce another product that is in higher demand. Thus, a cycle of supply and demand determines what and how much is to be produced.

As for greed, one might legitimately question whether it was not possible for individuals to become too greedy and charge excessively for a product? In answer, Smith contended that excessive greed is regulated by competition. In the marketplace, many entrepreneurs who compete against each other produce the same product. If one price is excessive, then people will buy from a competitor. Does the system really work this way? If the marketplace is open and free, the answer is yes. Take the case of computers; what was the cost of your first computer? What did your last computer cost? Is your present computer better than your first? The reality is that a business person that is not concerned with competition and price will not likely be around for very long.

Income of workers is also regulated by the marketplace. Workers compete for jobs given their desirability and pay. If the pay for a job is very high, it is likely that many workers will obtain the training necessary to work in the field but if the number of trained workers exceeds the demand for the job, the pay will decline as workers compete for positions. As the pay begins to fall, workers will seek employment in other fields. Likewise, if a job is undesirable or dangerous, then employers will be forced to offer higher wages to obtain the necessary workers. Adam Smith refers to all of this as "the invisible hand" that functions without the assistance, or meddling, as some might say, of the government.

Socialism

In socialism, it is the government that owns property and the means of production. In essence, socialism is the flip side of capitalism. For true socialism to exist, five elements are necessary.

Democracy. Many Americans mistakenly equate socialism with authoritative government. This is due mainly to the association of socialism to countries such as the former Soviet Union, China, and Cuba. In reality, nothing could be further from the truth. Unlike capitalism that can function smoothly in any governmental system, including a dictatorship, as was Germany under the leadership of Hitler, socialism demands a free and open society. If the government is to own property and control distribution, then the people must be free to elect public officials that will enact their will. Certainly, there are authoritative systems that have attempted to implement socialism. However, these were failed attempts because the system ultimately becomes more responsive to the needs of the few (leaders) and neglects those of the many. Ultimately, this is a recipe for failure. It should be noted that many of the world's democracies incorporate elements of socialism.

Egalitarianism. Derived from the root of the word equal, egalitarianism is an attempt to level the playing field so that everyone in the society has a chance to obtain the necessities of life: food, clothing, shelter, and employment. In extreme socialism there is an attempt to divide resources equally among citizens. However, most socialistic countries realize the impracticality of this goal and instead work to limit extreme inequality.

Community. To be successful there must be a commitment on the part of citizens to community. This implies that the members of society collectively cooperate to achieve desirable goals. Under capitalism, competition is not only necessary but also considered good. Under socialism, it is considered divisive and destructive.

Public Ownership. In capitalism, property and the means of production are privately held and utilized to create profits for individuals. In Socialism, property and the means of production are collectively owned and controlled by the government. The goal is not to create profit, but to serve the needs of all people in the society.

Public Planning. Under capitalism, the marketplace decides how resources are to be used through a system of supply and demand. In socialism, it is the government, acting on the wishes of the people, that make decisions on what is to be produced, how much, and who is to receive it. It is through planning that the first element of egalitarianism can be achieved.

Communism

Unlike capitalism and socialism, communism is more than an economic system. It is a secular religion. It calls for complete equality, a communal sharing of all goods, and an absence of government. For the true communist, the nature of humankind is good; it is, however, corrupted by the concept of property. Why else, maintain communists, do people lie, cheat, steal, and kill—for property. Governments exist to monitor conflict among people and nations. If private property is eliminated, then so is conflict and the need for government.

Although the concept of communism has been floating around since humans began debating politics, its modern-day champion is Karl Marx. A brilliant social thinker, Marx was born and educated in Germany. He received his doctorate in 1841 and began work as a newspaper editor. His editorials and comments quickly put him at odds with the governments of his day and he was soon exiled to Paris and then to London where he lived until his death in 1883.

At the time Marx lived, the Industrial Revolution was in full swing. It was Marx's observation that although industrialization held great promise for improving humankind's condition in practice, it created great inequality and misery among workers. Why was this true? Marx found the answer in the class struggle over society's scarce resources between the workers (**proletariats**) and the capitalists (**bourgeoisie**). In a capitalist system, workers provided the labor necessary for capitalists to produce a profit. Since the system is geared toward greed, the capitalist will attempt to extract as much labor from workers and pay them as little as possible to maximize profits. The system is exploitative and leads to the accumulation of vast wealth at the expense of the workers whose lives become deeply mired in poverty and hopelessness. Marx rejected the traditional argument of capitalism that workers could improve their lot by selling their labor to the highest bidder. As capitalism matures, he explained, the economy becomes more centralized; that is, successful companies gobble-up their competitors and grow. Carried to its extreme, only one company would survive and it, and it alone, would be in a position to dictate wages. Hence, the worker is hopelessly at the mercy of the capitalist.

For Marx this was not the end of the story. As the economy became more centralized and the wages of workers declined, it was inevitable that depression would occur because the workers could no longer buy the products of the capitalist. This is what Marx meant by his famous statement that capitalism produces its own "grave diggers." When the plight of workers becomes intolerable, Marx predicted that they would overcome their sense of **false consciousness** (the right of the capitalist to vast wealth because he earned it), and rise up in revolt. Immediately after the revolution, a dictatorship of the proletariat would be established to destroy the remnants of capitalist thought, and as the new ideas began to take hold in the minds of the people, the society would slip into the communistic state. For Marx, this was inevitable and was destined to occur worldwide. Once communism was established, humankind would live a utopian existence. Nations and governments would disappear.

No society, other than remote primitive societies, has ever practiced true communism. It is, in reality, a theoretical system. Even countries that have identified with it, such as the former Soviet Union, China, and Cuba, would admit to not having achieved communism. Rather, they would admit to being at the stage of "dictatorship of the proletariat." However, if Marx were alive today, he would undoubtedly take exception to that claim. He would undoubtedly see them in a feudal stage; they would have to pass through capitalism before communism could be achieved. For Marx the progression of economic cycles could not be broken. Capitalism was necessary before communism became a reality.

Mixed Economy

Today, neither pure capitalism nor pure socialism is practiced. Throughout the world, nations have borrowed a little of each in forming their economic systems. This is true even of the United States, which is commonly identified as being the world's greatest capitalistic economy. In reality, the economic system practiced by the United States is **welfare capitalism**. While not owning property, the government is actively involved in regulating it. Hence, monopolies, price-fixing, certain banking practices, discrimination in employment, as well as other practices are outlawed. Also, the government is very active in establishing social programs to promote social stability. A few examples include minimum wage, Social Security, unemployment compensation, Medicare, and welfare. In a purely capitalistic system the government would not be involved and individuals would have to fend for themselves. On the other hand, socialistic countries like Denmark and Sweden allow for private property and a certain degree of free market activity. Generally, these countries own and control what is termed the **commanding heights** of the economy—railways, airlines, energy plants, communication facilities, hospitals, etc.

Which system is best? To a large extent it depends on the culture and values of the society. In the United States, our value system favors liberty and individuality over egalitarianism. Additionally, citizens of this country have a long tradition of mistrusting the government. Consequently, a lean toward capitalism seems comfortable. Other countries in the world do not share our values of placing the individual first. For them, the good of the many preempts the needs of the individual, hence they lean toward socialism. All-in-all, each system has it strengths and weaknesses.

SOCIOLOGICAL PERSPECTIVES

Structural Functional

Central to the structural functionalist view of political institutions is societal survival. Sociologist Talcott Parsons used the term "goal attainment" as central to this process.

Structural functionalist theory suggests that societies that produce a surplus of goods have the responsibility to determine how to distribute or use those goods. Parsons maintained that successful societies utilize these goods to promote harmony. The first step to promoting harmony is goal determination. Domestic security, a goal crucial to promoting harmony in all societies, provides a good example. To achieve domestic security the government must undertake a series of steps. The *first* is to communicate the goal to the members of society. The *second* step is to establish institutions whose primary responsibility is to carry out tasks necessary to achieve the goal. This would be the military (National Guard), the Federal Bureau of Investigation, and state and local police departments. *Third*, the government must recruit individuals with the skill and dedication to work in the various institutions established for goal enforcement and provide for salaries, training, equipment, and so forth. *Finally*, the government must find ways to instill in people the beliefs, values, and attitudes necessary for goal attainment. Children in school being taught by their teachers to respect police officers and the law is an example.

Although this might appear on the surface to be a cold, determinist, one-way street with the government deciding policy and citizens knuckling under, structural functionalists maintain that the process is much more complex and participatory. A good example here would be education. In many societies, children at a very young age take an examination to determine their potential. Based on the examination, they are placed in curriculums leading either to a university or trade school. Could the government in this country introduce a similar plan? It is very doubtful. Embedded deep into the values of our society is the notion of opportunity. To foreclose on one's right to obtain an education and thereby be locked into a lower status position in society, might well cause civil unrest. Hence, the government establishes goals that are acceptable to society.

It is also true that in many cases it is not possible for all of the members of society to agree on the goal or how it should be carried out. The role of the government then, according to structural functionalist perspective, is that of mediation between conflicting views and the coordination of goal attainment. Without government, chaos would prevail.

Social Conflict

Unlike the structural functionalists who stress coordination and conflict mediation, the social conflict perspective focuses on the coercive and divisive aspects of government. The state, maintain these sociologists, is the major instrument of the powerful to maintain control and domination of the powerless.

The writings of Karl Marx provide the best source on this perspective, describing government as the ultimate instrument of class oppression. As noted previously, Marx determined that there were two major classes in society: the workers (proletariat) and the capitalists (bourgeoisie). The interests of these two groups are at odds since they compete for society's scarce resources. Workers demand higher wages, capitalists desire greater profits. Through their vast wealth, capitalists gained control of the political arena and utilized the power of the state to create laws that suppress the rights of workers. The argument that democracy altered this relationship by giving the worker more power was rejected by Marx as an example of "false consciousness," because although workers were able to vote, their lack of economic power prevented them from improving their lot through governmental action. Marx's observation was that capitalists used their vast wealth to manipulate the minds of workers and "buy" government offices or officials. The police, army, courts, and bureaucratic institutions of government were all at the beck-and-call of capitalists to suppress any threat to their power. So true is this, proclaimed Marx, that the only solution to improving the position of workers was to destroy the existing state. The revolution would be quick, the workers would seize the instruments of government in order to politically and economically reorganize the society.

Other sociologists take a less extreme view of the social conflict perspective. While agreeing with Marx on some principles, they usually part course with him on the necessity of revolution. They believe that needed and drastic changes can occur through the normal democratic process of elections and voting. However, before this can occur, the citizens of the nations must become aware of current exploitative processes within their government. Then, and only then, can they act in their own best interests to create a fair and more open society.

GOVERNMENT AND POLITICS IN THE UNITED STATES

If stability were a measure of success, then the United States would have to be considered the most successful practicing democracy in the world today. Unlike other countries, the United States has had but one revolution (the Civil War, 1861-1865), and despite such traumas as the Great Depression of the 1930s and the assassinations of four presidents, the government has remained on a stable course without disruption of the political process. In fact, even when confronted with massive political and economic woes after the Revolutionary War, our leaders leisurely took two full years to find a solution with a new constitution and, as De Tocqueville recounts, "... without it costing humanity a single tear or drop of blood."

Political Foundations of Democracy in the United States

American democracy rests upon the acceptance and practice of four major concepts. These are: constitutionalism, separation of powers, checks and balances, and judicial review.

Constitutionalism. The American government was the first to use the concept of a written constitution. Certainly, other countries have employed constitutions, but in an "unwritten" format. An unwritten constitution is not a single document but, rather, a series of laws, declarations, legislative acts, and commonly accepted customs. Similarly, an unwritten constitution is open-ended, meaning that each new act of legislature or parliament is automatically incorporated into the constitution. If conflicts exist, the newer act is taken as the current law. The first Americans were much more precise. To them, the Constitution was the supreme law of the land. Incorporated into a single document it set forth the parameters in which government could exercise power. All legislative acts and judicial decisions had to fit into the predetermined constitutional limits.

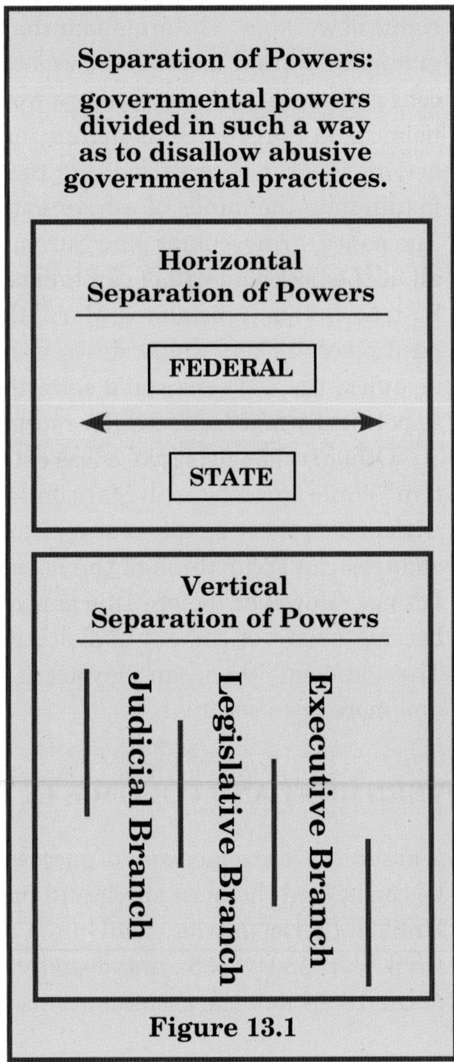

Figure 13.1

Separation of Powers. The American system of government separates governmental power horizontally and vertically. The first division is horizontal wherein power belongs to the federal (national) government and regional ones (the states). To hedge their odds against abusive government power at the national level, power is also vertically divided into three branches: legislative, executive, and judicial. Article I of the Constitution states that "all legislative powers herein granted shall be vested in a Congress of the United States." Article II, directs that "the executive power shall be vested in a President of the United States." And Article III, mandates that "the judicial power of the United States shall be vested in one supreme Court, and in such inferior Courts as the Congress may from time to time ordain and establish." The above arrangement is referred to as **separation of powers**. In essence, it provides additional insurance against one individual or group gaining too much power.

It should be mentioned that, constitutionally speaking, the states are not required to follow a similar arrangement in separating their power. However, all states have voluntarily chosen to follow the national model.

Checks and Balances. The Constitution also limits the power of government by means of a **checks and balances system.** The mechanics of this device are that it makes all three branches dependent upon one another to carry out their own responsibilities. See Figure 13.2. For example, Congress is assigned the responsibility to enact laws, but the president has the right to veto them. However, the power of the veto is not absolute. If Congress so chooses, it can override a presidential veto by a two-thirds vote in both houses. The Supreme Court can check the power of Congress by declaring that a law is unconstitutional. To curb this power, the Constitution provides for presidential appointment of federal court members. Thus, presidents exercise some influence on the court by appointing judges that agree with their political philosophy. But this power is restrained by the fact that the Senate must confirm all such appointments to the federal bench. Likewise, Congress controls the size and funds of the courts—a further check on the

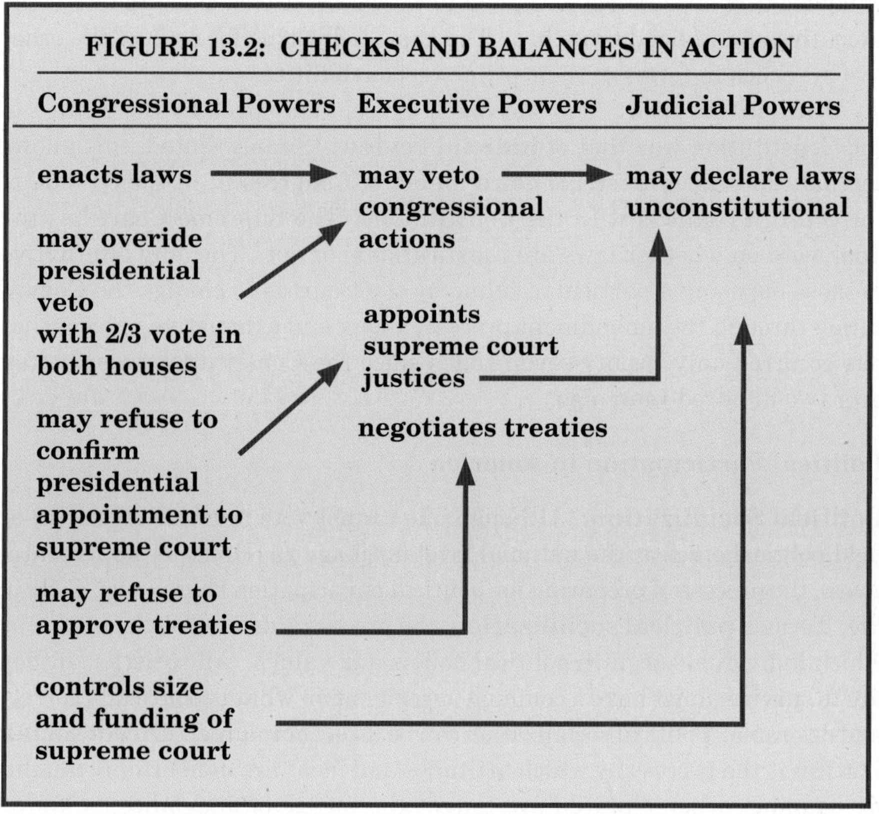

power of the judicial branch. The executive branch has the power to negotiate treaties, but final approval must be given by the Senate for them to be binding.

The electoral system itself is an example of checks and balances. The Constitution specifies that different constituencies select different elected officials in our government. For example, members of the House of Representatives are elected by voters from small districts within each state, whereas senators are chosen by the entire state. On the other hand, the entire nation is the constituency of the president. Moreover, the Constitution sets different terms for each—two years for a representative, six years for a senator, four years for the president, and life tenure for federal judges. The thinking of the writers of the Constitution was that, in staggering the terms of office, it would be difficult for any one group who might enjoy a brief period of popularity to capture the national government and dominate completely at the expense of others. Likewise, since they are elected at different times, it would be natural to assume that each group represents a different set of issues. The life tenure of judges was to insulate them from political pressure and provide a measure of continuity in the government.

Although numerous other examples can be offered, the point should be clear—under a system of checks and balances no one branch of the government is capable of carrying out its function without the support and cooperation of the others. Nor does any branch exercise its responsibility exclusively. This may well contradict the conception that the powers of each branch are rigidly and precisely defined. For example, although the responsibility of lawmaking is primarily assigned to Congress, it is also shared with the executive and judicial branches. The same holds true for each of the other two branches in terms of their prime responsibilities.

Judicial Review. The last major concept employed by the writers of the Constitution was that of **judicial review**. Simply stated, this allows the judicial branch to strike down an act of Congress if, in the opinion of the court, it conflicts with the Constitution. The Supreme Court has the final word on whether laws are constitutional or not. The only alternative to those opposing a particular ruling by the Court is to change the Constitution through the amendment process, a long and exhaustive process that has occurred only twenty-seven times since the Constitution was written over two hundred years ago.

Political Participation in America

Political Socialization. Although one cannot vote until the age of 18 or hold political office at the national level until age 25 (House of Representatives), the process of preparing for political participation begins very early in life. Termed **political socialization**, the process is defined as the means by which individuals acquire political beliefs and values. All societies, if they are to survive, must have a common agreement on what is politically correct and desirable. Political socialization can be direct or indirect. **Direct socialization** is the process by which attitudes and ideas are deliberately taught, for example, when children are taught the pledge of allegiance, or words to patriotic songs, such as the national anthem. **Indirect socialization** occurs by observing the behavior of others. Listening to parents discussing politics at the dinner table is only one of many examples that can be offered.

Political socialization begins at a very early age and starts in the home. Of all agents of political socialization—family, school, peers, etc., studies confirm that the family is the most important. If a child is raised in a warm and loving home that encourages autonomy and applies rules fairly, then he/she will generally develop an early trust toward authoritative figures and the system in general. Children between the ages of 8 and 13 begin to identify the government with individuals, principally, the president. Later, these initial associations give way to a more sophisticated understanding of the institutions of the political systems. Also, older children in this age group begin to identify with a political party, generally that of their parents.

An early study discovered political differences between boys and girls during preadolescent years (Iglitzen, 1974). Findings indicate that girls tended to express preferences for those candidates identified as being honest, sincere, and interested in peace. Boys, on the other hand, preferred candidates who emphasized economic issues. Studies confirm that these differences seem to carry through to adult life. The role of school in political socialization appears to be more of a reinforcer of established attitudes. However, Jennings and Niemi (1974) found that for students from economically deprived homes, school was instrumental in shaping political beliefs. Studies of political preference indicate that in some cases the peer group can override the early influence of family. This is particularly true of college students. In two separate classic studies, Theordore Newcomb (1958) and Martin Levin (1961) found that the political allegiance of students from Democratic Party backgrounds changed as more students enrolled at their institutions identified with the Republican Party.

Party Identification. Political socialization is best measured in terms of party identification. As mentioned previously, America lacks the ideological

A young boy expresses his wishes for change in the immigration policy of the U.S. Beliefs and attitudes about government and public policy are formed very early in life through political socialization.

Photo: Fibonacci Blue

diversity of other political systems in the world. In other words, we pretty much agree on what is important. This explains why we are basically a two-party system—Democrats and Republicans with the vast majority of citizens fitting comfortably into one of the two major parties.

As mentioned previously, the two political parties espouse the same fundamental ideological beliefs (equal opportunity and capitalism, among others). The only difference is their approach to implementing their beliefs. Of all differences, money seems to be a key factor in party identification. Republicans tend to be supported by the affluent, corporate leaders, physicians, and small business owners (including farmers). Democrats draw support from the working class, union workers, the poor, and racial minorities. Likewise, in terms of overall numbers, white males tend to support the Republican Party, whereas, women lean toward the Democrats. Catholics and Jews tend to vote Democratic while Protestants cast ballots for Republicans.

In terms of social issues, the Democratic Party historically has been more liberal than the Republican Party. This is seen in the support of the Democrats for abortion, gay rights, affirmative action, health care initiatives, and other issues requiring national funding. Republicans, on the other hand, stress traditional family values, individual initiative, local control, and an overall hands-off approach to "big government."

Despite these differences, overall support for political parties is weak and cross voting among Americans is common.

Voting. Perhaps the best indicator of political participation is voting. If one compares voting in America to that in other democracies, as shown in Figure 13.3, Americans come up on the short end.

Why is this true? A number of reasons help to explain the lack of voting in America. *First*, many political observers point to the voting process itself. Also, registration is complex and burdensome and elections are held on one day in the middle of the week. Both factors tend to suppress voting.

Figure 13.3: International Voter Turnout, 1991-2000
Source: International Institute for Democracy and Electoral Assistance

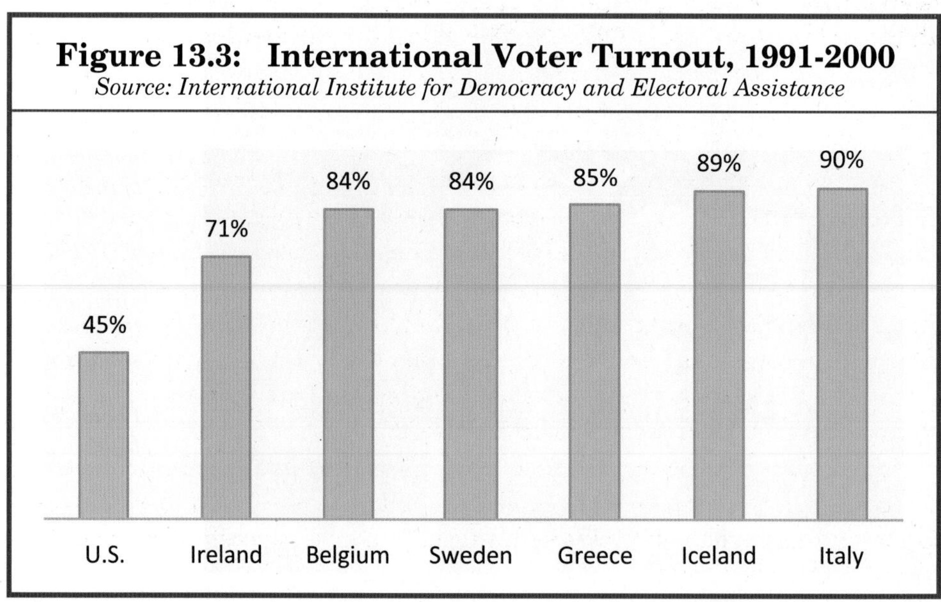

A *second* reason cited is that since the 1960s, Americans have become more mobile and more likely to be single. In combination, both factors tend to suppress voting. A *third* reason can be found in evidence demonstrating that we have become more cynical politically—people may tend to believe that voting really doesn't make a difference. Think about the fiasco of the missing, not counted, damaged, ballots in the 2000 presidential election. Although not as contentious, the following presidential election in 2004 had similar charges of vote manipulation and fraud. Finally, it may well be that the reason lies in the nature of our political system. In a system with ideologically different political parties, voting is important. Strong differences exist between parties and the election of one over another brings substantial changes in society. This is not true in America where both political parties represent the same ideological beliefs and where the Constitution protects us from sudden changes in society. Under these conditions, voting is not as critical because radical change is highly unlikely to occur regardless of who is elected.

Groups and Political Participation

Although individualism is highly valued in our society, we are, nevertheless, a nation of joiners. Nowhere is this more evident than in politics. In fact, the very nature of the political process in the United States encourages group membership.

An **interest group** is a collection of people who have organized to influence governmental action and legislation. Generally speaking special interest groups can be divided into those interested in ideological and non-ideological issues. **Ideological interest groups** are cause oriented. They seek action on the part of government in support of a cause that they feel intensely committed to. A recent newcomer to this category is the Tea Party Patriots. Spring up across the country, these groups advocate free enterprise, fiscal restraint, smaller government, and a balanced budget. Another not so glamorous example is the Ku Klux Klan who preaches the belief in white supremacy and separation of races. **Non-ideological interest groups** are economically oriented; the AFL-CIO, the American Medical Association, the American Bar Association and the National Peanut Growers Association are just a few examples.

Why have interest groups become so important in American politics? The reason can be found in the electoral process. In a media oriented age, the cost of running for office can cost hundreds of millions of dollars. The election of 2008 was one of the most costly in U.S. history with a record-shattering 5.3 billion in spending by candidates, political parties and interest groups for the congressional and presidential races. In their quest for the presidency, Democrat Barack Obama and Republican John McCain together spent more than one billion dollars (Politico, 2008).

Where does all this money come from? Certainly not from individual citizens dipping into their piggy banks. Candidates are forced to turn to special interest groups if they are to raise the necessary cash to compete successfully.

Due to recent changes in campaign laws, most special interest groups have organized PACs (political action committees). The sole purpose of PACs is to solicit funds to support political leaders favorable to their cause. As campaigns have become more costly, candidates have found themselves more dependent upon PACs. When questioned on the issue of accepting PAC funds, all will publicly state that they are not "for sale." But there is evidence to suggest that this may not be the case. Numerous studies have found that PAC money is carefully directed to congressional members who sit on committees responsible for awarding governmental contracts, writing legislation, or overseeing the activities of the interest group represented by the PAC. In the 2008 presidential election, just ten lobbying groups accounted for nearly 200 million dollars in campaign contributions to the campaigns of Barack Obama and John McCain (Capital Eye, 2008).

Many political scholars have raised serious concerns about the ability of interest groups and their PACs to subvert democracy. One of the *first* concerns is that it seriously undermines the importance of the "one man-one vote" principle that is deeply interwoven to the political fiber of this nation. Is the vote of one individual equal to another that has the potential to contribute hundreds of thousands of dollars to a candidate? Who is the legislator likely to listen to? *Second*, with modern technology and the accompanying host of political and psychological advisors, can money manipulate elections? Are issues presented in such a way that the voter can make intelligent decisions, or have elections become media contests? *Third*, there is concern lawmakers have become less responsive to the voters and their political parties. In the past political parties were broad based, representing a diverse set of interests. Political candidates worked closely with their political party to implement its goals. This is no longer true. Candidates can circumvent political parties and voters and go directly to interest groups. Hence, the number of people that they must respond to has narrowed considerably. And *finally*, interest groups tend to narrow the political differences between parties. Both parties need money to survive. The interest groups of the rich and powerful are in a dominant position here. Both the Democrats and Republicans are reliant upon the funds the PAC's have to distribute. Does accepting the money influence policies? There is sufficient evidence to believe that it does. Who then represents the disenfranchised—the poor, the sick, the children, etc.?

AMERICAN DEMOCRACY: THE ELITIST—PLURALIST DEBATE

The Elitist Position

C. Wright Mills is the founder of the elitist position which suggests that there is an unholy alliance between the military, the government and big business because the power elite, a term coined by Mills, held positions in all three interchangeably to further their own self interests. Arguing that the upper class holds the bulk of power, wealth, and prestige, he maintained that they use their position to further their own cause at the expense of the many. Likewise, the power of the elite is perpetuated through generations by linking business and marriage. They all belong to the same clubs, resorts, charitable and cultural organizations, and attend the same schools, churches, and social activities. All combined, this provides them with a distinctive lifestyle and perspective of the world.

These upper class families who constitute the power elite historically have dominated all three major sectors of the society - the military, the government, and the economy. The elites circulated through all the sectors and in the process consolidated their power as they went along. Dick Cheney illustrates this principle. As George W. Bush's vice president, Cheney was president of the Halliburton Corporation (and energy company). Alexander Haig, is another example. A retired army general, Haig held top corporate positions and served as Secretary of State under Ronald Reagan and then ran for president in 1988. Likewise, an examination of the Clinton cabinet found that millionaires occupied ten of the thirteen positions. Perhaps the best illustration supporting the elitist position is in the presidential candidacies of H. Ross Perot and Steve Forbes. Both multibillionaires, neither made any apologies for spending vast sums of their own wealth to further their political ambitions.

The importance of this is that it challenges the basic precepts of our democratic character, which suggest that we all have equal opportunity. In essence, the concentration of wealth and power in the hands of so few renders the voices of the many mute. As such, it is the ruling class of a small group of elites that make the economic, military, and political decisions affecting all of society.

The Pluralist Position

Taking exception to the elitist position, David Riesman (1950) stated that no single or small collective of individuals dominated American politics. Instead, the pluralist perspective suggested that power was spread among a plurality of competing groups from all corners of society: business, labor, farmers, doctors, educators, women, racial minorities, etc. Because their interests are narrow, no one group is able to rally enough people or power to dominate the political process. Rather, each group competed with each other for influence. Occasionally alliances between groups were established, but usually on single issues, and once the battle was over, alliances ended. Serving as one such example was the alliance between the ultra conservative Moral Majority and radical feminists to fight pornography. Once the issue was resolved the two groups departed company and resumed their fight against each other. Thus, as maintained by Riesman, power in America was fluid, changing constantly, and balanced by many groups capable of exercising a "veto power" over the other. The role of the government is more that of mediator. Decisions by Congress and the president are based upon the wishes of the "power majority"—those who happen to have the votes to exercise their will at a particular time.

Although it was impossible for Riesman to foresee the growth of powerful interest groups and the changes in the electoral process that have increased the importance of money and PACs, the pluralist argument is still relevant according to many sociologists and political scientists. The Civil Rights and anti-war movements of the 1960s are classic examples of the "power of the people." Likewise, recent victories in the fight for the environment demonstrate that money alone or the interest of the few does not dominate under the pressure of mass movements—the political system will respond in a democratic fashion.

AMERICAN POLITICS: THE FUTURE

There is reason to be concerned about the future of the American political system. Four areas of concern are most apparent.

First, as already mentioned, the influence of money in the political system continues to increase. There is little doubt that the growth of power PAC organizations has come at the expense of majority rule. Without controls, the power of the individual will be lost in a sea of money and influence. The continual denials that money does not influence votes are refuted by study after study that demonstrates an overwhelming attention by legislators to the needs and wishes of those from whom they accept campaign contributions. What is needed? It is the view of the writers of this text that elections require increased public funding. Only then will politicians be freed from the tremendous pressure of soliciting funds to run for office.

A *second* concern is the current (2008-2009) economic crisis and its cost to the American public. Political theorists have long noted the relationship between economic instability and political unrest. Beginning in 2006, with the burst in the housing bubble, Americans found that the value of their homes was rapidly dwindling. Values fell an average of 20 percent to 35 percent, depending on location. The housing collapse in turn caused trouble on Wall Street where stock values fell by as much as 40 percent by the end of 2008 (Business Journal, 2008). The financial institutions which created the problem in the housing market by engaging in risky subprime lending practices soon found themselves in serious trouble as millions of under qualified borrowers began defaulting on loans. This ultimately resulted in a credit freeze across the nation making borrowing money almost impossible for many individuals and businesses. Unable to find the credit they need to operate, businesses began to close. Concern over the future of their financial situation due to declining home values, losses in the stock market, and fears about unemployment, consumers cut back on spending. This created more failed businesses and more lost jobs and spiraling unemployment. At present, the unemployment rate is more than 9 percent and expected to continue to rise in the near future (Current Population Survey, 2010). One does not need a crystal ball to understand where all of this leads—severe economic recession or depression. To counter the crisis, which has spread globally, the U.S. government began a financial bailout, injecting cash into

A homeless man with his dog walks the streets in search of work. The severity of the 2008 recession coupled with cutbacks in industry has produced the highest unemployment rates since the Great Derpression.

Photo: flickr.com/photos/zormsk

the financial markets to the tune of one trillion dollars. Experts believe that before the crisis is over an additional one to two trillion dollars will be needed. Of course, all of this money is causing the national debt to increase at an alarming rate; a burden which will weigh heavily on our children. Will this strategy work? No one is quite sure. But what we are sure of, as stated earlier, is that it will produce major changes in the political structure of this nation and of the world. One such change occurred in the national congressional election of 2010. Concern over the economy and debt created a shift in voters to the right resulting in a historic shift of 63 House of Representative and 5 U.S. Senate seats to the Republican party. Additionally, Republicans picked up 6 more governorships.

A *third* concern, and one related to the above, is the disappearance of the middle class in America. As two major forces combine, the global economy (which forces the wages of U.S. workers down) and the current economic crisis (which has stripped away wealth from families) more and more Americans are being pulled out of the middle class and forced into the lower classes. In other words, we are becoming more stratified (Economist View, 2009) with a few people at the top, a few people in the middle, and the majority of people at the bottom. This is in sharp contrast to the 1990s when more American families moved up the socioeconomic ladder from the working class to the middle class. Now, as these families, and some of those who occupied the middle class before the economic boom, are forced to step down the economic ladder, there will be increased anxiety and disappointment, both of which will be expressed in the political arena. How will they be expressed? Although it is impossible to predict an outcome, one can speculate that it will lead to shifting loyalties or perhaps abandonment of political participation.

Finally, and again related, is the erosion of the confidence of the American people in the federal government which is at its lowest level in half a century. Just three percent of Americans say they trust the government to do what is right "just about always," and 19 percent indicating "most of the time" (Pew

Research, 2010). In light of the government's handing of Katrina and the Gulf Oil crisis, the wars in Iraq and Afhanistan, and the economic crisis, there is little wonder why Americans are so discontent with their political leaders and worried about the future.

In conclusion, we would not suggest that democracy in America is on the verge of collapse, but certainly there are indications that repair work is not only in order, but long overdue. President Obama was elected on a platform that promised change in the political process. Many Americans voted for him because they believed that the old quid-pro-quo ways had gotten us into trouble and a new approach was needed. We are hopefully watching and hope that Americans will express higher levels of confidence in their government and those who serve in elected positions.

Terms You Should Know:

Power	State	Nation-state
Sovereignty	Law	Nationalism
Coalition	Proletariat	Bourgeoisie
Welfare Capitalism	Coup	Veto
Interest Group	PAC	Power Majority

Can You Answer These Questions?

1. According to Max Weber, what are the three types of authority?
2. What is the difference between political and civil rights?
3. List and define the five types of governments noted in your book. Can you give an example country for each?
4. Using the definitions in your text, which type of democracy is the United States?
5. What is the purpose of an economic system? How would you characterize our economy in the United States?
6. How do "separation of powers" and "checks and balances" further democracy in our government?
7. What is "Judicial Review" and why is it important in our government?
8. Describe the difference between elitist and pluralist positions of government. Which do you think more adequately describes government in the United States?

Critical Thinking Exercises:

1. Karl Marx used the term "false consciousness" to describe how workers have been propagandized to believe that the rich have a right to their wealth. Do you believe there is any truth to this?
2. Would the political and civil rights of citizens in this country be better served if we moved to a direct democracy?
3. Do you think we could better our society by moving toward a strict form of capitalism in all parts of the economy?
4. After considering the pros and cons of interest groups in our political system, do you think they have done more harm or more good? What suggestions could you offer to improve the situation?
5. America is a federal system with a national government and fifty states. Given all the technological advances in communication and transportation, do we really need all of these states?

Photo: Treesftf

Work and Livelihood

Chapter 14

You've arrived.

Nervously you check your appearance in the reflecting glass of the door. A quick inventory tells you that everything is neat and in place. The expensive suit, the new haircut, the highly polished shoes, all perfect. A glance at your shoulders tells you that even the new dandruff shampoo you've been using seems to be doing its job. You smile, take a deep breath and feel your confidence swell. You're looking fine.

As you wander casually into the room, you look around and wave to some people you know. It's a beautiful setting. Leave it to your cousin Sean to pick the finest spot in town for his wedding. He always did have the best of everything: new BMW, top honors in his graduating class at college, immediate management position with a Fortune 500 company, and now, marrying into a wealthy family.

Speak of the devil, there he is.

Wow, look at that incredible woman in his group! This is looking better and better. Sure am glad I let mom buy this new suit for me so I wouldn't "embarrass" her. Just cause I'm not as perfect as Sean! I keep telling her there's nothing wrong with working at the grocery store. In a while I'll be making really good money. They might even make me manager one of these days.

OK, I'm heading over there. Looking good, looking good!

"Hey Sean! Congratulations, man."

"Jimmy! Great that you could make it. I was afraid you wouldn't be able to get off work. Listen, I want you to meet someone."

Here it comes, turn on the charm. She's gorgeous!

"Janice, this is my cousin Jimmy. He and I pretty much grew up together. He's a really great guy. And Jim, this is Janice, she's my new sister-in-law and the most promising new Assistant District Attorney we have in the state."

"Janice. Hi. New ADA, huh? Wow, brains and beauty, what more could a guy ask for?"

Janice laughs. What a great smile! "Hi Jimmy. You look pretty good yourself! What kind of work do you do?"

The single most often asked question that you will answer throughout your life is, "what do you do for a living?" Over and over again, literally thousands of times, you will be called upon to identify who you are by the work that you do. Make no mistake: the answer that you give will immediately identify and classify you in more ways than you can imagine—your education, the type of school you attended, your level of intelligence, your approximate income, probably your political orientation, your place in the community, what type of neighborhood you live in, and the people you most likely associate with. The list is endless. All of these calculations will flash though the mind of your inquirer as he/she analyzes information and begins the process of classifying and ranking your position (status) on the grand hierarchical scale of society.

Nothing defines who we are more than the work we choose or are compelled to do. Likewise, our work, if found challenging and rewarding, leads to personal satisfaction and happiness. On the flip side, if we fail to secure meaningful work, it can be the pathway to a host of psychological and physical problems—stress, loss of self-respect, depression, substance abuse, and early death.

It is also important to understand that while many people complain about their work, the need to work is so ingrained in our "psyche" that without it, good or bad, we would be lost. An example of this is illustrated by Morse and Weiss (1955) in a study where they asked people the question, "If by some chance you inherited enough money to live comfortably without working, do you think that you would work anyway, or not?" How would you respond? Over eighty percent of people who responded indicated that they would still work.

In this chapter we explore work. First we look at work in a historical context. We then move to understanding the nature of work and economic transformations in the Industrial Revolution as well as the new Post-industrial economy. And finally, we conclude with some current trends that could very well affect your future.

WORK: A BRIEF HISTORY

Not everyone throughout history has shared our current view of work. For most of history work was seen a negative light. The Greeks, for example, loathed the very thought of having to work for a living. For them, the mind and the noble pursuit of knowledge were all important. Aristotle echoed this sentiment when he stated that, "No man can practice virtue who is living the life of a mechanic or laborer." It was on this bit of philosophy that the Greeks justified the existence of slavery.

The Roman view of work paralleled that of the Greeks. With the exception of a few select professions, work was considered demeaning and those who had to perform it were afforded little, if any, dignity. Again, it was this attitude that supported the institution of slavery.

Moving on to the ancient Hebrews, we find that they had an equally distasteful attitude regarding work. In their view, work was a result of Adam and Eve's disobedience to God. Having been tossed from the Garden of Eden (no work), man was forced to toil in the fields and Eve was to bring forth her children in pain, hence, the connection between childbirth and labor. And wouldn't you know it, the rest of us, their children, were forced to pay for their transgression, or original sin, by "the sweat of our brow."

The image of work began to take on a more palatable taste with the early Christians. Although accepting the Biblical notion of original sin and the necessity of penance to atone for it, they also considered work to have some redeeming merit. Not only did hard work allow people to provide for themselves, but the accompanying wealth could also be used to help others in need. It was this association with "good works" that started us thinking of work as something other than a degrading necessity of life.

Though slightly elevated, work remained on shaky grounds for over sixteen hundred years until the dawn of the Protestant Reformation. Casting off all negative connotations, work was elevated to a spiritual virtue by Martin Luther, who asserted that one worked in servitude to God. The acceptance of this idea implied that work must be good because God's intention for man was good.

John Calvin, another Protestant reformer of the day, preached that not only was work the will of God, but it was His intention that people live frugally. Such a lifestyle enabled the accumulation of capital, which in turn, could be reinvested into the system for additional work-related ventures. Similarly, idleness which up until this time was considered a virtue, was now proclaimed to be sinful and the work of the devil.

Max Weber, in his great work *The Protestant Ethic and the Spirit of Capitalism* demonstrated the link between the concept of the spiritual value of work and the rise of capitalism in the West. The religious elevation of the status of work allowed for the development of a new value system that became the foundation upon which the Industrial Revolution would be built. Nowhere was this more evident than in the doctrine of **predestination** belief of early Puritans. According to this doctrine, people were pre-selected by God for salvation or damnation. The only catch was that it was impossible to know for certain whether one's direction of travel in the hereafter would be up or down. There were however, signs, the most important of which was financial success. The reasoning behind this was that: if work is God's will and man is predestined, then it only followed that God would show favor to those who would be riding the *up* elevator. With this belief system firmly in place, it is understandable why everyone worked very, very hard. Weber called this the **Protestant work ethic**. Today it is applied more to the concept of work than to religion.

THE NATURE OF WORK

Everyone talks about work, but do they all mean the same thing? One person talks of the work that they do at the office. Another speaks of work at home. Still another might indicate that he/she worked hard that day on the piano. Are all of these examples of work?

First, let's define what we mean by work. One definition used by a number of social scientists is that work is "any activity that produces something of *economic* value for other people." Under this definition all of the above could be considered work under the right circumstances. In the first case, the work done at the office would certainly qualify. It is work created in a **formal labor market** (outside of the home) and is produced for pay. The other two examples are more complicated. The work produced at home would also qualify. After all, someone must maintain the home, and doing so allows another the opportunity to work longer hours. This we classify as the **informal labor market**. Finally, our last example of piano practice would not be considered work unless it was done with the intention of producing economic value. Hence, it would be better referred to as a hobby. Later in this chapter we will return to the distinction between the formal and informal labor market.

ECONOMIC TRANSFORMATIONS

Economy and work are inseparable because the *type* of work people do is related to the *structure* of the economy. Sociologists are in general agreement in their identification of three major turning points in the economy. Two we have already passed through, and we are now in the process of achieving another major turning point.

Approximately 8,000 B.C.E. marks the beginning of the Neolithic Revolution. It was during this period that the nomadic ways of hunting and gathering societies gave way to farming and the domestication of animals. This, of course, had an impact on population size, and on the development of cities. The first known city, Jericho, dates back more than 8,000 years. This area in the Middle East is so unique that historians refer to it as the cradle of civilization, and to Jericho (Palestine) as the dawn of civilization. Land was cultivated, languages were developed, metallurgy was discovered, tools were created, and in general, humans began to reach across the world in search of other lands and riches. This age lasted for nearly ten thousand years.

The Industrial Revolution marks the beginning of our second turning point. Beginning with the invention of the steam engine by James Watts in 1776, the nature of work was irreversibly altered. The application of steam power to mechanical devices made the muscle power of man and beast obsolete. The introduction of mechanical power transformed society in four important ways:

> **Development of factories**. The small cottage-industries that had existed for thousands of years began to disappear. Work was taken out of the home and centered in large factories capable of utilizing the bulky and cumbersome mechanical engines that could generate the power of a hundred men in one stroke.
>
> **Possibility of mass production**. The development of mass production created a surplus of goods. Prior to this time human labor only barely produced a subsistence level of existence. Very little was left over for sale or trade with others. Likewise, with the newly found power a greater range of goods could be manufactured in a shorter time period.
>
> **Specialization in labor**. The skilled craftsman and old artisan practice gave way to specialization and the division of labor. With the advent of new machines and the assembly line, specialization was no longer necessary. Individuals were trained in a small task that they performed in a repetitive manner. Thus, where it took days and perhaps weeks and months, to create a product from start to finish, machines completed the process in a matter of hours.
>
> **Development of wage labor**. Before the Industrial Revolution, individuals produced goods for themselves and neighbors. To a large extent, a barter economy was the mode of exchange. With the development of factories, work became associated with wages. These wages were then in turn used to purchase items needed for survival.

As the steam engine marked a turning point for the economy, so did the computer establish our third turning point. In what is known as the Information Revolution, the United States and other industrial nations are in the process of shifting away from a manufacturing economy to a service economy. Here, the emphasis lies not in the production of goods, but rather in providing service in all areas, from advertising to banking to data management to public relations, etc. Likewise, as the Industrial Revolution centralized the workplace in the factory, the Information Revolution is decentralizing it to anywhere imaginable in the world. A computer and a phone line are all one needs. Work changes brought about by the service economy are discussed in greater detail toward the end of this chapter. For now, let us return to work as it was in the industrial society.

THE INDUSTRIAL SOCIETY AND WORK

Division of Labor

The single most distinguishing characteristic of modern industrialism is the division of labor. In his classical work on capitalism, *The Wealth of Nations*, Adam Smith openly lauded its advantage with an example of production in a pin factory. Here, working alone, a worker could produce pins at the rate of twenty per day. Dividing the labor into components, with a single worker performing one, and only one task, then passing it along to the next worker with a different task, the rate of production increased to 48,000 pins per day (Smith, 1776).

Scientific Management: Taylorism and Fordism

It would be a hundred years later, around 1900, before industry took full advantage of the industrial process under the guise of scientific management. As a management consultant, Frederick Taylor began detailed studies of various industrial processes with the expressed goal of breaking work down into its smallest and most efficient components for production. Also emphasized was the scientific study of a variety of tools necessary for increased production. Experiments were conducted in which management officials working under the direction of Taylor timed workers to precise seconds of production. From these studies, recommendations were made to leaders of industry on how to increase production. Invariably, this resulted in further division and specialization of the worker's task. Taylor's approach was to become so popular that eventually scientific management and the term **Taylorism** became synonymous.

While Taylor was preoccupied with efficiency, he paid little attention to its outcomes. However, without extended markets for the goods produced by mass production, efficiency meant little more than overstocked warehouses. It would be Henry Ford who would link the two—mass production and mass markets. Using an assembly line for the production of only one product, the Ford Model T, he was able to combine speed, precision, and efficiency and market his product to mass society. Likewise, Ford was concerned with his workers' pay rates. He reasoned that unless workers were paid more than subsistence wages, they would not be able to afford the products produced by mass production. He therefore increased the pay of workers to $5.00 per day, one of the highest wages for the period (Bryan, 1989)). As with Taylor, people began to use the term **Fordism** when referring to assembly-line production.

Benefits of Industrialization

Although it is easy to see the flaws and negative consequences of the Industrial Revolution, one must keep in mind that positive outcomes also occurred. Three of the most evident advantages are increased standard of living, a decrease in war and revolution, and increased social equality.

Increased standard of living. Although there is little doubt that workers during the early periods of industrialization suffered greatly, one

Workers strike for better wages and working conditions. Employed sparingly, a strike is considered the last resort in labor negotiations.

Photo: Roger Blackwell.

must remember that life in the period prior to capitalism was not a bed of roses. Humans labored long hours each day to scratch a living from the earth. Likewise, natural disasters such as harsh winters, famine, and floods claimed many lives. Industrialization, while not a miracle cure for all of life's problems, did increase the overall standard of living for humans. With increased production came surpluses and with surpluses came better diets, housing, medical care, clothing, and luxury items. For the first time in thousands of years, life expectancy began to increase.

Decrease in wars and revolutions. Industrialized societies, in comparison to pre-industrialized societies, are less likely to experience revolution. To a large extent this is the result of an overall increase in the standard of living. People who have jobs, are well fed, clothed and housed have less discontent. Hence, political regimes tend to be more stable. Likewise, nations have less incentive to go to war with neighbors. This is true for several reasons. *First*, having invested large sums of capital in the development of society (bridges, roads, factories, schools, hospitals, etc.), nations are less willing to risk losing that which they created. *Second*, industrial nations need markets for their goods. Consequently, they have more to gain by making friends rather than enemies. Also, the very nature of trade dictates a more friendly and tolerant attitude toward others. Some experts predict that in the not so distant future, globalization and interlocking economies will unite humans into one economy and one government. And *lastly*, with industrialization, weapons of mass destruction have become so apocalyptic that war is all but impossible. Humans turned this corner with the creation and development of nuclear weapons in the 1940s.

Increased social equality. Although the overall picture of capitalism painted by Karl Marx was bleak, there were a number of things about it that he admired. Based on his observations of industrialization in Europe, he concluded that capitalism was a dynamic and modernizing force. He predicted that with its advent, the older, rigid, autocratic systems of inequality would fall. Likewise, he believed industrialization inevitably would lead to the destruction of the feudal regimes and with it the aristocracy that had dominated governments and economy for so long. Marx was right in his predictions. With industrialization came new patterns of social mobility. The competitive nature of capitalism demanded talent. Those with talent, technical skills, knowledge and a strong work ethic were sought out regardless of family background. Today, while structural functionalist and social conflict theorists debate the extent of equality produced by capitalism, both sides would admit that it is a better system than that of pre-industrial society.

POST-INDUSTRIAL ECONOMY

Previously we indicated that there were three turning points in basic economy and that we have passed through two—the Neolithic Revolution and the Industrial Revolution. We are now in the midst of changing to the third—the Information Revolution. It is in this economy that you, your children, and their children will live and work. In this section we explore some distinguishing characteristics of this new economy.

The Rise of the Service Occupations

The rise of the service occupations came at the expense of farming and "blue collar" work. At the turn of the 20th century, forty percent of the population was engaged in farming and another forty percent worked in blue-collar factory jobs. Most of those who farmed owned their own land. Working with the equipment of the time, a farmer was capable of feeding five people. With the invention of better equipment, and the developments of scientific techniques and new fertilizers, the figure rose quickly. The typical farmer today can feed 100 people.

As production increased, the need for people in agriculture decreased. Likewise, with the development of new equipment, smaller farms were no longer profitable and many were combined into the mega-farms of today. A similar revolution was occurring in factories with the introduction of new equipment. Likewise, as global competition has accelerated, many manufacturing jobs have been shifted abroad to take advantage of cheaper labor. The statistic on this change is truly dramatic. Over the last third of the 20th

Through play, children learn to use a computer. With the rise of the service occupations and computer technology, it is essential that all students become computer competent.

Photo: Tim and Selena Middleton

century, the proportion of blue-collar workers in goods-producing industries was halved from 31 percent to 16.2 percent (U.S. Census Bureau, 1994B).

What happened to these workers? For the most part they were absorbed into the new service economy. Whereas employees in the service economy held two out of three jobs in the early 1970s, the figure increased to four out of five by the mid-1990s. And although a recent study demonstrates that over 70 percent of the work force identifies as working in a "white-collar" position, sociologists and economists are quick to point out that most of these jobs are not really white-collar, but service centered occupations. The difference between the two is that the latter is marked by a lack of prestige, security, and the financial benefits of jobs traditionally identified as white-collar (LeGrande, 1985).

The Rise of the Dual Labor Market

Global competition has resulted in the development of what one sociologist (Edwards, 1979) has identified as a dual labor market. The **primary labor market** consists of jobs that have been traditionally associated with white-collar work. The degree of education and skill necessary for entry into this labor market is high, and the competition for such jobs is fierce. However, workers are well paid, have high esteem and security, and are afforded benefits such as medical insurance and retirement plans. The **secondary labor market** is relatively new. Jobs in this market employ *contingent workers*—employees who work part-time or by contract. Both jobs are characterized by lower pay, few benefits, little security, and even lower esteem. For the most part, these are transient, dead-end occupations. Little education is required. Workers are forced to endure long hours of tedious and meaningless work. It is here where sociologists have discovered much alienation from work and discontentment with life. Even for workers who attain additional training and education, the prospects for advancement are slim. The following testimonies illustrate the difficulties of people trapped in this position:

> Montie Lavoie can't quite remember all the bad jobs she has held. She washed dishes when she was 16, worked as a barmaid when she came of age, and then found a full-time job making windows—for $6.00 an hour. Claudia Burrow has a longer list: fry cook, nurse's aide, sales clerk, security guard, housemaid... Sharon White went to work at 14 and spent ten years as a warehouse shipper before the company went out of business. She went back to school to become a childcare specialist. Then, needing more money, she got a job as an actress for a caterer. Life at or near minimum wage has been an unpleasant sameness everywhere in America. Lavoie, 36, and Burrow, 39, live on the high, empty, western plains of Montana. White, is from inner city Baltimore. All three provide living proof of one of the nation's most hallowed truths: Your can always get a job, if you really want one. But what kind of job?
>
> For $6.00 an hour you can't even pay the rent. These women, and 13 million more low wage workers in America have spent years—in some

Table 14.1: Occupations with the Fastest Growth

Occupations:	Percent Change	Number of New Jobs (in thousands)	Wages-May 2008 Median	Education/Training
Biomedical Engineers	72	11.6	$77,400	Bachelor's degree
Network Systems and Data Communications analysts	53	155.8	$71,100	Bachelor's degree
Home Health Aides	50	460.9	$20,460	Short-term on-the-job training
Personal and Home Care Aides	46	375.8	$19,180	Short-term on-the-job training
Financial Examiners	41	11.1	$70,930	Bachelor's degree
Medical Scientists, Except Epidemiologists	40	44.2	$72,590	Doctoral degree
Physician Assistants	39	29.2	$81,230	Master's degree
Skin Care Specialists	38	14.7	$28,730	Postsecondary vocational award
Biochemists and Biophysicists	37	8.7	$82,840	Doctoral degree
Athletic Trainers	37	6.0	$39,640	Bachelor's degree
Physical Therapist Aides	36	16.7	$23,760	Short-term on-the-job training
Dental Hygienists	36	62.9	$66,570	Associate degree
Veterinary Technologists	36	28.5	$28,900	Associate degree
Dental Assistants	36	105.6	$32,380	Moderate-term on-the-job training
Computer Software Engineers, applications	34	175.1	$85,430	Bachelor's degree
Medical Assistants	34	163.9	$28,300	Moderate-term on-the-job training
Physical Therapist assistants	33	21.2	$46,140	Associate degree
Veterinarians	33	19.7	$79,050	Professional degree
Self-enrichment education Teachers	32	81.3	$35,720	Work experience in related occupation
Compliance Officers*	31	80.8	$48,890	Long-term on-the-job training

* except agriculture, construction, health and safety, and transportation

SOURCE: BLS Occupational Employment Statistics and Division of Occupational Outlook

> cases decades—trapped in labor's twilight zone. They have added a bitter corollary to the old saw: Yes, you can always find a job, but much of the time you can't earn a living (Bugliotta, 1994).

Unfortunately, even though the number of jobs has risen rapidly with the Information Revolution, the vast majority (80 percent) of the newly created jobs are located in the secondary labor market (Mishel and Bernstein, 1994). On the average, these jobs earn one-fourth the salary of an employee in the primary labor market (Colatosti 1992). At one time, contingent workers were centralized in clerical occupations and the part-time service industry, while today employers seek contingent workers in education, as computer analysts, lab technicians, nurses, engineers, architects and so on.

Outsourcing

Why has employment been so slow to recover? Is the outsourcing of U.S. jobs to blame?

Two primary factors have caused the job market to trail the general economy: weakness in manufacturing and stellar productivity performance across all major sectors. Manufacturing has suffered through painful adjustments to over investment, a previously strong dollar, and migration of capacity overseas. Estimates of the actual number of jobs outsourced overseas are sketchy. Gardner Inc. contends that about 500,000 jobs in the technology sector could be sent abroad over the next two years, which would amount to a still moderate 5 percent of the total 10.3 million workers believed to work in the technology sector.

Adjustment is never easy, but American workers have demonstrated their flexibility and responsiveness to change over the past two decades. Our competitive advantage will continue in fields requiring higher skills and knowledge. This is why employment among college graduates has expanded by over two million jobs in the past year and why the jobless rate among these more educated workers is only around three percent (Reaser, 2004).

Bangalore, India represents the economy in fast forward, one that is growing at more than 8 percent annually, double the rate of the United States. Of course, India is still poor by comparison to the US. But the outsourcing wave from the United States has provided an outlet for thousands of technically astute, English speaking graduates pouring out of India's elite universities.

But an economic party like this one has its hangovers, such as BOSS, or burnout stress syndrome. When Ranit Bhalla, twenty-five, a software engineer, joined tech giant Wipro four years ago, the work was so intense he often found himself sleeping and bathing at the office. After six months of 16 hours days, 3 a.m. dinners and gastric problems, his exhausted body finally gave out. He spent fifteen days in a hospital and then needed counseling.

It is no easier on workers at the call centers that handle U.S. customer-service complaints. In a recent survey by India's Dataquest magazine,

40 percent said they suffer from sleep disorders, and 34 percent complained of digestive problems. Combine those factors with the ten to twelve hour night shifts that Indian IT workers pull so they can stay in synch with U.S. daytime hours (Rajan, 2004).

Green Economy

Finally, green industries may have arrived at the development stage that will allow them to capitalize on the technology revolution to move the nation forward. Energy independence was one of the most noted political promises of the Obama administration. Green promises have been historically linked to the Democratic Party. However, the market and political support for the Green Revolution may not be sustainable in the absence of continuous high energy prices, environmental disasters and threats to the economy. It seems unlikely that the financial support of the federal government will focus on the need to develop new jobs in unproven green industries.

Can the Green Revolution find the money to expand in a market strangled with credit restrictions? Can the demand for green energy be sustained in the face of dramatically reduced oil prices? It is palpable that universities, young and old environmentalists, and small business will be the source of the creative fuel that will drive the Green Revolution. The most frequently cited study generally in support of the green issue is a study conducted by the American Solar Energy Society, which estimated that 40 million green-collar jobs would be created by 2030.

The definition of a 'green-collar job' is still fluid and in most cases depends upon the product and its uses in the market. The reality is that green jobs are tied to an ambiguous mix of economic, social, and political goals that may or may not be closely linked to environmental concerns. A strategy of Alaskan and off-shore drilling may make the nation more energy independent and at the same time not environmentally friendly. Solar and wind power production efforts have been on the drawing board for decades, but have yet to be proven to be economically feasible alternatives to traditional fossil fuels, particularly in periods of declining fuel prices. The Renewable Fuels, Consumer Protection, and Energy Efficiency Acts of 2007 were a step in the right direction even though they all lack enforcement. The potential job growth numbers from the Green Revolution will help offset the recession's job losses but will not be sufficient to generate a new powerful force for economic expansion (Gnuschke, 2008).

Community Colleges: Training for Green Jobs

Community colleges are the key to sustainability for training individuals to partake in green jobs. New jobs in solar and wind power installation will require more than a high school education, but less than a four year degree. Van Jones, a community organizer in Oakland, California, advocated for millions of new environmental jobs to both combat global warming and lift underemployed people out of poverty. Jones postulated that solar panel installation is a low-skilled green-collar job that has the most immediate demand for workers. Manufacturing the thousands of machine parts that make up a wind turbine could likewise help rehabilitate the chronically depressed economy in Michigan which has the nation's highest unemployment rate having shed nearly 500,000 jobs since 2000. In that vein, Michigan's governor, Jennifer M. Granholm, a Democrat, started a No Worker Left Behind program in 2007 to offer up to two years of free tuition at any community college or university in the state to laid-off and low-paid workers. However, the state legislature only funded $15 million of the proposed $40 million requested by Governor Granholm. Until industry demonstrates more demand for green workers, many community colleges will be hard pressed to add new programs because solar technology is still much costlier than coal, and unreliable in indirect sunlight (McCandlish, 2008).

Diversity in the Workplace

The workforce in America has undergone major changes as a result of the post-industrial economy. In the early 1950s, white males constituted the majority of workers. This is no longer true for two reasons.

First, as discussed earlier in Chapter Eight, the number of minorities in the United States is growing. During the 1980s the population of African Americans increased by 13 percent in comparison to six percent for whites. Asian Americans—largely as a result of immigration—increased in population by over 100 percent. Today, Hispanics constitute the single largest majority in America comprising 12.5 percent of the population. New census data also indicates that nearly three-quarters of Hispanics lived in the West or South with half living in two states, California and Texas (U.S. Census, 2000).

Second, with the traditional role of women changing and the growing number of female-headed households, more and more women have entered the workforce. In the 1950s, the traditional role for women was to be a homemaker and stay-at-home mother. During this time fewer than thirty percent of adult women worked full-time. Today, nearly sixty percent of women sixteen and over worked for income outside the home (U.S. Department of Labor, 2008).

In summary, the 21st Century will see a workforce where women and racial minorities constitute the backbone of American labor. White males will account for slightly less than 40 percent of all workers. Experts are divided as to the impact this will have on wage differences between white males, racial minorities, and women.

The Rise of Telecommunication and The Virtual Workplace

Just as the Industrial Revolution changed the workplace from the home to the factory, the rise of technology and communication is taking work out of the company workplace. In the service economy an increasing amount of work is taking place in what has been termed: **the virtual workplace**. Here, rather than being *physically* connected to a client, work is *electronically* linked. Although there generally is a home office where the company is based, both workers and clients travel freely anywhere in the world while communicating and conducting business. Virtual workplaces have advantages for all involved in the work process. For business, the virtual workplace allows companies to become global by the flick of a switch. Likewise, rather than the large offices that were needed to house workers, companies now can reduce their requirements for work space and save money. Transportation and shipping costs are also reduced dramatically. For the employee, it is no longer necessary to commute to work. This allows additional time for other activities. Clients benefit because it is now possible to expand the pool of companies to select from, whereas in the past they were limited by geographic constraints.

It is currently estimated that 41 million workers in the United States utilize the virtual workplace to conduct a major portion of their business. Most of these are white-collar workers. However, an increasing number are women attempting to balance the demands of childrearing with the need for additional income. These jobs, generally in areas such as telemarketing, travel, and mail-order merchandising are poorly paid and have very few benefits. Although some experts have hailed the virtual workplace as a new and exciting frontier where many new opportunities have arisen, others point out that in many instances it is just a matter of converting higher wage jobs to lower wage ones. This is possible since industry can geographically move jobs from high cost metropolitan areas to lower cost areas with high unemployment rates where competition will force wages downward. Undoubtedly, this phenomenon has contributed to the declining middle class in the United States.

Employment & Population

Making informed career decisions requires reliable information about opportunities in the future. Opportunities result from the relationships between the population, labor force, and the demand for goods and services.

Population ultimately limits the size of the labor force—individuals working or looking for work—which limits the goods and services that can be produced. Demand for various goods and services is largely responsible for employment in the industries providing them. Employment opportunities, in turn, result from demand for skills needed within specific industries. Opportunities for medical assistants and other healthcare occupations, for example, have surged in response to rapid growth in demand for health services.

Population is the single most important factor in determining the size and composition of the labor force—people either working or looking for work. The civilian labor force is projected to increase by 12.8 million, or 8.5 percent, to 164.2 million over the 2006-2016 period.

The U.S. workforce will become more diverse by 2016. White, non-Hispanics will continue to make up a decreasing share of the labor force falling from 69.1 percent in 2006 to 64.6 percent in 2016 (see Figure 14.1). However, despite relatively slow growth, white non-Hispanics will remain the overwhelming majority of the labor force. Hispanics are also projected be the fastest growing ethnic group, increasing by 29.9 percent. By 2016,

Figure 14.1: Percentage of Labor Force by Race and Ethnic Origin, 2006 and projected 2016.

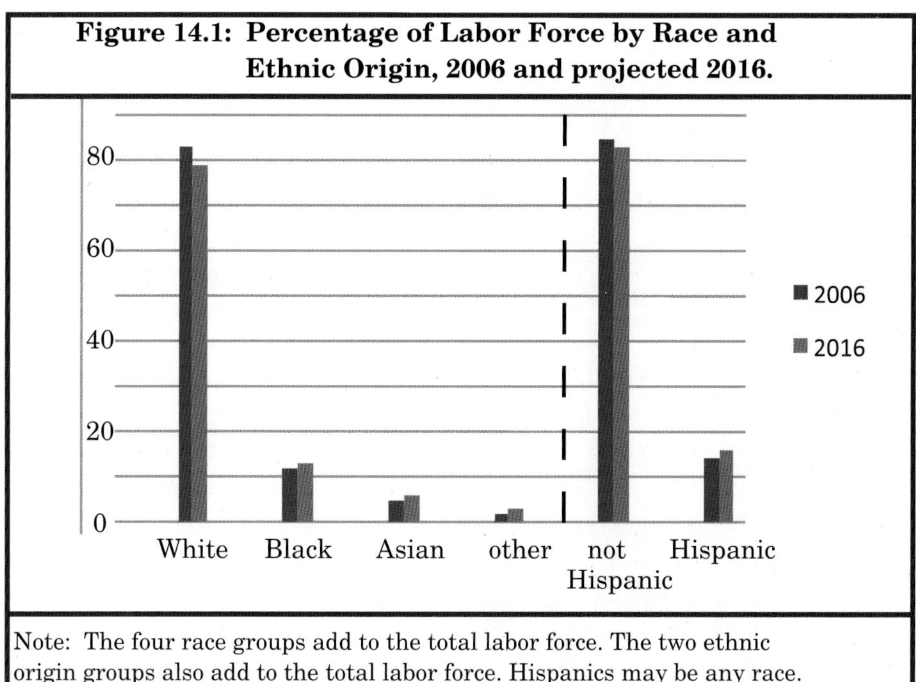

Note: The four race groups add to the total labor force. The two ethnic origin groups also add to the total labor force. Hispanics may be any race.

Hispanics will continue to constitute an increasing proportion of the labor force, growing from 13.7 percent to 16.4 percent. Asians are projected to account for an increasing share of the labor force by 2016, growing from 4.4 to 5.3 percent. Blacks will also increase their share of the labor force, growing from 11.4 percent to 12.3 percent (U.S. Bureau of Labor, 2008).

Unemployment

Unemployment rates have fluctuated throughout much of our history. At times they were high and at other times low. Economist John Maynard Keynes initially gave the common explanation for this. According to his theory, unemployment was the result of the inability of consumers to purchase products. This led to overstocks, which in turn led to layoffs. The new layoffs further aggravated problems by reducing the number of consumers capable of buying goods. You can see where this is going—more layoffs. Keynes' solution was for the government to intervene, stimulate the economy through control of interest rates, tax structures, and regulatory policies. Such action would stimulate the market to produce more jobs that in turn leads to increased consumer purchasing power (Piore and Sabel, 1984).

For a short time, the solution seemed to work. However, with economic globalization, the government has lost its ability to control economic conditions in this country. One consequence has been an increase in unemployment over the past two decades. In the 1960s, our unemployment rate averaged 4.8 percent. As of 2010, unemployment figures exceeded 9 percent (U.S. Department of Labor, 2010). Furthermore, it should be noted that many experts believe that this figure grossly underestimates the actual figure due

A sign protesting trade agreements which have lead to higher unemployment rates in America. Much of the discontent is directed at the G20 nations and their trade policies. Since 2008 unemployment in the U.S. has hovered around 9 percent.

Photo: Tim and Selena Middleton.

to the way in which unemployment is calculated. Unemployed workers are not counted as "unemployed" if they have become so discouraged that they have given-up hope and hence do not apply for work or are not entitled to benefits. Likewise, millions more work part-time as contingent workers in the secondary labor market in which they experience spells of joblessness (Breslow and Howard, 1995). One research study has placed the number of individuals in this category to be two-and-one-half to three times larger than the official unemployment rate. In any one year it is estimated that one out of five Americans will be out of work for a period of time.

Another serious problem not demonstrated by government statistics is that of **underemployment**; people who are employed part-time but who desire and seek full-time positions. At times, the number of underemployed individuals nearly equals the official unemployment rate. Many researchers believe that the only way to accurately measure joblessness is to report both figures. In 2003, the underemployment rate was 10.3 percent (Bernstien and Mishel). The seriousness of the problem is further demonstrated by a previous 1998 study estimating that 46 percent of the jobs with the most growth between 1994 and 2005 will pay less than $16,000 (1998 real dollars). Moreover, 76 percent of newly created jobs will pay below a living wage for a family of four (National Priorities Project, 1998).

What is surprising about the question of unemployment is that a number of economists consider it good for the economy because it acts as a means to reduce inflationary pressure. Likewise, a certain amount of unemployment is considered desirable by capitalists because it deflates high wages and thereby increases profits. Marx was first to predict that capitalists would utilize the, *"reserve army of the unemployed"* in this fashion. A current example is seen in a study tracking workers in the fast-food industry in central Harlem from 1992 to 1994. Despite the fact that jobs paid only minimum wage, there were fourteen applicants for every job opening. Even more astonishing was the study's finding of **creeping credentialism**—requiring degrees and certification for jobs in which the training is unrelated to the work. With a large pool of applicants to select from employers were hiring only high school graduates in their twenties (Newman and Lennon, 1995). Finally, capitalists have successfully used unemployment as a weapon against unions. When there are people who are willing to work for less, it is easier to control the demands of workers for higher wages and keep unruly employees relatively docile.

Table 14.1: Education Pays in Higher Earnings and Lower Unemployment Rates

Unemployment Rate (Percent)	Education Attained	Median Weekly Earnings in 2006 Dollars
1.4	Doctoral degree	1,441
1.1	Professional degree	1,474
1.7	Master's degree	1,140
2.3	Bachelor's degree	962
3.0	Associate degree	721
3.9	Some college, no degree	674
4.3	High-school graduate	595
6.8	Less than a high school diploma	419

Note: Data are 2006 annual averages for persons age 25 and over. Earnings are for full-time wage and salary workers.

Source: Bureau of Labor Statistics, Current Population Survey.

Education Pays

There is no disagreement among those who study the relationship between education and income stratification. Simply put, the more education one has the more likely he/she is to attain higher income. A correlation between education and unemployment has also been found. Table 14.1 clearly demonstrates the effects of education on both income and unemployment rates.

STRATIFICATION AND THE DECLINE OF WAGES

In the previous section we looked at a number of issues related to the post-industrial economy. However, these changes have not affected all workers in the same way. Society is made up of many groups and in this new economy current changes have affected different groups in different ways. The question we consider in this section is: what is the impact of the post-industrial economy on different groups?

Overall Decline

The Bureau of Labor Statistics that collects data for the nation's hourly work force has clearly documented a decline in overall wages of American workers. Statistics for 52 percent of the workforce which totals 76 million of all workers—from mangers, professionals, to factory and construction workers—show a disturbing downward trend. Experts calculate that in order to achieve a middle class income, a worker must now make an hourly rate of $20. Using an adjusted rate for inflation, the data demonstrates an overall decline of wages for workers of 18 percent from the period of 1979 to 2007. The Bureau also indicates that the wages of salaried workers showed a similar decline and, given the current economic crisis and climbing unemployment, the trend is likely to continue (Bureau of Labor Statistics, 2007). By comparison the top CEOs of the 500 biggest companies received a 38 percent salary increase in 2007 (Forbes, 2007).

Table 14.2: Occupations with the Fastest Decline				
Occupations:	**Percent Change**	**Number of New Jobs (in thousands)**	**Wages-May 2008 Median**	**Education/Training**
textile bleaching & dyeing machine operators & tenders	-45	-7.2	$23,680	moderate-term on-the-job training
textile winding, twisting & drawing out machine operators & tenders	-41	-14.2	$23,970	moderate-term on-the-job training
textile knitting & weaving machine operators & tenders	-39	-11.5	$25,400	long-term on-the-job training
shoe machine operators, tenders	-35	-1.7	$25,090	moderate-term on-the-job training
extruding, forming machine setters, operators & tenders	-34	-4.8	$31,160	moderate-term on-the-job training
sewing machine operators	-34	-71.5	$19,870	moderate-term on-the-job training
semiconductor processors	-32	-10.0	$32,230	Postsecondary vocational award
textile cutting machine operators & tenders	-31	-6.0	$22,620	moderate-term on-the-job training
Postal Service mail sorters, processors, & machine operators	-30	-54.5	$50,020	short-term on-the-job training
fabric menders, except garment	-30	-0.3	$28,470	moderate-term on-the-job training
Wellhead pumpers	-28	-5.3	$37,860	moderate-term on-the-job training
Fabric & apparel patternmakers	-27	-2.2	$37,760	long-term on-the-job training
drilling, boring machine tool setters, operators & tenders, metal & plastic	-27	-8.9	$30,850	moderate-term on-the-job training
lathe, turning machine tool setters, operators, tenders, metals & plastic	-27	-14.9	$32,940	moderate-term on-the-job training
order clerks	-26	-64.2	$27,990	short-term on-the-job training
coil winders, tapers & finishers	-25	-5.6	$27,730	short-term on-the-job training
photo processing machine operators	-24	-12.5	$20,360	short-term on-the-job training
file clerks	-23	-49.6	$23,800	short-term on-the-job training
derrick operators, oil,gas	-23	-5.8	$41,920	moderate-term on-the-job training
desktop publishers	-23	-5.9	$34,600.	Postsecondary vocational award
Source: BLS Occupational Employment Statistics and Division of Occupational Outlook.				

In examining income it is important to note the number of hours worked. Data here suggest that American workers are working longer hours for their wages. In 1980, the average American worker clocked 1,833 hours of work each year. By 1999, the average hours worked increased to 1,996 (The Des Moines Register, Sept. 1, 2003).

Gender

While income levels for working men have declined in the last three decades, the opposite appears to be true for women. Today, more and more women are entering the workforce. In part, this is due to changing attitudes allowing women more freedom to choose between home and careers. Another facet of this relatively recent phenomenon is that in a time of declining incomes for males, many women have found themselves forced into the workforce to shore-up slipping household incomes.

While it is still true that women earn less than men do, it is equally true that the gap has narrowed over the last forty years. In the late 1960s, full-time women workers earned 57 percent of what full-time male workers earned. In 2002, women's hourly wage was 78 percent of that of men. Some have suggested this is less than a real gain for women since corporations have eliminate more white males and replaced them with highly qualified women, but with less pay (Women's News, 2003). Data supporting this possibility shows that between 1973 and 1993 real income rose for women by 19.6 percent while that for men declined by 3.4 percent (Bianchi, 1995). As a result, both men and women lose. The real question is, who wins?

It is interesting to note that not all researches agree women are treated unfairly in the labor market. They suggest that if you factor into the equation all differences in age, occupational choice, and experience, the wage gap between men and women disappears. However, critics point out that women make different choices and have less experience due to socialization experiences that prepare them for childbirth and care. Likewise, they contend, even accounting for the above, women are at a disadvantage in the labor market due to gender discrimination (Women's E News, 2003).

In the late 1970s, sexual harassment was first defined as a form of sexual discrimination under Title VII of the Civil Rights Act of 1964. The guidelines defined sexual harassment as: Unwelcome sexual advances, requests for sexual favors, and other conduct of a sexual nature. . . when (1) submission to such conduct is either explicitly or implicitly a term or condition of an individual's employment. Quid pro quo sexual harassment occurs when decisions on hiring, firing, promotion, and salary are based on an employee's submission to sexual demands. If the demands are rejected and the employee suffers adverse consequences as a result, the employer has engaged in sexual harassment (Robinson, Jackson, Franklin & Hensley, 1998).

Race

It is difficult to accurately determine the effect of race on work and income since socioeconomic background and education are also factors in wage

As more and more jobs are shifted overseas, Americans are becoming increasingly sensitive to "outsourcing." Here, a small business owner vents his anger by posting a sign to indicate that his products are American made.

Photo: SPP.

earning. Generally, as seen in Chapter Eleven, minorities have lower levels of education and as a result are segregated into lower paying jobs. Also, minorities often live in economically depressed neighborhoods and lack access to jobs leading to upward social mobility. Despite this, there are indications that minorities, especially African Americans, have been less negatively impacted by the new economy than white males. In 1973, median male income (full-time) was $35,109 in constant 1993 dollars. By 1993, it decreased to $31,077—an eleven-percent drop in income. When African American workers were studied as a group, their decline was 3.2 percent; a decline, but not nearly as severe. On the positive side, African American women registered a 19 percent gain in less than two decades. However, since the earnings of full-time white women workers increased rapidly, the gap between African American women and white women actually increased by two percent.

A partial explanation for the above is that the sharpest decline in income has been in jobs typically not held by minorities (Breslow, 1995). However, in a group comparison of well educated, well paid African Americans, it was found that income had deteriorated more than that of whites. In 1999, African Americans with the same educational qualifications earned 16 percent less than did their white counterparts (U.S. Census Bureau, 2000). In 1976, the difference was six percent. Race appears to remain a major factor in wage disparity.

SOCIOLOGICAL PERSPECTIVES

Structural Functional

Structural functionalists regard the division of labor and work as major integrative factors for society. Not only does the division of labor allow for greater efficiency and production which ultimately leads to a better standard of living and longer life, it also provides the cohesive glue that unites diverse groups in modern society. With a division of labor, people must depend upon each other to meet their basic needs. No one is self-sufficient. As such, cooperation and tolerance is demanded. Through this process, harmonious relations are maintained. In terms of wealth inequality, structural functionalists see this as an inevitable occurrence. Individual differences in talent, motivation, and desire for success, ultimately lead to wage differences, which in turn, lead to wealth differences. Rather than a negative consequence, structural functionalists argue that wage differences are a useful tool for filling society's need for qualified and talented workers. If all jobs paid the same, who would want to do the difficult ones? Who would want to work harder than co-workers do? In the absence of financial rewards, who would attempt to better themselves?

In addition to providing for the physical necessities of life, structural functionalists point out that work in modern society is psychologically satisfying. More so than in pre-industrial society, individuals are able to express their creativity. With modern technology, there is no limit to what can be achieved. Similarly, modern society has allowed for an expansion of freedom in individual life and in the collective society. The efficiency of the modern society allows for more leisure time to pursue individual interests and for time with loved ones. Likewise, the overall trend in the world is for increased democracy and freedom of expression. This, for the structural functionalist, is credited to market economies and technological advances in communication, such as the Internet.

Structural functionalists will agree that many difficulties were encountered in the process of industrialization. Also, structural functionalists will admit that problems will be encountered in the new Information Revolution. This is to be expected. However, as these problems occur, the natural adaptive process of society will come into play to change society in ways to resolve the problems. These changes, though gradual, seek to reestablish order and cement members of society together.

Social Conflict

Social conflict theorists refute the base premise that division of labor is a cooperative, integrative force. In their view society is not cooperative and harmonious. Rather the bonds holding groups together are coercive and disintegrative. Workers have little power to control their lives in the workplace and are at the mercy of those who own and control production. The powerful use the competitive marketplace to pit worker against worker and to drive down wages and increase profits. Thus, cooperation between workers is all but impossible. Globalization of the economy and work has greatly aggravated the problem, not only for workers in this country, but for those abroad as well. Since the central focus of capitalism is the maximization of profit, the system is destined to be exploitative and destabilizing. This is obvious in the decline of overall wages in the United States and the disappearing middle class. As the profits of the powerful have greatly accelerated in the last two decades, real wages of workers have declined, further aggravating the division between the "haves" and the "have-nots." Likewise, as more and more families are forced into two-income situations, less and less time is available for parenting. Another very real and disintegrative effect of the new economy is that as the income-inequality/violence relationship increases so does crime. No industrialized country in the world has greater income disparity than the United States. Likewise, no other industrial country, other than South Africa, imprisons more of its people for crimes committed. Unlike structural functionalists who tout the democratization benefits of global capitalism, social conflict theorists argue the opposite: that global capitalism is a threat to democracy.

Social conflict theorists and structural functionalists both agree that work can be psychologically rewarding. Indeed, the relationship between work and self-esteem is well documented. Unfortunately, with the division of labor, workers have been alienated from their work. This leads to low self-esteem and discontent. From a social conflict perspective, this leads to the development of political instability and possible revolutionary change.

GLOBALIZATION: THE DEVELOPMENT OF A WORLD WORKPLACE

Increasingly, social scientists are coming to recognize the interdependence of world economies. The globalization of the economy, as it has come to be termed, has had a major impact on work, both in this country and abroad. The following are just a few of the major changes that have occurred.

First, the competition from workers abroad has increased dramatically. With the improvements in information technology and transportation, companies can now set-up shop virtually anywhere. Consider the following statistic. Presently, one out of every four workers in the world is from a first-world industrial nation. Due to increased globalization and the movement of manufacturing to Third World countries, this ratio is expected to decline. Estimates are that by the year 2050 it will only be one out of six (Bloom and Blender, 1993). What this means is that workers, including college graduates, in the United States will find it more difficult to secure employment.

Second, as we have already mentioned earlier, there will be an escalation in the loss of low-skill jobs. At one time in the United States the demand for physical labor was high. Hence, even if one did not possess much education, it was possible to find jobs that paid a viable wage working in various industries. With the advancement of technology, these jobs began to decline. Improvements in international transportation have accelerated the decline of such jobs. This trend is expected to continue as companies are forced to seek cheaper labor sources in order to effectively compete in the world economy.

Third, with increased competition from abroad, it is expected that wages will continue to decline in the United States. Intense international competition is directly responsible for this trend (Thurow, 1987). Today, over seven million workers from other nations, primarily Third World nations, are employed in manufacturing jobs that were once held by American workers (AFL-CIO, 2008). The implication of this is that a **global wage** is emerging in which wages are forced to the lowest possible denominator.

In other words, companies are saying to workers, "Either accept the new wage or your job goes abroad." While the global wage may in the short run help poorer nations, they wreak havoc in developed countries where the wages of workers have traditionally been high.

Two protest the move by Wisconsin Governor Walker to end collective bargaining rights of educators and public workers. The end of collective bargaining rights would essentially destroy unions and the power to bargain for wages and working conditions. Union membership in the U.S. has declined since the 1980s. Currently only about 12 percent of workers in the U.S. are union members. With the decline has come a decrease in wages and benefits for the average worker.

Photo: Maureen Madden.

Although the loss of jobs started with blue-collar workers, it has now spread to those in technical fields. Increasingly, people with technical skills from other nations are finding jobs in America. This is particularly true in the computer industry, where foreign workers sell their skills for a fraction of the wages demanded by technicians in the United States. The impact of low wages on the ability of workers to purchase goods has yet to be fully explored. Economists worry about the loss of discretionary income and the ability to buy the goods being produced. Such conditions have traditionally led to recessions.

A *fourth* consequence of the global economy is one we touched on earlier, that of downsizing. To compete in the global economy, companies are attempting to reduce expenses. The primary instrument used to accomplish this is reducing labor costs. Forrester Research, a financial consulting firm, predicts that within the next fifteen years, 3.3 million service jobs will be moved overseas (May, 2003).

Finally, the globalization of the economy has encouraged the development of multinational corporations. The simplest definition of a **multinational corporation** is a firm that owns and manages economic units in two or more countries. Although the size of these corporations varies, the end result is the same, a criss-crossing pattern of wealth and power. It is now estimated that one-quarter of the world's economic activity flows from only 200 companies in the world. This centralization of economic power in the hands of so few has enormous implications for **oligopoly** (few firms dominate the world market) and **monopolistic** (one firm dominates the world market) activity. With competing interests spread across the globe, multinational corporations have long ago lost their loyalty to any particular government. Moreover, they have used their wealth and power to control political situations in which they have economic interests, including control over wages and working conditions. It is highly unlikely that this situation will change in the near future.

Current Economic Problems and Changing Trends

At present, the economy of the United States is in crisis. With the collapse of the housing market and the ensuing bank failures, retirement and saving accounts of Americans have been devastated and hundreds of thousands have lost their jobs. In response to this crisis the government has allotted approximately a trillion dollars in bailouts and outright purchases of shares in financial institutions in an attempt to shore-up the economy.

In spite of this, experts predict that total employment is expected to increase from 150 million to 166 million by 2016, an increase of ten percent. The 15.6 million jobs that will be added will not be evenly distributed across major industrial and occupational groups, however. Changes in consumer demand, technology, and many other factors will contribute to the continually changing employment structure in the U.S. economy. Of the roughly 150 million jobs in the U.S. economy in 2006, wage and salary workers accounted for 138.3 million, self-employed workers accounted for 12.2 million, and unpaid family workers accounted for about 130,000. Secondary employment (second jobs) accounted for 1.8 million jobs. Self-employed workers held nearly nine out of ten secondary jobs and wage while salary workers held most of the remainder (U.S. Bureau of Labor Statistics, 2008).

SUMMARY

Total employment is expected to increase from 150.6 million in 2006 to 166.2 million in 2016, or by 10 percent. The 15.6 million jobs that will be added by 2016 will not be evenly distributed across major industrial and occupational groups. Changes in consumer demand, technology, and many other factors will contribute to the continually changing employment structure in the U.S. economy. Of the roughly 150 million jobs in 2006, wage and salary workers accounted for 138.3 million, self-employed workers accounted for 12.2 million, and unpaid family workers accounted for about 130,000. Secondary employment accounted for 1.8 million jobs. Self-employed workers held nearly 9 out of 10 secondary jobs and wage and salary workers held most of the remainder (U.S. Bureau of Labor Statistics, 2008).

It would be nice if we had a crystal ball so that we could take a quick peak at the future. But of course we don't, so we have to rely upon the past to give us directions for the future. In this chapter we have pointed to a number of significant trends that indicate a difficult future.

First we discussed two transformations of the economy. The *first* was the transition from agriculture to industrialization. The *second* major transformation was from an industrial economy to one centered on service and information. Each transformation has presented new challenges to workers. Unfortunately, the last one has had even more serious consequences than the first one. Current data clearly shows a serious decline in overall wages for American workers. Adjusting for inflation, the average American worker makes less now for the same hours worked than workers did in the 1970s. It is this factor that has led to a serious decline of the middle class in America. While it is true that some have profited handsomely from the new economy, many more have not. If this trend continues, America could well realize what Peter Glotz (1986) predicted we would become: the "two-third society." Here, only the top third of American workers, the technocrats, would be well paid. Glotz's two-thirds would include those in the middle who are not well paid and unsure of their jobs and the bottom third who consist of the unemployed and the underemployed.

Once, not so long ago, the American worker stood solidly on the top rung of the labor ladder. This is no longer true. How did it happen? As we saw in this chapter, the change resulted from the interplay between technology and competition abroad. This is the global economy and it has had a profound effect on the American worker. At one time we led the world in exports. The fact is we now import more goods than we export. As a result we were transformed from being the world's greatest creditor to the world's greatest debtor. This is what Harrison and Bluestone (1988) termed "the great American U-turn."

The great-unanswered question of course, is can we reverse the trend? To do so a number of events must occur. *First*, Americans must save more than they presently do. At one time Americans saved seven percent of their household income. Today, it is a mere four percent. This, of course, has a lot to do with declining incomes. *Second*, America must invest more in research and development and education. At present, due to the lack of educational opportunities (undoubtedly tied to class and racial discrimination) we must import people with computer skills from abroad to fill industry's technical positions. *Third*, government must find new ways, through economic planning, tax subsidies, and individual saving incentives, to aid economic growth.

Our ability to move forward is ultimately dependent on the global economy. What happens in one part of the world impacts all economies. This is all too clear as we nervously watch the Asian markets crumbling. Presently, we are in an unprecedented period of growth. This, as mentioned above, benefits some more than others. However, if the present at-risk global economies fail, it could create a world-wide domino effect in which all economies will suffer.

With all this in mind, the only prediction that we can reasonably be sure of is that major changes are ahead for workers. Based upon past experience, we know the readjustment will be difficult. Likewise, we can predict that changes in work will bring change to other institutions of society such as the family, education, politics, as well as others.

Terms You Should Know:

Outsourcing	Predestination	Decertify
Taylorism	Fordism	Division of Labor
Oligopoly	Multinational Corporation	Outsourcing
Green Revolution	Global Wage	Virtual Workplace

Can You Answer These Questions?

1. Describe the four major historic economic transformations.
2. What is the critical difference between Fordism and Taylorism?
3. How did Karl Marx view social inequality as a result of the Industrial Revolution?
4. What was Karl Marx's stance on the benefit(s) of industrialization?
5. How would a structural functionalist compare to a conflict theorist's view of work and livelihood?
6. What are the fundamental causes of outsourcing?
7. How is outsourcing detrimental to American workers employed in service and manufacturing areas?
8. List some of the advantages of multinational corporations.
9. What is the difference between primary and secondary labor markets?
10. Discuss some of the reasons for the decline of labor unions.

Critical Thinking Exercises:

1. Is it plausible that outsourcing may be curtailed by the middle of the century?
2. Why is sexual harassment still an issue in the workplace?
3. Chapter nine addressed the issue of the 'glass ceiling,' whereby individuals are not promoted because of their gender and/or race. Is it possible to eliminate that sort of action informally in the workplace?
4. What do you foresee as the next major industry to boom in the future?

Society and Change

Part Five

Chapter Fifteen: *Population*
Chapter Sixteen: *Urbanism*
Chapter Seventeen: *Collective Behavior & Social Change*

William Holinde, the maternal grandfather of one of your authors, was born in 1896. Growing up in Kansas, he married, purchased some acreage of land, raised seven children, and spent the remainder of his life working his farm until he retired at the age of seventy-six and moved to a small house in a nearby community. He died several years later. For the most part, there was nothing really unusual or remarkable about his life. However, if we look more closely using our sociological imagination, we discover that his life, and the lives of all those living during those years, was distinguished by the time in which he lived. Here was the first generation to experience the rapid onslaught of modern change, the pace at which this change occurred had never been known to anyone living before. Let's think about the life of William Holinde in the context of the time in which he lived. Here was a man who began to farm using the labor of animals. In his lifetime he saw the development of the automobile, the expansion of phone systems, the airplane, the invention of television, the computer, and by the time he died, space travel. What is striking about this is that it occurred in one lifetime—from the "horse and buggy" era to man walking on the moon!

Take a moment to think about the change that will occur in your own lifetime and that of your children. Although there is no way we can predict what will happen, we do know that rapid change is a part of our future. In this section we consider some aspects of that change. In Chapter Sixteen we look at population and examine factors that influence population growth and decline. We will see that with advances in technology life expectancy increases greatly. This will have a profound effect on human society. We note that while some nations have effectively worked to limit population growth, others, primarily those in third world countries, continue to experience an explosion of new births. How will the world handle this growth? In Chapter Seventeen, we examine the changes in our communities. Specifically, we will look at urbanization, the factors influencing the rise of cities, their problems, and how urban planners propose to resolve urban decay.

In our final chapter, we will explore social movements and change in society. We will see how social movements are formed and how they differ from one another. We will also examine the forces of social and technological change and how they impact our lives and the institutions of society.

In each of the chapters in this section the underlying theme is change. Although we cannot accurately predict the future, accepting the inevitability of change and attempting to anticipate new directions is critical for the future.

Renato Valenzuela, Jr.

Chapter 15

Population

One only has to look into the classrooms at most elementary schools in China to discover that something is missing. What's missing? Well, watch as children scamper through the doorway of schools in the early morning hours and you will see significantly more boys than girls. A normal sex ratio in society should be 106 boys for every 100 girls, but in China it is 120 boys to every 100 girls. How did this happen? It happened because in 1979 the Chinese government, faced with unsustainable population growth in a society of 1.3 billion people, launched an ambitious program to limit the number of future births. Termed the "one-child policy," it mandated that each urban family was limited to one child and those in rural communities were limited to two. To enforce the policy, the government used economic incentives along with forced sterilization and abortions. In extreme cases, for those who refused to be sterilized and fled, the government incarcerated parents, siblings, and relatives to apply pressure. Under heavy criticism from international groups, the Chinese government in 2002 moved away from forced sterilization and mandated abortions to achieve goals. These practices continue, however, in rural communities.

So, was China's one-child policy successful? Well, the answer is complicated. Although harsh, the one-child policy is credited as an important component in China's economic success by preventing the addition of hundreds of millions of new people to its population. In this sense it was a resounding success. On the other hand, two-and-a-half decades later, as we watch the children on their way to school, it is evident that the policy produced some serious latent consequences.

The *first* latent consequence was the result of a strong cultural preference for boys. Consequently, a number of methods were used to ensure that the family ended-up with a boy. This included female infanticide (killing of babies), abandoning girls along roadsides, and the use of ultrasound tests to determine sex and then aborting female fetuses. The result is an overabundance of boys in the society.

A *second* latent consequence is that since China has always relied heavily on family to care for aging parents, this tradition is in danger. With increased competition for wives, it is highly likely that many young men will leave their community and families in search of eligible women to marry. This will leave many of China's elderly without anyone to care for them.

A *third* latent consequence is that the shortage of women has resulted in trafficking of women. In a society where young, marriage-age women are scarce, their economic value has increased greatly. This has proven to be too great a temptation for poor families who sometimes sell their daughters to the highest bidder.

The *final* latent consequence of China's one child policy is just now coming to light. When all of these boys begin reaching adulthood, it will be impossible for all of them to find women to marry. This will lead to severe competition for wives. One estimate is that within 20 years China will have about 30 million unmarried men. These "bare branches" as they are called in China, will constitute the losers in the bride competition. Most likely, they will be poor and uneducated. This is a critical social problem since it is well established that males 15 to 35 years-of-age commit most crimes. This coupled with the fact that since these men will be stigmatized as losers and outsiders, it is highly probable that they will band together in anti-social groups.

China's one-child policy is now being played out in another of the world's most populated countries—India. As India's population topped the one billion mark, it was inevitable that a slowing of population growth was needed. However, given the experience of China, is there a better way to accomplish the goal? In this chapter we will explore the topic of population. When concluded, perhaps you can offer your own insights as to how to maintain a balanced, sustainable population.

DEMOGRAPHIC CONCEPTS

In social science, the study of population is termed **demography** and the individuals who study it are called **demographers**. The term itself is derived from the Greek language meaning "description of people" and describes the essential task of demographers, which is counting people. Although this might sound like a benign activity, its importance is fundamental to the major issues and conflicts throughout the world. For example, knowing the number and distribution of people in any one nation, or in the world, helps social scientists explain poverty, environmental problems, food distribution, crime, birth and death rates, migration patterns, disease, famines, and a host of other issues. Once tabulated, the information is a valuable source to governments in planning for schools, housing, hospitals, highways, communication networks, military recruitment, Social Security, and many more areas of governmental responsibility. Business relies heavily on population data to determine shifting markets and new products and technologies that need to be developed. And, though not in a technical sense, individuals use knowledge of population trends in determining when and if to marry, how many children they can afford, how much of family funds to allot to housing, food, education, and health care. So, you see, the study of population is crucial to every phase of life and human activity.

Like in any field of study, demographers have developed a special vocabulary and set of concepts to assist them in explaining their observations. In the following section we will examine the vocabulary and concepts demographers use and see how they help us to make sense of the information presented in this chapter.

Birth and Fertility Rates

One of the first concepts we will discuss is one that is most fundamental to the study of population — **birth rates**. This statistic is a measure of the number of births in a population each year. Birth rates are computed as births per 1000 people per year. Although this is a useful statistic, it does have its limitations. The most obvious one is that not everyone in the population is giving birth—only women and, more to the fact, only those of childbearing age. A more accurate measurement of population growth is the **fertility rate**, which is a measure of births per woman over a lifetime. Using these data, social scientists can chart average family sizes and changes in population rates within, and between, countries. For example, the fertility rate in Ethiopia is 6.17 while that in the United States is 2.1 (World Fact Book, 2008). Using this measure one can assume that the average family in Ethiopia has approximately six children, while the number of children in a typically American family would be two. For the most part, this is an accurate picture. Using this statistic, demographers can make predictions about the future for each country. For example, the population of the United States – located on one of the world's largest landmasses - is roughly 300 million. Ethiopia, on the other hand, has a population of about 68 million but is slightly less than twice the size of Texas (Siakhenn, 2005). Using this information, one can easily understand why Ethiopia will have difficulty sustaining its population in the near future unless its fertility rate declines.

Another term that is sometimes confused with fertility rates is **fecundity** or the number of children a woman is capable of bearing in her lifetime. Biologically, a woman can give birth to about 20 children in her reproductive lifetime although this rarely occurs anywhere in the world today. Worldwide the fertility rate is now 2.8.

Death Rates, Mortality Rates, and Life Expectancy

As important as they are, birth and fertility rates are only one piece of the population puzzle. Death and mortality rates are equally crucial to our understanding of population growth and decline. The **death rate** is the measure of deaths per thousand people each year. While this, like the birth rate, is important to know, it does not present a complete picture of who is dying, their age at death, and how those deaths affect a population. Are more older or younger people dying? At what age are they likely to die and how will this affect future growth or decline?

To overcome this limitation, demographers developed the **mortality rate**. This measure is age-specific, delineating the number of deaths in a specific age group per 1000 people in a population. Insurance companies use this measure to determine how much to charge for life insurance. This measure is also used to determine **infant mortality**, or the number of infants who die during their first year of life. Why is this important? Well, for one reason, if infant mortality is high, it could signal problems for the society down the road. Who will tend the crops or work in industry in a decade or two? How will such early deaths affect population growth? How will it impact governmental planning for schools, hospitals, resource distribution, and care of the elderly?

Also important to demographers is **life expectancy**, the number of years the average person can expect to live. In the United States, life expectancy has risen from 47 years in 1900 to its present figure of 78.06 years. While this dramatic increase is good news, it is also important to know that many other countries have significantly higher life expectancies. People live longest in Andorra, where the average number of years one can expect to live is 83.5; in Japan, it is 82.02 while Singapore's life expectancy is 81.8 and that for Sweden and Switzerland is 80.63 and 80.62 respectively. This information provides important insights about the health and culture of societies (CIA World Factbook, 2007).

Used together, these tools allow social scientist to compare societies and understand changes in population. Going back to our original example, you remember that Ethiopia has a very high fertility rate in comparison to that of the United States. However, it also has a very high infant mortality rate; 103.22 compared to 6.75 in the United States (www.geographyiq.com). Knowing this, it's not hard to understand why the fertility rate is so high among Ethiopian women. Since so many infants die, there is a huge burden placed on women to produce more babies so that families remain stable. This, of course, is true only as long as infant mortality remains high. What happens when the infant mortality rate begins to decline and the fertility rate remains the same? Would not this be a prescription for a population problem?

Figure 15.1 World Population Growth Rates 1950-2050

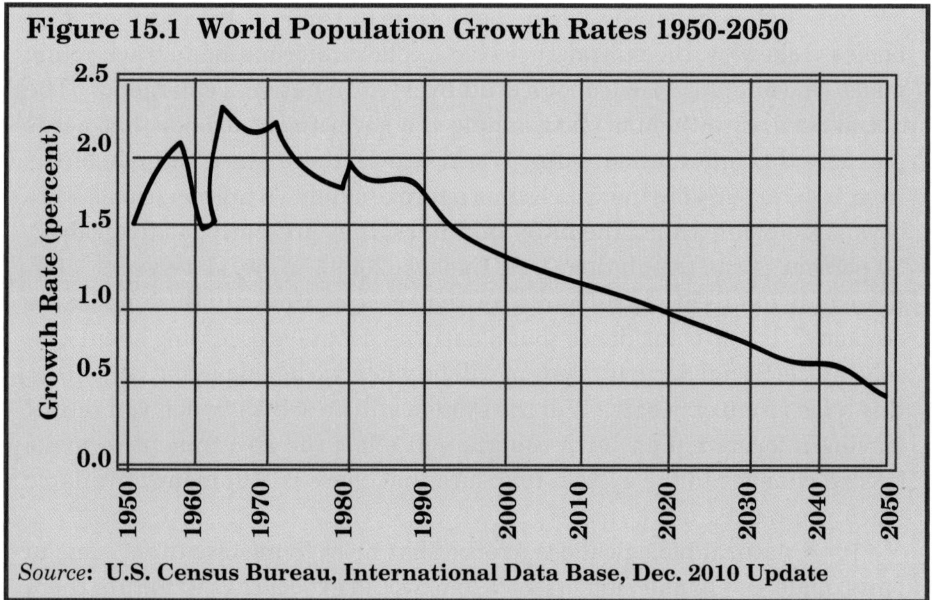

Source: **U.S. Census Bureau, International Data Base, Dec. 2010 Update**

Growth Rate

With the above concepts in mind, we are ready to understand how demographers calculate the growth rate for a society, as well as for the world. Simply stated, **growth rate** is the difference between the number of deaths and the number of births in a society, while accounting for immigration (people entering a country to become citizens) and migration (people leaving a country, relinquishing their citizenship). As with our other measures, this rate is expressed per 1,000 people in the population. While immigration and migration do not figure into the overall growth rate they do influence the growth rate of individual countries. As an example, although the fertility rate of American women is relative low, the country shows a positive growth rate, which is due to immigration. As seen in Figure 15.1, the world's growth rate is presently 1.2 percent per year and is expected to decline in the future.

Another easy way to gauge the population growth of a country is to take its growth rate and divide it into the number 70. This will yield the amount of time it will take to double a population. With a growth rate of 0.9 percent, Canada should double its population in about 78 years. Afghanistan, with a growth rate of 4.8 percent, will double its population in less than 15 years (Rosenberg, 2011). It is an unfortunate fact that worldwide those countries with the highest growth rates are also the ones who currently struggle to support their present population.

Cohort and Sex Ratio

In order to study populations, demographers have developed the concepts of birth cohort and sex ratio. **Birth cohort** simply refers to all of the people born in a particular year. This information allows for businesses and governments to plan for the future. For example, people who build homes are interested in knowing the number of young people coming into adulthood because that is generally when they begin to think of buying their first homes. Likewise, the military uses birth cohort information to track young males who might be needed for a draft in case of a national emergency. The Social Security system is one example of a government agency that needs and uses this information. After World War II, there was a surge in births from 1946 to 1964 during which time approximately 76 million people were born. Commonly called the **baby boomers,** they presently make up about 30 percent of the population (U.S. Census, 2009). Now, sixty years later, these individuals are coming into retirement age. How will this impact the economy? It's no coincidence that a national debate is occurring about how solvent the Social Security system will be when we begin paying benefits to this huge group of people. Will the system still be solvent when you retire? Having information on birth cohorts will allow the government to make needed changes to the system to insure that there is still money available when you retire.

It's a natural biological occurrence that most living creatures come in pairs, male and female, and as such, one would expect that in nature there would be equal numbers of each. Generally this is true, but not exactly. In human populations around the world there are about 100 girls born for every 105 boys. However, infant mortality for boys is slightly higher than it is for girls. Hence, the population is in balance. This calculation is referred to as the **sex ratio**. Unfortunately, humans can interfere in the natural order of events. It is well documented that female infanticide has been practiced throughout history due to cultural preferences for boys (Guttentag and Secord, 1983). Two countries that have received the most attention for female infanticide practices are China and India. As indicated in the opening section of this chapter, this manipulation of the sex ratio can have devastating consequences for society. In both countries, the government is attempting to deal with the problem though a series of legal and educational measures. However, the practice continues in many rural areas of both countries. In China, when a woman goes into labor, midwives often bring a bucket of water. If the baby is an unwanted girl, she is plunged into the

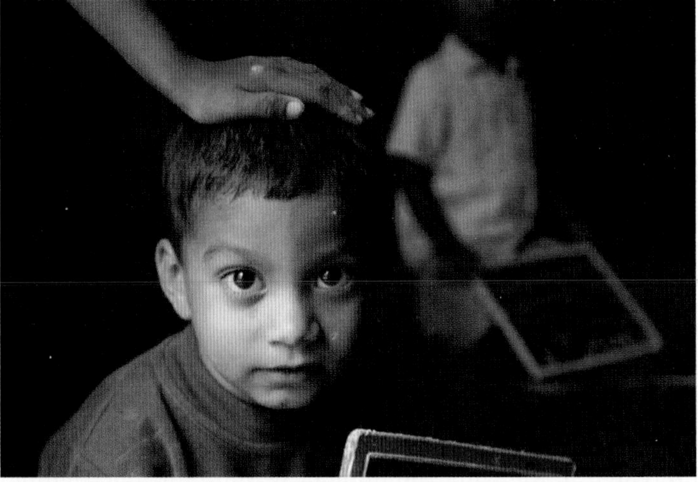

A proud parent pats the head of her child. Males are highly valued in both Indian and Chinese cultures. Attempts to control the population have resulted in the unintended consequences of female infanticide. UNICEF estimates that there are up to 50 million missing girls in India alone. In a generation, the ratio of males to females is expected to be 130 to 100, creating a severe shortage of females.

Photo: Pratham Books.

Figure 15.2: Population Pyramids - Sex and Age Distribution

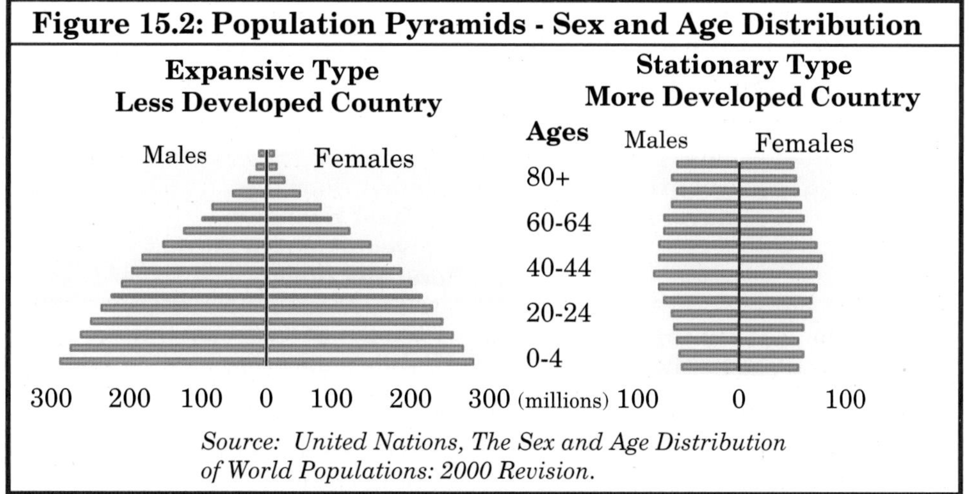

Source: United Nations, The Sex and Age Distribution of World Populations: 2000 Revision.

bucket before she draws her first breath. In India, unscrupulous doctors with portable ultra-sound machines travel from village to village, charging about $11 for each test, and if the fetus is an unwanted girl, they abort, charging an additional $44. This practice has resulted in an estimated 10 million abortions or murders over a twenty year period (Porras, 2007)). India will soon face the same dilemma as China. Wars and famine also contribute to an unbalanced sex ration.

To obtain a picture of a society, demographers use what is termed an age-sex pyramid. This is a graphic representation of the number of age-related males and females there are in society. This information can be used to gain an overall picture of the society and also help demographers understand future population trends. Of the two pyramids in Figure 15.2, the one of the left is an **expansive pyramid.** As you can see, the bottom of the pyramid is wide and narrows to the top. The implication is that there is a built-in momentum for future growth since a large segment of the population is below the age of 15. Expansive pyramids are more representative of lower-income nations. India is a nation with an expansive pyramid. At the beginning of the twenty-first century, India's population was nearly 1 billion. Even if birth rates began to decline to levels similar to North America and Europe, by 2025 their population would still reach 1.4 billion, making India the most populated country in the world (Constable, 1999). On the right of our illustration is a **stationary pyramid** where there are a relatively equal numbers in all age groups. The only exception is at the very top for older members of the society. The conclusion here would be that the population is relatively stable and will remain so for the future. Stationary pyramids are characteristic of more developed nations.

Population pyramids can also show distortion in the ratio of males to females. As we shall see later in this chapter, such a ratio has important implications for future births.

Table 15.1 Three Escalations in Human Populations

Year	Name	Reason for Growth
8000 B.C.E.	Neolithic Revolution	Global warming Animal Husbandry Development of pottery and Metallurgy
1750 C.E.	Industrial Transformation	Changes in Transportation Public sanitation Food supply and diet
1945 C.E.	Modern Era	Advances in Medicine and Pesticides

HISTORY OF WORLD POPULATION

As is true with most issues, it's only possible to understand the present if one has a sense of what has happened in the past. In this brief section, we will look at the history of population growth in the world. Demographers generally agree on three distinct periods of population growth: The Neolithic Revolution, The Industrial Transformation, and The Modern Era. See Table 15.1.

The Neolithic Revolution

Although no one is quite sure of the exact date when humans first appeared on earth, we do know that for most of the time our ancestors lived a nomadic existence, traveling from place to place in search of game, edible plants, and water. They consumed what they could and, when the supply ran out, they simply moved on to another location. Life was harsh and precarious. Death rates and infant mortality were high and life expectancy was short. As a result, there was great pressure to produce as many children as possible for survival. Even so, the population of the world grew very slowly.

Sometime around 8,000 BCE, with global warming on the rise, humans began to domesticate animals and developed the arts of horticulture and agriculture. With the ability to raise animals and crops, humans began to establish permanent settlements. Additionally, as they began to refine their techniques and develop better tools, they found that they could produce more food (a surplus) than was needed at any one given time. This surplus of food was the critical stage in population growth because it allowed for the feeding of more people. The surplus of food also allowed humans the ability to exert some control over death. More food meant better nutrition, which improved life expectancy. It was at this time that the world population began to climb.

It should be mentioned, however, that life was still far from easy. Populations did increase, but they also declined at times due to droughts, floods, insect plagues, and disease. So, the world population began to grow at this time, but it did so with sharp spurts and declines.

Industrial Transformation

Our second major escalation in population was brought about by the transformation of the economy relying heavily on agriculture to when industrial production became the focus. Starting in Europe in the 1700s, there began a shift from relying on animals and humans as a major source of energy to the use of inanimate power sources such as water and fossil fuels. This allowed for the production of goods far in excess of what was previously possible. In concert with this change came the development of new forms of transportation allowing for the exchange of goods from one geographic area to another. Harnessing this new energy, along with the development of new machines, allowed humans to produce even great qualities of food and to transport them to areas where shortages occurred.

It was also during this period that substantial improvements were made in sewer systems and sanitation, which allowed for the control of deadly diseases, like cholera, that are spread when waste enters the drinking water supply. Better sanitation and sewer systems encouraged the growth of cities that, in turn, supplied the labor for the factories that increased production. Consider two recent disasters—the Indian Ocean Tsunami in 2004 and the Haitian Earthquake in 2010. Although an exact figure in each is impossible to calculate, it is estimated over 200,000 people were killed. In both cases, a major fear was the outbreak of cholera, as well as other devastating bacteria-born illnesses, that could kill hundreds of thousands more. Had it not been for the swift action of world governments, supplying fresh water, food, and medicine, this surely would have occurred.

In summary, the two major factors that influenced the increase in population during the Industrial Transformation were the ability to produce and transport more food, and improvements in sanitation and sewer systems. In other words, fertility rates remained, for the most part, stable, while death rates declined.

The Modern Era

The modern era, beginning in the 1950s, is credited with increasing world population as a result of the development of modern medicine. Up until this period, the only check on some of the world's most dreaded diseases was improved sanitation. While this did help, it did not protect humans against major outbreaks capable of taking the lives of millions. As an example, consider the Spanish influenza outbreak of 1918-19 where over 50 million people worldwide, 500,000 in the United States alone, died as it spread from country to country, individual to individual. Today, with the development of antibiotics, immunizations, and insecticides (like DDT to stop malaria-bearing mosquitoes), modern medicine and technology has been able to either prevent or greatly control outbreaks of fatal diseases. Too, once developed, these medicines and technologies were transported to developing countries with high death rates. The result was a dramatic decrease in the death rate worldwide and that, of course, is good news. But, a new problem emerged because while the fertility rate in developed

Thomas Malthus

societies declined naturally as the people adjusted to their new reality, in developing nations the fertility rate remained high. Hence, the population of those countries began to rise dramatically, in many cases, way beyond the means of the society to support its increased members.

POPULATION THEORY

Concern with world population in not a recent phenomenon. A number of individuals began looking at potential problems with population growth as early as the sixteenth century. It was during this time, around 1750, that the Industrial Transformation caused the world's population to turn sharply upward, reaching one billion people by 1800. The first to take note of this alarming trend was Thomas Malthus.

Malthusian Theory

Malthusian theory developed from the writings of an English clergyman named Thomas Robert Malthus who spent his life teaching history and political economy. While he was an outspoken critic of two institutions in society, the church and slavery, it would be his theory on population growth that would distinguish his academic career. In 1798, he published a controversial work titled, *Essays on the Principle of Population.* Here, Malthus warned that the population of the world was increasing faster than the supply of food. According to his calculation the food supply increased in an arithmetically progression (1, 2, 3, 4, etc.), whereas population increased geometrically (1, 2, 4, 8, 16, etc.). Although Malthus conceded that improvements in agriculture could increase food supplies, he believed that it could never keep up with the geometric growth that he predicted in the population. Inevitably, demand would outstrip supply and result in mass starvation that, in turn, would wreak social chaos (Malthus, 1798).

Interestingly, while arguing for population control, Malthus steered away from birth control due to his religious beliefs. Instead, he proposed that people control the number of children they had by marrying later and practicing sexual abstinence in marriage. As you might guess, this idea failed to gain acceptance and since he had little else to offer in the way of population control, Malthus was tagged with an infamous title, that of being, "a dismal parson."

Karl Marx

At the time Karl Marx was formulating his theory on political philosophy, Malthusian theories were still being heavily debated throughout Europe. However, Malthusian theory sharply conflicted with the socialistic ideas that Marx promoted. According to Marx, overpopulation was not the cause of social unrest. Instead, he believed that social unrest was the result of the unequal distribution of resources, which is inherent in a capitalist society. Further, he maintained that there was no relationship between world population and the supply of resources. If societies were ordered fairly, any increase in population should lead to greater wealth, including in the production of food. Marx maintained that in capitalistic societies the relationship between the bourgeoisie (owners) and the proletariat (workers) was exploitive in favor of the former. Owners needed large pools of unemployed workers in order to hold down labor costs and increase their profits. Thus, overpopulation was a creation of capitalism for the benefit of the affluent class at the expense of those in the working class.

The importance of Marx's work is that it was the first to link overpopulation to the distribution of resources and the political system. Modern-day followers of Marxist views point out that worldwide hunger is not a result of overpopulation. There is, in fact, an abundance of food. The real problem is that those nations with low fertility rates consume a disproportionate share of the world's resources, including food. Hence, obesity is a problem for developed nations while for developing nations it is malnutrition and starvation. While this may be true, those who oppose Marxist thought on population point out that medical advances, which lower death rates, allow for greater numbers of people taxing a limited supply of arable land and fresh water supplies. No matter how fair the distribution of resources may become, increasing the population cannot continue without dire consequences. Whichever theory makes more sense to you, one can accurately state that both Malthus and Marx made valuable early contributions to our understanding of population.

Who is Correct?

Perhaps the answer to this question lies with a new theoretical branch sometimes refer to as **neo-Malthusians**. The popularity of this view began with the publication of *The Population Bomb* by Paul Ehrlich, in 1968. Neo-Malthusians bridge the gap between Malthus and Marx by accepting elements of both theories. On the one hand, they agree with Malthus that

Table 15.2: World Population Growth and the Time It Took to Double

Year	Population	Time to Double
8000 BCE	5-10 Million (est.)	Uncertain
1650 CE	500 Million	9,650 yrs.
1804	1 Billion	154 yrs.
1927	2 Billion	123 yrs.
1974	4 Billion	47 yrs.
2011	6.8 Billion	

Source: www.UN.org/esa/population/publications/6Billion

the world's population is dangerously out of control. As seen in Table 15.2, it took only forty-seven years for the world's population to double from 2 billion in 1927 to 4 billion in 1974. Demographers predict that the world's population will again double to 8 billion by the year 2025. At this rate, the population growth will exceed the world's natural resources. Here, neo-Malthusians seem to agree with Malthus. However, departing from Malthus original premise, they believe that humans are capable of controlling their own destiny through modern science, education, and birth control. In many ways, they tend to support demographic transition theory. Finally, neo-malthusians take on a Marxist flavor in their condemnation of developed nations that consume a disproportionate share of the earth's resources while doing little to assist underdeveloped nations in uplifting themselves. In fact, in many cases the policies of the developing nations can be viewed as exploitative. For instance, developed nations work with corrupt and brutal regimes in order to maintain a flow of vital resources to their nations. For neo-Malthusians, a more equitable distribution of resources is needed to insure that a sustainable existence can be provided to all of the world's citizens.

Demographic Transition Theory

In 1929, sociologist Warren S. Thompson proposed the **demographic transition theory**. According to this theory, population passes through a series of four stages as seen in Figure 15.3. In stage one, the *preindustrial stage*, both fertility and birth rates are high. Having many children is desirable since it guarantees the survival of the tribe and family. In this stage, children have economic value since human labor is a necessity of life. High fertility rates are also maintained because no effective means of controlling pregnancy is available. However, countering the high fertility and birth rates was a high death rate due to poor nutrition, disease, war, and accidental death, etc. Consequently, population was kept in check by the natural order of the times.

Figure 15.3 Demographic Transition Theory

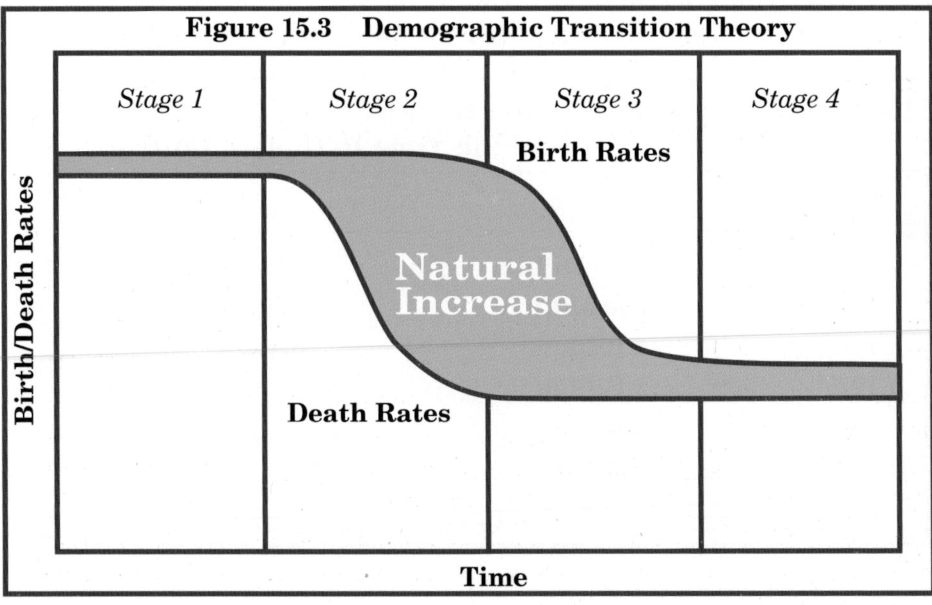

In stage two, the *transitional stage*, death rates begin to decline due to improvements in agriculture, sanitation, and medicine. However, fertility rates remain high and the population begins to climb dramatically. It was during this stage that Malthus and others began to take notice of expanding populations and the potential problem looming in the not too distant future.

In stage three, the *industrial stage*, fertility rates begin to decline as a result of a combination of factors. For one, more children reach adulthood, lessening the fear that parents could end up without children later in life. The economy evolves and the need for large families to farm declines. More and more people move to the cities to take jobs in factories. Suddenly, children become an economic liability rather than an asset. Moreover, science makes advances in birth control allowing families to plan the number of children they wish produce. As a result of these factors, and others, fertility rates come more in line with death rates and population growth begins to slow.

In stage four, the *post-industrial stage*, fertility rates decline further. Contributing to this decline are cultural and economic factors. *First*, our cultural attitudes about career-oriented women change. Prior to World War II, the appropriate role for women was that of mother and homemaker. After the war, more and more women began to make their way into the workplace. As this trend increased, women began to postpone pregnancy and limit the number of children they had so that they could pursue careers and income. In 1900, only 20 percent of adult women worked outside of the home (Kornblum and Julian, 1992). The number of dual income families increased to over 70 percent in 2000 (McGreger) and that number has not decreased. A *second* factor that has contributed to a declining fertility rate is the cost of raising children. Adjusting for inflation, a child born today will cost her family over $269,000 during the first eighteen years of life (USDA, 2007). With these figures in mind, it's understandable why many couples are choosing to become DINKS (Double Income No Kids).

FACTORS INFLUENCING POPULATION GROWTH

Population growth is not a natural event occurring evenly throughout the world. It is very much affected by economic, geographic, political, and cultural factors. In this section we will consider some of these factors.

Scarcity of Resources

Population growth cannot continue indefinitely; there is a limit to the number of humans that planet earth can support. Ecologists refer to this as the **carrying capacity**. The most common way to calculate the carrying capacity is to determine the net primary productivity (NPP), which is defined as the total amount of solar energy converted into biochemical energy through plant photosynthesis, minus the energy needed by those plants for their own life processes. Sounds complicated but, in essence, it is the total amount of food that the earth is capable of producing. Scientists calculate that using all plant growth on earth to support humans, the maximum carrying capacity of earth is 15 billion people.

Sudanese children from Darfur wait for food at a refugee camp. The crisis in Darfur is one of the worst humanitarian predicaments in recent time. The conflict is based not on religion, but race. Muslim Arabs living in Sudan have attacked black Sudanese in the west. It is estimated that 300,000 have died and over 2.5 million inhabitants of Darfur have been displaced. People in western Sudan have recently voted to secede to form a new country.

Photo: ned.com for social entrepreneurs.

Of course, our theoretical maximum carrying capacity could only be achieved under ideal conditions. When one looks at the distribution of people, land, and resources, the picture darkens considerably. First, 96 percent of the 3.6 billion of people that will be added between now and 2030 will occur in some of the most impoverished nations, those already exceeding their maximum carrying levels. The overpopulation of these areas has global consequences. Consider this: there is somewhere between one-third and one-half less forest on earth today than there was in the recent past. And at present, what remains is disappearing at an alarming annual rate of 32 million acres, equivalent to the size of Nova Scotia and New Brunswick combined (CBSNews, 2008). Lost are many species of plants and animals, not to mention clean water and breathable air. Imagine what this means to our future generations.

Droughts, Nationalism, War, and Genocide

The preceding information would most likely be advanced by the New Malthusians who contend that the world population is growing too rapidly and eventually will reach an unsustainable level. However, there are those, usually referred to as the Anti-Malthusians, who would refute this claim. For them, the problem lies in other factors. For instance, they would point to the developed countries where food is plentiful. In the United States and many other nations, the major concern of government is that its people are getting too fat. Medical experts have noted an alarming rise in obesity in the population for both children and adults, with a corresponding increase in many life-threatening illnesses such as diabetes and heart disease. In fact, statistics demonstrate that life expectancy is now on the decline for the current generation. Too, there is so much food that the U.S. government actually pays farmers not to plant fields. So, if there is so much food available, why do people die of hunger?

The answer to the above question is simply that not all nations are equally blessed. In many African nations a series of wars and droughts have created conditions that make it impossible for those countries to feed their people. This, of course, brings us to the problem of nationalism. If a particular country in Africa is in need and there is an overabundance of food in the United States, why don't we simply ship the food to the country in need? The answer is both political and economic. Farmers in the United States produce food to sell on the open market at a profit. If there is too much food, the profit margin declines. So, farmers restrict the amount of food they produce to maintain market value. Ok, but why not sell it to the nation in need? Well, in many cases, the nation in need lacks sufficient resources to pay market price. Of course, the United States government could step in to provide food to the needy nation. This would be considered foreign aid. But keep in mind that the government must pay the farmers for the food. The more a government gives in foreign aid, the more it must tax its own people. How many politicians do you think would relish the thought of going before their constituents to propose raising taxes? This is not to say that we don't give, we do. However, the act of giving must always be balanced with the reality of politics and economics—a reality that results in millions of people dying from malnutrition and starvation.

Another serious problem is war. Not all countries enjoy the stability of the United States or other developed democratic nations. On any given day you can turn to the news channel on your television and be confronted with a number of civil wars raging throughout the world. These wars naturally disrupt the supply of food. And even when other nations attempt to intervene and supply food, insurgents try to intercept the food for their own use or to prevent it from reaching the people who need it. It's an all too unfortunate fact that numerous aid workers have been murdered attempting to transport food to starving populations in war-torn nations. Too, in many cases, starvation has been used as a tool for genocide. In the Darfur region of Sudan, some 1.87 million individuals have been internally displaced as marauding Janjaweed militia groups have killed entire families, raped women and girls, burned homes, stolen cattle, and poisoned wells in an attempt to ethnically cleanse the region of non-Arabs (Unicef, 2005).

Industrialization

As stated above, there is a relationship between industrialization and fertility rates. Why is this true? Two main factors account for the relationship. *First*, in developing countries, family imparts additional status to both men and women. For women, who often have little education or opportunity, the number of children they bear determines personal value. Cultural values in developing countries generally demand that women bear children. Hence, the more children a woman bears, the higher her value. On the flip side, cultural values reward men for fathering many children. It is an expression of their manhood and, in many cases, a religious sign that they are blessed.

In many underdeveloped countries, culture and religious belief serve as barriers to the social advancement of women. One way to control population growth is for society to open educational and economical opportunities for women. In developed nations, women have fewer children.

Photo: Nicolas Rost for OCHA

Also, the more children a man fathers, the more likely he is able to fulfill another cultural obligation—maintaining the family name.

The *second* factor is expressed in terms of economics. In non-industrial societies, children are assets, providing labor in a subsistence economy. Having many children ensures that all the necessary work will be completed. Too, governmental services are limited or nonexistent so parents look to their children in later years to provide money, medical care, and physical support. In developed nations there is no need for an abundance of human labor. In industrialized societies much of the work has shifted to machines. Too, fewer individuals are needed for farming and many have moved to cities where land and homes are downsized. Here, children lose their economic value and, as a result, fertility rates drop. As stated previously, with the cost of raising a child to age seventeen at over a quarter of a million dollars, it is easy to understand why families limit the number of children they have.

Medical Advances and Birth Control

As we discovered earlier, in the transition phase of population growth there is a decrease in the death rate. This occurs when societies begin to industrialize, learn how to produce more food, learn modern methods of keeping water supplies clean and how to dispose of sewage and garbage in a sanitary way. While this alone contributes substantially to decreasing the death rate, it is not the entire story. Along with industrialization come improvements in technology and science—particularly in medical science. Diseases and plagues that once took millions of lives are now controlled through antibiotics, immunizations, and pesticides. Modern modes of transportation and communication allow medicines and chemicals to reach populations in developing nations, thus improving life expectancy. The problem, however, is that while death rates decline, the fertility rate remains high because of cultural values which give greater status to people with large families. Industrialization—which has not yet occurred—would change those values and fewer children would be born allowing for an improved standard of living.

Another major issue is the lack of access to birth control. In many countries, the use of birth control is discouraged or banned altogether. Both the Roman Catholic Church and some Islamic countries have hindered the dissemination of birth control knowledge and devices. For its part, the United States, under the Bush Administration, denied foreign aid to organizations that promote or perform abortions. Similarly, the United States has spoken out against provisions in the 1994 U.N. Conference in Cairo, which condoned abortion as well as sex education and condom use among teenagers (NOW, 2002). After his election, President Obama moved quickly to reverse the former president's policies (MSNBC, 2009).

Although much progress has been achieved in breaking cultural barriers to birth control, one must keep in mind that changes in population growth will not occur overnight. In many developing nations that have lowered their birth rates, a substantial part of the population base is young. For example, of the 840 million people living in sub-Saharan Africa half are under the age of eighteen (PRB, 2010). This large group, of course, will be having children of their own in the coming decades. An appropriate analogy here would be stopping an oil tanker at sea. You can stop the engines, but it's going to be a long while before the giant ship comes to a halt.

Empowering Women

Demographic experts have now come to realize that a key factor in controlling population in underdeveloped countries is equality for women. Dr. Nafis Sadiki, a United Nations expert on population control, captured the essence of this truth when she said, "Give women more life choices and they will have fewer babies" (Population Reference Bureau, 2002). However, to have more choices, women must first have access to quality education. Currently, two major factors deter women from achieving educational equality: scarcity of educational resources and local cultural values.

In the United States, as in most other developed western countries, education is considered a right for all citizens. This is not true of many developing nations where educational opportunities are scarce. When scarcity exists, a system of rationing develops with those at the top of the class system receiving the most of whatever there is to be rationed. Those at the bottom must then make choices. In the case of education, parents generally educate their boys rather than their girls in the belief that it is men who need education to best care for future families. Girls, on the other hand, are prepared for lives of being wives and mothers. Too, in developing nations with great fertility rates, young girls are kept close to home to help with household chores and to care for younger siblings.

In many nations religious beliefs, as expressed in cultural practices, place major restrictions on what a woman can and cannot do. Virtually all of the world's major religions are patriarchal institutions that subordinate women to men. In Christianity, the Bible declares, "Wives be subject to your husbands, as to the Lord. For the husband is the head of the wife as Christ is the head of the church." And, "Let a woman learn in silence with all submissiveness. I permit no woman to have authority over men; She is to be kept silent." In the Koran, it is stated that, "Men are in charge of women....Hence good women are obedient....As for those whose rebelliousness you fear, admonish them, banish them from your bed, and scourge them." In Judaism, a daily prayer recited by men is, "Blessed art thou, O Lord our God, King of the Universe, that I was not born a gentile. Blessed art thou, O Lord our God, King of the Universe that I was not born a slave. Blessed art thou, O lord our God, King of the Universe that I was not born a woman." Such values and beliefs have seriously limited the roles that women can perform in society. In essence, their only role is that of wife, mother, and homemaker. Under these limitations, it is little wonder that the education of girls seems unimportant.

Demographic experts have long noted a relationship between the education of women and the fertility rate. Providing women with more education allows them more opportunity to perform additional roles in society and thus lowers fertility. This fact is bore out in stark contrast between industrialized nations and those nations still developing.

AIDS/HIV

Although science has contributed much to life expectancy, we are still locked in a deadly war with bacteria and viruses. Perhaps the best example is that with HIV/AIDS. Prior to 1979 there were only eight reported cases. At the end of 1979, there were ten new cases. In 1980, 46 cases were reported; in 1981 it was 252. By 1989, the number of cases had risen to 105,990. According to estimates at the time, the "doubling rate" for AIDS was every five months. At this rate, and with no end in sight, the frightening possibility was that a worldwide pandemic was well on the way and beyond the means of science to control. Fortunately, the disease began to show signs of slowing in developing countries where the doubling rate went from five months to thirteen months in the mid-1900s (*U.S. News & World Report*, 1987). However, the original doubling rate of five months did take place in other less-developed countries, particularly those in what is termed sub-Saharan Africa. Although only ten percent of the world's population live in sub-Saharan Africa, it is home to more than 68 percent of all people living with HIV—some 25.4 million (Patton, 2009).

In 2009, it was estimated that 2.6 million new HIV infections occurred worldwide, including an estimated 370,000 children. Approximately one-half of all people who acquire HIV become infected before age 25. It is now the leading cause of death among 20-24 year olds (Patton, 2009). In this same year, roughly 1.8 million deaths were reported from AIDs or AIDs related causes (UNAIDS, 2010). In nine African countries in this region, life expectancy has dropped to below 40 years-of-age. One dramatic example is Swaziland, where in 2009 life expectancy at birth declined 20 years to age 31 (Avert, 2009).

Although women make up just a little over half of all persons infected worldwide with HIV, 98 percent live in developing countries where they comprise more than half of the HIV cases. For example, 2009 figures show that in sub-Saharan Africa, there were 12 million women living with HIV/AIDS compared to 8.2 million men (UNAIDS, 2010). Given this fact and the knowledge that the average lag time between infection and the development of AIDS is fifteen years, it is understandable why some demographers have predicted a catastrophic breakdown of the economic and social fabric of these countries.

Researchers have also noticed a sharp increase in AIDS infections in Asia. With 60 percent of the world's population, Asia has become home to the fastest-growing number of new infections. China, Indonesia and Viet Nam, which comprise 50 percent of Asia's population, are the leading countries with new infections (UNAIDS, 2010).

Although medical science has made progress in slowing the pace of this disease and in helping to prolong the lives of those affected, it remains a serious threat to world population. This is particularly true in developing countries where abject poverty and lack of adequate health care facilities hinder medical treatment. There is little doubt that the cultural and religious practices that disenfranchise women continue to play a major role in the spread of the disease.

International Migration

Births and deaths are not the only factors affecting the growth or decline in population. Demographic experts are also concerned with migration patterns. First, a definition of migration is in order. Migration refers to the permanent movement of people from one country to another. The reasons for migration are many and complex. For most people, the incentive to uproot and move to a different country is lack of economic opportunity in the country where they reside. This is certainly true of population growth in the United States, which began as a nation of immigrants. Even today, experts point out that up to 30 percent of our population growth is attributable to immigration. Seen another way, 12.6 percent of Americans today were born in some other country (Segal, UMA Anand, et. al., 2010). Although not everyone who immigrates to this country does so for economic opportunity, it is still safe to say that most impoverished people in the world still believe that the streets in America are paved with gold. Other countries that have experienced high rates of immigrations are Greece, Austria, Canada, and many Western European nations.

In many of these countries immigration has become a controversial issue. Many of the immigrants originate from Asian, African, and Middle Eastern countries and bring with them very different cultural patterns that often clash with existing values. As such, there is a period of unrest until the forces of assimilation unite the two cultures. Too, there are issues of unemployment, shortage of housing, increased educational expenses, and welfare assistance. These ultimately translate to a rise in anti-immigration feelings and, in some instances, violence. For example, in Germany, immigration has produced a rise in right-wing groups and major attacks on immigration. In the United States, the anti-immigration movement has been less violent and more political, calling for tougher immigration policies and stricter enforcement of existing laws regarding illegal immigrants.

Another important cause of immigration is escape from political, racial, and religious persecution. This has been especially true of Africa and Asia. Civil wars have caused literally millions of people to flee across borders in order to escape death. The United Nations estimates that there are over 21 million refugees in the world today (UNHCR, 2008).

POPULATION TRENDS IN THE UNITED STATES

Fertility Rates

The fertility rate in the United States has remained relatively low over the last few decades. This has motivated some demographers to predict that we could reach zero population growth. Under such a condition, deaths and births would balance out and the population would remain stable. Already, some thirty countries, most in Europe, have reached zero population growth. Although this might seem like a desirable condition, it does present problems. Declining fertility would mean an increasing number of older people in need of social services and medical care. This would place a strain on younger workers to provide the economic support necessary to support an older population. An example of this is Social Security. In 1950, the worker-to-beneficiary ratio was sixteen to one. Today, the ratio is 3.3 to one. And, according to some experts, within 40 years it will be two to one. Obviously, this is a problem!

However, while some demographers have expressed fears that we are approaching zero-population growth, most agree that the population of the United States will likely increase due to two major factors. *First*, while it is true that fertility rates have dropped among some segments of the population, fertility remains high among African Americans, Hispanics, and Asian Americans. *Second*, immigration rates are expected to increase over the next few decades. Data reveals that approximately one-third of the nation's population growth comes from immigration. By 2050, it is expected to account for 43 percent of our population growth. How does this compute in terms of numbers? Well, today the population of the United States has reached beyond the 300 million mark. By the year 2050, it is expected to increase to 391 million due to the combined forces of births, immigration, and increasing life expectancy.

Changing Immigration Patterns

Immigration is often referred to as the "bookend" demographic phenomenon of the twentieth century. In the first and last decade of the 20th Century over one million immigrants each year arrived in the United States to start a new life. In the decades between, immigration declined due to economic depressions and restrictive legislation. Although the numbers are comparable between the two decades, the origins and socioeconomic status of the immigrants differ greatly. At the turn of the twentieth century, immigrants originated from Italy, Austria-Hungary, Russia, Canada, Ireland, and England. New York City was the favored destination of European immigrants and at one time, around 1910, immigrants

Figure 15.4: Black Migration, by Region 1990-2000

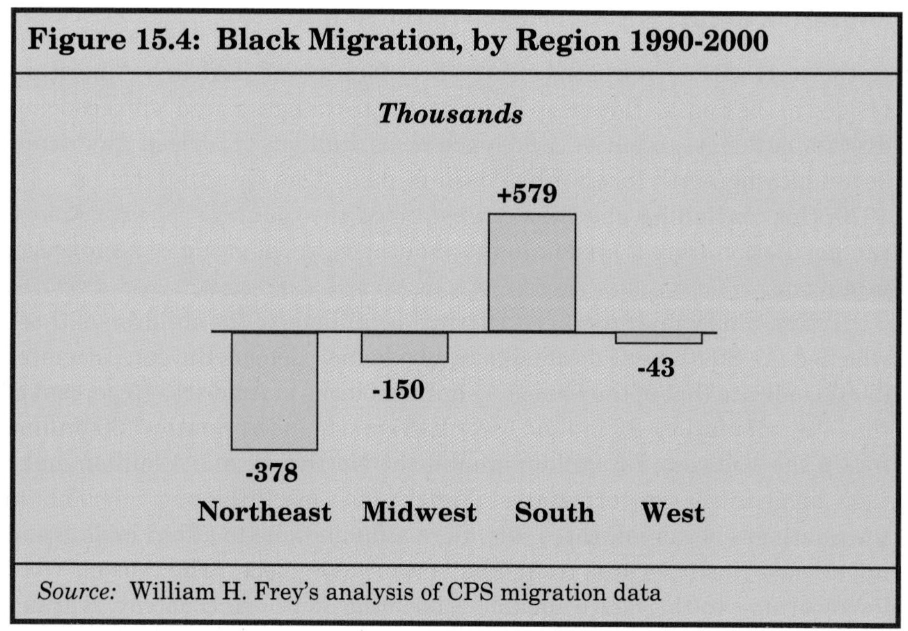

Source: William H. Frey's analysis of CPS migration data

accounted for 40 percent of the city's population. From the last decade of the twentieth century to the present, Central Americans and Asians have dominated immigration, arriving in Los Angeles, Chicago, and Miami; the most popular immigration destinations.

In terms of socioeconomic status, earlier immigrants, as expected, were less educated, held lower status jobs, and received less pay than the general public. With assimilation, however, one would expect these differences to decline and statistical data indicates that this has, in fact, occurred. Earlier immigrants have higher family incomes and higher status jobs than more recent immigrants. In fact, census data indicates that the median family income of those immigrants who arrived prior to 1980 is about the same as for native-born Americans (www.usinfo.sate.gov). The only anomaly appears to be educational attainment. On average, immigrants hold more educational degrees than native born Americans (Ohlemacher, 2007).

Changing immigration patterns have also been cited as a key factor in accelerating diversity in the United States. Past immigration trends created a predominately white and non-Hispanic society as evidenced by the fact that, in 1970, racial minorities comprised only 16 percent of total population. By 1998, the population of racial minorities rose dramatically to 27 percent. Furthermore, according to demographic experts, if the present trend continues, by the year 2050, approximately 53 percent of the population will belong to groups presently identified as racial minorities. Hispanics will become the largest minority group at 29 percent of the population, while African Americans will comprise 13 percent, and Asian Americans will increase from the current three percent to nine percent of the population (Pew Research Center, 2008).

Migration of African Americans to the South

At the start of the twentieth century, over 90 percent of African Americans resided in the South. However, this was soon to change. Faced with economic discrimination, segregation, and lynch mobs, millions of African Americans began moving north in what has been termed, "The Great Migration." By 1970, this continuing migration transformed the country's African American population from a predominately southern, rural group to a northern, urban one.

Today, a new migration is occurring as millions of the children of those who fled the South have decided to return home. Census Bureau estimates (2007) indicate that of the almost 41 million blacks in America (13 percent of the total population) 22 million (over half) reside in the South, 7.35 million live in the Midwest, 7.3 million inhabit the Northeast, and 4 million make their home in the western states. For the most part, the new migrants to the South are better educated and more affluent, able to afford middle and upper class lifestyles, and command better paying jobs. The reasons cited for returning to the South include a booming southern economy, warmer climate, improved racial relations, escape from the gangs and crime of northern cities, and a desire to rediscover their roots.

The Sun Belt Shift

In addition to the number of African Americans returning to the South, there has been a significant internal migration away from the Snow Belt (northeastern and north central states) to the Sun Belt (southern and western states). The 1970s marked the beginning of this trend, which has continued to the present date. In terms of numbers, the Sun Belt has attracted almost two-thirds of the new population growth in the United States. Many economists cite the movement of businesses to the Sun Belt as the catalyst for this migration. With cheaper energy costs, lower wages, and the absence of labor unions, businesses were able to operate more profitably. This in turn, produced more jobs luring workers away from the Snow Belt. Additionally, many seniors have moved to the Sun Belt in search of warmer climate and more affordable housing.

Baby Boomers

In 1946, the Census Bureau released a report predicting that the population of the United States would grow to approximately 165 million by the year 2000 (Jones, 1980). At that time, factors affecting population were relatively clear. Fertility rates were declining as more and more Americans moved from the farm, which required large families, to urban areas where smaller families were economically desirable. Thus, with demographic experts predicting declining death rates, fewer children, and stable sex ratios there was every reason to believe that zero population growth was on the horizon for the U.S. Of course, as we well know, this was not the case. Today,the population of the United States is more than 310 million (U.S. Census Bureau, 2011).

How did demographic experts miss the mark by such a large margin? The answer is quite simple—the baby boomers. This cohort represents everyone born between the end of World War II and the late 1950s. It is the largest group ever born in the United States, representing some 75 million people.

Rural Rebound

Throughout most of the twentieth century there was a steady movement of the population to major urban centers—those with populations of 50,000 or more. This trend suddenly began to reverse itself in the 1990s and continues today. For example, between 1980 and 1990, non-metropolitan areas grew by only 1.3 million residents while currently the rate of growth for such areas is 10.3 million. Likewise, in rural areas there was a net population loss in the 1980s whereas today there is a fourfold growth rate. Areas experiencing the greatest gains are in the Mountain West, Upper Great Lakes, Ozarks, parts of the South, and in rural areas of the Northeast. The only rural areas that posted a population loss are in the Great Plains, Western Corn Belt, and Mississippi Delta.

Several factors combine to contribute to the movement. The first is the peripheral growth of many metropolitan areas. With improvements in communication and transportation, many firms and families have discovered that they can enjoy the benefits of urban centers without having to deal with problems of congestion and high taxes. Too, concerns about crime, drug traffic, poor schools, gang activity, and pollution have driven many residents from the city. Another factor is the rebound of economic activity in rural communities. The recession of the 1980s has had a severe impact on the economy of rural communities resulting in the out-migration of many young rural residents to urban areas in search of work. This trend began to reverse itself in the late 1980s and continues today (AC, 2006). With more employment opportunities, young rural residents are electing to stay in the communities where they were raised (Johnson, 2001).

CONCLUSIONS

On the international front, the world exists in a schism. On the one hand there are a number of countries that have entered stage four of our demographic transition theory where fertility rates have declined in combination with improved mortality rates. As a result, they face a declining population, which presents problems; most particularly a shortage of workers to support an aging population. Likewise, with fewer workers, business and industry suffers which, in turn, produces perilous economic conditions for the whole of society. To augment its workforce, such countries have turned to immigration. However, this has created cultural clashes between newly arrived immigrants and the existing population. In Europe, particularly in France and Germany, there is bitter racial division between the two groups. So much so that a number of countries have turned to **pronatalist policies**. These policies encourage women to have more children through financial incentives. The ultimate hope here is that immigration can then be severely restricted to preserve the original culture. Of course, this is often counterproductive since the immigrants who have now become citizens of the country share in the incentive and tend to reproduce at a greater rate than do the women for whom the policy was intended.

On the other hand, third-world countries remain in the transitional stage with high birth rates and declining death rates. Each year the population of our planet grows by about 75 million people (U.S. Census Bureau, 2011). Most of this growth occurs in these underdeveloped countries which lack the food, housing, jobs, schools, medical care and political institutions to support their new citizens. Such conditions often engender internal strife and civil war, which only exacerbates the problem. Attempts to lower fertility rates, expand education, and expand opportunities for women fail more often than not, due to opposing cultural and political resistance.

What then, is the solution? Of course, there are no perfect solutions that will resolve all of the world's population problems. However, there are some actions that we can take that will put us on the right course. *First*, and foremost, the developed nations of the world must do more to reduce poverty in underdeveloped countries. Providing economic, educational, and medical assistance will enable these countries to begin on the road to self-sufficiency. *Second*, we must continue to encourage the leaders of these countries to move toward more open and democratic societies. It is a common observation that famine is rarely seen in a country with a true democratic government. Too, citizens rarely choose to emigrate when their native country provides for peace and economic opportunity. And third, governments must adopt policies that promote assimilation between its citizens and newly arrived immigrants. As the world continues to change, and the borders between countries become more fluid, it is inevitable that we will live among those from different lands and cultures. We desperately need to live together in peace and harmony recognizing that in the end, we all are citizens of the planet.

Let us now return to the question we asked at the beginning of this chapter. Given the experience of China's one-child policy, what advise could you offer to India in slowing its population to a balanced and sustainable level of growth?

Terms You Should Know:

Demography	Birth Rates	Fertility Rates
Death Rate	Mortality Rate	Infant Mortality
Life Expectancy	Growth Rate	Birth Cohort
Baby Boomers	Carrying Capacity	DINKS

Can You Answer These Questions?

1. Define the term "female infanticide." Where is it most likely to be practiced?
2. What is the difference between an expansive and a stationary age-sex pyramid? Which is more characteristic of developed countries?
3. Name and briefly discuss the three population growth periods.
4. How did Malthus and Marx differ in their theories of social unrest?
5. Who are the neo-Malthusians? How did they bridge the gap between the thinking of Malthus and Marx?
6. Name each of the four periods of the "demographic transition theory."
7. How is the "carrying capacity" of the earth calculated? According to this calculation, how many people can the earth support?
8. Why has the world's population growth slowed? Has growth slowed in all countries?
9. Where are most HIV/AIDS cases located? What are some factors that contribute to a higher HIV/AIDS infection rate in some countries rather than in others?
10. How is the immigration pattern of the United States changing?
11. What are some of the factors associated with the internal migration in the United States to the Sun Belt?
12. Define the term "pronatalist policy." How does it slow population growth?

Critical Thinking Exercises:

1. Technological advances in biology is bringing us closer to the time when couples can easily select the sex of their child. What might be some ramifications of this development?
2. The great forests of the world are rapidly disappearing. What can be done to encourage nations to preserve their forests?
3. Should the United States first require underdeveloped nations to adopt sound population policies before providing foreign aid? Can you suggest some policies that might be helpful?
4. In some countries the brith rate has reached a dangerously low level. What can societies do to encourage an increase in birth rates?

Photo: Chris Brown

Chapter 16

Urbanism

On a steamy Sunday afternoon, the residents of Mohawk North, an upscale condo development on the North side of Chicago, met for their third annual block party. About three dozen residents turned out to meet their new neighbors who had just moved in the week prior. The division lines were clearly evident. The African American residents, sixteen women with their children, sat in cheap plastic chairs with their backs against the wooden fence capturing what little shade there was. Across the courtyard, sat their affluent white neighbors. The contrast was inescapable, for although residents were separated by a distance measured in feet, their lives were a universe apart. Now, they were neighbors.

Bold and imaginative, Mohawk North represents an experiment in mixed-income housing that caught the attention and imagination of urban planners across the nation. Three years earlier, the CHA (Chicago Housing Authority) and developers of a piece of property located between the wealthy "Gold Coast" region and Cabrini Green, one Chicago's most notorious, crime-ridden housing projects, combined efforts. The plan was simple, 49 condos were built and sold from $200,000 and up. Seemingly high, the price of the condos was actually below market value and an exceptional buy. The only catch for those purchasing was that eventually, sixteen additional units would be rented to low-income, single families. These families, all sixteen, would come from

Cabrini Green, a housing project. CHA officials assured the resident-owners of Mohawk North that low-income families would be screened for criminal records and behavior characteristics. Likewise, all would be single parent families headed by a woman.

Developer Dan McLean and CHA officials defined the goals of the project. *First*, they wanted to show that all people regardless of race or background could live in harmony. *Second*, they wanted to demonstrate that scattered, low-income housing in affluent neighborhoods doesn't hurt real estate values.

On the owners' side, while there is hope, there is also trepidation. Concern has surfaced over a recent shooting of a girl at one of the schools, and a robbery of a resident at the front gate of the development. As one owner stated, "it's hard not to wonder if there is relationship." Also, many of the original owners feel that the renters pay too little for so much. Half of the low-income families are unemployed and pay as little as $3.00 per month in rent for a luxury condo. Others pay $230 or less (30 percent of their income).

On the renter's side, it's not been easy for the low-income families, either. At an initiation session before moving in, the Cabrini Green families were warned to expect some initial discrimination. CHA director, Wanda White, told the mothers, "the expectation is that you're gong to be loud, you're going to be raw, you're going to be bringing roaches." Having read the rules for all Mohawk North residents, one African American woman said, "I can see it already: If a white kid rides his bike on the sidewalk, it'll be fine. But if a black kid does—it's already in that rulebook that they can't."

Halfway into the block party the owners and their new neighbors remained separated. Finally, a woman from the owner's side walked up and grabbed one end of a jump rope with a mother from Cabrini on the other end and the woman's daughter began jumping. "This is all going to work out just as long as everyone plays by the rules." Thus began an experiment that may well become a model for the revitalization of our cities.

In this chapter we explore the urban community. First, we begin with a study of the origin of cities. Next, we move to urbanization and the theory of urban development. Too, in our reading, we will explore the relationship between urban environments and human behavior. Following this, we will consider the problems of cities, as well as some potential solutions. Finally, we will examine cities, as always, from the structural functionalist and social conflict perspectives.

THE ORIGIN OF THE CITY

The Emergence of the Village

Although it is impossible to pinpoint the exact date, anthropologists estimate that our species (Homo sapiens) first appeared about 50,000 years ago. These early modern humans were **nomadic**. They roamed the land in search of food and water. They hunted and foraged until the land could no longer provide for their needs and then move on in search of more promising lands. To say the least, life was precariously short and difficult. As such, population growth of our early ancestors was held in check by the forces of nature or battles between different bands competing for the same land and resources.

The condition of our ancestors did not improve until the *Neolithic revolution* that occurred approximately 10,000 years ago. It was during this time that humans discovered that they could greatly increase their supply of food with simple farming techniques—by planting seeds and harvesting grains. As simple as this might seem to us today, it was a monumental turning point in the development of our species. *First*, it freed early humans from the ineffective foraging and hunting way of life and allowed them to establish permanent settlements. A short time latter, humans began to domesticate animals to serve their needs for labor and for food. *Second*, with this surplus food supply from grains and domesticated animals, it was now possible to increase population. It was this combination of factors that led to the development of the village—a predecessor to the modern city.

Archeological investigation has unearthed some interesting details of these early villages. *First*, evidence reveals that villages appeared throughout the world at approximately the same time. *Second*, the population of villages was very small, somewhere in the neighborhood of 200 people. This was due to the fact that the cultivation and harvesting knowledge of early settlers was limited and thus unable to produce enough food to support larger populations. *Third*, almost everyone in the village was engaged in producing food. As such, only a very few individuals could branch out into specialized labor other than food production. And *finally*, for the most part, these early settlements were dominated by kinship patterns with most people being related to one another (Bairoch, 1988).

Why Cities Developed

Although no one knows for sure exactly why cities developed, three principle theories are advanced. The first is one that we have already alluded to—the agricultural **surplus theory**. Here, it is speculated that cities developed in response to the ability to produce a surplus of food. A surplus of food allowed some members of the village the freedom to develop specialties. These early artisans would then trade their products or services for food. Another, more controversial hypothesis, the **trading theory**, is advanced by Jane Jacobs (1982). Reversing accepted thought, Jacobs maintains it was trade that allowed for the development of specialties through the exchange of grains, livestock, and agriculture methods. This greatly revolutionized food production that in turn allowed the cities to flourish. As such, according to Jacobs, it was no accident that the first major cities sprang up along rivers and trading routes. Closely aligned with this latter theory is the **central place theory**. The core of this theory purports that people banded together in a central place to accommodate for a broader range of needs other than economic—their needs for government, religion, recreation, exchange of ideas, etc.

Preindustrial Cities

Regardless of which theory is correct, it wasn't until sometime around the year 3500 BCE that cities began to emerge. It is thought that the first cities developed in the rich, river valleys of the Nile in Egypt, the Euphrates and Tigris in Iraq, and the Indus in Pakistan. In differentiating these cities from earlier villages, Louis Wirth (1938), used four distinguishing characteristics—*size*, *density of population*, *permanency of location*, and *diversity of population*. A population of 10,000 people, although small by contemporary standards, would qualify for Wirth's definition of a city. Likewise, individuals would be concentrated in a definable and relatively compact area for an extended period of time. And finally, diversity of population would be evident. Here, those living within the confines of the city would extend beyond kinship ties. This diversity would lead to the need to develop new governments and legal systems. In addition to the above, Childe (1950) added *specialization* to the qualifications of what makes a city. Advances in agriculture freed others to pursue an array of economic and scientific endeavors. Artisans could develop their specialties offering a wide assortment of goods, service, and knowledge. Scholars were free to offer classes and seek scientific truth and as the sciences and trades advanced, so did the ability of the city to grow and prosper. This was demonstrated in the Mediterranean cities of Athens and Rome as well as in the Central American cities of the Inca, Aztec, and Mayan Indians.

Most of the large early cities had populations of 10,000 to 40,000 people living within a territory of three to four square miles. The largest of all early cities was Rome. At the height of its glory, around the second century C.E, Rome's population, within the city itself, is estimated to have been anywhere from 350,000 to 600,000 people. If one included what would now be termed the metropolitan area of the city, its population could have exceeded slightly over 2 million. The success of Rome was largely due to its military conquest. A series of Roman emperors devoted huge sums of money and human life in the conquest of much of Europe, the Near East, and North Africa. Those conquered were then forced into military duty or labor to extend the reach of the empire. The magnitude of this effort is demonstrated by the nearly 50 thousand miles of roads that were constructed by Rome to service its army and trade. In fact, many early European cities—London, Brussels, Utrecht, and Seville, were originally founded as forts and trading posts to service the Roman Empire.

Although Rome was by far the largest, other cities had significant populations. It is estimated that the Indian cities of Central and South America might well have reached 200,000. However, these large populations were rare due to logistical problems of food supply, sewage and waste control, transportation, governance, war, etc.

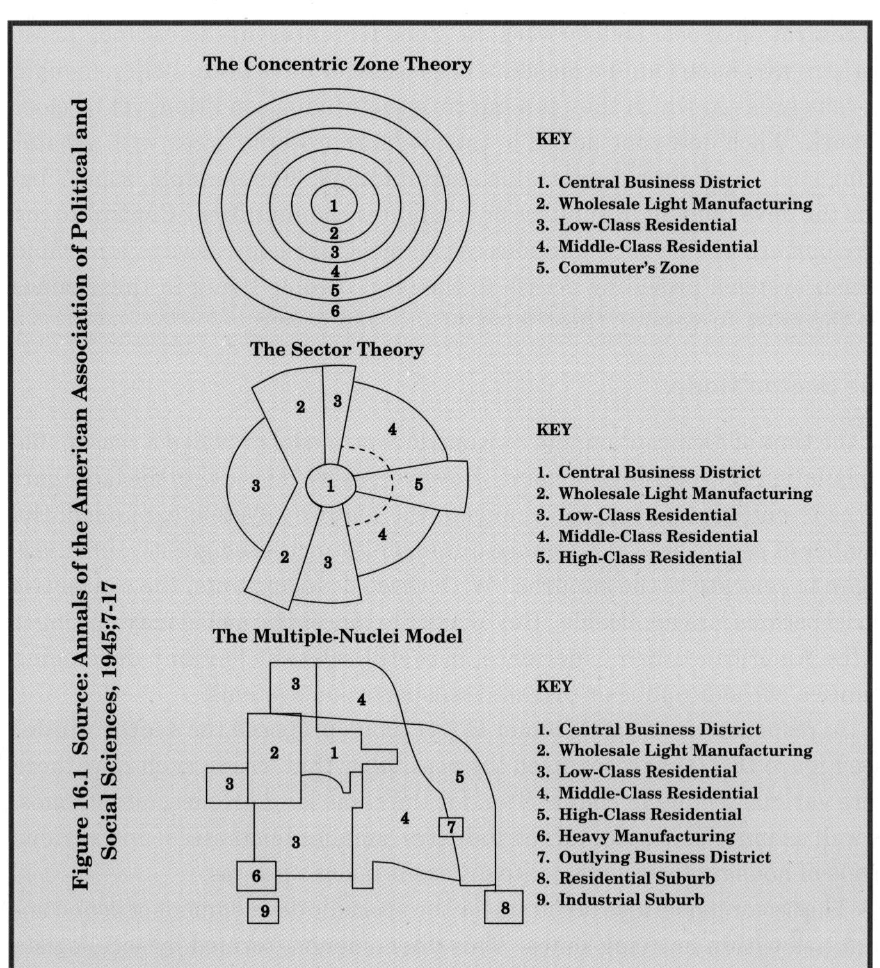

Figure 16.1 Source: Annals of the American Association of Political and Social Sciences, 1945;7-17

URBAN GROWTH

Not only do sociologists not agree on why cities evolved, they also do not agree on the dynamics of urban growth. In the following section we discuss four very different explanation of urban growth. Sociologists interested in the growth of cities are termed human ecologist. The term itself, **human ecology**, refers to the way in which individuals adapt to the environment in which they live.

The Concentric-Zone Model

Ernest Burgess (1925) presented the first theory of urban growth: the **concentric zone model**. As demonstrated in Figure 16.1, he believed that the development of a city expanded outward from the center. The pattern of growth takes place in rings or concentric zones. The first zone represents the downtown area or center of the city. It is the central business district. Immediately encircling this is zone II, an area of mixed light industry and manufacturing, and inexpensive housing. Burgess' noted that this zone is one of transition, characterized by deteriorating conditions and an extreme concentration of poor factory workers. Zone III represents an escape. Those workers who have found a measure of success, or have been thrifty enough, move to areas in which they can improve their living condition, yet be close to work. Each new zone added to the model represents areas with greater living space and more comfortable surroundings. For example, zone V begins the development of suburbs or commuter communities. Central to the development of this zone and successive ones, are expressways and rapid transit systems providing access to the city. People living in these zones are the most successful, those with wealth and power.

The Sector Model

At the time of its inception, the concentric zone model provided a reasonable explanation of urban development. However, as we moved into the later part of the twentieth century, life changed; the highway system expanded; the number of people able to purchase automobiles increased greatly; business began to relocate to the suburbs. With these developments, the concentric model became less applicable. But, while the concentric model may no longer fit the American urban experience, it is still relevant to many developing counties without public or private transportation systems.

In response, sociologist Homer Hoyt (1939), proposed the **sector model** (see Figure 16.1) that recognized the possibility that within each zone there were various sectors in competition for the same land. Hence, outer zones, as well as inner zones, contained industry, smaller businesses, and various levels of housing to accommodate different income groups.

The sector model also accounts for the sporadic development of poor communities within outlying zones. This phenomenon, termed by sociologists as **invasion-succession cycle**, occurs when newly arrived immigrants or racial minorities move into areas exclusively occupied by members of the dominant white majority. As tension mounts, the white majority begins to move out, a pattern identified as *white flight* in Chapter Eight. In extreme cases, an entire area can shift, with the end result being scattered pockets of poor within a suburban (or urban) setting. Additionally, sociologists have noticed that it is possible for an expressway or transit system to cut a path through an urban area from the city to the suburbs with the poor locating, for example, along a mass transit rail system because of their inability to purchase cars. The end result is a line of inexpensive housing from the inner city extending through several suburbs.

Multiple-Nuclei Model

The recent trend of grouping various types of businesses or neighborhoods in different locations of the community has given rise to the **multiple-nuclei model** (Harris and Ullman, 1945). Here, industrial plants, airports, landfills, etc. may be located in one part of the community while neighborhoods are situated in another, away from the noise and pollution. Surrounding the neighborhoods are commercial businesses that cater to the immediate needs of the home and apartment dwellers. These include supermarkets, restaurants, movie theaters, clothing stores, car washes, etc. Just outside this sector are other businesses not needed on a day-to-day basis but still required, such as auto dealers, lumberyards, brickyards, and others. As a result, there is a clustering effect with many different nuclei as shown in Figure 16.1. In some cases, the clustering has occurred because businesses have found it profitable to locate around each other as in the case of auto dealerships that chose to locate together so as to maximize their exposure. In other cases, city zoning ordinances dictate land usage to ensure orderly growth.

The Metropolitan Model

Within the past fifty years, the metropolitan model has gained more prominence. This model suggests that a metropolitan community is established when several or many cities begin to merge into one large functioning unit. This normally occurs when a large city expands outward to the boundary of several smaller towns or villages. When this occurs, there is a natural tendency for integration of functions and services to conserve dollars. An example of this integration can be seen with people who live in surrounding communities but commute to work or shop in the city. In a substantial way, the lives of both city and suburbanites are merged through shared concerns and resources.

A trend within the last twenty years is the merging of several metropolitan regions into one. Sociologists use the term **megalopolis** to describe this occurrence. The New York megalopolis is the largest in the United States with over 19 million people. With New York City as its hub, the megalopolis includes the urban areas of Long Island, western Connecticut, and the northern region of New Jersey. The second largest megalopolis is found in southern California with the merger of Los Angles, Anaheim, and Riverside. Here 15 million people reside. Today, over three-fourths of the population of the United States lives in one of 21 megalopolises. The grand exodus of the population to megalopolises has political scholars questioning the necessity or usefulness of maintaining the original boundaries of fifty states. In other words, do we really need fifty states? With so many people in New York or California, should Wyoming have the same number of votes in the Senate?

The Future

With this in mind, what do urban sociologists envision for the future? Certainly the movement will be for more concentrated growth. However, this growth will not be restricted to physical boundaries. With the information and the transportation revolutions, metropolitan cities around the world are beginning to connect. Computers, satellites, fax machines, cell phones, and many other devices have eliminated geography as a hindrance to cooperation and communication. Today, cities across the world are connecting in a dazzling array of networks. Likewise, the economy of any one city, indeed, a nation, is linked to what occurs in other major economic centers. In at-

Table 16.1: Largest Cities in the United States—2005

Rank	Place	Population	State
1	New York	8,143,179	New York
2	Los Angeles	3,844,829	California
3	Chicago	2,842,518	Illinois
4	Houston	2,016,582	Texas
5	Philadelphia	1,463,281	Pennsylvania

Source: U.S. Census Bureau, 2005

tempting to define what constitutes a global city, Saskia Sassen (1994) has delineated four qualifying characteristics:

1. Global cities serve as "command posts" for the organization of world business.
2. Instead of manufacturing, the central economic activity of global cities revolves around the new service economy of finance, accounting, marketing, design, and computing.
3. Global cities have become the Mecca's of innovation and creativity.
4. Global cities are the recognized market economies of the world.

Using the above criteria, New York, Los Angles, Mexico City, Hong Kong, Tokyo, London, and Singapore would qualify as global cities. Yet another distinguishing characteristic of global cities is their growing independence of governmental boundaries and reliance upon business decisions made in corporate headquarters, which in many cases are located in distant nations.

THEORIES OF URBAN SOCIOLOGY

Since sociology is the study of human interaction, it is only natural that sociologists take great interest in how behavior differs in an urban environment in comparison to smaller communities. The importance of this field of study ultimately led to the creation of urban sociology as a specialty within the discipline. The goal of **urban sociology** is to identify and explain specific traits of urban life. In this section we undertake a brief explain of some major theories of urban sociology.

Gemeinschaft and Gesellschaft (Ferdinand Toennies)

The first major work to define the difference between urban and rural living was developed by Ferdinand Toennies (1877). To him, each occupied an opposing position on a continuum. At one end was what he termed **gemeinschaft**, a smaller community of people bound together by kinship and tradition. Relationships between people were informal and social interaction was basically face to face. Division of labor occurred, but it was the commitment to a shared value system that provided the cohesive glue for community solidarity. **Gesellschaft**, on the other hand, was characteristic of large populations. The division of labor was complex, relationships between people were loose and fluid, and diversity of people and values necessitated a more rigid system of social controls.

Using Toennies definition, Gemeinschaft would fit our definition of primary relationships while Gesellschaft would better describe secondary relationships. In the larger view, Teonnies did not paint a very glamorous picture of city life. Urban environment, he believed, eroded primary relationships, made life less personal, and created an environment where self-interest was valued over community well being.

Mechanical and Organic Solidarity (Emile Durkheim)

Durkeim's (1893) approach to differences between urban and rural community embodies much of the thinking of Toennies. As a structural functionalist, Durkheim was interested in delineating those factors that held the community together and allowed it to function. In smaller, rural communities, social solidarity was maintained by the strong ties and shared values that were held in common by the people of the community. This, he termed **mechanical solidarity**. In larger communities, a higher degree or more complex division was necessary. Each individual performed a specialized task and no single individual was self-sufficient. Cooperation between and among individuals occurred because it was within self-interest to do so in order to survive. Durkheim regarded organic solidarity less desirable than mechanical solidarity, believing it to be less personal. He saw organic solidarity at the root of **anomie**, a condition of normlessness characterized by the loss of a sense of meaning and detachment from others in society. Anomie was recognized by Durkheim to be a major source of social unrest and pathological behavior.

Unlike Toennies, Durkheim found some positive aspects in living in an urban community. While less personal, urban dwellers had greater freedom to think and act in a manner different from those around them and moral tolerance was more evident. Additionally, urbanites enjoyed a greater degree of privacy than did their rural counterparts.

Urbanism as a Way of Life (Louis Wirth)

In 1914, sociologists at the University of Chicago established the School of **Urban Ecology**, a sociological specialty investigating the link between the physical and social aspects of urban environments. Louis Wirth, (1938) from this school, published his classical essay "Urbanism as a Way of Life" in which he asserted that a relationship exists between the physical dimensions of urban life—it's size, density, and structure—and human interaction. For urban dwellers, the constant bombardment of stimulation leads individuals to seek social isolation in which they become unconcerned about the existence and well-being of those around them. Aloofness, indifference, and abruptness with others replace personality traits such as empathy, kindness, gratitude, and sociability. Wirth's view may well explain the

Homeless men line up for a daily ration of bread. In the last three decades, and with the recent recession of 2008, the homeless population of urban centers is rapidly increasing.

Photo: Sara Lafleur-Vetter

murder of Kitty Genovese in New York City. Despite her pleas for help, she was repeatedly stabbed in front of dozens of people. Not one person intervened to help save her life. In fact, no one even called the police until after she had died. Although we might like to think that this was a separate incident, similar cases can be found in all major urban cities.

Urban Types (Herbert Gans)

Up until now, the views of urban life we have considered are rather pessimistic. Not all sociologists share this perspective, however. Herbert Gans (1962) argues that these views arise out of a preexisting cultural American bias *for* rural life. He asserts that pessimistic views on urban life were arrived at without taking into account the lives of all urban dwellers. In his work he identified five types of people who inhabit cities:

Cosmopolites: Included in this category are writers, artists, intellectuals, musicians, and professionals. They choose the city because of the variety of experiences and cultural activities available.

Childless couples: Many people who do not have to worry about education, playgrounds, and all other activities associated with childrearing choose the city for its excitement and proximity to work.

Ethnic Villagers: Included here are those newly immigrated to the country or those with strong attachment to the traditions of their homeland. Living together in enclaves surrounded by people like themselves, they are able to maintain kinship and cultural ties.

Deprived People: These are the poor, minorities, and the disabled who are unable to obtain affordable housing in other communities.

Trapped People: Included here would be the retired or those without the financial means to leave decaying neighborhoods. In general, people at the lower end of the stratification ladder.

Gans would argue that of the above, the first three categories view the city as positive and exhibit no social malaise. He also asserts that age and social class affect how one views their surroundings.

Subcultures (Claude Fischer)

In the mid-1970s, Claude Fischer published his urban theory of subcultures. Agreeing with Wirth that urban communities produce major social and psychological effects, he departed with him on how the process occurred. Wirth asserted that these effects were produced by a breakdown of existing social groups. Fisher, on the other hand, believed the loosening of community bonds was created by the formation of new groups. By the nature of size, urban communities promote diversity. The existence of diversity, and the tolerance of urban communities for diverse culture, only serves to encourage more diversity. Hence, subcultures grow and flourish. This is not only true for racial and ethnic minorities, but for a whole host of other subcultures—artists, juvenile gangs, homosexuals, lawyers, doctors, musicians, etc.

Another important element in Fischer's thinking is that not all subcultures are necessarily bad. The values and actions of some are beneficial to the community. In this way, Fischer is more aligned with the thinking of Gans.

URBANISM IN THE UNITED STATES

Settlement: The Birth of a Nation

While sharing some of the common experiences of all countries that have undergone urbanization, the United States experience is unique. This is due primarily to the colonial arrangement and the way in which the U.S. was settled. Unlike other countries, the United States was isolated from much of the world until its discovery by the Europeans in the late 1400s. Up until then, the continent was inhabited by a large number of distinct Native American tribes who were, for the most part, migratory, moving from location to location in search of food and shelter. As such, no permanent settlements were established until the arrival of the Europeans who colonized different parts of the country.

Many historians (of course, there is disagreement) consider the first attempt at colonization to have occurred in 1565 when the Spanish established St. Augustine in what is now the state of Florida. In 1607, the English founded Jamestown. A short time later, in 1624, the Dutch established New Amsterdam, which soon became the largest settlement in North America. New Amsterdam later changed its name to New York. The success of New York is attributed to its strategic location for trade and industry.

Another difference in the urbanization of the U.S. is the manner in which towns evolved. As mentioned previously, towns developed as people became more skilled at the production of food. This, again as mentioned previously, allowed others the freedom to specialize and trade their skills for food. Towns then grew as trading centers. Using this theory, the development of cities occurred from "outside" (rural) to "in" (town). In contrast, the North American experience was exactly the opposite. Towns were created first and only later did people begin to venture outward. Undoubtedly, this was due to the prior experience of Europeans with urban areas, the lack of knowledge of the land, and the necessity for fortification and security. Only later, as they became more familiar with the land and the inhabitants, did people venture farther out into the wilderness.

Another difference can be found in the colony experience itself. During our settlement period, the European nations were colonizing the world. The purpose, or incentive, of colonization was to exploit the great wealth of other nations. At first, it was minerals and trading goods, later, raw materials for manufacturing became important. It was during this phase that the colonies of North America became increasingly important to the Europeans, particularly the British, who were well advanced at industrialization. From the European perspective, the colonies of North America existed primarily to supply raw materials to the factories of the mother country (for example, England). These raw materials were turned into finished products for trade with other, more advanced nations. Under to terms of colonization, the colonies were prevented from establishing their own industries or trading with other nations. If they had been allowed to trade, it would in essence, be like creating your own competitors. In return, the mother country provided protection from hostile Native Americans and other European aggressors. However, without the right to industrialize or trade, growth was limited. Many historians believe this to be the central reason for the American Revolution—economic, not political, freedom. After the revolution, Americans were free to compete openly in the world market. This forever altered the character of American cities.

PROBLEMS OF URBAN AREAS

The problems that we encounter everywhere in modern life—crime, pollution, fiscal restraints, divorce, mental illness, drug addiction, juvenile delinquency, social alienation, domestic violence, etc.—appear to be magnified by urban growth. In other words, although all of these problems exist in every corner of our society, they appear to be much bigger in the cities. Not only is this true today, it was a common perception even as our nation began to take shape. It was reflected in the writings of Thomas Jefferson who stated that cities were, "pestilential to the morals, the health, and the liberties of man." Commenting further, he added, "The mobs of great cities add just so much to the support of pure government, as sores do to the strength of the human body" (Jefferson, 1780). A recent poll indicates that Jefferson's view of cities is as contemporary today as when he first penned them in 1780. When asked where they would live if they had a choice, only 13 percent of those responding chose the city (Zastrow, 1996). Similarly, a Harris poll found that an overwhelming majority of those presently living in the city (two-thirds) would prefer the suburbs, small towns, or a farm (Zastrow, 1996).

In this section, we will consider urban problems. Before beginning, it is important to stress again that these problems are not unique to cities. They are common to all communities. However, due to the sheer size of many cities, problems tend to stand out in a glaring fashion that tends to capture our attention. Nevertheless, there is little doubt that compacting many people into limited space presents an additive or accelerating effect to urban problems. One additional point needs to be made before proceeding.

Table 16.2 Urban Growth in America

Year	Population	Percent Urban
1790	3,900,000	5.1
1800	5,300,000	6.1
1820	9,600,000	7.3
1840	17,100,000	10.5
1860	31,400,000	19.7
1880	50,200,000	28.1
1900	76,000,000	39.7
1920	105,700,000	51.3
1940	131,700,000	56.5
1960	179,300,000	69.9
1980	226,500,000	73.7
1990	253,000,000	75.2
2000	281,400,000	80.3

U.S. Census, 2000

The problems presented below are not independent or exclusive. They are connected and in some cases, sequential. Hence, to solve one problem, one must work on all problems.

Declining Populations: Flight to the Suburbs

As mentioned earlier, when people became more affluent, they moved away from the city to distance themselves from the immigrating masses and increasingly crowded conditions of the inner city. At first, this was just a trickle, those who had found success. The baby boom, following the end of World War II, coupled with the prosperous, postwar economy, greatly increased the flow of people to the suburbs in search of the grand American dream: a home, a car, clean air, good education, and safe neighborhoods. Facilitating this trend were politically connected developers capable of getting government to fund expressways for easy access to the city, utility services, as well as guaranteed bank loans for homes at reasonable prices.

One might leap to the conclusion that this is a positive trend, after all, isn't overcrowding a major problem in cities? While this may be true, the problem is not the population decline itself, but rather, who is moving and who is staying. For the most part, those who leave the city are the professional and skilled workers. Those with jobs and taxable income to pay for all of the services that government must offer—police and fire protection, road and infrastructure maintenance, education, social welfare, sewage control, recreational facilities, libraries, and many more. The flight of these workers only serves to increase the proportion of lower-paid workers, those who are chronically under or unemployed.

However, since the economic downturn which began in 2008, and the subsequent housing woes, the pace of migration from cities to suburban communities has declined dramatically (Frey, 2011). Though a bright spot for cities, it is doubtful that this trend will continue once the economy improves.

Housing and Homelessness

Increasingly, the urban areas of our nation are being abandoned to the poor and minorities. Economic prosperity for some, combined with white flight (whites moving out of neighborhoods with racially diverse populations), has accelerated urban decay. Today, a majority of the poor of this nation reside in the inner city in housing units plagued by inadequate heat in winter, constant gas leaks, peeling lead paint, poor lighting, clogged and leaking toilets, rat and cockroach infestations, and numerous fire hazards. Given the economic condition of their renters, landlords have little incentives to invest money into their units. The poor, given their inability to earn, have little choice but to accept their plight. The magnitude of the problem is seen in the rising costs of housing for the poor. Current data reveals that 4.2 million working families, are paying fifty percent or more their income for housing (Center for Housing Policy, 2005). Thirty-five percent of households served by Feeding America Network had to choose between paying for food and paying their rent or mortgage (America's Second Harvest, 2006). One might think this would force the government to respond with housing subsidies, but the opposite has occurred. From 1997 to 2003, the number of low to moderate income working family households with critical housing needs increased from 3 million to 5 million. Much of this is due to deep cuts in HUD (Housing and Urban Development) housing by the Bush Administration.

At the same time that cuts were being made to HUD's budget, the Bush administration also instituted cuts in other safety net programs. As a result, more families found themselves endanger of becoming homeless. Although it is impossible to accurately estimate, current data do provide a reasonable picture of the homeless. Current estimates indicate that on any given day 800,000 Americans will find themselves on the streets. Included within this figure are over 200,000 children of which 42 percent are under the age of five. Additionally, within a given year, over three million adults and 1.5 million children will, at sometime, find themselves homeless (National Center on Family Homelessness, 2007). Given the unprecedented economic crisis in the housing market and declining stockmarket of 2007-08, it is highly unlikely the situation will improve in the near future.

Dwindling Fiscal Resources

The combined effects of racism and flight to the suburbs have left cities in a fiscal quandary. The chief sources of income for cities have traditionally been from taxes levied on property, sales, and corporations. However, as more skilled labor moved to the suburbs, so did many businesses in pursuit of more qualified workers. From their vantage point it was easier and more economical to do business in less congested areas with lower crime rates. Those corporations who have remained in the city have been able to exert enormous pressure on city hall not to raise business and sales taxes by threatening to move if rates increase. As for property taxes, the citizens of many states have been successful in implementing tax caps limiting government to cost of living increases. And, to top it all off, suburbanites have placed increasing strain on tax dollars by using the city for work and recreation while avoiding paying their fair share for the cost of roads, police and fire protection, garbage collection, emergency health care, utilities, etc. While it is possible to institute user fees, cities have been slow to take full advantage of these for fear of losing more business to the suburbs.

With all these restraints in place, cities have been forced to turn to the federal and state government for assistance. In the 1960s, huge sums of money were channeled to cities in the form of grants-in-aid for urban renewal and a variety of social programs. The magnitude of this effort can be seen in that between 1970 and 1980 federal outlays to states and cites increased fourfold, from $24 billion to $91 billion. The situation improved in the 1990s. However, since then, the War on Terror, and tax cuts by the Bush administration, has resulted in record-setting federal deficits. This has forced the federal government to severely cut back aid to state and local governments. These cuts, along with the declining stock market (loss of state investments), have resulted in the reduction or elimination of many social programs that the state and federal government provided for cities.

Urban Decay

Nowhere are the signs of urban decline more visible than with the seemingly endless numbers of abandoned buildings that pose numerous problems for city residents. They are dangerous playgrounds for children, hangouts for addicts and gangs, targets for arsonists and vandals, a breeding grounds for rats and other stray, disease carrying animals, shelters for vagrants, and isolated grounds well-suited for the commission of violent crimes.

Sociologist John Palen (Henslin, 1981) has noted that once a city begins its decline, financial institutions (banks, savings and loans, etc.) help to accelerate the process through **redlining**. Here, a red line is drawn around a deteriorating neighborhood with decreasing financial resources—usually an area with a high number of unskilled minority people—and refuse to lend money for home mortgages and business ventures. Once the process begins, it creates a self-fulfilling prophecy. Unable to obtain loans, business begins to relocate to areas where money can be secured. Homeowners, unable to find jobs, have difficulty keeping up with mortgage obligations or the funds to keep up their properties. As the appearance of property declines, so does the value of the neighborhood. This, in turn, discourages potential new homeowners from buying property in the neighborhood. As the deteriorating of the neighborhood nears completion, bankers and financial lenders applaud themselves for the good judgment of not having wasted institutional money investing in a "bad neighborhood."

Legislation enacted by Congress declared redlining illegal. However, like segregation, it is practiced covertly and remains a major problem of urban communities. Again, its practice is evident in the abandoned build-

Graffiti has become a constant and costly problem for city officials. To some it is a matter of art, to others it is nothing short of vandalism. Gangs use graffiti to mark their territories resulting in turf wars and violence.

Photo: Jeffery E. Pott.

ings that plague inner cities. Each year, owners abandon 150,000 housing units, apartments, and homes. Why do they abandon rather than sell their properties? The answer is that they are unable to find a buyer. Although it would be easy to fault individuals as uncaring and irresponsible, the truth is much more complicated. Faced with high taxes, low investment returns, increasingly costly repairs, difficult renters, slow and costly eviction procedures, and unresponsive city officials, even the most responsible owner may throw in the towel and walk away from his building.

While city officials would deny any complicity or responsibility for the above conditions, they do play a major role in the deterioration of communities by spending a disproportionate amount of funds in affluent neighborhoods in comparison to poor ones. In Chicago, the city spends enormous funds to maintain the downtown business area known as the "Gold Coast" and the lake-front properties. City officials defend the expenditures as necessary to maintain a thriving commercial area that can compete with the suburbs and other cities. Unfortunately, these efforts are not duplicated in poor areas. Similarly, politicians can influence the distributions of funds and benefits. An example is the casino gambling industry in Illinois. Although serious reservations were voiced when the idea to allow gambling was first raised, objections were overcome with arguments that the revenues created by gambling would fund education and provide urban renewal for poor communities. As part of the agreement to allow gambling, a deal was struck to allow casino gambling as long as economically deprived areas were selected as casino sites. However, once gambling was established, political pressure was directed at state legislators to allow affluent communities to build casinos.

Why did this happen? The answer lies within the political process. To remain in office, elected officials must continually be attuned to the demands of voters. Statistics on voting reveal that those most likely to vote are affluent and educated. Those least likely to vote are poor and uneducated. Likewise, campaigns cost money, lots of it. It's highly unlikely that a candidate can run an effective campaign from the dollar bills collected in poor neighborhoods. Thus, candidates are forced to turn to wealthy contributors and businesses for support. Once elected, it is impossible for public officials not to respond to the wishes of those who were most influential in placing them in office. In sum, the electoral process is a game that the poor are ill equipped to play; they lack both the knowledge and the means to be effective competitors.

Crime and Gangs

Are urban areas inherently more violent than rural areas or the suburbs? Sociological investigations reveal a positive correlation between crime and urban living. In comparison to suburbs, urban communities experience four times as much violent crime. A similar comparison to rural communities reveals an even greater disparity—violent crime is six times greater in urban settings (Kornblum and Julian, 1992). Other studies indicate a similar pattern for property crimes (Zastrow, 1996).

The fear of crime controls the daily activities of many that live in the city. City residents often arrange their schedules and daily activities to avoid being the victims of crime. In one study, half of those responding to a survey stated that they avoided walking at night for fear of being robbed, raped, or murdered. Responding to the same survey, only twenty percent of suburban residents confessed to such fears. An explanation for this may lie in the functionalist theory of mechanical solidarity discussed earlier. According to this theory, smaller communities are more cohesive and united by an accepted set of core values. Likewise, there is greater familiarity with neighbors and a sense of general concern for others. Those who stray from the "straight and narrow" are likely to face immediate informal punishment or be socially ostracized. On the other hand, in urban communities, diversity and density of the population tends to weaken community bonds and compliance to value systems is more formalized, being enforced by law and the legal system.

Another major problem of the city is youth gang activity that accounts for much of the crime in urban areas. Sociologists who have studied gang activity have reported a number of interesting findings concerning the formation and activities of gangs. Originally, the formation of gangs developed because groups of youths were competing for limited play space in densely populated areas of inner cities. The boys perceived themselves as having something in common and, conversely, perceive all others as outsiders. Banding together gave them a sense of security and identity (Cohen, 1955).

Although middle-class gangs do exist (generally "wannabe's"), membership in youth gangs is predominately confined to lower class, urban males. Some female gangs also exist, and they can be as violent as their male counterparts, but they function in a supportive role for male gang members. Why is gang activity predominately a male activity? Miller (1958, 1975) addressed this question in a classical study. Using symbolic interactionalist analysis, he found that lower class male competition for status revolves

Gang members display their body art. Urban areas have always attracted gangs. However, with the drug trade, gangs have become more violent as they war over boundaries and product.

Photo: Leon B. Dista.

around six core values: trouble, toughness, smartness, excitement, fate, and autonomy. According to Miller, the monotony felt in daily existence is relieved by trouble. Additionally, trouble allows males to challenge a system they perceive degrades them and allows them to assert their autonomy. Toughness is measured by violence; the more violent one is the greater status one has in the gang hierarchy. And finally, there is a strong belief in fate that allows gang members to accept the risk of violent activities. Simply put, getting "popped" means nothing more than your number came up. Increasingly, females exhibit these same values.

School Violence and Segregation

In the classic 1950s film, *Rebel Without a Cause,* the late James Dean portrays a trouble teen alienated by society and school. In one scene, there is a knife fight between Dean and another youth where the rules are not to kill, but to cut. School officials assured shocked parents who saw the film that the events in the movie were the product of an over imaginative screenwriter. Or, if such activity did exist in reality, incidents were rare and isolated. Few school officials today would attempt to sell that line to parents. Educators and parents have joined ranks demanding protection against school violence as more and more kids are toting, not the old fashion switchblades to school, but handguns. In 2009, eight percent of students in grades 10-12 reported to having been threatened by a gun (IES, 2010). Nowhere is the perception of violence greater than in the inner cities where gang turf fights are carried from the streets to the classrooms and school hallways. In spite of the fact that violent school episodes have occurred in rural and suburban communities, there is still the predominant belief that inner city schools are more violent. This perception has some validity if possession of weapons is used as criteria to measure potential violence. In a nationwide poll of 2,500 sixth through twelfth grade students in suburban and rural schools, only 4 percent said they had carried a gun to school in the past year (Vic Cox, 1997). A similar study of inner schools revealed 9 percent had carried guns to school at least "now and then" (Sheley and Wright, 1993). Furthermore, kids who want guns have little difficulty in obtaining them. Over sixty percent of inner city students stated that they could obtain a weapon if they wanted. In Houston, where gang battles have erupted in or near schools, police found students renting guns to other students for the day (Senate Committee on the Judiciary, 1992).

Violence has become so commonplace that many students who have no intentions of harming others carry weapons for self-defense. Alfred Blumstein, a noted criminologist, has compared the situation to an arms race among inner city students (in Simonetti, 1995.) School quality is perhaps the greatest single concern of parents when seeking a community in which to reside. Given current perceptions about where violence is most likely to occur and statistics and studies that tend to back up parental beliefs, the move to the suburbs is likely to continue.

In addition to violence, another factor undermining the growth and revitalization of cities is the overwhelming racial segregation of public schools. The flight to the suburbs, coupled with the preference for private schools for those with the financial means to afford them, have radically depleted the number of white students in urban public schools. According to recent data, black and Latino students in large urban schools are twice as likely to attend school with less than 10 percent of white students than their non-urban counterparts (Christian Science Monitor, 2008). In Chicago, for example, over 85 percent of all public school children exist below the poverty line (Catalist Chicago, 2011). This added to the fact that suburban school expenditures per pupil far out-weigh those for urban schools, it is little wonder that inner city public school students have lower standardized test scores and a higher dropout rate. In the late 1970s and early 1980s, courts and state officials attempted to alleviate the problem with **metropolitanization**, or busing between the suburbs and the city. However, not only was busing extremely costly, it also was ineffective, generating more white flight and a rush to private schools in targeted communities. Additionally, few parents supported the concept. In the end, the plan was abandoned.

Transportation

Americans have always had a love affair with the automobile. There are more cars in the United States per capita than any other country in the world. Part of this relates to our belief in the core values of freedom and self-reliance. Another important element is that to many, a car, an expensive car, is a symbol of wealth and status. To facilitate our obsession, the national government has spent hundreds of billions of dollars building superhighways and expressway systems. Additionally, federal and state government has worked diligently to limit the cost of gasoline. Is this a problem or a wonderful service provided by the government? It depends, of course, on which side of the tracks you're on. From the standpoint of cities, it has created three serious problems: flight, congestion, and inadequate public transportation.

Originally conceived, the creation of a massive highway and expressway system was supposed to bring people to the city and make travel between cities easier. In reality, the opposite has occurred. *First*, getting to the city during rush hour can be a nightmarish experience. Although Americans may like their comfort, cars are the least efficient means of transportation for moving people from one destination to another. In a comparative study it was found that car in a single lane of traffic moved 2,400 people per hour, while a bus moved 9,000, a train 40,000, and a subway 60,000 people. Upon reaching the city, drivers then have to contend with the glut of cars clogging city streets (Horton, Leslie, and Larson, 1991). One study estimated that 65 percent of the land in cities is now devoted to cars (Zastrow, 1996). This figure includes parking spaces, garages, service stations, repair shops, car washes, etc. Not only has this created a huge pollution problem, it is also a source of enormous frustration and cost to people who might well like to use city services. Forced to drive around for lengthy periods searching for a spot to park or pay a hefty price for parking at a garage, many people have abandoned the city altogether.

An even more devastating consequence of our devotion to the automobile is the lack of development of public transportation. Those who possess cars, generally the more affluent, have little interest in public transportation. Again, since the affluent exercise a disproportionate amount of political influence, politicians have little incentive to allocate tax dollars to the development of safe, efficient mass transportation. Additionally, the glut of automobiles in the city makes mass transit even less efficient and frustrating to those who do attempt to utilize it. Inadequate mass transit serves as an obstacle for the unemployed poor. Unable to afford a car and unable to get to areas of employment, they end up on the welfare roles, increasing the city's swelling tax burdens.

RESTRATIFICATION

Demographic and urban experts have noticed a major shift in the population of this nation. The term applied to denote this shift is **restratification**. Nowhere is restratification more noticeable than in the cities. As seen in Table 16.3, the ten fastest growing cities are in the South and the West. Three factors have accounted for this change. The *first*, and probably most important, is a shift in the economy from an industrial base to a service base. At the turn of the century, the North and Midwest were heavily industrialized and large numbers of immigrants seeking jobs settled in the industrial cities upon arriving in America. Also, large numbers of African Americans relocated to the North and Midwest in search of work that was readily available and to lessen the burdens of discrimination they found in the South. This created the huge cities in the North and Midwest. *Second*, the flow of migration steadily slowed and is now reversed with many African

Table 16.3: Cities With The Largest Growth

Rank	City	State	Population	Growth
1	New Orleans	Louisiana	239,124	13.8%
2	Victorville	California	107,221	9.5%
3	McKinney	Texas	115,620	8.0%
4	N. Las Vegas	Nevada	212,114	7.4%
5	Cary	North Carolina	121,796	7.3%
6	Killeen	Texas	112,434	6.5%
7	Port St. Lucie	Florida	151,391	6.3%
8	Gilbert	Arizona	207,550	5.8%
9	Clarksville	Tennessee	119,284	4.8%
10	Denton	Texas	115,506	4.7%

Source: CNNMoney.com., "The Big Easy Picks up the Pace, July 10, 2008." U.S. Census statistics.

Americans returning to the South to escape the segregation, discrimination, and limited job opportunities they now experience in the large urban centers of the North and Midwest. *Third*, as we moved into a service economy, many firms began to move their businesses to the West and the South to escape the congestion, high taxes, and union problems they experienced in northern states. An additional factor is that as the population has aged, increasing numbers of elderly are seeking refuge from the hard winters by moving to warmer climates.

The implication of this population shift is enormous. In our federal arrangement, states are allocated representation (political power) and tax dollars (federal programs) based upon population. As such, the South and the West are experiencing growth in dollars and power while the Northeast and Midwest are experiencing a decline. While this is a favorable windfall of benefits for the sunbelt states, they now experience many of the unpleasant problems formerly associated with cities located in the snowbelt—air pollution, traffic congestion, higher crime rates, drug and gang problems, urban sprawl, higher taxes, increased pressure on educational systems, etc.

TROUBLE IN SUBURBIA

As indicated earlier, the race to the suburbs was an attempt to escape the noise, pollution, crime, and congestion of the city. The reality today is that many suburbanites are facing the same urban problems as the inhabitants of the city from which they fled. Why is this true? In part, the growth of the suburbs occurred at such a rapid pace that local communities were unable or unready to handle the flow of new residents. At first, row-upon-row of single-family homes were built by contractors eager to attract new buyers. As the demand for housing increased and land became scarce, builders began converting property that was originally designed for single family

Once confined to the city, illegal drugs have become an increasing problem for suburbs as gangs move outward to attract new customers, increase profits, and enlarge boundaries.

photo: Token Blue Young.

units into apartments and condominiums. Inevitably, this resulted in overcrowding which in turn led to noise, pollution, crime, and congestion.

One factor attributed to the growth of the suburbs is "white flight." As the city's population of minorities increased, many whites moved to the suburbs to escape integration. In a short time, minorities, for the same reasons as whites, began an exodus to the suburbs. This created racial tension. Soon, many whites were selling homes in the suburbs to which they originally moved, to move even farther out, away from minority populations. The net effect was not integrated communities but dispersed pockets of segregated suburbs.

As the population of the suburbs increased, entrepreneurs eager to cash-in overbuilt commercial sites. Many of these failed, leaving suburbs with vacant and abandoned buildings to contend with. In many cases, even when a shopping mall was successful, it drained customers from downtown suburban stores. As a result, the downtown areas of many suburban communities face the same problems as the big cities did when the population moved to the suburbs. Today, one of the hottest topics for city officials in the suburbs is how to revive their downtown commercial districts.

As with the city, many suburban communities struggle with the issue of gangs. Today, gangs are not confined to the inner city. Their appeal reaches out to the suburbs. Likewise, many gangs find the suburbs an economic gold mine for drugs and other illegal activities. As such, more and more suburban communities find themselves scrambling to develop anti-gang programs.

Finally, many communities failed to plan for the rapid growth in population. The end product was a "mishmash" of commercial shops, light industry, single family homes, and multi-family units, all thrown together without any real thought to human ecology. Although many suburbs are now attempting to regulate and zone their communities, only time can resolves some of the old mistakes.

SOCIOLOGICAL PERSPECTIVES

It should come as no surprise that considerable disagreement is to be found on urban life between structural functionalists and social conflict theorists. In this section, we briefly discuss how each perspective sees the origins of urban problems and the future of cities.

Structural Functional

Perhaps the best description of is perspective's view on the problem and future of cities is that which was presented earlier, in the work of Ernest Burgess. As you recall, he presented the concentric zone theory. Here, the development of the city resembles a series of concentric circles. The first circle represents the central business district. As the city grows, it expands outward, developing new zones. Burgess noted that the zone that has the greatest mobility also has the most severe problems. This, he identified as zone two. High mobility is the source of demoralization that produces promiscuity, crime, gangs, poverty, and dysfunctional family life. He tabbed this zone as "the purgatory of lost souls" (Burgess, 1925).

Lest one jump to the conclusion that all is negative, structural functionalists would be quick to point out that the zones do have a function. Remember, structural functionalists look to see what functions best for society. Although the city is in constant transition, these transitory stages develop and exist for the benefit of society—development of new housing, establishment of new business, promotion of economic growth, etc. As for urban problems, structural functionalists point out that these, too, will be addressed by society as their dysfunction become so great that they cannot be ignored. In part, structural functionalists maintain that this is already occurring with urban renewal programs from the government and gentrification. Urban renewal has resulted in the construction of office building, financial centers, stadiums, and luxury hotels in downtown areas to promote growth and increase the tax base. Gentrification—the buying of older and rundown properties in poor and working class neighborhoods and revamping them into luxury homes, condominiums, town houses, lofts, and apartments—has initiated a movement of middle-class suburbanites back to the city.

The above two examples are illustrative of the structural functionalist position. While they admit that problems exist, they maintain that society is self-adjusting and problems will be address in a gradual process that is functional to society.

Social Conflict

According to social conflict theorists, the above explanation does not adequately explain the decline of the city or the potential to resolve its problems. Conflict theorists Tabb and Sawer (1984) refuted the structural functionalist explanation stating that the real problem of the city was inherent to the true nature of capitalism. In the early stages of economic growth, the market place was dominated by many small companies located within the city. In the "dog-eat-dog" marketplace some companies survived and gobbled-up smaller ones creating a process of centralization where a few companies grew large and powerful. These companies used their power to influence governmental policies favorable to them. Examples of such policies are those already mentioned in this chapter—government subsidies to land development (away from the cities), home mortgages (away from the city), and mass transportation systems (out of the city). Not only did these policies provide immediately enrichment to the affluent, they also solved a major problem of industry. Early in the industrial process, multistory buildings were constructed in the city. New manufacturing techniques made these buildings obsolete because it was inefficient to haul materials up and down different levels of a building. To convert these older plants would have required extreme outlays of capital. Likewise, there was tremendous competition for space to expand in the city. The solution was simply to abandon the old buildings in favor of newer, one-story plants with sufficient land to accommodate storage for materials and inventory (the suburbs). In essence, business leaders were successful in getting government to enact policies that favored their expansion and movement to the suburbs. In the process, businesses were able to avoid the twin problems of central cities higher taxes and powerful labor unions. While this benefited business, it devastated the cities of our nation by encouraging middle class and skilled workers to move out of the cities. Not only did this destroy the tax base, it created a huge reservoir of urban poor for a crippled government to contend with (Gottdiener, 1994).

Once the move was complete, business further enhanced its position by adopting anti-urban policies. Today, we see the rural and suburban areas politically united against programs that bring tax dollars and relief to the cities. While businesses have supported some programs like urban renewal and gentrification, they have done so only because it is in their financial interest. Few benefits actually "trickle-down" to the poor. In fact, gentrification has been shown to diminish affordable housing to the poor (Levine, 1987). In reality, the rich push the poor from their homes with little consideration of where the poor might find adequate shelter. For social conflict theorists, the problems of the city will only be solved with the major revamping of the political and economic institutions of this nation.

THE FUTURE OF CITIES

Saving the Cities—Why?

Before we begin to assess what the future holds for our cities, it is important to address the question of *why* it is important to save our cities. Three basic reasons can be offered. The *first* is that we, as a nation, owe it to those millions living in the city to provide a decent and safe place to live.

A *second* reason is that we have an obligation to the cities themselves. Although a substantial number of people live in suburban communities, they rely upon the city as a place of employment and a major source for participating in cultural, intellectual, and recreational activities. Even if we were never to step foot in one of America's major cities, we would still benefit from its economic and cultural activities. Indeed, it would be impossible for our nation to prosper or even exist without the big city.

A *third* reason for saving the city is that it provides a more efficient and ecologically correct alternative to urban sprawl. The concentration of larger numbers of people and shops in smaller areas, accomplished by building up, saves land for ecological purposes. Economically, it is cheaper to repair the existing infrastructure of cities rather than abandon, build new, and shift mass populations in the process. *Finally*, the concentration of people in smaller areas makes mass transit systems economically feasible, thus controlling the pollution now resulting from tens of millions of automobiles.

And finally, researchers have demonstrated that ultimately, by saving the city we save ourselves. Larry Ledebur of Wayne State University and William Barnes of the National League of Cities have found that there is a direct correlation between the health of the city and the health of the suburbs that directly surround it. In essence, their research suggests that a declining city produces a ripple effect that the surrounding suburbs are sure to feel. Conversely, if a city prospers, so does its' suburbs.

Saving the Cities—How?

What can be done to save our cities? Several suggestions have been offered to improve cities in the United States (and in other parts of the world). One of the first, was the idea of **urban homesteading**, a program already underway in a number of cities. Here, abandoned buildings and homes are offered for sale by the city for as little as one dollar. The buyer then promises to refurbish the existing structure and occupy it (business or home) for a specified period of time. The theory behind this program is that the repair of decaying buildings and homes will generate confidence in the neighborhood and thus create an incentive for others to improve their property and remain in the community.

Similar to this is a program to assist landlords to maintain their properties rather than abandon them. Assistance comes in two forms. The *first* is to provide tax breaks so as to make investments in at-risk urban properties more profitable. The *second* is to provide rent assistance to those most in need so that they can afford to live in newly repaired properties. The hope here is to save neighborhoods, provide decent housing, and prevent urban decay. Along with the above, cities also increase police and fire protection, street maintenance, garbage pick-up, and other services to encourage residents to stay and convince others to move in.

Still another idea revolves around creating **enterprise zones**. Combining a market-based philosophy with tax incentives, governments designate certain areas as enterprise zones in which tax credits are given to a business or industry that relocates into the zone. The relocation of businesses stimulates economic activity and provides jobs. To further boost economic activity, businesses are given additional tax credits for each new, full-time employee hired; with higher incentives awarded for new employees that come from low-income families. While this is being tried, critics maintain that it simply replaces one decaying area with another, as business and industry moves from one zone to another in search of tax relief. Other criticisms include that costs outweigh the benefits to society with the real winner being business.

One idea that is gaining acceptance, but is yet to be put into effect, is expanded use of regional authority. At present, authority is fragmented into thousands of competing political entities (towns, villages, school boards, park district, etc.) All of these are creations of the State. It is within the power of the State to consolidate or force competing units to work together for the betterment of all, rather than pursuing separate interests while zealously guarding turf. This would allow for regional planning for services such as police and fire protection, water and sewage systems, building codes, educational systems, libraries, parks, etc. Not only would this save taxpayers millions of dollars for overlapping services, but it would also allow state and local leaders to better plan for future growth.

One of the most important factors any family considers in deciding where to live is the quality of the community's school system. In most states, schools are financed by means of local real estate taxes. This allows for enormous disparity in quality between school districts. Wealthy districts with greater home values are able to out spend poor communities with lower property values. Nowhere is this disparity more obvious than between the suburbs and the city. To reduce the disparity, the State needs to find an alternative method to fund education in which city schools can compete with their suburban counterparts. As long as the disparity exists, there is little hope of attracting middle class families to move back to the city.

Finally, a way must be found to provide affordable housing in outlying suburban communities. At present, most suburbs resist the development of low-income housing, fearing that undesirable elements will move into their communities. The end result is the isolation of the poor in urban areas unable to compete for jobs that are available in suburban communities. It is reasonable to assume that suburban communities will continue to resist low-income housing. Therefore, it is up to state to mandate change.

There is little doubt that the above programs are controversial and will be difficult to implement. Fragmentation of authority and self-interest will continue to be the stumbling blocks of change. However, what is clear is that unless bold and new alternatives to present day policies are found, we all will suffer by the further decline of the cities of this nation.

Terms You Should Know:

Nomadic
Gemeinschaft
Anomie
Redlining
Resegregation
Human Ecology
Gesellschaft
Urban Ecology
Metropolitanization
Urban Homesteading
Megalopolis
Mechanical Solidarity
White Flight
Restratification
Enterprise Zones

Can You Answer These Questions?

1. How did the Neolithic Revolution contribute to the development of the modern city?
2. List and explain the three basic theories of why cities developed.
3. Discuss the four theories of urban growth? Which do you believe is most relevant today?
4. Why did Ferdinand Toennies believe that cities were not the most stable of social arrangements?
5. List and describe each of Herbert Gans' urban dwellers. Which would you most likely be?
6. Why did Claude Fischer believe the formation of subcultures was destructive to urban communities?
7. Of all the urban problems listed in the textbook, which do you think is the most serious?
8. Why is the tax base of cities declining? What can be done about it?
9. Is racial segregation increasing or decreasing? How does segregation differ in urban areas than in smaller communities?
10. What are the factors that lead to the growth of suburbs?
11. List some of the problems suburbs are currently facing.
12. Discuss some ways that can keep cities from further deterioration.

Critical Thinking Excercises:

1. Do you believe that people living in urban communities are less responsive to the needs of those living around them? Why?
2 There are advantages and disadvantages to living in large urban areas. What are some of these and do you believe the advantages outweigh the disadvantages?
3. In every urban community, there are areas of racial segregation. Is it possible for government to break this pattern?
4. Gang violence seems to be a reoccurring problem in large urban areas. What suggestions could you offer to help alleviate the problem?
5. What types of incentives could government offer to lure suburbanites back to the city or keep current residents of the city from leaving?
6. How do structural functionalists and social conflict theorists differ over the decline of urban communities? Which one do you think is most relevant?

Ivar Husevac Doskeland

Chapter 17

Collective Behavior and Social Change

We, as individuals, live in only the briefest moment of endless time. We are born, we develop as human beings, we leave our families and strike out on our own—we marry, go to work, have children, try to insulate ourselves from the tragedies of life, grow old, and eventually die, leaving the world to those who come after us. Rarely, in the midst of our busy lives, do we give thought to what life was like for those who came before us and what it will be for those in the future. In fact, we hardly have time to think about our own lives, how they have changed, and what lies ahead. However, we do, even at a subconscious level, understand that our lives are continually changing and with each change we are required to make new adjustments in how we live our lives, how we think about life, and our reaction to change.

In earlier chapters of our textbook we examined concepts like culture, norms, roles, and societal institutions. Likewise, we examined the forces of social statics and social dynamics. As you recall, **social statics** are those forces in society that seek to maintain the existing status quo. On the opposite side, we have **social dynamics**, or the forces that seek change. The clash between these two opposing forces ultimately results in what we term **social change**—a transformation in the social order and in institutions of society.

Sociologists who have spent time observing and analyzing social change have noted a number of traits associated with it. Although there are many, most can agree on four basic characteristics. *First* and foremost, is that social change is inevitable. Perhaps you have heard the expression, "the more things change, the more they stay the same." From the perspective of a sociologist who studies social change, nothing could be further from the truth. Our society is in a constant state of change. One only has to reflect on the changes they have experienced in their own lifetime to understand this truth. Take for example music. One can see the enormous change from the early days of "rock and roll" to the sounds of today. Although this might seem like a frivolous example, think about the social impact inherent in this change; from the lyrics, the sound, dress, values, and social structure. Technological changes have been even more dramatic. Most young people today could not recognize an eight-track tape. But in a few years we have gone from records, to tapes, to discs, to I-Pods. Musical technology invented today has a lifespan of only a few years before being swept away to the basement of history.

Second, social change is contentious and divisive. As we have mentioned, social change is brought about by the clash between those seeking change and those who wish to maintain the existing social order. Any change, regardless of how small it might seem, produces losers and winners. Those who benefit from the existing social order wish to maintain their advantage as opposed those who would benefit from the change. In our example of music, social institutions such as the family and church first perceived (and perhaps still do) the new sounds and lyrics as a threat to the normative structure of society, predicting rampant promiscuity, the breakdown of families, and a surge of out-of-wedlock children. Those advocating change viewed rock and roll as an expression of personal freedom to exercise their creative talents and express their views on the social and political culture.

Third, social change can have **latent consequences**. As we learned in Chapter One, latent consequences are those that are not intended or recognized as occurring at the time of change or those that might occur in the future. Moving away from our example of music, let's turn to one in medical technology. Scientists have been working to develop technology that would enable parents to pre-select the sex of their child. Presently, there are some methods available to assist in sex-selection, but they are not foolproof and they are expensive. Scientists agree that new, less expensive methods will be available in the near future. While this might seem a blessing to some couples, the latent consequences could be very disruptive to the social order. According to the most recent poll of Americans there exists a preference for boys over girls (Gallop, 2007). If the ability to pre-select were as simple as taking a blue pill or a pink pill, there would most certainly be an abundance of boys conceived. The impact to the social order and structure of our institutions, such as marriage, would forever be altered.

Finally, not all changes are equal in their impact on society. Some changes can transform society in minor ways, as our example in music shows. Other changes have a greater impact. One change with the potential of a great impact for the future of our society is the rapid advancements made in automation. If you could be transported a mere forty years into the past to an automotive plant, you would see thousands of workers on an assembly line. Today, what you would see is something akin to a sci-fi movie, rows upon rows of robots. In one task alone, the moving and positioning of a chassis from one assembly line to another once required sixteen workers. Today, with the aid of robots, only four human workers are needed (Bleicher, 2009). Everywhere you look, from checkout counters in grocery stores, to kiosks at airports, automation is replacing workers. Today, scientists are racing toward the holy grail of computer technology—artificial intelligence. And with each step in that direction, robots will be capable of taking over more tasks currently performed by humans. What will be left for humans to do? What happens when there is not enough work to go around? How do we define ourselves without work? What changes will occur in the social structure and in the institutions of society to cope with this change? And what will our relationship to the newly created machines be?

TYPES OF COLLECTIVE BEHAVIOR

The term **collective behavior** was first employed by sociologist Robert E. Parks, and later refined by Herbert Blumer, to describe a social process in which spontaneous actions emerge by individuals trying to cope with stressful situations or unclear conditions. These actions are generally unstructured, highly volatile, and violate the established social norms or existing institutions of society (Blumer, 1951). Collective behavior is generally divided into two categories: Dispersed and localized.

Dispersed Behavior

Dispersed collective behavior does not require large numbers of people to gather in a common setting. In fact, it does not, in its purest form, require any physical presence of individuals. Rather, it is an emotional response by individuals within a society to a similar stimulus. Listed below are some of the more common forms of this type of behavior.

Rumors. A rumor occurs when one person communicates false or unverified information to others within a social group. Since the origins of rumors are almost impossible to identify and their content difficult to verify, they are easily exaggerated with the passage of time. One example of an ongoing rumor in society today is concerning the religion of President Obama. Prior to election, a rumor started that Barack Obama, then a presidential candidate, was a Muslim. The rumor quickly spread through word-of-mouth and went viral on the Internet. Although numerous attempts were made to correct this misconception by the candidate and his supporters, the rumor persisted. Even after his election, a recent poll showed that nearly one in five Americans still believe he is a Muslim (Pew Forum, 2010).

Gossip. This is a form of behavior that is specific in its target and purpose. The target is an individual or a group and the intended purpose is social control. Gossip can be used as either praise or shame. Gossip is widespread and at some point in each of our lives we have been both a victim and a perpetrator of it. In the larger society, gossip has become a major industry in print, radio, and television covering the lives of celebrities.

Urban Legends. All of us, at some time or another, have heard stories so preposterous that it's hard to believe that anyone could believe them. These, sociologists refer to as urban legends. Perhaps you have heard the one where a traveler to Las Vegas is drugged and then wakes up in a bathtub only to find that his kidneys have been surgically removed. Another popular one is the scuba diver scooped up by a fire-fighting plane and dumped along with gallons of water onto a burning forest. Although there is no such record of either event occurring, the myths persist.

Mass Hysteria. Although not as common as other forms of dispersed collective behavior, mass hysteria occurs when a community reacts emotionally and irrationally to a real or perceived threat. The best example of this occurred in 1938 with the Orson Welles radio broadcast of, "The War of the Worlds." Although listeners were told prior to broadcast that the event was fictional, many either did not hear it or were swept away by the performance and believed that Martians were actually invading the earth. Another more recent example can be seen in the belief that vaccinating one's child from common childhood diseases could result in autism. Today, many parents refuse to vaccinate their children even in the face of scientific evidence that no such threat exists.

Fads, Fashions, and Crazes. These forms of social behavior are fast developing and have a short life span. **Fads** are temporary activities or behaviors that are enthusiastically copied by large numbers of society's members for a variety of reasons; emotional excitement, peer influence, or a desire to be outside of the prevailing norms. Two common examples are the number of new diets suddenly discovered then quickly debunked or a phrase, such as, "*Hey, Bro*" which is suddenly heard everywhere. Fads rarely have a lasting impact on society. While **fashion** is generally associated with clothing, it also includes a wide variety of things such as popular color schemes, music genres, automobiles, furniture, and numerous other items. Fashion is distinguished from fads in that items tend to have a longer lifespan. Take blue jeans, for example, once inexpensive but durable work clothing, you can now buy designer jeans for hundreds of dollars. They've been around for a hundred years and have morphed in every way possible, from blue cotton to every imaginable fabric and color. You can buy them in classic form or skinny, cropped, dressy, stretchy, low riders, with wide legs or boot-cut. **Crazes** are similar to fads and fashion but tend to have a bigger impact on society. Another distinction is that crazes are generally rooted in some form of economic activity. The housing bubble is one good example. Here, motivated by quick profits, investors began buying up properties and then quickly reselling them at higher prices in a matter of weeks. Of course,

An Algerian police officer watches over demonstrators. What started out as a peaceful protest soon turned violent. Mob behavior has long interested sociologists.

Photo: magharebia.

this lead to highly inflated prices and ultimately became one factor in the collapse of the housing market.

Localized Behavior

Localized collective behavior occurs when people who share a common concern or goal gather together in close proximity. Gatherings can be either planned or arise spontaneously. Four types of this form of collective behavior are crowds, mobs, riots, and panics.

Crowds. A crowd is defined as a temporary group of people brought together on the basis of a shared interest and whose collectivity influences individual action. That is to say, that an individual's behavior when he is in a crowd may be radically different from when he is alone. Crowds can be casual, such as those coming together to listen to a concert, or highly organized for the expressed purpose of changing the political or social structure. Past civil rights marches are one example; recent gatherings to protest the war in Afghanistan are another.

Mobs. This form of localized behavior is associated with intense levels of emotion and violence. Mob activity is generally directed at a specific target—either an individual or a group. In their purest form, mobs are leaderless, with no sense of purpose, and lack the boundaries of what is right or wrong. A tragic historical example of mob activity can be seen in the lynching era following the Civil War. Here, hundreds, if not thousands, of African Americans were dragged from their homes and hanged by angry white mobs. More recently, thousands of fans have taken to the streets to celebrate or protest the outcome of a sporting event. While starting out peacefully, they have often turned violent with loss of life and property damage.

Riots. Sometimes social and economic conditions in a society produce a level of frustration and anger that eventually drives people to violent acts that they would not normally commit under more equitable situations. In comparison to mobs, riots are comprised of a greater number of people, cover more area, and last longer. Riots generally begin with a single incident that people perceive as a shared injustice in the social structure. Although American history is rich with labor riots, race has more recently sparked urban violence. One example can be seen in the 1992 riots in Los Angles. Videotape of police officers beating Rodney King was televised nationwide. One year later, when the four police officers were acquitted of any wrongdoing, the city erupted in violence that lasted for six days. Before it was over, 53 people had died and thousands were injured.

Panics. In this form of collective behavior a crowd reacts irrationally to a serious threat. In 2003, the band Great White was playing at The Station, a nightclub in West Warwick, Rhode Island. A fire started when the band's manger set off pyrotechnics used as a backdrop to the performance. The fire quickly spread setting off panic among the 462 people in attendance who stampeded to the narrow hallways and blocked exits. Over 100 people died from burns, smoke inhalation, and being trampled. A key distinction between panics and mobs and riots is that in the latter two people rush toward an event or situation whereas in the former they rush away from it.

COLLECTIVE BEHAVIOR THEORY

Three main theories have been developed by sociologists to explain collective behavior: contagion theory, convergence theory, and emergent norm theory. In the past, we have used the ideas behind structural functionalism, social conflict, and symbolic interaction to shape our thoughts on social thinking. However, the theories of collective behavior do not easily fit into any one of these models and will be considered apart from them.

Contagion Theory. The first social researcher to attempt understanding why crowds form and why their behavior often flows to the irrational was Gustave LeBon. In his book, *The Crowd: a Study of the Popular Mind*, LeBon postulated that early on in crowd formation people develop a collective mind that functions at the lowest level of intelligence and social responsibility. Like a contagion, an intense emotional fervor sweeps through the crowd and renders participants incapable of individual thought or action. In essence, individuals develop a herd mentality and conform to the wishes of the collective irrational mind (LeBon, 1895). Later, in the twentieth century, Robert Parks and Earnest Burgess added to contagion theory by introducing the idea of *circular reaction*. Individuals, they suggest, mindlessly model their behavior on other participants in the crowd. Behavior is circulated throughout the crowd until all members behave exactly the same. In essence, the circulated behavior forms a feedback loop that further amplifies the destructive behavior (Parks and Burgess, 1921).

Convergence Theory. While contagion theory postulates that crowds adopt a collective behavior that is different from the participating individuals, convergence theory assumes that members of a crowd possess similar values and attitudes prior to their formation. Here, individuals converge for a particular reason and their unity or identity is due to their pre-existing like-mindedness. An example of this can be seen in some pro-life demonstrations where people gather to protest a clinic performing abortions. Suddenly, the mood turns ugly. Someone throws a rock and, in the excitement, the clinic is stormed and vandalized. The key here is that the members of the group did not develop a different mindset. They share a similar set of values and purpose. The only difference is that one irrational act of vandalism changes everything.

Emergent Norm Theory. Developed by Ralph Turner (1996), this theory accepts some aspects of contagion theory. However, it rejects the basic premise that individuals in the crowd become irrational or insane. Instead, it suggests that, for the most part, crowds follow an established set of social norms. As individuals we are norm following beings and conform to societal expectations whether in a crowd or alone. We have seen examples of this at various Tea Party gatherings. For the most part the norms of social civility have prevailed. Occasionally, when a member becomes obnoxious or unruly he/she is booed and chastised by other members of the crowd for unacceptable normative behavior. However, in some cases, a new norm, one of intolerance, has emerged and the behavior of the crowd changed dramatically with the shouting of racial slurs and violently striking out against anti-Tea Party participants. The key here is that this behavior is not normless, it occurred because a new norm, intolerance, emerged and individuals followed the emergent norm. Generally, emergent norms arise in situations where there is confusion about what norms are appropriate and/or where conventional norms do not appear adequate. Such conditions are fertile ground for the emergence of a new set of norms.

SOCIAL MOVEMENTS

Social movements are another important aspect of collective behavior. For our purposes we will define social movements as a large, collective, non-institutionalized group of individuals or organizations with the intent of effecting social or political change in the social structure. Unlike crowds, social movements are highly organized and goal oriented.

Types of Social Movements

Not all social movements are alike. Generally, sociologists classify social movements on the basis of their goals. In this section we will briefly examine four different types of social movements: reform movements, revolutionary movements, resistive movements, and expressive movements.

Reform Movements. In a reform movement the central goal is to alter or change a specific practice or social policy in the society. As such, its goal is narrowly defined and limited. It does not seek to overthrow the existing social order; it only seeks to change it. A good example is the international movement to abolish the practice of female circumcision where tradition and religion prescribe the practice of surgically removing the clitoris of young girls. Women across the world have formed organizations and created movements to abolish this practice. Although these movements have seen some success, the practice is ongoing in many rural and poverty stricken areas of the world. A few examples of reform movements in this country include those seeking changes in laws concerning public smoking, drinking and driving, and the legalization of marijuana.

Revolutionary Movements. Movements classified as revolutionary seek to overthrow the existing social or political order and replace it with a new order. Most notable among revolutionary movements are those concerning the political structure. Recently, in Tunisia and Egypt, people took to the streets demanding the resignation of their leaders and the creation of new political structures guaranteeing the economic and political rights of citizens. Although in both cases the government initially offered reform, the demonstrators refused settling for anything less than a complete overhaul of the political structure. Examples closer to home are the American Revolution and Civil War. Revolutionary movements are most likely to occur under conditions of extreme poverty or political alienation.

Resistive Movements. Resistive movements form in opposition to a change that has occurred in the social or political structure. A current example of this can be seen with the attempt to repeal the Patient Protection and Af-

A reform movement is one type of social movement. Here a young California woman urges support of Proposition 19 which would allow state residents, 21 years of age or older, to possess, cultivate, and transport marijuana for personal use. It would also allow the state government to regulate and tax commercial production. Proposition 19 failed to gain enough support to pass.

Photo: Cannabis Culture.

fordable Care Act, commonly referred to as Health Care Reform or Obama Care. The passage of the Act infuriated and energized conservatives across the nation and when the Republican Party won control of the House of Representatives in the 2010 midterm election, they openly targeted the Act for repeal. Another hard fought and ongoing resistive movement in the United States is the effort to repeal current abortion laws.

Expressive Movements. The major focus of expressive movements is self-fulfillment and gratification. There is no intent here to alter the social or normative structure of society. Instead, the main focus is on the individual. Religions typically have their roots in expressive movements. An example can be seen in the conservative Christian movement of "Promise Keepers," in which millions of men have pledged to uphold their religious beliefs and family obligations. A final example is the movement to allow men to reconnect to their masculinity through ceremonial drum beating and other male bonding exercises set in the wilderness.

Theories of Social Movements

Now, we turn to theories that attempt to explain the origins of social movements. Although many theories can be found, we will examine three of the most commonly cited: relative deprivation, resource-mobilization, and mass society.

Relative Deprivation Theory. Perhaps you have heard someone comment that they always seem to get "the short end of the stick." This expression lies at the core of what Denton Morrison (1971) referred to as relative deprivation, a feeling that somehow one is not getting their fair share of what they think they deserve. It is important to note that we are not talking about reality, but the perception of reality. For example, many people living in poverty in the United States have it far better than the majority of people in third world countries. But, in the eye of the beholder, poverty is *relative*. The poor in this country do not compare their situation to those living in third world countries, but to their immediate reference group—the middle and upper class here in the United States. By comparison, they feel deprived. Another key concept of this theory is *legitimate expectations*. It is not simply that people want what others have; it is a matter of legitimate expectations. They believe they deserve what everyone else has but somehow their opportunity to achieve it is being blocked. If such perceptions become widespread they can become the source of a social movement.

Resource-Mobilization Theory. A key problem with the theory of relative deprivation is that in all societies, particularly industrialized nations, stratification is present. Given this fact, one has to wonder why mass movements to correct perceived inequalities are not an ongoing and endless process. In other words, why do so many people living in poverty accept their position in life? Anthony Obershall (1973) theorized that resources avail-

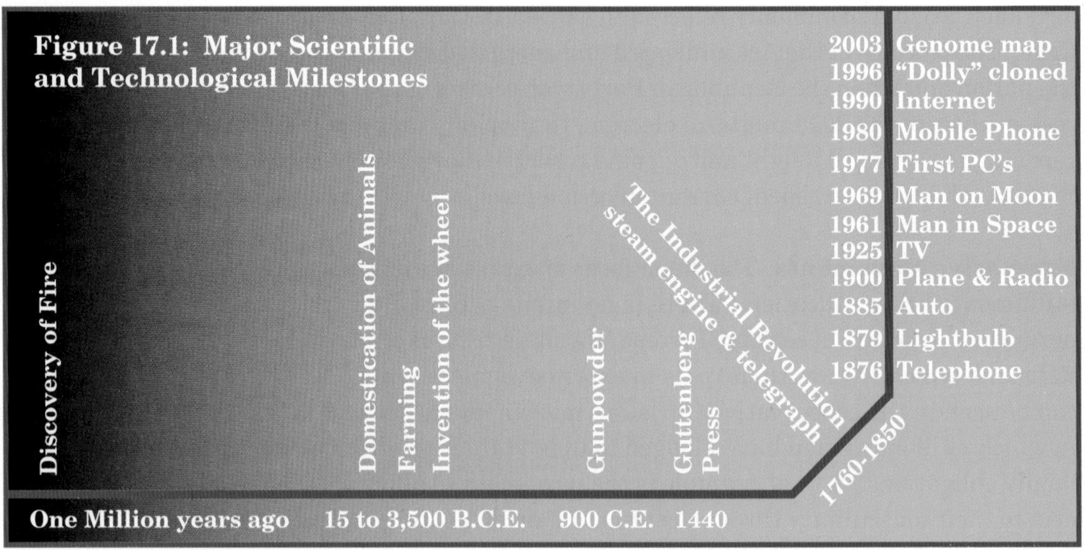

able to initiate and maintain a movement were the key. Social movements require not only people but also money, leadership, bases of operation, and communication networks to survive. Anyone who has ever participated in a labor strike understands the importance of resources. Many strikes have failed not because strikers lacked will or lost belief in their cause—they simply ran out of resources.

Mass Society Theory. In Chapter One we discussed the concepts of mechanical and organic solidarity. According to Durkheim (1893), as societies became more industrialized, they moved away from communal ties (*mechanical solidarity*) to ties based on functional interdependence (*organic solidarity*). These ties were less personal and, in extreme cases, lead to *anomie*, a loss of meaningfulness and a sense of detachment from society. Karl Marx describes a similar condition that he called *alienation*, a sense of despair resulting from being cut off from individual creativity and imagination in the workplace. Mass society theory argues that people join movements for a sense of purpose and to reconnect with society in a more meaningful way. The success of humanitarian movements like Habitat for Humanity and environmental movements such as Greenpeace can be explained by mass society theory.

SOCIAL CHANGE

Our lives are so filled with the day-to-day tasks of living that we rarely stop to think about how things are changing around us, almost on a daily basis. If we do think about change, our thoughts are at best fleeting. Picking up a disc we purchased just a year or two ago, we transfer the music or video to our I-Pod and think—well, that didn't last long. We then relegate the disc to the closet for storage, perhaps never to be used again. And then, we're off to our busy lives. In the process, we fail to recognize and understand the larger implications that even a small change can make in our daily lives and the social structure in which we live.

In this section, we take time to examine the impact of social change in our lives. We begin with a clear definition of social change and look at the levels at which change occurs. We then turn to theories of social change to understand why people resist or embrace change. We will also briefly examine the relationship between social change and social movements. And finally, we consider some future changes that have the potential to dramatically alter the way we think and live.

Defining Social Change

Social change is defined as the alteration, or variation of mechanisms, of the social structure. Change to the social structure produces change in social organizations, cultural norms, and even to the symbols important to society. These changes can be evolutionary, such as changes in religion. They can occur gradually or rapidly, like the developments in technology and labor markets. The change can be at the individual (micro) level or more systemic (macro) to social structure in general. In any case, we can see and analyze the reaction of individuals and groups to change. Change can be resisted or it can be embraced. Either way, the single universal truth about change is—it's inevitable.

Theories of Social Change

When it comes to explaining social change, there is no shortage of theories. In this section we will consider a number of the more prominent ones.

Evolutionary Change Theory. Many of the early social scientists that studied change in society were influenced by the earlier writings of Charles Darwin. It was Darwin who laid the groundwork for the evolution of species. Central to his thesis was the idea that there has been a steady and progressive evolution in all life forms, each change leading to a more advanced and efficient creation. Newly developed traits that were more efficient survived and were passed along in the gene pool while those that were outdated or inefficient died out and were eliminated. For Darwin, the progression toward a more advanced life was linear in form.

Early theorists such as August Comte and Emile Durkheim saw similarities between Darwin's work and the progression of change in society. These theorists developed what is now called **unilinear evolutionary theory**. They postulated that change in the social structure consists of progressive stages of development, each one more advanced than the previous one. The theory of Karl Marx could fit comfortably into this unilinear evolutionary theory. Though rooted in economic thought, Marx believed that the economy would pass through a number of stages, each bringing major changes to the social structure. He believed that the transition from one stage to another would be progressive and each stage would be more advanced until the achievement of the ultimate stage—communism.

More modern social scientists that subscribe to the concept of evolutionary theory believe that the progression is not so linear. Their **Multilinear evolutionary theory** suggests that social change is progressive but does not necessarily follow a straight linear path. They believe that change can originate in a number of different ways and can alter social structures in varying ways. For example, Karl Marx theorized that in capitalism, the industrialists would increasingly gain power over the workers through a centralization of the economy. For their part, workers would be forced to accept lower wages as jobs became scarce and unemployment increased. Marx believed that this would follow a progressive path until such time as the condition of workers would become so desperate that they would revolt and usher in a communist society. In the earlier stages of the Industrial Revolution, Marx's vision seem to be coming true; the economy centralized and the power of the industrialists was growing. But then something else happened that Marx did not anticipate—the rise of unions. Workers united and forced industrialists to improve wages and working condition. So while society progressed, it was not in the strict linear fashion envisioned by Marx.

Structural Functional Theory and Change. The main focus of structural functionists is on those behaviors and institutions that tend to maintain the smooth function of society. To survive in modern society we must depend upon the specialized talents and work of others. This necessitates cooperation and cooperation is the cohesive glue of society. Institutions within society function in much the same way. To survive, an institution, be it a school or a steel factory, must be functional and cooperate with other institutions and members of society. Thus, all aspects of social structure are integrative.

So how does this apply to social change? Talcott Parsons (1966) maintained that societies tend to gravitate to a state of equilibrium. In other words, society seeks stability and balance. But as we have stated previously, change is inevitable. Recognizing this, Parsons laid forth his ***equilibrium model*** in which he postulated that should a change occur in one part of the social structure it would necessitate change in other parts. If resisted, the social structure would experience increasing levels of stress until such time that what Parsons termed *stress consensus* happened—society would accept and adjust to the changes and thereby once again achieve equilibrium.

Structural functionalists offer numerous examples in our own society to illustrate their point. One example is women in the workforce. At one time, prior to World War II, it was uncommon for women to work outside of the home. Their role was restricted to childcare and homemaking. During the war women were recruited into the workforce to take the place of men fighting in combat. After the war, there was an attempt to push women back into their traditional roles. However, many women resisted. Initially, this was seen as a threat to the traditional institutions of family and marriage, as well as a threat to existing gender roles. The resulting social strain was very much evident. Eventually, the institutions of society adapted and values changed so that today women have far more life choices than did those in the past. Another example can be seen in the Civil Rights Movement of the 1960s. After the historic *Brown v. Board of Education* court case, segregation of public places was outlawed. However, the resistance to the Court's decision produced enormous stain in the social system. Eventually, the strain and resulting conflict was resolved as the attitudes of people and institutions changed to acceptance and the social system again regained equilibrium.

Social Conflict Theory and Social Change. Even though structural functionalists see societal strain as the initial phase of social change, they argue that eventually society does change through consensus and cooperation. Social conflict theorists would disagree with this line of thinking. For them, society is in a constant state of strain and conflict where the powerful attempt to maintain their control over the powerless so as to retain their advantages. Change occurs when disadvantaged individuals or groups rise up in resistance and demand changes. Change occurs, but not because those in control are suddenly shamed by their own greed or behaviors of inequality. Things change because those demanding change have gained power and the powerful are forced to accommodate the demands of those seeking change; to do otherwise would lead to self-destruction. Stratification and inequality are ongoing realities of modern life and the social system is in an ongoing and perpetual state of strain.

While structural functionalists (see above) explain the normalization of race relations as a result of strain in the social system followed by eventual equilibrium, social conflict theorists point to the time when African Americans, along with others, stood up for more just treatment through marches and demonstrations, often enduring violent and murderous acts. They would point to the race riots of the 1960s when entire neighborhoods went up in flames. Eventually, they point out, the system was forced to enact changes and the historic Civil Rights Act of 1964 was enacted by Congress and signed by President Lyndon Johnson.

Another example, though smaller in scale, can be seen in what became known as, "The Sonewall Riots." In 1969, a little bar in Manhattan's West Village became the center of an uprising by gays against the establishment. Raided by police on a regular basis, the gay patrons finally revolted. As the bartender, the doorman, and a few drag queens were arrested, chants of "gay power" rose up from the crowd. Soon, beer bottles, trash cans, and chairs began flying and a full-scale riot was underway. So too, was the birth of the Gay Rights Movement.

Symbolic Interaction Theory and Social Change. As we have seen throughout our text, symbolic interaction is a micro level theory. It focuses on the patterns of interactions of individuals in specific social situations. It is rooted in the belief that both the individual and the entirety of society is the collective sum of human interaction based on language and other symbols. Following this line of thought, symbolic interactionists believe that all social change originates from, and can be explained by, individual behaviors. Society is a collection of individuals. In the process of day-to-day interactions, individuals are confronted with a seemingly endless stream of interactions with individuals, groups, institutions, and objects in the material culture. With each interaction the individual decides how he/she will interpret the encounter and how to react to it. Since human beings have the capacity of higher cognitive thinking they also have the ability to interpret events differently from others around them. It is this divergence of thought about various interactions, this difference in interpretation of events, which symbolic interactionists see as the fertile ground for change.

The 1960s Women's Rights Movement in the United States serves as an example. At one time in our culture terms such as "dear," "honey," "dollface," "sweetie," etc. were used as endearing ways to address a woman. And, it is fair to say, that at one time many women accepted and appreciated being referenced in this way. Then a shift began to occur in the way women interpreted such remarks. Instead of endearing, women came to see the terms as objectification. As this interpretation spread, a movement was born resulting in dramatic changes in the social structure. Another example is that of relative poverty. The poor in this country do not compare themselves with people living in an impoverished nation; they compare themselves to middle and upper class people living in this society. As a result of that comparison, they perceive themselves as being poor and disadvantaged and conclude that they are in some way being blocked from the position and goods they want. The sum of these perceptions and the resulting actions then form the basis of a social movement directed at change.

Resistance to Change

As we have mentioned in this chapter, change is a constant and ongoing process in society. So too is the resistance to change. Here, we consider some of the obstacles to change.

Resistance to Shifts in Power Structures. It was Thorstein Veblen (1857-1929) who first used the term **vested interests** to describe those who resisted social change because it threatened their position of power and influence within the system. In a perfect example of vested interests we now see major changes occurring in the Middle East. The wave of revolts began in January 2011, when a college educated Tunisian street vendor named Mohamed Bouazizi set himself on fire after being humiliated by police. His self-immolation sparked a social movement protesting the lack of freedom, joblessness, and government corruption. In a matter of days the entire country was beset by protests that ultimately forced autocratic ruler, Zine El Abidine Ben Ali, to flee the country ending his 23-year rule. Within days of the successful Tunisian revolution, similar revolutions occurred throughout the region in Egypt, Libya, Jordan, Syria, Yemen, Bahrain, and Iran. In many cases, those who benefited from the rule of autocratic leaders organized counter demonstrations. In each country, the rulers had resisted calls for democracy because it threatened their vested interests in authority and power and any movement toward an open and democratic society poses a threat to the position of the affluent people who supported them.

We can also see resistance to change in our own society. On a national level, organizations like the medical community and labor unions try to protect their advantage by opposing proposed changes to their work and profession. Throughout the years, a number of attempts have been made to alter how we provide medical treatment in this country. The recent passage of "The Patient Protection and Affordable Care Act," commonly referred to as Health Care Reform or *ObamaCare* was a major struggle between those resisting change—insurance companies and medical providers—and progressives seeking to extend health care to citizens who were either uninsured or underinsured. Likewise, attempts to alter laws governing the right of workers to collective bargaining have met with resistance by unions. Although each provides supporting arguments in resisting change, there is, nevertheless, the reality that change alters existing power relationships and provides a strong case for maintaining the status quo by those in power.

Resistance to Technology Advancement. Whether simple or complex, technological advancement has been an important part of the rise of humans to the top of the evolutionary ladder. Sociologists have noted that innovations in technology always occur in an environment of resistance. Karl Marx, writing on the Industrial Revolution, described the process of alienation of workers from their work. Prior to the Industrial Revolution workers were highly skilled craftsmen who took pride in their craft and in starting and

As we become more technologically advanced, more and more jobs will disappear. Here a woman uses an automated checkout machine in a grocery store. Such machines are becoming increasingly common and with them fewer check-out clerks are needed.

Photo: SPP.

finishing a job. With industrialization, this was no longer possible and, Marx claimed, that it robbed workers of their creativity and imagination and ultimately would lead to despair which, in turn, would lead to revolution.

Today, we live in a world where technological advancements are a daily occurrence. Automation has brought to the workplace machines capable of streamlining the manufacturing process and producing higher levels of efficiency and profits. But, in the process, it also has displaced workers. Within a ten-year period the United States manufacturing output advanced from 1.1 trillion to 1.4 trillion dollars with an eleven percent job decline (Miklovic, 2003). And, this was just in manufacturing. The Internet and high-speed computers have displaced millions of other workers in the service economy. How have workers reacted to this? In the early nineteenth century British textile artisans, known as the Luddites, rebelled against innovations in their field by destroying mechanized looms. Today, resistance is seen more in political arenas where workers try to win concessions through labor unions by negotiating job security or by lobbying the government to restrict the import of foreign goods.

Resistance to technology has not been restricted to workers. Industry, for their part, has demonstrated a propensity to resist technology when it affects their markets and profits. The oil and automotive industries resisted investing in new technologies to improve fuel efficiency for decades. Likewise, energy companies have been notorious in their attempt to prevent government restriction on pollution controls as well as refusing to invest in alternative energy sources.

Despite resistance, technological innovation is destined to win out in the long run. Unions have made concessions. The automotive industry was forced to produce energy efficient and alternative fuel cars because of competition from overseas. And, with energy costs climbing, there is a renewed interest in investing in alternative energy sources for the future.

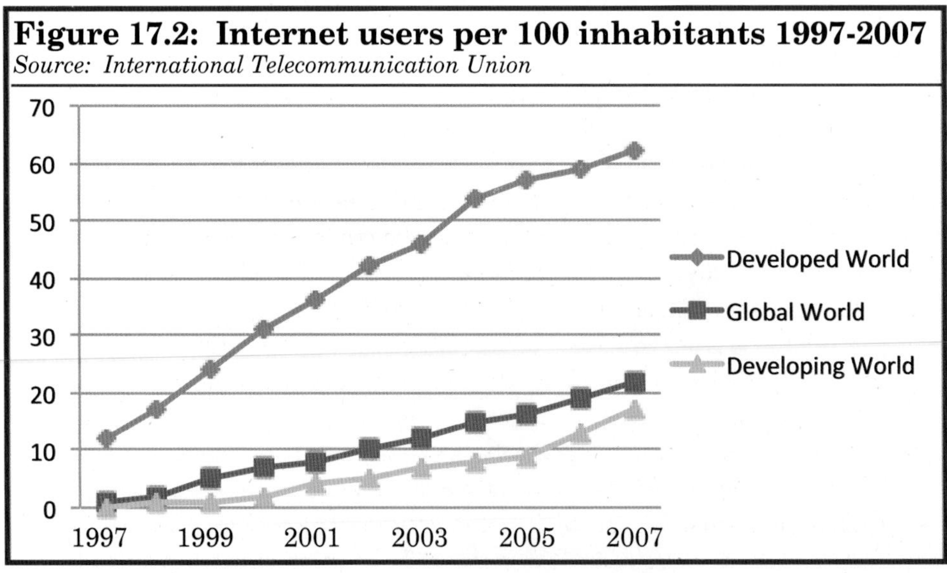

Figure 17.2: Internet users per 100 inhabitants 1997-2007
Source: International Telecommunication Union

Entrenched cultural and religious values hinder the acceptance of change. Here, two citizens apologize for ultra conservatives who hail from their state; particularly they express their disagreement with the State Board of Eduction in Kansas for mandating that creationist theories be taught along side of evolution in the classroom.

Photo: David Shankbone.

Resistance to Change in Cultural Values. Not all resistance to change can be explained in terms of power and economics. In many cases the resistance is simply because whatever change is occurring challenges the belief system of society. Galileo was quick to discover this when he began championing Copernicanism, the idea that placed the sun, rather than the earth, at the center of the universe.

In Chapter Three we discussed the concept of **cultural lag**. This is where changes in the material culture occur at a faster pace than changes in the non-material culture. Conflict develops because people have a desire to hang on to cherished beliefs and ways of life. In society today, we see constant conflict between religion and science. New discoveries challenge our beliefs about how the world was created and how humans have evolved over time. These discoveries sometimes lay in stark contrast to accepted religious beliefs. Conflict develops and, over time, new interpretations and ways of looking at sacred writings emerge. In some cases, the lag between science and belief can be lengthy, as that with evolution. Some religions now recognize evolution as a scientific fact while others reject the concept and maintain a belief in "creationism" or "intelligent design" where God is held directly and personally responsible for all creation.

As our concept of race and racial relations began to change, many people were reluctant to move to a desegregated society. In the 1950s and 1960s, federal troops were called into the South to forcibly desegregate schools. Angry white mobs gathered at school bus stops to verbally, and sometimes physically, attack black school children. Similarly, many communities were reluctant to give up the practice of segregating public and private facilities or to change laws forbidding marriage between whites and racial minorities.

Yet another example is the current debate over stem cell research. To many, embryonic stem cell research violates the sanctity of life. They maintain that human life begins at the moment of conception when a sperm cell fertilizes an egg cell to form a single new cell; the destruction of an embryo is nothing short of murder. Also, many opponents of this research maintain that embryonic stem cell research will lead to the creation of embryos for the sole purpose of servicing the living—a grievous breach of human morality. This was the concern that prompted President George W. Bush to place a ban on the use of federal funds for embryonic stem cell research. President Obama later rescinded this ban.

Gay marriage is another example of resistance to change due to cultural beliefs. Up until recently, homosexuality was thought to be an individual preference or choice. Biological and social research is now questioning this belief and increasingly more and more people are coming to view homosexuality not as a choice, but as an orientation one is born with. Based on this idea and the fact that marriage, from a legal standpoint, is a matter of state law, the question arises whether it is constitutionally legal to prohibit marriage between two same sex partners. At this point in time, the research is not absolutely definitive and as such there remains much controversy about the moral and legal rights of gays to marry. Many states have passed anti-gay marriage laws and other states have either passed laws allowing gay marriage or their courts have ruled prohibitions against gay marriage as illegal.

The above are only a few examples of resistance to change. Many more, too many to discuss here, can be found in everyday life. We conclude this section by restating that change is inevitable. It is a part of the human condition. It is not a matter of if change will occur it is only a matter of how quickly it will happen and what lies ahead. It is this topic that we take up next.

THE FUTURE

Now it's time to relax and let our minds wander down the road to the future. In this final section we consider some distant probabilities and some not so far off changes that have the potential to alter society and human interaction in dramatic ways.

Internet. We would be remiss if we did not begin with a discussion of the **Internet** and its impact on the human condition. Originally developed for military communication, the Internet spread to the public in the 1990s eventually linking billions of people worldwide and spawning social websites such as Facebook, Twitter, and MySpace. These websites, along with many others, have provided a way for individuals to transcend geographical boundaries and interact socially with others worldwide. One growing trend is the creation of alternative identities that allows people to create a cyberworld, such as *FarmVille*, where they live alternative lives. In addition to social networking, the Internet has freed workers from the workplace. More and more companies are moving away from the brick and mortar physical plant and allowing workers the freedom to work in a variety of settings. And finally, the Internet has been instrumental in facilitating mass movements such as social protests, organizing voters in elections, and even overthrowing governments. Before the Internet, governments were able to control what people listened to, read, and viewed; today, this is no longer possible.

Genetic Engineering. Ongoing work and experiments in **genetic engineering** offers great potential benefits but also confounding questions for society to work out. Current work with humans involves replacing defective genes with functional ones to prevent or to cure a variety of human malaises such as diabetes, arthritis, Parkinson disease, etc. There are medical breakthroughs on every horizon and we will soon be capable of using advanced technology for human enhancement. For example, we may soon be able to alter the appearance and intelligence, as well as personality traits, of human beings. Who will be the benefactors of such science? Who will be the losers? How will this advancement change our lives? Our society?

Cloning. Another line of research with the potential to alter the human condition is cloning. Scientifically termed "somatic cell nuclear transfer" (SCNT), the process is used to create identical organisms through asexual reproduction. The first mammal that was successfully cloned was a Finn-Dorset ewe in 1996 who lived for six years. Reports of other cloned mammals have since surfaced. It is only a matter of time before the first human is cloned. What then? Is it human? Does it have rights? And, what of the religious implications? Take a moment to ponder what happens when we have the capability to reproduce entirely asexually. At some time in the future will women abandon the risks and restrictions of pregnancy? What will become of marriage and family?

Artificial Intelligence. Since the advent of the computer, scientists have been chasing the dream of creating Artificial Intelligence (AI). Now, after 50 years of research, machines have been created that can mimic human thought, understand speech, and beat humans at tasks never before thought possible. Although these machines do not currently match the complexity of human intelligence, it is only a matter of time, perhaps in the next twenty years, when artificial intelligence will be achieved. The achievement of AI will dramatically transform the way humans live and work. In fact, there may be a time when there is no work for humans to do. Certainly robots with AI will be able to outperform humans in almost every job in the workplace. As humans leave or are forced out of the workplace, major adjustments in society will be required; how we define ourselves, how we relate to others, how resources are divided, how we spend our time, and many more equally complicated life and living questions. Finally, what will our relationship to these new machines be, if and when, they achieve consciousness?

Achieving Immortality. Since the beginning of time man has sought the "Fountain of Youth." You may recall, Ponce de Leone, traveled halfway around the world in search of the magical waters that would make him imortal. For most of human existence, this has been just a dream. Today, more and more scientific breakthroughs have brought us to the realization that humans may be able to significantly extend their lives. Recent advances in stem cell research and the replacement of aging organs through transplants is offered by some as a possible way to extend life. A number of scientists are working to achieve immortality by tricking our aging genes into thinking our body is still young. The central thesis is that our bodies are composed of genes that switch on and off during our lifetime—some are "on" only while we are young and others turn "on" or "off" as we age. Through gene modification, some scientists believe that we can prevent aging by understanding and eventually manipulating this genetic on-off switch so that our bodies are always in an optimal phase of life (Dawkins, 2006). Another, more radical, futurist vision is that humans will one day be able to transfer their memories and thoughts to a computer. Termed **singularity**, some researchers believe that in the near future, perhaps even by the middle of this century, we will be able to transfer our consciousness to a computer and in this way transcend our biology (Kurzweil, 2005). What then?

The above represents only a sampling of the many changes that will ultimately confront you as an individual and the social structure at large. Now it's time for you to contemplate the future. What changes will occur in your lifetime? How might these changes impact your life and the society in which you live?

Terms You Should Know:

Social Statics	Social Dynamics	Social Change
Collective Behavior	Rumor	Gossip
Urban Legend	Fads	Fashion
Crazes	Crowd	Mob
Social Movement	Legitimate Expectation	Relative Poverty
Anomie	Alienation	Vested Interest
Copernicanism	Cultural Lag	Genetic Engineering
Cloning	AI	Singularity

Can You Answer These Questions?

1. According to your textbook, what forces create social change?
2. Why is social change so contentious?
3. How does rumor differ from gossip? Who is most likely to engage in gossip?
4. What is the central difference between dispersed and localized collective behavior?
5. Discuss the three major theories of collective behavior presented in your textbook.
6. List and differentiate between the four types of social movements. Give an example of each.
7. What are the three major theories attempting to explain the origins of social movements?
8. How does unilinear evolutionary theory differ from multilinear evolutionary theory? Which would Karl Marx most likely subscribe to?
9. What is the main theory of the equilibrium model of social change?
10. List and discuss why there is so much resistance to social change. What is the biggest obstacle to social change?
11. How has the internet changed the world?
12. List some major technological advancements that have changed society.

Critical Thinking Exercises:

1. Identify a current social movement either in our society or internationally and discuss how society might be changed by it.
2. What do you think is the underlying reason people are prone to the sway of fashion and crazes?
3. Do you believe that technology will provide more or less freedom for humans?
4. Ultimately science, through genetic engineering, will be able to alter the physical and psychological characteristics of humans before birth. Given this option, would you as a prospective parent want to have your child "tuned-up"?
5. Imagine a world where robots with artificial intelligence are capable of doing all work. What changes in the social structure will this necessitate?
6. Let's say that science one day allows us to transcend our biology and live forever. Is this a good thing?

Works Cited and References

Chapter One

Bauman, Zygmunt. 1990. *Thinking Sociologically*. Cambridge, MA: Basil Blackwell.

Du Bois, W. E. B. 1967. *The Philadelphia Negro: A Social Study*. New York: Schocken (orig. pub. 1899).

Durkheim, Emile. 1893. *The Division of Labor in Society*. New York: Free Press.

Martineau, Harriet. 1962. *Society in America* (edited, abridged). Garden City, NY: Doubleday (orig. pub. 1837).

Mark, Karl. 1967. *Capital: A Critique of Political Economy*. Ed. Friedrich Engels. New York: International (orig. pub. 1867).

Mead, George Herbert. 1934. *Mind, Self, and Society*. Chicago: University of Chicago Press.

Merton, Robert. 1968. *Social Theory and Social Structure*. New York: Free Press.

Mills, C. Wright. 1959. *The Sociological Imagination*. London: Oxford University Press.

Parks, Robert and Ernest W. Burgess. 1921. *Human Ecology*. Chicago: University of Chicago Press.

Meacham, Andrew. 2009, Nov. 29. "Sexting-related Bullying cited in Hillsborough Teen's Suicide," *St. Petersburg Times*, A1. *www.tampabay.com/news/humaninterest/article1054895.ece*

Weber, Max. 1968. *Economy and Society: An Outline of Interpretive Sociology*. Trans. G. Roth and G. Wittich. New York: Bedminister (orig. pub. 1922).

Chapter Two

Becker, Gary. 1991. *A Treatise on the Family*. Harvard University Press.

Coleman, James S., Hoffer, Thomas, and Kilgore, Sally. 1982. *High School Achievement: Public, Catholic, and Private Schools Compared*. New York: Basic Books.

Coontz, Stephanie. 1996. "Where Are The Good Old Days?" *Modern Maturity*. May - June, pp. 36 - 53.

Dubin, Robert. 1978. *Theory Building*. Revised edition. Free Press.

Durkheim, Emile. Reissue edition 1997. *Suicide: A Study in Sociology*. Free Press.

Durkheim, Emile. 1982. *The Rules of Sociological Method, and Selected Texts on Sociology and its Method*. Edited with an introduction by Steven Lukes. Translated by W.D. Halls. The Free Press.

Hakim, Catherine. 1982. *Secondary Analysis in Social Research*. London: Allen and Unwin: London, UK.

Harding, David and Jencks, Christopher, "Changing Attitudes Toward Premarital Sex: Cohort, Period and Aging Effects," *Public Opinion Quarterly* 67, no.2 (2003).

Hart, Betty and Risley Todd R. 1995. *Meaningful Differences in the Everyday Experience of Young American Children*. Baltimore, MD: Paul H Brookes Publishing Co.

Johnson, William A. Jr., Rettig, Richard P. Gregory M. Scott, and Stephen M. Garrison. 2010. *The Sociology Student Writer's Manual*. 6th ed. Pearson

Lewis, Oscar. 1959 (1975). *Five Families: Mexican Case Studies in the Culture of Poverty*. NY: Basic Books.

Liebow, Elliot. 1967 [2003]. *Tally's Corner: A Study of Negro Street Corner Men*. Rowman & Littlefield Publishing Group.

Liebow, Elliot. 1993. *Tell Them Who I am: The lives of Homeless Women*. NY: Simon & Schuster.

Lofland, John. 1984. *Analyzing Social Settings*. Belmont, CA. Wadsworth.

Marshood, Nabil. 2010. *Voices from the Camps: A People's History of Palestinian Refugees in Jordan*, 2006. University Press of America.

Turner, Jonathan H., (ed.). 1989. *Theory Building in Sociology: Assessing Theoretical Cumulation*. Newbury Park, CA: Sage.

Waltz, Kenneth N. 1979. *Theory of International Theory*. Addison-Wesley

Weber, Max. [1904] 1949. *The Methodology of the Social Sciences*. Translate and edited by Edward A. Shils and Henry A. Finch. New York: Free Press.

Weber, Max. *Essays in Sociology*. Edited and translated, H.H. Gerth and C.Wright Mills. Copyright 1946 by Oxford University Press. Reviewed 1973 by H.H. Gerth.

Chapter Three

Alfvin, Carolyn. "Smooching Through History. Chicago Tribune 19 Apr. 1998: Section 13. April 19: pp.1, 9.

Christenson, H.T. 1960. "Cultural Relativism and Premarital Sex Norms." *American Sociological Review*. Vol. 25: pp. 31-39.

Crane, William. 1995. *The Art of Kissing*. New York: St. Martin's Press.

Giddens, Anthony. 1992. *The Transformation of Intimacy: Sexuality, Love, and Eroticism in Modern Societies*. Stanford, CA: Stanford University Press.

Gold, Rachel Benson, and Lehrman, Dorothy. 1989. "Fetal Research Under Fire: The Influence of Abortion Politics." *Family Planning Perspectives*, 21(1), January-February 6-11, 38.

Greenberg, J.H. 1968. *Anthropological Linguistics: An Introduction*. New York: Random House.

Harris, Marvin. 1975. *Cows, Pigs, Wars, and Witches: The Riddles of Culture*. New York: Random House.

Kinsey, Alfred C. 1948. *Sexual Behavior in the Human Male*. Philadelphia: Saunders.

Kinsey, Alfred C. 1953. *Sexual Behavior in the Human Female*. Philadelphia: Saunders.

Marx, Karl. *The Marx-Engels Reader*. Robert C. Tucker (ed.). New York: Norton, 1977.

McGinley, Laurie. "Research That Uses Human Embryos Should Get U.S. Funding, Panel Says." *Wall Street Journal* 28 September *1994*, Section B8. *https://tspace.library.utoronto.ca/html/1807/23394/nl94050.html*

Murdock, George. 1956. "How Culture Changes." In Harry L. Shapiro (ed.), *Man Culture & Society*. New York: Oxford University Press.

NPR. 2001. "Poverty in America." NPR/Kaiser/Kennedy School Poll. http://www.npr.org/programs/specials/poll/

OrganDonor.Gov. 2010. "Access to U.S. government Information on Organ & Tissue Donation and Transplantation. http://www.organdonor.gov/

Parker, Stephen. 1990. *Informal Marriage: Cohabitation and the Law*. New York: St. Martin's Press.

Pew Research Center. 2003. "Religious Beliefs Underpin Opposition to Homosexuality." *Pew Research Center for the People & the Press*. 18 November 2003.

Pew Research Center. 2007. "A Nation of "Haves" and "Have-Nots"? *Pew Research Center for the People & the Press,* 13 September 2007.

Rippy, Alyssa E., and Elana Newman, "Discrimination Against Muslim Women." ACLU, Women's Rights Project, 2008.

Roszak, Theodore. 1969. *The Making of Counterculture: Reflections of the Technocratic Society and Its Youthful Opposition*. New York: Doubleday.

San Francisco Chronicle. 1994. "Helms Loses Bid to Ban Talk of Gays in Schools." September 24: p. 4.

Spates, James L. 1976. *Countercultural and Dominant Cultural Values: A Cross-national Analysis of the Undergroup Press and Dominant Cultural Magazines.*

The Pew Forum, "A Stable Majority: "Most Americans Still Oppose Same-Sex Marriage." April 1, 2008.

Williams, R. M., Jr. 1979. *American Values—A Sociological Perspective*. New York: Knopf.

Woodward, Kenneth L. 1992. "Talking To God." *Newsweek* 6 January 1992: Vol. 119, No 1.

Chapter Four

Aldrich, Howard E., and Peter V. Marsden. 1988. "Environments and Organizations." In Neil J. Smelser (ed.), *Handbook of Sociology*. Newbury Park, CA: Sage.

Asch, Solomon. 1952. *Social Psychology*. Englewood Cliffs, N.J.: Prentice Hall.

Cooley, Charles Horton. 1909. *Social Organization*. New York: Scribner's.

Durkheim, Emile. 1951, original 1897. *Suicide*. New York: Free Press.

Durkheim, Emile. (1964, original 1893). *The Division of Labor in Society*. New York: Free Press.

Ebaugh, Helen Rose Funch. 1988. *Becoming an EX: The Process of Role Exit*. Chicago: University of Chicago Press.

Etzioni, Amitai. 1975. *A Comparative Analysis of Complex Organizations*, rev. ed. New York: Free Press.

Goffman, E. 1961. *Asylums: Essays on the Social Situations of Mental Patients and Other Inmates*. New York: Anchor Books.

Goffman, E. 1961b. Encounters: *Two Studies in the Sociology of Interaction*. London: Routledge and Kegan Paul.

Knoke, David. 1990. *Political Networks: The Structural Perspective*. New York: Cambridge University Press.

Marsden, Peter, V., and Nan Lin. 1982. *Social Structure and Network Analysis*. Beverly Hills, CA: Sage.

Marsden, Peter. 1987. "Core Discussion Networks of Americans." *American Sociological Review* 52, February: pp. 122-131.

Michels, Robert. 1967 (Originally published in 1911). *Political Parties: A Sociological Study of the Oligarchical Tendencies in Modern Democracy*. New York: Free Press.

Millgram, Stanley. 1963. "Behavioral Study of Obedience." *Journal of Abnormal and Social Psychology*. Vol. 67, No. 4, pp. 371-76.

Simmel, George. 1955. *Conflict and the Web of Group Affiliations*, Kurt Wolf, trans. Glencoe, IL: Free Press.

Stoner, J.A. F. 1961. "A Comparison of Individual and Group Decisions Involving Risk." Master's thesis, Massachusetts Institute of Technology, School of Industrial Management.

Summers, Jr., Harry. 1985. *Vietnam War Almanac*. New York: Facts of File

Veblen, Thorstein. 1912. *The Theory of the Leisure Class*. New York: Macmillan.

Wallace, Jim. 2010. "Girls charged with street gang terrorism." Retrieved from www.street-gangs.com/news/120210_girls_gang_terrorism.

Wallach, Michael A., Nathan Kogan, and Daryl J. Bem. 1962. "Group Influence on Individual Risk Taking." *Journal of Abnormal and Social Psychology* 65; pp. 75-86.

Weber, Max. 1946, original 1919. "Bureaucracy," in H. H. Gerth and C. Wright Mills, eds. *From Max Weber: Essays in Sociology*. New York: Oxford University Press, pp. 196-244.

Wellman, Barry, Peter J. Carrington, and Alan Hall. 1988. *Social Structures: A Network Approach*. Cambridge: Cambridge University Press.

Whitlock, Gaig. 2010. "Members of Stryker combat Brigade in Afghanistan accused of killing civilians for sport." Retrieved from http://washingtonpost.com/wp_dyn/content/article/2010.

Chapter Five

Bandura, Albert. 1977. *Social Learning Theory*. Englewood Cliffs, NJ: Prentice Hall.

Barwise, Patrick and Andrew Ehrenberg. 1988. *Television and Its Audience*. Beverly Hills, CA: Sage

Bowles, Samuel, and Herbert Gintis. 1976. *Schooling in Capitalist America*. New York: Basic Books.

Boxer, Paul, L. Rowell Huesmann, Brad J. Bushman, Maureen O'Brien and Dominic Moceri. 2009. "The Role of Violent Media Preference in Cumulative Developmental Risk for Violence and General Aggression." *Journal of Youth and Adolescence*. Volume 33(3), pp. 417-428.

Bronfenbrenner, Urie. 1992. "Principles for the Healthy Growth and Development of Children." *In Marriage and Family in a Changing Society*, 4th ed., James M. Henslin, ed. pp. 243-249. New York: Free Press.

Corsaro, William A., and Donna Eder. 1995. "Development and Socialization of Children and Adolescents." in Karen S. Cook, Gary Alan Fine, and James S. House (eds.) *Sociological Perspectives on Social Psychology*. Boston: Allyn & Bacon.

Davis, Kingsley. 1947. "Final Notes a Case of Extreme Isolation." *American Journal of Sociology*, Volume 52, pp. 432-437.

Donnerstein, E., & Barrett, G. 1978. "Effects of Erotic Stimuli on Male Aggression Toward Females." *Journal of Personality and Social Psychology*, Volume 36, pp. 180-188.

Donnerstein, E.I., & Berkowitz, L. 1981. "Victim Reactions in Aggressive Erotic Films as a Factor in Violence Against Women." *Journal of Personality and Social Psychology*, Volume 41, pp. 710-724.

Donnerstein, E. 1983. "Erotica and Human Aggression." In R. G. Green & Donnerstein (Eds.), *Aggression: Theoretical and Empirical Reviews* (Vol. 1). New York: Academic Press.

Donnerstein, E., Linz, D., & Penrod, S. 1987. *The Question of Pornography*. London: Free Press.

Eagly, A. H., R. D., Makhijani, M. G., & Long, L. C. 1991. "What is Beautiful is Good, but . . .: A Eta-analytic Review on the Physical Attractiveness Stereotype." *Psychological Bulletin*, Volume 110, pp. 109-128.

Eron, L. D., Huesmann, R, Lefkowitz, M. M., & Walder, L. O. (1972). "Does Television Violence Cause Aggression?" *American Psychologist*, Volume 27, pp. 253-263.

Freedman, Jonathan L. 2002. *Media Violence and Its Effect on Aggression: Assessing the Scientific Evidence*. Toronto, Canada: University of Toronto Press.

Gecas, Viktor. 1981. "Contexts of Socialization." Morris Rosenberg and Ralph H. Turner (eds.) *Social Psychology: Sociological Perspectives*. New York: Basic Books.

Goffman, Erving. 1961. *Asylums: Essays on the Social Situation of Mental Patients and Other Inmates*. Chicago: Aldine.

Hadaway, C. Kirk, and Penny Long Marler. 2005. "How Many Americans Attend Worship Each Week? An Alternative Approach to Measurement." *Journal for the Scientific Study of Religion*. Volume 44(3): pp. 307-322.

Hammermesh, Daniel S. 2006. "Changing looks and changing 'discrimination': The beauty of economists." *ScienceDirect*. Economic Letters 93: pp. 505-412.

_____ 2007. Quoted in online paper title "To those that have, shall be given.' http://www.economist_com/node/10311266?story_id=10311266.

Huesmann, L. R. 1982. "Television violence and aggressive behavior." In D. Pearl & L. Bouthilet (eds.), *Television and Behavior: Ten Years of Scientific Progress and Implications for the 80's*. Washington, D.C.: U.S. Government Printing Office.

Huesmann, L. R., & Eron, L. D. 1986. *Television and the Aggressive Child: A Cross-National Comparison*. eds. Hillsdale, NJ: Erlbaum.

Itard, Jean-Marc. 1962. *The Wild Boy of Aveyron*. New York: Harper & Row.

Itzin, Catherine. 1993. *Pornography: Women, Violence, and Civil Liberties*. Oxford: Clarendon Press.

Josephson, W. D. 1987. "Television Violence and Children's Aggression: Testing the Priming, Social Script, and Disinhibition Prediction." *Journal of Personality and Social Psychology*. Volume 53, pp. 882-890.

Kimmel, Michael, S., and Annulla Linders. 1996. "Does Censorship Make a Difference? An Aggregate Empirical Analysis of Pornography and Rape," *Journal of Psychology and Human Sexuality. Volume* 8, pp. 1-20.

Kohlbert, Lawrence, and Carol Gilligan. 1971. "The Adolescent as a Philosopher: The Discovery of the Self in a Postconventional World." *Daedalus*, Volume 100 (4), pp. 1051-1086.

Linz, Daniel, G., and Edward Donnerstein. 1989. "The Effects of Violent Messages on the mass media." In James Bradac (ed.), *Message Effects in communication Science. Sage Annual Reviews of Communication Research*, Vol. 17. Beverly Hills, Calif.: Sage.

Phillips, John L., Jr. 1969. *The Origins of Intellect: Piaget's Theory*. San Francisco: Freeman.

Piaget, Jean. 1956. *The Origins of Intelligence in Children.* New York: Norton.

Pines, Maya. 1981. "The Civilization of Genie." *Psychology Today*, September, pp. 28-34.

Rushton, J. Philippe. 1975. "Generosity in Children: Immediate and Long-Term Effects of Modeling, Preaching, and Moral Judgment." *Journal of Personality and Social Psychology. Volume* 31, pp. 459-466.

Snyder, M., Tanke, E. D., & Berscheid, E. 1977. "Social Perception and Interpersonal Behavior," *Journal of Personality and Social Psychology*. Volume 35, pp. 656-666.

Strossen, Nadine. *Defending Pornography*. New York: New York University Press, 2000.

Wrong, Dennis H. 1961. "The oversocialized conception of man in modern sociology." *American Sociological Review." Volume 26, pp. 183-193.*

Chapter Six

Anderson, David A.. "The Aggrate Burden of Crime". Journal of Law and Economics. Oct. 1999.

Anderson, Margaret L. 1997. *Thinking About Women: Sociological Perspectives on Sex and Gender,* Fourth Edition. Boston: Allyn and Bacon.

Bartollas, Clemens. 1997. *Juvenile Delinquency.* Fourth Edition. Boston: Allyn and Bacon.

Blau, Judith and Peter M. Blau. 1982. "The Cost of Inequality; Metropolitan Structure and Violent Crime." *American Sociological Review.* Volume 47 pp. 114-29.

Blumstein, Alfred. 1995. "Violence by Young People: Why the Deadly Nexus?" *National Institute of Justice Journal*. August, pp. 2-9.

Bryiak, George J. and Michael P. Soroka. 1977. *Sociology: Cultural Diversity in a Changing World.* Boston: Allyn and Bacon.

Bullough, Vern and Bonnie Bullough. 1987. *Women and Prostitution: A Social History.* Buffalo: Promethius Books.

Cohen, Jon. "Trust in Congress Scrapes the Bottom of the Barrel." *The Trail*, June 20, 2008.

Cohen, Stanley. 1972. *Folk Devils and Moral Panics.* London: MacGibbon and Kee.

Diamond, David. 1997. *USA Weekend.* Feb. 14-66.

Durkheim, Emile. 1993. Original 1895. *The Division of Labor in Society.* New York: Macmillan.

Federal Bureau of Investigation. 2007. *Crime Report,* Washington, D.C.: U.S. Government Printing Office

Freund, Matthew, Ph.D., Leanord, Terri L., M.A. and Lee, Nancy, MSW. 1989. "Sexual Behavior of Resident Street Prostitutes with their Clients in Camden, New Jersey." *Journal of Sex Research.* Vol. 26. No 4. pp. 460-478.

Garfinkel, H. 1956. "Conditions of a Successful Degradation Ceremony." *American Journal of Sociology.* Volume 61, pp. 420-424.

Goode, Erich and Nachman, Ben-Yehuda. 1994. *Moral Panics.* UK: Blackwell.

Janis, I.L. 1983. Groupthink. In H.H. Blumberg, A.P. Hare, V. Kent, and M.F. Davis (editors), *Small Groups and Social Interaction* (Vol. 2, pp.39-46). Chinchester, England: Wiley.

"Japan's Gangsters-Honourable Mob." 1990. *Economist,* April 21.

Kamel, G.W. Levi. 1983. *Downtown Street Hustlers.* San Diego: University of California. (Dissertation).

Kellerman, Christopher. "Children Behind Bars". 12/1/98.www.come-over.to/fasstar/juvcrime1.htm

Lemert, Edwin. 1972. *Human Deviance, Social Problems, and Social Control.* 2nd. ed., Englewood Cliffs, N.J.: Prentice Hall.

Lombroso-Ferrero, G. 1972. *Lombroso's Criminal Man.* New York: Patterson Smith.

Merton, R. 1957. *Social Theory and Social Structure.* New York: Free Press.

Miller, E.M. 1948. *Street Woman.* Philadelphia: Temple University Press.

Parrillo, Vincent N., Stimson, John and Stimson, Ardyth. *Contemporary Social Problems.* Third Edition. Boston: Allyn and Bacon.

Pollak, Otto. 1950. *The Criminology of Women.* Pennsylvania Press: Philadelphia.

Smart, C. 1977. *Women, Crime and Criminology: A Feminist Critique.* London: Routland and Kegan Paul.

Streissguth, Ann Ph.D. 1998. "Understanding the Occurrence of Secondary Disabilities in Clients With FAS and FAE." Getal Alcohol Drug Unit, University of Washington. Vol. 4 November. http://depts.washington.edu/fadu

Sutherland, E.H. and Cressey, D.R. 1970. *Criminology.* Philadelphia: Lippincott.

The Sentencing Project. 2006. *Rates of Incaration in Selected Nations.* Research for Advocacy for Reform.

Thio, Alex. 2003. *Sociology: A Brief Introduction.* Boston: Ally & Bacon.

Thomas, W.I. 1923 *The Unadjusted Girl.* Boston: Little, Brown.

Young, Jock. 1971 "The Role of Police as Amplifiers of Deviance." In Stanley Cohen (ed.) *Images of Deviance.* England: Penguin Books.

Chapter Seven

Abramovitz, Mimi. 1996. *Under Attack, Fighting Back: Women and Welfare in the United States.* N.Y.: Cornerstone Books, Monthly Review Press.

Aronowitz, Stanley. 2003. *How Class Works: Power and Social Movement.* New Haven and London: Yale University Press.

Barrett, Michele. 1980. *Women's Oppression Today: Problems In Marxist Feminist Analysis.* London: Verso.

Berger, Peter L. 1963. *Invitation To Sociology: A Human Perspective.* N.Y: Anchor Books.

Blauner, Robert. 1972. *Racial Oppression In America.* N.Y.: Harper and Row.

Braun, Denny. 1997. *The Rich get Richer: The Rise of Income Inequality in the United State and the World.* Chicago: Nelson-Hall Publishers.

Bullard, Robert D., Paul Mohai, Robin Saha & Beverly Wright. *Toxic Wastes and Race at Twenty: 1987-2007.* Cleveland, Oh.: United Church of Christ, March 2007.

California Newsreel, April 2006. "Interview with Sir Michael Marmot: Edited Transcript of Interview," Unnatural Causes: Is Inequality Making Us Sick? http://www.unnaturalcauses.org.

Cloward, Richard, and Lloyd Ohlin. 1960. *Delinquency and Opportunity: A theory of Delinquent Gangs.* N.Y.: Free Press.

Cobb, James C. 1984. *Industrialization and Southern Society, 1877-1984.* Lexington: University of Kentucky Press.

Cushing, Robert and Bill Bishop, "The Rural War," July 20, 2005, *The New York Times.*

Dahrendorf, R. 1979. *Life Chances.* London: Weidenfeld and Nicholson.

Davis, Kingsley, and Wilbert E. Moore. 1998 (orig. 1945). "Some Principles of Stratification," *American Sociological Review*, 10, April, pp. 242-249, cited in Robert Thompson, ed. *The Essential Sociology Reader.* Boston: Allyn and Bacon.

Democracy Now. January 18, 2008. "Free Lunch: How the Wealthiest Americans Enrich Themselves at Government Expense (And Stick You with the Bill)" http://www.democracynow.org/2008/1/18/free_lunch_how_the_wealthiest_americans

DeNavas-Walt, Carmen, Bernadette D. Proctor, and Jessica Smith. 2007. U.S. Census Bureau, Current Population Reports, P60-233, Income, Poverty, and Health Insurance Coverage in the United States: 2006, Washington, D.C.: U.S. Government Printing Office, http://www.census.gov/prod/2007pubs/p60-233.pdf

Durkheim, Emile. 1984. *The Division of Labour in Society.* N.Y.: Macmillian.

Eitzen, D. Stanly. March-April 2000, "Public Teams, Private Profits: How pro sports owners run up the score on fans and taxpayers." *Dollars & Sense*, 228, Cambridge, Ma.

Fisher, Gordon M. 1992. "The Development and History of the Poverty Thresholds." *Social Security Bulletin,* Vol. 55 No. 4, Winter, pp. 3-14.

Fletcher, Jr. Bill. "Can U.S. Workers Embrace Anit-Imperialism?". *Monthly Review,* July-August, 2003, Volume 55, Number 3. p. 104.

Giddens, Anthony. 1991. *Introduction To Sociology.* N.Y.: W.W. Norton & Company.

Gonzalez, Juan. September 12th 2008. "Yanks land deal ain't fair ball," *New York Daily News,* http://www.nydailynews.com/money/2008/09/11/2008-09-11 yanks land deal aint fair ball.html

Gouldner, Alvin W. 1970. *The Coming Crisis of Western Sociology.* N.Y.: Avon Books.

Harrington, Michael. 1962. *The other America: Poverty in the United States.* Baltimore: Penguin.

Herrnstein, Richard J. and Charles Murray. 1994. *The Bell Curve: Intelligence and Class Structure in American Life*. N.Y.: Free Press.

Johnston, David. 2007. *Free Lunch: How The Wealthiest Americans Enrich Themselves At Government Expense (And Stick You With The Bill)*. N.Y.: Portfollio.

Keddie, Nell, ed., 1973. *The Myth of Cultural Deprivation*. Baltimore, Md.: Penguin Education.

Kennickell, Arthur B. March 3, 2003, "A Rolling Tide: Changes in Distribution of Wealth in the U.S., 1989-2001" Federal Reserve Board, Washngton, D.C. 20551, http://www.federalreserve.gov/pub/oss2/scfindex.html

Kessler-Harris, Alice. 1982. *Out to Work: A History of Wage-Earning Women in the United States*. N.Y.: Oxford University Press.

Lewis, Oscar. 1970. *Anthropological Essays*. N.Y.: Random House.

Lewis, Oscar. 1959. *Five Families: Mexican Case Studies in the Culture of Poverty*. N.Y.: Oxford University Press.

Liebow, Elliot. 1967. *Tally's Corner*. Boston: Little, Brown.

Los Angles Times. June 26, 2003, Wire Reports, "IRS Report Confirms Rich Are Getting Richer." http://latimes.com/news/nationsworld/nation/la-na-briefs26.2jun26,1,2443432.story?coll=la-headlines-nation.

MacLeod, Jay. 1995 (orig. 1987). *Ain't No Makin' It: Aspirations and Attainment in a Low-Income Neighborhood*. Boulder, Co.: Westview Press.

Marmot, M.G., M.J. Shipley and Geoffrey Rose. 1984. "Inequalities in Death Specific Explanations of General Pattern?" *The Lancet* 5 May, pp. 1003-1006.

Marsh, Dave. 1987. *Glory Days: Bruce Springsteen in the 1980s*. N.Y.: Patheon Books.

Marx, Karl and Friedrich Engles. 1976. *The German Ideology*. Moscow: Progress Publishers.

Marx, Karl. 1954. *Capital: A Critique of Political Economy, Volume I*. Moscow: Progress Publishers.

Marx, Karl and Friedrich Engles. 1964. *Manifesto of the Communist Party*. Peking: People's Publishing House.

Newman, Katherine S. And Victor Tan Chen. 2007. *The Missing Class: Portraits of the Near Poor in America*. Boston, Ma.: Beacon Press.

Oliver, Melvin L. and Thomas M. Shapiro. 1995. *Black Wealth / White: A New Perspective on Racial Inequality*. N.Y.: Routledge.

Piven, Frances Fox and Richard A. Cloward. 1971. *Regulating the Poor: The Functions of Public Welfare*. N.Y.: Vintage Books.

Public Citizen. 2003. http://www.citizen.org/congress/welfare/index.cfm

Ryan, William. 1971. *Blaming the Victim*. N.Y.: Vintage Books.

Saez, Emmanuel. March 2008. "Striking it Richer: The Evolution of Top Incomes in the United States," http://emlab.berkeley.edu/users/saez/saez-UStopinomces-2006prel.pdf

Schott, Liz. March 19, 2009. "Policy Basics: An Introduction to TANF." The Center on Budget and Policy Priorities, http://www.cbpp.org/cms/index.cfm?fa=view&id=936

Sherman, Arloc. 1994. *Wasting America's Future: The Chldren's Defense Fund Report on the Costs of Child Poverty*. Boston: Beacon Press.

Sloggett, Andre and Heather Joshi. 1994. "Higher mortality in deprived areas: community or personal disadvantage?" *British Medical Journal*. Volume 309, 3 December, pp. 1470-1474.

Slivinski, Stephen. October 10, 2001, "The Corporate Welfare Budget Bigger Than Ever." *Policy Analysis*, No. 415.

Spencer, Herbert. 1913. *Social Statics*. N.Y.: Appleton and Company.

Spencer, Herbert. 1961. *The Study of Sociology*. Ann Arbor: University of Michigan Press.

Sydie, Rosalind Ann. 1987. *Natural Women, Cultured Men: A Feminist Perspective On Sociological Theory*. N.Y.: New York University Press.

Tabb, William K. June 2007. "Wage Stagnation, Growing Insecurity, and the Future of the U.S. Working Class." *Monthly Review*, Volume 59, Number 2 http://monthlyreview.org/0607wkt.htm.

Thompson, E. P. 1963. *The Making of The English Working Class*. N.Y.: Vintage.

Thompson, Kenneth, ed., 1985. *Readings from Emile Durkheim*. N.Y.: Tavistock Publications.

Tumin, Melvin M. 1953. "Some Principles of Stratification: A Critical Analysis," *American Sociological Review*. 18, 4, pp. 387- 393, cited in Robert Thompson, ed., 1998. *The Essential Sociology Reader*. Boston: Allyn and Bacon.

U.S. Census Bureau, http://www.census.gov/hhes/www/income/income.html, http://www.census.gov/hhes/www/poverty/poverty.html & http://www.census.gov/hhes/www/wealth.html

U.S. Census, Income, Poverty, & Health Insurance Coverage in the United States: 2007, 2009, (P60-238)

U.S. Department of Agriculture, 2009. Food Security in the United States: Key Statistics ad Graphics, http://www.ers.usda.gov/briefing/foodsecurity/stats_graphs.htm

Weber, Max. 1947. *The Theory of Social and Economic Organization*. N.Y.: The Free Press.

White, Brain K. Bucks, Arthur B. Kennickell, and Kevin B. Moore. February 2006. "Recent Changes in U.S. Family Finances: Evidence from the 2001 and 2004 Survey of Consumer Finances," Federal Reserve Bulletin, vol. 92, Table 3. African American and Hispanic.

Wilkinson, Richard. 2005. *The Impact of Inequality: How to make Societies Healthier*, N.Y.: The New Press.

Williams, Raymond. 1976. *Keywords: A Vocabulary of Culture and Society*. N.Y.: Oxford University Press.

Wilson, William Julius. 1987. *The Truly Disadvantaged: The Inner City, the Underclass, and Public Policy*. Chicago: The University of Chicago Press.

Wilson, William Julius. 1978. *The Declining Significance of Race: Blacks and Changing American Institutions*. Chicago: University Chicago Press.

Wolff, Edward N. "Recent Trends in Household Wealth in the United States: Rising Debt and the Middle-Class Squeeze—an Update to 2007," Working Paper No. 589, Levy Economics Institute of Bard College, March 2010.

Yates, Michael D. Ed. 2007. *More Unequal: Aspects of Class in the United States*, N.Y.: Monthly Review Press.

Zinn, Howard. 1995 (orig. 1980). *A Peoples' History of The United States, 1492 to Present. N.Y.: Harper Perennial.*

Chapter Eight

AMERICAN INDIAN REPORT. "National American Indian Heritage Month: Facts and Figures from the Census Bureau," Nov. 4, 2010.

AOA (Administration on Aging. 2010. "AOA Information for African American Elders. http://seniorhealth.about.com/library/news/blafa.htm. Retrieved 1/20/11.

Blauner, Robert. 1972. *Racial Oppression in America*. New York: Harper & Row

Braun, Denny. 1997. *The Rich Get Richer: The Rise of Income Inequality in the United States and the World*. 2nd ed. Chicago, IL: Nelson-Hall Publishers.

Butterfield, Fox. "Prison Rates Among Blacks Reach a Peak, Report Finds." *New York Times*. 7 April 2003. *www.nytimes.com/2003/04/07/.../07PRIS.html*

Celis, William. "Colleges Battle Culture and Poverty to Swell Hispanic Enrollments." *New York Times. 23* February 1993, B6.

Children's Defense Fund. 1995. *America's Children*. p. 29.

Current Population Reports, "School Enrollment in the United States: 2006." Issued August 2008.

Domhoff, William, G. "Who Rules American: Wealth, Income and Power." September 2005 (updated December 2010). http://Sociology.ucsc.edu/whorulesamerican/power/wealth.html.

Dunne, Diane Weaver. 2001. "Reporter's Notebook: Native Americans Struggle, Build Pride," *Education World*. 6 September. http://www.educationworld.com/a_issues/schools/schools012.shtml

Estrada, L.F., et al. 1981. "Chicanos in the United States: A History of Exploitation and Resistance," *Daedalus*, Vol. 110 (Spring), pp. 107-126.

Feagain, Joe R., and Clairece Booher Feagain. 1993. *Racial and Ethic Relations*. 3rd. ed. Englewood Cliffs, N.J.: Prentice Hall.

Folbre, Nancy. 1995. *The New Field Guide to the U.S. Economy*. New York: The New Press.

Fry, Richard. 2010. "Hispanics: High School Dropout and GED." Washington, D.C. Pew Hispanic Center.

Hamilton, Janice Outtz. 1995. "Higher Education and the New Demographic Reality," *Educational Record* 76, nos. 2,3, (Spring/Summer): p. 68.

Herrnstein, Richard. 1973. *I.Q. in the Meritocracy*. Boston: Little, Brown.

Hraba, Joseph. 1979. *American Ethnicity*. p. 298 Itasca, Il: F.E. Peacock Publishers, Inc.

Huntley, Steve. "America's Indians: Beggars in Our Own Land." *U.S. News & World Report 23* May 1983: p. 70.

Popescu et al. 2007. "Differences in Mortality and Use of Revascularization in Black and White Patients with Acute MI Admitted to Hospitals With and Without Revascularization Services." *Journal of the American Medical Association*. Volume 297(22): pp. 2481-2488.

Jensen, Arthur R. 1969. "How Much Can We Boost IQ and Scholastic Achievement?" *Harvard Educational Review Volume* 39 (Winter).

Keil, Julian E., et al. 1993. "Mortality Rates and Risk Factors for Coronary Disease in Black as Compared with White Men and Women," *New England Journal of Medicine* 329 (July 8): 73-78.

Le, C.N. 2008. "14 Important Statistics About Asian Americans" *Asian-Nation: The Landscape of Asian America*." http://www.asian-nation.org/14-statistics.shtml (October 8, 2008).

_____. 2011. "Population Statistics & Demographics" Asian-Nation: The Landscape of Asian America." http://www.asian-nation.org/population.shtml (January 21, 2011).

_____. 2011. "Socioeconomic Statistics & Demographics" Asian-Nation: The Landscape of Asian America." <http://www.asian-nation.org.

Leavitt, Judy W., and Ronald L. Numbers. 1985. *Sickness and Health in America*. Madison: University of Wisconsin Press.

McDermott. 2008. *Working-Class White*. University of California Press.

Merton, Robert K., "Discrimination and the American Creed," in *Discrimination and National Welfare,* Ed. R.M. MacIver. New York: Harper & Bothers, 1949, pp. 99-126.

Meyer, Dylan S. 1971. *Uprooted American: The Japanese-American and the War Relocation Authority During World War II*. Tucson: University of Arizona Press.

Myrdal, Gunnar. 1944. *An American Dilemma: The Negro Problem and Modern Democracy*. New York: Harper & Row.

National Committee on Pay Equity, "The wage gap: Myths and facts." In P.S. Rothenberg (Ed.), *Race, Class and Gender in the United States*. New York: St. Martin's Press, 2009. Online reference www.bls/cps/cpsaat11.pdf.

National Center for Health Statistics, National Vital Statistics Reports, vol. 54, no 19, June 28, 2006.

National Center for Health Statistics: 2004 data: Population Reference Bureau, analysis of data from the Multiple Causes of Death Public Use, 2004 Natality Data Set CD Series 21, number 17Ha. Data update in 2007.

Ong, Paul M. 1994. "The State of Asia Pacific America: Economic Diversity, Issues, and Policies." Los Angeles: University of California Asian-American Studies Center and LEAP: Asian Pacific American Public Policy Institute.

Purdum, Todd S. "Dinkins Goes to Korean Stores in Defiance of Boycott by Blacks." September 22, 1990, *New York Times*.

Paisano, "The American Indian, Eskimo, and Aleut Population," *U.S. Census Bureau*, 2003.

Reich, Michael. 1977. "The Economics of Racism." in David M. Gordon (ed.), *Problems in Political Economy*. Lexington, MA: D.C. Heath, pp. 183-188.

Rosenberg, Paul. "Unemployment by Education and Race." *Open Left*. 14 February 2010.

ScienceDaily. Retrieved January 20, 2011, from http://www.sciencedaily.com- /releases/2010/03/100329075909.htm

Statistical Abstract, 2002: Tables 36, 37, 38, 40.

Teitelbaum, Michael. 2004. *Chinese Immigrants: Immigration to the United States*. ISBN 0816056870 & U.S. Census, "Estimates of US-Census for year 2004."

The Journal of Blacks in Higher Education. "Black Student College Inches Higher But a Large Racial Gap Persists." Source of Statistics; NCAA. 2006 Data. http://www.jbhe.com/preview/winter07preview.html

Thurm, Scott. "Hispanic Employment Slips," *Denver Post* January 27, 1995: E1, E5.

Time, "The LA Riots: 15 Years After Rodney King," November 23, 2008. http://www.time.com/time/specials/packages/completelist/0,29569,1614117,00.html

U.S. Bureau of Census. 1991. "Annual Income and Poverty Reports." Washington, Government Printing Office (October 4).

U.S. Census Bureau, 1993.

_____. 1999. Money Income in the United States: 1998. Washington, DC: U.S. Bureau of the Census. Retrieved Mar. 18, 1999. Online.

_____. "Population Change and Distribution: 1990-2000", April 2001 (C2KBR/01-2).

_____. "Household Data Annual Averages, Table 17: Employment by Industry, Sex, Race, and Occupation." 2002.

Census Bureau Reports," September 24, 2002.

_____. "Current Population Survey, March 2001, Ethnic and Hispanic Statistics Branch, Population Division." Internet Release date June 18, 2003.

_____. "Table PINC-10. Wage and Salary Workers—People 15 Years Old and Over, by Total Wage and Salary Income in 2001, Work Experience in 2001, Race, Hispanic Origin and Sex," September 23, 2002.

_____. "Educational Attainment by Race and Hispanic Origin," 2010. Table 226. http://www.census.gov/population/wwww/socdemo/edc-attn.html.

U.S. Bureas of the Census, *American Fact Finder*, 2003: Tables GCT-P12, P14

_____. American Community Survey, 2006.

_____. Facts for Feature, March 27, 2006.

_____. "Total Population". 2006 American Community Survey. United States Census Bureau. Retrieved on 2008-01-24.

_____. (2006), Personal Income and Educational Attainment. http://en.wikipedia.org/wiki/Income_inequality_in_the_United_States.

_____. "Income, Poverty, and Health Insurance Coverage in the United States: 2006," August, 2007.

_____. Selected Population Profile in the United States. United States Census Bureau, retrieved 2007-09. S0201.

_____. "45 Percent of Puerto Ricans Living Below Poverty line," September 7, 2008.

_____. American Community Surveys, 2008 and 2009, Puerto Rico Community Surveys, 2008 and 2009.

U.S. Census, 2000. http://www.census.gov/hhes/wwwhousing/housing_patterns/pdf/ch5.pdf.

U.S. Department of Education, National Center for Educational Statistics. 2010. The Condition of Eduction 2010 (NCES 2010--028).

U.S. Department of Labor. Bureau of Labor Statistics, "Economy at a Glance." Data extracted Jan. 14, 2011. http://bls.gov/eag.pr.htm#eag-_pr.f.1.

_____. U.S. Department of Labor. Bureau of Labor Statistics, "Employment Status of the Civilian noninstitutional Population 16 to 24 Years of age by Sex, Race, and Hispanic or Latino Ethnicity." July 2007-2010. Table 2.

_____. "U.S. Interim Projections by Age, Sex, Race, and Hispanic Origin, 2004 & 2008." http://www.census.gov/ipc/www/usinterimproj/

_____, "American Community Survey, 2009" 2009. http:factfinder.census.gov/

_____. "Current Population Survey." September 10, 2009. htpp://www.census.gov/cps/

U.S. Census Bureau, Current Population Reports, PPL-148, P-20, and earlier reports; and "School Enrollment." Internet release date: 12/15/2010.

U.S. Commission on Civil Rights. 1988. *The Economic Status of Americans of Asian Descent*. Washington, D.C.: Clearinghouse Publications.

U.S. Department of Commerce, Bureau of the Census, U.S. Census of Population, 1960, Vol. 1, part 1; Current Population Reports, Series P-20 and unpublished data; and 1960 Census Monograph, "Education of the American Population," by John K. Folger and Charles B. Nam. From U.S. Dept. of Education, National Center for Education Statistics, *Digest of Education Statistics* 2002

U.S. Dept. of Education, National Center for Education Statistics, *Digest of Education Statistics 2007*, and _____, Current Population Survey, March 2007.

U.S. National Center for Health Satistics. 2001. "Life Expectancy for U.S. Children Born in 2000.

Whittle, Jeff, et al. 1993. "Treatment of Black and White Heart in a VA Hospital." *New England Journal of Medicine. August 25: pp. 621-627.*

Chapter Nine

Alan Guttmacher Institute. 1994. *Sex and America's Teenagers*. The Alan Guttmacher Institute.

Amato, Paul R. 1995. University of Nebraska, Lincoln; and Alan Booth, Pennsylvania State University. "Changes in Gender Role Attitudes and Perceived Marital Quality." *The American Sociological Review*. Vol. 60, No. 1, February: pp. 58-66.

Bellas, Marcia B. University of Cincinnati. 1994. "Comparable Worth in Academia: The Effects of Faculty Salaries of the Sex Composition and Labor-Market Conditions of Academic Disciplines." *The American Sociological Review*. Vol. 59, No. 6, December: pp. 807-821.

Bernard, Jessie. 1971. *Women and the Public Interest: An Essay on Policy and Protest*. Chicago: Aldine-Atherton.

Bernard, Jessie S. 1981. *The Female World*. New York: The Free Press.

Bonner, Jane. 1984. Research presented in "The Two Brains." Public Broadcast System Telecast.

Boulding, Elise. 1976. *The Underside of History*. Boulder, Colorado: Westview Press.

Buetel, Ann M. and Margaret Mooney Marini, University of Minnesota. 1995. "Gender and Values." *The American Sociological Review*. Vol. 60, No. 3. June: pp. 436-448.

Bureau of Labor Statistics, 2005, U.S. Department of Labor.

Burford, Heather C., Linda A. Foley, Patricia G. Rollins, and Kimberly S. Rosario. 1996. "Gender Differences in Preschoolers' Sharing Behavior." *Handbook of Gender Research, Journal of Social Behavior and Personality*. (Special Issue) Edited by Rick Crandall, Ph.D. Volume 11, No. 5. pp. 17-26.

Current Population Survey, Household Data, Annual Averages 2008. www.BLS.gov/cps/cpsaat37.pdf

Denoon, Daniel, "Only Happy Marriage is Healthy for Women," cited in WebMD, Nov. 2008.

Ehrenreich, Barbara, Elizabeth Hess, and Gloria Jacabos. 1987. *Re-Making Love: The Feminization of Sex*. Garden City, New York: Anchor/Doubleday.

Engels, Friedrich. 1902 (orig. 1884). *The Origin of the Family*. Chicago: Charles Hr. Kerr & Co.

Entwisle, Doris R., Karl L. Alexander, and Linda Steffel Olson, John Hopkins University. 1994. "The Gender Gap In Math: Its Possible Origins in Neighborhood Effects." *The American Sociological Review*. Vol 59, No. 6, (December) p. 822-838.

Ford, Clellan S., and Frank A. Beach. 1972. *Patterns of Sexual Behavior*. New York: Harper Colophon Books.

Freud, Sigmund. 1960 (orig. 1923). *The Ego and The Id*. translated by Joan Riviere. New York: W. W. Norton.

Gagnon, John. 1973. *Sexual Conduct: The Social Sources of Human Sexuality*. Chicago, Il: Aldine Publishing Co.

Gagnon, John. 1995. *Conceiving Sexuality: Approaches to Sex Research in a Postmodern World*. New York: Routledge.

Gilligan, Carol. 1982. *In a Different Voice: Psychological Theory and Women's Development*. Cambridge, Mass: Harvard University Press.

Gier, Nick, "Hate Crimes Against Gays Continue," *New West*, November 5, 2008.

Hugick, Larry, and Jennifer Leonard. 1991. *Sex in America*. The Gallup Poll Monthly. p. 60-73.

icasualties.org 2008

Kinsey, Alfred C., W.B. Pmoeroy, C.E. Martin, and P.H. Gebbard. 1948. *Sexual Behavior in the Human Male*. Philadelphia: W. B. Saunders.

Kinsey, Alfred C., W. B. Pmoeroy, C. E. Martin, and P. Gebbard. 1953. *Sexual Behavior in the Human Female*. Philadelphia; W. B. Saunders.

Laumann, Edward O., John H. Gagnon, Robert T. Michael, and Stuart Michaels. 1994. *The Social Organization of Sexuality: Sexual Practices in the United States*. Chicago; University of Chicago Press.

Lenski, Gerhard and Jean Lenski. 1982. *Human Societies: An Introduction to Macrosociology*. 4th ed. New York: McGraw-Hill.

Linton, Ralph. *On Status and Role. Sociology; The Classic Statements.* Edited by Marcello Truzzi. University of Michigan. McGraw-Hill, Inc.

Livingston, Mary M., Kim Burley, and Thomas P. Springer. 1996. "The Importance of Being Feminine: Gender, Sex Role, Occupational and Marital Role Commitment, and Their Relationship to Anticipated Work-Family Conflict." *Handbook of Gender Research, Journal of Social Behavior and Personality.* (Special Issue) Edited by Rick Crandall, Ph.D. Volume 11, No. 5. pp. 179-192.

Masters, William H., and Virginia E. Johnson. 1966. *Human Sexual Response.* Boston: Little, Brown.

Mead, Margaret. 1963, (Orig. 1935). *Sex and Temperament In Three Primitive Societies.* New York; William Morrow.

Mettrick, Jon and Gloria Cowan. 1996. "Gender Stereotypes and Predictions of Performance: Women in Air Combat." *Handbook of Gender Research, Journal of Social Behavior and Personality.* (Special Issue) Edited by Rick Crandall, Ph.D. Volume 11, No. 5. pp. 105-120.

Money, John. 1988. *Gay, Straight, and In-Between: The Sexology of Erotic Orientation.* New York: Oxford University Press.

Nauert, Rick, "Health Benefits of a Happy Marriage." *PsychCentral*, March 20, 2008.

Parsons, Talcott. 1942. "Age and Sex in the Social Structure of the United States." *The American Sociological Review.* Vol 7. No. 4, August: pp. 42-45.

Phillips, Adam. 1994. *On Flirtation.* Cambridge, MA: Harvard University Press.

Presser, Harriet B. University of Maryland, 1994. "Employment Schedules, Gender, and Household Labor." *The American Sociological Review.* Vol. 59, No. 3, (June) p. 348-364.

Rist, Darrell Yates. 1992. "Are Homosexuals Born That Way?" *The Nation* #255 (October 14) p. 424-429.

Sadker, Myra, and David Sadker. 1984. *Year 3: Final Report, Promoting Effectiveness in Classroom Instruction.* Washington, D.C: National Institute of Education.

Sadker, Myra, and David Sadker. 1994. *Failing at Fairness: How America's Schools Cheat Girls.* New York: Scribner.

Shilts, Randy. 1988. *And The Band Played On.* New York: Penguin.

Sommers, Christina Hoff. 2008. "Why Can't Women be More Like Men?" *The American,* March/April issue.

South, Scott J. and Glenna Spitze. 1994. "Gender and Housework: Housework in Marital and Nonmarital Households." *The American Sociological Review.* Vol. 59, No. 3, June: p. 327-347.

Speilvogel, Jackson J. 1997. *Western Civilization Vol. II: Since 1950.* St. Paul, MN: West Publishing.

Steinmetz, Suzanne K., Clavan, Sylvia, and Stein, Karen F. 1990. *Marriage and Family Realities: Historical and Contemporary Perspectives.* New York: Harper and Row.

Chicago Tribune. 1998. "Sex Change Challenges Gender Identity Theory." July, 7th. As reported in *Pediatrics* July issue.

United States Bureau of the Census. 1975. *Historical Statistics of the U.S. Colonial Times to 1970, Part 1.* Bicentennial ed. Washington, DC: Government Printing Office.

_____. 1993. *Current Population Reports.* Washington, DC: Government Printing Office.

_____. 1994. *Statistical Abstracts of the United States.* Washington, DC: Government Printing Office.

_____. 1995. *Current Population Reports.* Washington, DC: Government Printing Office.

Valiam, Virginia. 2008. Quoted from the article "Why Can't a Woman be More Like a Man?" *The American*, March/April issue, 2008.

Weitzman, Lenore J., Deborah Eifler, Elizabeth Hodaka, and Catherine Ross. 1973. "Sex-Role Socialization in Picture Books for Preschool Children." *American Journal of Sociology.* Vol. 79, No. 3, November: pp. 665-685

Williams, Robin M., Jr. 1970 *American Society: A Sociological Interpretation.* 3rd edition. New York: Alfred A. Knopf

Chapter Ten

Adam, Barry D. 1986. "Age, Structure, and Sexuality: Reflections on the Anthropological Evidence on Homosexual Relations." In *The Many Faces of Homosexuality: Anthropological Approaches to Homosexual Behavior*. Edited by Evelyn Blackwood. New York: Harrington Park Press, Inc.

Ahrons, Constance R. and Roy H. Rodgers. 1994. "The Remarriage Transition." *Family in Transition Eighth Edition.* Edited by Arlene Skolnick and Jerome Skolnick. New York: Harper Collins.

Amato, Paul R., David R. Johnson, Alan Booth, and Stacy J. Rogers. 2003. "Continuity and Change in Marital Quality Between 1980 and 2000." *Journal of Marriage and Family*, Vol. 65, Issue 1, February 2003, pages 1-22. Full text accessed through EBSCO, March 26, 2003.

Amato, Paul R., David R. Johnson, Alan Booth, and Stacy J. Rogers. 2007. *Alone Together: How Marriage in America is Changing.* Cambridge, Massachusetts: Harvard University Press.

Bane, Mary Jo. "Household Composition and Poverty" in *Fighting Poverty: What Works and What Doesn't.* Edited by Sheldon H. Danziger and Daniel H. Weinberb. Cambridge, Massachusetts: Harvard University Press. Pp. 209-231.

Beaver, Patricia D. 1986. *Rural Community in the Appalachian South.* Prospect Heights, Illinois: Waveland Press, Inc.

Becker, Gary S. 1981. *A Treatise on the Family.* Cambridge, Mass: Harvard University Press.

Beige, Kathy. 2005. "Where Can Gays Legally Marry" from *Your Guide to Lesbian Life*, on About.com, Accessed July 19, 2005. URL: http://lesbianlife.about.com/cs/wedding/a/wher-emarriage.htm

Bergmann, Barbara R. 1986. *The Economic Emergence of Women.* New York: Basic Books.

Bokemeir, Janet. 1997. "Rediscovering Families and Households: Restructuring Rural Society and Rural Sociology." *Rural Sociology.* Vol. 62, no. 1; pp. 1-20.

Bramlett, Matthew D. and William d. Mosher. 2001. "First Marriage Dissolution, Divorce and Remarriage: United States." Advance Data from Vital and Health Statistics, Number 323, May 31, 2001, Hyattsville, Maryland: National Center for Health Statistics. PHS 2001-1250

Bureau of Labor Statistics. 2005a. "Average Hours Per Day Spent in Primary Activities for Total Population." United States Department of Labor. Accessed July 14, 2005. URL: http://www.bls.gov/news.release/atus.t01.htm

Bureau of Labor Statistics. 2005b. "Employment Status by Sex, Presence of Children, and Age of Children, Race and Hispanic or Latino Ethnicity, 2004." Department of Labor. URL: http://www.bls.gov/sps/wlf-table5-2005.pdf. Accessed July 14, 2005.

Bureau of Labor Statistics. 2005c. "Median Usual Weekly Earnings of Full-time Wage and Salary Workers in Current Dollars, 1979-2004." Accessed July 14, 2005. URL: http://www.bls.gov/cps/wlf-table16-2005.pdf: http://wwww.bls.gov/cps/wlf-table16-2005.pdf

Bureau of Labor Statistics. 2008. Working in the 21st Century. U.S. Department of Labor. URL: http://pubdb3.census.gov/macro/032007/pov/new04_100_01.htm. Accessed July 21, 2008.

Campaign for Our Children. 1997. "Campaign for Our Children Website." Accessed July 1997. URL: http://www.cfoc.org/main.html

Carr, Lois Green and Lorena S. Walsh. 1979. "The Planters Wife: The Experience of White Women in Seventeenth Century Maryland" in *A Heritage of Her Own: Towards a New Social History of American Women*. Edited by Nancy F. Cott and Elizabeth H. Peck. New York: Simon and Schuster, Touchstone Books.

Centers for Disease Control and Prevention. 2006. National Youth Risk Behavior Survey: 2006. Department of Health and Human Services. Accessed February 8, 2008. URL: http://www.cdc.gov/mmwr/PDF/SS/SS5505.pdf

Chandra A, Martinez GM, Mosher WD, Abma JC, Jones J. 2005. Fertility, family planning, and reproductive health of U.S. women: Data from the 2002 National Survey of Family Growth. National Center for Health Statistics. Vital Health Stat 23(25).

Cherlin, Andrew. 1981. *Marriage, Divorce, Remarriage*. Cambridge, Mass: Harvard University Press.

Clarke, Sally C. 1995. "Advance Report of Final Marriage Statistics, 1989 and 1990." Monthly Vital Statistics Report. Vol. 43, no. 12. July 14. United States Department of Health and Human Services, National Center for Health Statistics.

Collins, Randall and Scott Coltrane. 1991. *Sociology of Marriage and the Family: Gender, Love and Property*. Third Edition. Chicago: Nelson Hall Publishers.

Coltrane, Scott, and Michele Adams. 2003. "The Social Construction of the Divorce 'Problem': Morality, Child Victims, and the Politics of Gender." *Family Relations*, Vol. 52, Issue 4, pages 363-373.

Coontz, Stephanie. 1997. *The Way We Really Are: Coming to Terms with America's Changing Families*. New York: Basic Books, a division of Harper Collins Publishers, Inc.

Coontz, Stephanie. 2005. *Marriage, a History: From Obedience to Intimacy or How Love Conquered Marriage*. New York, NY: Viking, Penguin Group.

Crittenden, Ann. 2001. *The Price of Motherhood: Why the Most Important Job in the World Is Still the Least Valued*. New York: Henry Holt and Company.

Darling, Jon and L. Sue Greer. 1986. *Johnstown, Pennsylvania 1986: Selected Community and Family Reactions to Chronic Hard Times*. Prepared for the Center for Technology, Training and Development of the Southern Alleghenies (CENTECH). Pennsylvania Department of Commerce Grant #85-054.

Day, Randal D. 1995. "Family Systems Theory" in *Research and Theory in Family Science*, edited by Randal Day, Kathleen Gilbert, Barbara Settles, Wesley Burr. Pacific Grove, California: Brooks/Cole Publishing Company.

Degler, Carl N. 1980. *At Odds: Women and the Family in America from the Revolution to the Present*. Oxford, England: Oxford University Press.

Eshanova, Zamira. 2002. "Central Asia: Increase in Polygamy Attributed to Economic Hardship, Return to Tradition." Eurasianet.org. http://www.eurasianet.org/departments/culture/articles/eav102002_pr.shtml Posted October 20, 2002, accessed May 26, 2003.

Etzioni, Amatai. 1983. *An Immodest Agenda: Rebuilding America Before the 21st Century*. New York: McGraw-Hill Book Company. Ford, C. S., and Beach, F. A. 1951. *Patterns of Sexual Behavior*, New York: Harper and Brothers.

Foust, Michael, "Gallup Poll: 58 percent oppose 'gay mariage,' half support amend, *Bapist Press*, 2006-May-22, at http//www.bpnews.net/

Gelles, Richard J. 1994. "Ten Risk Factors." *Newsweek*, July 4, p. 29. Gilligan, Carol. 1982. *In a Different Voice: Psychological Theory and Women's Development*. Cambridge, Massachusetts: Harvard University Press.

Goldstein, Joshua R. 1999. "The Leveling of Divorce in the United States." *Demography*, Vol. 36, no. 3, August. Pages 409-414.

Harvey, David L. 1993. *Potter Addition: Poverty, Family, and Kinship in a Heartland Community*. New York: Aldine de Gruyter.

Harvey, Elizabeth. 1999. "Short-Term and Long-Term Effects of Early Parental Employment on Children of the National Longitudinal Survey of Youth." *Developmental Psychology* vol.35, no.2: pp.445-459.

Hewlett, Sylvia Ann. 1986. *A Lesser Life: The Myth of Women's Liberation in America*. New York: Warner Books.

Hewlett, Sylvia Ann. 2002. *Creating a Life: Professional Women and the Quest for Children*. New York: Talk Miramx Books, Hyperion.

Hoschild, Arlie and Ann Machung. 1989. *The Second Shift: Working Parents and the Revolution at Home*. New York: Viking Press.

Katz, Michael B. 1989. *The Undeserving Poor: From the War on Poverty to the War on Welfare*. New York: Pantheon Press.

Kingsolver, Barbara. 1995. *High Tide in Tucson*. New York: Harper Collins.

Lamana, Mary Ann and Agnes Riedmann. 2003. *Marriages and Families: Making Choices in a Diverse Society*, Eighth Edition. Belmont, CA: Wadsworth/Thompson Learning.

Lerner, Gerda. 1979. "The Lady and the Mill Girl: Changes in the Status of Women in the Age of Jackson, 1800-1840." in *A Heritage of Her Own: Towards a New Social History of American Women*. Edited by Nancy F. Cott and Elizabeth H. Peck. New York: Simon and Schuster, Touchstone Books.

LeVine, Robert A. and Merry White. 1987. "The Social Transformation of Childhood" in *Parenting Across the Life Span: Biosocial Dimensions*. Edited by Jane B. Lancaster, et al. New York: Aldine De Gruyter.

London, Kathryn A. 1991. "Advance Data Number 194: Cohabitation, Marriage, Marital Dissolution and Remarriage: United States, 1988." United States Department of Health and Human Services: Vital and Health Statistics of the National Center. January 4.

Macartney, Jane. 1994. "China Lashes Out at Resurgence of Tibet Polyandry." World Tibet Network News, Posted Wednesday December 28, 1994. Accessed May 26, 2003. http://www.Tibet.ca/wtnarchive/1994/12/28_1.html

Mountain Comprehensive Healthcare Corporation. 1997. "June 1997 Birth Announcements, Whitesburg Medical Clinic" *The Mountain Eagle*. July 16. P. B5

Moynihan, Daniel P. 1965. *The Negro Family: The case for national action*. Washington, D.C.: United States Department of Labor, Office of Family Planning and Research.

National Center for Health Statistics. 1995. "Advance Report on Final Divorce Statistics, 1989 and 1990." *Monthly Vital Statistics Report*, Vol. 43, no. 9, supplement. March 22.

National Center for Health Statistics. 2002. "New Report Sheds Light on Trends and Patterns in Marriage, Divorce, and Cohabitation." News Release. July 24, 2002. Hyattsville, Maryland: National Center for Health Statistics. http://www.cdc.gov/nchs/relaeases/02news/div_mar_cohab.htm. Accessed June 9, 2003.

National Vital Statistics Reports. 2008. "Births, Marriages, Divorces and Deaths: Provisional Data for 2007. Volume 56, no. 21, Hyattsville, MD: National Center for Health Statistics. Accessed July 21, 2008, http://www.cdc.gov/nchs/data/nvsr/nvsr56/nvsr56_21.htm

Norton, Arthur and Louisa Miller. 1992. *Marriage, Divorce and Remarriage in the 1990's* Current Population Reports Series P23-180. Washington, DC: Bureau of the Census. October.

Orthner, Dennis. 1996. "Families in Transition: Changing Values and Norms" in *Research and Theory in Family Science* Edited by Randall Day, Kathleen Gilbert, Barbara Settles, Wesley Burr. Pacific Grove, California: Brooks/Cole Publishing.

Parsons, Talcott and Robert F. Bales. 1955. *Family, Socialization, and Interaction Process*. Glencoe, Il: Free Press.

Peters, H. Elizabeth. 1986. "Marriage and Divorce: Informational constraints and Private Contracting." *American Economic Review* Vol. 76: pp. 437-454.

Peterson, Richard R. 1996a. "A re-evaluation of the economic consequences of divorce." *American Sociological Review* vol. 61, no. 3, June: pp 528 - 536.

Pogrebin, Letty Cottin. 1983. *Family Politics: Love and Power on an Intimate Frontier*. New York: McGraw-Hill Book Company.

Popenoe, David. 1996. *Life Without Father*. New York: Martin Kessler Books, The Free Press.

Queen, Stuart A., Robert W. Habenstein, and Jill Sobel Quadagno. 1985. *The Family in Various Cultures*. Fifth Edition. New York: Harper Collins Publishers, Inc.

Raschke, Helen. 1987. "Divorce" in *The Handbook of Marriage and the Family*, edited by Marvin B. Sussman and Suzanne K Steinmetz. New York: Plenum. Pp. 597-624.

Riley, Matilda White. 1994. "The Family in an Aging Society: A Matrix of Latent Relationships." in *Family in Transition*. Eighth Edition, edited by Arlene S. Skolnick and Jerome H. Skolnick, New York: Harper Collins College Publishers.

Rogers, Susan M. and Charles F. Turner. 1991. "Male/Female Sexual Contact in the USA.: Findings from Five Sample Surveys, 1970-1990." *The Journal of Sex Research*. Vol. 28, no. 4: pp. 491-519.

Simmons, Tavia and Martin O'Connell. 2003. "Married-Couple and Unmarried Partner Households: 2000." Washington, DC: United States Census Bureau, Department of Commerce. February 2003.

Smith, Kristin E. and Amara Bachu. 1999. "Women's Labor Force Attachment Patterns and Maternity Leave: A Review of the Literature." Population Division Working Paper No. 32, U.S. Bureau of the Census, Washington, D.C. January 1999.

Smith, Tom W. 1999. *The Emerging 21st Century American Family*. GSS Social Change Report No. 42. Chicago: University of Chicago, National Opinion Research Center.

Stack, Carol B. 1974. *All Our Kin: Strategies for Survival in a Black Community*. New York: Harper and Row, Publishers.

Straus, Murray A., Richard Gelles, and Suzanne K. Steinmetz. 1980. *Behind Closed Doors: Violence in the American Family*. New York: Doubleday and Company.

The First Measured Century. www. pbs.org/fmc/book/2worrk8.htm

Thornton, Arland and L. Young-DeMarco. 2001 "Four Decades of Trends in Attitudes Toward Family Issues in the United States" The 1960's through the 1990's" *Journal of Marriage and the Family*, Vol. 63, no. 4, pages 1990-1037.

Uhlenberg, Peter. 1989. "Death and the Family" in *Family in Transition*. Sixth Edition. Edited by Arlene S. Skolnick and Jerome H. Skolnick. Originally printed in *Journal of Family History*. Fall 1980.

United States Census Bureau. 1997. "Sixty Five Plus in the United States." Statistical Brief, March 1995. Economic and Statistics Administration. United States Department of Commerce. Accessed July 1997. URL: http://www.census.gov/socdemo/www/agebrief.html

United States Census Bureau. 1997b. *Statistical Abstract of the United States* 1997. 117th Edition. The National Data Book. United States Department of Commerce. Washington, D.C.

United States Census Bureau. 2003. "Primary Child Care Arrangements Used by Employed Mothers of Preschoolers: 1985 to 1999." Current Population Reports, Washington, DC: Department of Commerce. Internet release January 24, 2003. http://www.census.gov/population/www/socdemo/child/ppl-168.html Accessed: June 17, 2003.

United States Census Bureau. 2004. Annual Social and Economic Supplement, 2003." Current Population Survey, Current Population Reports, Series P20-553. URL: http://www.census.gov/population/socdemo/hh-fam/tabms-2.xls Accessed May 5, 2005.

United States Census Bureau. 2004. "Table C2 Household Relationship and Arrangements of Children Under 18" Current Population Reports, Washington, DC Department of Commerce. Internet release: March 2004. Accessed:April 16, 2005. http://www.census.gov/population/www/socdemo/hh-fam/cps2003/tablC2-all.xls

United States Census Bureau. 2005. "Martial History for People 15 years and over, by age, sex, race and Hispanic origin, 2001." Survey of Income and Programs Participation, 2001 Panel, Wave 2, Topical Module. Accessed July 13, 2005. http://www.census.gov/population/socdemo/marital-hist/p70-97/tab01-white.xls

United States Department of Health and Human Services. 2004. "Health, United States, 2004: With Chartbook on Trends in the Health of Americans." Hyattsville, MD: Centers for Disease Control and Prevention, National Center for Health Statistics. Publication #2004-1232.

United States Department of Justice. 1994. "Violence Between Intimates." *Bureau of Justice Statistics Selected Findings: Domestic Violence*. November. No. NCJ-149259. Washington, DC: United States Department of Justice, Office of Justice Programs.

Vanek, Joann. 1979. "Time Spent in Housework" in *A Heritage of Her Own: Towards a New Social History of American Women*. Edited by Nancy F. Cott and Elizabeth H. Peck. New York: Simon and Schuster, Touchstone Books.

Ventura, Stephanie J. Brady E. Hamilton, and Paul D. Sutton. 2003. "Revised Birth and Fertility Rates for the United States 2000 and 2001" National Vital Statistics Reports, Vol. 51, no. 4. February 6, 2003. http://www.cdc.gov/nchs/data/nvsr/nvsr51/nvs451_04.pdf

Wallerstein, Judith and Sandra Blakeslee. 1995. *The Good Marriage: How and Why Love Lasts*. Boston: Houghton Mifflin.

Weed, James A. 1980. "National Estimates of Marriage Dissolution and Survivorship: United States." Vital and Health Statistics Series 3, Analytical Studies, no. 19. United States Department of Health and Human Services Publication No. (PHS) 81-1403. November.

Winton, Chester A. 1995. *Frameworks for Studying Families*. Guilford, Connecticut: The Dushkin Publishing Group.

World Almanac and Book of Facts. 2005. "Recent Trends in Vital Statistics" page 73. URL: http://search.epnet.com/login.aspx?direct=true&db=afhtan=16987936. Accessed June 24, 2005.

Zelizer, Viviana K. 1985. *Pricing the Priceless Child: The changing social value of children*. New York: Basic Books.

Chapter Eleven

American Association of State Colleges and Universities. "Enrollment Trends at AASCU Campuses, 1994-2004, Vol. 3, No. 5, May 2006

CAPE. "Projections of Education Statistics to 2016." Research from the National Center for Educational Statistics, 2008. http://nces.ed.gov/programs/projections/projections2016/tables/table_01.asp?referrer=list

College Board, "Trends in College Pricing 2006." Based on data collected in the *College Board's Annual Survey of Colleges*, 2006-2007.

Banfield, Edward. 1974. *The Unheavenly City Revisited*. Boston: Little, Brown.

Bowles, Samuel, and Herbert Gintis. 1976. *Schooling in Capitalist America*. New York: Basic Books.

Carey, Kevin and Erin Dillon. 2008. "College Access and Social Class: The A.J. Soprano Factor." *EDUCATIONSECTOR*. February 19th.

Carnegie Task Force, *Starting Point: Meeting the Needs of Young Children,* 1994. New York: Carnegie Corporation pp. 3-22.

Chicago Tribune, "Most in failing schools will be denied tutors." Section A, p. 1, September 13, 2003.

Coleman, James S., and Thomas Hoffer. 1987. *Pubic and Private High Schools: The Impact of Communities*. New York: Basic Books.

Coleman, James S., Campbell, Ernest Q., Hobson, Carol J., McPartland, James, Mood, Alexander, Weinfield, Frederick D., and York, Robert L. 1966. *Equality of Educational Opportunity* Washington, DC: U.S. Government Printing Office.

Coleman, James s., and Lee Rainwater. 1978. *Social Standing in America: New Dimensions of Class*. New York: Basic Books.

Entwisle, Doris R., and Karl L. Alexander, 1992. "Summer Setback: Race, Poverty, School Composition, and Achievement." *American Sociological Review* 57: pp. 72-84.

Famighetti, Robert. 1997. *The World Almanac and Book of Facts 1997.* New York: St. Martin's.

Gilbert, Dennis L. 1998. *The American Class Structure* (5th Ed.). Belmont, CA: Wadsworth.

Hedges, Larry V., Laine, Richard D., Greenwald, Rob. 1994 "Does Money Matter? A Meta-Analysis of Studies of the Effects of Differential School Inputs on Student Outcomes." *Educational Researchers* 14 (April): 5-14.

Feldman, Bob. "Savage Inequalities Revisited." *Dollars and Sense Magazine*, January/February 2003.

Fox, M.A., B.A. Connolly, and T.D. Snyder. 2005. Youth Indicators 2005: Trends in the Well-Being of American Youth. Washington, D.C.U.S. Department of Education. National Center for Education Statistics. Table 21. htt://nes.ed.gov/pubs2005/2005050.pdf [http://nces.ed.gov/pubs2005/2005050.pdf].

Hanushek, Eric, A. and Ludger Woessman. 2005. "Does Educational Tracking Affect Performance and Inequality? Differences-in-Differences Evidence Across Countries." Discussion Paper No. 1901. Dec. 2005. Forschungsinstitut Zur Zukunft der Arbeit (Institute for Study of Labor).

Herrenstein, Richard. 1971. *IQ in the Meritocracy*. Boston: Little, Brown.

Herrenstein, Richard J. and Murray, Charles. 1994 *The Bell Curve: Intelligence and Class Structure in American Life*. New York: The Free Press.

Hoekstra, Mark. 2009. "The Effects of Attending the Flagship State University on Earnings: A Discontinuity-Based Approach," *Review of Economics and Statistics*, 91 (4): pp. 717-724.

Jencks, Christopher, et al. 1973. *Inequality: A Reassessment of the Effects of Family and Schooling in America*. New York: Basic Books.

Jensen, Arthur R. 1969. "How Much Can We Boost IQ and Scholastic Achievement?" *Harvard Educational Review,* 39 (Winter): 1-123.

McKinsey & Company. 2009. "The Economic Impact of the Achievement Gap in America's Schools: Summary of Findings. http://www.mckinsey.com/app_media/images/page_images/offices/socialsector/pdf/achievement_gap_report.pdf

Leacock, Eleanor, ed., 1971. The *Culture of Poverty: A Critique.* New York: Simon and Schuster.

Lewis, Oscar. 1971. *The Culture of Poverty: A Critique.* New York: Simon and Schuster.

Liu, Goodwin, Ross Wiener, and Eli Pristoop. "Funding Gaps 2006." *The Education Trust.* 20 Dec. 2006. 26 Mar. 2007. Path: http://www2.edtrust.org/EdTrust/Press+Room/Funding+Gap+2006.htm.

Mortenson, Thomas G. 1995. *Postsecondary Education Opportunity: The Mortenson Research Letter on Public Policy Analysis for Postsecondary Education* 41:5 (November).

New American Foundation. Federal Budget Project: National Ranks Per Pupil Expenditures 2008. http://febp.newamerica.net/k12/rankings

Science and Engineering Indicators. April 2, 2002.

Orfield, Gary, and Franklin Monfort. 1988. *Racial Formation in the United States from the 1960s to the 1980s.* New York: Routledge, Chapman & Hall.

Plomin, Robert and DeFries, John C. 1989. *Scientific America.* May.

Rachlin, Jill. "The Label That Sticks." *U.S. News & World Report* 3 July 1989: pp. 51-52.

Rist, Ray C. 1978. *The Invisible children: School Integration in American Society.* Cambridge, MA: Harvard University Press.

Schnept, Sylke V. 2003. "Inequalities in Secondary School Attendance in Germany." S3RI Applications Working Paper A03116, South Hampton: South Hampton Statistical Science Research Institute.

Sewell, William H., and Robert M. Hauser. 1980. "The Wisconsin Longitudinal Study of Social and Psychological Factors in Aspirations and Achievements." *Research in Sociology of Education and Socialization* vol 1: pp. 59-99.

The Educational Trust. "Charting a Necessary Path: The Baseline Report of Public Higher Education Systems in the Access to Success Initiative." December, 2009.

_____. "An Annual Survey of America's Charter Schools, 2008." Center for Educational Reform, July 28, 2008. Retrieved September 19, 2009.

_____. "Opportunity Adrift: Our Flagship Universities are Straying from their Public Mission," January 2010.

Thurow, Lester. 1980. *The Zero Sum Society.* New York: Basic Books.

U.S. Department of Education. 1990. National Center for Educational Statistics, National Education Longitudinal Study of 1988, Washington, DC: U.S. Government Printing Office.

_____. 2010. "The Evaluation of Charter School Impacts: Final Report." NCEE-4029. June, 2010.

U.S. Census. 2010. "Educational Attainment by Race and Hispanic Origin," 2010. Table 226. http://www.census.gov/population/wwww/socdemo/edc-attn.html.

U.S. Census. The 2011 Statistical Abstract: The National Data Book. "College Enrollments of Recent High School Graduates." Table 272. Internet Release Date: 2010. http://www.census.gov/compendia/statab/cats/education.html

U.S. Census Bureau, 2000. URL: http://ferret.bls.census.gov/macro/032000/perinc/new03_001.htm

U.S. Census Bureau, 2000. "School Enrollment: Social and Economic Characteristics of Students." October 2001.

U.S. Census Bureau, 2004. "Educational Attainment in the United States: 2004."

U.S. Census Bureau, Current Population Survey, 2007 Annual Social and Economic Supplement. Numbers in thousands.

U.S. Census Bureau, 2007. "Educational Attainment in the United States," Current Population Survey, 2007 Annual Social and Economic Supplement. Internet release date January 10, 2008.

National Center for Education Statistics (NCES) and Census, 2005-2006.

U.S. Census Bureau, 2006, *Current Population Survey,* "ED4 High school completion: Percentage of adults ages 18–24a who have completed high school by race and Hispanic origin, and method of completion, 1980–2006."

U.S. Department of Education, National Center for Education Statistics. 2002. "The Condition of Education 2002" (NCES 2002-025), Indicator 25.

U.S. Dept. of Education, National Center for Education Statistics, Digest of Education Statistics 2007, and U.S. Census Bureau, Current Population Survey, March 2007.

U.S. Department of Education, National Center for Education Statistics. (2010). "Condition of Education 2010." Table A-23-2,(NCES 2010-028).

Verhovek, Sam Howe. "Rich Schools, Poor Schools, Never-Ending Legislation." *New York Times* 30 May 1993: pp. 57-63.

Wadsworth, Gordon. 2010. "Sky Rocketing College Costs," InflationData.com. http://inflationdata.com/inflation/Inflation_Articles/Education_Inflation.asp. Retrieved: Jan. 12, 2011.

Wilson, Franklin D. 1985. "The Impact of School Desegregation Programs on White Public enrollment, 1968-1976." *Sociology of Education* 58: pp. 137-153.

Wilson, Kathryn, Lambhright, Kristina, and Smeeding, Timothy. 2004. Internet Paper: School Fiance, Equivalent Educational Expenditures and Income Distribution: Equal Dollars or Equal Chances for Success?" 222-cpr.maxwell.syr.edu/faculty/.../pdf/school finances-6.25.04pdf

Wortman, Paul M., and Fred B. Bryant. 1985. "School Desegregation and Black Achievement: An Integrative Review." *Sociological Methods and Research vol. 13: pp. 289-324.*

Chapter Twelve

Alexander, Pat. 1994. *Eerdmans' Handbook to the World's Religions*. Grand Rapids: William B. Eerdmans Publishing Company.

Armstrong, Karen, Susannah Heschel, Jim Wallis. 2002. "Fundamentalism in the Modern World." *Sojouners*. Vol. 31. No. 2 March/April: pp. 20-26.

Barnes PM, Bloom B, Nahin R. Complementary and alternative medicine use among adults and children: United States, 2007 (PDF). CDC National Health Statistics Report #12. 2008.

Berger, Peter L. 1967. "Religious Institutions." In Neil J. Smelser (ed.), *Sociology: An Introduction*. New York: Wiley.

Durkheim, E. 1954 (Original work published in 1915). *The Elementary Forms of Religious Life* (J. Swain, Trans.) New York: Free Press.

Finke, Roger, and Rodney Stark. 1992. *The Churching of America*. New Brunswick, NJ: Rutgers University Press.

Gallup and Newport. 1991. Cited in David Popenoe, *Sociology*. 10th ed., 1995, Englewood Cliffs, NJ: Simon & Schuster Company.

Hadaway, C. Kirk, Penny Long Marler. 2002. "Being Religious or Being Spiritual in America: A Zero-Sum Proposition?" *Journal for the Scientific Study of Religion*. Vol. 41. No. 2 June: pp. 289-300.

Hadaway, C. Kirk, Penny Long Marler, and Mark Chaves. 1993. "What the Polls Don't Show: A Closer Look at U.S. Church Attendance." *American Sociological Review*. Vol. 58. No. 6 December: pp. 741-52.

Hall, Holly. "Donations to Religious Groups Were Virtually Flat Last Year." *The Chronicle of Philanthropy* 8 June 2010.

Hammond, Phillip E. 1992. *Religion and Personal Autonomy: The Third Disestablishment in America*. Columbia: University of South Carolina Press.

Hyat, Kamila, 2008. "No Room for Doubt and Division." *The New International*. Retrieved 2008-09-25.

Lamb, Christina. 2002. *The Sewing Circles of Herat: A Personal Voyage Through Afghanistan*. New York: Harper Collins.

Lampman, Jane. 2002. "How America Prays." *The Christian Science Monitor 12 September*.

Marx, Karl, and Friedrich Engels. 1969 (Originally published in German in 1848.). *The Communist Manifesto*. Baltimore: Penguin.

Melton, J. Gordon. 1989. *The Encyclopedia of American Religions*. 3rd ed. Detroit: Gale Research.

Noss, John B. 1980. *Man's Religions*. 6th ed. New York: Macmillan.

Parsons, Talcott. 1966. *Societies: Evolutionary and Comparative Perspectives*. Englewood Cliffs, NJ: Prentice-Hall.

Robinson, George. "Religion in America." *U.S. News and World Report* Vol. 132. No. 6 November/December 2002: pp. 14-15.

Roof, Wade Clark. 1993. *A Generation of Seekers. The Spiritual Journeys of the Baby Boom Generation*. San Francisco: Harper San Francisco.

The Gallup Poll. 2007. *Public Opinion*. Rowman & Littlefield Publishers, Inc., Lanham, Maryland.

The Pew Forum. "Pew Forum U.S. Religious Landscape Survey." Pew Research Center Publications. Conducted in 2007, released in 2008.

_____. " Prayer in America." *Pew Research Center Publications*. May 7, 2009. http://pewresearch.org/pubs/1211/pray-daily-demographics-religion

_____. The Pew Forum on Religion & Public Life. "The Future of the Global Muslim Population: Projections for 2010-2030." 27 January, 2011.

Warner, Steve. 1993. "Work in Progress Toward a New Paradigm for the Sociological Study of Religion in the United States." *American Journal of Sociology* vol. 98 March: pp. 1044:1093.

Chapter Thirteen

Althaus, Scott, L., 2005. "How Exceptional was Turnout in 2004?" *International Communication Association & American Political Science Association* Vol. 15 No. 1, Winter.

Capital Eye, "Cost of Presidential Race Already Tops all Elections Prior to 2004," February 4, 2008.

Cook, Timothy E. and Paul Gronke, "Trust, Distrust, Confidence, Lack of Confidence: New Evidence of Public Opinion toward Government in Institutions from 2002." Paper prepared for delivery at the annual meeting of the Southern Political Science Association, Savannah, Georgia, November 2002.

Current Population Survey. 2010. http://www.bls.gov/cps.

Economist View. 2009. "The Shrinking Middle Class?" 10 March. http://economistsview.typepad.com/economistsview/2009/03/the-shrinking-middle-class.html

Scan, Mark. Forbes, "Lines grow at unemployment Offices." Forbes 20 November 2008. http://www.forbes.com/2008/11/20/weekly-jobless-claims-markets-econ-cx_md_1119markets08.html

Gallup Poll, September 5-6, 2005. http://en.wikipedia.org/wiki/Hurricane_Katrina#Political_effects

Hall, R.L. and R.W. Wayman. 1990. "Buying Time: Moneyed Interest and the Mobilization of Bias in Congressional Committees." *American Political Science Review*. Vol. 84: pp. 797.

Iglitzin, L.B. 1974. "The making of the apolitical woman: Femininity and sex-stereotyping in girls." In J.S. Jaquette, ed., *Women in Politics*. New York: John Wiley.

International Institute for Democracy and Electoral Assistance. Center for Voting and Democracy, "International Voter Turnout, 1991-2000. http://archive.fairvote.org/turnout/intturnout.htm

Jennings, M.K., and R.G. Niemi. 1974. *The Political Character of Adolescence: The Influence of Families and Schools*. Princeton, J.J.: Princeton University Press, 1974.

OSC. 2011. National Commission on the BP Deepwater Horizon Oil Spill and Offshore Drilling. http://www.oilspillcommission.gov/final-report.

Mills, C.W. 1956. *The Power Elite*. New York: Oxford University Press.

NBC/WST Polls: "Obama Bouncing Back." 19 January 2011. http://www.msnbc.msn.com/id/41161439/ns/politics-more_politics/

Newcomb, T.M. 1958. "Attitude Development as a Function of Reference Groups: The Bennington Study." In E. Maccoby, T.M. Newcomb, and E.L. Hartley, eds. *Readings in Social Psychology* (3rd. ed.). New York: Holt, Rinehart and Winston.

Pew Research Center for the People and the Press. 2010. "Distrust, Discontent, Anger and Partisan Rancor." 18 Apr. 2010.

Phillips, Kevin. 1993. *Boiling Point: Democrats, Republicans, and the Decline of the Middle-Class Prosperity*. New York: Harper Collins.

Riesman, D., N. Glazer and R. Denney. 1950. *The Lonely Crowd: A Study in the Changing American Character*. New Haven, Conn: Yale University Press.

Skocpol, Theda. 1979. *States and Social Revolutions: A Comparative Analysis of France, Russia, and China*. Cambridge: Cambridge University Press.

Tocqueville, Alexis de. 1980. *Democracy in America*, Vol. 1, Phillip Bradley (trans. and ed.). New York: Knopf.

Valelly, Richard. 1990. "Vanishing voters." *The American Prospect* Spring: pp. 140-150.

Weber, Max. 1947. *The Theory of Social and Political Organization*. Translated by A.M. Henderson and Talcott Parsons. New York: Oxford University Press.

Weber, Max. 1946. *From Max Weber: Essays in Sociology. Hans Gerth and C. Wright Mills. trans. and eds. New York: Oxford University Press.*

Chapter Fourteen

AFL-CIO website: www.aficio.org/issues/jobseconomy/exportingamerica/outsourcing_problems.cfm

Aristotle *Politics*. Book 3, Section V.

Barnet, Richard, J. 1994. "Lords of the Global Economy: Stateless Corporations," *The Nation* 19 December: pp. 75ff.

Bernstien, Jared and Lawrence Mishel. "Labor Market Left Behind." *Economic Policy Institute: Briefing Paper*, Washington, D.C. 2003

Bianchi, Suzanne M., "Changing Economic Roles of Women and Men," in Reynolds Farley (ed.) 1995. *State of the Union: America in the 1990s*, Vol. 1: Economic Trends p. 127. New York: Russell Sage Foundation.

Bloom, David E., and Brender, Aldi. 1993. "Labor and the Emerging World Economy." *Population Bulletin* 48 October: pp. 1-39.

Boston Herald, "White-Collar workers feel the pain: Study: Grads bore brunt of recession." Wednesday, 27 August 2003.

Breslow, Marc, and Howard Matthew. "The Real Un(der)employment Rate," *Dollars and Sense* vol. 199 May/June 1995: p. 35.

Bryan, Ford R. 1989. *The Fords of Dearborn*. Detroit: Harlo.

Bugliotta, Guy. "The Minimum Wage Culture," *The Washington Post National Weekly Edition*, 10-16 October 1994.

Colatosti, Camille. 1992. "A Job Without a Future: Temporary and Contract Workers Battle Permanent Insecurity," *Dollars and Sense,* vol. 176 May 1992: p. 9.

Edwards, Richard. 1979. *Contested Terrain: The Transformation of the Workplace in the Twentieth Century*. New York: Basic Books.

Forbes.com. Special Report "CEO Compensation." 3 May 2007.

Gallagher, Daniel and George Strauss. 2008. Paper provided by Institute of Industrial Relations, UC Berkeley in its series Institute for Research on Labor and Employment, Working Paper Series with number 1057.

Glotz, Peter. "Forward to Europe." *Dissent* vol. 33 no. 3 Summer 1986: pp. 327-339.

Harrison, Bennett, and Barry Bluestone. 1988. *The Great U-Turn: Corporate Restructuring and the Polarizing of America*. New York: Basic Books.

Hochschild, Arlie R. 1997. *The Time Bind*. New York: Henry Holt.

LeGrande, Linda, *The Service Sector: Employment and Earnings in the 1980s*. Congressional Research Service, Library of Congress, Report No. 85-167 E, 15 August 1985.

Levy, Frank. 1987. *Dollars and Dreams: The Changing American Income Distribution*. New York: Russell Sage Foundation, pp. 3-4.

May, David. 2003. "White-Collar Workers Feeling the Chill of Recession: For a Planned Economy." <www.socialistappeal.org/econnews/white_collar_workers.html>

Mills, C. Wright. 1951. *White Collar: The American Middle Class*. New York: Oxford University Press.

Mishel, Lawrence and Bernstein, Jared. 1994. The St*ate of Working America: 1994-95*. p.109-153. New York: M.E. Sharpe.

Morse, Nancy C. and Weiss, Robert S. 1955. "The Function and Meaning of Work," *American Sociological Review* Vol. 20: pp. 191:198.

Multinational Monitor. "Wealth and Income Inequality in the USA: Inequality and Corporate Power." Vol. 24-Number 5, May 2003.

National Priorities Project and Jobs with Justice. Working Hard, Earning Less: The Future of Job Growth in America. Available for the National Priorities Project, 17 New South Street, Suite 301, Northampton, MA 01060.

Newman, Katherine, and Lennon, Chauncey. "The Job Ghetto." *The American Prospect* Vol. 22 Summer 1995: pp. 66-67.

New York Times/CBS News Poll. 1996. "The Downsizing of America: Layoffs." *The New York Times* World Wide Web site (March 9).

Nie, Norman H. 1999. "Tracking our techno-future." *American Demographics* July: pp. 50-52.

Pearlstein, Steven. "Recessions Fade, But Downsizings Are Forever." *The Washington Post National Weekly Edition*, 3-9 October 1994: pp. 21.

Piore, Michael, and Charles Sabel. 1984. *The Second Industrial Divide*. New York: Basic Books.

Rajan, Sara. "Prosperity and its Perils." *Time* 1 March 1 2004: pp. 34

Reaser, Lynn. "Outsourcing of U.S. jobs: threat or benefit?" *ABA Banking Journal* vol 96, no. 2 February 2004: p. 96.

Robinson, Robert K. and William T. Jackson, Geralyn McClure Franklin, Diana Hensley. "US sexual harassment law: Implications for small businesses." *Journal of Small Business Management*, vol. 36, no. 2 April 1998: pp. 1-12.

Smith, Adam. 1982. *The Wealth of Nations*. New York (Originally Published in 1776): Penguin.

Sweeney, John J. 1996. *America Needs a Raise*. Boston: Houghton Mifflin.

The Des Moines Register, "Does America Really Honor Workers?" 1 September 2003: p. 8A.

The Economist. 1997. "Not Striking." 342: p. 73.

Thurow, Lester. 1987. "A Surge in Inequality." *Scientific American* vol. 256 May: pp. 30-37.

U.S. Bureau of Labor Statistics, "Unemployment Situation Summary," 5 September 2003.

U.S. Census Bureau, Statistical Abstract of the United States: 2000, Table 252: Earnings by Highest Degree Earned: 1999, p. 158.

U.S. Census Bureau. 1993. *Income and Poverty* CD-ROM Table P19.

U.S. Census Bureau. 1994B. *Statistical Abstract of the United States.* CD-ROM, Table 654.

U.S. Department of Labor. October, 2008. Bureau of Labor Statistics, Washington, D.C. 20212

U.S. Department of Labor. Women's Bureau, Statistics & Data, *"Quick Stats 2007"*, Novemeber 22, 2008.

Walker, Blair, S. "Small PC Firms Reaps Big Profits," *USA Today* 13 May 1992.

Women's E News, "Lower Male Income Causes Tightest Wage Gap," 14 September 2003.

Work in America. 1973. Department of Health Education and Welfare, pp. 4-5.

Chapter Fifteen

Associate Content (AC), "Rural Relocation: Is moving to the country for you?" April 9, 2006.

Avert. 2009. "The Impact of HIV and AIDS in Africa. International HIV and AIDS Charity. http://www.avert.org/aids-impact-africa.htm

CBSNews. 2008. "Is Thee Hope for the World's Vanishing Forests?" http://www.cbc.ca/world/story/2008/06/24/f-vanishing-forests.html

Constable, Pamela. "India's Clock Just Keeps on Ticking." *Washington Post National Weekly Edition* 30 August 1999: p. 16.

Greenhalgh, Susan, and Jiali Li. "Engendering Reproductive Policy and Practice in Peasant China: For a Feminist Demography of Reproduction." *Signs*, vol. 20, no. 3, Spring 1995: pp. 601-640.

Guttentag, Marcia and Paul F. Secord. 1983. *Too Many Women? The Sex Ratio Question.* Beverly Hills, CA: Sage.

Haub, Carl, and Deana Cornelious. 1999. *1999 World Population Data Sheet.* Washington, DC: Population Reference.

CIA World Factbook, "List of countries by life expectancy," 2007.

Johnson, K.M. 2001. "Recent Population Redistribution Trends in the United States." Paper presented at the Annual Meetings of the Population Association of America, Washington, D.C.

Jones, Landon Y. 1980. *Great Expectations.* New York: Ballantine.

Kornblum and Julian, *Social Problems.* 7th Ed. (Englewood Cliffs, NJ: Prentice-Hall, 1992.

McGreger, Sue L.T. 2000. *Changing Family Structure and Demographics.* Working paper.

Malthus, Thomas Robert, 1798. *Essays on the Principle of Population.* New York: Augustus Kelly, Bookseller; reprinted in 1965.

MSNBC. "Obama Reverses Abortion-Fund Policy." January 1, 2009. http://www.msnbc.msn.com/id/28812519/

National Organization for Women. 2002. "U.N. Population Conference Rejects Bush Administration's Anti-Abortion Stance." December 30, 2002.

Patton, G. et. al. 2009. "Global Patterns of Martality in Young People: A Systematic Analysis of Population Health Data."

PRB. "Improving the Reproductive Health of sub-Saharan African Youth." Population Reference Bureau. May, 2010. http://www.prb.org/Topics/Youth.aspx.

Peterson, R. Dan, Delores F. Wunder, and Harlan L Mueller. 1999. *Social Problems: Globalization in the Twenty-First Century*. Upper Saddle River, N.J.:Prentice Hall.

The Pew Research Center. *Û.S. Population Projections*. 2008.

Population Reference Bureau. *2002 World Data Sheet*. Washington, D.C. Population Reference Bureau, 2002.

Population Reference Bureau. 2003. 2003 world population data sheet, July 23, 2003.

Porras, Marina. 2007. End the Biggest Holocaust in Human History: Female Infanticide/ Feticide!" Go Petition: Changing the World. http://www.gopetition.com/petitions/end-the-holocaust-of-female-infanticide-feticide.html

Raghunathan, V. K. "Millions of Baby Girls Killed in India." *The Straits Times*, 8 February 2003.

Rosenberg, M. 2011. "Population Growth Rates: Population Growth Rates and Doubling Time." *About.com Geography*. http://geography.about.com/od/populationgeography/a/population-grow.htm.

Segal, Uma Anand, Doreen Elliot, and Nazneen Sada Mayadas (eds.). 2010. *Immigration Worldwide: Policies, Practices and Trends*. Oxford University Press, Inc., New York, New York.

Statistically Abstracts of the United States, Washington, D.C.: Bureau of the Census, 2002. Table 41.

Ohlemacher, Stephen. (2007, September 12). "Number of Immigrants Hits Record 37.5 Million." *The Washington Post*. http://www.washingtonpost.com/wp-dyn/content/article/2007/09/12/AR2007091200071.html

UNHCR, The UN Refugee Agency, June 2008.

UNAIDS. 2010. Global Report: UNAIDS Report on Global AIDS Epidemic. http://www.unaids.org/globalreport/

UNICEF. www.unicef.org/emerg/darfur/

United Nations. 2010. Estimates reported by Martin Nesirky, spokesperson for Secretary General, and Jean Victor Nkolo, spokesperson for President of General Assembly. United Nations. January 13, 2010.

U.S. Bureau of the Census, 2002d. *Statistical Abstract of the United States*. Washington, DC: U.S. Government Printing Office.

U.S. Census Bureau. 2011. World Vital Events: World Vital Events Per Time Unit: 2011. http://www.census.gov/cgi-bin/ipc/pcwe

U.S. Census. "Annual Estimates of the Resident Population of the United States, Regions, States, and Puerto Rico: April 1, 2000 to July 1, 2009 (NST-EST2009-01)." http://www.census.gov/popest/states/NST-ann-est.html

_____. "World Population: 1950-2050." U.S. Census Bureau, Population Division. http://www.census.gov/ipc/www/idb/worldpopgraph.html

_____.U.S. Census Bureau. "World Population Growth Rates: 1050-2050." http://www.census.gov/ipc/www/idb/worldgrgraph.php.

USDA. 2007. "Expenditures on Children by Families." Center for Nutrition Policy and Promotion: Miscellaneous Publication 1528-2007.

U.S. News & World Report, 12 January 1987: p. 61.

World Factbook, "Rank Order—Total Fertility," 23 Oct. 2008.

www.geographyiq.com/ranking/ranking_infant_mortality_rate_aall.html

www.Siakhenn.tripod.com/fertility.html

www.usinfo.state.gov/journals/itsv/0699/ijse/spain.htm

www.unaids.org/EN/Geographic+Area/ByRegion/sub-saharan+africa.asp

www.usda.gov/cnpp. ("Expenditures on Children by Families").

Chapter Sixteen

America's Second Harvest, Hunger In America, 2006

Bairoch, Paul. 1988. *Cities and Economic Development from the Dawn to the Present*. Chicago: University of Chicago Press.

Burgess, Ernest W. 1925. "The Growth of the City: An Introduction to a Research Project." In *The City*, Robert E. Park, Ernest W. Burgess, and Roderick D. McKenzie (eds.) Chicago: University of Chicago Press (1967 edition).

Catalyst Chicago. "More Illinois Living in Poverty, at Ricks of School Failure." 17 February 2011.

Center for Housing Policy, "The Housing Landscape for America's Working Families." 2005.

Childe, V. Gordon. 1951. *Social Evolution*. Cleveland: World.

Children's Defense Fund. 1994. *The State of America's Children Yearbook 1994*. Washington, DC: Children's Defense Fund.

Christian Science Monitor. "Resegregation of Schools Deepening: Districts in Big Cities of Midwest and Northeast Undergo the Most Change." 28 January 2008.

Cohen, Albert K. 1955. *Delinquent Boys: The Culture of the Gang*. New York: Free Press.

Cox, Vic. 1997. *Guns, Violence, and Teens*, Springfield, NJ: Enslow Publisher, Inc., p. 22.

Durkheim, Emile. 1964. *The Division of Labor in Society*, George Simpson (trans.). New York: Free Press (originally published in 1897).

Fischer, Claude S. 1976. *The Urban Experience*. New York: Harcourt.

Frey, William H. 2011. "Migration Declines Further: Stalling Brain Gains and Ambitions." http://www.brookings.edu/opinions/2011/0112_migration_frey.aspx.

Gans, Herbert j. 1962. *The Urban Villagers*. New York: Free Press.

Gottdiener, Mark. 1994. *The New Urban Sociology*. New York: McGraw-Hill.

Harris, Chauncy, and Edward Ullman. 1945. "The Nature of Cities." *Annals of the American Academy of Political and Social Science* vol 242, November: pp. 7-17.

Horton, Paul B., Gerald R. Leslie, and Richard F. Larson. 1991. *The Sociology of Social Problems*. Englewood Cliffs, NJ: Prentice-Hall. p. 274.

Hoyt, Homer. 1939. *The Structure and Growth of Residential Neighborhoods in American Cities*. Washington, D.C.: U.S. Federal Housing Administration.

IES. 2010. Indictors of School Crime and Safety: 2010. NCES 2011-002, November 2010.

Jacobs, Jane. 1970. *The Economy of Cities*. New York: Vintage Books.

Jefferson, Thomas. 1780. Quoted in Kornblum and Joseph Julian, *Social Problems*. 7th ed. Englewood Cliffs, NJ: Prentice-Hall, 1992, p. 421.

Law Center for Homelessness and Poverty. 2003. Reported online at http://www.homeless.org/do/Home.

Miller, Walter. 1958. "Lower-Class Culture as a Generating Milieu of Gang Delinquency" *Journal of Social Issues* vol. 14: pp. 5-19.

Miller, Walter. 1975. *Violence by Youth Gangs and Youth Groups as a Crime Problem in Major American Cities*. Washington, D.C.: U.S. Government Printing Office.

Levine,MarcV. 1987. "Downtown Redevelopment as an urban Growth Strategy: A Critical Appraisal of http://feedingamerica.org/ the Baltimore Renaissance." *Journal of Urban Affairs* vol. 9: pp. 103-123.

Palen, J. John. 1981. *The Urban World*. 2nd ed. New York: McGraw-Hill.

Sassen, Saskia. 1994. *Cities in a World Economy*. Thousand Oaks, CA: Pine Forge, 1994.

Senate Committee on the Judiciary Hearing before the October 1, 1992, second session. Children carrying weapons: Why the Recent Increase," Washington, D.C., p. 26.

Sheley, Joseph F. and James D. Wright, "Gun Acquisition and Possession in Selected Juvenile Samples," Research in Brief, National Institute of Justice. December 1993, pp. 5-6.

Simonetti, Rosen Marie. "A LEN interview with Professor Alfred Blumstein of Carnegie Mellon University," *Law Enforcement News*, 30 April 1995.

Tabb, William, and Larry Sawers (eds) 1984. *Marxism and the Metropolis*. New York: Osford University Press.

Tonnies, Ferdinand. 1957. *Community and Society*. East Lansing: Michigan State University (originally published in 1887).

U.S. Census Bureau. 1996. *Statistical Abstract of the United States*. Washington, D.C.: Government Printing Office.

U.S. Bureau of Census, 2001. Table 31.

U.S. Bureau of the Census, *Statistical Abstract of the United States* 1994, CD-.ROM. Washington, DC: U.S. Government Printing Office, 1994

U.S. Census Bureau, "Population of 50 Largest Cities, 1900-2005."

Wirth, Louis. 1938. "Urbanism as a Way of Life." *American Journal of Sociology* vol. 44: pp. 1-24.

Zastrow, Charles, 1996. *Social Problems: Issues and Solutions*. 4th Edition. Chicago: Nelson-Hall Publishers.

Chapter Seventeen

Bleicher, Matthew, "So Are Robots Stealing Our Jobs? And is this a Bad Thing?" Robots, FTW, 11 August 2009. http://robotsftw.com/2009/08/so-are-robots-stealing-our-jobs/

Blumer, Herbert G. 1969. Collective Behavior." In Alfred M. Lee, (ed), *Principles of Sociology*, 3rd ed. New York: Barnes and Noble.

Blumer, Herbert, "Collective Behavior," in A. M. Lee, ed., *Principles of Sociology*. New York, Barnes & Noble, 1951, pp. 67-121.

Dawkins, Richard. 2006. *The Selfish Gene*. New York: Oxford University Press.

Durkheim, Emile. 1966. *The Division of Labor in Society*. New York: Free Press. Originally Published in 1893.

Gallup Poll. 2007. "American Continue to Express a Slight Preference for Boys. http://www.gallup.com/poll/28045/americans-continue-express-slight-preference-boys.aspx

Kurzweil, Ray, 2005. *The Singularity is Near: When Humans Transcend Biology*. Penguin Books, New York, New York.

LeBon, Gustave. 1960. The Crowd: *A Study of the Popular Mind*. New York: Viking. Originally Published in 1896.

Marx, Karl. 1967. *Capital: A Critique of Political Economy*. Ed. Friedrich Engels, New york: International (orig. pub. 1867).

Miklovic, Dan. 2003. "Outsourcing not the Culprit in Manufacturing Job loss." *Automation-World*, 9 December 2003.

Morrison, Denton. 1971. "Some Notes Toward Theory on Relative Deprivation, Social Movements, and Social Change." *The American Behavior Scientist* May-June: pp. 675-690.

Obershall, Anthony. 1973. *Social Conflict and Social Movements*. Englewood Cliffs: Prentice Hall.

Parks, Robert E., and Earnest W. Burgess. 1921. *Introduction to the Science of Sociology*. Chicago: University of Chicago Press.

The Pew Form. "Growing Number of Americans Say Obama is a Muslim." Religion, Politics, and the President. Poll, August 18, 2010.

Turner, Ralph H. 1996. "The Moral Issue in Collective Behavior and Collective Action." *Mobilization* 1:1-15.

GLOSSARY

Achieved status. The status or position in society that one achieves through his/her own efforts.

Acculturation. The voluntary adoption of the norms, values and lifestyle of the dominant culture.

Affirmative action. Governmental policy and programs that grant preference to minorities in order to make-up for past and present discrimination. The purpose of affirmative action is to achieve economic equality.

Agnosticism. A belief that does not deny or affirm the existence of a god.

Alienation. A Marxian concept describing the process whereby workers are robbed of their creativity and imagination through industrialization.

Altruistic suicide. Emile Durkheim's term for a person who sacrifices his/her life for the good of the group.

Androgyny. A gender role that combines male and female characteristics.

Animism. A belief that supernatural being or beings, spirits, or deceased ancestors actively exist in the bodies of present-day people or in creatures or physical objects in the natural environment.

Anomic suicide. Emile Durkheim's term for suicides that are the result of an absence of norms in society.

Anomie. A state of normlessness characterized by the loss of a sense of meaning and detachment from others in the society.

Artificial Intelligence. Intelligence that is similar to humans, but created by means of computer technology.

Atheism. The belief that God does not exist.

Ascribed status. The status that comes to an individual through birth or through a condition over which he/she has no control over.

Assimilation. The process of absorption into the dominant culture.

Authoritative leadership. An individual who exercises leadership in a strong and individual fashion.

Authority. The right to exercise power.

Baby Boomers. An extraordinarily large cohort born in the United States during the period of time following World War II and lasting 15 years.

Barter. An economic exchange of one item for another. No money is involved in the transaction.

Battered wife syndrome. A post traumatic stress disorder cause by repeated physical abuse. It has been used as a legal defense by women accused of murdering their abusers.

Behaviorism. A theory that argues that pattern behavior is not biologically determined, but learned.

Bias theory. A theory that blames prejudice for the secondary status of minority groups.

Birth cohort. The number of people born in a specific year.

Birthrates. The average number of children born to women.

Born again. A Christian concept held by some religions that one must accepting Jesus Christ as savior in order to enter heaven. Generally applied, this marks a life-transforming period for the individual and is accompanied by ritual rights of passage.

Bourgeoisie. A term meaning capitalist employed by Karl Marx.

Bureaucracy. A formal organization with clear objectives and a hierarchy of administrators who possess the power to achieve organizational goals. Within the organization there is an established division of labor, rules of conduct, and means to keep records.

Capitalism. An economic system founded by Adam Smith whose central features are private property, profit, and competition. Private property means that all (or almost all) property, from land to the means of production (industry), is owned privately by individuals. The motivating force behind capitalism is the desire to create profit through competition.

Charismatic authority. Authority that derives its source of power from the magnetic personality of the leader.

Checks and balances. A structural feature of government in the United States where all three branches of government—legislative, executive, and judicial—are dependent upon one another to carry out their individual responsibilities.

Church. A formal organization devoted to religious belief and worship.

Civil rights. Rights that ensure that citizens are protected from harm by other citizens of the state and from the government itself.

Class. A stratification system in which members of a society are hierarchically ranked according to money, education, race, etc.

Class consciousness. A collective awareness by workers that they have been manipulated by the ideology of the elite to serve their personal interests.

Coalition. A government where two or more political parties join forces to form a voting majority in the legislative branch. Having formed this majority the coalition is then termed "the government."

Cohabitation. A household in which those living together are not married or related.

Cohort. A demographic term for group.

Collective behavior. A social process in which spontaneous actions emerge by individuals trying to cope with stressful situations or unclear conditions.

Cloning. Scientifically termed "somatic cell nuclear transfer," or a process that is used to create identical organisms through asexual reproduction.

Collective conscience. The shared common values, outlooks, interpretations of events, languages and dialects of a society or social group.

Commune. A small group of individual who voluntarily live together and collectively share resources and work.

Communism. An economic system that calls for complete equality, a communal sharing of all goods, and in its ultimate form, an absence of government.

Concept. A term use to describe or refer to an object in terms of specific qualities, traits, and attributes.

Constitutionalism. A feature of the American system of government whereby power is exercised via a written constitution and any attempt to exercise power outside of the bounds of the constitution is unlawful.

Coercive organization. An organization to which membership is not voluntary. An example of a coercive organization is a prison.

Correlation. The relationship between two variables where change in one is associated with change in the other.

Counterculture. A culture created in opposition to the dominant culture.

Crazes. Fast developing forms of social behavior similar to fads, but with a greater impact on society.

Creeping credentialism. Requiring degrees and certification for jobs in which education is unrelated to the work.

Crowd. A temporary group of people brought together on the basis of a shared interest and whose collectivity influences individual action.

Crude divorce rate. Measures the number of divorces per 1,000 of the total population. This measure includes many individuals who are not eligible for divorce due to their age or non-married status.

Cultural diversity. The differences found among cultures.

Cultural universals. A concept referring to social structures and events that seem to be shared across cultures.

Culture. A term referring to all of the shared knowledge, values, rules of behavior, and the objects that make-up the way of life of a people.

Cultural lag. A condition created when changes in the material culture occur at a faster pace than the non-material culture.

Cultural relativity. An attempt to understand the beliefs and practices of a people in the context of their culture.

Culture of poverty. A theory associated with victim-blame that holds that individuals and groups in poverty are responsible for their own plight and maintains that the central problem is that years of dependency and lower-class values lead to failure.

Death rate. The number of deaths per 1000 people per year.

Decertification. The process of forcing union representation out of corporations.

De facto segregation. The separation of races by residential patterns.

De jure segregation. The separation of races by law.

Deferred gratification. The willingness to put off the satisfaction of present desires in order for a greater gain in the future.

Democratic leadership. A leader that seeks the advice and input from members of the group.

Demography. The study of human populations.

Deviance. Behavior or characteristics that violate important social norms.

Dharma. A belief in a moral force with which all Hindus must act in concert.

Dictatorship of the proletariat. A Marxian theory describing the political events following a worker revolution. According to Marx, this inevitable revolution would ultimately lead to the creation of a classless, communist society characterized by harmony and equality.

Direct Democracy. The purest form of a democratic government in which all citizens participate in all governmental functions and decisions.

Discrimination. When an individual acts upon his/her prejudice by denying rights and benefits to others.

Domestic partnership. The legal recognition of an unwed couple whose purpose is to grant the same rights to unwed couples that is enjoyed by those legally married.

Dual-career marriage. A marriage where both partners are employed outside of the home.

Dyad. A two-person group.

Dysfunction consequence. An unintended and opposite consequence of an action.

Educational attainment. The amount of formal education a person has achieved.

Egalitarianism. A belief in the equality of all people.

Ego. The part of the subconscious that Freud believed regulates and balances the needs of the id and superego.

Egoistic suicide. Emile Durkheim's description of people who take their own life due to the lack of ties to a group or the community.

Elitist position. A position suggesting that governmental power is exercised by a few elite individuals who are interchangeably members of the military, big business, and the government for the sole purpose of perpetuating their own interests.

Ethnicity. A group of people whom share a common cultural heritage such as language, geographic origins, religion, values, food and dress.

Ethnocentrism. A belief that one's own culture is superior to that of others.

Eurocentrism. A belief that European culture is superior to all other world cultures.**Experimental group**. The group in a study that is subjected to the independent variable. (The variable being investigated.)

Extended family. Family arrangement with three or more generations (grandparents, parents and children). The extended family was the dominant form in pre-industrial societies.

Fads. Form of social behavior that is fast developing and short-lived.

False consciousness. A Marxian theory describing the process whereby the worker is led to believe that his/her share in life is the outcome of a just and fair competitive system—capitalism.

Fashion. A form of social behavior, usually, but not always, associated with clothing in which some trend or object becomes popular in society.

Feminist. One who advocates social and economic equality for women in opposition to the male dominated system of patriarchy.

Feminization of poverty. The fact that more women end up below the poverty line due to discriminatory behavior in society's institutions.

Fertility rates. A computation of how many births per lifetime the average woman will have.

Folkways. Norms that constitute the customary patterns of our lives.

Fordism. A management of labor developed by Henry Ford linking mass production to mass markets.

Formal labor market. Work that produces pay.

Formal organization. A secondary group charged with the responsibility of achieving explicit objectives.

Gay. A term used to identify a male homosexual.

Gender. The socially constructed attitudes, meanings, beliefs, and behaviors associated with the sex differences of being born male or female that are learned through the process of socialization.

Gender identity. Thinking of oneself as either male or female in accordance with the cultural norms associated with those roles.

Gender roles. Sex roles that are learned and reinforced through associated behaviors and attitudes with the help of socializing agents such as family, schools, peers, media, politics, and religion.

Genetic Engineering. Manipulation of the genetic structure of living organisms.

Global wage. A condition of the global economy in which wages are forced to the lowest possible denominator through worldwide competition for jobs.

Gossip. A form of social behavior in which an individual or group is targeted with information for the purpose of shame or praise.

Government crime. Crimes committed by the government.

Grim Rule of Three. A phrase used to describe the life chances of children in poverty. Specifically it details how the children of the poor are three time more likely to suffer diseases and death than those of the non-poor.

Group. Collection of people whom consciously and regularly interact with each other.

Group cohesion. The strength of the bond uniting group members.

Group conformity. The tendency of the members of the group to follow rules and expected behaviors.

Group dynamics. A term describing how a group works.

Group polarization. The process through which a group arrives at a more extreme decision than any one member would support individually.

Groupthink. The process whereby a group arrives at a decision that they privately know is wrong, but feel that they cannot challenge.

Hermaphrodite. A person with a combination of male and female internal and external genitalia.

Heterogeneous societies. Societies that are highly diverse in their social, religious, racial and ethnic makeup.

Heterosexuality. Refers to being emotionally and/or sexually attracted to the opposite sex.

Historical materialism. A Marxian theory that all values and social institutions flow from the economy.

Homogeneous societies. Societies that are highly similar in their social, religious, racial and ethnical makeup.

Homophobia. The irrational fear of homosexuals.

Homosexuality. Refers to being emotionally and/or sexually attracted to the same sex.

Hypothesis. A statement of prediction that sets forth the basis for testing the relationship between variables in an attempt to link theory to reality.

Id. Freud's term for the pleasure-seeking part of our subconscious that represents our innate drives.

Ideal culture. The beliefs, values, and attitudes that the members of a culture hold but do not necessarily follow.

Independent variable. In a research study, the variable manipulated to study its affect on other (dependent) variables.

Individual blame theories. Theories that essentially blame individuals for their own shortcomings or failures.

Individual racism. Overt and direct forms of racism in which individuals hold extreme prejudices and act in discriminatory ways.

Informal labor market. Work that does not produce pay such as volunteerism, housework and childcare.

Ingroup. Groups with which we identify and to which we are strongly attached and loyal to.

Innovations. A concept created by Robert Merton to describe the way norms assist in achieving goals.

Instincts. The inborn skills of creatures.

Institutional racism. A form of racism deeply embedded in the customs and operational practices of social institutions that serves as an obstacle to minorities and keeps them from moving out of their subordinate positions and into the economic and social mainstream.

Intelligence. Our capacity for intellectual and mental achievement.

Interest group. A collection of people who have organized to influence government action and legislation.

Internet. Electronic means of communication through a computer network.

Judicial review. The right of the judicial branch to strike down an act of Congress if, in the opinion of the court, it conflicts with the Constitution.

Karma. A belief that all beings of life—gods included—are subject to the same hopeless cycle of pain, suffering, and rebirth.

Labeling. The identification or stereotyping individuals or groups in a negative light that keeps them from achieving their potential.

Labor power. A term used by Karl Marx to describe the aggregate of mental and physical capabilities which workers use to create products.

Laissez-faire leadership. A leader who exercises minimal control.

Language. A shared system of symbols used in verbal and written communication.

Law. A binding custom or practice of society that is codified (written down) and enforced by legitimate governmental authority.

Leader. Someone who exercises formal or informal influence over those within the group.

Learning. The process of acquiring knowledge about the world and society.

Legal-rational authority. Where the right to exercise power is derived from the members of a society who create positions of authority. In such authority, rules are created which limit the scope of power of those occupying the powerful positions.

Lesbian. A term used to identify a female homosexual.

Life Chances. The opportunities and choices made available by society to people in a particular social position.

Life expectancy. The average number of years of life remaining for persons of a given age.

Linguistic Relativity Hypothesis. A proposition that language acts as a mental filter, shaping the way we see the world.

Looking-glass self. A theory advanced by Charles Horton Cooley stating that personality formation is a matter of interpreting other people's perceptions of how we look and act.

Macro level research. Investigation of large-scale social interactions including social institutions, making cross-cultural comparisons, and studying the effects of global issues.

Malthusian theory. A theory advanced by Thomas Malthus that held that food production increased arithmetically (from 1 to 2 to 3 to 4 and so forth) while population grew geometrically (from 2 to 4 to 8 to 16 and so forth).

Manifest consequences. The *intended* consequence of an action.

Marriage. A socially and legally approve mating arrangement.

Mass education. The widespread expansion of formal education in the larger society.

Master status. The most important of all of our statuses as it defines who we are to other members of society.

Material culture. A term referring to all the things that people make and use in society.

Matriarchy. A stratification system favoring women.

Means of production. The ability to produce goods. Generally applied to industrial societies.

Mechanical solidarity. Strong social ties and shared values that are based in common beliefs.

Meritocracy. A belief that rewards should be allocated commensurate with talent, effort and output.

Micro level research. Investigations of small-scale social interactions including relationships between individuals, friends, co-workers, students, family and others.

Military juntas. A government run by the military. Typically, military juntas come to power by means of a coup.

Minority group. A status reserved for those groups singled out by the dominant or more powerful members of society for differential treatment.

Mob. Localized behavior that is associated with intense levels of emotion and violence.

Modeling. The attempt to imitate behavior of others.

Monarchy. A government in which power is passed down from generation to generation on the basis of family lineage. The leader is all-powerful and any rights granted to citizens are the sole discretion of the leader.

Monogamy. The marriage of one man to one woman.

Monopoly. A condition where, for a particular product, one firm dominates the world or regional market.

Monotheism. The belief in the existence of only one god.

Moral panics. Responses to exaggerated fears and concerns of a particular group in society.

Mores. Strongly held beliefs about acceptable behavior.

Morality rate. A measure of the number of deaths per 1000 people within a specific age group.

Multiculturalism. A concept referring to the diversity of values in society.

Multinational corporation. A firm that owns and manages economic units in two or more countries.

Nationalism. A shared sense of identification that stems from a commitment to a common ideology and shared values.

Nature. In the "nature versus nurture" expression it refers to what we bring into the world at birth.

Norms. The rules of society that prescribe how its members are to behave in given situations.

Normative organizations. An organization established to pursue an altruistic (worthy) objective. One example of a normative organization would be MADD.

Nuclear family. Family structure containing only two generations—parents and children.

Nurture. In the "nature versus nurture" expression it refers to what we learn or gain through social interaction.

Objective knowledge. An area of knowledge that refers to that type of information that is considered factual.

Oligarchies. A form of government in which the exercise of power is divided among a small group.

Oligopoly. A situation that exists when a few firms dominate the world market for a particular product.

Organic solidarity. Social ties based on a functional interdependence of the members of society.

Outgroup. As opposed to ingroup, one toward which we express resentment and competition, and sometimes outright hatred.

Panics. A form of collective behavior in which a crowd reacts irrationally to a serious threat or perceived threat.

Patriarchy. A stratification system favoring men.

Pattern. Refers to a regular and systematic repetition of the same behavior(s) not occurring by chance.

Peer groups. A social group containing individuals who are similar in age or social position.

Peter principle. A bureaucratic principle that suggests that workers are promoted within an organization until they reach a level of incompetence.

Pluralist perspective. A view that holds that government power is spread among a plurality of competing groups from all corners of the society: business, labor, farmers, doctors, educators, women, racial minorities, etc.

Polyandry. Marital arrangement where a woman has more than one husband.

Polygamy. A form of marriage allowing for more than one marriage partner.

Polygyny. Marital arrangement where one man is married to two or more women at the same time.

Political rights. Rights that guarantee citizens the opportunity to participate in the political process.

Political socialization. The means by which individuals acquire political beliefs and values.

Polytheism. The belief in many gods and/or goddesses.

Poverty. A condition in which people lack the resources to obtain the basic standard of living in a society.

Poverty line. The government's official calculation of poverty; measured at three times the cost of the economy food plan.

Power. The ability to obtain through a variety of means what one wants from others.

Predestination. A belief that people were pre-selected by God for salvation or damnation.

Primary deviance. An act of deviance by an individual that either is not discovered or is excused.

Primary group. The most important of our group memberships. An example would be our family.

Primary labor market. Jobs that have been traditionally associated with white-collar work, are secure, offer good benefits and pay, and the opportunity for advancement and training.

Primary socialization. The socialization we received in small primary groups such as the family.

Profane. That which relates to everyday life.

Protestant Work Ethic. Max Weber's term describing the ideal of a hard working, self-denying, and high moral life that was essential to the development of capitalism.

Race. A cultural perception that an individual belongs to a group of people who others *believe* to be physically and genetically unique.

Racism. A term describing a particular type of prejudice and discrimination in which individuals believe that people are divided into distinct groups based upon heredity.

Rationalization. A term developed by Max Weber to describe the process whereby traditional thinking (craftsmanship) was replaced by thinking dominated by efficiency, control, and effectiveness in goal accomplishment.

Real culture. The actual beliefs, values, and practices of society members.

Rebel. According to Merton, a person who not only disagrees with the values and norms of society, but also deliberately attempts to destroy the system and replace it with a new one.

Recidivism. The probability that those incarcerated and then released are likely to return to prison for the commission of new crimes.

Reference group. A group used to help us define our identity. Examples of reference groups are family, friends, and work colleagues.

Refined divorce rate. Measures the number of divorces in a year for every 1,000 married women over age 15.

Reform schools. Institutions for the incarceration and rehabilitation of juvenile offenders.

Relative Poverty. The depravation felt by some members of a particular society who perceive themselves as possessing a lifesytle below others who have more.

Religion. A unified system of beliefs and practices relative to sacred ideology.

Religiosity. A sociological concept referring to the importance of religion in individuals lives.

Representative Democracy. A government in which citizens elect or appoint others to make decisions for them.

Resocialization. The process of stripping away old values and patterns of behavior so that new ones may be introduced. Occurs most frequently in what is termed the "total institution."

Retreatists. Those who refuse to follow the socially accepted means to achieve their goals.

Ritualism. A practice by people who conscientiously follow the norms of society even when there is no hope that they will achieve their goals via those norms.

Risky behavior. Used in a sexual sense, it implies behavior or actions that may be sincere and seemingly innocent but by design send signals that may be misinterpreted by others.

Riots. Violent group behavior associated with intense levels of frustration and anger in the community.

Role. A set of expected behaviors attached to a status.

Role conflict. A situation in which two or more roles, possibly work and family, occupied by an individual are in conflict.

Role strain. A condition that results when it is not possible to successfully fulfill all the expectations of a role.

Role taking process. Advanced by George Herbert Mead, this theory states that personality formation is the product of social interaction occurring at different life ages by taking on the roles of others.

Rumor. False or unverified information that is passed to others within a social group.

Sample. Individuals chosen to represent the population in a research study.

Schools. Specific institutions expressly designed to teach individuals through professional instruction.

Scientific method. A systematic method of investigation used in research.

Secondary deviance. If an individual is caught and punished while in the process of deviant behavior, he/she may be labeled as deviant and often, as a result, will continue the deviance.

Secondary groups. These groups are large, impersonal, and formal. An example would be a political interest group or a professional occupational group.

Secondary labor market. The market in which contingent or part-time workers are employed.

Secularization. The process whereby the power and influence of religious thought and organizations is lessened in favor of worldly thought.

Self-fulfilling prophecy. A concept identified by Robert Merton that suggests that behavior can result simply because it was predicted by others.

Separation of Powers. An American structural concept of government in which power is horizontally and vertically divided so that no one unit of government becomes too powerful.

Serial monogamy. A process whereby individuals marry more than one person in the course of their lifetime. Each new marriage, however, follows the end of the previous one.

Sex. Biological characteristics that distinguish males from females.

Sex ratio. A ratio arrived at by dividing the number of males by the number of females.

Sexual harassment. Unwelcomed sexual advances, requests for sexual favors, and other verbal or physical conduct of a sexual nature.

Sexuality. Refers to how society views sex and how we feel about ourselves as sexual beings.

Shamans. The individual in a preliterate tribe who attempts to heal group members by calling upon spirits to help control or heal diseases.

Singularity. The achievement of immortality by humans through biology or transfer of consciousness to computers.

Situational constraints. Obstacles encountered by the poor that prevent their upward social mobility.

Social aggregate. A collection of people who find themselves gathered together at a particular time and location but who do not interact or share a common sense of identity. An example would be a group of people waiting for a train.

Social category. A collection of people who share something in common but do not interact with each other. An example would be all the students in the United States.

Social change. Alteration, or variation of mechanisms, of the social structure.

Social channeling. A social conflict theory describing how upper class parents prepare their children for positions of wealth and power.

Social Darwinism. A theory stating that individuals are born with different abilities—some leading to success, others leading to failure.

Social dynamics. The forces in society that provide for change and/or conflict.

Social mobility. The movement of an individual to another social or status group.

Social networks. The links formed between individuals, families, cliques, and other groups.

Social statics. Forces in society that attempt to maintain the existing status quo (that which currently exists).

Social solidarity. The social bonds that unite a society.

Social Stratification. The ranking of individuals in a hierarchy system according to a distribution of economic resources, social statuses, and power.

Social structure. How society is organized and constructed.

Socialism. An economic system in which the government (the people as a collective) owns all or most of the property. The central feature of socialism is that the government plans for the production of goods and use of resources for the benefit of all people.

Society. A self-contained group of humans who share a common territory, and have organized themselves for the purpose of survival and perpetuation of a certain way of life.

Sociobiology. A discipline of sociology that assigns a large role to biology (nature) in explaining behavior and the development of personality.

Sociological imagination. A term developed by C. Wright Mills to describe a way of thinking that provides individuals with an understanding of how societal forces shape our lives.

Sociology. The scientific and systematic study of society and social interaction.

State. An entity possessing the legitimate monopoly over the use of force within its territory.

Status. The position that one holds in a group or society.

Status offenses. Violation of norms associated with status.

Status quo. A term used to describe that which currently exists. In a sociological sense, it generally applies to maintaining or changing the existing social structure and values.

Stereotyping. A process whereby a trait, usually negative, is generalized to all members of a particular group.

Subculture. A group that while identifying with a substantial portion of the dominant culture holds values, beliefs, and traits and customs that are distinct and separate from the rest of society.

Subjective knowledge. Personal knowledge that is dependent upon and interpreted by our personal experience.

Superego. Freudian term for that part of the subconscious that contains all teachings of society and that insists that we follow the societal rules.

Surplus value. This was Marx's term for profit in the capitalistic system.

Symbol. Something having cultural significance and thereby the capacity to elicit a meaningful response.

System blame theories. Theories that blame society and its institutions for social problems such as racism gender inequality, and poverty.

Taboos. A classification of mores that refer to forbidden or unthinkable behavior.

Taylorism. A principle of work management in which work is broken down into the smallest and most efficient components for production.

Technology. The tools and machines used by society to achieve greater practical application of knowledge to increase power and conserve human energy.

Theory. A systematic explanation for observations that relate to a particular aspect of life such as poverty, crime, social class, status, and many others.

Total institutions. Formal institutions designed for the purpose of resocializing individuals.

Totalitarian governments. Authoritative governments that attempt to control every aspect of people's lives.

Totemism. A religious belief of many preliterate societies where animals were seen as both gods and ancestors.

Tracking. The process of placing students into various categories based on their perceived or assumed academic ability.

Traditional authority. Authority where rule is legitimized by birthright or because the religion of the society has conferred upon the leader a divine right.

Transsexuals. People who feel they are one sex, though biologically they are the other.

Transvestitism. The practice of wearing clothing appropriate to the opposite sex.

Triad. A three person group.

Underclass. A term used to describe those in poverty.

Underemployment. A condition of having to work part-time when full-time work is desired and sought after.

Urban legend. Stories circulated in society about an event that are outlandish and based in myth only.

Utilitarian organizations. Organizations established for the purpose of economic gain.

Validity. In a research study, validity refers to the fact that the researcher is indeed measuring what he/she intends to measure.

Values. A common set of beliefs about what is right and what is wrong.

Variable. Any item that can be measured and represent different values.

Virtual workplace. Workplace that is linked electronically to anywhere in the world rather than physically to a specific site of operation.

Voucher. A grant of tax dollars allocated to parents for sending their children to the private or public school of their choice.

War on Poverty. A term used to describe an overall effort of the government through federal programs to eliminate poverty in the 1960s.

Wealth. Describes all economic assets owned by an individual.

Wealthfare. Governmental aid or benefits given to the wealthy.

White collar crimes. Crimes committed by professionals and other white-collar workers.

White ethnics. Those who identify their ancestry as originating in nations predominately populated by white people.

White flight. The migration of whites from all-white communities to escape forced integration.

Work. An activity that produces something of economic value.

Name Index

E

F

G

H

I

J

K

L

M

N

O

P

R

S

T, U, V

W

Y, Z

Subject Index

A

B

C

D

E

F

G

H

I

J

K

L

S

T

U

V

W, Y, Z